067-0895-80
8

RT 43.70

G. MIRANDA & SONS
1887 Claro M. Recto Avenue
P. O. Box 2930, Manila

INDUSTRIAL PSYCHOLOGY

McGraw-Hill Series in Psychology

Consulting Editors

NORMAN GARMEZY

HARRY F. HARLOW

LYLE V. JONES

HAROLD W. STEVENSON

INDUSTRIAL PSYCHOLOGY

Second Edition

B. von Haller Gilmer
Carnegie Institute of Technology

With the collaboration of:

W. J. E. Crissy
Michigan State University

Robert Glaser
University of Pittsburgh

Lee W. Gregg
Carnegie Institute of Technology

Thomas L. Hilton
Educational Testing Service

Myron L. Joseph
Carnegie Institute of Technology

Harry W. Karn
Carnegie Institute of Technology

Robert E. Krug
Peace Corps

R. J. Lewis
Michigan State University

Robert B. Miller
International Business Machines Corporation

McGraw-Hill Book Company
New York, St. Louis, San Francisco, Toronto, London, Sydney

Dedicated to
Walter VanDyke Bingham

Preface

There is now a field of *general industrial psychology*. It is composed of the contributions of experimental, social, counseling, and clinical psychology, and of the researches found scattered throughout a broad literature of the behavioral sciences and of business. This revised edition pulls together the content of the field much in the manner of other introductory texts in psychology.

Realizing that no one psychologist has the depth of knowledge and feeling for each area of specialization to write a well-balanced text, we have combined the resources of several. The contributors have from the beginning been keenly aware that a text written by several people would lack uniformity of style and organization unless one person took the responsibility for putting the entire manuscript into a single style. To achieve this, the senior author has worked closely with each contributor in the writing and the rewriting of the chapters. The final product is a uniform presentation. Each contributor's name appears on the chapter(s) he prepared.

The basic changes from the first edition are twofold. First, each chapter has been rewritten to bring in selected new research-oriented material. Second, the text has been reorganized to provide for expansion of subject matter into a pattern better facilitating teaching. Two chapters on mental health have been removed, and new subject matter has been inserted in appropriate places through the book. The chapter on business procedures in the first edition has been omitted, along with a lengthy chapter on the early development of industrial psychology. Two new subject areas are introduced as chapters in an industrial psychology text for the first time. One is a chapter on the psychological climates of organizations. Another, the final chapter, pulls together an array of material from researches and interviews on career development, dealing with the decision-making problems individuals face in an organizational environment.

In describing the human aspects of the industrial setting, we have borne in mind the fact that many students taking courses in industrial psychology are not psychology majors. We have kept in mind that there are those who will use the text for a reference in various programs of continuing education. And we have tried to remember also that this text has distribution overseas. Effort has been made to include intercultural studies where appropriate. Since this is a general text, we realize that the inclusion of materials on techniques and methods must be limited. References to these are given at the end of each chapter for those readers who wish to dig deeper into specifics. These references, for the most part, are limited to books. They have been chosen to reflect levels of difficulty from the easily readable to the sophisticated specialties. These suggested readings expand subject matter beyond the limits of each chapter and in general do not duplicate the text material. Chapter bibliographies at the back of the book contain some references not specifically cited in the text. These tangential citations are included as background material for readers who may wish to get a feel for the wide variety of researches underlying general industrial psychology. Literature-summary references are given where available. To make reading of the text smoother, some reference numbers are given at the end of a paragraph, and some references are given in a general form. These changes from the first edition are in response to suggestions from a number of users both overseas and in the United States.

To the many researchers and writers who could not be included in the bibliography because of space restrictions we wish to extend our appreciation for providing us with a base for planning the book. Through the direct and indirect communication we have had from several hundred users of the first edition of the text we wish to express our thanks for suggestions, many of which are reflected in this revision. And the senior author wishes to express his debt to his colleagues in psychology and the Institute of Industrial Relations at the University of California in Berkeley for providing a stimulating climate for completion of this revised edition during his tenure there as visiting professor. We wish also to recognize the following organizations which in one way or another contributed to the preparation of this volume:

Abilities, Inc., Allis-Chalmers Manufacturing Company, American Association of University Professors, American Federation of Labor and Congress of Industrial Organizations, American Federation of Teachers, American Federation of Television and Radio Artists, American Hospital Supply Corporation, American Institutes for Research, American Institute of Architects, American Management Association, American Medical

Association, American Psychological Association, Automobile Manufacturers Association, Bank of America, Bell Telephone Company of Pennsylvania, Brownell Tours, Canadian Pacific Railways, Carnegie Corporation, Chrysler Corporation, Coca-Cola Company, Coleman & Associates, Columbia Broadcasting System, Congo Tire and Rubber Company, Corning Glass Works, Craig House, Crown Zellerbach Corporation, Detroit Free Press, Draper Mercantile Company, E. I. du Pont de Nemours & Company, Inc., Eastman Kodak Company, Encyclopedia of the Social Sciences, Esso Standard Oil Company, Fisher Scientific Company, Ford Foundation, Ford Motor Company, *Fortune Magazine,* General Dynamics Corporation, General Electric Company, General Motors Corporation, General Motors Institute, Hale Manu Craft, Harless & Kirkpatrick Associates, Harper & Row, *Harvard Business Review,* Harvard University Press, Hawaii Tourist Bureau, Her Majesty's Stationery Office, Howard Chase Associates, Inc., Institute for Social Research at the University of Michigan, International Association of Applied Psychology, International Business Machines Corporation, John Roberts Associates, John Wiley & Sons, Kaiser Industries Corporation, Kennecott Copper Corporation, King Ranch, Kraft Foods Company, Life Insurance Agency Management Association, Litton Industries, Monsanto Chemical Company, National Association of Secondary Industrial Supplies, National Education Association, National Foreman's Institute, National Institutes of Health, National Safety Council, New York Life Insurance Company, *New York Times,* Office of Naval Research, Ohio State University, Operating Engineers, Local No. 3, San Francisco, P. & O.–Orient Lines, Pacific Telephone Company, Peace Corps, Pittsburgh Plate Glass Company, Polaroid Corporation, Princeton University Press, Procter & Gamble Company, Psychological Corporation, Psychological Service of Pittsburgh, Raytheon Manufacturing Company, Refractory Phase Farm, Robert Brunner, Inc., Ronald Press, Rotary International, Science Research Associates, Scientific Methods, Inc., Scientific Products, Inc., Shenango China Company, Stromberg-Carlson Company, Systems Development Corporation, Television City, Inc., *Time,* Inc., Triple G. Farms, Unilever, Ltd., United States Air Force, U.S. Department of Labor, U.S. Department of State, United Automobile Workers, United States Steel Corporation, Universal Manufacturing Corporation, University of Chicago Press, Veterans Administration, Wells Fargo Bank, Western Maryland Railway Company, Westinghouse Airbrake Company, Westinghouse Broadcasting Company, Westinghouse Electric Corporation.

Appreciation is expressed to Professor J. Marshall Brown who prepared the *Instructor's Manual* to accompany this text.

B. von Haller Gilmer

Contents

I.

PSYCHOLOGY IN INDUSTRY

1

General Industrial Psychology

B. von Haller Gilmer

Organizations include people, and people are important. There is hardly a phase in the daily life of the man or woman associated with modern industry that is not in some way related to the study of human behavior. Industrial psychology is interested not only in the man at work on the production line but also in the salesman on the road and the girl at the desk in the office. It is the study of people whose work is selling insurance, laying bricks, supervising the people producing goods, or directing the activities of the large corporation.

The man who drives to work in America is guided by green and white road signs, and the tourist in Europe finds the use of pictograms advantageous in facilitating understanding beyond language barriers. These perceptual forms are used because research and practical experience have proved their value. The same is true with the tests administered in selecting the insurance salesman, the procedures used to study efficiency in laying bricks, the methods applied in training supervisors, and the programs involved in evaluating leadership.

INDUSTRY—A PLACE TO STUDY BEHAVIOR

Industry, at the present time, provides a good field in which to study the wants and needs of human beings. What does the psychologist in industry do? An answer to this question, of course, depends upon the size of the industrial organization, upon what the organization does, and upon the attitude of any given management toward psychology. There is hardly a nationally known corporation that does not employ the services of psychologists. Many smaller companies work with psychologists on a part-time-consulting basis.

The psychologist working in industry does far more than give tests, a job popularly believed to be his activity. True, he has designed the tests and has validated them to see if they are accurately predicting what they are supposed to. But in the main the psychologist in industry has turned the testing program over to others. He is now advising the industrial relations department on the company's pending contract negotiations with the union, or he is designing a study to determine the buying habits of a suburban housewife as she walks through her local supermarket. One hour the industrial psychologist may be discussing the psychology of learning with the company's training director; the next hour he may be participating in a conference on a morale survey to be conducted in an out-of-town plant.

The Psychologist's Staff Position. The industrial psychologist usually holds a staff position, largely advisory, which enables him to apply his talents wherever they are needed. He helps to improve safety programs, and he works with engineers on the human aspects of equipment design. He assists the office of public relations in its interactions with consumers and with the community in which the company operates. He engages in the varied programs dealing with the mental health of the worker, and he assists management in finding ways to reduce absenteeism. The industrial psychologist may draw up a plan for the executive development of the newly hired college graduate on one day and discuss the problems of aging employees the next. From personnel selection to training, from supervision to job evaluation, from career planning to labor relations, the industrial psychologist moves in a wide and ever-varying scene.

WHY STUDY INDUSTRIAL PSYCHOLOGY?

"I do not plan to be a psychologist. Why then should I study industrial psychology?" This is a fair question, and quite possibly it has already occurred to the student reader. Here is our answer.

You and Industry. Most college graduates—whether they have specialized in the liberal arts, in science, in engineering, or in business administration—eventually find work in some branch of industry. One does not have to be involved in personnel administration, labor relations, or other phases of management to be confronted with human problems. From the hour the college graduate starts his new job in the small company or enters the training program of the large corporation, he moves in an environment swarming with human problems. Induction and training in this new job comprise an involved human problem for the individual as well as for the company. It will help the student if he can find out in advance what he is getting into when he enters modern industry. Career planning today is much more involved than it was just a few years ago. Our first answer to the question, "Why should I study industrial psychology?" arises from surveys which reveal that students today more than ever before want to know what they are getting into. There is no better way to find out about the psychological climate of a work situation than to discuss the scientific and clinical studies about people who work in this climate.

A second reason for studying about human behavior in industry arises from the fact that more and more leaders of modern industry are coming from the ranks of college graduates. Leadership in business is becoming more demanding, and the person without a liberal education is handicapped in getting the kind of position from which he can move upward in any business organization. The study of the human side of management, of supervision, is the province of psychology. It serves as a counterpart to the study of economic man.

The technical student, for example, the engineer, may ask, "Why take psychology?" Studies show that five years after graduation only about one-half of engineering college graduates are in engineering. A few years later most are out of technical work altogether. What are they doing? Many advance to administration, a portion move into sales, some become entrepreneurs, but all seem to get more and more involved with the human side of industry. In one survey, for example, the graduates of a large engineering school who had reached supervisory or administrative positions in industry reported that more than three-fourths of their time was taken up by working with people. The importance of having skill in human relations can be illustrated by a study of over four thousand white-collar workers from seventy-six different companies. Here it was found that 10.1 per cent were fired from their jobs because of a lack of technical competence. In contrast, 89.9 per cent were dismissed because they couldn't work with people [5].

Finally, whether we work directly in industry or not, as consumers and as citizens we find our lives influenced on every side by industrial changes. We are concerned with labor-management conflicts because the consequences often touch our pocketbooks; we are concerned with technological advances and their effect on the production of goods because these determine our material welfare; and we are concerned with the problems in industry, to at least some degree, because many of the people we know work there.

Man's behavior plays a part in all phases of industrial life. As educated people we should be aware of the significance of this force.

WHAT PSYCHOLOGISTS DO IN INDUSTRY

It is quite natural that people are confused about the function of psychology in industry. One writer [19] has suggested why this is so by saying that "psychology is probably misunderstood for the same reason it is so popular: it deals with a subject on which people have always considered themselves to be authorities." No place is this more true than in the general area of business and industry, where managers have prided themselves on being able to solve practical problems, to manage men. How can a science largely born and bred in ivory-tower lecture halls and attic laboratories attract the attention and money of the hard-boiled executive? A description of one typical research will provide the answer [16].

The publication describes a simple training experiment which saved money for the company. In a factory where new employees were customarily broken in on the job, the company wanted to know whether a part-time training program would pay. Under the psychologist's direction, one group of new employees was sent directly to work, and a comparable group was sent into a training program. The performances of both groups were recorded, and costs were evaluated by the accounting department. It was found that even after six months' experience, the untrained workers took twenty-nine minutes to change knives on a flying shears, whereas the group that had been trained properly was doing the job in only eighteen minutes. The eleven minutes saved in labor costs amounted to $20,880 a year. Furthermore, it was found that during the first thirty days of employment, accidents were 19 per cent fewer among the workers in the trained group than among those broken in on the floor. Waste and breakages were lower, labor turnover was not so great, and absenteeism was 51 per cent less among those given training under the direction of the industrial psychologist.

Applications of Basic Principles. From laboratory work the psychologist has found out how people learn and how they can be trained more economically. In clinical situations he has found out how people feel and how they react to frustration. On the job the psychologist has discovered the basic principles underlying good supervision. The psychologist knows other things about human behavior that can be applied to product design, manufacture, and distribution; his knowledge not only is of economic value to the industrialist but also can make the conditions of work more pleasant for the employee.

Out of many psychological experiments have come answers to practical problems in the management of men and proof that many of the strong beliefs of the old-fashioned businessman are wrong. The idea that a "good judge of men" could look at the job applicant, talk to him, and tell right away what he could do and if he was a good worker has been disproved. Gone is the notion that being a good foreman means being tough and the belief that pay is the only thing the worker is after.

Today many psychologists, along with other behavioral scientists, are regularly employed in industry; others serve as consultants. They work with engineers on problems in the design of equipment. They help design the home telephone to reduce errors in dialing; they suggest changes in the cockpit of the airplane to make it less confusing for the pilot. The psychologist has helped change the aim of industrial design from what is easiest to make to what is best for the man.

Psychologists, along with other researchers, have discovered that human stress may be influenced more by one's emotional state than by hard work. A standard prescription for the harassed executive is to take a vacation. But the enforced idleness of an unwanted vacation may be the worst possible course for some people. Psychologists have studied the executive as well as the worker, and they know why he has been described as the most lonesome man in the organization.

The psychologist has uncovered many things about the needs of the worker in his struggle for status, for recognition, and for other elements that lead to job satisfaction. He knows that, contrary to some popular opinion, high morale does not always bring about high productivity. More importantly, he knows in part why.

Some Limitations in Psychology. Psychologists in industry have to spend some of their time restraining the enthusiastic administrator who believes that psychology has the answer to more problems than it really has. He has been impressed with the effectiveness of the company's program of selecting office workers and machinists and expects the psychologist to be able to do an equally good job predicting which of his younger men are the best bets for executive development. But for this problem the psychologist is not yet ready to supply all the answers. Nor is he able to select good salesmen. There are limitations as to what he can do in the areas of mental health. The well-trained psychologist knows the present limitations of his science and its applications.

A particularly controversial area of industrial psychology is consumer research and advertising. Among the techniques attracting attention is what is called *motivation research*. Some people in the advertising business believe they can get at the unconscious motives in people, and they gear advertisements to do so. For example, marketing people have called deep freezers "frozen islands of security," and have spoken of the automobile as "an extension of one's personality."

Long-range Studies. The psychologist who works in industry is interested
not only in day-to-day problems but also in long-range programs dealing
with the effective utilization of human resources. Although he does not
have as complete control over the variables as does the psychologist working in the experimental laboratory or the clinician working in the confines
of a therapeutic situation, the industrial psychologist is interested in basic
problems as well as applications. Fortunately for the profession of psychology, the spirit of the laboratory and the clinic has been carried into
industry.

Fundamental research is being carried on today in industrial, governmental, and military settings. We have learned that psychology does not
have to be locked in a laboratory in order to be scientific.

Psychology Itself as Big Business. Not only do psychologists work for other
people; in some ways psychology itself is big business. For example, one
company alone, Science Research Associates, had over eleven thousand
industrial clients in 1962 for its tests, a threefold gain over 1957, and it
has been predicted that this figure will be more than doubled by the late
sixties. Surveys by *Fortune Magazine* and other industrial organizations
indicate that some 60 per cent of the largest corporations are using tests for
selection or promotion. Let us use testing as our example of psychology in
business.

Testing has a long history. According to the studies of DuBois [10] it
began as early as 2200 B.C., seventeen centuries before Confucius. By
1115 B.C. the Chan dynasty introduced formal job-sample tests for posts
in the government. Rudimentary selection procedures involving tests were
conducted for hunters, writers, and measurements of horsemanship skill.

Although tests are of ancient lineage and research, development, and the
practical use of psychological tests classify testing and test publishing as a
multimillion-dollar industry, there has always been some controversy about
testing programs. In reviewing a long history of this controversy, Tuddenham
[48] concludes that tests, rightly used, can be the best and most impartial
means we have yet found for meshing the needs of society with the talents
of individual men. But tests also lend themselves to abuses of many kinds
and are far from perfect in application. They are sometimes bad, and for
two reasons: that they do not work well enough and that they work too
well. The shortcomings of tests are probably better known to their inventors than to anyone else. Critics often evaluate tests against a standard
of perfection rather than against alternatives. But when viewed in terms of
alternatives, proper tests used wisely pay dividends. In modern industry
errors of vocational choice, errors of personnel selection, and errors of
upgrading are becoming increasingly costly. Training and retraining become
related to measurements of individual differences. As problems of automation add to the complexity of man-machine systems, it becomes fairly

predictable that more and more aspects of the application of psychology to industry will become big business in themselves.

Illustrations, other than the example of testing used here, will be given in coming chapters showing how psychology itself is expanding rapidly. One reason is found in the fact that psychology concentrates so much research effort in studying cause-effect relationships.

CAUSE AND EFFECT IN BEHAVIOR

No action, no emotion, no thought of a person ever occurs really spontaneously. Human behavior does not just happen; it is caused. Every act that a person performs is the result of sufficient antecedent causes. The antecedents of a thought are often hard to discover, but causal factors are always present even for the most evanescent of psychological phenomena.

The Individual and the Situation. How an individual responds to any particular situation depends upon what he brings into the situation in terms of his abilities, attitudes, skills, desires, understandings, and habits. Picture, if you will, the differences between what the union representative brings into the labor-contract negotiations and what the representative of management brings in. Chances are that each has about the same abilities and many of the same skills for negotiation. But one thing is certain: the two men bring in different attitudes and desires from their respective backgrounds of experience. They have distinctly different economic goals. Labor is interested in job security and in high wages and certain related fringe benefits. Management is interested in profits. The importance of this difference is sometimes overlooked. One study showed that over two-thirds of a group of people surveyed had the opinion that in an average year few companies operate at a loss. However, the United States Treasury Department reports that in almost every peacetime year since 1913 at least 40 per cent of American corporations have shown no net income, and that the record of all American corporations over the past thirty years shows a profit on sales of less than 4 per cent. It may also be of interest to know that since the first automobile was produced in 1893, some 1,850 United States auto firms have gone out of business. It is therefore understandable that the goals of labor and management are in conflict. The solution of their problem hinges on a fair division of income from the goods produced. But what is fair raises the problem of who determines. Understanding the basic differences of attitude each faction brings to the negotiations is important in determining cause and effect. Both are aware that most businesses are here today and gone tomorrow, the average life expectancy of a business being only six years.

For labor to accept management's initial offer in negotiations is practically unheard of, because labor has its position of prestige and power to maintain. The labor leader must prove to the workers that he truly represents them in their demands, that he understands their feelings. Similarly, the representative of management has responsibility to his superiors, who in turn represent the stockholders. Although each recognizes the other's position, clearly each faction in the dispute tries to sell its particular side to the public. Misunderstandings are almost inevitable. It is of great help that the industrial psychologist who is working in this area knows what each side brings into the situation. He knows that the individuals representing labor and management come with somewhat prejudiced backgrounds as *individuals,* and he knows that the *situation* itself accentuates the differences in their points of view.

Finding the Cause. Sometimes the cause of a person's behavior is concealed. He may take an intense dislike to someone he has just met, without apparent cause until he is made aware that this person acts just like someone with whom he has had unpleasant experiences. The worker who is reprimanded may feel that his foreman spoke without cause, whereas the concealed but quite real cause may be that the foreman is worried about a problem at home.

One may miss seeing the actual cause for behavior when something else seems more apparent. The apparent cause of a strike may be failure to get a raise in wages; this may even be the cause that is stated publicly. But often it is found that the real cause is something less easy to see, such as loss of status of the union leaders or dissatisfaction with supervision.

Sometimes we miss seeing the cause of behavior because of a prejudice we hold or because we wish to see some particular cause-effect relationship. We may see a situation as a cause of something when the real cause does not lie within the situation but within the person involved. One may blame his lack of promotion on office politics rather than on his own lack of ability.

Cause-Effect Complexities. One pitfall in practical problem solving comes from transferring a cause-effect relationship which appears in one situation to another situation in which it is not valid. For instance, in considering a problem of absenteeism, it is possible to assume too quickly that the first cause suspected is the real one. Perhaps it has been found that improving the physical working conditions will reduce absenteeism among women; yet it may be a costly error to assume that such improvements will have the same effect upon men. The fact that most heavy drinkers are frequently absent from work should not lead one to generalize that this is the major cause of absenteeism; we may discover that most workers who have frequent absences are not heavy drinkers. High rates of absence on Monday in some plants may lead us to suspect that the workers have indulged in a big week end, but in actuality the cause may be poor supervision.

The psychologist working in industry has a particularly difficult job ascertaining cause and effect relationships. For one thing he is often dealing with multiple causation, and he does not have many conditions favoring well-controlled experimentation. Whereas industry is willing to spend time and money on product research, it is still not completely sold on human behavior research. But there is growing evidence that psychology itself is being accepted more and more in industry as managers are learning what the behavioral sciences have to offer. The field of industrial psychology, say Dunnette and Kirchner [11], is probably growing more rapidly than any other in psychology.

PSYCHOLOGY AS A BEHAVIORAL SCIENCE

The behavioral sciences include a number of disciplines, such as anthropology, economics, political science, sociology, and psychology. Other specialties which are closely related to the behavioral sciences have a bearing on industrial psychology, namely, management engineering, industrial administration, industrial design, and labor relations. Differences among the behavioral sciences are not always clearly demarcated, but this does not cause confusion when a given discipline is problem-oriented. Both anthropology and sociology are concerned with groups of people, and in both disciplines emphasis is given to the study of the cultures of various societies or groups. Social anthropology is particularly interested in primitive cultures and how societies have developed from them.

The events that make history are primarily events of human behavior. Economics touches on behavior as it deals with the making and distribution of goods, market analyses, and predictions of what people may do next in buying stocks and bonds. Political science is closely related to industry through its studies of institutionalized governments.

By understanding how businesses are organized, how they are managed, and the complexities of the power struggles between management and labor, we get a wider view of how industrial psychology is related to many other specialties.

A Four-way Function. Industrial psychology is concerned with four relationships of man as he functions in industry. It is interested in relations between person and person, between person and group, and between person and object; and it is interested in problems of the inner man himself.

The salesman who tries to get you to buy his company's product or service functions in a *person-to-person* relationship. The supervisor who gives orders to his workers is functioning in a *person-to-group* relationship, just as is the man who deals with groups in the school or in the community. The worker who operates a machine is engaged in a *person-to-object* relationship, the source of many psychological problems in industry. Perhaps most important of all are the problems of *intrapersonal* relations which arise when a man tries to understand his own desires, abilities, and frustrations.

Industrial psychology borrows from a number of fields within psychology itself, utilizing the facts, theories, and methods of experimental, social, counseling, and clinical psychology. Industrial psychology also is interested in problems beyond the scope of the business firm; it moves into extended social areas in looking at people with abilities and people with handicaps.

Some Newer Questions. From some recent intercultural studies of managerial talent, at one end, and a large-scale measurement program of culturally handicapped people from underdeveloped countries, at the other, comes the conclusion that talent at all levels—worker, supervisor, manager, professional—is not an exclusive commodity of any section of the world or of any ethnic group. As a result of these types of studies, psychologists are now asking research questions about selection instruments that exclude minority groups. Furthermore, many social scientists are now writing to the effect that the concept of individual differences is in for redefinition. Societies went through the historical phase of status by the inheritance of title and property and by so doing failed to give opportunity to much potential talent. More recently, we North Americans went overboard in search of people with high mental ability and found them at all levels of our culture. But we also found there is a difference between inherent potential and what a person may actually accomplish. Today, particularly in industry, a new additive has been given to the pursuit of excellence—how does the person *perform?* Equally important, how does he perform *toward a particular end?* And *within what environmental context* is he required to perform? There are data that show some culturally handicapped people can become productive when given a chance, but this involves programming, selection, and training.

In the chapters to follow we shall describe a number of new areas that industrial psychology is expanding into.

THE METHODS OF PSYCHOLOGY APPLIED TO INDUSTRY

The experimental method of psychology teaches us to define the real problem, relate it to known principles, vary certain aspects in the conditions while holding others constant, make hypotheses, collect and analyze data, and verify our hypotheses. The experimental method requires that we conduct experiments in ways that allow for repetition and for control. It requires that we understand the variables involved.

Designing Experiments in Industry. In the laboratory it is relatively easy to design experiments so that they can be repeated. Let us say we are interested in the effects of exposure of white rats to gamma irradiation from cobalt, perhaps the effects this may have on learning ability. It is a simple matter to get animals that can be paired off into test groups and control groups, to describe and control precisely each aspect of the experimental situation, and to collect and analyze the data in standard ways. Such an experiment can be set up and repeated wherever appropriate animals and physical conditions exist. Many experiments of this kind have been reported in the literature, and each one is of a nature allowing for repetition. Indeed, a few of the studies have been repetitions, some by the same people, some by others.

Some experiments in industrial psychology can be repeated anywhere as easily as the one just described. For example, one can determine with high certainty whether horizontal-type meters can be read with any greater degree of accuracy than vertical-type meters. However, many industrial problems are so involved and so complex that repetition under exactly similar conditions often is not possible. This does not mean that we should not try to apply the experimental method to the problems. It does mean that we have to be aware of the limitations of our study. It is not possible, for example, to learn with any great degree of accuracy just how effective human relations courses in supervision are in specific terms. We can, however, get some fairly good approximations by applying problem-solving methods to our studies.

A second limitation in applying the experimental method to industrial human problems is that the experiment itself may interfere with the very thing we are trying to study. For example, we may wish to determine whether the severe noise generated by a jet plane has any effect on the performance of the mechanics testing the aircraft. If the people know they are subjects in an experiment, the results may be affected by that awareness. But the situation may be such that if we are to get answers at all, the subjects will have to know what we are doing. This is, of course, a limitation in our experiment. Nevertheless, important findings can be obtained even under such limitations.

Another limitation of an experiment may be that it has some artificial arrangement in it. In an attempt to discover which variables are important to a problem, the psychologist must select the ones he wants to control. He may select the variables which will give him results of importance. On the other hand, he may go through the motions of an experiment that leads nowhere. Sometimes he may get negative results because the wrong questions were asked when he set the experiment up; yet he may find later that the results opened up a whole new set of important problems not considered before.

But do not let these limitations of the scientific method discourage you. They are present in all the sciences—in physics and in chemistry and in the biological sciences. They just appear more frequently in the behavioral sciences. In the chemistry laboratory a person can be given an unknown solution to analyze. If he cannot run his tests on Friday, he stores the solution in an appropriate place where temperature and pressure are controlled and waits until Monday to make the analysis. On Monday the solution is just the same, and the analysis can be made just as accurately. But if someone comes to you on Friday with a personal problem, you cannot defer listening until Monday. Neither he nor his problem can be put into cold storage.

Experimental Variables. Our picture of the experimental method is clearer when we consider the part played by variables and by the *control* of variables. To do an experiment we must have at least two variables. For example, suppose we want to find out whether there is any relationship between taking salt pills and increasing productivity in making steel ingots under conditions of extreme temperature. Several things may be involved, but one important possibility is that the men may be influenced by suggestion. We therefore design our experiment to control this possibility. We select two groups of steelworkers, comparable in age, productivity, safety records, and a dozen other things, and give one group genuine salt pills and the other group pills with only an outer coating of salt. The latter group is our control group; the group which gets the salt pills is the experimental group.

In this study we are dealing with two variables: the number of salt pills and the amount of productivity. In more technical language, we call the salt an *independent variable,* because we can, if we wish, vary the amount independently of other factors in the experiment. Productivity, on the other hand, is our *dependent variable,* because we are interested in whether or not variations in productivity of ingots depend upon the use of salt pills.

It is sometimes difficult in experiments to determine which is the independent and which the dependent variable. In setting up an experiment, we usually have at least one independent variable and one or more dependent variables. Our problem becomes a little more confused when we include *intervening variables.* In our example, it is possible that the amount of water in the worker's body at any given time is related to the effects that salt may have on fatigue and hence on productivity. Often it is these in-between variables that we have difficulty knowing about. Let us consider, for example, a question which on the surface seems simple to answer: What is the relationship between the intensity of illumination and productivity? How would you design an experiment to answer this? What variables would you have to deal with?

Surveys and Clinical Information. Valuable data about human problems in industry come from surveys and from clinical observations. Much of what we know about the problems of labor-management relations, advertising and selling, human relations in supervision, and mental health has been learned by using these procedures.

One of the big contributions of industrial psychology has been to coordinate the methods of the experimenter, the survey psychologist, and the clinician into a resourceful attack on the problems of the people who work in industry, who live in the industrial community.

THE HISTORY OF INDUSTRIAL PSYCHOLOGY

Industrial psychology began in America in 1901 [13, 14] and in England not long thereafter [12, 41]. It received some of its directional trends from the kinds of practical problems presented to psychologists during World Wars I and II. Following World War II psychology in industry spread over Europe and into parts of Africa and Asia. The development of industrial psychology in its early days was other-directed, and to a large extent it continues to deal with the practical problems presented by administrators and planners not only of industrial organizations but of government and military organizations as well.

Beginning with problems in advertising and selling, psychology expanded into researches centering on personnel selection, training, and vocational guidance. By 1925 industrial social psychology entered the picture with investigations and theories of motivation, communication, and group behavior. By 1945 engineering psychology became a part of industrial psychology, and has broadened into studies of human factors in man-machine systems. The early sixties saw the addition of organizational psychology to the traditional field still called industrial psychology after some two decades of growth.

The early development of industrial psychology centers around men, books, and organizations, and present-day developments to a large extent are programmed around multidisciplinary approaches to problems. Many of these are supported by foundation grants and government contracts added to institutional researches carried on within organizations themselves.

Among the early names is that of Walter Dill Scott who opened up the beginnings of industrial psychology in America by showing how psychology could be applied to advertising and selling. He became the first man to hold the title of professor of applied psychology. He was appointed to this position by the man who established the first graduate school of industrial psychology, Walter VanDyke Bingham, at the Carnegie Institute of Technology in 1915. The first Ph.D. in the field was given by this institution in 1921 to Bruce V. Moore.

Edward K. Strong, Jr., branched industrial psychology into guidance with his researches on vocational interests. Hugo Münsterberg, with his researches into industrial accidents and his book *Psychology and Industrial Efficiency,* published in 1913, put psychology into the study of the worker. Such books as Whiting Williams's *What's on the Worker's Mind* and *Mainsprings of Men* started an emphasis on studying the worker. This emphasis remained major until the sixties, when the manager and the professional man began to receive the investigator's attention. The Scott and Clothier *Personnel Management* was published in 1923; for years this was, and in its revised editions still is, a standard work of the personnel movement.

Other books and other people important to this early history can be found in the writings of Ferguson [13, 14]. The Viteles text, *Industrial Psychology,* defined the field of industrial psychology in 1932; since then over one hundred texts have been published [49].

Consulting organizations have always played an important part in the development of industrial psychology. The first such psychological profit-making enterprise was the Scott Company, founded in 1919; it survived until the Depression of 1923. The Psychological Corporation, organized in 1921 by Cattell and a group of prominent American psychologists, became the second psychological-consulting firm, and it is still functioning with vigor. Today there are several hundred such firms in the United States. In 1946 the Tavistock Institute in England became important as a consulting firm, serving many local industries and such world-wide corporations as Unilever, Ltd. There are today a number of psychological-consulting firms throughout Europe and in parts of Asia.

Journals and professional organizations have added their bit to the history. In 1945 what is now called the Division of Industrial Psychology of the American Psychological Association was established and gave professional recognition to the field in a formal way, and in 1962 the Division of Consumer Psychology got underway. Today industrial psychology is international in scope and becoming intercultural in design of some studies. An array of psychologists is presently organized as the International Association of Applied Psychology.

No history of industrial psychology, however brief, is complete without the story of the Hawthorne studies, investigations which have opened up a host of problems, generated theories and controversies, and filled volumes of references. Let us give a brief account of these investigations which brought the social aspects of industrial psychology into focus.

THE CLASSICAL HAWTHORNE STUDIES

In 1927 the Hawthorne (Chicago) plant of the Western Electric Company began a study designed to ascertain "the relations between conditions of work and the incidence of fatigue and monotony among employees." The work began with an attempt to determine the relationship between changes in plant illumination intensity and production. It was begun by, among others, Elton Mayo and a group from Harvard composed of Roethlisberger, Dickson, Whitehead, and Homans. In the beginning the study was conceived to be a one-year project, but it extended year after year as the maze of human problems affecting productivity became more and more involved. In 1939 Roethlisberger and Dickson published *Management and the Worker* —a classic in showing the nature of refinement in experimental methodology and how a dozen new problems in human behavior evolve as solutions to one are being sought [39].

The series of experiments comprising the Hawthorne studies started by varying factors such as lighting, temperature, humidity, hours of sleep, and the like in order to see their effect on the workers' output. There were studies to determine the effect of rest periods, a shorter workweek, and wage incentives and production. The results were surprising; they opened up a new field of research on employee attitudes, a field which has grown so rapidly in recent years that a review of the writing on job attitudes published in 1957 records almost two thousand references. The Hawthorne studies led to a change of methodology from the direct to the indirect method of interviewing, and they led to new approaches in the study of leadership. Studies began to show the importance of social organizations and their effect on production. The problems of communication became apparent. The beginning of industrial counseling came as a result of these studies. Although it soon became clear that no specific relationship existed between visual illumination and production, this original problem opened up an array of motivational problems still being worked on in industry.

A New Era in Psychology. In succeeding chapters, references will be made to parts of the Hawthorne studies. Let us record only the first study that was made, because here we find negative results that initiated a new era in industrial psychology.

The illumination experiment was conducted in three selected departments. In the first department small parts were inspected. In the second, relays were assembled, and in the third, the work involved winding coils.

For the control situation, production was measured under the existing lighting.

In the first department illumination was arranged so that the various levels of intensity averaged 3, 6, 14, and 23 foot-candles. In this department the production of the workers did vary, *but not in direct relation* to the amount of illumination.

The illumination intensities in the second department were 5, 12, 25, and 44 foot-candles. Production in this department increased during the study, but not entirely as a result of the changes in illumination.

Observations of the third department showed similar results, and the experimenters began to see the necessity of controlling or eliminating various additional factors which affected production output.

Here was a problem that was not so simple as it looked. The study was replanned, and a second experiment was conducted with more refined techniques. It was set up in only one department with two groups of workers participating, equated for numbers, experience, and average production. The control group worked under relatively constant illumination, and the test group worked under three different illumination intensities. Competition was eliminated between the groups by having them work in different buildings.

What happened? *Both* the test group and the control group increased production appreciably *and* to an almost identical degree. These perplexing results brought forth a third experiment in which further refinements in procedure were introduced.

In this experiment only artificial light was used to illuminate the working areas; all daylight was excluded. The control group worked under a constant intensity of 10 foot-candles. The test group began with an illumination of 10 foot-candles, and this was reduced 1 foot-candle per period until they were working under only 3 foot-candles of light. Despite the discomfort and handicap of insufficient illumination, this group of employees maintained their efficiency of work.

In a fourth experiment two volunteer girls worked in a light-controlled room until the intensity was reduced to that of ordinary moonlight. At this stage they were able to maintain production, they reported no eyestrain, and they showed even less fatigue than when working under bright lights.

A fifth experiment was conducted with girls whose job involved winding coils; during this experiment there was no real change in production. At first the intensity of the lights was increased each day; the girls reported that they liked the brighter lights. An electrician then changed the light bulbs but kept the same intensity. The girls commented favorably on the "increased illumination." Finally, in the latter part of this experiment the illumination was decreased. For this condition the girls said the lesser amount of light was not so pleasant, *but* they reported feeling the same way when the lights remained constant, even though the electrician was supposedly reducing the illumination!

A Change in Thinking. As the publications from the several Hawthorne studies emerged, thinking about industrial psychology problems changed. No longer were problems in production conceived to be simply a function of illumination, physical fatigue, or working temperature. No longer was labor turnover thought of as being caused by the amount of dollar income. Questions about leadership, about supervision, about human relations began to emerge. As a result of these and other studies and of the demands placed on psychologists by the practical problems of World War II, applied psychology entered a new and bigger phase.

HUMAN PROBLEMS IN ORGANIZATIONS

Of the many things affecting human performance, none is currently having more impact than technological change. Change, as well as accommodation or resistance to it, is having its effect in terms of retraining of the worker to give him new skills and causing the manager to wonder how he can best use the computer in decision making. One problem is the relation between automation, which is spreading, and the labor supply and demand, which is fluctuating. Unskilled jobs are becoming a smaller and smaller fraction of all jobs, and only continuously higher levels of education and retraining can steer the technologically unemployed into the skilled and service-trained jobs where they are needed.

The psychologist is interested in how people react to change and why. A retraining program for the jobless launched with fanfare in one Appalachian town in West Virginia drew only 640 applications from the 8,000 jobless there, even though pay was offered during training; furthermore, only 200 of these applicants were found to be suitable for learning new jobs.

At the core of the manpower-upgrading problem is the psychology of motivation. One study reveals that social-psychological factors influence individual decisions in different ways for different people. Those workers less likely to volunteer for retraining are the poorly educated, the older employees, and high-seniority men. Industrial programs of skills upgrading have to be sold to the individual through a variety of appeals over and above economic threats. Basic attitudes regarding the age–learning-ability relationship will have to be modified if there is to be any hope for recruiting larger proportions of adult workers for retraining programs [40].

Technology is spreading irresistibly, but so are problems. Banks have computerized many operations but despite these laborsaving devices the number of bank employees has tripled in the last decade. It is predicted that in many areas employment will increase but that occupational patterns will also undergo significant changes. One survey found that while 3 million workers have second jobs, even more managers and professional people engage in moonlighting, because their services are needed and salable.

Economic survival depends on wiser use of new technology, one government official contends, and for the new world we must take a look at human capacities. We have to share action abroad with people of different levels of civilization and different historical pasts. Now man is making the most rapid progress in terms of technology that he has ever made, and human beings at all work levels must live through, absorb, and deal with greater changes than before. The man who is twenty years old can expect to make at least six job changes during the remainder of his working life and retire earlier than did his father. For the industrial psychologist, the impact of technological change often means dealing with conflicts between the things that are intellectual, on the one hand, and emotional, on the other. It is generally agreed that man has an enormous capacity for learning, and a number of writers make the point that every culture that has survived has found ways of channeling human behavior into creative endeavors. Basic to this is continuing education. It is predicted that soon one-third of the population will be in the process of being educated at any given time.

The industrial psychologist is interested in contrasting systems of work organization that pit the traditional autocratic climate against the participative, human relations approach, and he is interested in manpower and organizational planning. The psychologists, along with other behavioral scientists, are addressing themselves, with acceptance, to the human problems of business. The problems are many—how to get people to say what they think, to work together in problem solving; what kinds of information will contribute positively to the motivation of people; how organizations can be structured to better satisfy human needs. These and many similar types of problems make up the context of industrial psychology [3, 4, 24, 45, 48].

Psychologists are also interested in another level of problems—why people resist change. One telephone system was faced for months with whole communities of subscribers overpaying their bills by 1 cent just to interfere with accounting. Investigation showed they resisted change from letters to numbers on dials. Why people follow certain set patterns of behavior intrigues us all. Social Security records show that across the country Monday is the busiest day of the week in answering inquiries. Why do Americans look at and listen to an average of around twenty million commercials a year? Why are we forgetful? Chances are four out of ten that when you are packing for a trip, you will fail to put something in your suitcase. The fact that one family in five moves every year is of concern to the behavioral scientist, and he is interested in the statistic that 51 per cent of a group of investors did not know what their companies made. The psychologist is also interested in the fact that the average person does 137 basic things daily, such as brushing his teeth and walking around.

The psychologist is interested in why high-priced executives are so much in demand. He is interested also in John Doe, producer, and John Doe, consumer. And he is interested in researches from the laboratory that might tell him more about behavior. One laboratory experiment that bears on the problems of industrial psychology involved pairs of monkeys. Each animal in the pair had its own metal cage, but both cages in the pair were connected to the same electric circuit. Each cage was furnished with a switch, but only one switch in each pair was connected to the circuit. The psychologist conducting the experiment found that when the monkey with the functional switch learned to use it to prevent shocks to himself and his partner, he often developed ulcers. The partner, whose switch did not function, did not develop ulcers. The psychologist studying the experiment may conclude that the constant anxious tension of the "executive" monkey places him in a vulnerable position of responsibility and decision making not shared by his partner. But before he extrapolates these findings to people, he asks some further questions [6].

YOUR PERSONAL INTERESTS

Possibly most students of applied psychology, personnel psychology, human relations, or industrial psychology have elected this course. In a survey to determine some of the reasons students take such a course, it was found that a few did so simply because it fitted conveniently into their schedules or because they were interested in broadening their general education. Most students, however, reported that they chose the course because they planned to go into industry and they felt that a description of the human aspects of industry would help to prepare them for the job ahead.

This text has not been written to include just what the student wants. It has been prepared by professional men with firsthand experience in industry, either as part-time consultants or as full-time staff members, who have written on what they believe the student should know.

You will find that some of the problems described are familiar to you, particularly to those of you who have worked for pay. Few, if any, problems will be covered that are totally lacking in interest to you. You will possibly wish to project yourself into the situations and problems described. This is good. When we discuss the multiple roles of the supervisor, you are encouraged to picture yourself in his position and also in the role of worker. When executive-leadership problems are discussed, try to feel yourself in a position of having to make the right decision. Learn to look at advertisements within the framework of the psychology of influence, or consider what you would do about some strike situation you read about in the paper once you knew the real facts.

A Suggestion. The attitude one has as he reads a textbook strongly influences what he gets out of it. We suggest that you will get the most from this book if you ask yourself such questions as: How can learning about human behavior in industry apply to my personal experiences? How can I continue to learn about human behavior? How can I put to use what I will learn?

We suggest that when you sit down to read a chapter in the book, you first read the headings in order to get a rough idea of the organization of the chapter. After this, you may find it of value to formulate a few questions to ask yourself before you settle down to careful reading. In the chapter on executive leadership and development, over one thousand articles and books were studied before the author started to write the chapter. You may speculate on the kinds of questions about leadership that have led to so many writings on the subject. No doubt your questions are much the same as those which others have asked and tried to get answers to. What are the requirements of a good leader? Do I have what it takes to be a leader? Seeking out the answers to such questions, many of which may not be found in the text, is a good way to get an education. Asking good questions even without finding answers contributes to one's thinking. We hope that this book will stimulate your interest in the behavior of people who work in industry and in other organizations.

This text is focused on the understanding of psychological principles and their use in making the kinds of decisions businessmen must make in working with people. It is designed to help you acquire some specific understandings, skills, and desires which will prepare you to learn to work with others with increasing consideration, understanding, and effectiveness.

Many of the subtleties of the relations between individuals, and between the individual and the organization, are what have been called *psychological contracts*. These are the unwritten expectations, reciprocal in nature, not formally covered in agreements. They are somewhat comparable to the expected behavior between student and professor. For the student, the psychological contract may mean respect for learning and wisdom; for the professor, an understanding of youthful desire for change. For the employer, the contract may mean respect for age and years of loyalty; for the employee, it may mean support of the company image. In the chapters to follow, you may wish to think of these kinds of relations. They are important for sensing human feelings and perceiving conflicts.

II.

INDUSTRIAL ENVIRONMENTS

2

The Structures of Organizations

B. von Haller Gilmer

Most people work for a living, and most people work for industrial organizations. All organizations are structured and for different purposes, ranging from the military, which is structured for fighting and for keeping the peace, to educational institutions formally organized to provide intellectual stimulation and informally structured to occasionally induce frustrations. Few organizations function with a primary purpose of satisfying human needs, and this applies particularly to industry. Although there is no such thing as a typical industry, it is possible to describe in a general way modern business firms and labor organizations so that the reader can see the essential nature of business enterprise in our economy and can come to understand the part played by the human element in developing, producing, and marketing industrial goods. Perhaps he may also begin to see what parts he can play as an individual in an organization.

THE MEANING OF INDUSTRY

Business enterprises are usually called firms or companies, and they may differ in size as much as the family grocery store on Main Street differs from the United States Steel Corporation, with mills in many cities, iron and coal mines in several countries, and hundreds of ore ships sailing the lakes and high seas. The company, large or small, is owned and controlled as a unit, however scattered its parts may be. The company is thus a business unit under some form of coordinated management. The independently owned grocery store is managed by the proprietor. He makes the fundamental policy decisions about his store, and this function the economists call entrepreneurship.

In large and more complex forms of business it is more difficult to determine the entrepreneur. For example, who runs the American Telephone and Telegraph business? The million stockholders? The board of directors? The president? The answer is that no single person or even group of people acts as the entrepreneur; the functions of the entrepreneur are performed by various individuals and groups through an intricate system of coordination. For example, the Dearborn plant of the Ford Motor Company is operated somewhat differently from the Kansas City plant, although both are largely controlled and coordinated by the general office. A plant, being a group of buildings with more or less fixed physical equipment, has a specific location, and this allows it to function with varying degrees of independence from some central authority.

This leads us into a consideration of the term "industry." Economists use the term to denote the producing of any commodity and the rendering of services. Farmer Fritz Streff is a part of the beef industry if he raises cattle, a part of the corn industry if he produces corn. Some corporations engage in many industries. General Motors, for example, is in the auto industry, the appliance industry, and many others. Westinghouse is involved with a wide range of diversification, from building huge generators to operating radio and television stations. The process of researching, developing, making, and distributing a commodity is industry, whether the commodity is a concrete thing, like an automobile, or something entirely different, like an insurance policy.

In the nineteenth century, manufacturing plants were relatively small, and communication between the owner and the workman was comparatively easy. The workman was skilled in all the jobs required for the manufacture of the product. The owner was frequently the president, the manager, and the superintendent of the company all rolled into one, and the worker reported directly to him. Many firms of this type still exist, and in rural areas it is not uncommon to find a single business enterprise influencing the entire community. In southwest Virginia, for example, the Draper Mercantile Company runs not only the socially centered general store, a garage, television-repair shop, three farms, and the town's water system, but its owner, Bill Gannaway, is on the county school board and a director in the local bank. He is the fifth-generation proprietor of this organization, the store being the oldest business firm in the county.

In the fifteen hundred or so different industries in the United States, made up of some five million separate firms, many small firms still exist, but the rapid trend toward consolidation and merger has for the most part made owner management a thing of the past.

Today companies such as General Electric, General Motors, and some of the aircraft and oil industries operate in divisions scattered throughout the nation and in some foreign countries. Each division may employ 10,000 men, and often each division is an industrial enterprise within itself. Yet each one operates in coordination with all other divisions toward a common purpose, and each one conforms to established overall policies. This situation brings about complex problems of organization in which the human element is an important consideration. A modern industry may be said to be structured in terms of a formal anatomy, represented graphically by the flow-chart description of chains of command, of authority, and of responsibility. But it may also be structured in terms of the less formal psychological climate in which the people work.

THE ANATOMY OF THE MODERN COMPANY

The administrative anatomy of a company is designed for the purpose of making decisions most effectively. Only in the smallest of firms are decisions made by a single individual. Ordinarily, even though the final responsibility for taking an action may rest on one particular person, there are usually formal and informal preparations made by a number of people which lead to the decision situation.

The decision-making process of converting policy into practice necessitates an administrative setup in which each division of a company is headed by someone who has both authority and responsibility for its supervision and control. Similarly each division may be broken down into a framework of departments with an operating head for each.

No two companies are identical. Company organizations vary not only in size but also in the character of the people making up the company. However, there are five principal types of administrative organizations into which most firms can be placed.

Line Organization. This is a very simple structure. Responsibility and control stem directly from general manager to superintendent to foremen to workers.

Line and Staff Organization. As companies get larger, they become more complex, and top executives can no longer be personally responsible for such different functions as research, engineering, testing, planning, distribution, public relations, and other activities requiring special training and experience.

In this type of organization executives and supervisors retain authority and control over activities in their particular departments. But this *line* function is aided by *staff* assistance from engineers, budget officers, and other specialists.

Functional Organization. This structure is an extension of the line and staff organization; here more attention is given to specialized skills, mainly at the supervisory or foreman level. One foreman may serve as the production boss to meet quotas, another as inspector, and a third may be responsible for maintenance. In this system the clear-cut lines of responsibility and authority of the line organization have been lost, but gains have been made in terms of getting more specialized work supervision.

Line and Functional Staff Organization. This type of organization gives the functional staff more responsibility and authority in consultation with the line organization in such specialized functions as inspection, purchasing, and shipping.

Line, Functional Staff, and Committee Organization. In order to facilitate communication involving decision making, some large companies construct a network of committees to work with the line and staff organization. In certain companies these committees are permanent and meet regularly. In others they are organized to serve a temporary function only.

One of the psychological problem areas of large organizations centers on staff-line conflicts. Porter and Lawler [32] report that whereas line and staff managers do not differ in attitudes with respect to such things as pay, staff people are frequently unhappy because they lack decision-making power. The staff manager, for instance, is expected to be particularly knowledgeable about his specialty, with a high degree of education, and to spend considerable time with a variety of types of executives; yet he has little opportunity to use his knowledge for decision making unless he usurps the authority of the line. The line manager, on the other hand, is expected to take advice on decisions for which he has responsibility, often from a younger man who has been with the company a shorter period of time. Just how the anatomy of the company is related to psychological problems we shall amplify later as we discuss how some structures of firms are changing. Line-staff relationships are different between the old-line production-oriented company and the company heavily involved in research and development (R&D).

THE ORGANIZATION CHART

The organization flow chart of a large corporation is presented in Figure 2.1. Here we see in the top-management section that the stockholders are represented by a board of directors under a chairman. Responsible to the board is the president, who is charged with the formation and supervision of the policies of the corporation. In some companies the rank of the board chairman and the president is the same; in some the chairman is superior in authority to the president. Most frequently, however, the president is the ranking working officer of the company. He in turn delegates to the treas-

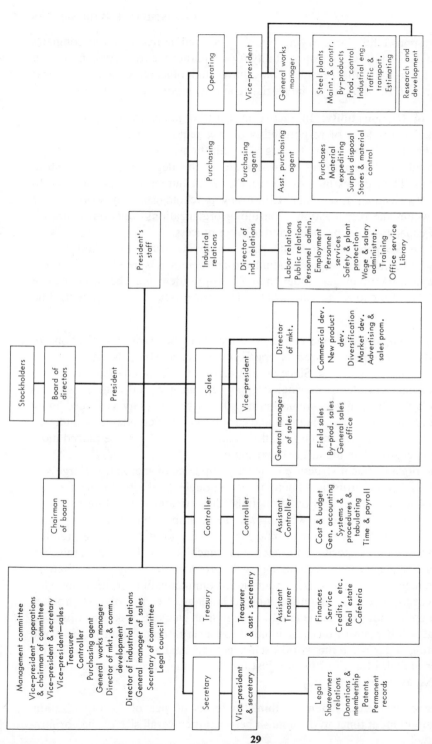

Fig. 2.1. This organization flow chart of a large steel-fabricating company indicates the chains of command and the lines of responsibility within the organization.

29

urer responsibility for carrying out the financial policies of the company and to the secretary the responsibility for corporate records. As can be seen from Figure 2.1, the president may have staff officers, such as the legal counsel and the director of industrial relations, reporting directly to him.

Lines of Responsibility. In theory at least, organizational structure demands that the lines of responsibility do not require too many men to report directly to one man. In large organizations, industrial psychologists employed by the company often operate in the department of industrial relations. Their duties may range from those of human-factors specialist to those of consumer researcher. Consulting psychologists may work at any level within the organization. Consulting organizations function in an advisory capacity to the president and to other officers.

In the company of moderate size, employing some two thousand or fewer personnel, the organizational structure is less spread out. For example, a works manager rather than a vice-president may be in control of such staff functions as industrial relations, product development, and purchasing.

Size of Company. As one comes to understand business organizations of different magnitudes it soon is apparent that each size has characteristic strengths and weaknesses. Since no one man in the large company can have the personal knowledge of what is going on and personal contact with his workers which an owner-manager has, the large company is forced more in the direction of coordination and group action. Personal ego interests, though always present in the so-called "company man," may be placed more in the background in the larger organization.

The organizational structure of most companies of medium or large size has an inherent problem. There is not enough flexibility to meet emergencies when perfect coordination fails. Supervision at the foreman level finds itself in a myriad of what appear to be impossible demands coming down from the top. There is insufficient flexibility to overcome the gremlins of distribution, material shortage, and machine breakdowns. However, modern management is attacking such problems with systems analysis, mathematical programming, automation, communication control, or what has recently been called information technology. Yet the biggest problem of the entire industrial scene involves the human element. Asks one observer, "What will happen to the individual? Most every organization in the world is getting larger while the world itself is getting smaller. . . . We will grow bigger and alas for all of us, not just for the young, facelessness will follow bigness, as the night, the day."

Size and Problems. When we think in terms of size of an organization, it is important at times to distinguish between the overall size of the corporation and the company's subunits, such as divisions or departments. In terms of overall size we can say that large companies have many technical and financial-resource advantages, more community and international prestige, and offer self-fulfillment opportunities for a small number of people in the middle and upper levels of management. Bigness also has disadvantages— delay in decisions, ego-satisfaction problems for a large majority of people, and problems of bureaucratic power for the subordinate. There is evidence that productivity and profitability are lower in the large divisions of a company than in the small divisions and that workers in small work groups or departments are better satisfied than workers in large groups or departments. More absences and turnover are found among larger work groups, but the general belief that communication is better in the smaller organization is not necessarily true. Size is a variable in identifying and handling people problems, but it is important to specify whether we are talking about company size or the size of subunits. To fail to do so can lead to some beliefs contrary to facts [1, 6, 9, 11, 14, 43].

Where is the so-called "organization man"? Common belief would have one simply conclude that he is the exclusive product of the large company, but Porter [30] has found that many empirical studies show otherwise. In studies of more than seventeen hundred managers in companies of all sizes, administrative jobs in large firms are generally seen as being more challenging, more difficult, and more competitive than jobs in small firms. The personality traits of the organization man are seen as being in greater demand in small than in large companies. In large and small organizations there are many similar psychological problems. For the manager large companies seem to satisfy as wide a variety of psychological needs as do smaller firms. For the worker this may or may not be true. Job satisfaction depends on so many things other than size of the organization that we must look at the many variables related to organization structure and human behavior. The chapters to follow do this.

THE STRUCTURES OF LABOR UNIONS

Some people have the opinion that a labor union is something extraneous to the structure of industry. In actuality the labor union can be and, with all but the smaller industries, is as much a part of the total industrial structure as is engineering, accounting, or any of the other functions organized within a framework of management.

Importance of Labor Unions. Labor unions are important in our economy, in industry, in politics, and socially. Most of us become aware of the economic part played by organized labor when we see it exercising vast pressures on wages, hours, and working conditions. Within industry, the labor union is the power behind the worker in his daily grievances with the foreman. This important contact between labor and management rarely reaches public attention save in instances usually associated with publicized strikes. On the political front, organized labor is becoming more and more of a force in the selection of officeholders, both local and national. As lobbyists, its representatives are most effective. Socially, labor unions satisfy the need for belongingness of millions of industrial workers. Union organizations vary in size; very small unions may have only a dozen or so members, whereas, the AFL–CIO has several million. The number of local unions in the United States approximates sixty thousand.

Structure of the AFL–CIO Union. The organizational structure of a large union does not differ very much from the company flow chart. A close look at Figure 2.2 reveals that the AFL–CIO union is in some ways larger than the mammoth General Motors empire. The large national and international unions are primarily concerned with such broad policies as membership qualifications, area and trade jurisdiction, national politics, and the sort of industry-wide bargaining which we shall describe in detail in a later chapter on labor-management relations.

Local Unions. It is the locals of the larger unions and the small company unions which function on the important day-to-day basis with management. The local in any one plant or department usually has a fairly simple structure. It has a chairman, an executive board, stewards, and general members.

The offices of the local are held by regular plant employees who are elected by the members. Depending on the particular practices of any given local, complaints or grievances may be taken to the steward, the executive committee, or its chairman. Since all the officers are working in the shops, they have direct contact with their fellow workers and often have a feel for the problems.

The Shop Steward. As a general rule the shop steward, or committeeman, as the union's representative in each shop or department of the plant is called, acts as the contact point between the members and the higher union leadership as well as the intermediary on complaints with the foreman. When complaints or grievances cannot be ironed out at this level, the steward may take them to the next level of management supervision directly. If the problem has to be carried to a higher level, the union executive board usually takes over.

Contact with Management. Administratively, the union serves as a link between management and the workers at three levels: (1) at the *com-*

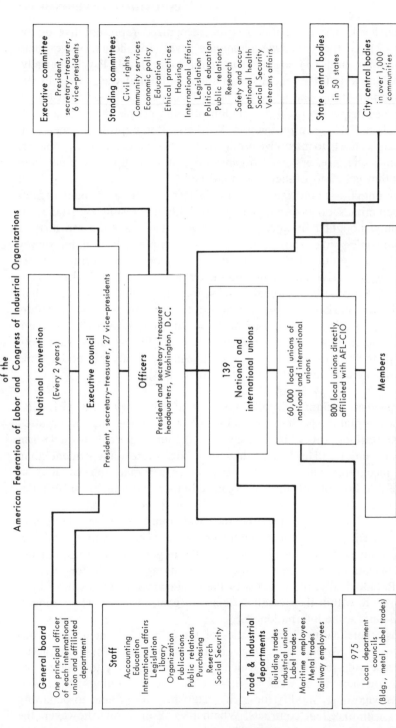

Structural Organization
of the
American Federation of Labor and Congress of Industrial Organizations

Executive committee
President, secretary-treasurer, 6 vice-presidents

Standing committees
Civil rights
Community services
Economic policy
Education
Ethical practices
Housing
International affairs
Legislation
Political education
Public relations
Research
Safety and occupational health
Social Security
Veterans affairs

State central bodies
in 50 states

City central bodies
in over 1,000 communities

National convention
(Every 2 years)

Executive council
President, secretary-treasurer, 27 vice-presidents

Officers
President and secretary-treasurer headquarters, Washington, D.C.

139 National and international unions

60,000 local unions of national and international unions

800 local unions directly affiliated with AFL-CIO

Members

General board
One principal officer of each international union and affiliated department

Staff
Accounting
Education
International affairs
Legislation
Library
Organization
Publications
Public relations
Purchasing
Research
Social Security

Trade & Industrial departments
Building trades
Industrial union
Label trades
Maritime employees
Metal trades
Railway employees

975 Local department councils
(Bldg., metal, label trades)

Fig. 2.2. The organizational structure of the AFL-CIO is similar to the company flow chart. This vast union is, however, much larger than any one corporation. It also operates differently in some respects from the company organization. (Courtesy AFL-CIO.)

33

munication level, where the union is the recognized representative of the workers; (2) at the *collective-bargaining* level, for hours, wages, and similar benefits; and (3) at the *worker-grievance* level. Psychologically, the union functions for its members in some additional ways. It gives the men recognition status and some feeling of belonging to a powerful group. Unionism has helped to break the notion of some people that workers are merely tools to be used in production. Workers often express the view that management's efforts to maximize profits ignores the men and their problems. The union is the workers' own organization, at least up to a point, and through it they get many of their needs satisfied.

Popular opinions about labor unions, just as with management organizations, sometimes do not completely jibe with the results of studies. It is commonly thought that workers rank wages at or near the top in their desires, but some studies show otherwise. For example, a local union survey at Ford in the middle 1960s showed that among fifteen critical issues workers ranked early retirement and better pensions first, higher wages thirteenth. Even paid coffee-break rest periods are included in nearly half of the collective-bargaining agreements negotiated in the sixties. And Purcell, in a large study involving the meat industry, has shown that unlike a few labor and management leaders, the rank-and-file workers want both their company and union to coexist. Dual allegiance *is* possible under some conditions, concludes this industrial psychologist [33].

The Independent Unions. Not all unions are affiliated with the AFL–CIO or with the internationals. Shostak [37] studied forty of these often forgotten labor organizations, thirty-six blue-collar and four white-collar single-firm independent unions. He found that they are more independent than generally recognized and that they have shown a remarkable capacity to survive despite hostility of most of organized labor and indifferent attitudes of employers.

Each of the forty organizations studied was found in varying degrees to be person-based, plant-oriented, employer-centered, conservative, and ideologically motivated. All this in contrast to the larger (and more powerful) union organizations, but these smaller organizations had a history of persistence. Paradoxically, the weakest of these independent unions have been the most secure within the overall system of organized labor. The strongest were good bait for the internationals.

The basic personality characteristics of these independent unions, concludes Shostak, have both advantages and disadvantages. These characteristics cover a wide range. Those which adhere most closely to keeping the *status quo* are likely to be weak agents in collective bargaining. The unions which most vigorously modify these characteristics were found to be strong bargainers with excellent contracts. Whether weak or strong, however, the single-firm unions still display personality characteristics which mark them as quite different from all other North American labor organizations.

Growth of a Union Local. One way we can see how psychology is related to a labor organization is to take a look at the growth of one union local. Following World War II, the building industry expanded enormously. For the men of Operating Engineers, Local No. 3 (AFL–CIO), San Francisco, it meant a growth from fifteen hundred members in 1945 to over thirty thousand in 1965. The members of Local 3 were at the very point of an expansion explosion. They skinned the cats and ran the rubber; they manned the blades and the pile drivers, the cranes and the shovels, the transits and the levels. They went from three to sixty-three business representatives, from one typed contract page to ninety pages, from a budget of a few hundred thousand dollars into several million. And problems expanded as Local 3 became involved with job-skill retraining and increased community responsibility. By the middle of the sixties, Local 3 was employing two consulting psychologists to help it with its own problems involved in the management of change, from leadership selection and supervisory training to setting up a road map for systems analysis.

THE INFORMAL ORGANIZATION

In the preceding sections we have discussed different formal organizations in industry. However, the flow charts and anatomic descriptions tell only part of the story of what life in industry is like. What of the difference between the way a company is actually managed and the way it is commonly described? In Figure 2.3 Stryker [38] gives an "insider's organization chart" showing some of the things which might happen to a formal organization chart if it were redrawn to reflect what *actually* goes on in a company. This company is hypothetical, but it is quite typical of the way many companies are run. Here the president is repeatedly asked to settle arguments among the manufacturing, purchasing, finance, and sales divisions, each of which wants its say on inventories. In this company, however, the most frequent conflicts occur between the people in line functions and those in the staff departments, such as engineering and marketing, who exercise authority over the line by virtue of their specialized knowledge.

Some Organizational Fictions. The managers of each department in this company are typically aggressive, and they pay scant attention to jurisdictional distinctions as defined on the formal organizational chart. For example, in this insider's organizational chart the authority of the industrial relations department completely overlaps that of the personnel department.

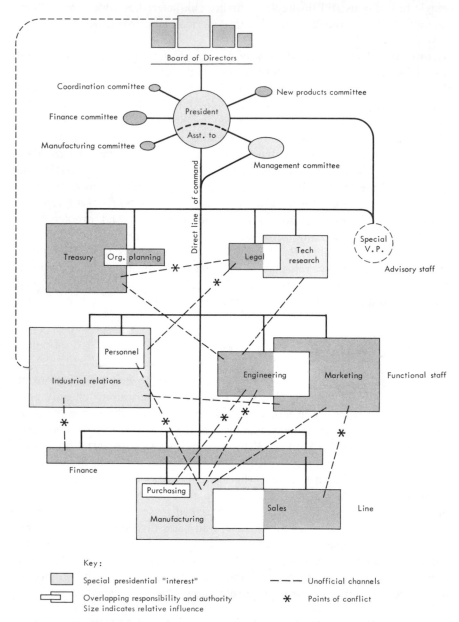

Key:

☐ Special presidential "interest"   --- Unofficial channels

▱ Overlapping responsibility and authority   ✳ Points of conflict
Size indicates relative influence

Fig. 2.3. This array of lines, squares, circles, lozenges, and rectangles demonstrates what might happen to an orthodox organization chart if it were redrawn to show what actually goes on in a company that needs organization planning. In this hypothetical company the president is repeatedly asked to settle arguments among the divisions. He is surrounded by committees, one of which is so

There are two reasons for this situation. First, the president shows an enthusiasm for industrial relations. Second, a dominant member of the board of directors makes much of labor relations in his public utterances. Similarly, the company's finance chief has so much influence with the president that his department cuts right across all decisions handed down the line of command. The dotted circle (upper right in Figure 2.3) symbolizes the post held by the fun-loving brother of the president, who is totally incapable of managerial functioning. The president is surrounded by committees, one so dominant that it not only advises him but can give orders down the line as well. His young assistant, in his confidential status, colors much of what the boss hears from the twelve executives who jealously insist on reporting directly to the chief.

Stryker makes the point that the statement that the president runs the company and is assisted by everyone under him is a fiction recognized by any manager who has experienced the politics and personalities of top management. The fiction is perpetuated in the formal organization chart whose neat little boxes and connecting lines strive to show who is running what and who reports to whom. The informal organization chart, which no one will dare to draw, is quite different; yet it is the hidden operating structure which gets the work done.

It is convenient to try to wrap up organizational structures into orderly packages. But often these straight lines connecting symmetrical boxes are nothing more than what one industrialist referred to as "the organizational chart we depart from." The stereotyped clichés expounded by some management organizations rarely fit the real situation. Compare a few of these with the insider's organization chart above:

1 Always define responsibilities clearly.
2 Always give authority along with responsibilities.
3 Never change a man's job responsibilities without informing all concerned.
4 Do not give the man more than one boss.
5 Do not give orders to another supervisor's subordinates.

---

dominant that it can give orders down the line as well as advice to him. His young "assistant to," in his confidential status, filters and colors much of what the boss hears. The dotted circle symbolizes the post held by the fun-loving brother of the president, who is ill equipped to handle managerial functions. A dominant board member, on the other hand, directly interferes in industrial relations. Note also the points of conflict between "line" functions, such as manufacturing, and "staff" departments, such as engineering and marketing. (Reprinted from the July, 1953, issue of *Fortune Magazine* by special permission; copyright 1953 by *Time*, Inc.)

6 Criticize subordinates only in private.

7 Settle promptly disputes over authority or responsibility.

8 Keep the man informed of his standing.

We do not wish to imply that formal organizations are valueless; far from it. We wish to stress the point that human behavior cannot be neatly put into a chart. Perhaps this is a good thing. At any rate, it is realistic.

The Organization's Social Structure. For better or worse the modern corporation has not only become the most efficient form for organizing large-scale production and distribution; it has virtually become a community within the community, manifesting a genuine social structure of its own.

The informal organization of the modern company has been called by various names: "the ropes," "the setup," "the system," or "our way of doing things." Basically it is a tissue of relationships which are never static and are revealed through symbols, subtle permissions, and taboos—the memo pad which reads "From the desk of . . . ," who sits with whom in the company dining room, whom you call by nickname, who has the key to the private washroom. One article introduces the problem of status hierarchies by this statement: "It is ambiguity of status and not over-emphasis that is most provoking—one has only to think of the subtle probing that goes on between two strangers in business to find out just where the other fits in."

STATUS HIERARCHIES IN INDUSTRY

An individual's status—who outranks whom—has long been a part of our culture. The GI is strongly conscious of status or rank because it is force-fully brought to his attention by the formalities of saluting and the clear-cut spelling out of what he can and can't do, including even certain restrictions placed on his family. It is certainly not customary for the wife of an en-listed man to associate with the wife of an officer in many situations.

The Nature of Status Differences. The tenet that all men are equal does not apply to military organizations, nor does it apply to industrial or-ganizations. As a matter of fact, it does not apply in the home, in the school, or in the community. Even in the most democratic of societies, status differences are found at every economic and social level. The lead-ing citizen in the political world may have much less status when he travels in financial circles. The lowly clerk may be Mr. Big on the public golf links. In many organizations, however, and particularly in industry, status position is more constant. The president of the company maintains his status position in the office and in the mill, at church and at the country club, whether or not he is a good golfer.

Within many business organizations, status not only is defined by the person's administrative rank but also is symbolized by rugs, pen sets, and other executive trappings. The visitor to the headquarters of a large modern corporation might well judge the relative importance of his vice-president acquaintance by whether he is taken to lunch in the executive dining room on the sixteenth floor or on the thirty-second floor.

Status Symbols and Need Satisfaction. Juggling for the perquisites of rank and the acquisition of status symbols is characteristic in many parts of modern industry. Certain needs of the executive are satisfied by attaining rank and status symbols. Often the little privileges that go with an office are more important to an executive than a raise in salary. Of course the men at the top get the best of everything in any case, so they do not have to play the game of "going one up on" the other fellow. The real struggle occurs among vice-presidents and those in middle management. One observer reports that a major crisis arose in a large company when it bought a new type of posture chair to test on a few of its executives. Those left out were so miserable that one man, to save face, bought a chair with his own money and smuggled it into the office. Another reporter tells of a group of foremen who walked out on their job until management agreed to provide them with a separate table in the workers' dining room adorned with a tablecloth and other appointments symbolizing their superior status.

One large corporation changed job titles and then made a study of the effects on the people involved. It was found, for example, that changing a title from "staff engineer" to "plant engineering associate" enhanced the status of the man involved. Other changes in a positive direction included changing the title "clerk" to "confidential clerk," "motor vehicle inspector" to "motor vehicle supervisor," "general plant employment supervisor" to "general plant personnel supervisor." When a title was changed from "draftsman" to "tracer," the study showed a loss rather than a gain in status. It was also found that even changing the name of the place where people worked was important. For example, employees preferred to say they worked "on the lower level" rather than "in the basement." Some workers prefer "incentive pay" to "piece rate." Even the word "company" often evokes a friendlier association than that of "corporation." However, some executives prefer to say that they work for a "corporation" because it sounds more prestigious. The word "company" sounds less harsh. The word "corporation" sounds harder and more powerful, and this is an association made by high-level leaders. It has been experimentally demonstrated in laboratory studies that people tend to match sounds with particular referents [19].

Upgrading job status is spreading. Says one psychologist ". . . the problem of household servants may be made better by new management and new status. The people who go into domestic service dislike having to deal with the middle-class housewife as a person and being subject to her directions. They prefer to work in teams, wear uniforms which help define their on-the-job roles, and to have an office through which the work is scheduled."

People themselves sometimes change their titles. It is, for example, common to hear real estate salesmen refer to themselves as "counselors." Even the United States Government is interested in semantics: the Post Office Department sends out notices on the use of words. For example, it is suggested that employees not refer to "junk mail," but rather speak of "advertising media."

Other semantic differences show "news analyst" carries higher status than "reporter." The word "salesman" gives way to "sales executive," and it is most common to find "engineer" applied to a variety of routine jobs. Caste-like social distinctions are found in many different places, for example, "officers and their ladies" versus "enlisted men and their wives," and in this technical age one may hear the accident of a space shot called an "engineering failure" as opposed to a "scientific success."

The struggle for status has been around a long time. The businessman's lunch has been traced back to 40 B.C., beginning when a Roman innkeeper served a special meal for ship brokers "too busy to return to their villas." This venture prospered early because, in part, the lunch symbolized success. Studies by the National Restaurant Association say that 69 per cent of corporate executives play host at a business luncheon from one to three times a week and 53 per cent are guests once or twice a week. And the symbols of success may completely reverse themselves in time. Overseas travel via jet airplane became a symbol for "the executive who had to save time." Three years later, as jet travel became commonplace, to go by ship was the thing to do; it gave the executive "time to think." The unlisted phone number, long a hallmark of distinction for the few, has become nearly as common as a credit card.

Status symbols certainly are not restricted to business. Consider the names of farms, the pictures of bulls and horses painted on doors of station wagons, large block letters on sweaters, fraternity pins on blouses, ornamental lodge pins, and colorful military ribbons. Even pregnancy is sometimes a status symbol for the middle-aged woman, says one physician. We all struggle for status, whether we are high or low in any given hierarchy. One observer found many more people will cross illegally against the light at a busy traffic corner when a prosperous-looking man leads the way than when the same man repeats the performance dressed like a bum. Status seeking appears to be a universal form of behavior which we must consider in our attempts to understand human relations in industry and to cope with the many manifestations of status anxiety. One writer commenting on hierarchy structures in colleges concluded that even in such an intellectually oriented environment it is impossible to escape the implications of status.

Professional people no doubt use words at times as much for their status value as for communication, and the manager does the same. Words have a way of becoming habitual, sometimes even hindering communication. No matter how carefully management may think it says it, workers often do not understand what the boss is trying to get across to them. One survey showed that only 12 per cent of the workers fully comprehend the average company house-organ.

Often terms that management uses mean little to the workers, but could be put in words that they can grasp. Some suggestions would include the use of "company earnings" for "company revenues," "sales tax" for "excise tax," "efficient production" for "productivity" and "interest you have to pay" instead of "discount rate." The worker may be unaffected by the word "strike" but become upset with "work stoppage," even as does the professor who feels someone is attacking his status when questions are raised about "academic freedom." One commentator has made the point that when men are released from some of the artificialities of a stratified society, great individual differences in performance will emerge, and may lead to peaks and valleys of status as dramatic as those produced by hereditary stratification.

Status and Structure. One kind of status in business comes as a result of the administrative structure in which one man is boss and the other is subordinate to him. This status relationship establishes differences in rank and designates the right (and often the obligation) to give orders. In another kind of status relationship the executive is deferred to by the worker, but he has no right to command the worker. The worker may step back and hold the door open for the manager, but the latter, as a general rule, has no right to demand such service unless the worker's job involves opening doors. A third kind of status relationship is found among men of equal rank. Here conflict often arises as the men compete for subtle indications of status dominance. One may observe this by watching two foremen vie for the attention of the superintendent; the one who gets told things first may feel himself more in the know and hence feel that he is in the position of more prestige.

Illogical Status Differences. Many of the status distinctions of our society do not make logical sense. The highly skilled master mechanic who works in the shop may be more important to the company than the clerk in the accounting office, and he may command much more pay. However, his status is generally considered inferior to that of the office worker. In effect, status hierarchy places the white-collar position above the blue-collar job, which in turn is higher than that of the day laborer.

The relationship between status and wages is sometimes paradoxical. The $10,000-a-year manager is expected to have a higher status than the $5,000-a-year man. On the other hand, the $15,000-a-year union official may not command the social status of either. Within the framework of most industries, however, status hierarchies are associated with wage gradations and job classifications, and the man who makes more money holds more status prestige.

Some aspects of status differences within a company make sense, and others do not. Most people would agree that the seniority of the older worker entitles him to a higher status than that held by a young worker even though the younger person may be more apt in his job than the man with the longer service. However, it can hardly be considered logical that the office boy who works in the research department has a higher status than the office boy who works in the engineering testing department. But in many instances he is made to feel superior. An even more illogical status differential has grown up in some industries where women doing the same work as men are regarded as inferior to them. In one plant a strike was called when women were placed beside men on an assembly line, doing the same kind of work. The men maintained that this lowered the status of the job.

STATUS AT DIFFERENT RANKS

One way to portray status hierarchies in industry is to describe in detail the work situation of men in different ranks. For comparative purposes we shall describe the job of the foreman, the department head, the superintendent, the vice-president, and the president of a mythical manufacturing company. This will be followed by a description of the status differentials within the labor-union structure, where the worker finds what little status he has.

The Foreman. The foreman is the first-line supervisor of the workers. In some companies he is definitely accepted as a part of management; in some he feels he is a part of labor. In other companies the foreman is in the awkward position of not being quite accepted by either management or labor. He spends a good part of the day on the floor, carrying out orders from above and seeing that work gets done. Though technically considered the first level of management, the foreman often feels that he really isn't in the know. At the same time, the foreman is not accepted as a worker. Rarely does he belong to the workers' union, and he must maintain a status position above those whom he supervises. His ability to maintain a distance from the workers and an identification with them at the same time is an indication of his degree of success as a foreman.

The foreman usually starts the day at his desk looking over the work orders. After he has done his turn around the shop, getting work started, he sometimes talks with neighboring foremen and with his department head about plans for the day and about yesterday's difficulties. Much of the foreman's time is taken up listening to problems and making decisions as he circulates among the workers. To the workers, the foreman is the boss. He judges their work, maintains discipline, enforces the rules, gives orders, listens to their troubles, and tries to maintain smooth relations with the shop steward (the workers' union spokesman).

The foreman often finds himself in a position so close to the work and the workers that he fails to get an overall view and becomes impatient with those in the hierarchies above him. He feels that many of the orders which come down from above are unreasonable, while at the same time he feels that the workers do not understand the company's problems. The foreman is usually as impatient with paper work as is the enlisted man in the army.

Of course, foremen differ widely in their personalities and attitudes. Some of them try to cover up for their men and their mistakes and resist putting in changes that upset established routine. Other foremen play the company-man role and are critical of the workers.

Management often claims that the foreman needs more training, particularly in the area of human relations. (The foreman's superiors often fail to tell him that what they mean by "human relations" is that he is to follow orders, get the work done, and keep the problems at a minimum.)

As the workers see him, the foreman is to represent their views to management and to protect them from excessive pressures from above. He is viewed as the vital first link in labor-management relations and is expected to know all the answers.

And what does the foreman think about his status? There seems to be one universal attitude: he feels that he never has enough authority to carry out his responsibilities.

The Department Head. The department head, or chief, as he is sometimes called, is unquestionably a part of management. His relationship to the workers is quite different from that of the foreman. Whereas the foreman deals directly with the workers in getting the job done, the department head uses the foreman as the buffer for his demands. In problems of discipline of the workers, failure to meet production quotas, or worker complaints, the department head centers his attention on the foreman. He thus avoids becoming involved in many energy-sapping frictions with the men, while at the same time he can play the role of the big boss.

The department head spends much of his time at his desk away from the work location. He reads reports, screens the type of information that should be passed up the line, and filters out the communications coming down which he feels should be passed along to the foreman. The head is in a position to know what is going on, since he spends a great deal of time in conferences with other department heads, with design and test engineers, with inspectors, and with other staff people. He has his ego boosted by showing VIPs through the department and by having his advice sought as a line officer.

The department head is actually too busy to find out firsthand what is going on in the shop. Hence he is quite dependent upon the foremen to keep him informed. This dependency is a club which the foremen may hold over the chief in order to get his cooperation when it is most needed. It is through the department head that foremen indirectly have a voice in the lower-level decision making.

The workers see just enough of the department head to know that he exists; hence they often let the foreman know that he, too, has a boss. The head can overrule the foreman, or he can make a decision without having to cope with its consequences. If the chief is friendly, the workers feel he is a last resort to hear serious complaints. If he is unfriendly, then the workmen feel that no one will listen to them directly, and they turn their complaints into formal channels through their union steward.

Psychologically, the department head is in an awkward position. He frequently does not possess as much formal education as the engineers with whom he works, but he is above the level of the foremen, the group from which he was most likely chosen for his present job. He is the last visible authority for the workers. He is consulted in some decisions and left out of others. Though primarily management-minded and officially a part of management, the department head is nevertheless in the quandary of not quite knowing just where he does stand. The brass decide at any given time whether or not he is to be included in making policy or procedural changes.

The Superintendent. The superintendent, or works manager, is in the top-management bracket. Psychologically, at least, he is quite far away from the actual work of the plant. He keeps in touch with its activities through conferences, reports from department heads, memos, and data sheets. In the larger companies the superintendent often functions under the vice-president in charge of manufacturing and so is the eyes and the ears for his boss, helping to make policy recommendations above the level of everyday details. He is in a status position which allows him to disagree with the ideas of vice-presidents (up to a point!) as he upholds the importance of getting the work turned out. The manufacturing super-intendent is often a case-hardened old-timer who has risen through the ranks from foreman. He may or may not have much formal education, but he knows the plant and as a consequence has good cause for feeling secure in his job. At the same time the superintendent sometimes shows defensive behavior in resisting changes suggested by the top brass. In some respects the superintendent holds a status position, at least in the plant, above that of vice-presidents, even though they outrank him.

The Vice-president. Vice-presidents are frequently in an awkward status position. They have often come into the company from outside or have come up through staff positions in sales, engineering, accounting, or some other specialty, and hence do not have a detailed knowledge of the opera-tions of the company as a whole. Vice-presidents sometimes hold the rank for public relations reasons (this is particularly true at the assistant-vice-president level) and are the attenders of meetings and luncheons. They are often active in community affairs. Vice-presidents, save those who merely hold the title for prestige reasons, are in policy-making positions and hence have much power. By the time a man has reached the level of vice-president, he "is high enough to be shot at," as one observer put it. He has status, but he has to continue the competition game to hold his power—a situation clearly portrayed in the novel *Executive Suite*. It is at the vice-president level, as well as at certain lower executive levels, that we find the man's industrial status carrying over into the community. He is named to important civic committees and to boards of directors, and he usually expends much energy in playing the role of the important man around town.

The President. "The most lonesome man in the organization" is one way this man has been described. He has status, and he possesses so many symbols of his status that he can afford not to flourish his rank for prestige purposes. Most presidents are professional managers and have attained their position because they have real ability and a strong constitution. The president is a lonesome man for several reasons. In the first place, he faces certain problems that only he can deal with. Not only does he have to steer his organization so that it will meet the ever-present problems of competition; also, he must keep abreast of the social, economic, and political changes that affect business. Second, the president has virtually no one of his own status who can listen to his complaints or share his frustrations. He cannot become too confidential with other people in the organization for fear of revealing some of his own weaknesses. He must

be very cautious of his statements because his every word may be interpreted as a commitment or policy indication. The new president soon finds
that his old vice-presidential acquaintances gradually begin seeing less and
less of him as he expands outward, as he attends more and more dinners
and business meetings. These outside contacts, which make it possible for
him to get to know other top executives in other companies, mean that he
has less time for his old friends.

Although the president's attention is focused outward, he still must keep
informed about how things are going within the company. Although he
receives information prepared especially for him and is given advice by
his staff, much of the problem solving is still his. With all that he has to do
to keep up with his many jobs and the demands placed on him by his
status as well as by the company shareholders, the president soon finds
his time and energy taxed to the limit.

Janney [17] asked 200 company presidents to look at themselves, and
they came up with many common problems, likes, and dislikes. Problems
centered on having to make that final decision, having to play a role as a
model for the rest of management, and being unable to afford the luxury of
competing with anyone else in the firm. In general, almost every man,
regardless of the size of his company, reported that he did not know what
it was to be president until after he had settled down into the job. On
the positive side, the job of president carries with it satisfaction of self-
realization; on the negative side, it brings the distaste of being treated
as an office instead of a person, and often as the symbolic whipping boy.
Opportunity to build, innovate, and receive the rewards of prestige and
income help to offset the intangibles of accomplishment.

As one president remarked, "When I was farther down in the hierarchy
I wanted more status. Now that I have it, I do not have time to recognize
it nor the energy to enjoy it."

STATUS WITHIN THE UNION

One mistake commonly made by the lay person is to believe that unions
are organized along the same lines as management. To be sure, the usual
structure of a union local presents a hierarchy made up of members,
stewards, executive board, and a chairman of the board; the organizational
chart of the large international union may look like that of any sizable
corporation. But the union functions quite differently.

Power-status Paradox. In the local union the hierarchy is not one of
authority where the steward is over the members, and the chairman is boss.
The chairman does not give orders or make decisions which can be forced

on those below him. Although the chairman of the local may have status in one way, he does not have power status as does the foreman, the department head, or the superintendent in management. The workers do not have to take orders from the officials of their local unions, and locals do not have to follow the dictates of any higher headquarters. The president of a large union, such as the AFL–CIO, and his executive board may have the official right to negotiate contracts and to function in many ways in collective bargaining. They may agree to a new contract with a company, and they may use all the prestige of their office to get the locals to agree to it; but they cannot guarantee that the union membership will accept it. One of the frustrating situations facing management in negotiating with a union is that it must work out agreements which not only satisfy the union officials but are also acceptable to the union membership. Although unions are becoming better organized, they still are rather loosely coordinated. It is not just window dressing when we hear that the larger international unions at times refer problems down to the lowest levels for decision. They have to.

Worker Status. It is through his identification with the union that the worker has status. It is through the union that he feels strength and has a means to fight power with power. Whereas the man in management possesses symbols of status represented by titles, executive dining rooms, and company airplanes, the union man identifies himself with the heroic figures of union movements and the folklore of struggle. He can express himself through such traditional songs as "I'm a Union Man." The union leader, regardless of his power and prestige, is never allowed to forget that he has risen to his position through his ability to get and maintain the support of his fellow union members. This is quite a contrast to the management executive who attains position through the approval of his superiors. We shall elaborate on this important point in a later chapter dealing with labor-management relations.

The Union Officers. When the union leader moves up from the local through regional and district offices into headquarters, he moves into a different world. While in the local, whether he was a steward or chairman of the executive board, he was still a worker, paid for his work. Union activities were extracurricular. As he moves up and his union activities demand full attention, the union officer goes entirely on the union payroll. In a psychological sense he has moved up above the rank and file and is no longer accepted as one of them. Consequently, even the most popular union leaders feel insecure when they lose touch with the boys in overalls. If a union official becomes too friendly with management, he jeopardizes his leadership role, unless at the same time he continues to make gains for the workers. Herein lies at least one basic cause of so much industrial conflict.

At most levels, union salaries are modest compared to executive jobs in industry, save at the very highest levels. (The salaries of the top officers of the AFL–CIO, for example, are above those of many top officers in business.) Men who work their way to the top of the union ladder and *hold their positions* are as much the executive type as any that may be found in high positions in industry. The rabble-rousing-organizer type rarely, if ever, reaches a high union position. But however skillful the top union official becomes socially, economically, or politically, the system which put him into his status position constantly reminds him that his power comes from the group.

ORGANIZATIONAL COMPLEXITY AND HUMAN RELATIONS

The administrative organization of most companies is in effect a more complicated structure in terms of the responsibilities of its leaders than we are accustomed to thinking. Men in management now supervise expenditures of money on a scale that would have financed ancient wars or supported large kingdoms. They must, at least to some extent, understand the design and operation of specialized equipment and the complexities of modern accounting procedures; they must understand something of the importance of product research, the mechanisms of mass production, and the basic assumptions underlying the marketing of manufactured goods. The modern manager should know at least the fundamental principles underlying personnel selection, training, the division of labor, and the apportioning of rewards. Modern management must provide storage facilities, utilize transportation, set prices, scrutinize credits, direct publicity, and energize salesmanship. Management must raise funds, market securities, account for values, watch costs, meet liabilities, pay dividends, and stand answerable to public opinion. The evolution of business has compelled the formulation of principles and the invention of administrative mechanisms to aid proprietors in the task of management. The aim of an administrative organization is to establish such a series of relationships between the individuals involved in an enterprise that joint action without conflict is possible in the accomplishment of a common task.

A Problem of Ego Identification. The preceding paragraph was paraphrased from a textbook on industrial organization published in 1925 [18]. The problems of administrative organization are even more complex today than they were three decades ago. Worthy, writing on organizational structure and employee morale, says that the most important and fundamental cause of poor management-employee relationships is overcomplexity of organizational structure [42].

In viewing many business enterprises, one cannot but be impressed by the number of different departments and sub-departments into which they are divided, and the extent to which the activities of both individuals and groups have been highly specialized. In a very large number of cases, employees perform only elementary, routine functions because jobs have been broken down "scientifically" into their most elementary components. The resulting specialization undoubtedly has certain advantages, such as requiring less skilled people, shorter training time, etc. In many cases, however, the process has been carried to such extremes that jobs have little inherent interest or challenge; operations have been reduced to the simplest possible repetitive level and the worker makes nothing he can identify as a product of his own skill.

To a large extent employees in industry today have been deprived of the sense of doing interesting, significant work. They often feel little responsibility for the work tasks they are assigned. Increasing supervisory pressure to maintain production often creates resistance. At times the workers show only passive resistance by failing to respond to pressure or by finding some means to avoid it. In strongly unionized companies, however, resistance takes a more active form; the employees band together to exert pressure against supervision and management. In short, one of the basic human relations problems in industry is establishing some ego identification with the end product of the work the individual performs.

TOWARD A GLOBAL VIEW OF HUMAN PROBLEMS

The behavioral scientist must function within a complex organizational setting. Before turning to the following chapters which detail what the psychologist in industry does, let us take a more global look at the types of human problems which face organizational leaders in industry.

Lest the reader get the impression that it is a form of weakness to be concerned about human relations, let him ponder a significant statement by an executive vice-president of a modern industrial corporation.

While I am very definitely *pro* human relations, I am also *pro* toughmindedness, making practical decisions, self-discipline, profit consciousness, high standards of performance, individual initiative, creative imagination, hiring able men, firing misfits, and above all getting results. What is more, I do not see any conflict between one and the other [36].

To understand organizational behavior one must recognize that it is a product of human sentiments, sometimes nonlogical, affected by personal hopes and aspirations, and complicated by customs and traditions.

It is a matter of record that orientation of leaders toward the understanding of human behavior will make cooperative action easier, bring about better understanding between people, and reduce human frustration and conflict. Understanding human behavior has been shown in organization after organization to be the essential force in promoting group purposes without bringing about a loss of personal identity. In short, establishing effective human relations promotes not conformity, but individual integrity; not happiness, but the right to work out one's own salvation.

Elements of Effective Human Relations. What are the basic elements necessary for the establishment of effective human relations in industry? Schoen [36] lists ten aspects of behavior which the effective industrial leader has learned to be concerned with in everyday practical situations:

1 An underlying element of his approach to other people is an attempt to understand them; that is, he tends to accept people as they are.

2 He has an awareness of and sensitivity to differences between his outlook and another man's yet is able to maintain his own point of view in the face of such differences.

3 He has an ability to respond to and understand not only the logical content of what other people say but also the feelings and sentiments implied by their words and their behavior.

4 He has some awareness of his own nature and of the impact of his behavior on other people.

5 He understands clearly the nature of the social structure or social system of which he is a part.

6 He is realistic about the existence of a hierarchy of authority, responsibility, status, and position in his particular organization and is alert to how this hierarchy affects people's behavior, including his own.

7 In taking action in an organizational situation, he is able to predict (within limits) how the organization will respond.

8 In taking action, he makes use of those generalizations about social phenomena which he has constructed and tested by his own experience, and at the same time he continually watches for the unique elements in every concrete situation.

9 He realizes that human relations and its point of view are *not* concerned with making everyone happy or sugar-coating harsh reality.

10 He knows that human relations are *not,* and should not be equated in toto with, the job of management or executive leadership.

These ideas were written by a business executive in a business magazine. They cover, of course, only a small segment of what we regard as the subject area of industrial psychology. They are presented here to illustrate the point that the scientific and clinical approach to problems of human behavior is vitally important to modern industry. They are included also to show that the inherent problems of organizational complexities may be at least to a degree, better understood when we can spell out more about human nature.

ORGANIZATIONAL CHANGE AND THEORY

From the time of the fifteenth-century notebooks of Leonardo da Vinci, dealing with analyses of shoveling operations of workers, to modern-day automation, man has been concerned with the human consequences of technical change. The so-called "scientific management" movement, typically associated with Taylor and the Gilbreths in the early twentieth century, dealt with time-and-motion study [39, 13]. Their studies made attempts to specify, to standardize, and to improve the rules for performing routine clerical and production-line tasks. In this era industrial engineering came on the scene as more and more companies put into use the stop watch and employed various techniques for specifying job performance. Although it is subject to methodological limitations and not supported by some recent human-factors research and has only limited acceptance by organized labor, time-and-motion study is still used in many places to establish work rules and to provide a standard for setting up wage rates.

Traditional organizational theory, which described the layout of jobs and how workers should perform their tasks, largely ignored man's psychological life. The early scientific managers made the error of assuming that people on the job try to satisfy only one kind of need, physical need; they assumed that there is an automatic sharing of goals among members of the organization and that people try rationally to seek the best solution to a problem. These industrial engineers confused what people should do, as they saw it, with what they actually do. The principles of traditional organization theory do not resemble reality above easily programmed levels. To a large extent management creates its own unique set of human problems, from active resistance to the more subtle defensive behaviors, when it describes a given work flow and division of labor. Whereas the classical theorists, with their emphasis on chain of command and job specializations, placed emphasis on structure, the modern theorists have stressed structure less. One writer summed up the differences by saying that classical theorists talked about "organizations without people" while many modern theorists have talked about "people without organizations."

Though they are not yet fully developed, new ideas are coming into the picture which may help eliminate some problems while, no doubt, establishing other ones. These ideas come from mathematicians, engineers, computer technologists, psychologists, sociologists, economists, and other behavioral scientists. They deal with problems of social environments, of systems complexities, of informal organizations, of work groups, communication, and decision making. On the cutting edge of new researches, with some applications in industry, are the contributions of psychologists interested in mathematical models. There is some reopening of problems dealing with mental abilities, attitudes, and personality.

During the first two decades of this century, the influence of Taylorism brought about a shift in the position of the production worker. Instead of being completely independent, he was now being told the "what," the "how," and the "when" to do. Gradually organizations moved toward participative management, still leaving the worker in the position of having someone else plan for him. More recently, a third phase of organizational change has appeared, that of *information technology*. What will this new additive mean to organizations and to men?

Information technology is epitomized by the high-speed computer and represented by techniques like mathematical programming and methodologies like operations research. It is introducing a vast new array of variables in communication, systems of work flow, and people's jobs. With a growing acceleration in technology (it is estimated that about 90 per cent of all scientists and engineers since the beginning of time are alive today), what of these human problems? In the Athens of Pericles in the fifth century B.C. full-time intellectuals numbered about 1 for every 1500 people. In the United States today the ratio approximates 1 for every 200 persons.

Whereas scientific management concentrated on the hourly worker, taking much initiative from him, participative management aimed higher, giving increased status to the people in middle management. This had the effect of relegating the worker to an even lower position in the hierarchy. With the coming of information technology, and the many aspects of automation in general, it now appears that the man in middle management may himself be pushed down in importance, separating the production worker still farther from the rest of the organization. Even top management is more and more affected by automation; the top executive is being forced to do more "systems thinking." In effect the use of machines promises to allow fewer people to do more work, but in a way which will cause the worker to become "programmed" more than ever.

Management can and must work toward an integration between technology and organization by changing the technology, by changing the organization, and by introducing new mechanisms. Predictions of things to come take wide range. One behavioral scientist predicts that in factory and office the business organization is likely to become a highly automated man-machine system where perhaps the "automated" executive will have a great deal in common with the automated worker or clerk. He believes that human employment will become smaller relative to the total labor force in those kinds of occupations and activities in which automated devices have the greatest comparative advantage over human beings and that employment will become relatively greater in those occupations and activities in which automated devices have the least comparative advantage. Automation does not necessarily mean dehumanizing work, but it will probably mean fewer manual workers, more men in maintenance, with increasing numbers operating on professional levels. It may be that certain interpersonal relations in supervision will be reduced in importance. One engineer predicts that by "augmenting human intellect" the problem solving of executives, scientists, and other professional people will lead to increased capabilities in decision making, necessitating some new model of executive superstructure. If the computer takes over more of the routine of intellectual functions, man may have more time to devote to working on social problems. The future seems to be more than just an enlargement of the present.

Success in management in the not too distant future may well carry smaller rewards in ego satisfaction and in status than it now does. As the decision-making function becomes more computerized, there may be fewer outlets for man's creative drives, he may have more time on his hands, and he may have to look beyond the company for much of his need satisfaction. At least it seems safe to make the prediction that there will be no dearth of psychological problems for the individual, and most certainly there will be many changes in the psychological climates of organizations. The challenge of change may be identified as both threat and opportunity [5, 10, 40].

A New Additive—Organizational Psychology. Psychology in industry, both in theory and in practice, appears to be moving in the direction of including a new emphasis called organizational psychology. Basically, the human problems of governments, the military, and even the community are much the same as those of business organizations and unions. Much as traditional industrial psychology, with its emphasis on personnel problems, added social industrial psychology, then engineering psychology, it now appears to be absorbing organizational psychology. In tracing the history of applied organizational change in industry relative to psychology, Leavitt [22] points out that following World War II engineering psychology, clinical psychology, and social psychology joined forces in coming to the aid of the personnel man, the training director, and the general line manager. Gradually the classical industrial psychologists, allies of Taylorism and scientific management in the development of the measurement of abilities and in working on problems of job analysis and on noise and monotony, joined with the human relations psychologists. And these in turn joined with the game theorists, the operations researchers, and the computer people. Organizational psychology is allied to classical industrial psychology and to human relations psychology, but it differs from both of them in its greater concern with descriptive and experimental research, with emphasis on understanding organizations as well as improving them. We have now reached the stage of applying psychology in industry on an ever-broadening scale [23, 24].

Organizations are changing, and rapidly. On the one hand, they are influenced by the physical aspects of technology; on the other, they are influenced by a new look from behavioral scientists at the people problems. Here, says Gardner [12], a basic part of the problem is to achieve some measure of excellence in this society, "with all its beloved and exasperating clutter, with all of its exciting and debilitating confusion of standards, with all the stubborn problems that won't be solved and the equally stubborn ones that might be."

Industrial psychology, as it faces the effects of organizations on individual goals and individual perceptions of the environment, is becoming multidisciplinary. The operating procedures of any business or any other organization are closely related to the needs of people within the organization; at least there are those who think they should be.

Organizations and People—A Perspective. In projecting a vision of the future of organizational life pieced together by detecting certain trends of the past and certain changes in the present, Bennis [3] has set forth some of the conditions that he believes will influence organizational life in the next few decades. The environment will feature interdependence rather than competition, turbulent rather than steady enterprises, and large rather than small ones. Increased level of education and rate of mobility will bring about certain changes in the values people hold about work. Bennis predicts that there will be movement away from oversimplified clichés ("increasing profits," "raising productivity") toward goals having to do with more innovative and creative things and that there will be an increase in goal conflict, not unlike the dilemma found in universities today where there is conflict between the goal of teaching and the goal of research.

In terms of structure it is predicted that organizations will become adaptive, rapidly changing temporary systems functioning around problems to be solved by relative groups of strangers who represent a diverse set of skills. Leadership and influence will fall to those who seem most able to solve the problem rather than follow some set of role expectations. People will be differentiated, says Bennis, not according to rank or roles, but according to their particular skills and training. The individual may have to get his social satisfaction off the job or learn to develop quick and intense relationships on the job.

If one can predict from the volume of predictions about organizational change, it seems safe to say that for some individuals there will be a measure of agonizing indecision as to how to relate to psychological as well as to structural environmental changes. Some people may thrive on the efforts involved in coping with change.

SUGGESTIONS FOR SELECTIVE READING

Ad Hoc Committee. The triple revolution. *Adv. Age,* Apr. 6, 1964. (Reprint of 15 pages from Box 4068, Santa Barbara, Calif.) An overall view of human problems related to cybernetics, weaponry, and human rights written by people from many professions.

Adams, R. N., & Preiss, J. J. (Eds.) *Human organization research.* Homewood, Ill.: Dorsey, 1960. Methodology for the sophisticated reader.

Backstrom, C. H., & Hursh, G. D. *Survey research.* Evanston, Ill.: Northwestern University Press, 1963. Methods and techniques, from surveys to interviewing.

Bass, B. M. *Organizational psychology.* Boston: Allyn and Bacon, 1965. Work, communications, and conflict in industrial organizations.

Baulding, K. *The organizational revolution.* New York: Harper & Row, 1953. The emergence of the management consultant.

Bennis, W. G., et al. (Eds.) *The planning of change: Readings in the applied behavioral sciences.* New York: Holt, 1961. Shows how planned change is created, implemented, evaluated, and maintained.

Buckingham, W. *Automation: Its impact on business and people.* New York: Harper & Row, 1961. One picture of industrial change.

Bunting, J. R. *The hidden face of free enterprise.* New York: McGraw-Hill, 1964. Some thinking on the size and power of the large corporation.

Burns, T., & Stalker, G. M. *The management of innovation.* Chicago: Quadrangle Books, 1962. Impact and rate of change in the field of organizational theory.

Cornell, W. B. *Organization and management in industry and business.* New York: Ronald, 1958. A nonpsychological description of a modern company.

Cyert, R. M., & March, J. G. *A behavioral theory of the firm.* Englewood Cliffs, N.J.: Prentice-Hall, 1963. A sophisticated treatment of theory and procedures found in organizations.

Dahl, R. A., et al. (Eds.) *Social science research on business: Product and potential.* New York: Columbia, 1959. Applications of behavioral sciences in industry; readable to sophisticated.

Ginsberg, E. (Ed.) *Technology and social change.* New York: Columbia, 1964. Sophisticated papers on organizational change and theory.

Grimshaw, A., & Hennessey, J. W. (Eds.) *Organizational behavior: Cases and readings.* New York: McGraw-Hill, 1960. Decision-making problems at various levels of the industrial organization.

Haire, M. (Ed.) *Modern organizational theory.* New York: Wiley, 1959. Theories on objectives and decision making through sophisticated readings.

Haire, M. *Organization theory in industrial practice.* New York: Wiley, 1962. A provocative book on organizational theory.

Litterer, J. A. (Ed.) *Organizations: Structures and behavior.* New York: Wiley, 1963. A book of readings extending discussion of this chapter.

McGregor, D. *The human side of enterprise.* New York: McGraw-Hill, 1960. The classical versus the human relations approach in management of human resources—theory X versus theory Y.

March, J. G., & Simon, H. A. *Organizations.* New York: Wiley, 1958. A classic on the ways decisions are made; some chapters readable, others sophisticated.

Rubenstein, A. H., & Haberstroh, C. J. (Eds.) *Some theories of organization.* Homewood, Ill.: Dorsey, 1960. Selected readings on how people behave in organizations.

Schein, E. H. *Organizational psychology.* Englewood Cliffs, N.J.: Prentice-Hall, 1965. Intergroup relations in organizations.

Standard Oil Company of New Jersey. *Social science research reports.* New York: Author, Employee Relations Department, 30 Rockefeller Plaza, 1962, 1963, 1964, and 1965. Practical reports on selection, training, organizational practices, etc.

Strother, G. B. (Ed.) *Social science approaches to business behavior.* Homewood, Ill.: Dorsey, 1962. Researches affecting structures.

Superintendent of Documents. *United States Government Organizational Manual,* 1965–66. Washington: Government Printing Office, 1965. Handbook of Federal Government Organization. New edition each year.

Webb, W. B. (Ed.) *The profession of psychology.* New York: Holt, 1962. Some material on psychology in industry.

Wolf, W. B. (Ed.) *Management: Readings toward a general theory.* Belmont, Calif.: Wadsworth, 1964. For another view of organizational theory.

3

Psychological Climates of Organizations

B. von Haller Gilmer

Organizations differ not only in physical structure but also in the attitudes and behavior they elicit in people, and these differences are related to psychological structures. Some people like where they work and sometimes for the same environmental reasons that lead others to express dislike. Individual personalities and job requirements interact to produce a *climate* that can be significant to both the individual and to the organization.

Some people experience feelings of uncertainty upon going into a new environment, and there is good reason to believe that the failure of many people to adjust to the industrial scene is due to the fact that they do not know the nature of the climate they are getting into. On the other hand, many people who find success in industry attribute it, in great part, to an early discovery of what the industrial environment consists of. In this chapter, we shall extend the description of the nature of organizations to include the *psychological* structures. The professional literature is increasingly using such descriptive terms as "organizational culture," "psychological climate," and "company personality." By climate we mean *those characteristics that distinguish the organization from other organizations and that influence the behavior of people in the organization.* It is in effect what we react to—the whole context of stimulation and confusion where we work. Psychological, or organizational, climate affects not only the behavior of individuals but also how organizations themselves interact. For industrial psychology the postulate that behavior is a function of the interaction of the organism and the environment is relevant to problems in selection, training, job satisfaction, and mental health in general.

Among the questions of possible interest to the reader of this chapter are: What kinds of organizational climates have been studied? How can climates be measured? What effect does climate have on the individual?

EXAMPLES OF DIFFERING INDUSTRIAL CLIMATES

"Company personalities, like individual ones, do not fall readily into neatly ordered categories—each is unique in many ways." With these words Gellerman [29] in 1960 introduced the problem of psychological climates as seen by a professional industrial psychologist, thus giving modern emphasis to a very old problem which has been viewed by philosophers, playwrights, and novelists since the times of the early Greeks. We shall begin our presentation of the problem by giving examples of four types of company personalities described in Gellerman's book, *People, Problems, and Profits*. Although we do not have completely adequate ways of measuring organization personality, more and more behavioral scientists are becoming interested in this emerging specialty. The perplexities of a changing order demand that we seek at least some sample pictures of the social environmental influences on the individual in his work. The descriptions below are disguised, but they are all real, as are the others presented throughout the chapter.

A Paternal, Passive Company. A metropolitan transit company grew up with its city, and by the time it passed its hundredth birthday, it had long since been regarded as an established local institution—more like the public library or a hospital than like a private commercial enterprise. The company is ably but conservatively run and has a reputation for lifetime employment of its men.

Since it has already expanded about as much as it can be expected to, the company offers very slow advancement for its employees. Only death, disability, and retirement create vacancies for promotion. There is no mandatory retirement age. While the company has no trouble attracting qualified new employees, it tends to lose a heavy percentage of them before they have completed ten years of service. Unfortunately, the losses include many of the more promising younger men, who leave because they feel that is the only way to advance before they become old. They are easily replaced, but the caliber of seasoned young employees from whom future supervisors will have to be chosen is getting discernibly lower.

Over the years the employees are slowly splitting into two large camps—the older and the younger—with a relatively small group of younger veterans in between. The younger men complain that the "grandfathers" dominate employee committees and look after their own interests first.

A Paternal, Aggressive Company. An established manufacturer of woodworking tools entered the do-it-yourself market and acquired, for the first time in its history, a national sales force. Backed by a vigorous leadership and an imaginative sales policy, these men soon captured a substantial share of the hobby-tool market for the company. Management expects a lot of its men, but it also rewards them handsomely: in addition to liberal commissions, it awards surprise gifts and bonuses to salesmen who are doing very well. District, local, and national meetings are held regularly, in which top-level executives join the men in shirt-sleeve planning and review sessions.

Each salesman is carefully chosen, and management makes it clear that it considers its salesmen an elite corps—and it treats them accordingly. Men who start to flounder are given immediate help, and if the difficulty isn't cleared up after a reasonable period, they are quietly and unceremoniously replaced. Turnover is very low, and sales volume has risen steadily from year to year. "Every man on my team," boasts the national sales manager, "is a pro."

An Impersonal, Aggressive Company. It is interesting to compare the tool company described above with a firm in a closely related field—one that had a similar sales policy but a crucially different working atmosphere. This company made paints and varnishes, and it also went after the do-it-yourself market in a big way. Salesmen were chosen for their aggressive manner and were schooled in hard-sell tactics. District managers kept close tabs on their men and were instructed to keep the pressure on at all times.

Salesmen could (and did) make a great deal of money, but the personal touch was missing. Bonus checks arrived at their homes by mail without even a note from the home-office executives. The men seldom had contact with anyone in the company other than their immediate superior; once the initial training was over, the men who judged their performance did so from afar. Some men became demoralized by the absence of management interest and accepted jobs with other firms (sometimes at a financial loss).

The men who survived were a very hard-boiled breed—independent to a fault. Through them the company earned a reputation for relentless competitive pushing. Turnover was fairly high, but the company looked upon this as an effective winnowing-out process that corrected its hiring mistakes and gradually filled its ranks with hardy veterans who neither wanted nor needed management to take a personal interest in them.

Despite the similarity of the sales problems these companies faced, it is quite clear that a man who had done well in the tool firm would probably have been a misfit in the paint firm, and vice versa. (There were, in fact, a number of cases on record which substantiated this.) *Compatibility with the company personality is as much a requisite for success for employees as aptitude, experience, and other personal qualifications.*

An Impersonal, Passive Company. A large, diversified corporation in the consumer-products field had developed so many divisions that each, in effect, had a personality of its own. Nevertheless, the corporation exerted a central control over sales, production, and financial policy, so that the differences in working atmosphere between divisions were watered down and tended to revolve around purely local issues. The net effect of this centralized control was not a sameness in the divisions but a common denominator of apathy that underlay the differences.

One division, for example, was widely known for its research and development work, and attracted many brilliant young men to its laboratories. Here they could learn from outstanding scientists and experiment with elaborate equipment. But there was very little room for advancement, and even senior scientists were organized into task forces that devoted themselves to assigned problems only, rather than being free to follow the leads and hunches that were generated by their findings. Each team dealt with a fragment of a major project and did not follow it beyond the point it had been assigned to reach. It became commonplace for the majority of the younger scientists to leave the division after a few years. They were usually able to command high salaries, for the company had a reputation for giving excellent training. In fact, it was running a training program for other companies at its own expense—without knowing it.

Another division produced an item that was generally recognized as the top-quality product in its field. It was priced competitively with other brands. After World War II, competing items were brought out which did not match it in quality but were more appealingly packaged and more effectively promoted. The division's management people reacted to these challenges rather slowly, in part because they were lulled by the fact that their reputation for quality was as strong as ever even though their sales weren't. Among competitors, the word got around that they were asleep at the switch—too complacent to move quickly.

Gellerman listed five steps for analyzing the character of a company. First, identify the men in the organization whose attitudes count. Second, study these men and determine their goals, tactics, and blind spots. Third, analyze the economic challenges facing the company in terms of policy decisions. Fourth, review the company history, giving particular attention to the careers of its leaders. Fifth, integrate the total picture with the aim of extracting common denominators instead of adding up all the parts to get a sum.

PERSONALITIES WITHIN THE ORGANIZATION

The personality of a company, in many respects, is a composite of the varied behaviors of the people within it. This of course complicates, but at the same time gives meaning to, any analysis of organizational climates. In the English language alone, some eighteen thousand terms have been compiled that serve to distinguish people behaviorally, and there is no dearth of difficulties in coming to grips with the concept of personality. About a quarter of these terms cover such traits as aggressiveness, sociability, and introversions. Another quarter deal with the more transient behaviors, the temporary states or moods. Others among these descriptions relate to such evaluative judgments as "insignificant" or "worthy." Other words cover the descriptions of physique and capacities. And there have been numerous attempts to specify aggregates of individual traits. Historically we have Plato's "philosopher-kings," "guardians," and "workers"; Jung's "intro-extrovert" distinctions; and William James's "tender-minded" versus "tough-minded." We have had Riesman's analysis of the "inner-directed" and the "other-directed" and, more recently, the experimental work of Forehand and Guetzkow dealing with the "people-oriented" versus the "system-oriented" in bureaucratic organizations [26]. Brogden [10] has found a dichotomy between "practicality" and "idealism" which corresponds to the analysis given by James. The practical individual accepts business rules and customs as they are; the idealist is concerned with how things ought to be.

In an interdisciplinary analysis of organizations, how they grow, and how they exert their influence upon individuals who work in them, Presthus speaks of three general types of personalities in the average bureaucratic structure [60]. Found at or near the top of the organization pyramid are the "upward mobiles," who react positively to the large bureaucratic situation and succeed in it. The uncommitted majority in the organization are the "indifferents," who see their jobs as mere instruments to obtain off-work satisfactions. Then there is a small, perpetually disturbed minority composed of persons who can neither renounce their claims for status and power nor play the disciplined role to get them. The author states that these types are oversimplified and idealized but useful in better understanding organizations and people.

While one may not wish to rigidly place people in pigeonholes, their behaviors do differ in *pointing in directions* that can lead to the assumption that the large organization provides a more sympathetic workplace for the upward mobile (who is less critical of some of those values that lead to success) than for the type of person who wishes to escape through indifference or the person who wishes to contest the *status quo*. We shall give some generalized descriptions of these three personality types, possibly not quite adequate in describing any one individual. It might be well, also, to keep in mind that there are perhaps individuals who combine some of the characteristics of all three types. One person may play an upward-mobile role to reach a position of relative security where he can afford to be indifferent to the job yet induce change by indirect means.

Many researchers say that both upward mobility and indifference are functions of class and education as well as personality and that attitudes toward pyramid climbing are complex and contradictory. Many of the writers referred to in later chapters stress the importance of seeking compatibility between individual and organization in spite of our difficulties in coming to grips with the concept of personality. Within this frame of reference we give the following brief descriptions.

Upward Mobiles. These people have tendencies toward high job satisfaction and identify strongly with the organization. Typically they get a disproportionate share of the organization's rewards in power, income, and ego reinforcement. A lack of success is more likely to be interpreted by them as personal failure than as system failure. The upward mobile is an organization man, a conformist who can act without much self-analysis. He plays at human relations as a career utility, is sensitive to feedback, and behaves accordingly. This driving type thinks in strategic terms and will use ritualistic behavior to conceal resentments.

The upward mobile is rule- and procedure-oriented and often views individuals in detached terms. He places personal advancement before group acceptance, feels little sense of conflict, and goes in heavily for the paraphernalia of organizations. His interests and aspirations are tied to the organization so much that he finds little difficulty in rationalizing organizational claims. Often he lacks broad or national perspective on problems.

Indifferents. The great mass of wage and salary employees comes within the category of the indifferents who withdraw from system participation when possible. In one sense they sometimes regard organizations, especially large ones, as planned systems of frustration. Compared to the upward mobiles, they do not compete strongly for rewards. Since this is a typical pattern of the majority in an organization, the upward mobiles get more chance to operate. In effect, then, the indifferent shares in neither the ownership and profits nor the ego involvements of the organization. He must therefore seek off-the-job satisfaction and reject the values of success and power, paying lip service to the system only when he has to.

Many indifferents, both blue-collar and white-collar, pay lip service to mobility but transfer their expectations to their children. They "expect less" and, therefore, may be "less disappointed." Status anxiety, success striving, and self-discipline, which are characteristic of the upward mobile, are rejected by the indifferent. After he puts in his required hours of work, he jealously guards the remaining time as his, because he separates his work from his personal life.

It is noticeable in the mass-production type of industry that the indifferent may depreciate the things he makes. ("If people only knew how shabby those things are they wouldn't buy them.") He has become conditioned not to expect much from the organization and not to identify strongly with it. This may be related to the fact that he gradually becomes immune to discipline and seeks to identify himself with his immediate work companions. Labor economists say this attitude allows the small group to play a protective role and thus, through the union, shields this man from the real or imaginary threats from management.

Sometimes, as his organization changes, the formally upward-mobile person shifts to a role of indifference. This is related in some respects to the middle-age revolt. The man may reject advancement because of the added responsibility it entails. The indifferent frequently has generally satisfactory interpersonal relations, since he is not perceived as a threat by his colleagues. Even in his large union, the indifferent worker only helps provide numerical support for decisions made by others. For the indifferent person, blue-collar or white-collar, people, jobs, and organizations are not much different—he tends to adjust to each.

Ambivalents. These people are described as being both creative and anxious, and usually find themselves marginal, with somewhat limited career chances. They can neither reject the organization's promise of success and power nor play the varied roles required to compete for these. While upward-mobile anxiety is usually adaptive, the ambivalent tends toward the neurotic. While the upward mobile likes the *status quo* and the indifferent accepts it, the ambivalent wants to change it.

Intellectual interests of the ambivalent tend to run high, and he is frequently found with limited interpersonal facility. He is often subjective, withdrawn, or introverted, but may attack "the system" when sufficiently shaken up. The ambivalent honors theory and knowledge, and he has a high verbal skill. He is in no way system-oriented, even resisting bureaucratic rules and procedures. His career expectations are idealistic, often unrealistic, and he often finds himself unable to bargain effectively. Repeated frustration on the job tends to increase the *psychological distance* between the ambivalent individual and the organization.

The ambivalent rejects authority and cannot bring himself to believe that those who reach authoritative positions merit them in terms of talent, wisdom, and morality. This may be related to the finding that in a number of companies studied, there was no relationship found between intelligence and aptitude, on the one hand, and rank and salary, on the other.

Instead of playing a role, the ambivalent plays himself and consequently may be out of step with the system. He cannot conform to folkways, often rejects work-group values, and cannot condone the compromise people make in status seeking. Whereas the upward mobile is sustained by status rewards and expectations and the indifferent adjusts by limiting his aspirations, the ambivalent becomes disturbed. He may develop a compulsive interest in his work, not primarily for its intrinsic value, but as a means of obtaining sufficient recognition to set him off from the rank and file. The ambivalent is not good in practical decision making and in a sense is unsuited for the large organization in all but one respect—his critical function as an agent of change.

Personality Configurations. McMurry [50] interviewed some nine hundred banking and investment-house employees, two-thirds of whom were given tests of mental ability, interest, and values, and concluded that there is a functional relationship between the structured, routinized character of banking operations and organization and the personality configurations of most bank employees. Typically, banking offers security, slow advancement, limited opportunity for initiative and responsibility, and an emphasis upon status rewards rather than economic ones. Banks tend to attract people with high dependency needs.

One of the values of studies of personalities within organizations is that they point up a changing need for appropriate recruitment and selection procedures. McMurry concludes from his study that selective criteria can prove dysfunctional since such employees do not always meet the organization's needs of management succession on a promotion-from-within basis. Banks must come to recognize that employees of the "right type" are not going to keep them competitive in our changing economic climate. Banks must give up their status as an "institution," must recruit strong executive officers, supported by a creative staff, and must introduce more automation. And most important, concludes this investigator, banks must recognize that personnel policy is a *line* rather than a staff function.

Deutsch [19] found that company images affect recruiting. Sometimes the vague and quasi-fictitious reputations that companies acquire tend to attract disproportionately from certain applicant populations and to repel others. For example, conformism of the organization man. Many a business is not as overpowering nor as dreadful as it has been depicted. Some statements, however, carry more weight in memory than do statistics. "I came, I saw, I concurred." This remark omits the point that some people talk back and survive, even get promoted. In a research review of leadership and influence, Hollander [38] has shown how leaders can be conformers to group norms while also being innovators. What may be nonconforming to one member of a group may not be so to another.

VARIETIES OF ORGANIZATIONAL CLIMATES

In the paragraphs to follow we shall give several examples that show climates in a variety of organizations, ranging from the built-in conflicts found in some production plants to descriptions taken from studies of university climates.

Conflict between Staff and Line Officers. Within a large production-type organization, one climate common to many old-line companies is created by conflict between staff and line managerial officers. Economic competition, scientific advance, technological change, expansion, and the growth of the labor movement have caused rapid changes and resulting unstable conditions. Over the past four decades industry has had to call more and more on specialists to help with the problems of management. These specialists, including chemists, statisticians, lawyers, industrial relations officers, psychologists, accountants, and a great variety of engineers, are usually known as staff people. Their functions, for the most part, are quite necessary and deal with specialized problems. They also advise the line officers, who have authority over production and "get things done."

It has been assumed that efficiency will result from having staff experts advise busy administrators, but experience has shown there are real problems here of the people nature. The assumptions that staff specialists would be reasonably content to function without a measure of formal authority over production and that their suggestions for improvement of processes, their development of new products, and their techniques for control over production would be welcomed by line officers both require closer examination. In practice, staff-line cooperation varies a great deal and serves as an important dimension of the organizational climate. Often there is much conflict between industrial staff and line organizations. This is particularly true where there are age, education, and social differences between the two groups.

Dalton [17] has made an analysis of data dealing with staff-line tensions drawn from three industrial plants. These plants, which were in related industries, ranged in size from forty-five hundred to twenty thousand employees. The managerial groups numbered from two hundred to nearly one thousand. Dalton found three conditions basic to the staff-line struggles: (1) the conspicuous ambition and individualistic behavior among the staff officers; (2) the complication arising from efforts by the staff to justify its existence and to get acceptance of its contributions; and (3) the fact that incumbency of the higher staff officers was dependent on line approval.

As a group the staff personnel were ambitious, restless, individualistic, and concerned with getting rapid promotion, making the right impressions, and receiving individual recognition. The situation was further complicated by the fact that the staff officers were younger than the line officers. The latter disliked what they perceived as the younger men telling them what to do. In meetings the staff officers frequently had their ideas slighted or even treated with amusement by the line men.

These younger, less experienced staff officers had been selected because of their outstanding academic records. They had entered industry with the belief that they had much to contribute and that their efforts would win early recognition and rapid advancement. Certainly they had not considered that their contributions would be in any degree unwelcome. This naïveté was due to a lack of firsthand experience in industry and to the omission in their academic education of learning about the people type of problems.

The shifting and expedient arrangements between the staff and the line came as a shock to the unsophisticated staff man. He had entered industry prepared to engage in logical, well-formulated relations with the managerial hierarchy and to carry out precise, methodical functions for which his training had equipped him. He soon had to learn that his freedom of function was caught in a web of informal commitments, that his academic specialty was often not relevant to his job assignments, and that he would have to engage in a subtle game of selling his ideas and himself.

The usual reaction of the staff man to this climate is to look elsewhere for a job or find a niche for himself with some degree of security where he can work out his own status-increasing devices. Unable to move up vertically in the organization, the staff officer often moves in a direction of lateral expansion by increasing his personnel. A few, of course, gain satisfaction by switching from staff to line. The line officer reacts to this expansion and movement toward a line position as a direct threat to his own authority and security. The fact that top line officers determine promotions causes many subtle behaviors to develop among both line and staff officers currying favor from above. And, more recently, a new threat has been added to the scene with research and development operations increasing in importance. The line man resents the well-financed research programs now under the control of the staff people.

In contrast to the descriptions above, there are some climates more favorable to staff-line cooperation. With the growth of highly technical kinds of production industries—electronics, technical instruments, space programs—new organization structures have evolved. Some of these industries began with staff specialists who later became line officers. In such a climate, the newly graduated engineer, with all of his ambition, restlessness, individualism, and naïveté, may find a more satisfying climate. In some of the evolving organizational structures, those with primary emphasis on R&D, staff personnel sometimes hold a dominating position over line officers, but conflict still remains as a built-in variable.

A Comparative Study of Technical Groups. The formulas around which organizations develop generally lead to some uniformity of organization structure in terms of operating procedures, records and reports, task-performance rules, and plans and planning rules. Thus we usually see, in a business organization, a division of work by function as well as a management hierarchy to assure the achievement of the objectives. Knowingly or unknowingly, however, management also imposes certain values and concepts about people. This, of course, is related to company climate. It is easy to find climate differences between companies that are in different kinds of businesses. But what about separate companies in the same line of business? Barnes [5] has made a study bearing on this question by comparing two engineering work groups in two different companies. We shall speak of these as department A and department B.

Department A is organized as a *closed system*, where there are little or no member autonomy, few opportunities for social interaction, and low upward influence by employees on management. Basically, top management sets the department values and goals in a highly structured manner. Department B is organized as an *open system*, where individual autonomy is encouraged, and social interactions are a part of the daily routine. There is a high degree of mutual influence between different levels of the organization. What of the differences found between these two psychological climates?

In department A, it was found, as predicted, that individual employees were very status-conscious and tended to cluster in groups of similar status and interests. This had the effect of bringing about high competition within the department, where small groups pursued different objectives. There was found an inverse relationship between job performance and job satisfaction. Those groups with the best performance had the lowest job satisfaction. Salary levels were related to such status indicators as education, age, and seniority.

In department B the climate was found to be different, as predicted. There were less concern from the engineers with status as such, generally higher job satisfaction, and greater concern by individuals with the overall objectives of the department. Salary was found to be related more to job performance and less to such factors as age and seniority.

Although it was difficult to compare the two departments directly, Barnes reports that "management and customer productivity expectations were better met in Department B than in Department A."

This study, comparable to others, shows that engineers are primarily professionally oriented. They identify more with their work than with the organization per se. Attempts on the part of management to overstress the business values of practicality and productivity meet with strong resistance. This resistance mounts rapidly and tends to persist, accompanied by low morale. It is suggested from this study that emphasis should be placed on engineering so that there will be a climate of mutual influence between the management and engineering values.

Interpersonal Relations—A Study of Competitiveness. In a different study of climates, we turn to office situations in two small sections of a public employment agency, situations involving interviewers. The interviewers received requests for workers over the phone. After they interviewed a given client, the files were searched for suitable vacancies. If an acceptable job was found, the interviewer referred the client to it and later phoned the employer to determine whether the client had been hired.

"The statistics which show how many interviews and how many placements each person in the section did are passed around to all interviewers.

Of course, you look at them and see how you compare with others. This creates a competitive spirit," said one of the interviewers. In a period of job shortages, competition took the form of trying to utilize job openings before anyone else did. Interviewers were so anxious to make placements they even resorted to illicit methods.

Within this type of setting Blau [9] found two diverse sections which he could study for cooperation and competition. Section A was highly competitive. Hoarding of jobs was an effective way to improve an interviewer's placement record. The members of section B were more cooperative. When they learned about interesting vacancies, they often told one another. Any interviewer who manifested competitive tendencies was excluded from the network of reciprocal information and lost the respect of his coworkers.

Within this setting, a comparison of the two groups of interviewers revealed that the more competitive group was *less* productive, whereas the more competitive individuals in the competitive group were relatively *more* productive. Anxiety over production and the consequent competitive practices interfered with efficient performance in section A. In section B, by contrast, conditions gave rise to cooperative norms which fostered friendly personal relations. This group was found to be more productive and to have more cohesiveness, accompanied by a reduced anxiety.

Blau found that in the absence of social cohesiveness, competitive striving for outstanding performance was an alternative way of relieving anxiety over status. This study exemplifies the occasionally found apparent paradox that competitiveness and productivity may be *inversely* related for *groups* but *directly* related for *individuals* in the competitive group.

Hotel Climates. One of the common ways in which differences in psychological climates can be observed is by comparing hotels and individual reactions to them. One person may like a hotel because it is "sophisticated"; another may dislike it for the same reason. Tour agencies have long been aware of the importance of matching individuals with appropriate accommodations suitable to their status, demands, and pocketbooks. One worldwide travel agency which has recorded the climates of hotels for over half a century concludes that environments vary along such dimensions as size, local culture, economic competition, sensitivity to criticism, sophistication of clients, attitude toward tourists, and the current pattern of acceptability.

Architecture has changed along with customs. Thus, thirty years ago top-class American hotels were stately, even if slightly too ornate; today they have given ground to "Hiltonization." The chauffeurs' waiting room has given way to a drive-yourself rental agency. The success of a modern American hotel depends more on a judicious use of space than on luxury. Reading rooms, writing rooms, and tearooms have passed on, casualties of today's living and today's economics.

University Climates. Colleges and universities have climates, as most students, alumni, and professors know, and the climates of many of these institutions have changed markedly in the past decade. They have changed in some measure because of the large-scale financing (mostly for research) by tax-free foundations and by state and Federal governments. Increasing enrollment is having its effect, and so are efforts in the direction of the pursuit of excellence. The self-image of the university itself is changing and is now being studied on a wide scale. Individual research in the larger institutions is giving way to programs of research, and the aggressive academic man has moved in to run the show. We now have vice-presidents of research, development professionals, and other entrepreneur types. Major rewards tend to go to people who are skillful at playing the game of "grantsmanship." Sometimes only lip service is given to teaching, with occasional pellets being passed out to quiet those stubborn individualists who believe that undergraduate instruction is still a vital part of the academic organization. In large universities, size and urbanization often encourage indifference among faculty members and students alike [1, 12, 14, 41, 45].

On the student level much attention is being given to personality factors on the college campus. Studies are being made to consider ways in which faculty members can have more effective contact with students and how larger colleges may be broken down into smaller units where peer-group influence can be enhanced and where teachers and students can find a give-and-take climate less dominated by judicial robes. And descriptive studies of college climates are expanding rapidly. Some of the more sophisticated industrial recruiting people are becoming interested in these climates in their attempts to match people better with jobs [54, 63].

Student Subcultures. The most widely held stereotype of college life pictures the "collegiate culture" as a world of football, fraternities and sororities, dates, cars, and campus fun. In content, this system of values and activities is not hostile to the college, to which, in fact, it generates strong loyalties and attachments. It is, however, indifferent and resistant to the serious demands of the faculty. Part-time work, intense vocational interests, an urban location, and commuter students all work against the full flowering of this collegiate subculture, as do student aspirations for graduate or professional school and the more serious interests on the part of students and faculty.

Economic pressures on the students, combined with their serious interests, help define the "vocational culture" found often in the urban colleges which recruit the ambitious, mobility-oriented persons who do not have the time or money to go collegiate. These students have very little attachment to the college, which is just an adjunct to the world of jobs. To some of these hard-driven students, ideas and scholarship may be as much a luxury as sports and fraternities.

Present on every college campus, although dominant on some while marginal and almost invisible on others, is the wonderful subculture of serious students, the "academic culture." Where the collegiates pursue fun and the job-oriented seek skills, these students seek knowledge. Their symbols are the library, laboratory, and seminar. These students are often oriented toward vocations; they are seriously involved in their course work beyond the minimum required for passing and graduation. These academic-minded students do identify themselves with their college, particularly with its faculty.

And then there is the "nonconformist culture." Students in this group are often deeply involved with ideas, both the ideas they encounter in the classroom and those that are current in the underrealm of art, literature, and politics. They seek to be different. Some are phonies. To a greater degree than their academically oriented classmates, these nonconformists use off-campus groups and currents of thought as points of reference over against the official college culture in developing strategies for independence, criticism, and no doubt, in some cases, getting attention. In the aggressive nonconformists there exist a critical detachment from the college they attend and its faculty and a generalized hostility to the college administration. The precise form this style takes varies from campus to campus, but where it exists it has a visibility and influence far beyond its usually small membership. The nonconformist may seek as his or her status symbol some distinctive style of dress, speech, and attitude [63, 68].

SOME INDICATORS OF CLIMATE

Organizational climates, to some extent, may be indicated by the physical environment. No doubt some change in banking institutions toward a feeling of friendliness and informality was instituted a few years ago with the removal of barred teller cages and armed guards. To some extent the prepared speeches of officers, the reports to stockholders, and national advertising may give some indications of company personality. But for the most part a combination of certain little indicators within the organization may reveal as much about the true nature of a company as the direct and indirect releases from formal reports and public relations. These little indicators may vary greatly; any one may be found in some organizations, absent in others. They can number in the hundreds. Some are positive, and others are negative. Here we shall describe a common one, the office memo. The particular memorandum quoted is not presented because it is typical of the several hundred we have in our files; as a matter of fact, it is not.

It is presented here because it represents a contrast to the more positive supervisory climates to be described in the chapter on human relations in industry.

An Office Memo. The memorandum quoted below is from the general supervisor of a large manufacturing company to office personnel in the production section. It is presented here without editing, save for the deletion of an introductory paragraph and one name.

1 Tardiness in the morning or at noon is unexcused absence and is to be made up or the offending individual's pay will be docked.

2 Work is to start promptly on time. Reading of newspapers, magazines, etc. is not to carry over into working hours.

3 Work is to end at the established quitting time, not five (5) minutes or more before that time. Employees are not to stand poised at their desk while they watch the clock.

4 Company policy dictates personal illness is excused. Other absence is unexcused and time is to be made up or the employee's pay will be docked. Absence may be excused at the option of the squad supervisor but such excuse will not be automatic for any flimsy reason. Exempt employees are expected to make up their lost time.

5 Non-business conversation is to be kept to a minimum. There is an excess of such at present.

6 Singing, whistling or humming is not considered necessary to production section work.

7 All newspapers and non-technical magazines are to be kept off tables or desks during working hours. This does not mean they are to be kept or read in the rest room.

8 "Pools" are not condoned by the company since time is wasted in preparation, determination of winner, and lengthy discussions.

9 There is no "coffee break" either official or unofficial.

This is a business office operated for profit. Such profit—or lack of it—directly affects each individual. Men working for a living should act like grown, responsible individuals. Those few who do not bring restrictions and reprimands to all.

Management asks and expects efficiency to improve. A stricter work policy is being instituted. Those who will not, or do not want to work under such policy, may discuss the subject with the writer.

The Image. Quite often the public view of a company is presented by the men at the top, and for the most part favorably. However, since the early days of big business, some top executives have shown an inability to influence or even to help mold a favorable corporate image. Even lack of skill in facing television cameras and inquiring reporters on the part of a ranking officer of a large corporation may have its negative influence on the image so carefully built up over the years by public relations.

The top executive is necessarily a generalist, with little specific *expertise* in many disciplines on which he must rely. His time for communication in detail is limited. He gets reports and news in digest, prepared especially for him and often filtered. Within this climate the executive may well soon get out of touch. And when this brand of isolation filters farther and farther down the line, as it may well do, cloistered climates can become established even inadvertently, in spite of attempts at appropriate image making.

Interesting as the descriptive aspects of organizational climates may be, analysis must go deeper. We need to know more about the organization as a complex system in which *task* variables (production of goods and services), *structural* variables (systems of authority), *technological* variables (drill presses and computers), and *people* variables interact. Some indication of this interaction can come through taking a look at the problems of measuring climate and determining its dimensions.

MEASUREMENT OF ORGANIZATIONAL VARIATION

The measurement of organizational climate is similar in some respects to the measurement of individual personality. At one level of information we have *informal descriptions,* which involve personal accounts (at times perhaps biased) of the activities of organizations taken from observations of conferences, records, correspondence, memos, and even interpretations based on such things as locks placed on office telephones. Descriptions are sometimes wrapped up in such closure words as "democratic," "authoritarian," "conservative," and "noncommunicative." Such *field studies* of the actual, ongoing activities of organizations help provide both the keen observer and the researcher with the feel of the climate studies. On the one hand, we have had studies examining behavior in contrasting organizations, such as the open and closed authority systems described above (see page 67). A second approach has involved investigation of organizational correlates of observed differences in behavior in two firms with marked differences in the degree of personal autonomy of their members. Dill [20] found, for example, that it is quite possible to measure differences in the way information from external sources is handled when dealing with suppliers, customers, and competitors, as opposed to the handling of internal restraints which are self-imposed. One firm may stress the use of formal rules and procedures; another may be less formal in its business-operating procedures. In one firm the observer may find extensive top-management involvement in routine activities that are completely delegated in another firm.

Another level of information involves systematically selected *perceptions of people* in the organization. Any given number of participants may perceive the climate differently in terms of how they accept or reject rules and regulations and how they view the general social environment. Likert [48], in describing what he calls the new patterns of management, shows that the way the individual perceives his company and the roles he plays in it is important. He finds it is possible to measure climate indirectly via the perceptions of the individuals whose behavior is being studied. Much has been learned by studying such perceptually based measures as rule-centered and group-centered behavior. Scales have been developed to provide indices of climates.

Objective indices of climate have covered a wide range of variables, from size and profit-sharing plans to union representations to facts on absenteeism, accident rates, and productivity. Just as we put together, with varying degrees of success, the traits of an individual and come up with some personality description, we attempt to get at the total integration of the company. And as in the measurement of the individual, the accuracy of measurement of company personality is related to the sophistication of the examiner and his instruments.

Evan [23], for example, has approached the problem of measurement in terms of hierarchies of skills, rewards, and authority in organizations. Found important to understanding climate differences are such things as ratio of higher-level supervisors to foreman, number of levels of authority from top management to workers, and the ratio of administrative to production personnel. Another approach has made use of statistical techniques in the analysis of organizational properties. Katzell *et al.* [44] studied five situational characteristics of seventy-two wholesale-warehousing divisions of a firm and found it possible to utilize for climate study such variables as size of work force, city size, wage rate, unionization, and percentage of male employees. Palmer [56] analyzed such organization conditions as pension plans and such personal behaviors as lateness and turnover in 188 manufacturing firms and found these variables useful as objective indices of climate.

The *experimental manipulation of climate* in leadership style, in small-group behavior, in industrial human relations situations, and through simulations has offered various ways of creating climates for study. At the training level and the executive-development level, business games and other techniques are now including organizational-climate variables to be considered in decision-making procedures.

These and a wide variety of studies have led to several dimensions of climate possibly useful to the individual in his career thinking. Let us look at five primary dimensions of organizational climates.

DIMENSIONS OF ORGANIZATIONAL CLIMATES

In a sense, the study of industrial psychology itself is a study of psychological climates. Organizations react differently to hard times and to prosperity somewhat as individuals do. They differ in respect to the influences of geographical location, the way they face competition, and the way they meet contingencies. It is useful to try to compare companies according to their resources, growth potential, earnings, dividends, and other economic variables. It is also useful to compare companies along climate dimensions. Throughout the remainder of this text we shall talk from time to time about variables that go to make up climates. In order to set the stage for later discussion of individual needs and of the kinds of information we must obtain to better understand the industrial world, we shall talk about how companies vary in size and shape, leadership patterns, communication networks, goal directions, and decision-making procedures. These and possibly other dimensions interact to help determine the totality of a psychological climate. Just how they interact is not now completely understood, but several researches show these five dimensions to be important [31].

Size and Shape. One may easily appreciate the difference in size between the 160-acre farm and the vast million-acre spread of the King cattle ranch in Texas. But it may be more difficult to get the full impact of the fact that the Federal government employs more people in engineering than in typing jobs and that more and more people are going to work for the larger industries. In the past two decades the number of self-employed declined; during the same period the number of private wage and salary workers almost doubled, and the number of government workers increased more than twofold. The chief merit of the large organization, be it an industrial, governmental, or research bureaucracy, is its technical efficiency, with a premium on precision, speed, and control. Today, big corporations and the Federal government account for 70 per cent of all patents issued.

Haire [36] points out that as the business grows, the old face-to-face techniques are no longer adequate; new and different ones are required. Such things as the kinds of skill and the location of pools of skill within the organization, the decentralization of authority, and the development of new kinds of communication networks may change radically as the company grows. Often there is a tendency to perpetuate solutions that were successful in the past, "trying to solve tomorrow's problems with the techniques that worked yesterday." Size, of itself, is not necessarily harmful; however, the appearance of size has a seductive quality in that it may lead to the belief that the organization is strong and powerful just because it is big. Whereas the smaller organization may be able to maintain an agility and flexibility in adapting to changed conditions, the larger one may be handicapped in this respect, thus hindering some individuals within the organization.

The shape of the organization in some companies is changing from pyramidal—workers in the majority at the base—to hexagonal—where the blue-collar workers represented at the base about equal the number of men in the management teams at the top, and the majority portion includes large numbers of professional staff people. Certainly the vertical communication system of the old up-and-down pyramid is in for changes, no small part of the problem involving effective supervision and coordination of these highly individualistic staff professionals. Where bureaucracy is the end product of increased size and complexity and where the personality pattern of the bureaucrat is often centered on impersonality, one can easily see how conflict is going to be easy to arouse within the organization as well as with customers and the public.

Psychologically, size of the organization may be thought of as one dimension of organizational climates where the individual is treated more and more impersonally the larger the organization becomes. Yet, as we shall note in a later chapter, size alone does not determine job satisfactions, as important as it may be. The level at which a person finds himself in the organizational structure, be the organization large or small, is a most important variable, as is the size of the subunit in which the individual finds himself.

Leadership Patterns. After years of research, psychologists have concluded that there is no simple relationship between morale and productivity, in the office, the plant, or the laboratory. High job satisfaction does not necessarily mean high productivity. Much depends on other variables—types of incentives, supervision, hierarchy status, personal need achievement, occupational levels, and a host of others. We know well that good supervisory practices must be the concern of all levels of the organization. A local foreman will have some difficulty trying to exert a democratic type of leadership pattern where his bosses and the structure above him are autocratic. One plant superintendent, speaking before an assembly of lower supervisors gathered to take a course in human relations, passed out a set of specific rules telling the men how they were to become more permissive in their leadership roles. He concluded, with emphasis, "We will have good human relations in this plant even if I have to demote each of you." Certainly here is a situation where, to say the least, a democratically-oriented instructor may experience difficulty.

In a study of four managerial levels it was concluded that the leadership hierarchy, like any other social structure, has role differentiation. Each role player, whether he be a foreman or a top manager, contributes only a segment of the necessary conditions that will lead to organizational effectiveness. We seem to be heading toward a condition where leaders will be judged more on how well each performs his personal obligations and less on how well the organization as a whole performs. This may be one reason why industries are now laying so much emphasis on individual performance appraisal. It must be recognized that not every promising recruit is a potential member of top management. Some people will become outstanding leaders as foremen, as plant superintendents, or as professional specialists, but not necessarily in top management. We should seek to enable people at all levels to develop to the fullest their potentialities in the role they can fill best. It must also be recognized that in an era of computers, expert teams, and government by consensus, leadership patterns are changing in ways that put new demands on the individual.

There is some evidence to support a situational approach to leadership. In one study, for example, employees in small work groups, which were characterized by a great deal of interaction among workers and between workers and their supervisor and by a high degree of interdependence, had more positive attitudes toward equalitarian leaders. On the other hand, employees in large work groups, in which opportunities for interaction among workers and between workers and their supervisor were greatly restricted and in which individual employees were highly independent, were found to have more positive attitudes toward authoritarian leadership.

At one extreme, the leadership pattern may be a very rule-centered and bureaucratic one. At the other extreme, it may be very group-centered and democratic. In between are found authority-centered or autocratic patterns of leadership and individual-centered or ideocratic leadership patterns. There is growing evidence that organizations, in considerable measure, can be reliably described in terms of typical leadership practices.

Communication Networks. The consultant frequently asks the department head, "What do *you* think is the main problem here in the plant?" Quite often he gets the reply, "Communications." One writer points up the problem by concluding that what we call communication problems are often only symptoms of other difficulties which exist among persons and groups in an organization; communication, other than the most formal kinds, flows along friendship channels. When trust exists, content is more freely communicated and more accurately perceived by the recipient. When individuals have different goals and value systems, it is important to create understanding about needs and motives. Often the free flow of ideas and information is restricted by the feeling that one may not receive credit for the contribution or by fear that his idea will be stolen. Basic to free (and accurate) communication in an organization are questions of task assignments, authority and responsibility, status relationships, and "where *I* stand." One observer reports the instance in a university of a status professor who, though for years he had been a good source of information, good sounding board, and a champion of unpopular causes, literally stopped communicating. Later he explained that he wanted to see where he fitted into a yet ill-defined climate. He had a new department head, a new dean, and the president had just announced his own retirement.

Basically the firm, as a communication system, can be defined in terms of four elements. First, there are the characteristics of the information taken into the firm from the outside in a wide variety of ways, ranging from sales orders and reports of salesmen about competitors to a family problem told to a foreman. Second, there are the firm's rules for doing something about the information. What happens to the sales order? What will be done about the word about the competitors? What will be done, if anything, about the worker's family problem? Third, there are rules about handling information generated from inside the organization. What parts of the organization make decisions, issue orders? How does the information move through the firm? Fourth, there are the characteristics of information leaving the firm, through orders to suppliers, deliveries to customers, and public relations releases. It makes a difference who gathers the information, who filters it and for what purpose, and how various people perceive and interpret the information [51].

Getting accurate information upward through the organization is a particularly difficult problem. The foreman may sense the feelings of a group of workers, filter out that which makes him look at fault, and pass the information to his boss, who in turn follows a similar screening procedure. The use of the problem-solving approach not only stimulates less-filtered upward communication but also helps to create a climate more favorable to decision making and helps remove sources of resistance to change. When people near the bottom of the pyramid feel their views are getting to the top unaltered, they are more receptive to the orders coming down through channels.

An important question to ask about the best way of communication is, "Communication for what?" One experimenter set up a laboratory situation in which A talked to B without return talk, which he termed one-way communication. Two-way communication was set up similarly; this time there was conversation, that is, communication from A to B and from B back to A. Later the same format was followed involving more people. Several practical findings emerged from the studies. One-way communication was much *faster,* but two-way communication was *more accurate,* and the receivers felt more sure of themselves in the two-way system. The sender found himself more vulnerable in the two-way condition because the receiver picked up his mistakes and oversights and told him about them. The two-way system, in some college classrooms, for example, is more noisy and disorderly; there are interruptions, expression of feelings, asking for clarifications, and so on. The one-way method, on the other hand, appears neat and efficient to the outside observer, but communication is less accurate. The same patterns have been found in real-life situations. If speed alone is of primary importance, then one-way communication has the edge, for example, a military situation. If appearance is important, where one wishes to look orderly and businesslike, then the one-way system is preferable. The same is true if the sender wishes to keep his mistakes from being recognized or wants to protect his own power by blaming the receiver for not getting the message. In a two-way system the sender may be criticized, but he will also get his message across. Said one observer, "It's easier to give a speech than to induce appropriate behavior in others." No doubt feedback types of communication are sometimes avoided because of the psychological risks that may get involved [33].

There are some barriers to good communication where several people are involved. There is the status barrier, as between superior and subordinate, and at times there is even interpersonal hostility. And some people allow organization rules to become barriers to really effective communication. Later we shall give details of studies of communication networks involved in group problem solving, concluding that a centralized position of autonomy in making and passing along decisions may be efficient, but where morale is involved as an important constituent, a noncentralized network is superior.

Goal Directions. In the American culture there is an image of respect for size, quantitative indices, power structures, and personal competitive ability. At the same time our culture demands that the individual develop satisfactory methods of adjustment, of avoiding anxiety, and of gaining approval. The fear of failure often leads to compulsive attempts to achieve security by controlling one's environment and by achieving ever-greater success.

Organizations have a tendency to persist. Taking a look at the past history of a company, and particularly its leaders, gives at least one index of an organization's goals. Over a period of time individual responses become somewhat patterned. In the North American culture, for example, deference to authority may come more slowly than in Middle East cultures. But even in the most permissive of American organizations, criticisms, dissent, and feelings are often confined within the company. Internal differences are sometimes repressed in an effort to develop a public image of unity. Once a decision has been made, there is an effort to have everyone go along.

What underlies a company's approach to human relations? Can the management and the union have common goals? What are the ways in which the organization seeks change? How does the organization react to utilizing new techniques such as mathematical programming, operations research, and the use of computers? Does the company actually help the individual to grow? Does the company seek decentralization in power? Who sets the goals in the organization? Does the company adhere to the more classical merit-rating devices, or is some self-evaluation of performance allowed, where the individual sets his own targets? How strong are the pressures for uniformity within the firm? How does the company, the plant, the department, react to change?

These are some of the questions that need to be asked as one takes an overall look at the goals of an organization. Questions and answers vary with other dimensions, but particularly with size. The small company may be able to specify its goals more clearly and in effecting change be able to relate cause and effect more closely. Still, large organizations are not unvaryingly monolithic. Subunits within them pursue different goals and often impose different standards on employees. Certainly profits have a great effect on changes in the company at the top level, and where there are local dissatisfactions with current achievement, changes will be made. One of the big problems, at all levels of the organization, is resistance to changes. In a study by Scott [66] it was found that men who are willing to make changes, men who conceive their job to be more flexible than do many middle-management people, may get the rewards of status and top appointments. Whereas many managers feel their role in the organization is to "follow the rules," some able men become mavericks and succeed; others, just as able, may actually lose their jobs. Scott, after a ten-year study of leadership in the Gulf Oil Corporation, concludes that the "behavior that may lead a person to a vice-presidency in one climate may get the same man fired in another." The creative man, the man who is dissatisfied with the *status quo,* has a better chance of getting ahead in the company where the goals involve progressive change.

How a company initiates change from within and reacts to outside influences in problem solving gives some indication of organizational goals. A main consideration centers on the degree of support *actually given* to research and development. In the space-exploration industries this consideration is primary.

Decision-making Procedures. Centralization of decision-making power, long established on the management side of single organizations, seems to be increasingly characteristic of industrial unions. And more recently companies have united, to some extent, in industry-wide bargaining. University scholars are giving more attention to the basic problems of the nature of decision making, and some industrial organizations are studying their own structures to determine the hierarchy of influence in both policy and operating decisions. For example, a study in one large corporation led to the conclusion that decision influence is multidimensional; no single individual actually makes a company-wide decision.

Psychologists have long been interested in problems about the impersonal quality of a decision, on the one hand, and its degree of acceptance, on the other hand. Many studies have been conducted on leader behaviors and the amount of influence which various persons have in decision making and on both the systems and personality variables involved. Hundreds of studies have dealt with such problems as group participation in problem solving, authoritarianism of supervisors, concepts of autocratic, democratic, and laissez-faire leaders, locus of organization control, decision rules, individual adjustment patterns, and a host of other problems about decisions and what they do to people. Top management recognizes the need for large hierarchic structures, and sometimes it recognizes the problems that such structures impose on individuals. And recently there has been some concern about the place of the computer in decision making. "It is of great value *below my level*" is not an uncommon reaction.

EFFECTS OF CLIMATE

Familiar to the student is the accuracy with which a sophisticated upperclassman can describe the diverse environments between the authoritarian class situation and the permissive one where the instructor encourages class argument. The worker's reaction to a new supervisor and the speculation that goes on in middle management when a vice-president has a heart attack are both illustrations of the fact that people react to climates and climate changes. It is not uncommon at any level to hear words to this effect: "I did not object so much to *what* was done, but I did object to *how* it was done." Organizations sometimes change because individuals change. A modification of climate also offers one good way to observe the effects climate has on the people in the organization.

How Psychological Climates Can Change. The psychological climates of organizations change sometimes for good and sometimes for bad. A change may happen even where there is no turnover in company personnel. Let us illustrate how the character of one organization became quite different as the president modified his behavior over a period of some five years. The president initially worked cooperatively with his executives, often taking their advice and sharing in the give-and-take of conference behavior. The business expanded, profits increased markedly, and so did problems. Then gradually the climate of the organization began to change from permissive to autocratic. Fewer and fewer conferences were held, and the president made more and more decisions without consultation. One observer described the process as "decision by desperation." Both staff and line officers, who had previously been quite free and open with constructive criticisms, now found that not only were criticisms not wanted, they were in effect forbidden.

What had happened? When the president began his term of office, he never considered suggestions and criticism to be a reflection on his ability. A few years later, however, he was taking all such comments personally. He read into them an implication that he personally had failed for not having foreseen and forestalled the situation which was being criticized. Whether he also suffered from the ego inflation that goes with prolonged occupancy of a top administrative post is not so clear. It may be that he just grew tired of facing new disruptive problems.

The effect on the organization all the way down the line was one of clamming up. People began to censor what they would say and consider to whom they would talk. A few of the top people resigned, but on the whole the organization became adapted to the new climate.

Some recent studies aimed at determining the main variables which differentiate the activities of organization have shown that individual labor-union locals show differences in character. Sometimes a clash in personalities between the company and the union may be a precipitating cause for strikes. Sometimes such clashes may change the climates of both organizations. There is evidence that certain industries are consistently strike-proof, while others are consistently strike-happy. Keen observers of the labor-management scene report that some regions of the United States are known to be strike-happy, while others are relatively strike-free. Often these strike-happy communities are the cities or towns where industry has not been very progressive in research on human relations.

The Influence of Climate. Conflict between individuals and organizations is inevitable. People with strong needs to be independent find that most organizations do not provide a proper setting. Learning theorists and training directors have long known that in general rewards are better motivators than punishments, yet most industrial organizations include much of the latter. One training program may succeed because it is operating in a climate of rigid and formal rules with people who are rules-oriented. In the same climate the program may fail if the trainees involved are unstructured and ambivalent. With some people conflict increases with the number and concreteness of regulations; with others it may even decrease. The training director who receives the assignment to help develop a future executive might well ask, "For what kind of climate?"

Two kinds of influence of climate on individuals may be distinguished. First, there is a *direct influence* that affects all or almost all members of the company or some subunit. The second kind of effect is termed *interactive influence,* which exists when a climate has a certain effect upon the behavior of some people, a different effect on others, and possibly no effect at all on still others.

Some behaviors never occur because the stimuli that would elicit them are never presented. Organizations themselves place constraints on people through rules and regulations, routine practices, and taboos. It is not uncommon for the ambitious person to find himself in a climate that puts restraints upon freedom, thus narrowing his alternatives of action. Bavelas [8] has emphasized the point that in any organization of human beings there accumulates through time a common fund of experience. Out of it develop ways of behaving, ways of working, ways of loafing, ways of cooperating and ways of resisting. A newcomer to an established subculture may rebuke the old-timers as being cynical about the system, apparently unaware that there is at times a thin line between cynicism and wisdom. He may find to his embarrassment that hasty evaluation of people and established practices can backfire.

Individual Perceptions. Organizational goals, the personal goals of leaders and the goals of members of the organization sometimes are in conflict. The newly appointed leader may not fully understand the implications of the organization's goals nearly as well as the older employees. Although organization goals may be specified and may actually make logical sense, old-timer members may see these goals from different viewpoints. The extent to which the individual perceives and understands the organization's goals may depend upon his own experiences, skills, and attitudes. The individual who, for one reason or another, responds to his own goals, ignoring those of his organization, can succeed to the extent that his goals coincide with those of the organization and to some extent with those of the membership itself. The person who responds to both his own and his organization's goals faces the possibility of conflict, depending upon what his own goals are. In a review of a large literature centering on the study of psychological climates, Forehand and Gilmer [25] conclude that adjustments are made in terms of how the individual *perceives* his climate. This perception to a large extent is governed by personality factors and how they are related to the satisfaction of one's needs.

SUGGESTIONS FOR SELECTIVE READING

Blau, P. M., & Scott, W. R. *Formal organizations: A comparative approach.* San Francisco: Chandler, 1962. For a view of researches on organizational climates.

Bristol, L. (Ed.) *Developing the corporate image: A management guide to public relations.* New York: Scribner, 1960. Articles on the rapidly expanding field of public relations.

Cheit, E. F. (Ed.) *The business establishment.* New York: Wiley, 1964. Indirectly gives information on climates.

Clark, J. M. *Alternative to serfdom.* New York: Vintage Books, 1960. The economic case for competition related to climates.

Costello, T. W., & Zalkind, S. S. (Eds.) *Psychology in administration: A research orientation.* Englewood Cliffs, N.J.: Prentice-Hall, 1963. A text with integrated readings covering perceptions of people and situations, needs, stress, learning, attitudes, and decision making.

Farber, S. M., & Wilson, R. H. L. (Eds.) *Conflict and creativity.* New York: McGraw-Hill, 1963. A collection of articles for the sophisticated reader, on such subjects as independent thought in a conformist world.

Fisk, G. (Ed.) *The frontiers of management psychology.* New York: Harper & Row, 1964. A symposium dealing with the problems of management in a changing technological climate.

Hollander, E. P. (Ed.) *Leaders, groups, and influence.* Fair Lawn, N.J.: Oxford University Press, 1964. A resource book covering innovation, status, and conformity as related to leadership.

Ingraham, M. H., & King, F. P. *The outer fringe: Faculty benefits other than annuities and insurance.* Madison, Wis.: University of Wisconsin Press, 1964. Some of the determinants of university climates.

Jennings, E. E. *An anatomy of leadership: Princes, heroes, and supermen.* New York: Harper & Row, 1960. Organizational climates in terms of leaders driven to dominate, men dedicated to causes, and iron-willed individuals.

Kahn, R. L., & Katz, D. *Social psychology of organizations.* New York: Wiley, 1964. Two psychologists describe aspects of climates.

Kilpatrick, F. P., et al. *The image of the Federal service.* Washington, D.C.: Brookings, 1964. A source book that gives a climate picture.

Maccoby, Eleanor, et al. (Eds.) *Readings in social psychology.* New York: Holt, 1958. A range of readings on social perception.

Riesman, D., et al. *The lonely crowd.* New Haven, Conn.: Yale, 1950. A readable book about people in climates.

Sanford, N. *College and character.* New York: Wiley, 1964. The organizational climates of colleges.

Sells, S. B. (Ed.) *Stimulus determinants of behavior.* New York: Ronald, 1963. A technically oriented collection of writings related to organizational climates.

Smelser, N. J., & Smelser, W. T. (Eds.) *Personality and social systems.* New York: Wiley, 1963. Articles on the influence of personality and social variables on behavior.

Thompson, G. *Aeschylus and Athens.* London: Lawrence & Wishart, 1941. How the ancient Greek dramas described organizational climates.

White, W. S. *The professional: Lyndon B. Johnson.* Boston: Houghton Mifflin, 1964. Especially Chapter 10 for organization climate.

4

Psychology in the Marketing Environment

W. J. E. Crissy and R. J. Lewis

The American economy is unique in the business history of the world. Our gross national product is more than half a trillion dollars! At the same time the American businessman is becoming increasingly conscious of competition from overseas. New markets must be found both at home and abroad to keep pace with research and development and with mass production. It is to be remembered that industrial psychology had its beginnings in the areas of advertising and selling before turning its emphasis to personnel psychology. Psychology in advertising and selling is now receiving more attention as marketing becomes even better recognized as a part of the industrial environment.

As never before, the behavior of the consumer is being viewed by both huckster and researcher, spurred on by the fact that consumer spending soaks up about two-thirds of our nation's economic output. From the "six-year-old purchasing agent" to "middle-age impulse buying," the psychologist is taking a look at the behavior of people. Copywriters are finding that expansion of advertising to attract the foreign market involves something more than the translation of the successful General Motors slogan "Body by Fisher" (the Flemish version of which had to be revised when it came out "Corpse by Fisher").

The psychological factors of perception, cognition, and affection in advertising require deeper understanding than the mere discovery that color in advertising can create problems. Purple is a noble shade in Japan but represents death in Burma. The African's admiration of anything new from America sometimes evokes literal reactions. For example, Gillette was discovered to be a heavy seller because it used wrappers that depict a razor blade slicing a crocodile in half to emphasize sharpness. Literal-mindedness can be a problem. After her first glimpse of television, one native woman asked, "When all the good men have killed all the bad men, why do they rush off to clean their teeth?"

THE GENERAL CLIMATE

Born of big business, advertising and selling have changed much since World War II. The advertising dollar volume alone doubled between 1950 and 1960, and bids fair to double again by 1970. The average United States business now spends $1 on advertising for every $70 in sales, as against 50 cents for every $100 at the close of World War II. As advertising becomes more pervasive, so does debate about it. Is Madison Avenue corrupting the standards of Main Street? Do the fifty major organizations of nearly six hundred agencies wield too much influence on the behaviors of people? Around a decade ago, 1 million dollars was a respectable year's advertising budget for anyone but a major consumer-goods manufacturer; today a single TV spectacular may cost that much. Virtually every United States corporation of any size is a heavy advertiser and, on the average, changes its ad agency every seven years. One survey of admen revealed that only 8 per cent of those polled considered their fellow admen to be completely sincere. There are many questions of why people buy what and where, and many answers are given. Questionnaires to 12,000 American housewives indicated that most prefer one store over another, not because of stamps or contests, but because of polite and helpful clerks. Statistics related to where the consumer puts his money abound, from Americans who place 90 billion telephone calls per year to the failure of people to respond to things that will benefit them personally. For example, it had been expected that 70 per cent of some 1½ million veterans sent literature on higher benefits would respond, but only 19 per cent did. Americans use some 20 tons of aspirin daily, and the figure increases with economic recessions. Some 40 per cent of all passports issued go to people over fifty, and in a modern supermarket, an average of seven new products are put on the shelves each week, and four are taken off. And there are instances of products being advertised and evoking responses before they are even invented—certainly one way to evaluate a potential market. The researcher is interested in the statistic that the average housewife spends 45 minutes a week in the supermarket and makes up to 30 decisions. And he is interested in attention and influence. A study by the American Association of Advertising Agencies says that with 1,500 ads per day assaulting his eyes and ears, the American consumer has built up a "crust of indifference." He shuts out more than 1,400 of the daily ad pitches, reacts to only 13. [4, 7, 28, 34, 84].

The American consumer is being peeped at, shadowed and grilled, and even analyzed in terms of his personal habits during the hour and half-hour station breaks on TV. Researchers are using mathematics and high-speed computers to help manufacturers understand why people buy or do not buy a particular brand or product. Let us illustrate by one experiment. Kuehn [48] tested the effects of retail-shelf display upon buying behavior and how it is related to habit. Canned soups were arranged in alphabetic order by the type of soup—asparagus, bean, etc.—retaining the original amount of display space for each brand and type. Previously, canned soups had been grouped by brand ("block" or "billboard" display) rather than type.

Although several signs were placed at the soup section telling the customers that the cans had been rearranged alphabetically, 60 per cent of the customers were foiled by the new arrangement and their own habits. Half of the customers who already had canned soup in their shopping carts said, when asked, that the soups were in their usual order. When told of the change, many checked their purchases to see if they had taken the right can from the shelf. Half of the balance were just plain confused, despite explicit information on the signs. Only one-quarter of the women who bought soup were able to cope with the new arrangement. Infrequent customers of the store—men and children and women who generally shopped elsewhere, for example—who were unfamiliar with the layout of the store and were looking for clues were less susceptible to habit patterns in their buying.

The power of habit, reports Kuehn, was further underlined by other evidence. Under the original shelf arrangement there was no indication that consumers switched brands when the leading brand of tomato soup went out of stock. When the soup display was rearranged as described above, however, and the leading brand was out of stock, sales indicated that the next leading brand picked up from 50 to 80 per cent of the sales which normally went to the leader. The only difference was in the arrangement of cans on the shelf.

This study and similar ones illustrate the use of developing mathematical descriptions of the influence of competitive merchandising factors upon brand choice—models that can be tested, modified, or refined in the continuing effort to develop greater understanding of buying behavior. A model may contain two opposing forces, habitual purchase behavior and the influence of merchandising variables designed to modify or strengthen this behavior. For example, the success of a new product depends on its inducing consumers to shift away from their former brands ("new low cost" or "new standard of performance"); the continued success of an established leading brand depends on its strengthening existing habits ("the taste to stay with").

The marketing environment is a climate of big money and big decisions, of studies of why complacency brings order and order has a tendency to bring resistance to change. What people say they will buy is not always what they actually purchase. Marketing involves both guesswork and science. The consumer psychologist certainly works in the climate of a living laboratory which is multidimensional: a climate in which one experienced investigator estimates that $1 worth of basic research requires $10 of product development and $100 to promote and gain acceptance of the product. Over twenty-five thousand new products are introduced each year in the United States at a cost of many millions of dollars in research and development expenditures. Even in the medical field many R&D products never find a market. For example, in one year the American Hospital Supply Corporation looked critically at 1,098 new products and placed 214 on the market.

Perceptions and Product Image. It is most difficult to get at what people really think about a product or what induces certain buying behavior. One can be misled in a door-to-door survey if the assumption is made that the housewife will reveal all about herself in such a casual way. Attitudes, rationalizations, and other behaviors get involved. We shall discuss perceptions later, but for now let us illustrate how difficult it is to build up a desired new product image when from the beginning old attitudes may be involved.

One investigator made two "shopping lists" which were shown to housewives [35]. The lists contained a series of everyday household-purchase items such as a pound and a half of hamburger, two cans of Del Monte peaches, etc. One list contained Nescafé, while the second, otherwise identical with the first, substituted Maxwell House regular for the instant coffee. When the surveyor asked a matched group of housewives to describe the type of woman who would purchase each list of products, he found that a considerable proportion mentioned "lazy" housewives and "women who don't plan well" for the list containing instant coffee. Direct questioning gave no indication that this was a connotation associated with the perception of the new product. Sometimes overcoming built-in attitudes, feelings, or even rationalizations is essential for success in introducing a new product. In this particular instance the product was successfully introduced. Certainly, the marketing environment is a stimulating place to study human behavior.

THE BUSINESS AND ITS EXTERNAL ENVIRONMENT

As a first step in understanding a company's marketing and distribution effort, it is necessary to consider the external environment with which it interacts. This total environment may be thought of as six-dimensional. It includes stockholders, those who provide the money ingredients needed; vendors, those who provide the goods and services needed for the company to fulfill its mission; government, especially the tax-collecting and regulatory aspects; the community, the places where the company does business; the industry, the firms with which the company competes for business directly or indirectly; and, most important, the customers and prospective customers comprising the market place.

Just as each individual finds the surrounding social environment varied and complex, so does the business. The well-adjusted person seeks to carry on a favorable interrelationship with people and groups around him; a business firm has a similar adjustment objective. The actions taken and the decisions made in conducting the affairs of a business must take the complex external environment into account.

In a competitive economy the one public which must be considered above all else is the market place or, more exactly, the public is the market place. It has been said with considerable truth that the customer has veto power over the very survival of the firm. If a company is to survive and prosper, it must conduct its affairs in such a way that it projects an image of uniqueness. It must be viewed as a distinctive and desirable place to do business. Its products and services must be perceived as unique, different and better than other products and services. Its people must be viewed as unique, good folks with whom to do business. This projection of a unique image is the universal and pervasive strategic objective of every company's marketing effort. This holds true whether the company is a small proprietorship doing business in a local community or a publicly held corporation doing many millions of dollars worth of business in a world-wide market place [3, 12, 28, 47, 81].

Strategy and Tactics. The term "strategy," whether used in a military setting or in marketing, has certain connotations. It is future-oriented. It is related to the style or stance taken in carrying out objectives. It includes both what to do and what to avoid doing. There is an interrelationship between strategy and planning. Just as in the military, it is true in the market place that if strategy were successful whenever used, there would be no need for tactics. Seldom, however, are battles fought as contemplated; seldom if ever do events occur in the market place exactly as planned. Hence there *is* need for tactics. Tactics are of the *now*. They are the modifications made in strategy in view of the unforeseen, unexpected, or uncontrolled. The principal reason for marketing tactics is competitive strategic behavior. As a competing firm makes a move, the company must be prepared to make a countermove. Psychology has much to contribute to marketing strategy and marketing tactics. Buying behavior must be influenced without authority and without coercion. In a free economy each company must strive, not to sell, but to induce purchase. Let us see how this is accomplished.

The Five Steps in Marketing Strategy. A paperback on how to get rich gives the sage and psychologically sound advice, "Find a need and meet it." Many years ago the eminent psychologist E. K. Strong concerned himself with the selling process [73]. His early model of this aspect of business stands the test of time and reflects the five sequential steps needed to complete the marketing process. Set forth below is an adaptation of the early model by Strong:

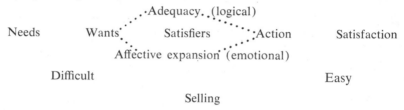

$$\text{Needs} \qquad \text{Wants} \overset{\cdots\text{Adequacy}\cdots\text{(logical)}}{\underset{\text{Affective expansion (emotional)}}{\text{Satisfiers}}} \text{Action} \qquad \text{Satisfaction}$$

| Difficult | | Easy |

Selling

The above diagram suggests that the beginning of the marketing process is needs, human and corporate. Needs have peculiar properties. They are vague, generalized, internally focused, and hard to talk about. More importantly, however, from the standpoint of marketing strategy, needs tend to a condition of homeostasis or dynamic balance. The first step in marketing strategy is *to disturb homeostasis.* Unless the firm is able to disturb the *status quo,* it is not likely to induce buying behavior.

When homeostasis is disturbed, wants emerge. Both corporate and individual wants are specific, concrete, externally focused, and easy to think about and talk about. They are conceptualized in terms of what satisfies them. Thus, the second step in marketing strategy involves *cataloging wants* and how they are satisfied. Each company must have a current picture of customers' and prospects' wants and how they are being met. This step in marketing strategy can be thought of as the marketing intelligence function within the business enterprise. Data must be made available concerning how people perceive, think, and feel with respect to their wants and how they are satisfying them if the company is to be successful in a competitive economy. Notice that the word "adequacy" and the words "affective expansion" are placed in loose relationship to wants and action. This suggests that both a logical and psychological approach must be made to learn about wants and satisfiers. How a company feels about its present supplier may be more important in inducing purchasing action than an evaluation of the supplier on a logical basis.

The third step suggested by the diagram is that each company must *view its goods and services, its personnel, and itself as a construct of want satisfiers.* From a strategic standpoint the company has the task of presenting this array of want satisfiers in a fashion that meets certain criteria. This presentation must be understandable, believable, interesting, and persuasive. Only if it meets those four tests can the company move to the next step in the marketing process.

Notice that in the diagram the fourth step suggested is *action*. What action? Purchase, not sale. In a competitive market place coercion is inappropriate; subtle persuasion is the rule. The process, however, does not stop when a business transaction occurs. Notice that the diagram suggests a fifth step, *satisfaction*. Part of any company's marketing strategy is an ongoing buyer-seller relationship which ensures satisfaction to the customer. The old cliché "The customer is always right," provides a rule of business living where competition prevails.

THE MIX

To understand the planning and direction behind a firm's behavior in the market place there are three interrelated areas that must be understood. They are the perceptions which the business has of its *customer-product mix, product-service mix,* and *marketing mix.* The interrelationships are depicted in Figure 4.1.

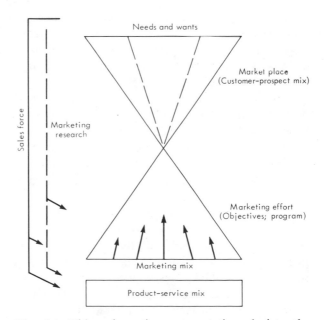

Fig. 4.1. This schematic representation depicts the relation between human needs and wants and the marketing environment.

Customer-prospect and Product-service Mix. The firm begins its activities by determining the needs and wants of customers and prospects. To do this a firm has two possible information systems—its sales force and marketing research. Having identified the needs and wants in the market place, the firm then evaluates its customer-prospect mix. Here the firm must decide which of the needs and wants in the market place it is capable and desirous of serving. This provides the prime determiner for defining the firm's market place. After the market of the firm has been determined and the specific needs and wants identified, the firm must structure its product-service mix to provide the satisfiers for the needs and wants of its customers and prospects. The questions to be asked are: What satisfiers are we now providing? What satisfiers should we be providing? It should be remembered that the needs and wants found in the market place are not static but are dynamic; hence the firm needs a continuous informational system in the market place and a continuous reevaluation of its product-service mix based on the information obtained.

Ingredients of the Marketing Mix. Of special concern to industrial psychology is the marketing mix. In this area there has been an increased awareness on the part of industrialists that the marketing and distribution of goods and services involve careful planning and administration of many diverse but *interdependent* activities—advertising, personal selling, sales promotion, merchandising, customer service, public relations, credit, pricing, transportation and delivery, and market and marketing research. None of these can stand alone; hence a system approach recognizing their interdependence must be used in marketing planning. In combination these activities comprise the company's marketing mix.

Obviously the mix will vary depending on the customer-prospect mix being served, the product-service mix being produced, current economic conditions, and the men and money allocable to the marketing and distribution function. In view of the many determinants of the marketing mix, it is not surprising that companies producing competitive lines often differ in their marketing mixes. One may stress intensive advertising coverage and direct-mail promotion with minimal personal selling. Another may do relatively little advertising but reach the market with a large sales force. The more competitive the industry, the more challenge there is to each company to utilize fully all its interrelated demand-creating forces. In general, though, all companies have a common objective for the marketing mix, that is, profitable distribution of goods or services by marrying their product-service mix to the needs and wants of the customer-prospect mix.

What is involved in each ingredient of the mix?

Advertising. Advertising is commonly defined as any paid form of non-personal presentation and promotion of ideas, goods, or services by an identified sponsor. The media of advertising include magazine and newspaper space, trade papers, billboards, throwaways, programs and menus, car cards, skywriting, catalogs, and local and national radio and television. Each firm must determine which combination of media will be most effective for marketing its goods and services and the extent to which each is to be used. An example of a research hypothesis which might be tested by the psychologist would be, "Advertising in printed media is more believable than advertising presented by radio or TV."

Personal Selling. Personal selling involves interpersonal communication between an individual member of the firm's sales organization and a customer or prospect, with an objective of inducing purchase. For some companies the prospect is the ultimate user of the goods or services. For others the prospect is a wholesaler, distributor, or agent who, in turn, has his own marketing mix for the distribution of his goods. A testable hypothesis might be, "Empathy as a personal characteristic of the salesman is a correlate of his sales effectiveness."

Sales Promotion. Sales promotion includes those marketing activities other than personal selling, advertising, and publicity that stimulate consumer purchasing and dealer effectiveness, such as displays, shows and exhibitions, demonstrations, and various nonrecurrent selling efforts not in the ordinary routine. A research investigation might involve determining the extent to which the surprise element enhances the effectiveness of the promotional effort.

Merchandising. The term "merchandising" refers to the activities of manufacturers and middlemen designed to adjust the merchandise produced or offered for sale to customer demand. An alternative definition is the planning and supervision involved in marketing the particular merchandise or service at the places, times, and prices and in the quantities which will best serve to realize the marketing objectives of the business. An example of the potential contribution of psychology might be to determine how various types of retail outlets are perceived by prospective clients in order to determine the best place to locate particular goods and services.

Customer Service. Depending on the nature of the product, customer service may be a nonexistent or a major mix ingredient. Service activities include maintenance and repair of products, technical and professional assistance in problem solving, help in training the customer's personnel in operating the equipment, and market and marketing research on the customer's products.

Public Relations. Since the reputation the company has in its industry, in the business world, and in the community markedly influences the sales of its products, public relations is an important ingredient of the marketing mix. All employees informally contribute to the public relations of the company. Some companies employ a specialized staff or an outside agency to coordinate this aspect of the marketing mix.

Credit. This ingredient varies in importance from company to company, depending on the goods or services sold, policy with regard to payment, and precedent within the industry. In general, the acceptance of a customer's credit becomes more important in the marketing mix as the value of the unit purchase increases. In many cases a firm has the option of directly accepting the customer's credit and financing the purchase or using some private outside agency and acting as an intermediary to acquire financing for its customer. In recent years this demand-creating force has increased in importance. A firm might test the hypothesis that extension of credit increases the size of the average purchase.

Pricing. With a product or service for which there is an elastic demand, pricing can become a powerful ingredient in the marketing mix. Indeed, the other demand-creating forces have as an objective to demonstrate that the potential value of the goods and services to the purchaser is worth more than the money asked. It would be grossly oversimplified to think of pricing as a mere economic concept. It is interrelated with value, particularly the value the prospective customer puts on goods and services. Thus it can have psychological and sociological significance. An importer and marketer of French perfume might test the hypothesis that the perceived superiority of his products is correlated with higher prices.

Transportation and Delivery. Promptness, cost, and customer convenience must all be considered in this mix ingredient. In a highly competitive industry this often becomes the crucial factor in the customer's decision to buy or not to buy from a particular supplier. Its importance varies considerably from industry to industry and even among companies selling similar lines.

Market and Marketing Research. As shown earlier, this is one of the two informational systems which can be used to provide information about the market place. The objective here is to substitute facts and data for guesswork in the marketing and distribution of goods or services.

PURCHASE BEHAVIOR

In substituting facts and data for guesswork, business is usually interested in what the various types of behavior in the market place are and what prompts such behavior. One writer suggests that a company that is marketing-oriented sees itself as in the business of creating customers rather than building or manufacturing goods. Let us review the viewpoints and methodologies that have been used to gain more insight into the purchase behavior of customers and prospects. Whether the company markets to ultimate consumers, to middlemen, or to industrial users, the common goal of marketing in studying the purchase behavior of customers is to understand better what the various influences are which collectively affect purchase behavior. There are three approaches and viewpoints firms take to solve this continuing marketing problem.

The Economic Approach. This approach is based on the assumption that people are basically rational in their decision-making behavior. From this viewpoint the "why" of purchase behavior would be that the individual is attempting to maximize utility. The economist John M. Keynes illustrates this viewpoint. He held that the purchase behavior by the ultimate consumer is primarily governed by his "absolute" income level. In contrast, Milton Freedman, another economist, holds that it is the "permanent" income level that determines the ultimate consumer's purchases and that transitory ups and downs do not affect his behavior. James Dusenberry illustrates a third economic view. He believes in a "relative" income hypothesis that explains the ultimate consumer's purchase behavior in terms of his position relative to those ahead of his income bracket and what their behavior is like.

The Statistical Approach. In this view purchase behavior is studied by amassing and analyzing data and seeking predictive variables. These studies may encompass:

1 Demographic factors, such as age and occupation
2 Status striving and mobility between classes
3 Budget information on the planning of past and future expenditures
4 Life styles, relating purchase behavior to the study of the family unit and its mode of adjustment
5 Life cycle, relating the purchase behavior to the study of the family unit and its relative position on a life-span continuum ranging from mate selection to widowhood or widowerhood and death

The Motivational-analysis Approach. This type of approach is generally characterized by an attempt to determine more of the "why" of behavior and less of the "what is" of behavior. This is uniquely the domain where the psychologist operates, not that he has a monopoly. Increasingly, sociologists and anthropologists are concerning themselves with the "why" of purchasing behavior. Fundamentally, reasons for buying or not buying are sought in the personality dynamics of the individual. Characteristic of the methods used are projective techniques, word and sentence free association, and the like.

Regardless of the approach taken, it is clear that what is being studied and, hopefully, being explained is the decision-making process of an individual in the market place. This is not to imply that every time a consumer enters the market place, a complete cycle of decision making is undertaken, for as Katona has pointed out, some purchases become relegated to habit [45]. And beliefs are important. In a study on consumer preferences for beef, two different displays were put on the counter. One was an economical concentrate from cattle fed on grass; the other was more expensively grain-fed. The fat from the grass-fed cattle was slightly offwhite in color in contrast to the grain-fed beef. When the more expensive "grain-fed" beef was identified as such it outsold the "cheaper" brand. But when neither was identified, and both marked at the same price, each sold equally well. In a follow-up study, customers said there was no difference in taste in the beef bought from unidentified racks. But when identified, the customers said there was a difference—favoring grain-fed beef. Maybe it pays to *tell* people what they like.

Having examined illustratively approaches to understanding purchasing behavior, let us now direct our attention to two major demand-creating forces in marketing—advertising and selling.

ADVERTISING

Today we can correctly refer to an advertising *industry*. Approximately 12 billion dollars is spent annually in North America on this ingredient of the marketing mix. Over 350 companies spend 1 million dollars or more on their advertising each year. What a far cry from the announcements painted on the bathhouse walls in ancient Rome!

Kinds of Advertising. What kinds of advertising are there? There are many bases of classification—by media, coverage of the market, source of the money, size, and frequency—but perhaps the soundest method of classi-fication for the psychologist is by the objectives to be met.

The great bulk of advertising is in the *direct-sell* category. This adver-tising is designed to influence directly the purchase of goods or services. A department store's full-page spread in your Sunday newspaper and the spot commercial on your local television station urging you to buy an album of hit-tune records are commonplace examples.

During the twentieth century there has been a phenomenal increase in emphasis on *buying by brand*. Advertising has brought this about, and today a large segment of consumer-goods advertising is designed to re-inforce the brand name. Examples abound in the advertising of clothing, foods, and appliances. A variant of this type of advertising is aimed at reinforcing the company name as a guide to the purchaser.

Many companies, particularly those which do not have consumer prod-ucts for sale, use a large portion of their advertising dollars to establish themselves as good corporate citizens. Examples of such *institutional advertising* include an oil company's campaign stressing safety on the road, a major life insurance company's award-winning series of advertise-ments furnishing career information, and the dramatic program on net-work television sponsored by a nationally renowned steel company. In this kind of advertising one or more companies often furnish publicity for national or community endeavors, including car cards and newspaper, radio, and television announcements for fund raising.

All advertising, regardless of kind, is aimed at triggering perceptual, cognitive, and affective responses in each individual reached. Although we respond as total beings and these processes are interactive, we can, for discussion and analysis, consider each of them separately.

FACTORS IN ADVERTISING

Printed advertisements, regardless of media, involve visual perceptual processes exclusively. Radio advertising, in contrast, depends exclusively on auditory perception. The advent of television complicated matters. In this increasingly important advertising medium an optimal combination of visual and auditory stimulation must be used if the message is to be maximally effective. Our first consideration, then, deals with *perceptual factors*.

Such perceptual variables as the following have undergone research scrutiny: size, color, kind of illustration, amount of copy, and frequency and duration in the case of radio and television commercial spots. Some of the research is done under the precise conditions of the laboratory; *much of it must be conducted in the field with some sacrifice of accuracy*. Set forth below are synopses of several studies which will serve as illustrations of how perceptual factors in advertising are studied.

Investigators [44] studied the influence of color on legibility of copy; they used a procedure similar to that of visual-acuity tests except that the subject moved forward until he could just read the characters correctly. Forty-two color combinations were employed, and it was found that legibility depends on the brightness difference between the color of the lettering and that of the background. Further, dark-colored lettering on a light background is more legible in daylight than the reverse. Gray was found to form the best background for the legibility of colored lettering. A fairly high positive rank-difference correlation (rho .54) exists between legibility and affective preference of color combinations. For example, blue lettering on a gray background was given an average legibility rank of 1.0 and an average affective-preference rank of 1.0; red lettering on a gray background was given an average legibility rank of 4.0 and an average affective-preference rank of 3.0. In this connection, it was also found that color-combination preference depends more on brightness difference than on legibility.

In another study, the same authors measured the relevance of illustrations to copy in thirty-nine advertisements from *House Beautiful, House and Garden,* and *The Saturday Evening Post.* The pictures were cut from the copy and mounted on a white-cardboard background. The subjects, ninety-four college students, were instructed to indicate whether they had or had not seen each of the pictures before, what commodity was featured in the picture, and what desirable feature or features of the commodity were in evidence. It was found that in those pictures in which commodity had a high relevance to copy (those judged correctly by 80 to 100 per cent of the subjects), the commodity was the conspicuous, and in most cases the centermost, object. Additional features of highly relevant-to-copy illustrations included the label or trademark on the commodity and lack of an excessive number of extraneous objects surrounding the commodity. In those illustrations in which desirable features of the commodity had a very high relevance to copy (those judged correctly by 80 to 100 per cent of the subjects), the plain and unambiguous representation of the product features was characteristic. Further, these pictures contained within their borders printed words which tersely informed the reader of the desirable features, and the human subjects of the illustrations reflected happiness and contentment in their faces. The investigators concluded that the relevance of pictures to copy was lower than it should be since the average reader rarely reads the copy and pays only fleeting attention to the illustrations.

Not only must each advertisement be perceived; its message must be understood. Hence *cognitive factors* involve word choice and sentence structure as key variables to ensure understanding on the part of the audience or reader.

Determination of Readership and Comprehension. The Psychological Corporation, a consulting firm, undertook the determination of readership and comprehension of Union Carbide and Carbon newspaper advertising in Charleston, West Virginia. Interviewers questioned 363 men and women on the Sunday the advertisement appeared in the two local papers as well as on the following Monday. Of those who reported having read either of the two newspapers 74 per cent reported having seen the advertising, and 40 per cent of that group reported having read it. Of these latter 145 cases, 84 per cent gave at least one idea which showed a good or fair understanding of the advertisements; 12 per cent had only a poor understanding; and 4 per cent had no idea whatsoever. These figures are based on answers to the question, "What ideas did you get from that advertisement?" which was put to the respondents after the newspaper had been taken out of sight. It is interesting to note that 86 per cent of those who reported having read the advertisement thought it was worthwhile; that is, they had gained something from reading it.

In an effort to determine the optimum length of advertisement headlines, researchers investigated the ability of the reader to remember headlines under varying conditions [52]. Headlines ranging from four to fifteen words, each set in a uniform size and style of type face, were presented to 100 university students for recall and recognition. The results indicated that brevity had a decided advantage if readers spent a uniform, brief period of time on each headline. When a variable exposure time was allowed, almost all the advantages of brevity disappeared. It is a matter of conjecture whether the shorter headlines were better remembered because they could be read so much more quickly and easily or the apparent advantage was due to other factors influencing ease of recall, as illustrated by the fact that the immediate-recall scores for some of the shorter headlines were low, and others were high. It is reasonable to assume that the length of time spent on a headline is influenced greatly by context and length of the headline itself. The study did not indicate clearly exactly how long a good headline may be. However, it was found that almost nine-tenths of the subjects remembered one headline containing nine words. Since the subjects were all college students, these results cannot be applied to average magazine readers without allowance for the more limited buying interests of students and the lower average memory span of the population as a whole.

Spot-advertising Study. A packaged-drugs firm was interested in determining the effectiveness of its spot advertising in printed media. To study the impact of the copy, key words were extracted from sample advertisements, and respondents were asked to free-associate to each, to give a definition, and to indicate the degree of affectivity (strong dislike, dislike, strong like, and like). The phrase setting in which the word occurred was then mentioned and the interviewee again asked to free-associate. The final question posed was, "What product or service does this remind you of?" For example, when seventeen male and fourteen female subjects were asked to free-associate to the word "membrane," 42 per cent responded with "form of skin or tissue." This phrase was also the modal definition given. A mixed emotional attitude was found; 57 per cent of the subjects expressed like and 42 per cent dislike. The modal response to the captive phrase "shrinks swollen nasal membranes" was "colds." Further, the word had a high brand-associative value for the company. The research indicated that very favorable affective attitudes existed toward such words and phrases as "penetrating ingredient," "stimulates," and "gives you a lift." Such words as "antispetic," "aromatic," and "medicates" aroused predominantly favorable reactions, whereas unfavorable affective reactions were elicited by "bacteria," "congestion," and "inflamed." The investigators note that when negative emotional reactions are involved, the advertisement should "provide a way out."

The importance of affective factors in advertising is exemplified by other, unpublished research available to the authors. An artist was commissioned to prepare some illustrations suitable for insurance advertisements. Safety, protection, and security were to be the central themes. One picture showed a mother fastening a safety gate in front of a small boy as the father descended the stairs. Pretesting of the illustration through depth interviewing revealed that the man was regarded as the focal point and that the family was breaking up; hence respondents failed to relate the picture to insurance. When the father was removed and the illustration depicted a child playing while the mother fastened the safety gate, the desired safety theme became apparent to the viewers.

Following perception and cognition in advertising, we must deal with how people feel, the *affective factors*. Regardless of type of advertising or of product or service for sale, affective responses must be considered. Feelings can be aroused by the illustration, the wording, even by the location of the advertisement in the medium. A leading manufacturer of perfumes pays a premium rate to ensure that his advertisements appear on a page with a love story! Two unpublished research projects, done for client companies by the writers and an associate, serve to indicate how affective factors can be studied. Let us consider these next in showing the importance of pretesting advertisements.

Pretesting. Advertisements are usually tested before they are used. This testing may involve people's reactions to each advertisement as a whole or to its component parts. It may be done under laboratory conditions within the agency or in the field. Often alternative forms of the advertisement are tested in order to choose the most effective one.

If advertisements are checked within the agency, an intensive study is made, using a relatively small number of subjects. Three pieces of laboratory equipment are valuable aids—the tachistoscope, the chronoscope, and the eye camera. The first is used to present split-second exposures of the whole ad, the illustration, or the headline. The purpose is to determine whether the material presented can be perceived speedily. For example, there is a consistent finding that more than six words in a headline prevent its perception in a single act of attention. The chronoscope is useful in measuring precisely the time needed for forming associations with stimulus words or illustrations, for reading the body copy, etc. The eye camera, often used in combination with a device for turning pages at a constant, known speed, provides a means for determining the attention-getting parts of the advertisement. It is also used for studying this factor in an entire issue of a magazine or newspaper.

To systematize the collection of data on people's reactions to advertisements as wholes, several advertisement tests or checklists have been developed. The most elaborate one is the Thompson-Luce test, which consists of thirty-five factors found to contribute to reader interest in an advertisement. These variables include "page," "color," "visual emphasis," "baby," "animal," "food," "shock," "pathos," "danger," "news," "slogan," etc. When analysis of several thousand advertisements on the basis of these controlled factors was compared with later consumer-readership reports, the Thompson-Luce preevaluation was found to be accurate within 2 per cent in predicting the ratings later reported by advertisement-checking services. Further, the Thompson-Luce factors were weighted on the basis of statistical studies of good and poor advertisements. Results indicated, for example, that babies appeared in the illustrations of high-ranking advertisements four times more frequently than in the low; and visual emphasis, lack of confusion in the advertisement's appearance, was found eight times more often.

A number of people have suggested rating advertisements on the basis of "attention," "meaning," "feeling," "memory," and "action."

Consumer Panels. When advertisements are taken into the field for pretesting, less intensive data are obtained from larger numbers of subjects. Inherent in field testing is the problem of ensuring an appropriate sampling of the desired segment of the population. This factor has caused many large advertising agencies to maintain a consumer panel, that is, people who have been selected on the basis of prescribed criteria and who may be used, as need arises, for testing purposes.

There are four common types of panels.

1 *The consumer jury.* A group who may be asked to give judgment on pieces of copy, to listen to radio programs, or to act as advisers on other matters of interest to an advertiser.

2 *The consumer testing group.* Individuals who are available to make blind tests of products.

3 *The opinion panel.* A group of persons or families who can be relied upon to answer questionnaires on various subjects, ranging from product-use habits to opinions on public affairs.

4 *The continuous-purchase-record type of panel.* Individuals or families who keep adequate records of their purchases of specified products over a period of time. Thus a continuous case history of certain kinds of purchases is provided.

Information may be obtained from the panel members by mail, personal interviews, or group meetings. Individuals are carefully chosen to include representative samplings of the population with regard to age, income, education, and any other identifying characteristics of importance to the sponsoring advertiser. Panel members are often compensated for their cooperation by points, which may be used in selecting premiums or merchandise from a special catalog. An alternative in this procedure is to draw a prescribed sample from each study. If this method is used, the field interviewers are given criteria to be met in selecting respondents.

Obviously, the advertisements which can be taken for testing to the interviewee's home or place of business are limited to printed media. Pretesting of radio and television advertising involves bringing the subjects to a central location. However, there is one important exception to this. In the last few years such advertising has been pretested over a single local station prior to widespread use.

Posttesting. Testing advertising after use is easier to accomplish than pretesting. However, once the advertising money is spent, it is too late to make changes! Yet this after-the-fact evaluation is useful in several ways:

1 It provides a guide for the formulation of future advertising.

2 If several advertisements have been used, it yields data concerning their relative effectiveness.

3 If several media have been used, the relative merits of the media can be appraised.

4 It furnishes information on the yield of advertising in the company's marketing mix.

The most precise posttesting method is *direct return*. If a printed medium is used, a coupon is provided for answering the advertisement. Often a prize or premium is offered the respondent. With an estimate of readership or audience, it is possible to determine percentage of response. If radio or television is used, a phone number or a mailing address is presented. A variant of this method is *split run*. If the company has alternative forms of the advertisement, these can be run alternatively in a particular issue of the magazine or newspaper and the relative effectiveness of each determined.

Another method is similar to field pretesting. Either a consumer panel or a sample is interviewed. If unprompted recall is sought, the respondent is asked which advertisements he remembers in a particular issue of a magazine or newspaper. If radio or television commercials are being studied, he is asked which ones he remembers on a particular channel or station or on a designated program. Those who recall the advertisements being tested are then interrogated in detail. If prompted recall is desired, the interviewee may be shown the advertisement and then asked detailed questions concerning his reactions to it.

Since the advertiser usually wants to know how his messages are faring with competition, posttesting is done by outside research organizations. Interest in this type of research has grown. The advertiser can obtain readership and listenership information on his own advertising as well as on that of his competitors by subscribing to such services as Starch and Gallup in printed media and Nielsen, Trendex, Pulse, and American Research Bureau in broadcast media. As a specific example, a Starch report reveals for half-page and larger ads those which have been noted, seen-associated, and read most.

The ultimate test of direct-sell advertising is the profitable sale of goods or services. For this reason an important posttesting method is the advertisement's impact on sales volume. A nationally known manufacturer of cold remedies places newspapers, radio, and television spots depending on local weather conditions. Whenever colds are likely, the advertising is intensified. An immediate follow-up on retail outlets is then made to determine the effect on sales of the company's products.

The following is illustrative of the methods used in posttesting advertisements. In its study to determine the effectiveness of the advertising of the detergent Silver Dust, the Psychological Corporation employed a pretested questionnaire which encompassed three basic approaches. The sample consisted of 400 cases. The interviewees lived in one- two-, or three-family houses rather than apartment houses, and the bulk of them were in the $2,000-to-$5,000 income bracket. In the *recognition* test five advertisements were shown simultaneously, and the interviewees were asked whether they had seen them. This is a variation of the usual recognition test in which only one advertisement is shown at a time and the interviewee required to answer "yes," "no," or "don't know." The latter method tends to produce a higher percentage of "yes" answers, while the method used in this study is more conservative. The *aided-recall* segment of the study utilized an introductory question designed to eliminate confusion with the advertising of other soaps, followed by the question, "Have you noticed any other wash soap advertising recently?" This was the most rigorous test, since the individual is asked to produce from all the competitive advertising influences the one brand that stood out. The succeeding questions dealt with the outstanding features of the Silver Dust advertisements. Finally, the *controlled-opinion,* or *consumer-jury, test* was employed to get some idea about the different advertisements themselves. The respondents were asked to look at and read the advertisements again, to choose the one which was most interesting, and to describe what they liked about it.

SELLING

In most companies, selling comprises the largest part of the marketing mix, whether viewed in terms of dollars spent or people employed. Selling is classifiable in three ways—by what is sold, by channel of distribution, and by ultimate purchaser.

When we approach the subject of what is sold, the simplest classification of selling consists of industrial goods, consumer goods, and intangibles. Examples of each of these would be selling steel to the automobile manufacturer, selling vacuum cleaners door to door, and selling air travel to newlyweds. Obviously each of these general groupings can be made more specific, depending on the needs of the person who is describing selling. A common practice in business with regard to industrial goods is to categorize such selling by industries—rubber, chemicals, steel, etc. Another practice is to subdivide consumer goods into hard and soft, the latter being expendable items. Similarly, intangibles may be broken down into such subcategories as investments, insurance, etc.

Kinds of Selling. Should the approach to classification be through channel of distribution, three kinds of selling can be distinguished—direct to purchaser, wholesale, and retail. Each of these in turn admits of further refinement. Thus the direct sale of consumer goods may be accomplished by personal selling or by direct mail. In the case of industrial goods, direct selling may be subdivided into selling an established line of products or selling goods made to customer specifications. Similarly, wholesale selling can be subdivided into selling through jobbers or selling through exclusive agents or franchises that are independent businesses, though they sell only one company's products. In the industrial field there is still another grouping which cuts across both wholesale and direct selling: manufacturers' representatives. Such persons do direct selling, but for several companies, and are in many ways independent businessmen. Retail selling can be broken down, depending on the goods or services sold, to department store, specialty shop, and miscellaneous kinds of retail outlets. The characteristic factor of retail selling is that the customer is induced to come to the outlet for the goods or services.

When an attempt is made to classify selling by kind of customer, obviously the simplest classification is whether an individual or a company is the purchaser. Some firms sell goods and services to a wide range of both individuals and companies. For example, an automobile manufacturer may distribute his cars through dealers to a wide range of people of both sexes. The same company may make a large number of fleet sales, that is, sell quantities of automobiles to companies for use by their sales and executive personnel. Other businesses may find the market for their goods exclusively in a small and homogeneous group of individuals. An example of the latter would be a firm selling hearing aids. Still other companies may have no individuals as customers, and their market may be limited to homogeneous groups of companies. An example of this would be a tool-steel manufacturer; the product is sold only to a restricted number of companies for making tools, dies, and the like.

Still another way of classifying selling might be the mode of payment. Our economy is characterized by a tremendous amount of credit buying. Many retail outlets sell for both cash and credit. Others operate exclusively on a cash basis or exclusively on a credit basis.

Since the above classifications are not mutually exclusive, the best way to describe a particular field of selling is to make a composite description, using all the above categories. For example, the selling engaged in by the Polychemicals Department of E. I. du Pont de Nemours & Company can be classified, in terms of the above, as industrial, direct, and company. Yet even when a composite description such as this is made, little insight is gained concerning the nature of the selling process itself and the relation of the principles and techniques of psychology to it [17, 54, 79].

ANALYSIS OF THE SELLING PROCESS

Selling represents the uniquely personal and individualized part of the firm's marketing effort. A fundamental consideration is the extent to which the salesman follows a set sales presentation or, at the other extreme, individualizes what he says and does to each person in each account. Obviously, it is more difficult to personalize a fully structured sales presentation than it is to handle the sales call as an informal interview. Many considerations will govern the degree of structuring effectiveness for the individual company. From a personnel standpoint the knowledge, skill, and sophistication of the men comprising the sales force will markedly influence this kind of decision. Generally speaking, the lower the knowledge, skill, and sophistication level, the more appropriate it is for the company to prescribe what is to be said and done. A kindred consideration involves the knowledge and sophistication of the customer or prospect. The more knowledgeable the customer or prospect, the more likely it is that questions will be raised and objections voiced. Conversely, with less sophisticated people a set presentation may be more effective. The company will certainly consider other matters in arriving at its policy in this aspect of selling—dollar value of the purchase, the relative complexity of the products and services, the cost-revenue relationships, and the degree to which other demand-creating forces have presold prospects and customers. Still another consideration involves the likelihood of repeat business. If the nature of the products and services is such that ongoing account relationships are developed, it is likely that the customers and prospects will expect individualized treatment. On the other hand, if the one-time purchase is the prevalent pattern, it may not be commercially feasible to invest time and effort studying the individual needs of the account and how these can be met, particularly if the unit sale is small.

Clearly, to the extent that the sales presentation is individualized by the salesman, he is in effect made responsible for the strategy used in each account and the tactics whenever he is face to face. This means that he is literally selling himself along with the products and services. He bears a role relationship in each customer-prospect account as a problem solver and idea man. He must carefully consider such matters as the nature of the customer's business, the key problems where his products and services may be of assistance, who the people are who make the buying decisions, and what their individual and collective idiosyncrasies are. He must also be concerned with who the competitors are and what share of the business each one is enjoying, what the competitive strategies and tactics are, and what the likelihood of future business is.

At the other extreme, when the presentation is fully structured, the salesman's manner, or style, becomes the key way in which he can influence a favorable reception to what he says and does. He must pace himself to the reactions he observes in the other person. He must avoid sounding like a phonograph record. There is a tremendous difference between a fully structured sales presentation and a so-called "canned" presentation. The latter term has an adverse affective association, for the implication is that the salesman spouts his message like an automaton [9, 17, 22, 50].

Because selling is uniquely personal as contrasted with advertising, sales promotion, merchandising, and other demand-creating forces, the salesman must be aware that he is a prime stimulus eliciting reactions in the customer or prospect. This places a premium on social perceptiveness. When a sale is consummated, the other person literally perceives, thinks, and feels the act of buying. Thus the salesman must take into account the customer's perceptive process in what he says and does. He must also take account of affective reactions. Finally, he must be capable of directing the thought processes of the other person toward the objective he has in mind.

In a very real sense the effective salesman does not sell; he induces people to buy.

FACTORS IN SELLING

As in advertising, the factors in selling involve the sequence of perceiving, understanding, and feeling. The importance of *perception* in selling stems from the fact that the sales interview involves a unique interaction between the salesman and the customer. Each provides a continuing stimulus for the other. What the salesman says and does must be perceived by the customer and responded to favorably if a sale is to take place. For this reason the focus of the salesman's attention is the customer. He must catch the small cues in the customer's behavior which tell him which points to stress, which ones to gloss over.

Many aspects of perception have a direct application in selling— selectivity of attention, span of attention, subjectivity of perception, and sensory reinforcement. Examples will illustrate these.

Selectivity of Attention. The well-prepared salesman is likely to have hundreds of sales points he can make about his company and its products. However, on any particular call he must choose a few salient points to stress. The key factor in making his choice of points will be what the other person is most likely to attend to selectively.

Span of Attention. An office-supplies salesman was getting along fine with a prospect until he spread out several selling aids, leaflets describing in detail the quality and benefits of the line. The prospect leafed through them and said, "I don't have time to read these now. Leave them with me and I'll give you a ring."

Subjectivity of Perception. It has often been said that we see what we want to see, hear what we want to hear. The purchaser of an electric typewriter complained bitterly when he was billed for his service contract. He thought that a year's service was included in the price of the typewriter. The salesman was certain he had made the point clear in his presentation. Further, the purchase agreement signed by the customer clearly mentioned the service and cited the price for it.

Sensory Reinforcement. A good many years ago when the dairy companies first introduced bottled fruit juice on their milk routes, one firm set up an excellent sales presentation. The route man was instructed to ring the bell, and, as the housewife opened the door, to hand her a bottle of the juice. Then he was to say, "Pardon me, please hold this for me." Imagine the impact of feeling the cold bottle, seeing the contents, and hearing the sales story!

The *affective factors* involving feelings and emotions can significantly influence the outcome of a sales call. Three characteristics of affective responses have particular application in selling:

1 Such responses tend to radiate to other aspects of the physical and social environment than to those which provoked them.

2 Once aroused, they are likely to last for a substantial period of time.

3 They can be positive (euphoric) or negative.

In everyday conversation these three points are alluded to when a person is described as being in a good or bad mood.

The following incident illustrates the significance of feelings in buying. The president of a small firm was a hot prospect for some key-man insurance. The insurance company's representative called for an appointment, arrived promptly, and gave an adequate presentation, but the president did not buy because of an unfavorable gut reaction to the salesman. The two men sat in the president's office, smoking as they discussed the proposition; however, the salesman failed to use the ash tray provided. His ashes grew longer and longer; they finally fell down the front of his shirt and onto the freshly waxed floor. As the refuse collected on the floor, the president became more and more certain he would not buy from that company even if it were the only one in the business. Once triggered off, his response generalized to the salesman as a person, to the company, even to the sales proposition itself!

The salesman as a person and his conduct provide the primary stimulation of the prospect's and customer's feeling during the sales call. It is incumbent upon the salesman to arouse positive affective reactions. These do much to ensure his success with the prospective customer.

The proper handling of a complaint offers a dramatic application of what has been discussed. The following incident is illustrative. An electric typewriter had been purchased. The secretary had just begun to use it when she noticed that it skipped as she typed. She became irritated (negative affective response) and complained to her supervisor. The salesman was called, and very shortly a serviceman arrived. As the serviceman entered the office he asked, "Is this the typewriter?" (It was the only one in the room.) "Yes, and it's a lemon," the secretary replied. The serviceman quickly made an adjustment on it and said, "You could have done that yourself if you had read the manual." The secretary, angrier than ever, said, "If it were a good machine, it wouldn't need fixing. I'm a secretary, not a mechanic." It is doubtful whether this customer will ever buy another typewriter from that firm. The serviceman adjusted the typewriter but ignored completely the feelings of the customer.

The customer's mental processes induced by the salesman must also be considered in selling. These *cognitive factors* are important. Obviously, the sales presentation must be made so that it is understandable to each prospect or customer. Particularly in industrial sales work, technical features and properties of the line must often be explained to purchasing agents without technical or professional educational background. Concreteness of language and aptness of illustrations or examples often spell the difference between success or failure in a sales call.

A key characteristic of thought process relevant to the above statements is reification. The mind literally works like a motion-picture camera. It abhors abstractions. When the stimulus word or phrase is abstract, the individual hearing it translates it according to his own perceptual, affective, and cognitive set. For example, if a salesman says of his product that it is of high quality, the person hearing him might have any number of associations—"too expensive for me," "overengineered for the application I intend," "long lasting," "trouble-free." The important caution is that the salesman must pick his examples, illustrations, and comparisons according to what he knows of the other person's background.

Too frequently, salesmen interject trade jargon during a presentation. The prospect or customer, though not understanding it, is reluctant to betray his ignorance. As the call continues, the person becomes more confused, and the end result may be a lost sale.

Because the customer's needs and wants are the focus of the sale, the presentation should center upon customer benefits to be derived from the purchase rather than upon features and qualities of the product. An automobile salesman is likely to be more successful saying, "The horsepower of this car gives you a fast pickup at a light," than saying, "This car has 315 horsepower." In general, benefits are more easily understood than product features. There is a personal stake in the former!

COMPARISON OF ADVERTISING AND SELLING

Table 1 summarizes the perceptual, affective, and cognitive differences between advertising and selling. The reader might find it a valuable exercise to make a table setting forth ways in which they are similar.

**Table 1 / Perceptual, Affective, and Cognitive
Differences between Advertising and Selling**

Advertising	Selling
Perceptual	
1 Most media, except television, stimulate only one sensory modality.	1 Vision and audition and sometimes other senses are stimulated.
2 Attention is voluntary once arrested.	2 Once salesman gets to see prospect, he has a captive audience.
3 Message must be perceived in short time period, may be reinforced by repetition.	3 Message developed over a long time period, often on basis of several calls.
4 Often the full message is not perceived; e.g., dial is turned to another channel.	4 Salesman can leave with customer reminders of his visit, e.g., samples, descriptive literature.
Affective	
1 Once feelings are aroused, either positively or negatively, no immediate way to exploit or change them.	1 Feelings can be aroused *and changed* by the salesman during the call.
2 Negative feelings may permanently block purchase.	2 Negative feelings, if changed by salesman, may result in purchase.
3 Primary affective stimulus is the ad and its components.	3 Primary affective stimulus is the salesman and his behavior.
Cognitive	
1 Vocabulary, sentence structure, etc., must be understandable to *all* prospective purchasers.	1 Except in canned sales talks, language and expression can be related to each prospect's background.
2 No direct method of knowing whether message is understood.	2 Prospect's responses indicate to the salesman whether his message is being received.
3 Brevity is at a premium.	3 Message can be expanded and stated in different ways.

There is one other fundamental psychological difference between the two which warrants discussion. Necessarily, advertising is designed to influence a mass audience; selling is most often directed to an individual prospect or customer. The former must, therefore, employ a *type* approach to human behavior. The latter can and should utilize a *trait* approach. A particular advertisement for a household detergent may contain a repertoire of appeals (stimuli) designed to influence all housewives who see it to purchase the product. The appeals may include economy, ease of storage, and use with all kinds of fabrics. On the other hand, a housewife who has not seen the advertisement may be induced to buy the product by her local storekeeper primarily because she wishes something to wash her new Dacron dress. In this case, mention of the economy appeal might have blocked the sale. She might not have wanted to use an inexpensive detergent on her expensive dress.

The advertiser has to determine the characteristics held in common by those persons comprising the market for his products or services. This by inference reduces the market to a type. In contrast, the salesman has to learn the traits of each individual prospect or customer. Each must be treated uniquely.

PSYCHOLOGICAL PRINCIPLES AND CONCEPTS
APPLIED TO ADVERTISING AND SELLING

Since this book is devoted to the application of psychology to business, it will be helpful to see concretely how various psychological principles and concepts are applied to advertising and selling.

Learning, an Active Process. Learning, as well as forgetting, involves active response to stimulation, as we shall discuss in the chapter on training. Thus it is not surprising that advertising, whatever the medium, repetitively suggests action, real or simulated. "Try some today." "Road-test it and see." "Imagine yourself basking on the sands of Waikiki." "Let your taste be the judge."

The effective salesman uses this principle every day in his work. When he uses a questioning approach in his calls, he induces action in the form of responses to his inquiries. During his presentation he urges the prospect to handle the sample, to operate the machine. He knows that the prospect must get into the act if a sale is to take place.

In both advertising and selling it is safe to say that the more action induced, the greater the conviction or belief on the part of the prospect or customer. Ultimately, this means more sales.

Overlearning. The jingle used to advertise Pepsi-Cola had such an impact that the company found it could play the tune and omit the words and still get its message across. This is a dramatic example of overlearning. Brand-reinforcement advertising is designed to cause overlearning. Once a particular need is felt, it is hoped that the company's brand line will be sought as *the* satisfier.

In successful selling it is necessary for the salesman to overlearn his products, especially the benefits to be derived from their use. If he has learned his product information only to the point of bare recall, he is likely to encounter difficulty. An unexpected question or reaction on the part of the customer may cause a mental block just when he needs a ready answer. If the salesman has to interrupt his presentation to check his price list or to find technical information, he is likely to lose the prospect's attention. Worse still, the customer's confidence in him as the knower may be undermined.

Similarly, it is important for the salesman who expects repeat sales to overlearn the relevant facts about each of his accounts. Basically, this is a twofold body of knowledge. He has to know who's who and the traits of each person with whom he has contact. He also must know the uses the company makes of his products and the related production and marketing problems that require solution.

Temporal Summation. A commonplace example of this phenomenon is to be absorbed in a book when the telephone rings. We may not be consciously aware of the sound until the phone has rung several times. We rush to answer it before it stops. All our sensory modalities are subject to temporal summation.

In advertising, repetition is used to penetrate the awareness of readers or listeners. It is no happenstance that repetitive jingles are effective in inducing the purchase of goods. Most companies keep their logo (special name plate of an advertiser, usually cast in unique lettering) the same over a period of years in advertising and packaging. The familiar *Coca-Cola* scroll is an effective example.* Similarly, companies maintain the same package shape and color to utilize temporal summation.

The salesman makes general applications of this principle during each call and on repeat calls. In the course of his sales presentation he may make the same point in several different ways. For example, a paper salesman calling on an industrial prospect wished to stress the shelf life of his product in inventory. He said, "The last ream you draw from the storeroom will be as good as the first." "Our paper is treated so it won't fade." "The wrappers are sealed to keep out dust and moisture." "This paper won't curl and ripple after it's around for awhile."

In another instance, a salesman said, "I don't know what happened to that fellow today. I finally got an order. This was my fifth call on him."

* *Coca-Cola* is the registered trademark which distinguishes the product of The Coca-Cola Company. It is reproduced here by special permission.

Perhaps the salesman honestly felt that the successful call was the last one. A more likely explanation, however, is that the successive calls had a *summating* effect on the prospect. The message finally got through to him. Where the nature of the business requires repeated calls to close the sale or where repeat orders are sought, temporal summation is an important principle to employ. On each call the salesman should review with the prospect or customer the ground previously covered and then build his presentation on that foundation.

Spatial Summation. The world around us is perceived through our several senses. Our nervous system is so structured that when the same stimulus is received through two or more of the senses, reinforcement of the message occurs.

Only television among the major advertising media illustrates this perceptual phenomenon. The TV commercial reaches the listener through both the eyes and the ears. Radio, magazines, newspapers, and billboards all depend on one sense to convey the advertising message. An important research problem exists in television: how to maximize perception with visual and auditory stimuli available for simultaneous presentation.

In selling, the application of this principle is more widespread. Remember the dairy-route man and his orange juice? This is an illustrative example of spatial summation. Most salesmen are provided with visual aids in the form of pictures, diagrams, descriptive literature, etc. When these are used to reinforce the oral presentation, the chance of getting the message across is increased, and the likelihood of a sale is enhanced. However, if visuals are in sight at inappropriate times, they may only serve to distract the prospect's or customer's attention from the salesman's message.

Affective Expansion. This peculiarity of human emotions and feelings has direct application in all forms of advertising. The testimonial of an attractive movie star may influence thousands of young girls to buy a particular cosmetic. If they love her, by affective expansion they like the product she uses. The chairman of the board of a well-known advertising agency once declared, "With a baby and a kitten for illustrations I can sell anything." This statement may be an exaggeration, but the fact remains that emotional appeals do induce people to buy.

It is important for the salesman to be aware of this characteristic of the feelings and emotions. His primary application of this principle is to customer behavior. However, he can also better understand his own adjustments if he is aware of affective expansion. Every salesman is likely to have discouraging days when, despite his efforts, he fails to close a single sale. He must guard against letting his ill feelings become cumulative; otherwise he is apt to express them toward customers and prospects. It is sound planning for a salesman to make his first call on a satisfied customer even if no order is in prospect. It will serve to build up his positive feelings and to bolster him for the more difficult calls that must be made later in the day.

Projection. People tend to perceive their own strengths and weaknesses, likes and dislikes, virtues and vices in others. Think about the gifts you have purchased for your family and friends. Didn't you buy things you would like to receive? If you have been in an automobile accident or have witnessed one, you may have observed each driver blaming the other fellow, perhaps even accusing him of committing the very fault he himself was guilty of. Moyer and Gilmer found that adults buying toys for children often buy those with parent appeal rather than those which have child appeal [56].

The advertising agency that bypasses research and structures a campaign on appeals that agency personnel like instead of determining the likes and wants of the market is using projection. The manufacturer of a well-known home permanent sought to enter the Latin American market. Erroneously the advertising campaign emphasized economy because this appeal had proven effective in the United States. Had research been done in advance, the advertiser would have known that the product did not compete in price with a wave done at the beauty parlor in any Latin American country. When sales proved disappointing, subsequent research revealed that safety was an effective appeal because of the ineptness of beauticians in that market. The same research, incidentally, revealed that there was an untapped market for home permanents, namely, young girls preparing for Communion and Confirmation. A modification of the product was manufactured for this juvenile market and subsequently also marketed in the United States.

Too often the salesman is likely to stress in his presentation what he would like to hear were he the customer. The following anecdote from *The American Salesman* is illustrative:

A Manhattan real estate salesman and his wife were planning to have a family in the next few years and felt they should acquire a home in the suburbs and pay for it before the wife left her job. Their chief concern about a home in the suburbs was that it be located so as to ensure easy transportation to the heart of the city. They finally found one that met their needs. After a few months in their new residence, the salesman decided to sell suburban real estate rather than continue working in the city. As he showed various pieces of property to prospects, he continually pointed out the convenience of travel to and from the city. One of his prospects was completely unimpressed by his presentation and, as a result, sought the services of another real estate broker. Information later obtained indicated that the prospect was moving to the suburbs to get away from his troublesome mother-in-law; consequently, the last thing he wanted in a new home was to make it easy for her to reach him.

Rationalization. It is part of human adjustment to justify our behavior in our own eyes. Few persons can claim never to have used after-the-fact reasons for doing something. The extreme example of rationalization is the alibi artist. He always has a ready excuse for anything he says or does. This mechanism is illustrated daily in consumer advertising. "Limited quantity." "Order some now before the supply is exhausted." "Buy now; prices are going up." "These coats would cost twice as much in the regular season." As an experiment, scan the ads in your daily newspaper. See how many examples of rationalization you find. The advertiser who uses this principle attempts to provide reasons *in advance* for the purchase of his product. It is especially effective with luxury items.

The salesman bases part of his strategy on rationalization. It is his job to furnish the prospect or customer with reasons justifying the purchase of the goods or services he has for sale. An automobile salesman closed a sale with a customer just before the model change-over by using these points: "At this price your first year of depreciation is already deducted from the list price." "The new models have only minor changes." "Financing rates are going up." "Think of the trips you can take before winter sets in." "The amount you save will pay your youngster's tuition for a whole year."

Functional Autonomy of Habits. Nowhere is this principle better illustrated in advertising and selling than in the cigarette industry. Well over two-thirds of the adolescent and adult population smoke cigarettes. Yet few people can tell you why they smoke. Heavy smokers often light up without being conscious of it. Companies in the industry strive to "brand-lock" their customers. The marketing objective is to have the customer think not of a cigarette, but of Fumos!

A considerable amount of our behavior is a matter of habit. Habits, once established, are difficult to break. Brand-reinforcing advertising is designed to make a brand name a matter of habit in buying a particular item or line of goods. Often advertising copy contains such phrases as "Make it a habit to buy at . . . "; "fiftieth anniversary sale"; "a way of life for knowing people."

The salesman with a long-established account has a concrete example of the force of habit. His competitors have a difficult task in any efforts to take away such a customer. The longer the seller-buyer relationship lasts, the less likely the customer is to change to another source of supply.

It is sound sales strategy to study carefully the habits of each customer. To the extent that the salesman knows them he is able to make buying from him a habit which fits into the habitual behavior of the customer. A salesman learned that a particular purchasing agent obtained purchase requisitions from the various departments of the plant each Friday afternoon. Habitually the purchasing agent took them home with him to study over the week end. The salesman also found out that he and the purchasing agent attended the same church. The salesman, without being obvious about it, arranged to meet the purchasing agent almost every Sunday and to chat with him on these occasions. The salesman also rearranged his call schedule so that he saw the purchasing agent on Monday mornings. The salesman reasoned that through the Sunday contacts he would become a part of the purchasing agent's thought processes regarding prospective purchases. The Monday morning calls provided the salesman an opportunity to interview him before his competitors got there.

Frequency of Purchases. Habits also function in the matter of purchase frequencies. Figure 4.2 shows that the probability of a consumer's buying the same brand on two consecutive purchases of frozen orange juice decreases exponentially with an increase in time between those purchases. In his studies of consumer brand choice as a learning process Kuehn [48] emphasizes there is a "time rate of decay of purchase probability." Buying habits must be reinforced; recency is an important variable.

The Life Insurance Agency Management Association [27] has shown that although ownership or regular life insurance is strongly related to such variables as income and education, exposure to a recent sales interview is

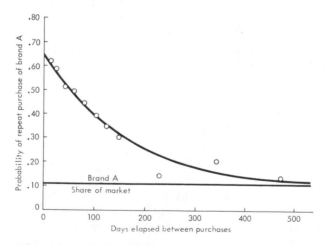

Fig. 4.2. Effect of consumer purchase frequencies. The probability of a consumer's buying the same brand on two consecutive purchases of frozen orange juice decreases exponentially with an increase in time between those purchases. (From Kuehn, A. A. Consumer brand choice as a learning process. *J. Adver. Research,* 1962, 2, 10–17.)

important. In an extensive study of prospects between thirty and forty-nine years old, LIAMA found the probability that the interview resulted in a sale was almost constant.

UNANSWERED QUESTIONS

Human behavior being as complex as it is, it is not too surprising that when principles and methods from psychology are applied to any phase of business, results are not always up to expectations. Certainly this is true in marketing. In a free economy the customer or prospect has veto power over the very survival of the business enterprise. He cannot be coerced. There is no power relationship that can be exercised to force him to buy a particular product from a particular company. Yet increasingly business is becoming more scientific and systematic in its approaches to marketing problems. Set forth below are some of the unanswered questions—problems which are worthy of psychological research if the body of knowledge called marketing is to increase and be more precise.

First, we need to refine our research methodology by measuring the relative strengths of demand-creating forces under given marketing conditions in specific segments of our economy and under specific conditions of supply and demand. For example, when a particular person buys something, what were the relative impacts of advertising, packaging, pricing, sales promotion, and selling on the decision?

Second, and related to the above question, when a particular person buys something, what values did he place upon the particular company making the product, the brand, the product, the attendant service, and the person with whom he dealt? For example, when a housewife buys a can of Campbell's tomato soup, what is the relative influence on her decision of the store where she deals, the brand name Campbell's, and the way the soup is packaged? Third, how can business close the gap between stated intentions to purchase and actual purchasing behavior? Recurrently, marketing research studies indicate varying degrees of discrepancy. Fourth, how can the company assess more effectively the relevant personality and motivational factors in the individual which may bear upon his buying decisions? In recent years great emphasis has been placed upon motivation research as a necessary complement to marketing research.

Motivation research is not a substitute for market research. It adds meaning to cold statistics, such as the percentage of teen-agers who use home permanents, by indicating the satisfactions the users derive, the unique features they perceive in the brands they use, or what improvements they feel might be made in the product. Motivation research has helped to indicate why particular products have not gained acceptance. Some advertising agencies use it to stimulate copywriting ideas. It has shed considerable light on "product personality," i.e., the characteristics users attribute to a particular product. For example, motivation research revealed that a particular cigarette was feminine. An advertising campaign featuring he-men smokers complete with tattoos changed its gender in the minds and feelings of the smoking public.

For the future, we predict that marketing will demand more and more attention from the behavioral scientist as we advance farther in the direction of becoming a nation of consumers. As industrial psychology becomes more concerned with the consumer, we predict it will play an increasing role in the study of the marketing environment.

SUGGESTIONS FOR SELECTIVE READING

Abelson, H. I. *Persuasion.* New York: Springer, 1959. A book for practising persuaders written by a psychologist.

Anastasi, Anne. *Fields of applied psychology.* New York: McGraw-Hill, 1964. Part IV, on consumer psychology, covers methodology, buying behavior, and the perceptual-cognitive factors in advertising.

Bliss, P. (Ed.) *Marketing and the behavioral sciences.* Boston: Allyn and Bacon, 1963. A book of readings on the applications of the behavioral sciences to marketing decisions.

Britt, S. H. *The spenders.* New York: McGraw-Hill, 1960. A former Madison Avenue psychologist looks at the marketing mix.

Coleman, L. R. *The practice of successful advertising.* Sydney, Australia: Pydge, 1959. Psychology in advertising at the practical level.

Crawford, J. W. *Advertising: Communications from management.* Boston: Allyn and Bacon, 1960. An aspect of the marketing mix.

Dichter, E. *The strategy of desire.* Garden City, N.Y.: Doubleday, 1960. For a description of motivation research in marketing.

Dichter, E. *Handbook of consumer motivations.* New York: McGraw-Hill, 1964. Motivation research in the marketing mix.

Ferber, R., & Wales, H. G. (Eds.) *Motivation and market behavior.* Homewood, Ill.: Irwin, 1958. Readings on methods and techniques used in determining consumer motivation and purchase behavior.

Flesch, R. *A new way to better English.* New York: Harper & Row, 1958. Applications of reading research, in part related to advertising.

Grossack, M. M. (Ed.) *Understanding consumer behavior.* Boston: Christopher, 1963. A look at the marketing mix, from tourist reactions to furniture buying.

Hepner, H. W. *Modern advertising: Practices and principles.* New York: McGraw-Hill, 1956. Fundamentals of advertising and selling by a psychologist.

Karn, H. W., & Gilmer, B. v. H. (Eds.) *Readings in industrial and business psychology.* (2d ed.) New York: McGraw-Hill, 1962. Section XII has five articles on marketing and consumer research.

Katona, G. *The powerful consumer.* New York: McGraw-Hill, 1960. Economic psychology related to consumer attitudes, social groupings, levels of aspiration, and economic fluctuations.

Katona, G. *Psychological analysis of economic behavior.* New York: McGraw-Hill, 1951. An economic psychologist looks at the marketing mix.

Katona, G. *The mass consumption society.* New York: McGraw-Hill, 1964. An overall view of the marketing environments at the consumer level.

Katz, E., & Lazarfeld, P. F. *Personal influence.* Glencoe, Ill.: Free Press, 1955. The "opinion leader" concept in advertising.

Lucas, D. B., & Britt, S. H. *Measuring advertising effectiveness.* New York: McGraw-Hill, 1963. Another aspect of the problem of criteria.

Mayer, M. *Madison Avenue USA.* New York: Pocket, 1959. A popularized image of American advertising.

Nielsen, G. S. (Ed.) *Industrial and business psychology.* Copenhagen: Munksgaard, 1962. Some readings are related to the marketing mix.

Rich, S. U. *Shopping behavior of department store customers.* Boston: Harvard Graduate School of Business Administration, 1963. Problems of everyday buying.

Sandage, C. H. (Ed.) *The promise of advertising.* Homewood, Ill.: Irwin, 1961. Covers an area from studies of buying behavior to image building.

Starch, D. *Measuring product sales made by advertising.* Mamaroneck, N.Y.: Daniel Starch, 1961. Techniques in studying advertising effectiveness.

Steiner, G. A. *The people look at TV.* New York: Knopf, 1963. For a general discussion of television in the marketing mix.

Stephan, F. F., & McCarthy, P. J. *Sampling opinions: An analysis of survey procedures.* New York: Wiley, 1958. Technical aspects of opinion surveys.

Wall Street Journal Editors. *Americans and their pocketbooks.* Chicopee, Mass.: Dow Jones Books, 1964. A popular account of how your neighbors earn and spend their money.

Weiss, E. B. *The vanishing salesman.* New York: McGraw-Hill, 1962. How the functions of selling are changing.

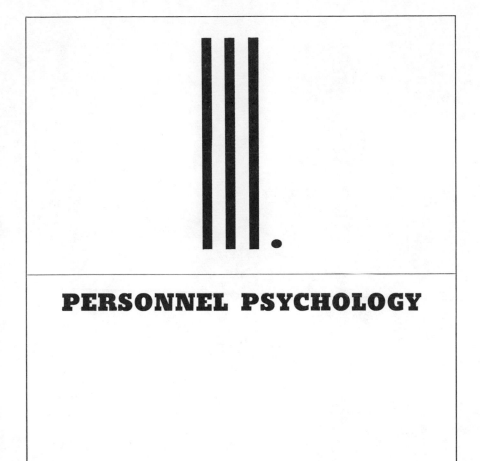

PERSONNEL PSYCHOLOGY

5

Human Needs in Industry

B. von Haller Gilmer

Human beings want many things. All of us must have air, food, shelter. Other needs, which are just as real, include status, recognition for our efforts, and a feeling of belongingness; but these needs are often more difficult to satisfy. It is important to consider how they are related to the work environment of the person in industry.

Industry has made much progress in helping the worker as well as the executive satisfy some of his economic needs and obtain many of the physical comforts of life. But progress has been slower in other respects— in helping the man feel that he belongs, that he has the opportunity to measure up to his own ambitions. One reason for our lack of progress in helping motivate the man to acquire skill and use it in the development of his full potential lies in the fact that what a man needs changes with time and with circumstances. In youth, men look more for opportunity, in old age, for security.

A BASIC MODEL OF BEHAVIOR

In this chapter we will describe some of the more common needs and raise some practical questions of why people behave as they do. We hope that the presentation here, which will be amplified in later chapters, will help the reader to understand the sources of behavior. In developing need structures there is often a delicate balance between dependency and independence in human behavior. In most organizations the individual's superiors control many of the paths to need satisfaction, and within such a framework we shall describe variations within individuals and how reactions to frustration and common defensive behaviors indicate the nature of our struggle for need satisfaction, both individually and as an achieving society. Let us begin by taking a look at a basic model of behavior for the individual relevant to personnel psychology.

The student of psychology is familiar with three interrelated assumptions about human behavior: Behavior is *caused*. Behavior is *motivated*. Behavior is *goal-directed*. We will present these three assumptions in terms of a basic model of behavior described by Leavitt [26]. This model is represented in Figure 5.1.

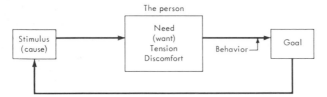

Fig. 5.1. A basic closed-circuit model of behavior, showing relationships between causality, motivation, and goal direction. Obtaining a goal eliminates the cause, which in turn eliminates the motive and, finally, the behavior. (From Leavitt, H. J. *Managerial psychology*. Courtesy of the University of Chicago Press; copyright 1964 by the University of Chicago.)

In this closed-circuit model, obtaining a goal eliminates the cause, which in turn eliminates the motive, which consequently eliminates the behavior. When one's stomach is empty, the emptiness stimulates a feeling of hunger, and this feeling stimulates action in the direction of food. When obtained, the food fills the stomach, causing cessation of the hunger impulses, and this in turn terminates the behavior in search of food. The description seems simple, but at this point Leavitt emphasizes that the closed-circuit conception has a limitation of which we should be aware. Whereas one can consume enough food to stop hunger and food seeking temporarily, it does not follow that one can consume a given quantity of prestige, for example, and feel satiated. This is important to remember if we are to understand the drives of people in industry.

Often human behavior does fit in with the system just described. Behavior may be an effort to eliminate tensions by seeking goals that neutralize the causes of tensions. For instance, a man thinks that he has a need for a new car. The more he considers the proposition, the more his tension increases. He explores the market and finds the car that will meet his needs. The more he thinks about a new car, the more he is influenced by advertising and the more a desire to obtain one builds up in him. Finally, when arrangements are made to buy the car, the tension is resolved.

Understanding something of the general nature of human wants sets the stage for dealing with many of the problems to be described later in chapters dealing with personnel management, work, and social and personal adjustments.

VARIATIONS WITHIN INDIVIDUALS

One of the main influences on a man's needs is his age. It is quite apparent that the needs of the child differ greatly from those of the adult. Similarly, the satisfactions that we expect from our job depend, in part, on the age and experience bracket we are in. Most industrial workers range in age from eighteen through sixty-five, and those in management range from the early twenties to retirement. There is evidence that the range of individual differences within the limits of man's working span is so great that one man may be as youthful biologically and psychologically as another who is fifteen or twenty years younger. But in spite of these individual differences, we can still say that psychological needs change with age, and these changes affect our attitudes toward work.

Needs in Youth. The youth is aware of and welcomes change. The individual is growing, his world is widening. The man just out of college, entering an industrial career in engineering, salesmanship, or some like field, seizes every opportunity to get ahead, and he has the stamina to take the competition. He wants and expects challenge, for herein lies the path to recognition. In old age, change is unwelcomed and resisted. The dreams of better days ahead are over, and the world is narrowing. Competition is shunned because few have the stamina to keep up the pace.

The problems of early youth are numerous. The college student in his senior year must decide whether to take a job or to enter graduate school and study for a profession. When he begins working, he must try to adjust his psychological needs to meet new economic necessities. He must look for an opportunity where his anticipations can be realized and his enthusiasms rewarded. He may not succeed at first. But youth has one big advantage; disappointments are soon overcome by hopes for a better future. Dissatisfaction with one job may be remedied by taking another. The opportunities for youth in our expanding economy build up attitudes of both confidence and defiance—just the reverse of the kind found in the older person. A youth at the worker level, regardless of his limitations in education, is optimistic about the future. His physical strength and vitality to some degree make up for his lack of training and experience. Desires that are not readily fulfilled today are projected in terms of satisfaction in the future.

Needs in Middle Age. In middle age, status becomes of great importance; in this age, a man is determining whether or not he will be a success, as measured by his own goals. In occupations in which long professional training is essential to productive activity and economic independence, such as engineering and science, men who have not yet been admitted to full standing may identify themselves as being young. On the other hand, a laborer, who may be the same chronological age as the newly licensed company lawyer may feel himself old at thirty-five. A steelworker or coal miner may feel he has reached his economic peak just at the age that the engineer and accountant are ready for promotion and their best work.

Along with decreases in physical stamina and sexual activity, such things as vanishing hairlines indicate the passing of youth, a stage soon to be followed in some people by what has been termed a "middle-age revolt" [5]. This usually comes earlier in the case of the worker, later with the manager or professional man; but it comes to many in terms of lost dreams and failure to meet cutthroat competition. This revolt comes when the man cannot plead the inexperience of youth or the frailties of age. The middle-ager sometimes expresses guilt feelings of failure and blames himself for not having gone into the right job. He frequently wonders whether he married the right woman. He may see his weight climbing and his hair thinning. When youngsters call him "sir" and the lone courtesy candle appears on his birthday cake, the middle-aged man is quite ready to magnify his problems. His ego suffers another blow when he moves into the bifocal stage and finds that his insurance rates are going up. It is in this stage that the middle-aged man sometimes begins to aggress against his family and against his job. During this period of emotional second adolescence, the middle-aged worker may be difficult to deal with and the manager may be hard to work for.

Perplexing are the problems of motivation which emerge in adult life, problems not discontinuous with those of college-age students. We know something about the individual crises of middle age brought on by early commitment to values too shallow to endure for a lifetime—"where many people have not prepared to go all the way" [12]. To some middle age is a stage where sophistication lessens the thrill of discovery, where there is a realization that there are problems ahead that the person didn't have as a youth, and he is not sure whether he can handle them or not. On the more positive side, middle age is for other people a time when they are both experienced enough and vigorous enough to extend themselves, when the first anxieties of responsibility have passed, when they feel on top of their jobs, when they have stopped worrying so much about tactics and images, and when they begin to go for more satisfying objectives. For some, middle age is losing the tyranny of "what people will think."

Middle age is a time when the individual has already committed himself to an occupation and a way of life. The conservatism that frequently sets in around middle age may involve protection of "what little I have left." This may be important in coping with the problems of old age, which will be covered in a later chapter.

VARIATIONS BETWEEN INDIVIDUALS

Another factor influencing human needs involves class differences. A job considered good by the son of a dayworker might be thought of as poor by the son of a vice-president. Job satisfaction has a relation to job expectancy. The young man who comes from the working-class family may regard the job of a toolmaker or bricklayer as very satisfactory. This class of job would probably be considered inferior by the young man from a higher social status. Thus job status and social status go hand in hand where there is some permanence involved. The president may brag that his college son is spending the summer with a drag crew in the steel mill. The worker may also brag about his son having a similar job. However, the needs being satisfied in the two cases are quite different.

When we think in terms of needs being satisfied, we must think in terms of goal expectancy. One young man from a lower-class family may be dissatisfied with the same job his neighbor likes because he or his family has set higher goals for him.

The level of aspiration of any given person in relation to his feelings of accomplishment determines in large measure his attitudes. The son of the worker who aspires to work his way up from the bottom, who pictures himself becoming a part of management, may play just such a role until he experiences failure and rebuff time after time. Being thus thwarted, he may turn his attention to union activities. If he is encouraged with success here, he may well go on to become a leader and a strong union man. Some of the outstanding union leaders today, men with proved leadership and executive ability, have become union rather than management men because in the union they found the recognition they had been seeking.

Status Anxiety. The acceptance or rejection of a person and his consequent attitude toward his work are frequently a matter of status. Ours is one of the few societies in history in which performance is a primary determinant of status. The college man who may be competing with a high school man for recognition on the job may feel that he is in an advantageous position.

He may well be taken aback to find that being known as a college man who works with noncollege people can have its disadvantages. The author has several instances in his files of engineering students who have had to buck the problem of being accepted on the job where their coworkers had never been to college. The thing that may make a person "belong" in one situation may well be a handicap in another. A Ph.D. in psychology is a union card in academic circles, and it can serve as an entree on many occasions. Any experienced consultant, however, can verify the statement that this advanced degree can be a handicap in being accepted in the shop. Status anxiety is found in every part of our culture, but it is particularly noticeable in industry. Here we can observe human tensions in a clear-cut way as one man compares himself with another in terms of the recognition he has received and the advancements he gets.

Differences in Ambition. Although we have seen how social status, age, and education determine, in part, an individual's ambitions and job satisfactions, it is important to remember that the drives of some people differ regardless of the influence of these factors. Many people seem quite adjusted to their job situation though it be of comparatively low status and low financial return. It is hard for the highly motivated person to realize that some people are not as ambitious as he. In one industrial situation, psychologists were employed to study the attitudes of people who had several times been passed over in promotions. Some were quite indignant because they had not received recognition, but a surprising number seemed quite content to remain at their particular level. One man, who gave evidence of having more ability than he had used, was asked why he was content with his medium-status job. He pointed out that he valued other things in life more highly than job success. "I know what you are thinking," he said during the interview. "I don't have hypertension, I don't have an ulcer, I'm a failure!"

We know that there are variations of human needs from person to person and also that the needs of any individual change from time to time. We know that these variations are in some instances related to age, in others to status, experience, and education. But there are many changes of needs in the human being for which we cannot account. Industry has laid primary emphasis on improving the workers' environment, but only indirectly has it studied the worker himself to determine his needs.

Need Variation across Groups. Not only do needs vary from one person to another; sometimes they vary from group to group. A study [29] made during World War II offers us a good example. In an industrial plant, blue-green lighting had been installed after research had indicated that this would reduce eyestrain. Careful records of production were kept, and after the blue-green lighting had been installed, the output of male workers increased. There were many comments about less eyestrain from the men. They were very happy with the new lighting. But with women employees the story was quite different. Output fell off, and absenteeism hit its highest peak. The women's production was greatly reduced. Why? Because they felt that the new type of lighting made them look ghastly; and, in fact, it did. In this particular instance, an environmental situation which motivated one group of people in one way had just the opposite effect on another group with different specific needs.

REACTIONS TO FRUSTRATION

Attempts to obtain satisfaction of needs and desires frequently meet with obstacles regardless of one's status or job. Many times these blockages are only temporary and are overcome easily. At other times, however, attempts to attain a goal are blocked time and time again, with the result that there is an accumulation of tension within the individual. The work environment in our highly competitive North American industrial system is in itself particularly frustration-inducing for workers and managers alike. The examples given below, all taken from industrial settings, illustrate several kinds of reactions to frustrations that normal people show.

Elementary Aggression. Elementary aggression as shown by the adult looks somewhat like the behavior of a naughty child. In an Eastern city, a union local called a strike which shut down all truck deliveries to and from the five largest department stores. As the strike, which involved hundreds of drivers, went into its second year, such childlike behavior was engaged in as heaving paint bombs into the homes of the store supervisors and breaking plate-glass windows in the stores by throwing steel balls at them from moving automobiles.

Displaced Aggression. Displaced-aggression reactions are shown in indirect and subtle ways; they are so named because the behavior is directed against some object or person other than the real source of the frustration. For example, the frustrated worker who is sore at the boss, may rant and rave at his family. He cannot tell off the boss for fear of losing his job, so his wife and children become the innocent victims of his displaced aggression. The following example illustrates this kind of behavior.

A middle-aged woman employee was transferred from her regular operation of assembling parts in a metals-fabrication plant to a new operation in the same department. The new job consisted of a repetitive type of task, machining springs for toy motors. After a day the woman became adept at the job and was able to produce about 250 pieces an hour, and after another day at the job, 350. The amount of production asked by the gang boss was 500 units per hour. The worker reported that she could not reach this requirement. The boss insisted that she could raise her production if she wanted to and that she was holding back purposely because she wanted her old job back. Her name was reported to the foreman as being one of several workers who balked at meeting production requirements. The foreman spoke to her in harsh tones, telling her, in effect, to produce or else.

The woman became upset and was able to do hardly any work for the remainder of the day. She did not say anything to the foreman. During the next three days her work improved slightly in quantity but decreased in quality. It was also discovered later that she had been the one responsible for stopping up the toilet in the ladies' rest room on three successive days following the instance. On each occasion she had placed a whole orange in the commode. Certainly this was displaced aggression!

Organized Aggression. Organized aggression may come about through well-laid planning, as is often found in prolonged labor-management conflict. But often closer to the real feelings of people is the aggression that becomes organized more informally. An example of this type of reaction to frustration is found in writings about the famous Western Electric researches [19].

In the study of a wage-incentive scheme, it became apparent that the majority of a group of workers, regardless of other differences, shared some common feelings. If an individual turned out too much work he became a "rate buster"; too little work labeled him a "chiseler." The person who would say anything to injure a fellow member of the group was a "squealer." It was also accepted practice that no member of the work group should act officiously.

The wage-incentive scheme was planned to encourage output by setting pay rates on the basis of group earnings. The experts who devised the scheme assumed that the group would bring pressure to bear upon the slower workers to make them work harder and so increase the earnings of the group. Actually what happened was practically the reverse. The workers put pressure not only on the slower workers but upon the faster ones as well. Pressure was applied in various ways. One informally organized aggression was "binging," as the men called it. If one of the workers did something which the group did not consider proper, a fellow worker had the right to bing him. This consisted of a quick, stiff blow on the upper arm. The worker who was struck got the idea and did not strike back. The punishment was psychological, not physical.

Why was such behavior engaged in? For one thing, the industrial worker has his own ways of doing his job, his own traditions of skill, and his own satisfactions from achieving goals set according to his own standards—this, of course, within certain practical limits. The worker hates to be "told" or to be "planned for" by experts. In a sense he rejects authority, particularly when customs of work are challenged by innovations put in without his approval. The resulting frustration brings out aggression. The aggression frequently becomes organized when the majority of the group feels the same way about the source of the frustration.

Work as Escape. Another kind of reaction to frustration, frequently found with the harassed executive, is the attempt to escape through excessive work, more or less routine in nature. Such was the case with an executive vice-president of a large corporation whom we shall call Mr. Gregory.

Mr. Gregory was in his early fifties. He was a graduate of an engineering school and had worked his way up in the company over a period of some thirty years. Now he had held the position of executive vice-president for four years. To all outside appearances he was a highly successful executive; in the office before eight, he was the last to leave in the evening, carrying a loaded brief case. It gradually became apparent to Gregory's superiors that he was working harder and harder and accomplishing less and less. There seemed to be no family or outside problems causing his difficulty. During a routine clinical examination held periodically for top executives, the following facts appeared. Gregory had been successful as an engineer, and he had made notable progress as the vice-president of manufacturing. In fact, his success in the latter position led to his appointment as executive vice-president. About two years after this promotion, the corporation expanded, and the job became too big for Gregory, though he did not realize it at the time. He began to postpone more and more decisions and to become harder to see. He spent his time primarily on details of a clerical nature, working evenings and sometimes on week ends. When pressed for decisions, particularly from the lower echelons, he made it known that he was too busy, not verbally but by actually being busy.

Here is a type of reaction to a frustration caused by inability to cope with the important parts of a job; the reaction is to seek escape by concentrating on the unimportant things.

Excuses for Failure. One of the most common ways of reacting to frustration caused by failure to reach a goal is indulging in rationalization. The person tries for a way out by coming up with a plausible or good excuse for failure; he tries to justify his behavior. This is illustrated by the industrial clerk whom we shall call Harold.

Upon graduation from high school, Harold was employed by the ABC Company as a general clerical worker in the office. During the ensuing five years he made satisfactory progress, and at the end of that time he was transferred into the accounting department. Shortly after beginning work in the accounting department, he married. Within the next few years Harold's family responsibilities increased until his salary was not sufficient to sustain the standard of living to which he and his wife had become accustomed and which they desired to maintain. Harold requested an increase in salary from his superior in the firm, and he was told that he was receiving all that the job was worth. The head of the accounting department told Harold that the only way in which he could hope to receive an increase in salary was to qualify himself for a higher-rated job. He advised Harold to enroll in an accounting course in a local night school.

Harold had not participated in any formal educational training since graduating from high school, where his work had been of only average quality. He enrolled for courses in accounting, but within a few months he began to experience difficulty with his schoolwork. His conduct in the office and at home became noticeably different. At the office he discoursed loudly and long to his fellow workers on the unnecessary attempts by accountants to make their work unduly hard for students and the unnecessary difficulty of standard accounting practices. At home also Harold's behavior showed a change. Whereas he had formerly taken considerable interest in his home and enjoyed playing with his children, he became surly toward his family.

As time wore on, Harold's behavior went from rationalization to withdrawal through daydreaming. Instead of working on his lessons for night school, he began spending more and more time hanging around the local beer parlor, drinking mildly, and making various plans to get a job in which he would make a great deal more money. No effort was ever made to carry through these plans.

Piling Up Frustration. Let us use one final example to show how frustration after frustration can accumulate to such an extent that a person will aggress in violent ways that may even lead to the loss of his job.

The XYZ Electrical Manufacturing Company decided to have a time-and-motion study made. Joe M. worked on the assembly line in one of the company plants. He was a hard worker and took pride in his speed on the job. Since he had skill and was fast, he received one of the largest pay checks in the department. One morning Joe got up late and, while rushing around to leave for work, had a severe argument with his wife. When he arrived at work, he found a man standing a few feet away from his table. No words were exchanged between them, but as Joe worked he saw that this man was checking his movements with a stop watch. Joe found that he was slowing down, and as he attempted to work fast, he began to drop some of the tiny parts making up the assembly. As time passed, Joe became more and more angry. Finally he lost control of himself and shoved the motion-study man to the floor.

One may at first interpret the aggression shown by Joe as resentment of this particular time-and-motion-study man. In the hearing that followed, however, it became clear that Joe had been frustrated all morning. It began with his getting up late and having words with his wife; the frustration was added to by Joe's having had a difficult time finding a parking space; and it was climaxed by the checking of the time-and-motion-study man. Any one instance in itself would probably not have induced the aggression, but the accumulation of pent-up tensions finally reached the explosion point.

COMMON DEFENSIVE BEHAVIORS

"If one waits patiently, everything will turn out all right." This statement is all too typical of the person who depends upon someone else to solve the problems. *Dependency* is perhaps more normal in a statistical sense than is self-reliance [13]. It has several manifestations, which are commonly related to what people *don't* do, such as unwillingness to make decisions, to exert extra effort. It is sometimes characteristic of the person who is satisfied with the *status quo*. Dependency is related to conformity in behavior. In some respects industry pays a higher price for inefficiency which comes through dependency than it does for the tensions produced by neurotics. It is hard to recognize but easy to rationalize, and it is certainly a roadblock to individual productivity. One of the dangers of obsolescence in industry, in research, or in teaching or learning, for that matter, is the failure of individuals to appraise their indifference to their personal progress or to prepare for problems to be faced.

One way to think of human behavior is that it can go in three directions —toward solution of the problem at hand, toward persistent nonadjustive behavior, and toward some halfway form of substitute adjustment. Some people feel they are solving their problems just by getting mad; others resort to defensive behavior. One of the dangers of technical obsolescence, which can happen to administrators and teachers as well as to engineers and scientists, is *rationalization*. Through excuses for failure one works toward believing what he wants to believe. Frequently *withdrawal* reactions provide escape for the dependent person, e.g., the secretary who may engage in an excessive amount of daydreaming and neglect her typing. Daydreaming, is one of the problems to be faced in accident prevention when the person is in a hazardous situation. Although daydreaming may include elements that can lead in positive directions, it often is defensive in nature.

Identification as a defense mechanism in industry is frequently overlooked. In the first place, it is a powerful and often useful tool in the training of new employees. The beginning employee, whether he be in the office or the plant, is in a stressful situation because he does not know exactly what is expected of him just when he wants to make a good impression. The new worker may identify with the worker at the next bench, learning more from him than from the formal instructions of a supervisor. He may, of course, seek identity with the union. The man in supervision will seek to identify with management. All of this may be perfectly normal behavior unless carried to excess. Identification may be good or bad for the individual depending upon the interaction of the person with his work climate and on the goals of the organization.

Another technique adjustment used by some people to reduce the stress they encounter from an environment is to *insulate* themselves by keeping away from others. The person may appear self-sufficient, detached, even cold, but the careful observer will notice that he maintains this behavior as a protection.

Compensation as a compromise reaction is quite commonly found in organizational settings. Here a person substitutes a second goal and satisfies it when the original one is blocked. Although a second choice, it still satisfies him and hence is often a handicap to the person and company as well. One may even overcompensate in seeking a compromise.

One may also cover up some weakness through *projection*. The man on the drill press who slows down because "no one else is beating his heart out for the company" is projecting his feelings onto others. The man who pads the expense account may ease his guilt by saying it is a part of the "culture of the organization." The supervisor who does not feel that he is getting due recognition for his efforts may project his feelings against "the system."

For some people the starting of *rumors* may be considered defensive behavior. Rumors may be started deliberately for political ends or they may be unintentionally inspired, serving a competitive need to increase one's own ego. Rumors tend to flow best horizontally. They spread more widely when they are ambiguous. Knowledgeable people are less likely to transmit rumors, particularly in crisis situations. Errors in relaying rumors are in the direction of what one expects to hear rather than what one actually hears.

Of the wide differences in adjustment patterns which people use in trying to reduce the unpleasant effects of stress one of the most subtle is *reaction formation*. Here we find the person, successful or otherwise, who attempts to conceal motives by publicly displaying attitudes that are their direct opposites. A feeling of hostility toward another may be expressed by excessive thoughtfulness where the other is concerned. One observer reports the case of a high-level executive in a department store who used every opportunity to extol the virtues of his superior, whom he disliked and distrusted. Such behaviors are often difficult to evaluate, but when combined with many other critical incidents that can be described, they are helpful in studying the effects of organizational climates on individuals.

PATTERNS OF ADJUSTIVE BEHAVIOR

The unintended effects of organizational life on physical and mental health are now receiving a wide array of research attention. Especially stressful in terms of adjustive behaviors are variables related to leadership roles, creative problem solving, and security and status in the organization. The skill mix of the individual and the content demands of the job become important as change involved with automation and technical obsolescence leads to tension, fluctuations in self-esteem, lowered morale, and anxiety—in some respects appearing as anxiety in search of a cause. For the individual there are no models of adjustment for universal emulation; each individual must find his own style. Anxiety may aid or distort any given person's perception of the organization [41].

Mental-health statistics abound in which it is shown that one out of every thirteen persons may spend part of his life in a mental hospital, one out of every three families having at least one member with a serious emotional problem. By no means do these figures tell the whole story. Only a small percentage of disturbed people find their way into a hospital or receive professional treatment. That half of the hospital beds in the United States are used by patients with neuropsychiatric illnesses only indicates one view of the problem. There are data from Europe indicating that the problem of mental and emotional disturbances is comparable to that in North America. Costs to industry alone in terms of absenteeism, accidents, disciplinary problems, and lost production have never been statistically determined, since there are no clear-cut criteria of what constitutes a mental-health problem for those who continue to work and never receive a clinical diagnosis. One study of adults aged twenty to fifty-nine living in midtown Manhattan concluded that only about 20 per cent could be considered essentially in good mental health [38]. As atypical as this special group may be, it does show one aspect of the problem in large urban situations. From studies of the worker and the manager have come some useful ways of thinking about the problems of the individual in an organization. Let us illustrate by example how change can affect people.

The impact of technological change on the work environment in one office was studied by Mann and Williams [31]. They found that the introduction of electronic data-processing equipment meant a general tightening of the task structure of the office. Changes in job requirements which involved more risk, a greater understanding of the total system, and a greater degree of interdependence brought on increased tension. The office workers felt that top management not only expected more of them but was less interested in them as individuals than before adopting the electronically controlled accounting procedures. Significantly higher proportions of these white-collar workers believed their future looked worse and worried about layoffs and general job insecurity. These people who had been at the vortex of the automation change-over, workers and supervisors alike, showed evidence of more psychological and physical anxiety than exists in similar white-collar groups in the nation.

Some people, of course, thrive on change and react differently in their attitudes. In one survey respondents were asked to choose between a job that paid a low income but had high security and a job that paid a high income but had low security. Most "professionals and executives" chose the latter type of job, whereas "salaried employees" and "factory workers" chose the former kind.

TOWARD SATISFYING NEEDS

Later in the book we shall describe job attitudes and satisfactions in considerable detail. However, it is important to introduce the subject here in order to emphasize the point that industry does have some control over need satisfactions.

Attitudes and Needs. Installing a bonus system in a plant may not increase production at all. The failure may lie, not in the inadequacy of the bonus system as such, but in the fact that no account is taken of the workers' attitude toward the system and their understanding of it. If the bonus system appears desirable to the workers and is meaningful to them, they are likely to increase production as a result. To know whether we can expect the horse to drink, we must know whether or not he is thirsty. To know whether or not a bonus system will increase production requires that we have information about the workers' reaction to such a system. The worker and the manager alike want to be included, to participate in what affects them. A number of experiments support this position. Let us briefly describe one from the meat industry [27].

During the meat conservation program in World War II, the government decided to try to convince housewives that they should use cheaper cuts of meat and thus stretch the supply. What was the best way to get them to change their old habits of buying choice cuts? Two kinds of test groups of housewives were organized—lecture groups and discussion groups.

The first test groups were exposed to lectures by competent speakers, who used excellent visual-aid charts and slides showing the various cuts of meat. The lecturers presented statistics to show that the family could get good nourishment from cheap cuts and save money at the same time. However, follow-up checks showed that, although the housewives listened attentively, they were not motivated to buy the cheaper cuts of meat.

For the second test groups, a different approach was used. There were no formal lectures. The group of housewives listened briefly to a leader who presented the facts and then let the women argue about prices, budgets, and health. Each member of the group had ample opportunity to express her opinion. The problem now belonged to the participants, not to some bureau in Washington. When the buying habits of this second group were checked and compared with those of the first group, it was found that the discussion group responded much more favorably.

We know that men want recognition; they want to feel that they belong. In one large industry with which the author is acquainted, the safety director told him that when the familiar "tell and repeat," "tell and repeat," was reinforced by giving more recognition to the workers—by having them submit suggestions on safety and serve on small safety committees—accidents declined more. He concluded by saying that although the safety problem was still of concern, he felt that the reduction in accidents was due partially to the fact that the safety program now belonged to the men. A need was being satisfied, at least in part. The men felt they had some status. How well a person's actual status in an organization matches what he expects it to be is important in need satisfaction. The effects of low status congruence, for example, may be a cause for job dissatisfaction, lowered productivity, and failure to work well with others [37].

Getting at Feelings. People working in industrial relations have found that one of the key problems in labor-management communication involves the understanding of feelings. No one knows better than the contract negotiator that employees want more than what they find in the pay envelope. Often negotiators have seen workers become angry and go on strike and then look around for something to demand. Higher wages, fringe benefits, and shorter hours are ready demands, neat and easy to formulate. But in many cases they are only secondary demands substituted for wants or needs which the workers have difficulty describing. Both employers and employees frequently are not conscious of their real motives. Some of these needs may even be as simple as that stated by a union official speaking of a strike in a Midwest factory. Asked what the real issue was, he replied, "The real issue wasn't the 15 cents an hour we asked for, or the 5 cents we got. The real cause of the strike was that we had to convince that guy he couldn't be a dictator any longer." One of the big issues in a recent nationwide strike of a large corporation was found to be essentially psychological. The company had made a substantial offer to the union for a long-term contract, but it was refused by both the leaders and the majority of the membership of the union. The strike went on for weeks, indeed, for months, and was finally settled for what was basically the original offer, plus a few face-saving agreements. What had happened was that the company itself had worked out all the details of what it would give the union. Little or nothing was left for the union negotiators to do. They had not participated in framing the offer. As the strike wore on, management was forced into letting the union officials have their way and argue *their* points. A psychological need had now been met, and with full public relations fanfare it was announced that a new contract had been signed, that *pay* demands had been met!

One of the best places to observe the nature of human needs is in any labor-management–bargaining situation where there are quite diverse interests involved and where both management and labor bring into the situation both similar and different needs. During the conflict that results, we see that man is interested in seeking psychological satisfactions as well as economic ones.

Feelings of Accomplishment. To assume that all the problems of men working in industry can be solved entirely through wage systems is oversimplifying the nature of human needs. Just as we have evidence that high morale and high production do not necessarily go hand in hand, so we must say that wage incentives per se do not always result in enthusiasm for efficient work. Let us illustrate this point by describing an industrial study summarized in Figure 5.2. Here we see that when time rates, bonus rates, and piece rates were compared, some tasks (wrapping, for instance) increased in output as much as 46 per cent when bonus rate replaced time rate; there was a further increase of 30 per cent in production when a

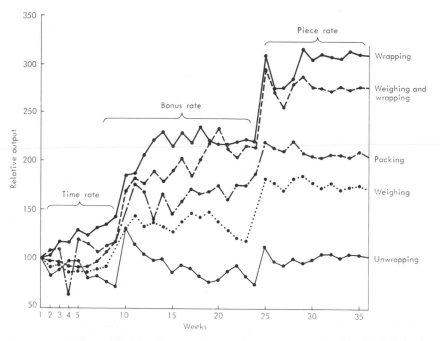

Fig. 5.2. Wage incentives in work per se do not always result in enthusiasm for work. We see in this illustration that, when time, bonus, and piece rates were compared, some tasks increased appreciably in output (wrapping), but others did not (unwrapping). (From Wyatt, S., Frost, L., & Stock, F. G. L. *Incentives in repetitive work.* London: Industrial Health Research Board, No. 69, 1934; courtesy Controller of Her Majesty's Stationery Office.)

piece rate replaced the bonus system. Note, however, that one task (un-wrapping) showed no appreciable difference in production regardless of the pay system. The authors of this controlled study [47] on work output also recorded the feelings of the workers toward their jobs. They pointed out that the most marked improvement in production came in tasks, such as wrapping, which involved behavior that aroused favorable feelings in the workers. There was no improvement when the task was disliked, where no feelings of accomplishment were evidenced, such as unwrapping.

There is no doubt, according to experimental studies and practical ob-servations, that there is some relationship between wage systems and the incentive to work. But wage systems alone are not sufficient to stimulate the will to work. If the work required seems aimless, futile, and unchallenging to a man, the economic incentive may have little or no effect upon him.

Need Satisfactions on the Job. Let us look at how a supervisor may apply effective human relations skills in a practical way. Let us assume that a plant worker comes to his foreman with a problem. He is obviously upset. If the foreman is well trained in the principles of human relations, he will try to get the man to see his own problem [30].

First, the supervisor will act as a sounding board for the man's frustra-tions. This means that he must get the man to talk about what is bothering him, to reveal his real feelings. It is wise for him to avoid making any sug-gestions to the man in this stage, because it is known that the frustrated person regards any suggestions as an attack on him and that this leads him to some form of defensive behavior. The result is merely further frustration on his part. The effective supervisor will act only as a listener in this first stage of working with the man. He will encourage him to get his frustra-tions off his chest.

Second, the good supervisor will try to help the employee locate the cause of the trouble. He will try to discover whether the problem is re-stricted to the man or is more general. If it is the man's alone, he will encourage him to talk about what he thinks is the cause of the difficulty; the supervisor will try to get him to locate the problem, to state it.

Third, the supervisor will try to get the worker himself involved in finding a solution to his problem. The employee is more likely to modify his behavior or his attitude if *he* decides to do something about the prob-lem rather than if he is told what to do. He will be asked to tell what he thinks the facts are, what he thinks should be done. The effective super-visor will encourage the worker to give several possible solutions and then to choose the best one to try first. This makes the employee consider the consequences of his suggestions. Thus by listening and by asking questions, the supervisor helps the man to be less emotional and more ready to work the problem out along rational lines.

We may now ask what needs in the man have been satisfied in this situation. First of all, he has received recognition; the supervisor has listened to his problem. Second, frustrations have been relieved. Tension has been reduced, and the worker feels more secure in the situation. Finally, the worker's ego has been boosted; he has gained the feeling of belonging. His thinking was asked for, and the supervisor considered it seriously.

It is possible that some people who get little notice on the job may even behave in ways to bring a reprimand (and attention). One supervisor tells of how a clerk who made her first error in twelve years started a new pattern of behavior. Following discovery of the error she was called in and spoken to harshly. On subsequent days she made more errors, later explaining that she had been working for the supervisor three years and he apparently never noticed her until she started making mistakes.

One of the ways in which industry can help human beings to satisfy their needs, at least to a small degree, is to place the right person in the right job.

SUGGESTIONS FOR SELECTIVE READING

Bergler, E. *The revolt of the middle-age man.* New York: Wyn, 1954. A psychoanalyst looks at needs in middle age.

Berne, E. *Games people play: The psychology of human relations.* New York: Grove Press, 1964. A medical doctor writes about "life games" that are related to needs.

Cofer, C. N., & Appley, M. H. *Motivation: Theory and research.* New York: Wiley, 1964. For the sophisticated reader.

David, H. P. *Population and mental health.* New York: Springer, 1964. Nineteen experts from ten countries discuss industrialization and mental health.

Davis, J. A. *Education for positive mental health.* Chicago: University of Chicago, National Opinion Research Center, Report 88, 1963. A technical review of literature on the many aspects of mental health from child to community.

Guetzkow, H., & Bowman, P. H. *Men and hunger.* Elgin, Ill.: Brethren Publishing House, 1946. A psychological experiment in semistarvation.

Kagan, J., & Moss, H. A. *Birth to maturity: A study in psychological development.* New York: Wiley, 1962. Relationship between child and adult behavior and how needs change.

Lauttit, R. T. (Ed.) *Research in physiological psychology.* Belmont, Calif.: Wadsworth, 1965. Sec. 1 exemplifies current research on thirst as a basic need.

Levinson, H. *Emotional health in the world of work.* New York: Harper & Row, 1964. A description of emotional illness common to the world of work.

Lindzey, G. (Ed.) *Assessment of human motives.* New York: Grove Press, 1960. Cross section of contemporary thought and research through sophisticated readings.

McClelland, D. C. *The achieving society.* Princeton, N.J.: Van Nostrand, 1961. Evidence is drawn from history and from some forty contemporary nations to show how need for achievement precedes periods of rapid economic growth.

McKinney, F. *Understanding personality: Cases in counseling.* Boston: Houghton-Mifflin, 1965. Twenty readable college student cases.

Miller, D. R., & Swanson, G. E. *Inner conflict and defense.* New York: Holt, 1960. Frustration and defensive behaviors.

Neugarten, Bernice L., et al. *Personality in middle and late life.* Englewood Cliffs, N.J.: Prentice-Hall, 1964. Empirical studies of ego functions in middle age; configurations of older people.

Olmsted, M. S. *The small group.* New York: Random House, 1959. Findings from research on small groups.

Rogers, C. R. *On becoming a person.* Boston: Houghton Mifflin, 1961. Deals with "Who am I?"

Stacey, C. L., & De Martino, M. F. (Eds.) *Understanding human motivation.* Cleveland: Howard Allen, 1963. Readings covering levels of aspiration, frustration and aggression, and unconscious motivation. Not directly related to industry.

Stewart, G. R. *Ordeal by hunger.* Boston: Houghton-Mifflin, 1960. The history of the Donner party tragedy in 1846. An account of extreme individual and group needs related to decision making.

Stoodley, B. H. *Society and self.* New York: Free Press, 1962. Raises some involved, sometimes sophisticated, questions.

Terman, L. M., & Oden, M. H. *The gifted group at mid-life: Thirty-five years follow up of the superior child.* Stanford, Calif.: Stanford, 1959. A rare study in the sense of following a group into middle age.

Worchel, P., & Byrne, D. (Eds.) *Personality change.* New York: Wiley, 1964. Papers on variables related to needs and change; sophisticated in places.

6

Personnel Selection

Robert E. Krug

We all are continually participating in selection. We are selected for the high school band, the football team, and the class play. We are selected as pin mate, friend, and listener to someone's problem. From among the many we are selected as college entrant, officer candidate, employee, supervisor, or chairman of the board. For all practical purposes, selection is a continuing series of processes which operate throughout most of the life span. Most of us find ourselves from time to time in the role of selectee and in the role of selector. Selection ranges widely, from picking the best twenty out of thirty heifer calves to keep for cows to choosing the president for a corporation.

Selection may be careful or careless, systematic or haphazard. In some instances selection follow-up may be planned from the beginning; in others it may end after the administration of a few tests and an interview. In the sophisticated organization, validation of selection procedures to find out how effective the selection program really is has become a standardized practice. One function of industrial psychology is to help develop plans for selecting people carefully and systematically, to check on how well the procedures hold up, and to recommend when changes need to be made.

Personnel selection is one of the traditional areas of industrial psychology, an area increasing in importance as modern technology adds to the complexity of jobs at all levels of the industrial organization. It takes place not only when the individual is first hired by a company but also each time he is promoted, transferred, or reassigned. Recently, selection has become related to problems of retraining workers whose old jobs have been made obsolete by technological changes. By its very nature the selection system is actuarial. It is a safe bet that the rancher will make some mistakes in selecting his future breeding herd because he must deal with a multitude of variables. The same holds true in the selection of the executive. The industrial psychologist recognizes these problems, and he is also aware of the fact that more and more companies are using psychological techniques in their prediction because few, if any, other procedures have worked out as well over the long haul. In selection the psychologist is also aware of his obligations to society and to the dignity and welfare of the individuals involved.

Intentional selection is at least as old as recorded history. The writings of antiquity counsel us on the traits desired in the leader, the apprentice, and the warrior, but we search in vain for an unbiased accounting of the degree of success actually attained in their selection. In fact, acceptable evidence on personnel selection is limited almost entirely to the twentieth century, and its development is almost the exclusive property of the psychologist. It has been asserted that the development of psychological tests and the consequent quantitative investigation of relationships between human abilities and various criterion behaviors represent one of the outstanding achievements of the behavioral sciences to date. While this development is far from complete and our current practices of using tests, along with other procedures, contain some error, there can be no serious doubt that we are accomplishing the task more successfully than at any time in the past. There can also be little doubt, despite occasional published opinion to the contrary, that psychological tests used properly are the most practical tools available in developing an adequate solution to most selection problems [6, 18, 26, 34, 37, 39].

THE SELECTION PROBLEM

Suppose we have three positions to fill and thirty applicants for the positions. Within that group of thirty it is to be expected that there will be three persons whose combined job performance would be superior to that of any other group of three candidates. Of course, we cannot know just who those three would be unless we can put all of the applicants to work and see who does the best job. Short of that, what could we do? We might just choose three applicants at random or choose the three handsomest, the three tallest, or the three most articulate of the applicants. We probably would make mistakes using any of these approaches; no approach that we could adopt could perfectly predict future events. Our problem, then, is to adopt an approach that would identify the three individuals whose performance would be superior to that of any other candidates that we might select by any other approach.

The process of selection is the same, of course, whether we have one, two, or a hundred slots to fill, and whether we have two or three or hundreds of candidates for the slots. In the special case where we wish to select but one person, the goal of a selection procedure is to identify that one person whose job performance will be superior to that of any individual identified by any other procedure. Whether we are selecting one person or many, the test of a procedure is how well it would stack up against any other procedure over the long run and, of course, against the objectives of the sponsor. The test of a procedure thus emphasizes how the procedure would select a number of people rather than an individual case. This derives from the fact that selection is based on probabilities and that we treat the individual in terms of some class membership.

There are advantages to using a selection model in which we either select or reject each applicant, but many situations are more complicated, as we shall see. When we are selecting for a number of jobs simultaneously, the problem can be viewed in terms of attempting to maximize the total effectiveness of the organization. Rather than attend to the aggregate performance on one job, we must then sum these aggregates over many jobs. For example, one individual may be adequate for several jobs. Rather than assign him to the job which would be optimal for him, we must consider the relative availability of talent for the several jobs, and the optimal assignment for the organization may require that he be assigned to some job other than the one for which he is best suited. This *classification* or *assignment* problem is far more difficult to handle. It characterizes most military-selection situations and is, for illustration, reasonably descriptive of industry's assignment of new-hire engineers. Another complication of the simple select-or-reject model occurs when we consider *placement*. This is a special case of classification, where our interest is in making differential assignments along a single dimension, as in placing college students in advanced, regular, or basement sections of freshman mathematics. Here again, the selector has several decisions to make other than "reject." Often an organization may have special reasons for keeping an employee on the payroll. Hence, in practice, things are seldom either–or.

Most employment situations are mixed; they are neither pure selection nor pure classification, and they involve at least three aspects of the process of selection. First, the evaluation of effectiveness of any selection procedure requires an agreed-upon index of job success which will permit at least a crude quantification, or ordering, of job performance. Second, to actually establish the value of a procedure, we must measure the job success of those individuals who would not be selected as well as the success of those who would be selected. Third, the relative effectiveness of various selection procedures must be put to empirical test. Should there be argument over the objectives, neither debate nor empirical evaluation can be fruitful. If there is agreement on what it is that we wish to accomplish, then an unambiguous verdict can be reached by collecting the evidence if it is available. This involves, first of all, beginning with the standards by which we determine success and failure in selection.

THE PROBLEM OF CRITERIA

A criterion is a standard. It is an index against which other indices may be compared and evaluated. In our context, a criterion is some measure of job success and therefore defines a desired end product of selection. Clearly, a program of personnel selection can be no better than the criteria which define it. It will be well to indicate at the outset that the selection of criteria always involves an arbitrary judgment at some point. In one sense, the definition of success is always a policy decision made by the leaders of an organization. This decision may be stated formally as a series of objectives or informally as a general goal; or it may exist only as a vague generality about "staying in business" [10, 44].

An Example of Establishing a Criterion Measure. Let us consider for a moment the objective of selling soap, as a first formulation of a criterion of success of a salesman. At first thought we might consider that the gross value of sales per unit time is easy to obtain and directly relevant to the objective. This measure is quantitative and offers to rank all salesmen from best to worst. By deciding that some level is necessary to continued operation, we might designate a critical point as separating the successful from the unsuccessful. But is the problem so clearly cut? No! What kinds of error are associated with this easily obtained measure? First, we might note that the unit of time selected is critical. Are we concerned with the amount sold per hour, per day, per week, per month, per year, or over some still longer period? Or does any one of these units give us information about all? This latter question is one to which we can get an answer. We may investigate the relationship which exists between measures gathered on a daily, weekly, monthly, and yearly basis. By considering such additional factors as the cost of hiring and training a new salesman, we may establish a minimal period of time to be taken as the unit in our criterion measurement. But let us look again at the problem.

While the traditional methods of correlational analysis are available as aids to this subproblem of studying relationships, it is also true that arbitrary decisions may weigh considerably. For example, an organization may feel that for purposes of good customer relations, it is desirable to have a low turnover among salesmen even if turnover is not associated with high costs in hiring and training. As a consequence, the organization may prefer a longer period of time for the definition of success than that demonstrated necessary for adequate reliability and relevance of the measure. As a result of such considerations, we may select various units of time as criteria along a time dimension. Thus a practically useful period, such as six months or a year may be employed.

We must also take into consideration the differences in experience existing within the group of salesmen. If the organization is sufficiently large, an adequate sample may be available for preliminary study within which experience is equal, but this will certainly not always be the case. If adequate sales-performance records are maintained, it may be possible to establish norms for various amounts of experience, but this will not always be possible either. Let us assume that we can by some method equate or allow for differences in experience and that we have settled on a time period upon which to base the once corrected gross-sales measure; we must still consider some very practical and common sources of error.

Sources of Error in Criteria. One noticeable source of error might be termed *situational*. For example, one neighborhood may be dirty and another relatively clean. The amount of soap used per person for laundering purposes should be greater in a heavily industrialized city than in a mountain-resort community. We might correct for this factor by obtaining data on the total amount of soap sold by retailers in each sales district, and interpreting our gross-sales figure as a per cent of the available market. This twice-corrected figure assumes that all competing companies apportion their sales effort, e.g., advertising dollars, similarly in regard to geographical area, so that the relative competition is equal for all salesmen. This is almost certainly not true, so we combat error of one variety only to introduce error in another form. The concentration of population will also vary widely over sales districts, so that one salesman may contact more consumers per retailer visited. We would have to correct our measure for both absolute differences in population and for population density.

It is possible for a salesman to overstock a retail outlet. This can result in return of goods and in loss of good will and of future sales. We should also consider the soap company's position in a specific area when a given salesman entered. A high sales figure may reflect the good work accomplished by the salesman's predecessor. Conversely, low figures may obscure the slow rebuilding of good will in an area where the organization's share of the market was reduced by the performance of a previous salesman. The point of all this is simply that considerable refinement may be necessary before the easily obtained gross-sales figure is transformed into a useful measure of sales performance. The relationship between the original and final measure may be low or even negative. If our measure is to stand for success on the job, all pertinent questions must be asked of the situation. Success is really multidimensional when several different goals are involved.

Steps in Criterion Development. Let us demonstrate the importance of developing standards by having the reader work through an example for himself from some field which he knows. It might be enlightening, for example, for the college student to consider seriously the criterion problem involved in defining the successful college student. In this way we can illustrate the essential tasks of the personnel psychologist in regard to criterion development.

First, the student should construct a detailed, comprehensive, and systematic definition of successful job performance on and off the campus which encompasses all agreed-upon objectives. For an organization which has stated its objectives essentially as policy decisions, this task is one of translation, with the psychologist determining behavioral referents of each goal statement. In most cases, however, the goals are likely to be inferences from objective descriptions of successful and unsuccessful job performance collected by the psychologist or job analyst. In the university setting the office of the dean may be the focal point for analysis.

Second, the student should attempt to construct a measure, acceptable to all parties, for each statement in the definition. At this point also, the task requires assistance from the dean; indeed, this is really a cooperative effort of the student and the dean. In industry similar cooperation is necessary between the psychologist and the policy maker. The first attempt at measurement will often clarify statements in the definition. Third, the measures must be refined by removing vague language, misunderstandings, and sources of error. Fourth, the interrelationships between the separate measures must be determined. Practical as well as scientific goals call for parsimony. The final criterion should contain the minimum number of dimensions necessary for an adequate representation of the original definition. We can therefore eliminate measures which, upon inquiry, turn out to be duplicated by others.

Fifth, we must establish appropriate *weighting systems* which will enable us to deal with the total criterion field. This problem cannot be avoided. If we say, "Each measure is essential, and all are equally important," we imply that no combination of measures can take place but that, instead, each facet of the criterion is a hurdle which must be passed. If, on the other hand, we decide that certain dimensions are mutually compensatory (strength on one compensates for weakness on another), then an additive combination will be permitted. The college student may find more weight should be given to the grade factor than to athletic participation. The industrialist may find cost consciousness outweighs the public image although both are of importance.

Sixth, we must investigate time as a dimension underlying our criteria. On this basis we select measures available early as representative of measures which can be obtained only at a much later date. Seventh, we may revise measures according to considerations of economy, reliability, and validity. It is important to note that these final matters engage our attention at the end rather than at the beginning of our program of criterion development. The ultimate consideration concerning any measurement technique is its validity, i.e., the extent to which it measures what it purports to measure. The validity of a technique is dependent in an intimate way upon its reliability, i.e., the extent to which it yields consistent measures.

SOME AVAILABLE CRITERIA

In practice, the criteria employed in the industrial setting tend to be most available when the selection program is installed. Often subsequent development involves little more than improving the record-keeping process so that the measures are complete and are collected under reasonably standardized circumstances.

Practical industrial problems are frequently accompanied by demands of immediacy; solutions are needed now, not in five years. In addition, sponsors of the research are sometimes naïve regarding the problem. The uninitiated person tends to view the difference between successful and unsuccessful as roughly analogous to the difference between good and bad, and is consequently surprised that the psychologist views the matter as a problem at all.

Using Company Records. A variety of measures are available in company records, all of which seem related to the objectives of most organizations, many of which are easily amenable to quantification, and most of which can be gathered routinely. Wherry [45] lists the following as suggestive of the measures which one might collect from the records of most industrial organizations:

1 *Items bearing on output per unit time,* such as units produced, number of sales, items coded, commissions earned, words typed

2 *Items bearing on quality of production,* such as number of rejects, cost of spoiled work, coding or filing errors, returned goods (sales), complaints filed

3 *Items bearing on lost time,* such as days absent, times tardy, days sick, visits to medical department, unauthorized rest pauses

4 *Items bearing on turnover,* such as length of service, quits, discharges, transfers

5 *Items bearing on training time and promotability,* such as training time to reach standard production, cost of material spoiled during training, rate of advancement, merit ratings

6 *Items bearing on employee satisfaction,* such as number of grievances, morale-survey results, visits to plant psychiatrist, participation in plant athletic programs, suggestions registered

The above list contains measures of potential utility for a variety of jobs. It would provide a first approximation for a wide range of clerical, sales, and production jobs, sampling six potentially relevant facets of a complete criterion. In many programs of criterion development, the simple records of performance already available provide a reasonable starting point. Their most serious deficiency is incompleteness. It is important that they reflect all of the critical *behaviors* which distinguish the successful from the unsuccessful worker. Distinguishing between the promotable and unpromotable manager usually requires even more complete criteria.

The Use of Ratings. Not all jobs leave a highly visible record of performance. We hesitate to treat a department's production record as indicating the same thing for a foreman that an individual production record indicates for a worker. Most of the items in the above list may be relevant to supervisory jobs if we take a departmental aggregate as the supervisor's criterion score. Such a score clearly possesses some relevance; the supervisor's goal *is* to increase production both in quantity and quality, to reduce lost time, to keep within certain cost limits. However, as we move upward in an organizational hierarchy, we become increasingly dependent for criteria upon the evaluative judgments of men occupying the next higher position, and sometimes there is bias involved. Fortunately, however, two developments in rating-scale construction have shown success in controlling the error or bias which characterized earlier scales. These have been proved in practical usage, but equally importantly, each has helped to stimulate extended research into the problems of criteria. Let us describe them here to illustrate ways of getting practical answers to everyday problems.

The Critical-incident Technique. Flanagan's critical-incident technique is a set of procedures designed to collect and make use of direct observations of human behavior on a job [10]. A critical incident is a reported *specific action* that led to a notably effective or ineffective consequence. It is an event that actually occurred at a definite time and place. And it is given by those persons who are in the best position to contribute relevant job information, namely the supervisors and workers on a given job. While one incident reveals little, several hundred or a thousand incidents properly compiled can provide a useful overall description of an activity in terms of specific critical behaviors. A pool of critical incidents may provide the foundation for a variety of personnel procedures. In the practical setting critical incidents apply directly to the rating problem by providing a checklist of observable behaviors. For the person using such a checklist, the frame of reference is descriptive rather than evaluative. He is not asked to decide whether the ratee *would* behave as a certain phrase suggests, but instead simply checks those behaviors which *actually occurred* during the period being reviewed. Most error in rating systems is due to the rater's inability to make accurate judgments about traits which are imperfectly defined and which have imperfectly understood behavioral referents. The critical-incident checklist requires no such inferences. The evidence from a number of industries makes it clear that the supervisor must be trained to adopt the descriptive frame of reference and to view performance evaluation as a problem requiring continuous observation rather than once-a-year recall. Given this training, the technique provides a means of assessing performance which avoids the weaknesses of many rating schemes.

The Forced-choice Technique. The critical-incident technique was an outgrowth of the Aviation Psychology Program of the United States Army Air Force in World War II. A different approach to the control of bias in ratings was developed by psychologists of the Adjutant General's Office, United States Army, during the same period. The rationale of the forced-choice technique is to present the rater with alternative descriptions which are equally favorable in some general sense but which have differential significance in regard to success on a given job. This is another attempt to remove the evaluative frame of reference, in this instance by making it impossible to evaluate the alternatives in each choice. Since within a matched set of alternatives all elements are equally good or bad as general descriptions, the rater is free to describe the rate by those elements which are most applicable to him as an individual. The construction of forced-choice rating scales involves the determination of favorableness (general preference, goodness, or desirability) for each item as well as the relationship of the item to successful job performance. Forced-choice scales have been used successfully in a number of large industrial organizations. There have also been attempts at constructing forced-choice scales using critical incidents as the stimuli, in order to capitalize on the unique advantages of each. In addition, there is evidence that a general overall rating, made after completing a critical-incident checklist or a forced-choice scale, is more valid than one made without using the more objective scale. We shall consider additional rating procedures in a later chapter [35, 37, 46].

THE PREDICTION OF SUCCESS

Let us assume that our criterion problem is solved and that we have an adequate quantitative definition or measure of success. Logically, the next step is to obtain an estimate of ultimate performance for each applicant, be he student, supervisor, accountant, or professor. Obtaining such an estimate will involve three steps. First, we must isolate a series of measures of attributes which are related to job success. We call these *predictor variables*. Second, we must establish weights to assign each predictor which will reflect its relative contribution. As a third step, we must specify the rules for combining the predictor measures. In other words, we want to determine an equation in which criterion performance is expressed as some function of weighted-predictor scores.

The Definition of a Predictor Field. As indicated, our first step is to isolate the variables to be used as predictors. How is the initial pool of potential predictors defined? Throughout most of the history of personnel selection this definition has been achieved rather casually. In most instances, the basis for initial selection of predictors is "general knowledge of the job," which represents an unspecified blend of observations, personal experience on the job, interviews with workers and supervisors, knowledge of what has worked in the past, and sometimes pet ideas of the boss. If considerable information is available from previous studies of the criterion, one can attempt to define the predictor field by matching each criterion component with a predictor.

A promising approach to this problem is the *method of rationales* growing out of the use of critical incidents. The central feature of the method is the preparation of detailed and comprehensive rationales which make explicit the several steps and inferences which lead from knowledge of job behavior to the writing of a set of test items. A rationale consists of three parts. First is a description of the behaviors found to be critical on the job, behaviors which, when classified, form the basis for a critical requirement. A second section is concerned with an analysis of this behavior in terms of known principles or inferred variables which the psychologist believes to be basic to the performance. This section is thus a tentative definition of the needed predictor field. The third section of the rationale details the implications of the analysis for test construction, including item specifications. One advantage of the method lies in the fact that the thinking of the psychologist is thus made public and can be evaluated. The rationale thus provides an explicit hypothesis concerning an expected test-criterion relationship which can be tested empirically.

Given that testing time is not a major problem for the early stages of research on defining a predictor field, errors of commission, in including a measure which turns out to be of no value, are not harmful. Omitting a measure that would show validity if included may be serious. As a consequence, our definition of the field is likely to contain more rather than fewer characteristics to be measured. Some of the characteristics may suggest existing instruments as measures. A statement about "manipulation of verbal symbols," for example, suggests a test of verbal intelligence, and many such tests are available. Presumably, a test would be chosen on the basis of applicability to the group to be tested, time required, economy, and other such factors, given that several tests were adequate as measures of the required characteristics. However, one cannot assume that all tests labeled "verbal intelligence," for example, are measures of the same thing. How do we find out what any given test is for? How can we know if the test is any good for our particular purpose?

Evaluation of Tests. The personnel psychologist does not start from scratch in his evaluation of tests. Such evaluation has been going on for a long time, and the results are available to anyone who knows where and how to look. Certain tests acquire status as standards by virtue of their demonstrated excellence; others see decreasing usage or usage different from that intended by the developer of the test. Sometimes status tests get out of date but continue to be sold. Profitable as this may be, continued sale of outdated tests is not good professional practice. The psychologist is usually aware of this problem, but the lay personnel man sometimes is not. The former publisher of a test developed four decades ago and long out of print says he still receives frequent orders for it from nonprofessional people.

There are several standard sources in which one may seek information about a test. One such source is the manual published for the test itself. In evaluating a test by reading its manual, one should be influenced not by the claims made but by the data cited in support of such claims. The increasing adequacy of test manuals is a sign of progress in the field of testing. In learning about specific tests additional sources are (1) the "Validity Information Exchange," published in *Personnel Psychology,* a quarterly journal devoted to personnel research, (2) the "Validity Studies" section of *Educational and Psychological Measurement,* another quarterly, (3) Buros's *Mental Measurements Yearbook,* published at somewhat irregular intervals by Rutgers University Press [4], which contains reviews of standardized tests as well as bibliographic information, and (4) standard texts on psychological testing. In our suggested readings other sources of information about tests are given, and information may be gathered by reference to standards of the American Psychological Association.

What information should one seek from such sources? A guide to the interpretation of a test may be found in the relationships that have been demonstrated to exist between the test and other tests and between the test and nontest variables. If one were interested in test X, for example, whose manual says it measures "verbal intelligence," he might ask three questions. (1) What is the relationship between test X and other measures of verbal intelligence? If the relationship in previous studies has been consistently low, this may indicate that test X is not a good measure of verbal intelligence; but if the relationship has been positive, the interpretation of test X as a test of verbal intelligence is supported. (2) What is the relationship between test X and tests intended to measure other factors? If test X has been highly related to tests of number skill or of visual ability, for example, this may indicate that some other explanation of test X's meaning is possible. (3) What relationships have been demonstrated between test X and measures assumed to reflect or not reflect verbal intelligence? For example, has the test been related to criteria of success in other fields requiring ability to manipulate verbal symbols or to grades in language courses? If so, such results may provide a guide for anticipating the relevance of test X to the situation for which it is being considered [2, 11, 16, 22].

Other Selection Measures. While some elements of the predictor field may be assessed by using existing tests, other elements may require use of non-test variables or the construction of new tests. For some aspects of background experience the application blank or work-history record may provide needed data. It should be noted that information gathered through these means is treated in the same fashion as a test score. For example, something from the work-history record itself becomes a "score" on a potential predictor yet to be validated. If some aspect of the definition concerns a personality variable for which no adequate test measure exists and the personnel man doubts that he can construct an adequate one, the decision may be made to assess the characteristics in an interview. In this instance, the interview is to be considered as a measuring device which provides a score on certain characteristics.

There are critics who have headlined the obvious, namely, that there are aspects of human behavior which are not currently measurable by psychological tests. The sometimes intended corollary, that these characteristics can be assessed by other means, does not necessarily follow. Reasonableness demands that a required characteristic be represented by the best measure available, consistent with considerations of economy and practicability. All measurements resulting from whatever operation are evaluated according to the same rule; namely, that which predicts success is kept, the rest is dross. Fortunately, industrial psychologists find perceptive personnel men readily grasp this important point even if it throws out some of their pet predictors.

Job-application Blank. As a selection instrument the application form is included in the initial battery of predictors, not because this is the traditional way to start the employment process, but rather because there are certain pieces of predictor information which can be collected most conveniently from such a blank. Since an organization hires for many jobs and since one application blank is preferable to many, the blank may collect information from an applicant that is not presumed relevant to the job for which he is being considered. Likewise, an interview schedule may be more or less flexible to fit a variety of jobs.

Interviewing. There can be little question that many hiring procedures are maintained primarily because of the lag of culture. A face-to-face interview has been a part of the process for so long that it is often continued even though there may be no clearly stated objective indicating what it is to accomplish. This is not a critique of the interview; it simply calls attention to the fact that some of our procedures are at times permitted to remain outside the rules of the game as viewed by personnel psychologists. A face-to-face interview may well be justified in terms of the human relations value involved; as such it is a legitimate part of the induction program but may be extraneous to the selection process. There are five fairly common forms of the interview. The *traditional* selection interview is haphazard and usually impressionistic. At the other extreme is the *standardized* interview, which sometimes is little more than an orally administered questionnaire. Between these two extremes is the *patterned,* or *guided,* interview getting information about such things as financial condition and social activities. There are also *stress* interviews, and *group* interviews which merit use under certain conditions. Unilever, Ltd., an international company, reports that the group interview, used in conjunction with an appropriate testing program, has much value in its world-wide selection program.

In order for the interview to qualify as a part of the selection process, we must specify the characteristics which are to be measured by it and then show that these measurements are related to subsequent criterion performance. That the interview can be useful has been demonstrated by the recent work of Ghiselli and his associates, who find one can uncover managerial talent through the use of appropriate interview procedures combined with certain objective data such as intelligence-test scores. The interview is most successful when dealing with personal relations and career motivation.

THE ANALYSIS OF PREDICTOR–CRITERION RELATIONSHIPS

Here we wish to show graphically how we go about relating predictors to criteria in order to acquaint the reader with a technique used in expressing relationships.

The Correlation Coefficient. Given scores on all predictors, test scores, interview ratings, etc., and all criteria for all members of our group, we are ready to construct a first approximation to a selection equation. The standard procedure for constructing this equation is via multiple regression. While the formulas involved appear complex, the essential idea in multiple regression is no more difficult than that involved in the simple correlation coefficient.

The correlation coefficient (r) is an index of the strength of relationship between two variables. It can vary from $+1.00$ (a perfect positive correlation) through 0 (no relationship) to -1.00 (a perfect negative, or inverse,

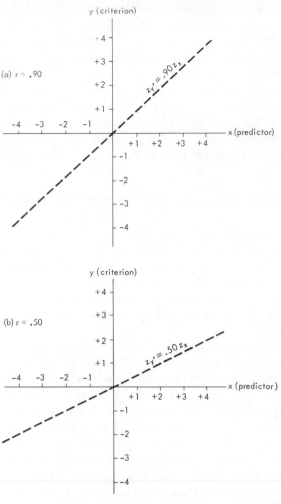

Fig. 6.1. Prediction via these regression-equation graphs shows the regression line (dashes) that relates a predictor and a criterion measure for two levels of correlation. In each case, the best estimate of criterion performance may be obtained by constructing the perpendiculars from the point on the x axis indicating the individual's predictor score. For example, a person with a predictor score of $+2$ is estimated to have a criterion score of $+1.8$ if $r = .90$, or $+1.0$ if $r = .50$.

correlation). It can be pictured as the slope of the straight line which best represents this relationship. For the two-variable problem, then, the *best estimate* of the criterion performance is equal to the correlation coefficient multiplied by the predictor score $(Z_y^1 = rZ_x)$. This use of the correlation coefficient is represented in the two examples of Figure 6.1. For any standard value of the predictor, the best estimate of criterion performance is determined in these examples. A graph showing the relationship between predicted and achieved scores in a multiple-regression problem (one where many variables are used to predict the criterion) would look like those in Figure 6.1. The difference would be that the predictor would be a composite of several independent variables. Some readers may find it useful to think about correlation coefficients in terms of regression lines as well as in terms of numbers.

THE CURRENT STATUS OF THE SELECTION PROCESS

How successful is the personnel psychologist in his attempts to improve the selection process? What benefits may the employer reasonably expect? Should he adopt the procedures we have described? These are reasonable questions. Let us answer by practical examples. From many studies we have chosen four varied ones. One study is taken from a military-selection program, one from an academic setting, and two from industry.

Selection of Airplane Pilots. The first example is a frequently cited result of the Aviation Psychology Program of the United States Army Air Force during World War II. Figure 6.2 shows the result of using a battery of tests to select pilots. The figure illustrates the percentage eliminated from primary flight training for each of nine aptitude areas (pilot stanine). These results, based on a sample of over 153,000 cases, were obtained in a very large-scale program employing the talents of many of the nation's leading psychologists, in a situation where a failure in training was extremely expensive compared to costs of testing. From Figure 6.2 it is evident that by selecting only those candidates whose pilot stanine was 6 or above, 70 per cent of the potential failures would have been eliminated. The picture is actually a very conservative representation of the effectiveness of selection in this case. A civilian adaptation of the Air Force test battery remains useful in selecting airline pilots for a number of domestic and foreign airlines, and the basic research conducted during and following World War II is finding current application in the space program.

Selection of College Students. The second example is taken from an academic-selection situation and is representative of the level of success generally attained in such programs. The predictor is a composite of three College Board achievement tests and high school standing, the four variables being weighted to produce the maximal multiple correlation for a previous sample of students. In this example the prediction equation has been in use for over a decade, with yearly validity checks giving values con-

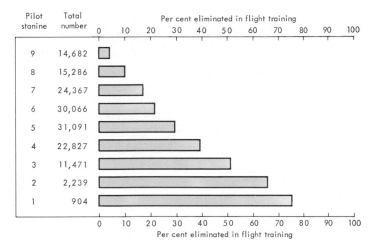

Fig. 6.2. This selection-of-airplane-pilots graph shows the relationship between the pilots' stanine (Aptitude Index) and the successful completion of flight training. (From Staff, AAF Training Command. Psychological activities in the training command. *Psychol. Bull.,* 1945, 42, 46.)

sistently in the .60 to .68 range. Figure 6.3 illustrates the practical value of the equation by graphing the relationship between the aptitude index and two indices of achievement. One index is the percentage at each level who graduated after eight semesters, which is par for the course. The second index reflects the level of achievement (grade-point average) representative of each predicted level.

It can be seen from these graphs that an increase in selectivity on the part of the college would result in a decreased attrition rate and an increase in the percentage of students earning superior grades. It is also evident that this procedure would eliminate some students who would have been successful had they been permitted to attend, but let us remember that all methods of selection are imperfect whether we are selecting cows, pilots, or students.

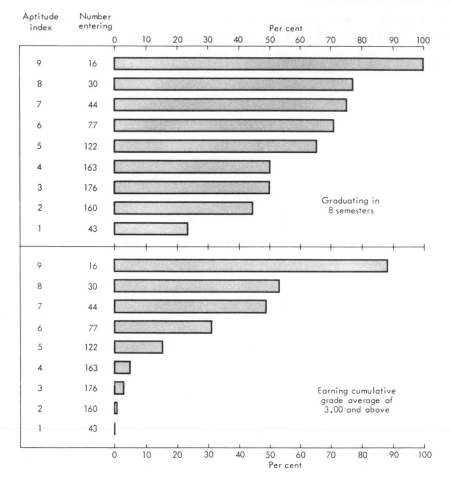

Fig. 6.3. This academic-selection graph shows the relationship between Aptitude Index and two different criteria of success in college. (Courtesy Bureau of Measurement and Guidance, Carnegie Institute of Technology.)

Selection of Life Insurance Agents. The selection of salesmen was one of the first practical problems to receive attention by the industrial psychologist. The Life Insurance Sales Research Bureau and its successor, the Life Insurance Agency Management Association, have been active in this field for around forty years. While LIAMA is concerned with a wide range of research problems, the aptitude index which it maintains is of practical value and represents the importance of maintaining a continuing research program for the improvement of personnel selection. The results of this long-range program of research are summarized in Figure 6.4, which relates the index to a sales-performance criterion. Here again we see evidence that significant gains can be produced by hiring only those applicants who earn high index scores.

Classification of Technical Personnel. Our final example, used here to show a different kind of practical selection problem, differs from the preceding ones in two ways. First, the test battery was designed as a classification instrument rather than as a selection test. Second, the study reports concurrent rather than predictive validation. What does this mean? A predictive study tests an applicant population at time 1 and then collects criterion data at time 2. If our interest is in selecting executives, twenty years may intervene between times 1 and 2, which makes test validation a lengthy process. Using samples of workers whose criterion performance is already available allows us to collect predictor and criterion information simultaneously. Promising findings from such a study justify the expense of a subsequent predictive study. Results indicate that the tests do measure factors associated with on-the-job success of current employees. There is no guarantee, however, that these factors will have identical meaning when assessed in an applicant group. We cite the study because the results do appear quite promising and may help set a pattern for continuing research in this area. It is of note that several large organizations are currently undertaking long-range research studies of professional and managerial

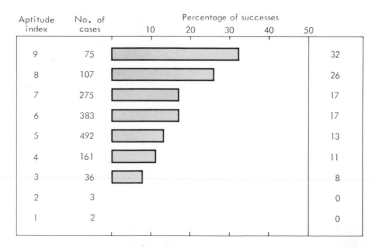

Fig. 6.4. The sample involved consists of inexperienced, company-financed men tested with Form 7 in Canada between July 1, 1960, and September 30, 1961. A man is considered a "success" if he survives his first year and ranks in the top half of his company's first-year survivors in terms of his volume of ordinary production. (From mimeographed LIAMA bulletin dated August 16, 1963.)

performance which will ultimately contribute some much-needed data in this area [11].

Figure 6.5 reports several comparisons based on four groups of engineers from a major aircraft company who completed an extensive test battery. This battery attempts to measure thirty-eight variables clustered in six areas

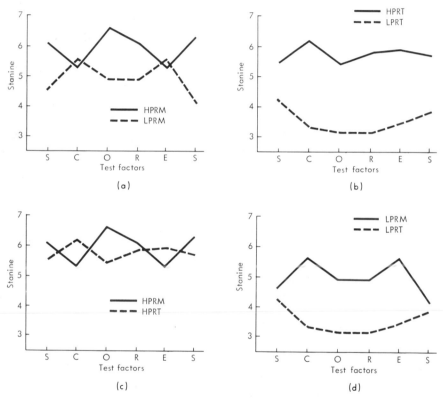

Fig. 6.5. Comparison of four groups of engineers; see text for explanation. (From Flanagan, J. C., & Krug, R. E. Testing in management selection: state of the art. *Personnel Admin.*, 1964, 27, 3–5, 36–39.)

(**S**upervision, **C**reativity, **O**rganization, **R**esearch, **E**ngineering and **S**alesmanship), various combinations of which indicate the degree of success expected in each of a number of possible job assignments.

In this study, a group was carefully selected to provide four relatively homogeneous subgroups. The subgroups were as equally matched as possible on three input variables (age, education, and company experience) and differed on two criterion dimensions (supervisory versus nonsupervisory position and high versus low rate of advancement). The four groups are designated High Promotion Rate Manager (HPRM), High Promotion Rate Technical (HPRT), Low Promotion Rate Manager (LPRM), and Low Promotion Rate Technical (LPRT).

Inspection of these graphs reveals several important findings. Within both Manager and Technical samples, groups with different promotion rates earn clearly distinguishable profiles (graphs *a* and *b*). Considering the two Low Promotion Rate groups (graph *d*), the Technical subgroup earns a generally low profile, while the Manager group is not low overall but is low on precisely those factors which are critical for success in supervisory activities. The two High groups show equally high profiles (graph *c*) but differ significantly in profile shape. This comparison reveals the potential of a classification instrument in making useful differential predictions for highly competent personnel. It is also interesting to compare HPRT with LPRM. Here we see that there is considerable similarity in profile shape. It is probable that this similarity would be duplicated in many engineering organizations. High technical competence is a prerequisite for advancement to a supervisory position, and some highly competent technical people lack the skills necessary for successful supervisory performance; hence some good technical people become poor supervisors. The importance of these types of data for supervisory practices will be covered in a following chapter on human relations in supervision.

The Utility of Current Selection Procedures. We have pictured the current state of personnel selection through four examples which represent a considerable range of human performance. The graphic presentations which accompanied the examples give some idea of the usefulness of procedures currently available. We should not, however, be dismayed by the fact that the value of a validity coefficient depends on the particular situation; the same is true of any numerical index. What is the value, for example, of a gain of fifteen words of French vocabulary? The answer depends upon how difficult it was to obtain the gain, how the gain relates to some objective, what the original vocabulary was, and many other contingencies. Careful interpretation of a validity coefficient, similarly, requires a close examination of what the value of that coefficient *depends on*. Let us consider this for practical purposes in industry.

Imagine a situation where the demand for employees is exactly equal to the number of applicants. If everyone must be hired, no improvement will result from a selection process regardless of the validity of the predictors employed. We noted, in examining the pilot-selection results, that selecting only those candidates whose stanines were 6 and above would radically alter the average performance of the selected group. Similar statements would apply to the student and life-insurance-salesman examples. Thus one factor becomes important, namely, the *selection ratio*. That is to say, we must know the percentage of applicants who must be accepted in order to fill the job quota. Even a low correlation may be useful with a small selection ratio.

The amount of improvement in performance attributable to selection is also a function of the *base rate,* defined as the percentage of people in an unselected population who would be successful on the given job. Clearly, a job which can be handled adequately by 95 per cent of the total population will leave little room for improvement and would not justify the expenditure of funds for researching the selection problem.

There are other ways to evaluate the effectiveness of selection programs. In considering the Air Force example, we noted the expense involved in accepting candidates for training who were potential failures. Turnover is always associated with cost to the industrial employer, as well as to the unsuccessful employee. In most selection situations the monetary savings are relevant to the question. Even where a specific cost can be assigned to training, the number of candidates that must be accepted in order to meet a demanded output from the training program leads to a selection-cost figure which is meaningful to the employer. As a matter of fact, one advantage of a well-planned selection program is that it can be measured in personnel savings.

THE RECRUITMENT OF EMPLOYEES

We noted at the beginning of this chapter that one of the requirements for effective selection is to have available a sufficient number of potentially successful workers to satisfy the demand. How can we recruit enough people to allow us to pick the best? There are several familiar ways for getting job applicants. At the worker level little more than the presence of an employment office or a union-member friend is needed except in time of manpower shortage. Occasionally a newspaper announcement of openings is added. At higher levels, newspaper advertising is almost certain, listing with an employment agency likely, and advertising in professional journals or campus recruitment visits possible. Being added to the picture are the more subtle attempts to lure students and trainees through career opportunities presented on television or through various public relations releases. "Recruitment by influence" at the higher technical levels, such as for the new profession of health physics, is becoming more commonplace. During the post–World War II years we have witnessed a vigorous campaign on the part of industry to obtain the services of technical, scientific, and executive personnel. The visit of recruiting teams to campuses has taken on the aspects of selling as much as selection. Still greater effort is expended in the recruitment of higher-level executive personnel. Agencies exist which specialize in providing candidates for such openings, and if we can believe popularized accounts, competition between companies is intense, even including some reports of pirating.

At the worker level some companies have labor contracts specifying that all recruiting be done by the union. This throws a burden of selection to the union in some respects, certainly at a level of initial screening. This is a problem that is becoming increasingly important as workers are selected for programs of retraining, many of which are managed by the unions.

How good are present recruiting practices? Most companies really do not know the answer or are keeping the information to themselves. It is not too surprising that there is no published evidence of the success of most recruiting efforts. We are unable to compare the relative effectiveness of newspaper and magazine advertising, personal visits and impersonal ads, agency referrals and the nominations of current employees. A large company could compare the success of employees obtained by each device and evaluate the cost per criterion gain. This we know has been done in a number of companies, but the data remain the private possession of the particular organization. For the majority of jobs, recruitment does not appear to be a problem save at the levels of technical and professional specialties. For the unemployed, for the handicapped, and for aging persons placement is still a grave problem. Personnel-selection practices are slowly moving in the direction of aiding with these national problems by helping determine abilities, laying stress on what the individual can do ıather than on his disabilities per se. At both the worker and managerial levels, technological advancement is giving a reemphasis to personnel selection and is beginning to have its effects on recruitment practices, particularly at the professional level.

THE FUTURE OF PERSONNEL SELECTION

There are several current trends which suggest some future directions of personnel selection. While foreseeing the future is always somewhat hazardous, it is, after all, the stock in trade of personnel selection.

Personnel Selection in the Developing Nations. Several recent writers note that ability testing is to a considerable extent an American development. While research on testing and selection has long history in England and in South Africa, it has been really within the last decade that psychologists in Europe and the Far East have extended the use of psychological procedures into industry. And it was not until the early sixties that the American government began to call upon the psychologist to help foreign nations in selection problems. It is now being demonstrated that the technology of test development and the procedures of personnel selection represent important and exportable services to assist the United States programs of technical aid to the developing nations. These programs are also giving us information useful in testing the culturally handicapped in the United States. The key problem of economic advancement in developing countries lies in the development of human resources. Education represents a primary solution to this problem, and a major world-wide effort is under way to greatly increase the quantity and quality of mass education. Educational expansion is necessarily a long-range development. If school buildings can be erected overnight, instructors cannot be created so quickly. During the long period of educational development, it is essential that effective use be made of available facilities and teachers. This requirement makes severe demands on the procedures for selecting and placing the trainees.

One example of the export of American know-how came recently when the United States Agency for International Development initiated a program to adapt modern selection methods to the needs of west Africa. The American Institutes for Research was given the job of conducting a study to assess the feasibility of devising and implementing suitable screening techniques for Nigeria and other countries of sub-Saharan Africa.

A first task was to find out *why* standard test procedures were so ineffective in Africa. It was discovered that African examinees, including English-speaking ones, were handicapped, not by absence of relevant skills, but by the complete strangeness of the test situation. It is easy to see that certain test items depend on cultural responses but less simple to perceive (trapped as we North Americans are by our own cultural background) that nearly every aspect of standard test administration is loaded with culturally biased assumptions about expected behavior.

To create more suitable tests, some of these strange elements were eliminated, while some were replaced by equivalents valid in the African context; however, many could be neither replaced nor eliminated. The solution was to teach the test-taking procedure as a part of the normal administration. Special methods for training the examinees became an integral part of each test. The monograph by Schwarz [33] which reports the results of this feasibility study shows the tremendous contribution which these newly devised instruments can make toward solving the manpower problems in the west African setting.

As a result of these findings, the study was greatly enlarged. A team of psychologists spent many months in Africa expanding the battery, developing large-sample norms, and demonstrating the validity in a wide variety of selection situations. The final battery contained twenty-one aptitude tests, various composites being devoted to technical, clerical, scientific, and semiskilled trades and to academic selection. It seems clear that developments such as this will be expanded to provide selection solutions to similar problems in many parts of the world. United States assistance of this kind represents a relatively small-scale financial investment with both immediate and long-range payoff in terms of increased effective utilization of personnel. Professionally, these and similar studies illustrate once again that psychology is rapidly expanding its influence for international betterment.

Other Developments in the International Area. It seems certain that the personnel psychologist will become involved in several other activities related to our country's increased role in international affairs. Let us mention three of these briefly as illustrations.

First, psychologists will be concerned with the training and education of foreign psychologists and personnel technicians to maintain and improve the programs which we install. Second, we will become increasingly concerned with the selection of Americans for nonmilitary overseas service. Psychologists, some on loan from industry, have been deeply involved in the selection and training of Peace Corps volunteers, and this will continue. Many United States industries have long been active in selecting personnel from their organizations to work in overseas installations; this will increase in scope as more and more companies enter the foreign market. Third, personnel psychologists whose major interests are in selection, training, leadership, human factors, and safety will find in the international field a new arena which presents challenging problems in adapting well-tested procedures to new cultural settings.

Criterion Development. Our technical capacity to construct adequate and representative criterion measures has outdistanced our actual development of such measures. There are probably two reasons for this. First, it was much simpler to take the readily available criterion than to construct a better one. This, we predict, will remain true. Second, the easily obtained measure usually turned out to be predictable, and the apparent success was salable. There is reason to believe that this will not remain true. As we tackle more complex jobs where the critical behavior is less visible (the executive, the Peace Corps volunteer, the research scientist), our easy criteria will probably be both less predictable and less convincing. We will therefore invest a more appropriate share of our energy in developing criteria which are both predictable and convincing. And there should be new thinking about criteria at the level of theory, says Wallace [42].

Development of Nonintellective Measures. The early development and subsequent wide acceptance of psychological tests were concerned almost exclusively with general ability. Naturally enough, further development centered on the structuring and refining of this area. Pioneering work by the factor analysts suggested that it would be useful to consider intelligence as composed of several independent abilities, such as verbal ability, number, space, etc. In the cognitive area as many as forty such dimensions are reasonably well established. Aside from the area of mental abilities, most of the progress evidenced has been in other ability or aptitude areas. Tests of mechanical aptitude, manual dexterity, clerical speed and accuracy, and the like have been a part of the psychometrist's kit for a considerable period of time, and are included in most effective industrial selection batteries. Our record in the areas of interest, personality, and motivation has been less impressive. The Strong Vocational Interest Blank, developed in the early days of industrial psychology, might be offered as an exception to the generalization. The blank has seen extensive and careful use for around forty years, and a number of relationships are well established. Even here, however, the blank is of demonstrated usefulness as a *selective device* in only a few occupations, the best known of which is life insurance salesman. While personality inventories have occasionally demonstrated apparent validity in job prediction, there is a dearth of cross-validated positive results. A tremendous amount of work in this field is current, and we can confidently expect its continuation. It is evident that the ultimate validities probable from tests of ability are not significantly greater than those already obtained; validities have indeed leveled off. Improvement is probable only by extending our range of predictors [6, 7, 19, 28].

Emphasis on Higher-level Personnel. Within industry, most of our early progress in selection was with jobs in the semiskilled to skilled levels. For higher-level jobs, the task was left primarily to educational institutions. The presence of a college degree was sufficient to warrant favorable prognosis. Within the executive framework, selection occurred internally via promotion, a survival-of-the-fittest approach which appeared adequate. The factor responsible for change was the increased complexity of the jobs. As technology grew, specialization became commonplace. An engineering graduate might be capable of excelling in one job but of doing only mediocre or failing work in another. For the executive, the range of knowledge and experience demanded by the job could not be gained casually but needed to be planned. This required that the potential executive be identified early in his career. Increasing effort may be expected in the area of executive and professional selection, with added attention given to the problem of choosing leaders who must be responsive to many publics.

The Matching of Persons and Jobs. Personnel strategies have traditionally taken one of two directions. Attention has been given either to the design of the job so that any or almost any person could handle it or to the selection of persons to fit an already defined job. The former has been the approach of engineering psychology, the latter of personnel selection. There is increasing realization that these strategies need not be either–or;

one may consider both the job and the person simultaneously and investigate strategies that involve both selection of persons and adaptation of jobs. The strategy might be extended beyond the concept of "job" as usually defined and might consider the interaction of the person and the complex social milieu, or climate, of the working situation. Thus the work now being developed on the measurement and analysis of organizational climate will eventually influence, and may help improve, the process of personnel selection.

The long-range researches now under way on the identification of leadership and of talent, on evaluation studies in career development, and on the immensity of the problems related to training and retraining bid fair to confirm the prediction that personnel selection will continue as a major area in the applications of psychology in industry. But in a technological world rocking with change we must also be ready to predict the selection problems for the managerial and worker skills that will be needed in the decade ahead.

SUGGESTIONS FOR SELECTIVE READING

Albright, L. E., et al. *The use of psychological tests in industry*. Cleveland: Howard Allen, 1964. Techniques, "how" and "where" sources.

Amrine, M. (Guest Ed.) Testing and public policy. *American Psychologist*, 1965, *20,* 857–993. A "where-we-stand" issue about the many problems of "uses and abuses" of psychological tests.

Barnette, W. L. (Ed.) *Readings in psychological tests and measurements*. Homewood, Ill.: Dorsey, 1964. Articles ranging from personality to synthetic validity.

Bingham, W. V., et al. *How to interview*. (4th ed.) New York: Harper & Row, 1959. A classical book.

Cronbach, L. J. *Essentials of psychological testing*. New York: Harper & Row, 1960. A readable text on testing in general.

Davis, F. B. *Educational measurements and their interpretation*. Belmont, California: Wadsworth, 1964. A general book on scholastic selection; not related to industry.

DuBois, P. H. *An introduction to psychological statistics*. New York: Harper & Row, 1965. Methods of measuring human characteristics and their interrelationships; sophisticated but readable.

Dunnette, M. D., & Kirchner, W. K. *Psychology applied to industry*. New York: Appleton-Century-Crofts, 1965. A paperback on the methods applied to problems of psychology in industry, ranging from selection techniques to human-factors procedures.

Fear, R. A. *The evaluation interview: Predicting job performance in business and industry*. New York: McGraw-Hill, 1958. The uses of interviewing.

Ghiselli, E. E. *Theory of psychological measurement.* New York: McGraw-Hill, 1964. Statistical techniques and theoretical concepts basic to psychological measurement presented in understandable style.

Guion, R. M. *Personnel testing.* New York: McGraw-Hill, 1965. Emphasis on research; from worker to executive.

Helmstadter, G. C. *Principles of psychological measurement.* New York: Appleton-Century-Crofts, 1964. Covers principles of testing rather than instruments.

Jenkins, J. J., & Paterson, D. G. (Eds.) *Studies in individual differences: The search for intelligence.* New York: Appleton-Century-Crofts, 1961. A selection of articles on history, from Galton to Guilford.

Kahn, R. L., & Cannell, C. F. *The dynamics of interviewing.* New York: Wiley, 1957. Theory, techniques, and cases of interviewing.

Lyman, H. B. *Test scores and what they mean.* Englewood Cliffs, N.J.: Prentice-Hall, 1963. A trade book about testing.

McLaughlin, K. F. *Interpretation of test results.* Washington, D.C.: GPO, 1964. A readable 63-page bulletin which explains use and limitations of tests for guidance and counseling of students.

Maier, N. R. F. *The appraisal interview: Objectives, methods and skills.* New York: Wiley, 1958. A practical discussion of interviewing.

Porter, E. H. *Manpower development.* New York: Harper & Row, 1964. The problems of manpower development for large-scale military operations.

Richardson, S. A., et al. *Interviewing: Its forms and functions.* New York: Basic Books, 1965. Guide for planning and executing interviews.

Sidney, E., & Brown, M. *The skills of interviewing.* London: Tavistock Press, Tavistock Institute, 1961. Methods and procedures in interviewing worked out in large corporations.

Super, D. E. & Crites, J. O. *Appraising vocational fitness: By means of psychological tests.* New York: Harper & Row, 1962. A practical guide in using tests.

Thorndike, R. L., & Hagen, Elizabeth. *Measurement and evaluation in psychology and education.* New York: Wiley, 1961. Techniques and procedures in selection and evaluation.

Torre, M. (Ed.) *The selection of personnel for international service.* New York: World Federation of Mental Health, 1963. Job descriptions, testing, and screening of people for international missions.

Tyler, Leona E. *Tests and measurements.* Englewood Cliffs, N.J.: Prentice-Hall, 1963. Extension of material of this chapter at technical level.

Wood, Dorothy Adkins. *Test construction.* Columbus, Ohio: Charles E. Merrill Books, 1961. For the reader lacking formal background in statistical-evaluation methods.

7

Training in Industry

Robert Glaser

When we speak of the utilization of human resources in an industrial organization, or in a nation for that matter, we are almost inevitably led to think of training. We recognize that individuals need to be taught to perform in specific ways in order to accomplish certain aims. The aims must be specified, and the behavior of individuals must be shaped and modified so that they can perform the tasks required as members of an organization. "Shaping" and "modifying" are key words. They define the meaning of training and, indeed, of all education. This is what training is, and this is what training agencies and educational systems do: *they begin with individuals who behave in certain ways and modify this behavior so that these individuals behave in ways which are defined as the end products of the training program.*

An organization is fortunate if the skills it requires exist in adequate quantities in the manpower resources available. An industry is even more fortunate if all it needs to do is pick out the appropriately trained individuals on its own roster. However, the widespread and firmly established existence of training departments in industrial and governmental organizations attests to the fact that things are not so simple. With both machines and operating procedures becoming more complex, training within industry is becoming more and more essential.

With the passing of the Manpower Development and Training Act by Congress in the early sixties, interest in industrial training has expanded [21]. Researches from within military settings have also added many problems of relating training and the principles of learning [7, 18, 29]. More and varied people are becoming interested in training and retraining problems and in viewing their impact on society. In this chapter we shall give a background for understanding both the basic and applied aspects of training in industry.

THE SPECIFICATION OF TRAINING OBJECTIVES

The first step in establishing a training program is to state the objectives of the program in operational terms. The behaviors to be learned as a result of training should be specified in terms of the particular actions and operations that men must perform. It is not enough to state that the objective of a training program is to produce a good executive or supervisor, a good salesman, a proficient repairman, or a loyal employee. The particular skills and attitudes that make up these job performances need to be analyzed specifically and set down as training objectives. These then constitute the behaviors which are the goals, or end products, of the shaping and modifying learning processes involved in training. In specifying training objectives it is important to get answers to questions such as:

1 What are the requirements for proficient job performance?

2 What are the special characteristics of a job with respect to the organizational structure in which it is performed?

3 How can the job be engineered, or organized, so that it fits into the general system most effectively? Can it be simplified? Can it be combined with other jobs?

4 To what extent is a man being trained not only for skill in an immediate job but for possible conversion to other or future jobs?

5 What logistics problems are involved? That is, do we have the right number of people to be trained? Do we have equipment available for training?

Determination of the Requirements for Proficient Job Performance. Some ways of doing things are better than others, and certain ways in which people behave lead to more successful accomplishments than do other ways. In specifying the objectives of a training program, these behaviors must be identified. The ease with which they can be identified is, to a large extent, related to the ease with which they can be observed. This ease of observation is further related to the complexity of the behavior involved. Consider, for example, the differences between a training program for typists and a training program for first-line supervisors. The specific behaviors and skills of a proficient typist are relatively easy to define in terms of typing speed, accuracy, correct letter form, and neatness. Specification of a similar set of defining characteristics of supervisory proficiency in a particular organization is obviously more difficult, as we shall see in Chapter 8. Even more complex is the difficulty of defining the objectives of a course designed to develop good company executives.

Job Analyses. Although the specification of training objectives for certain jobs is difficult, techniques for carrying out systematic job analyses can provide a basic tool for accomplishing this task. With specific reference to training, the essential aim of job analysis is to specify the ultimate and immediate objectives of the training program. More directly, the aim is to specify the knowledges and skills which constitute the behavior to be displayed by an individual at the end of a course of training. It is unsatisfactory to say that an individual is being trained so that sometime in the future he will be able to become an executive or an experienced technician. The subobjectives, or subgoals, of immediate training that are related to long-term and eventual job proficiency should be specified in detail as far as possible. Some of the best research in this area has been done by military psychologists. An example of the detail that is often required for

Table 2 / Sample Format for Describing a Maintenance Task

Operator: *Line Mechanic—Fire-control System*
Work Cycle: 1 *Adjust System Voltages.* Performed every 25 hours of aircraft operation.
Task: 1.1 *Adjust Power-supply-regulated Voltages.* Requires 40 minutes. If any of the specified indications cannot be obtained, replace power-supply unit.

	Control	Action	Indication	Alternatives and/or Precautions
J1.1.1	POWER switch	Turn to WARM UP.	Inverter hums, pilot light comes on.	Make sure covers are on high-voltage units before starting task.
1.1.2	AC VOLTAGE (screwdriver)	Turn as required.	AC voltmeter aligns to 117 ± 4 volts.	
1.1.3		Wait maximum of 5 minutes.	READY light comes on.	If READY light does not come on, use press to test button. If light is burned out, replace it.
1.1.4	METER SELECTOR switch	Turn to 300.		
1.1.5	+300 VOLTS ADJ. (screwdriver)	Turn as required.	Meter indicates within green area.	
1.1.6	METER SELECTOR switch	Turn to −150.		
1.1.7	−150 VOLTS ADJ. (screwdriver)	Turn as required.	Meter indicates within green area.	

specification of job characteristics, appears in job analyses of Air Force tasks carried out as a basis for equipment and job redesign, and for establishing training programs with appropriate course content, manuals, and training devices. Table 2 presents a segment of a task analysis for a maintenance task. Table 3 presents a similar description for a pilot task [51]. These tables are presented here merely to show the amount of detail required for the specification of the job characteristics for a single task. However, this detail is similar to that required for the more comprehensive time-and-motion studies in industrial engineering work. To the extent that the objectives of training (the end-product behaviors) are known, they should be stated so that we can have definite behaviors which we want our

Table 3 / Sample Format for Describing a Pilot Task

Operator: *Pilot F–100 Interceptor*
Work Cycle: 1 *Climbing to Altitude as Directed by Ground Control.*
Task: 1.1 *Accelerate to Climb Speed* (in shortest possible time and in most favorable position to intercept and destroy unidentified aircraft).

Job-element Variables

Inputs

Needed input information
1 Position, speed, and direction of unidentified aircraft (provided by Ground Control)
2 Friendly or unfriendly aircraft
3 Amount of fuel
4 Position, speed, and heating of interceptor

Disruptive or irrelevant inputs
1 Air turbulence
2 Background chatter from Ground Control
3 Radio static
4 Enemy jamming

Critical time characteristics of inputs
1 If fuel is limited, intercept may have to be made before the most favorable position for attack can be reached.

Decisions

1 Best course to follow in accelerating to climb speed
2 When climb speed has been reached

Required Control Actions

Controls	Actions
1 Control stick	Standard-power boost and artificial back pressure
2 Rudder pedals	Standard-power boost and artificial back pressure
3 Throttle	Standard

Table 3 (*Continued*)

Feedback

Indications of adequacy of actions
1 Airspeed indicator reads attained speed.
2 Direction indicator reads desired heading.
3 Attitude indicator shows level flight.

Delay action to indication
1 Airspeed indicator lags about 2 seconds during rapid acceleration.
2 Direction and attitude indicators have lag of less than 0.5 second.

Characteristic Errors and Malfunctions

Climb may be started later than is efficient because of airspeed-indicator lag.

Contingencies Which Will Affect Task

Contingencies	Effects on task
1 Ground Control loses target.	Pilot must decide whether to attempt unaided intercept or return to base.
2 Target changes course.	Acceleration course may have to be revised.
3 Ground Control detects target escorts.	Attack attitude revised, changing point at which climb to altitude is started.
4 Malfunction occurs.	Must decide whether or not to abort.

---

trainees to learn. To the extent that we do not or cannot specify these behaviors, we must *guess* about the content of a training program.

How to Describe a Job. The crucial problem is how to describe a job in a detailed manner which is meaningful for training. Many of the job-analysis schemes now in use in industry and elsewhere are not satisfactory for this purpose. One type of job-analysis procedure directly infers underlying abilities from observation of the job. According to this method, jobs are described in terms of abilities, such as numerical facility, verbal fluency, color vision, or ability to recall details. These terms, however, are ambiguous and are subject to different interpretations from job to job. For example, the presence of colored signals may not mean that color vision is involved. One should observe whether the operator must respond to the presence of a light regardless of its color or whether he must discriminate between differently colored signals. The specification of the kinds of discriminations an individual has to make among numerical, verbal, or other visual signals can help pinpoint the skills which must be learned. Another method of job description comes from time-and-motion study in which physical descriptions of movement are employed, such as "moves lever forward," "loads vehicle," "empties vehicle," and so forth. This kind of description is convenient to use and is unambiguous. However, it provides no indication of the behavior involved in initiating or terminating the movement. Moving a lever to shift gears in a truck requires different kinds of discriminations from those involved in moving a lever to start a production line rolling.

What the training specialist requires is a set of descriptive categories which tell him how to proceed. For certain kinds of tasks, such categories as the following have been suggested by Gagné and Bolles [20].

Identifying. Examples are pointing to or locating objects and locations, naming them, or identifying what goes with what, either physically or in words or symbols. This includes much of what is meant by learning "facts."

Knowing Principles and Relationships. This means understanding a statement relationship, as shown by being able to state, illustrate, and recognize its implications. Often this is a statement that tells how a cause produces an effect or how a result can be predicted from several component factors. It may involve knowing arbitrary rules of contingent procedure; e.g., if such and such is observed, do thus and so.

Following Procedures. Examples are knowing how to perform a set of operations that must be carried out in a rather fixed sequence, such as a preflight check, starting a car, or making a well-defined type of calculation.

Making Decisions or Choosing Courses of Action. This involves the application of conceptual rules or principles as a basis for making the kinds of decisions that are involved in diagnosing or interpreting complex situations. However, sometimes it involves perceptual discriminations that are learned or acted on directly without reasoning.

Performing Skilled Perceptual-Motor Acts. These may be quite simple (using basic hand tools) or quite difficult (manipulating the controls of an airplane or performing a sensitive adjustment that requires precise timing). Often the simpler skills provide necessary steps in more complex tasks that require the following of lengthy procedures.

Six Job-analysis Methods. The advantages and limitations of various methods of obtaining task information for training purposes have been investigated. One study compared job practices with training-course content using six job-analysis methods. The different methods were *direct observation,* an activity *checklist* filled in by the job analyst and job supervisors, a job *questionnaire* filled out by the technician, investigation of maintenance *records* for each job, *reports* to the observer of jobs just completed, and *sorting* of descriptive task statements prepared by the observer [6].

These methods were compared in terms of the amount of observer time required, the amount of technician time required, the amount of time required for observer training, the amount of technical job knowledge required by the observer, the amount of total job coverage possible in one week, the type of data analysis required of the information obtained, and the difficulty of this analysis. The study showed that some combination of routine checklist and questionnaire, supplemented with a large measure of concentrated on-the-spot observation, is valuable for getting information for training purposes. Many industrial training problems could be dealt with more economically if just a little more time were given to the problem of determining what information will be most useful.

Procedures for the specification of the behaviors to be developed in a training program are extremely important because on the basis of these specifications the entire program is established, as shown by Miller [39].

Determination of the Structure and Organization of a Job. Certain considerations about the nature of a job and its relation to an organization are of value for training. It is most important in industry that the distinction be made between training and education. Training is usually defined as the teaching of specific skills. Education usually refers to a broader type of teaching in which the objectives relate to proficiency in future situations by providing a basis for learning through experience or future training. It is often important for an organization to decide upon the goal of its training program. Within the limits of training time, is it more worthwhile to train individuals for a high proficiency level in a particular phase of a job, or is it more worthwhile to provide a higher degree of general training? Specific training gets people on the job faster and usually at a relatively high level of competence. Broad general training usually means that men will be more adaptable to fluctuations in job procedure and new equipment, but in any event, they require a period of specific on-the-job training. Each kind of training has its place. Instruction given the mechanic in running a new machine meets our definition of training. The instruction given in our graduate schools of business to young executive trainees we consider education.

Job Simplification. As jobs in industry and in the military become involved with increasingly complex equipment, it often appears that lengthy training is required. One way of managing such a situation is by job simplification, or *shredout*. Shredout refers to the breaking up of jobs, or tasks, into more easily trainable units. Such units will then require shorter training periods and less background for the people entering training. These units can be developed by training specialists in cooperation with the persons responsible for the utilization of the trainees. Shredout may require that a job be reorganized or redesigned so that it is performed in a new way. With appropriate job design a trainer may find that much less training time or fewer training demands are required. Industry has done little research in this area, but the military has done a great deal. An example of this research is reported for a control tracking situation where the task was redesigned to provide the operator with more immediate and direct knowledge of the effects of his own motions. Subjects who performed without task redesign were incapable of controlling more than one dimension or coordinate. With task redesign, five out of six operators handled four coordinates with ease [3]. Studies of this kind highlight the principle that training should be considered in relation to equipment and job design. This will be exemplified in the chapter on human engineering factors.

INPUT CONTROL

A necessary aspect of the training process in industry is the selection of the raw material that is to be modified. Personnel for a training program are selected by a variety of procedures consisting of such devices as tests, interview judgments, personal history, previous training, and in some cases the whims of a supervisor or manager. Judgment based upon interview is an extensively used procedure, the effectiveness of which is not evaluated often enough. The more formal selection techniques, in comparison with other aspects of a training program, have quite a detailed body of methodology and relatively well-laid-out procedures, as was shown in the preceding chapter on personnel selection. However, some special considerations of these for training will be mentioned here.

Selection procedures and training methods are influenced by the adequacy of the manpower supply available. When there is a full manpower pool, less precise selection procedures can be employed in order to select the relatively small number of trainees with the desired qualifications. The precision of selection procedures becomes increasingly important as larger numbers need to be selected or as the amount of available manpower grows smaller [48].

Cost Considerations. Testing practice in industry is also related to the cost of training. If test scores are positively correlated with success in training and with subsequent job performance, then the selection of individuals with high test scores can decrease the average cost of training per satisfactory employee. However, setting too stringent a test score for acceptance into training may require the testing of a large number of applicants. Using such a procedure can increase testing costs so much that the combined cost for testing and training per satisfactory employee is higher than the average cost for training a group with a lower minimum test score. This is true because qualifying with a lower score would require fewer applicants from which selections could be made. In general, overall costs increase when very high test scores are demanded. Refined selection techniques are especially necessary if classification for input into a number of different training programs is required. Such a practice would take place, for example, if a large organization desired to select electrical engineers for placement in various company training programs leading to administrative, research, managerial, sales, or production careers [50].

Another aspect of input control is the determination of specific *training needs*. Training-needs tests can be of particular value for refresher courses and for on-the-job training courses to increase proficiency. On the basis of job-oriented knowledge and skill tests, individuals can be selected for refresher courses or advanced training. The main job of the training specialists in this connection is to develop a series of tests which can diagnose these training needs and assess levels of proficiency. Input for a training program often comes from the work force already employed in a company, and the problem becomes one of selection from this group. This kind of program entails the selection of foremen and higher-level supervisors who can benefit from training.

Selection and training procedures cannot be considered as relatively independent problems. The manpower available can determine the extent and nature of a training program. Similarly the time and cost of training is influenced by the kind of personnel selected. Attention to the interaction between testing and training permits evaluation of the relative utility of each function. If only applicants of high ability are accepted for training, then training can be less costly and perhaps be continued to a high terminal level. If lower-ability applicants are accepted, a longer training period and appropriate job reorganization may be required to reduce the need for high-level personnel.

LEARNING PRINCIPLES AND TRAINING PROCEDURES

We come now to the heart of the training process—the actual procedures and techniques used in shaping and modifying behavior, including the teaching of certain skills, knowledges, and attitudes. The instructor or the supervisor must determine the best procedures to use, recognizing the caliber of the input population and the nature and objectives of the organization.

Scientific Findings and New Applications. An individual learns as a result of certain events that take place in his environment. Determination of the characteristics of these events and the relationships of these events to how behavior is acquired comprise a primary study of the science of psychology. As psychology advances, it will probably be possible to state the kinds of training procedures required for particular kinds of behaviors and for particular kinds of individuals. At this future time training and education will have become the applied psychology of learning. In furthering this end, psychologists spend much time working to discover the relevant considerations and variables that make up the laws of learning. Applied practice often outruns cataloged knowledge, and so individuals are trained and educated on the basis of the informal knowledge gained by experience instead of on the basis of the more rigorous knowledge gained by formal experimentation. This is illustrated by the fact that bridges and steam engines were built before laws describing their underlying principles were formally specified. However, experience is neither an inexpensive nor an efficient guide, and it is likely that the individual who modifies traditional practice with available scientific knowledge can do a more effective job. It also may be that the individual who, on the basis of scientific findings, breaks with the practices built up from experience will discover new applications and techniques which far outdistance the old.

It seems clear that what is most needed for the advancement of training methods and the development of a psychology of training is fruitful and flexible interplay between the requirements of training programs in industry, government, and educational institutions and an experimental approach to the modification of behavior. To have "pure" and "applied" endeavors operating in close coordination is an important undertaking. An experimental and research approach to training may be in the long run as valuable to an organization as a research laboratory for product development. Within the past decade industry has shown quite a willingness to work with professional educators and psychologists in attacking the practical problems of human learning.

Variables in Learning. A number of psychologists have attempted to draw together the results of the accumulated knowledge about learning and to state general principles that apply to training. These principles should be regarded primarily as *relevant variables* to be considered in developing training methods. The specific application of these variables in relation to the behavioral modifications required is a matter of determining their particular value in a specific training situation. This may be no more unreasonable than saying that here are some important considerations for building a new piece of equipment, but the exact application for developing this equipment, with certain desired characteristics, must be determined by field tests. If a consideration or variable is found to influence learning in a training situation, then it is important to ensure its appropriate use.

Repetition and Practice. Repetition can facilitate the learning of a task. A training situation should be designed so that the repeated practice of skills is possible. The amount of practice required depends upon the kind of task involved, training techniques, and individual trainee differences. The influence of these variables in a practical situation should be determined by observation and investigation. Too often, in industry as well as in college, time limits are set for training programs without knowledge of the amount and kind of repetition required for learning the tasks involved. Repetitions that are separated by a period of time are often more effective than repetitions that occur close together. Spaced repetitions, as compared with massed or concentrated repetitions, appear to result in rapid learning and increased retention. The trainer must determine the optimal schedule of practice for the particular activities with which he is concerned, and he must also consider the size of practice units.

Task Guidance. Learning is facilitated when the behavior of the learner is controlled through guidance. The word "guidance" here refers to any procedure employed to ensure that the trainee performs a task or works through a problem in a way which the trainer considers correct. In many instances one of the most important functions of a trainer is to aid the learner in performing correct responses, such as selecting the best movement, using the correct form, or choosing the alternatives which give maximum information in making a decision. Training is most efficient, it seems, when the trainee is allowed to make only a minimum of incorrect or ineffective responses. As a task becomes learned and the associated responses become finely differentiated in the presence of task cues, guidance should be shifted to these new, more precise responses.

In relation to guidance, industrial psychologists often discuss the problem of training for accuracy versus training for speed. In general, it appears that the answer depends upon the extent to which fast task responses differ from slower responses. If the difference is great, it is probably best to approximate the speeded task to be learned at the outset of training. It is often pointed out that information to the trainee concerning the outcome of his efforts and the nature of his errors aids learning; this, too, can be considered a form of guidance. The trainer needs to determine the kind of information which, in particular training situations, can be best used by the learner, and he must decide upon the best method of presenting this information to him.

Reinforcement. The learning of a task is facilitated when the learner is stimulated by the successful consequences of his behavior. Reinforcement refers to the fact that new behavior is learned and old behavior is changed when the individual's actions produce a consequent event such as a reward. Put another way, when an event that follows the learner's activity results in an increase in that activity, that event is said to be a reinforcer, and the process involved is called reinforcement.

Psychologists refer to the reward that is contingent upon or follows from, the performance of a task as reinforcement. Reinforcement can take many forms in training and education; it can be information about successful results or achievement or about progress or improvement; it can be monetary reward, recognition, approval, or the feeling of accomplishment. In a particular training situation, it may be practical to make a survey of the events which are most reinforcing to the trainees. It is important that the trainee have realistic goals in the course of training. Unrealistic goals cause failure and are punishing rather than reinforcing. The appropriate establishment of realistic goals which are reinforcing is an important task of the trainer.

Positive and Negative Reinforcement. Another important task for the trainer is to determine the trainee's level of aspiration and to give the trainee practice in setting aspiration levels for himself which are reinforcing and contribute to learning. Certain training programs use permissive-discussion methods, which are designed to encourage the trainee to express his attitudes and viewpoints. Permissive discussion reinforces the trainee's behavior in expressing his views. The expression of these views is then reinforced by the acceptance or nonacceptance of the group and by the reaction of the instructor. Certain general classes of reinforcers are distinguished by psychologists—positive reinforcers and negative reinforcers. *Positive reinforcing events* are effective because they are presented as a consequence of a response. Familiar examples are a good test score, the praise of the instructor, or information that a task has been performed accurately. *Negative reinforcers* are effective because they are withdrawn as a consequence of task performance. Examples include removing a trainee from a job he dislikes as a result of the successful completion of a training course and transferring a trainee to a new task which is less monotonous than his former job.

Reinforcement Schedules. Reinforcement is most effective if it occurs immediately after a task has been performed. Waiting until the end of a training session to inform a trainee of his success may not be as effective as immediate reinforcement. Determination of how various techniques and conditions of reinforcement influence learning and task performance has long been an important area of study for psychologists. Of particular interest in training is the frequency and pattern of application of reinforcement. How often and according to what kind of schedule should reinforcement follow the tasks being learned? Different schedules yield different characteristics in the behavior acquired. The effects of various schedules or programs of reinforcement in training curricula is an interesting matter for investigation and application. Optimal schedules of reinforcement can be of much practical importance. Skinner, who developed the idea of reinforcement schedules, points out that one kind of schedule of reinforcement depends upon the behavior of the individual himself; that is, a reinforcement occurs only after a fixed number of responses. This is a common schedule in education, where the student is reinforced for completing a project or a paper or some other specific amount of work. It is essentially the basis of selling on commission or of piecework pay. In industry such a schedule can result in very high rates of responding, which set unduly high standards of performance and result in excessive fatigue and so are dangerous to health. In view of these results, piecework pay is frequently strenuously opposed. Investigation of the effects of reinforcement schedules in industry, e.g., schedules of pay and the use of bonuses and incentive wages, could result in generating optimal productivity with the increased morale and happiness of the employee [33, 44].

Reinforcement is not only an important consideration in the early stages of learning a task; it is equally important in shaping and maintaining the fine discriminations and fine behavioral modifications required for the increased effectiveness of task performance. At this stage of training, when a high level of skill is being obtained, the task of the instructor becomes critical in ensuring that appropriate behaviors are reinforced in the presence of appropriate cues.

Learning to Discriminate. It is important for the trainee to learn to discriminate between those aspects of a situation to which he must behave *differently* and those aspects to which he must respond in a *similar* fashion. In other words, whether he is learning to perform a fine motor skill or to make executive decisions, the trainee must learn to discriminate between certain classes of behavior and to respond similarly within these classes. This may be compared to what a child does when he learns to discriminate between a dog and a horse and learns to respond in a similar fashion by calling them both animals. Bringing out this within-class similarity of responses is called *generalization training*. Here the individual learns to generalize his performance to cues other than those on which he was initially trained. Learning to discriminate between classes and to generalize within classes is considered a basic learning process involved in the formation of concepts. Perhaps writers of training manuals have this kind of underlying learning process in mind when they point out that a training situation must contain an adequate variety of practice materials, that situations to be discriminated should be as little alike as possible, and that response interference is a function of the degree of proficiency attained in task performance. Other considerations of learning also indicate the desirability of a variety of practice material.

Experience shows that without guidance and without appropriate arrangement of the training situation, reinforcement may not be effective in the right way. As a result, accidental connections may be established between certain task responses and the reinforcing event. In this way the operator of a machine may in a sequence of control manipulations give his controls some superfluous movements which are unrelated to the success of the desired operation. A comparable situation exists in certain games and sports like bowling and billiards in which the trainee develops a response referred to as body English which accompanies the true movements that contribute to a successful throw of the ball or shot with the cue. In a similar fashion, accidental and wasteful behaviors may be learned in the course of learning to become a successful supervisor. Responses which are learned as a result of the accidental contingency of responses and reinforcement are often called "superstitious" responses. A trainer should be aware of this possibility in the course of training. Careful delineation and spacing of subtasks may avoid this situation.

Extinction. The modification of behavior through learning sometimes involves *removing* certain behaviors from a trainee's repertoire. In order to remove certain task responses from a learner's performance, reinforcement contingent upon the task can be withheld. When reinforcement is not forthcoming following a learned response, the response becomes less and less frequent and in effect becomes removed as a part of task performance. The process whereby a task response loses strength as a result of lack of reinforcement is called *response extinction*. Often the process of response extinction is slower than the process of acquiring a response through reinforcement.

Using the notion of extinction, trainers have often pointed out that bad habits, or incorrect responses, can be eliminated by practicing them in a situation where they are recognized as wrong and where reinforcement is withheld. It is also important to check on the growth and progress of trainees, because their falling behind may be the result of performing tasks for which they have not been appropriately reinforced. Lack of reinforcement may also lead to emotional behavior or frustration in the course of extinction. The trainer should be aware of this and make allowances for it; he should attempt to extinguish incorrect responses while at the same time reinforcing substitute behavior. Extreme lack of reinforcement which can lead to extreme discouragement and lack of will to continue is, of course, to be avoided. In the development of attitudes it is often advised that procedures be designed to permit trainees to express hostile attitudes, to let off steam. It is desirable in these procedures to permit no reinforcement to occur, so that these attitudes can undergo extinction. Otherwise, it may be that the release of the hostile expression is reinforcement enough to guarantee its continuance. This may be particularly true in an industrial climate where one's boss is excessively autocratic.

A trainee's present task performance is dependent upon his prior conditions of practice and reinforcement. The extent to which a task response will be resistant to extinction, i.e., persist in the face of little or no reinforcement, will be the result of past training procedures. It follows from this that for certain job situations where the occurrence of failure is highly probable at times, tolerance for failure is best taught by providing a backlog of success or a history of reinforcement. Certain patterns or schedules of reinforcement, where success comes only intermittently in the course of practice, result in greater resistance of task performance to extinction.

Forgetting is not equivalent to extinction. Extinction occurs when a response occurs and reinforcement does not follow. Forgetting refers to a decrease in response proficiency as a result of the nonoccurrence or disuse of the response over the course of time. Some psychologists believe that forgetting is the result of learning competing responses which take place in the situation where the originally learned responses would have occurred. In general, as a result of forgetting, performance losses are greater soon after the cessation of practice than later on.

Training Sequences. In the learning of a task, certain sequences of task performance are more effective for the learner than others. In fact, one of the major problems of effective training is not that of making training tasks similar to job tasks, but of *arranging successive tasks* in such a way that the behavior is efficiently learned. The systematic arrangement of practice on particular components of a complex motor skill may often lead to far greater improvement than direct practice on the task in its actual complexity. One investigator [35] found that requiring practice *first* on certain difficult visual-motor discriminations and later on the task itself was an efficient learning sequence. For some time, psychologists have debated the question of whether the whole method of learning an entire task is superior to the part method in the acquisition of a skill. It appears now that the answer depends upon the nature of the task and that a good trainer will organize a task into the most effective sequence for learning. The determination of effective learning sequences may be accomplished by careful job analysis and experimentation with suggested procedures.

In the course of learning complex behavior, the learner's performance progresses from unskilled, coarse responses to skilled, carefully differentiated behavior. The job of the trainer is to reinforce the correct responses in the correct sequence in a way that will lead to the desired behavior. He does this by reinforcing those task responses which approximate the behavior eventually desired and then continuing to reinforce behavior which gets closer to the performance of a skilled employee. The procedure of successively reinforcing a sequence of behavior approximating the finally desired task performance is called *successive approximation*. Thus, a trainer should not expect perfection too soon from a beginner; early in learning, he should often concentrate upon actions rather than upon the quality of the end product. An analogy given by one writer [44] is that this procedure of shaping and modifying behavior is like shaping a lump of clay, where the sculptor begins with gross approximations to the final figure. If the trainer waits for a complete task performance before reinforcing, he may not be effectively teaching the early basic responses required in the educational sequence.

Learning and Effort. It is important to point out that as a task response is learned and the learner becomes increasingly skillful, there is a *reduction in the amount of effort* required to perform it. In many tasks this occurs to such a degree that a skillful operator seems to work effortlessly with little apparent concentration upon or attention to what he is doing. A trainer should be aware of this stage of performance if it occurs in the tasks with which he is concerned, so that he can permit the learner to drop out unnecessary responses and cues which were required in early training. At this time the trainer may also find it desirable to introduce further tasks which the learner can now perform but which would have interfered with early task performance. A related consideration in training is what is called *response tolerance* or *response precision*. This refers to the range of precision that is permitted in responses during particular stages of training. Permitting practice on only the correct response restricts the range of tolerance so that the learner cannot make responses that are too fine or errors that are too gross. On the other hand, a wide range of response tolerances in the early stages of training allows the trainer to reinforce approximately correct responses and to refine his reinforcement through successive approximations. In deciding upon appropriate response tolerances, the trainer must consider the interacting influence of many of the variables previously described, such as guidance of the correct response, reinforcement, and extinction.

Meaningfulness of Material. Learning is facilitated when the tasks to be learned are meaningfully related. If some general principles which the learner understands (has previously learned) underlie a sequence of tasks, then these tasks will be learned more readily than tasks which are not meaningfully connected. Training sequences should therefore be organized around *connecting principles* whenever possible. The trainer should be aware of principles which do relate material meaningfully and those which do not. For example, the teaching of certain principles of basic electronics may assist a trainee in learning his job as a radio repairman. On the other hand, it may be that some principles which are traditionally a part of early training actually relate tasks only at more advanced job levels, e.g., at the level of radio-design engineer.

In attitude and morale training it appears that free exchange of opinion should be encouraged if such discussion helps develop meaningful relationships which facilitate future learning. One of the important characteristics of learning sequences may be that effective sequences define meaningful relationships among the task responses to be learned.

Aversive Consequences. For efficient learning, stimulation by *unsuccessful,* or aversive, consequences of the learner's behavior appears to be less effective than positive reinforcement. A trainer can expect better results by stressing praise and offering a suitable incentive for correct or nearly correct performance than by stressing reproof or enforcing penalties for incorrect performance. Training under the control of rewarding consequences is preferable to training under the control of punishment. In training programs, aversive controls may take the form of docking pay, withdrawing privileges, discharge from the course, return to a lower-status job, or threats of these consequences. Research findings indicate that the inmediate effect of aversive consequences is to eliminate the incorrect behavior. *However,* if the behavior is not removed by the process of extinction, the elimination may not be permanent. This may suggest that punishing consequences can be used to depress an incorrect behavior temporarily so that an incompatible correct response can be learned in its place. The term "incompatible" means that both responses cannot take place at the same time. An appropriate caution is that aversive consequences may often evoke emotional or defensive responses which are undesirable and which may be incorporated in the future job situation.

Plateaus. In many training situations involving complex behavior, the learner reaches a stage in which he exhibits no apparent learning progress or increase in task proficiency. Psychologists have called these stages plateaus because, in a curve showing learning progress, stages of no apparent learning result in flattened sections in the curve. An important function of the trainer is to analyze the characteristics of such stages of learning in his training program. The occurrence of a plateau may indicate both desirable and undesirable influences. With certain behaviors, a plateau or slowing down of learning may indicate that the learner is acquiring the responses and discriminations required for more proficient task performance. At the same time, early unskilled responses of the learner are undergoing extinction. These early responses may rely, for purposes of initial training, on certain training supports not required at advanced levels of proficiency. In such cases, learning and task proficiency following the plateau may increase at a greater rate than previously, since now a more efficient set of task responses is being learned and employed. In training circumstances of this kind, the trainer should be aware that learning is proceeding and that the apparent decrease in progress is temporary.

In some instances, stages of no learning may be quite real and may be influenced by a number of learning considerations, such as sequence, reinforcement, and motivation. A plateau may also indicate that the learner's limit of proficiency in the training situation has been reached. If there is a large discrepancy between this limit and the level of proficiency expected on the actual job, it is probable that the training situation has not adequately simulated the job conditions and the job equipment. If increased job simulation of the training task is not feasible, then it is necessary that the behaviors taught during training consist of responses that readily transfer to and provide a basis for increasing proficiency on the job.

Learning to Learn. Much can be gained in certain training programs if the learner is taught how to learn. Experimental studies indicate that when a trainee is presented with a series of different tasks, he often develops greater facility in learning the later tasks than he displayed in learning the earlier tasks. It has been pointed out that the training of a set to learn can be of important practical significance for job situations in which an individual must adjust rapidly to changing problems and changing equipment models [16, 30].

Factors in a training program which influence learning to learn may be an important consideration for the trainer. A significant influence appears to be systematic variations in the learning situations presented to the trainee. The variables that are important in establishing learning sets need to be determined. These may consist of such aspects of behavior as habits of attending to critical discriminative cues or habits of modifying behavior when learning difficulties are encountered.

Active Learning. Learning that takes place by active responding permits more effective control by the trainer than does that which takes place through passive observation. Guthrie [28] writes that "in order to make listening profitable . . . it is essential that the student be led to do what is to be learned. . . . A student does not learn what was in a lecture or a book. He learns only what a lecture or book caused him to do." In this regard athletic coaches have a great advantage over trainers concerned with other kinds of behaviors. Many of the skills with which an athletic coach is concerned consist of overt behaviors which can be readily observed and shaped by appropriate reinforcement and sequencing. He can see the results of his training procedures and modify them accordingly to produce the behavior desired. The critical point here is that an important part of a trainer's job is to make the behaviors with which he is concerned as overt as possible. Only in this way can he see what he is doing. In teaching problem-solving tasks, such as the troubleshooting of equipment, it is important to use techniques and performance measures which make the learner's behavior overt.

Specially developed training exercises which require reasoning and integration of knowledge are useful ways of making the performance of such behaviors more available to the trainer. Training procedures which require a trainee to respond actively by summarizing a problem in his own words may be effective learning procedures of this kind. Despite the apparent advantage for trainer control that active responding permits, many training programs rely almost exclusively on a lecture method, which does not make available to the trainer the behaviors he is interested in shaping.

Transfer of Training. The objective of a training program may not be to produce a highly skilled trainee capable of immediately performing the tasks required for a job. It may be, rather, to teach certain behaviors which will facilitate learning when the trainee is placed on the job. Often the aim of a training program is a dual one—to train for a specific task and also for transfer of training. Studies in the psychology of learning indicate that the validity of programs designed for transfer can never be taken for granted. It is necessary for the trainer to determine whether positive-transfer effects occur as a result of training procedures. This is an important endeavor because transfer effects can be positive or negative. They can either facilitate or hamper subsequent learning and performance. Furthermore, established behaviors which have an apparent similarity to subsequent task responses may show little if any positive-transfer value.

It is difficult to determine those training tasks which facilitate subsequent learning and performance. Nevertheless, the trainer has the job of investigating and checking on the transfer value of his training program. If he does this, he can identify the training tasks and training procedures which maximize transfer for the tasks with which he is concerned. It seems that the considerations which are important for learning in general are equally relevant for learning behaviors which facilitate positive transfer.

The necessity of establishing dual objectives for a training program is often a complicating factor. The military service, for example, recognizes the need to train men to operate and maintain certain specific pieces of equipment and at the same time to train them to adapt to frequent equipment changes. Training for a specific job requires certain kinds of input personnel and certain training procedures which demand a particular amount of time. Training for transfer and adaptability may require different considerations and usually requires a longer training time. Within the limits of a two-to-four-year service period for many military personnel, a compromise program is necessary. In industries which have a large personnel turnover the problem is similar.

Motivation and Motivating Conditions. The influence of the considerations for learning so far discussed are enhanced or depressed by motivating conditions. A good example is the way in which the effect of repetition or reinforcement is influenced by such conditions. For the practical purpose of modifying behavior, a trainer may distinguish between the motivational possibilities that a trainee brings to the learning situation as a result of his past experience and the motivational conditions that can be built into the training program. It is good practice for the trainer to assess the motivational states with which trainees enter a training program. For example, trainees can differ with respect to their desire to learn and their need for achievement. Also trainees can enter a training program with different degrees of anxiety or apprehension about aversive consequences that may occur in the training situation. The influence of anxiety upon learning has received considerable study. It appears that the learning of tasks at different levels of complexity is influenced differentially by varying degrees of anxiety. Although some degree of anxiety may be motivating, too intense a degree may result in emotional states which distract from learning. This may be true in industry where, let us say, the trainee may have some feelings of insecurity anyway [47, 49].

It is even more important for the trainer to determine what motivating conditions he can introduce into his training program in order to enhance the effect of such variables as reinforcement. Trainers often suggest that this can be accomplished by setting up conditions of competition and cooperation in a training program. However, the long-range effects of motivating conditions during training which differ from the actual motivating conditions present in the future work situation need more study, particularly in the industrial setting. Some experimental results do indicate, however, that learning under one type of motivating condition facilitates, or generalizes to, performance under another type of motivating condition [4, 34].

Individual Differences. Learning takes place on the foundation of existing behavior which a trainee brings to the learning situation, and trainees differ in this respect. An effective trainer will carefully evaluate the initial behavior of his trainees, since this comprises the raw material with which he must work. He should be aware of differences that exist between individual trainees or groups of trainees. As far as possible, training practices should allow for such considerations as differences in the initial ability of individuals to make certain required sensory discriminations, individual differences in the speed of learning, age differences which facilitate or retard learning, and the enhancing or hampering influences of the personality of a given instructor upon different individuals.

Emotional and Attitudinal Conditioning. The paradigm of Pavlov's dog should be described here to point out that during training emotional and attitudinal conditioning may take place which can persist in later job behavior. It will be remembered that in Pavlov's experiments, meat powder elicited salivation; then a tone was paired with the presentation of the meat powder over a number of repeated trials. After a time, the tone alone was sufficient to elicit salivation. Similarly, a pleasant instructor can elicit pleasant experiences. When the task to be learned is paired repeatedly with the instructor, then the training task alone can come to elicit pleasant experiences that will be elicited in the future job. In order, then, to contribute to good morale and to individual satisfaction, it is important for a trainer to be aware of this sort of conditioning.

TRAINING AIDS, TRAINING DEVICES, AND SIMULATORS

Training aids and devices are widely used in training programs, and psychologists have begun to study the characteristics of effective training aids. The military services, for example, have official policies which require the development of training devices to accompany the construction of new equipment. A major proportion of time in some training programs is spent using training devices. In industry, for example, commercial airlines have made sizable investments in flight simulators because they reduce costs greatly by keeping operational equipment in use and because they provide opportunity for training and proficiency checking under supervision and low-hazard conditions [16, 19, 36].

The task of the psychologist in this work is to ask and answer such questions as: What are the characteristics of a training device that result in effective transfer of training to the job situation? How can a training device be built which will provide reliable measures of proficiency level? To what extent does a device have to simulate actual job conditions in order to provide effective training? In addition, these questions are important: To what extent do actual job conditions have to be deliberately altered to provide effective learning and reliable proficiency measurement? Does the use of a particular training device result in better transfer skills than less expensive classroom training aids? How can present aids and devices be used more effectively? The answers to these questions can be found by application and concurrent experimental investigation. From the psychologist's point of view, a major attraction of training aids and devices is that they offer a means of automatically controlling many of the variables which facilitate learning and transfer.

PROGRAMMED INSTRUCTION AND TEACHING MACHINES

Recently the application of learning principles to training and instructional practice has been implemented through the concept of programmed instruction. This has been described by Hughes [32], by Lumsdaine and Glaser [38], and by Shoemaker and Holt [43]. Essentially, programmed instruction represents an attempt to organize the process of teaching according to what we know about human learning. Much research and development work is going on in this new field, and increasingly frequent application is being made in the military and in industry [1, 7, 9, 12]. Because this new field is developing rapidly, its principles and practices are constantly being refined. In its initial modern development, the basic principles involved have been described by Skinner [45]. Many of the principles that are incorporated in programmed instructional materials are those described earlier in this chapter.

The construction of programmed instructional materials takes very seriously the importance of the behavioral specification of training objectives and the significance of such learning variables as task guidance, immediate reinforcement, and active learning. An important principle is that of gradual progression; when teaching complex performance, the behavior the trainee brings to the situation is reinforced when it is only a slight approximation to the terminal behavior being taught. The program moves in graded steps, working from a simple level to higher and higher levels of complexity. This gradual progression serves to make the student correct as often as possible and helps maintain his motivation for learning. A short example of a programmed instructional sequence is shown in Figure 7.1. The student is exposed to material in the form of small steps which are designed in such a way as to encourage him to respond. Before beginning the program, the student is told to respond while he reads through the step, or frame, as it is called. He writes his answers either directly in the book where the frame appears, on a separate answer pad, or, if a teaching machine is used, on the exposed space. As soon as he has completed the response called for, the student can expose the correct answer either by turning the page or advancing the machine. In the example in Figure 7.1, you should begin with the top panel on page 1, i.e., step 1, respond to it, and turn to page 2 to get your answer confirmed in the top panel. You should then go on to the top panel of page 3 for step 2, respond to it, and confirm your answer by turning the page, and so on.

At the beginning of the program progression, the frames call for behavior which the student brings to the teaching situation, and this behavior is gradually developed in relation to new subject-matter content. In the course of constructing a program, each step is tested so that trainees can respond to it with a high probability of success. This maximizes the occurrence of positive reinforcement. The probability of success is increased by the use of prompting techniques which essentially are hinting and coaching procedures based upon what is known about the trainee's background. For example, consider a set of frames designed to teach the Greek number

AN EXAMPLE OF A PROGRAMMED TEXTBOOK; CONVERSION TO NUMBER BASES OTHER THAN 10—Page one

STEP 1: It has been said that the reason we use a **decimal** (from the Latin word for 10) system in our arithmetic is that primitive men probably counted on their fingers. The total number of fingers and thumbs on both hands is ____. This number is called the **base** of our ordinary arithmetic.

STEP 3: There is nothing magical or sacred about the base 10 system we employ. In fact, conversion to bases other than 10 often provides important advantages. Some people have suggested that a base 12 system would facilitate computation, since 5 numbers **less** than 12 divide into it **evenly.** These 5 numbers are ____, 2, ____, ____, ____. In our base 10 system, on the other hand, only the numbers ____, 2, and ____ are less than 10 and divide it evenly.

STEP 5: Since we are familiar with the digits 0, 1, 2, 3, 4, 5, 6, 7, 8, 9, we will use them as much as possible while converting to other bases. For example, if we wanted to convert to the base 3, we would use the digits 0, 1, 2. If we wish to convert to the base 5, we would use the digits 0, 1, 2, 3, 4. If we wished to convert to the base 7, we would use the digits,

____, ____, ____, ____, ____, ____, ____.

STEP 7: There is another base, the **binary** base, which is immensely important in the construction of modern high-speed computers. These computers use vacuum tubes and switches which can be either "ON" or "OFF." From this and from the word "binary," you might guess that the base of the binary system is ____.

Fig. 7.1.   Reprinted from Glaser, R., Homme, L. E., and Evans, J. L. An evaluation of textbooks in terms of learning principles. In A. A. Lumsdaine and R. Glaser (Eds.). *Teaching machines and programmed learning.* Washington, D.C.: National Education Association, 1960.

AN EXAMPLE OF A PROGRAMMED TEXTBOOK: CONVERSION TO NUMBER BASES OTHER THAN 10—Page two

STEP 1: Response Check
         10

STEP 3: Response Check
         1   1
         3   5
         4
         6

STEP 5: Response Check
         0
         1
         2
         3
         4
         5
         6

STEP 7: Response Check
         2

AN EXAMPLE OF A PROGRAMMED TEXTBOOK: CONVERSION TO NUMBER BASES OTHER THAN 10—Page three

STEP 2: If our primitive computers had had a different number of fingers on their hands, they may very well have had an arithmetic with a base other than 10. For instance, if they had had six fingers on each hand they might have developed an arithmetic with base _____.

STEP 4: Since we use a base 10 system, we need 10 different numbers or symbols, which we will call digits, to write out our values. These digits are 0, 1, 2, 3, 4, 5, 6, 7, 8, 9. Notice the 0 (zero). You will need to list the 0 when writing out the digits of **all** bases. We always need the **same** number of digits as the base we are using and one of these digits will alway be "0." If we use a base 5 system we would need _____ digits.

STEP 6: We have seen that conversion to the base 12 might provide some advantages in computation, especially in division. However, if we use base 12, we will need _____ different digits. Since the digits 0-9 provide only 10 digits we must make up 2 new ones. (We wouldn't want to use 10 and 11, since these are made up of other smaller digits and are therefore not distinct.) You could make these up yourself, but for convenience, let us use ∅ for the digit after 9 and ∅ for the digit after ∅. Therefore, the digits for the base 12 are _____, _____, _____, _____, _____, _____, _____, _____, _____, _____, _____, _____.

STEP 8: The binary system is base 2; therefore the digits we might use would be _____, _____.

AN EXAMPLE OF A PROGRAMMED TEXTBOOK: CONVERSION TO NUMBER BASES OTHER THAN 10—Page four

STEP 2: Response Check
        12
            Please return to Page One and go on to Step 3.

STEP 4: Response Check
        5
            Please return to Page One and go on to Step 5.

STEP 6: Response Check

12	6
0	7
1	8
2	9
3	Ø
4	Ø
5	

Please return to Page One and go on to Step 7.

STEP 8: Response Check
        0
        1

prefixes which might be used in teaching the technical vocabulary of chemistry [46]. The trainee must learn to correctly use such prefixes as *mono, di, tri, tetra,* and *penta* with respect to the subscripts in chemical notations. The background of the student can be exploited by using such a frame as "A *mono*cle is a lens for use in only _____ eye." Or, "The *five*-sided building in Washington used by the military is called the _____gon." Later in the program the trainee is transferred to a specific application when he is asked to compose the technical names for chemical compounds indicated with symbols; for example, "CF_4 is carbon _____fluoride." In the program progression prompting techniques are used to control error and to evoke relevant behavior so that it can be brought under the control of new subject-matter content. The immediate-answer feedback provided by a program can encourage careful attention to the material, since the student works to come up with the correct answer. Since prompts are learning crutches, they have to be removed so that by the time the lesson is completed the trainee is actually performing the real task. In the course of the program progression, prompts are gradually withdrawn so that eventually the trainee responds on his own. In a programmed sequence, provision is made for the appropriate scheduling of practice and review with a variety of subject-matter examples.

One of the most important aspects of programmed instruction is the way in which a program is constructed. It is tested and revised until proof can be given that it teaches the training objectives set for it. In the course of its construction, if a trainee does not learn, then the program is revised and modified. Each successive revision ensures that the student's performance is brought closer and closer to the training objectives of the program. Once it teaches satisfactorily, it can be used in operational training.

The relation between teaching machines and programmed instruction is similar to the relation between computers and computer programming. An instructional program must be developed which can be implemented by machine capability. Programmed instruction is being carried out in the form of programmed textbooks, as illustrated by Figure 7.1. However, the potential for the integration of instructional programming, computer processing, and machine display and response devices cannot be overlooked, says Coulson [10].

OUTPUT CONTROL THROUGH PROFICIENCY MEASUREMENT

At the end of a training program and during the course of training, it is important for the trainer to measure the performance of the trainee. In this way he can determine whether or not the trainee has learned the behaviors specified as training objectives to the level of proficiency required. For training purposes, proficiency measures have three primary uses: (1) They provide information about the trainee's performance in the course of training which can be used to decide upon the subsequent course of learning. (2) They provide standards of proficiency which must be attained at the end of training. (3) They can be used to diagnose inadequacies in training procedures so that training can be improved.

TESTS OF PROFICIENCY

The main concern of the trainer in the development of proficiency tests is to measure those behaviors which have been specified as the objectives of training. This assumes that the specification of objectives adequately describes the behaviors necessary for job performance and for transfer of training on the job.

The validity of a measure is determined by how well the training objectives have been built into the proficiency test. The type of validity required for proficiency measures of this kind is called *content validity*. In evaluating the content validity of a training-achievement test, one asks, "To what extent does this test require performance by the trainee of the behaviors which constitute the objectives of the training program?" The more completely and reliably a test measures the attainment of these objectives, the greater is its content validity [13].

The determination of content validity is usually, like job analysis, a qualitative matter in which an essentially qualitative comparison is made of training objectives and the behavior elicited by the test. One use of training-achievement tests should be to set standards of performance which most trainees can achieve by appropriate training. This could be accomplished by varying training procedures when necessary, for example, by repeating certain aspects of the course or by employing different-sized learning units for different individuals. Most trainees should then eventually perform satisfactorily on the established proficiency measures. In practice, however, training procedures and training time are relatively uniform, with the result that trainees perform with varying degrees of proficiency. A cutoff score is often decided upon below which achievement is unsatisfactory. This situation may require the estimation of predictive validity for appropriate use of the proficiency test. The predictive validity of a test refers to the extent to which it predicts future measures of behavior. This kind of validity is usually determined by correlating test scores with subsequent performance measures. With adequate validity of this kind, end-of-course–proficiency measures can be used to estimate future job proficiency, and job assignment can be made accordingly.

Much of the work relating to the construction and interpretation of proficiency measures has developed out of general test theory, which has emphasized individual differences. One emphasis in test interpretation in this context has been on relative measures, such as standard scores and percentiles which indicate the relative standing of an individual in a given group. In training, the emphasis is somewhat different. What is required is an indication of the level of attainment of training objectives. For example, a percentile or standard score on a test of a job skill would not indicate whether the trainee was highly competent or had little skill. The determination of proficiency attainment must be made in terms of training objectives. Levels of proficiency or achievement should be made by the training specialist and subject-matter experts on the basis of their judgments of observed performance and specified in terms of proficiency-test performance. Scores on such proficiency tests should indicate the degree to which training objectives have been attained by the trainee. These scores can then tell the trainer whether or not it is necessary to make changes in the training program in order to produce trainees with the desired proficiency levels.

THE ORGANIZATION OF TRAINING

This chapter has been concerned primarily with the principles which underlie training. In practice these principles need to be applied to many different types of training programs. Industrial training in general involves both on-the-job training and off-the-job training. In the former, a training program is organized to fit in with working operations and is carried out by experienced operators, foremen and supervisors, or special job trainers. Off-the-job training is carried on in a company school or by arrangement with outside technical schools and universities. Depending upon the job involved and the lines of employee development in an organization, training of many kinds can take place [15].

Training occurs at various levels in an organization and is concerned with shaping different areas of job behavior. For purposes of description, these areas can be classified in a meaningful way.

Orientation and Indoctrination Training. This training is concerned with new employees or employees who enter new job situations within a company. The objective is to provide information about the policies and goals of the organization and to develop attitudes such as pride, respect, and loyalty.

Vocational and Job-skill Training. Here the concern is to train novices or semiskilled individuals in the specific tasks required for skilled job performance. Many organizations have centralized training groups and well-defined procedures for accomplishing this.

Professional and Technical Training. In contrast to the vocational training just described, professional and technical training is primarily concerned with the acquisition of advanced job techniques and the learning of recent technological and scientific developments which are of direct or indirect benefit to the organization.

Managerial, Supervisory, and Executive Training. Although the special skills which contribute to success in jobs in this area are less well known than those in other areas, an increasing amount of training in industry is concerned with the development of executive skill. Training in human relations, supervisory procedures, and principles of scientific management takes place both on and off the job.

Specialized Training. An organization continuously requires a variety of specialized training programs such as job-rotation training, training in work simplification, salesmanship training, training in labor relations, safety training, training in employee evaluation, programs of general cultural and civic development, and so forth. As an individual and organization evolve, the need for specialized training appears to be ever present.

TRAINING AND EXPERIMENTATION

A training program in an organization has features throughout it which can be investigated by experimental study. The industrial psychologist can bring to it hypotheses based on research findings, as indicated in the section on training procedures. Training personnel involved in day-to-day training operations can bring to it the results of their experience. From whatever source the problems or hypotheses come, they should be set up to give an adequate test of the practical alternatives and the general training variables being studied. This requires close cooperation between psychologists and training personnel. The psychologist may require experience in an organization's training programs. At the same time, training personnel may require indoctrination in a research point of view toward the training process. This interplay can contribute to improved programs of training for specific organizations and to the further development of training as an applied discipline based upon a science of learning [52].

SUGGESTIONS FOR SELECTIVE READING

Bruner, J. S. *The process of education.* Cambridge, Mass.: Harvard University Press, 1960. Indirectly related to industry.

Costello, T. W., & Zalkind, S. S. *Psychology in administration.* Englewood Cliffs, N.J.: Prentice-Hall, 1963. Part Four includes articles on effecting change through learning.

De Cecco, J. P. (Ed.) *Educational technology: Readings in programmed instruction*. New York: Holt, 1964. Only indirectly related to industry.

Deterline, W. A. *An introduction to programmed instruction*. Englewood Cliffs, N.J.: Prentice-Hall, 1962. For the reader who wants a readable treatment of programmed learning.

Dolmatch, T. B., et al. (Eds.) *Revolution in training*. New York: American Management Association, 1962. The use of programmed instruction in industry.

Gagné, R. M. (Ed.) *Psychological principles in systems development*. New York: Holt, 1962. Contains five chapters on training.

Glaser, R. (Ed.) *Training research and education*. Pittsburgh, Pa.: University of Pittsburgh Press, 1962. Long-range training and research in universities and in the military.

Glaser, R. (Ed.) *Teaching machines and programmed learning*. Washington, D.C.: National Education Association, 1963. A review of articles in first decade after modern origin by Skinner.

Hartley, Ruth E., & Hartley, E. L. *Readings in psychology*. New York: Thomas Y. Crowell, 1965. Section 5 contains seven representative articles on research in learning.

Hughes, J. L. *Programmed learning: A critical evaluation*. Chicago: Educational Methods, Inc., 1964. Present and future problems, indirectly related to industry.

Karn, H. W., & Gilmer, B. v. H. (Eds.) *Readings in industrial and business psychology*. New York: McGraw-Hill, 1962. Section IV has six articles on training in industry.

Lumsdaine, A. A., & Glaser, R. (Eds.) *Teaching machines and programmed learning*. Washington, D.C.: National Education Association, 1960. A collection of papers showing the origins and ideas which launched the modern teaching and training movement.

McGehee, W., & Thayer, P. W. *Training in business and industry*. New York: Wiley, 1961. Practical and theoretical problems in industry.

McLarney, W. J. *Management training*. Homewood, Ill.: Irwin, 1962. Cases and principles of value to management training.

Proctor, J. H., & Thornton, W. M. *Training: a handbook for line managers*. New York: American Management Assoc., 1961. Method in training.

Ross, A. M. (Ed.) *Employment policy and the labor market*. Berkeley, Calif.: University of California Press, 1965. A collection of behavioral science articles ranging from training to discussions of unemployment as a way of life.

Schein, E. H., & Bennis, W. G. *Personal and organizational change through group methods*. New York: Wiley, 1965. The laboratory method of group training.

8

Human Relations in Supervision

B. von Haller Gilmer

The first direct contact between management and the workers is made by the foreman, or first-line supervisor, as he is also called. His position has been described in a number of ways: he is the key man in production; he is a man who always feels that he has more responsibility than authority; he is the pivotal factor in human relations; he is accepted neither by management nor by the worker. His lot is improving somewhat. He has been elevated from bull of the woods to a person who holds the key to industrial morale. However, he still faces the problems of multiple loyalty. In this chapter, we shall analyze the principles of human relations in industry as revealed through the problems of the foreman.

A HISTORICAL PERSPECTIVE

Around the turn of the century, the foreman held a position in industry quite different from that which he holds today. Almost alone he had the responsibility and authority for running the shop. He hired and fired at will, acted as timekeeper, controlled production, and was, in effect, his own wage and hour administrator.

All this changed rapidly with the growth of unions, with the expansion of companies in size and complexity, and with increasing automation. Engineers and other trained specialists became essential people as technology advanced. Hiring was taken over by the personnel department, and union stewards became buffers between the foreman and his men. As the supervisor's authority and responsibility split in varying directions, management, for the most part, did little to help the situation. The foreman was bypassed in the chain of command and the worker found himself taking orders from a dozen bosses instead of one.

A Change of Status. Then once again, as industry continued to grow in complexity, the supervisor's position became a key position. But this time it was different—the foreman was now an interpreter of policy, not a maker of policy. Training courses were established for him as he took on more and more responsibility for job instruction, accident prevention, and worker morale. This was the end of the bull of the woods who had become a supervisor only because he had been on the job a long time. The new pattern involves better selection and training of supervisors, men with more decision-making ability, with drive to move up. Commented one supervisor promoted from a single to a multiple department, "I didn't notice much change in my problems except they are multiplied. It is more difficult to move from one type of decision to another than from one type of work to another."

Whether the supervisor comes from the ranks (a yardmaster on the railroad, let us say, who slowly works his way up from trainman) or is given his supervisory post shortly after joining the company (for instance, a young college graduate, expertly trained in technology or science, who rises swiftly in the chemical industry), a new dimension is added to his job—human relations.

Human Relations Emphasis. Emphasis on human relations in supervision has become most pronounced since World War II. But the seeds had been planted back in the 1920s by reports on surveys of company policies on the human aspects of supervision, by the writings of Bingham on human relations skills, and by the experimental work in human behavior begun at the Western Electric Company.

In this chapter we shall describe the nature of good supervision, the roles of the modern supervisor, and the tools he uses in applying good human relations. Although the psychological principles of good supervision apply at any level of management, in this chapter we shall deal primarily with the first line of supervision—the foreman. Supervision in middle and top management will be covered later in the chapter on executive leadership and development.

THE NATURE OF GOOD SUPERVISION

Information on the nature of good supervisory practices has come in recent years from a number of sources. Programmed experimental research from such organizations as the Survey Research Center of the University of Michigan has given us answers to questions involving the relationships between supervision and productivity. Reports of the Foreman's Institute include analyses of numerous case studies of industrial relations problems. Personnel associations and training societies have concentrated much of their efforts on supervisory selection and training. The National Industrial Conference Board, the various associations of business colleges, and government agencies have been focusing more attention than before on human relations in supervision. Kay and Palmer [23] say we can define human relations in industry as "the adjustment of unique individuals to their work through selection, training, and control of their environments in order that they may achieve the greatest job satisfaction while rendering the greatest service to their employers and their society." In this section we shall review experimental and observational studies of the human aspects of supervision.

Measuring Supervisory Results. Often two groups of workers doing the same work under similar circumstances produce results that differ significantly both in quantity and quality. If other factors are about equal, researchers have tried to answer this question: How does the way these groups are supervised affect their productivity?

One writer [33] has summarized the results of supervision on high-producing and low-producing groups in two diverse kinds of work—clerical work in an insurance office and section-gang work on the railroad. He found that the more secure the first-line supervisor felt with his superiors, the greater the group productivity; but the greater the amount of pressure exerted on the supervisor from above, the less the section productivity. There was more productivity from the groups of workers where the supervisor assumed a leadership role than there was from groups where the supervisor acted as just another employee. Of particular interest was the finding that where supervision was employee-oriented, production was higher than where supervision was production-oriented. One has to interpret these findings with caution, however. There must always be some emphasis on production, or little will get done. But exclusive emphasis on production without consideration of the employees can be self-defeating. Other investigators report virtually the same results from studies made in a large utility company. Employees who felt free to discuss personal problems with supervisors were more highly motivated to turn out work than were employees who did not have such freedom. Being sensitive to employees' feelings, voluntarily letting the employees know where they stood in an informal way, and giving recognition were described as the behavioral evidences of employee orientation [37].

In a series of studies it was found that greater production resulted where the supervisor had influence with his superiors and used this power to help the employees achieve their goals. When power is used to block employees' achievement, the group's achievement suffers. These studies support the contention that close supervision of the section heads is not so effective for productivity as more general supervision, a factor related to the feelings of security of the supervisor [48].

An attempt to summarize the many findings of the Survey Research Center led to the observation that the effectiveness of the supervisor was not a problem to be solved only at the first-line supervisory level. If a superior emphasizes production with the supervisors beneath him, those supervisors are, in turn, more likely to emphasize production with their workers. This emphasis frequently results in a production record lower than that of supervisors and superiors who emphasize personal relationships with employees. Good supervisory practices must be the concern at all levels of the organization [20].

Other writers, in summarizing studies on office employees, forest personnel, and skilled tradesmen, concluded that supervisors in the more effective work groups were more democratic and more likely to share information with subordinates, who were thus kept in the know. Such supervisors were effective in planning, in organizing, and in demanding adherence to regulations. They made decisions consistently and decisively [66].

One industrial relations professor, reporting on several studies, concluded that supervisors who achieved good teamwork in their groups were also quite loyal to the company. Those supervisors who perceived and prepared for future needs were found to be good counselors and good organizers. In general, the more effective supervisor felt that his authority was commensurate with his responsibility. In decision making, the better supervisors were reported to have good judgment and to be consistent, whereas poorer supervisors were often considered overly cautious [49].

Supervisory Complexities. When over one thousand insurance agents from five different companies were asked for suggestions on how their managers could improve their jobs, the most frequent recommendations centered around closer and more understanding agent-manager relationships. Several studies have shown that the employee-oriented practices of the supervisor, combined with other skills, resulted in greater agent effectiveness. It was found that attitudes toward the company and how it is managed were favorable when attitudes toward the immediate supervisor were favorable [15, 42].

Permissiveness, democracy, and flexibility in supervision do not automatically lead to good supervision. A study of the engineering department of a company illustrates how a work environment can become too flexible. Supervisory practices may be ineffective when policy practices of top management do not concur with those of immediate supervision [1]. This study reported bad morale in an engineering department of a company with the reputation of being an engineers' paradise. The structure of the department was such that each man had almost complete freedom; the major source of supervision was a committee which passed on research plans and checked on progress. In effect, there was no supervision save the vague pattern of control from top management, which gave the engineers no chance for advancement in responsibility. In fact, the environment was so flexible that the men felt insecure in their positions.

Much has been written on the techniques of good supervision, and it is of interest to note that many of the do's and don't's accumulated through practical experience serve as behavior samples of good human relations principles. Almost every book written on industrial supervision includes such good suggestions as: avoid getting into arguments with your men; learn to say "no" without harming the man's ego; praise people in advance so they will try to work toward your expectations; be honest in admitting your errors; tell the employees in advance of impending changes that will affect them.

Whether one regards human relations as an art, as a science, or as a combination of both, there is evidence to show that good human relations in supervision come only with hard work. Maintaining good human relations is a continuing problem.

How well one can go from effectiveness on the verbal level to effectiveness on the behavior level depends in part upon one's depth of understanding and one's ability to sense the local psychological climate. Good supervision is found at the *behavior level on the job*. Some men talk better supervision than they practice. As one observer put it in describing a certain supervisor, "He is big talk, little do." No doubt a great deal of money and effort are wasted on training programs that get no further than the verbal level.

Effects of Training. It is doubtful that we will ever have a monetary measure of education. But the few studies which have been conducted on industrial training of personnel below the executive level give us an indication that we had better not expect too much from *individual* training when the *situational* setting for the person is not improved.

International Harvester Study. Fleishman et al. have reported on extensive efforts to evaluate a supervisory training program conducted under the supervision of the Personnel Research Board of Ohio State University with the cooperation of the International Harvester Company. This was the first attempt to obtain measures of certain leadership variables both before and after a training session and then to observe changes in the variables after the foremen returned to their jobs. The two-week training stressed principles of human relations and made use of role playing, visual aids, group discussion, and lectures [13].

Prior to the training the foremen were given a Foreman's Leadership Opinion Questionnaire which was designed to measure crucial aspects of leadership. A factor analysis of the instrument indicated that there were two important aspects of leadership. The first, which was labeled "consideration," appeared to be related to friendship, mutual trust, and warmth between the leader and his group; the second, "initiating structure," appeared to measure how much the foreman was concerned with "well-defined patterns of organization, channels of communication, and ways of getting the job done."

The day the foremen completed the course they were given the instrument again. The scores for consideration and initiating structure are given in Figure 8.1.

As expected, since the course concerned human relations, the foremen showed a general increase in consideration and a decrease in initiating structure. Most research in this area has stopped at this point, with all concerned happily assuming that an enduring change in the foremen's attitudes has been achieved. But Fleishman and his associates asked about the *permanent* effects of the leadership training. These were evaluated in a number of ways.

The researchers compared a group of foremen who had not attended the training school with a group of foremen who had; the latter were divided into subsamples according to the time elapsed since training. Contrary to their expectations they found that the most recently trained group were *lower* in consideration behavior than the untrained group, and that some of the trained groups *increased* in initiating structures. These disquieting results were explained partially on the grounds that "the course makes the foreman more concerned with human relations, the whole project makes him more aware of his part as a member of management." Apparently the researchers believed that this resulted in the foreman showing less consideration and more initiation of structure.

The Company Climate. An extensive additional study indicated that the company environment or climate to which the foremen returned was an important variable. The climate was measured by giving each foreman and his boss modifications of the instruments already described. "The results showed that foremen who operated under leadership climates high in consideration scored significantly higher themselves in both consideration attitudes and behavior." The trend for initiating structure was the same.

Fleishman and his associates asked whether it is good for foremen to be high in consideration and less so in initiating structure. Many researchers have simply taken it for granted that the answer is "yes," but the analyses of Fleishman and his associates indicated that the foremen whose workers

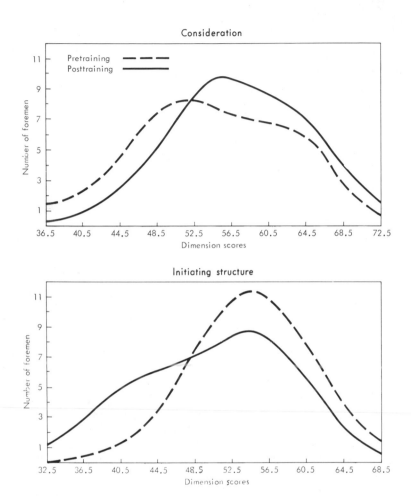

Fig. 8.1. Distribution of scores on the Foreman's Leadership Opinion Questionnaire before and after a course in human relations. The foremen showed an increase in "consideration" (friendship, mutual trust) and a decrease in "initiating structure" (getting job done, communication). (From Fleishman, E. A. Harris, E. F., & Burtt, H. E. *Leadership and supervision in industry: An evaluation of a supervisory training program.* Columbus: Ohio State University Bureau of Education Research, No. 33, 1955.)

had the highest morale were the most considerate and were less inclined to initiate structure. The correlations for rated proficiency were variable. Further analysis indicated that much depended on the extent to which a department was under the pressure of a time schedule. In those departments where pressure was high, proficiency and initiating of structure were highly related in a positive way, whereas in the low-urgency departments (the nonproduction departments), proficiency and consideration were positively related.

It was found that the foremen with the higher consideration scores had less absenteeism, whereas the opposite was true for initiation of structure. Finally, it was found that there was a tendency for more initiation of structure to go with more grievances.

Leadership and the Social Setting. One of the conclusions drawn from this study is a notable statement which should be impressed on the minds of all those who study leadership. Leadership behavior is not a thing apart but is imbedded in a social setting. In addition, the authors concluded that the ultimate answers as to what kind of leadership is most effective in various settings "may require an evaluation of long-range objectives as contrasted with those of short range."

This study raises some questions about the effects of human relations training. If nothing else, it shows that we must not blithely assume that the training will have the expected effects on the trainee.

THE MULTIPLE ROLES OF THE SUPERVISOR

The supervisor has been described as a man who plays a dozen roles. He always belongs to two organizational groups and sometimes to three. As management's representative to the employee, he must carry out company policy; as the employee's representative to management, he has a reverse role. Under some circumstances, the supervisor may find himself with a third loyalty—the foreman's union. In carrying through his major roles as a leader and key man of a communication network, the supervisor from time to time functions in selection, training, counseling, labor grievances, upgrading, record keeping, and public relations; in addition, he is something of a technologist.

Loyalty of the Supervisor. "Does your supervisor pull for the company or for the men?" This was one question asked of a group of employees by two investigators. At the same time, ratings were given on the supervisors' performances by their superiors. These authors found that the supervisor who could understand the objectives of *both* the company and the workers was rated highest by management. More supervisors who pulled for the company were rated less effective by management. Many of the employees felt it was possible for the supervisor to pull for both the company and the men. Most significantly, this study showed that dual loyalty posed no serious problem where the goals of the company and the goals of the employees were compatible. However, when management fails to recognize this duality, the foreman may lose his ability to act for the employees and eventually lose his effectiveness in helping management gain its objectives. Failure on the part of the workers to recognize the duality may inhibit the supervisor's success as a representative of management. Apparently one of the factors that brings foremen, union leaders, and union stewards to positions of leadership is the ability to see both sides of the dual position [37].

Concern has been voiced because it is difficult to upgrade a man from the rank and file and have him feel a balanced loyalty. A case in point came to the attention of this writer, who had been giving similar but separate courses in human relations to supervisors and to middle-management administrators. Each group brought up an instance of a recently appointed foreman who would not cross a workers' picket line. The management group felt that his duties demanded that he cross the line. The supervisory group maintained that it would have been a violation of the spirit of unionism, since the supervisor himself belonged to a foreman's union. The man himself confided to the instructor that he was in conflict and did not know what to do. A search of the psychological literature to find what consultants with long experience had to say about such problems showed that one psychologist [35] concluded that management needs to select and train supervisors more carefully, pay more attention to their dissatisfactions, make them feel more a part of management, and thereby forestall their joining a foreman's union. Another writer said that such problems are problems of communication between higher management and the supervisors [2]. A marked difference often exists between what management believes the responsibility of the supervisor is and what the foreman himself conceives it to be. Viteles [59] says it is a multidimensional problem involving status, pay, conceptions of authority and responsibility, and the opportunity to act and feel like management. Herzberg and his associates [20], in reviewing the literature on job attitudes, conclude that management must give proper attention to the supervisor if it expects him to identify with management. However, the relative value of such attention, its nature, and the conditions most appropriate for it are not yet known from concrete evidence. One psychologist reports that in his company it is general practice to move supervisors up and down in rank, a situation resulting in foremen asking questions about loyalty when demoted again and again to worker status.

EMPATHY IN SUPERVISION

Some psychologists believe that applications of the concept of empathy may lead to better selection and training of supervisors. Here empathy has been defined as "the ability to put oneself in the other person's position, establish rapport, and anticipate his reactions, feelings, and behaviors." Some writers attribute a part of the conflict between labor and management to a lack of empathy on the part of both groups [22].

An experienced investigator, in one of his studies on industrial conflict, found that facts are not the same for people with different attitudes and that leaders on both sides come to an industrial controversy ready to see only the good on one side and only the bad on the other. Studies with the widely used File and Remmers test How Supervise? and the Kerr and Speroff Empathy Test show that the abilities to perceive the feelings of others are related to supervisory success. But where does the balance in feelings come in? One psychologist found, for example, in a study of empathy among people working in a textile factory that the supervisors tended to overestimate the worker's knowledge of the best methods of supervision and to underestimate management's knowledge of the facts [11, 26, 47, 51, 56].

One writer who prefers the term "sensitivity" to "empathy" (since the word "empathy" carries a connotation of sympathy with the object empathized) found that, on the average, the better the supervisor is able to sense employee attitudes, the higher the productivity of the work group. He also found that supervisors were less sensitive to topics and attitudes in which they themselves might be ego-involved. For example, a foreman may be very sensitive about working conditions for his men but insensitive to his own acts of favoritism.

The supervisor must play an interpretative role that extends beyond the job situation itself. The tensions which arise in the worker must be understood by the supervisor. He must understand the nature of the man's resistance to authority, his fears, and the feelings of insecurity. In this respect, it has been found that the more considerate the foreman's own supervisor, the more considerate he is himself. There are reports of a relationship between the pressures put on the foreman by his superiors and similar anxieties he creates in his men. Hatch [16], using a forced-choice differential-accuracy approach to the measurement of supervisory empathy, found that the ability to predict the attitudes, opinions, and feelings of workers increases with increases in the degree of acquaintanceship between supervisor and subordinate.

SENSITIVITY TRAINING

At various leadership levels, sensitivity training (T groups) has been both a stimulating and a controversial subject for some time [7, 45]. As defined by Argyris [2] it is a program designed to provide experience where success, self-esteem, and interpersonal competence can be increased; where dependency and control can be decreased; and where emotional behavior, when and if it is relevant, can be as fit a subject for discussion as any "rational" topic. Sensitivity training provides group situations where leaders (frequently executives) expose their behavior as well as their thinking; they receive feedback about their behavior and give feedback about the behavior of others in an atmosphere where human beings are willing to expose themselves. The purpose of T groups is to become more aware of how one's behavior is interpreted by others. Advocates of sensitivity training believe it is valuable to know how others see you; critics believe it can be harmful. "What criteria?" ask others. Perhaps the researches on empathy now going on may provide some answers and some answers may be reported by the T-group people themselves.

In terms of methodology, sensitivity training involves small groups of fifteen to twenty people. Most groups begin with an embarrassing silence followed by rambling conversation during which feelings are expressed and the reactions of the members are aired. The trainer's role is one of keeping a free climate for hair-down expression. In theory, participants come to see themselves in a new light and begin to become aware of how they affect other people.

THE JOBS OF THE SUPERVISOR

Let us examine a little more extensively how thin the supervisor has to spread his talents and energies in carrying out the many roles of his position, how he has to be virtually a Jack-of-all-trades.

Inducting the New Worker. The supervisor's tact in getting the new man to talk about himself in a free and easy way is essential to good supervision. At this first session he must give the worker information about the company in general, its overall policies, and the relationship between the employee's specific department and the whole company. Departmental rules and regulations have to be explained in relation to the worker's specific duties. The supervisor must judge how extensive he should make introductions and how he can best make the man feel he belongs to the work group. All of this has to be done with the knowledge that the new man can take in only so much and that his first impressions will be important.

Training Responsibilities. Some training responsibility falls to the supervisor. He must know how to prepare the best instruction sequence for the job at hand. The good supervisor must learn firsthand the principles of transfer in training, the nature of habit interference, and what to do about it. In short, he finds himself in education, but often unprepared.

Safety. Good safety practice is the responsibility of everyone, but to the supervisor goes the job of checking on the environmental and personal causes of accidents in his department. He must be alert for the man who operates without authority or bypasses safety devices, who uses unsafe equipment or operates a machine when emotionally upset. When he sees a worker committing an unsafe act, the foreman must "stop-study-instruct" and sometimes apply discipline right on the spot. The supervisor often must apply the principle of repetition in safety education. He is frequently the one who must tell the family when a man has been injured or killed.

The Handling of Grievances. In their initial stage, grievances fall to the supervisor. He must examine them for cause, whether attributed to work climate, to wrong job placement, to inadequate job training, or to personal causes. The good supervisor soon learns that gripes are often safety valves, not grievances. In some situations, the supervisor finds a large part of his day taken up with the union steward, ironing out difficulties. He knows that the causes of grievances are legion—pay differentials, union-contract specifications, unguarded work hazards, uneven distribution of overtime, favoritism, strict rules, credit stealing, disciplinary action, etc. The supervisor must be alert to them all. Fleishman and Harris [12] have found that, in general, "low consideration" and "high structure" go with high grievances and turnover. There are, however, critical levels beyond which increased consideration and decreased structure have no effect. Workers under foremen who establish a climate of mutual trust, rapport, and tolerance for two-way communication with their work groups are more likely to accept higher levels of structure.

How to handle nonunion grievances is a problem because the employee may face frustration when he has a complaint. One survey of 171 companies found that 27 per cent say they make no provision at all to hear grievances of nonunion workers. This places an added burden on the supervisor that may be involved [9]. That grievances can be solved before they reach a stage of writing, where language and criteria and sometimes lawyers get involved, has been demonstrated. McKersie [34] describes some practical steps in keeping grievances at the oral level which have been worked out between the United Automobile Workers and International Harvester. It was found that problem solving is facilitated when a climate for free discussion exists, where both parties feel free to search for solutions, where discussion focuses on the issue rather than on precedent, and where solutions developed at the first step are not overturned too often by higher officials.

Discipline Handling. The supervisor often finds himself in a difficult position as he tries to break bad habits of his men and to prevent wrong actions from going unnoticed. He acts as an analyst as he seeks the reasons for absenteeism or lateness to work, as a problem solver as he interprets facts that lead to correction of behavior, encouragement, warning, penalty by layoff or demotion, or finally dismissal. And in strongly unionized plants he deals with discipline under the watchful eyes of the union committee. His problem is even more complicated in those situations where the committeemen like to foment trouble for management, and sometimes even rules themselves can get in the way. One slowdown among Canadian postmen following the rules to the absolute letter (because of a grievance) completely disrupted mail service. An army study in small-unit leadership showed that the effectiveness of discipline among enlisted men depended more on climate than on the person administering the discipline [21].

Worker Rating. How to rate the worker is a problem that has not been effectively solved anywhere along the line. Rating scales or critical-incident techniques, regardless of their merit, depend upon supervisor observations and judgment. Whether he likes it or not, the supervisor must make judgments where objective standards of judgment probably do not exist. His ratings are often hampered by labor-management conflicts of interpretation. In the judgment of the supervisor, a relatively new man may be superior to the man with seniority, but the latter must be favored according to most union-contract agreements. Rating, a rough problem even in the isolated confines of the ivory tower, is a most difficult task in the industrial complex, as we shall see in a later chapter.

Managing the Budget. And, lest we forget, the supervisor has the role of budget manager. He must keep records—material cost, manpower cost. He must have a working understanding of profits and loss and able to tell the difference between real work and soldiering. He must know how to plan for waiting time; he must know what to do with men who "make the job last." In one study the Home Builders Research Institute found a model home held up by 219 delay-causing problems—waiting for supplies and tools, for instructions, and for others to finish a given project— that were all preventable.

Communication. The supervisor is a key in the communication network, whether communication be up, down, or horizontal. From giving orders to satisfying customer and public relations, the supervisor plays both a formal and an informal role.

A Checklist of Supervisory Practices. One way to appreciate the many and varied demands placed on the supervisor in modern industry is to make a checklist of his day-to-day activities. A review by the author of several such checklists taken from large industries and small industries, from office situations and plant situations, from closely confined workplaces, and from the transportation industries show that the human relations problems are the same, though activities from job to job may vary extensively. The following checklist states questions to the supervisor in a straightforward way. Each question is phrased for a positive answer.

1 Do you know each of your men well enough to tell where he lives, where he came from, and what his interests are?

2 Do you know the general aims of the company?

3 Can you list in order your men who are ready for promotion?

4 Do your men work together well?

5 Do you know how to give an order?

6 Have you obtained better working conditions for your men?

7 Have you corrected the sources of grievances before they come up?

8 Do you listen to complaints?

9 Do you reprimand without building up ill feelings?

10 Do you avoid talking behind a man's back?

11 Do you reprimand in private rather than in public?

12 Do you have a check sheet for introducing a new man to his job?

13 Do you guide the new employee over rough spots?

14 Do you keep a progress chart on the new man?

15 Do you have a good criteria for judging performance?

16 Are you a good listener?

17 Are your records useful?

18 Do you know how to get a man to talk in an interview?

19 Do you keep up to date on company policies?

20 Do you keep up to date on union activities?

21 Do you plan work schedules in advance?

22 Do you have adequate inspection procedures?

23 Are you familiar with the technical side of the men's jobs?

24 Does work go on efficiently in your absence?

25 Do you keep your superiors informed of your department's activities?

26 Do you avoid taking up bothersome details with your boss?

27 Do you answer correspondence on time?

28 Do you see where your job fits into the overall organization?

29 Do you have a man who could take your job?

30 Do you know what the accident hazards are in your department?

31 Do you train for safety?

32 Do you give recognition to the man who does good work?

33 Do you ask workers for suggestions before attacking a new job?

34 Do you spread overtime work fairly?

35 Do you allow conversation at work on routine jobs?

36 Do you ever ask a worker to criticize his own work?

37 Do you admit your mistakes?

38 Do you believe that ability to handle workers is learned?

39 Do you know what goes on in departments other than your own?

40 Do you use conferences in getting ideas over to workers?

41 Do you keep cash and production records for your department?

42 Do you ever explain company policies to your men?

43 Do you keep your people informed on business conditions of the company?

44 Do you spend part of your time listening to worker complaints?

45 Do you believe the worker wants more from his job than just pay?

46 Do you believe most workers will cooperate in helping solve problems?

47 Do you believe that a worker who does not get promoted should be told why?

48 Do you believe in giving workers rest periods?

49 Do you believe people want to know where they stand on a job?

50 Do you believe in trying to sense how the worker feels?

Knowing what to do at the verbal level and actually carrying through at the behavior level is one of the big problems of supervision. Studies show that practically no supervisor does all the things which he knows should be done. For our purposes here the list is useful in emphasizing the many demands put on this man of many roles.

Supervisor-Worker Relationships. Studies made by Hersey [19], involving over six thousand people, have led to some very practical understandings about supervisor-worker relationships. When employees were asked about the most irritating factor in their work situation, 75 per cent of them responded that the boss was. The response was strongest where the boss was closest to the worker in distributing work, supervising training, handling grievances, and enforcing discipline. But to these same people, the boss was also something of a father figure who meant much in their daily lives.

A great deal has been said about the worker's need to get a feeling of accomplishment from his work. The importance of this need has long been recognized, but how can the person in the low-level unskilled job or the person who has reached his limits of job accomplishment feel that he is making progress? Studies of workers in such categories show that feelings of accomplishment do not have to be directly associated with the job itself. If the job helps the man to feel that he can buy a car or build a cabin, then some degree of satisfaction may be present. A good foreman looks for these signs of progress as well as for the feelings of satisfaction that may come from the act of work itself, the so-called "intrinsic" aspect of work.

Hersey has brought out consideration of another aspect of the supervisor-worker relationship not often voiced. He found that over a period of time workers build up an emotional resistance against the driving foreman which hinders production. However, emotional pressures brought on by unavoidable events are quite different in their long-range emotional impact on the worker. Since these events are impersonal, they are unlikely to arouse antagonism and a desire to fight back.

One experienced supervisor up from the ranks put the problem of supervisor-worker relationships thus: "It seems the lower a person is on the chain of command, the harder he is to supervise and the harder he is to motivate. It's hard for the supervisor to provide drive that isn't there."

Overgeneralizations in Supervision. One of the dangers involved in establishing do-don't rules of supervision comes from overgeneralization of selected facts. There is some evidence which supports the contention that a simple, repetitive operation involving no conscious thought produces in the worker a feeling of boredom or monotony and a consequent desire for change. This contention may well be true if the given worker is an intelligent, ambitious person who is made to stay on a simple, repetitive operation. On the other hand, a person of low intelligence may resist being taken off a job that is boring to others. Studies also show that workers performing the same simple, repetitive operations are less likely to be affected by monotony if they see others doing the same thing and if they are allowed to talk and laugh with fellow workers. Permission to talk and laugh, however, must be limited to such tasks as making simple machine parts, where there are no adverse effects on production; card-punch operators in accounting departments (a task boring to some people) would lose considerably productionwise if allowed to talk and laugh with fellow workers on the job.

One other overgeneralization that has led to some misunderstanding is the belief that restriction of output by workers is found only in strongly organized union plants. Nonunion workers have been found to be just as prone to restrict output whenever the conditions of their employment lead them to fear layoff or a cut in rate. The good supervisor understands such subtleties of human behavior. He knows the importance of telling the worker why he is doing a particular job. In most higher positions people know the "whys" without being specifically told. Workers often do not have the opportunity to learn about a job except through the foreman.

But what of the morale of the supervisor himself as he attempts to carry out his many jobs? Why do employees frequently turn down the chance to become foremen? Much of the answer lies in the lack of clarification of the supervisor's role, forced as he is to deal with his workers both individually and in groups. Sometimes the supervisor even has to play the part of instigator in getting some status award for the boss. One may wonder just how many executive awards come in this manner!

THE SUPERVISOR AND THE INDIVIDUAL

The supervisor's relationship with any given man may well follow a pattern of helping to hire him, induct him into the job, train him, place him, rate him, upgrade him, counsel him, or fire him. As he gets to know his men, the supervisor becomes a student of the subject of individual differences.

The New Man. Although selection is today a function of the employment office or the personnel department, the supervisor, in many instances, still passes final judgment on who shall be hired. This gives him prestige in the eyes of the man. He is recognized as having authority and representing management. With the personnel department having recruited and screened applicants, the foreman first gets to see the man in the interview. Here he initially establishes his relationship with the man, a step that leads to inducting the worker.

Some people are insecure as they start a new job. In such instances, the supervisor functions in two ways. First, he tries to make the new employee feel some degree of belonging. Second, he often must skillfully break down ways of working carried over from the last job, remaining ever mindful of man's resistence to change. Since first impressions tend to linger, the foreman can in this stage of induction "sell attitudes" as well as establish a cooperative relationship which will come in useful at a later date when the inevitable discipline problem arises.

Induction of the new worker is the beginning of his on-the-job training. The authors of a book on human relations in supervision maintain that the induction stage is crucial in helping to reduce costly employee turnover; about 80 per cent of all turnover takes place during the first three months of employment. The attitudes which promote individual job satisfaction, as well as group morale, get established in the induction process [46].

How Supervisory Responsibilities Have Grown. One of the most difficult problems in industry is evaluating how well a person performs. No matter what formal criteria are set up, whether a worker is promoted, transferred, retained, demoted, or fired, the supervisor is a key man in the process. Many of the problems in this area are literally dropped in the foreman's lap without any plan as to how he is to solve them.

We find, for example, the supervisor in an unenviable role as he becomes troubleshooter and attempts to solve grievances at his level of employee relations. If he has too much trouble with the union steward, both labor and management can project their frustrations upon him. He must not only hear complaints, seek the facts, define the problem, and work out a solution, but he must promote good morale, too.

As a counselor, one of the key roles of the supervisor, the foreman must learn to discriminate between helping with personal problem solving and wasting time on unnecessary complaints. Here he sometimes finds himself in the role of a therapist without the preparation of a therapist.

COUNSELING AND MENTAL HEALTH

Almost every individual relationship between the supervisor and the worker involves some form of counseling. By taking a look at the now classic Western Electric studies which were begun in 1927, we can get a picture of how counseling in industry took on at least a degree of formality.

Western Electric Studies. These studies set out to discover the effect of the working environment, e.g., illumination, working conditions, rest pauses, and the length of the working day, on production. Through a series of circumstances one investigator of the studies found himself in the role of a supervisor in a department. Trying to obtain information from the workers, he noticed, as their comments were solicited, that they began to lessen their unfavorable attitudes toward management. As time went on, it became apparent that factors other than working environment and working conditions were having an effect on the productivity of the employees. What was happening here?

At first, the investigators thought that asking workers about their job was the key thing. A series of systematized, structured interviews was set up, but with little success. Next came a more informal type of interviewing where the workers were allowed to discuss any topic of interest to them. The theory underlying this approach was that the worker would tend to talk about the thing that was bothering him most. But no ready-made system of effective counseling resulted from this approach; it did little more than give the workers a chance to get things off their chests. Finally, it was discovered that the key to the formalized employee counseling lay in giving the worker a chance to effect some *personal problem solving*. Thus in 1936 Western Electric instituted employee adjustment counseling by hiring full-time professional counselors [52].

In this program each counselor was assigned a given department or area within the plant. He had no supervisory or administrative responsibilities; his sole function was to acquaint himself with the employees with whom he was working and to counsel on personal problems in any informal situation—at the bench, at the desk, and in hallways and washrooms, as well as in private counseling rooms. Experience showed that the interviews averaged a little over an hour; the employees were not docked in pay for the time they spent in counseling sessions. Counseling could be initiated by the worker, his supervisor, or the counselor.

Evaluation of Formal Programs. How effective have these formal counseling programs been? Are they worth the money they cost? Answers to these questions, within and without Western Electric, are many. At one end of the continuum we find some in management highly endorsing such programs. At the other end, some managers have thrown the idea out. Some other companies have established formal programs of counseling; some have tried them and later dropped the idea. Union reaction has, by and large, been negative to formalized counseling services. Spokesmen for unions regard them as a sop on the part of management to get more out of the worker.

Perhaps one can conclude that the lack of adequate objective-evaluation procedures has led to the many pros and cons about formalized industrial counseling. There really is no clear answer to the question of the effectiveness of the formal programs. The author, in conversation with a plant manager where a program had been well received for several years, heard the explanation of the sudden discontinuance of the program in these words: "We got a new vice-president, and he has interests other than the counseling program instituted by his predecessor."

When Do We Have Counseling? Regardless of the pros and cons for specific programs of counseling, much has been learned about the psychology of industrial counseling. Whether formal or informal, counseling is an important aspect of management-worker communication. Let us take a look at this communication of feelings, bearing in mind that in most companies the counseling that does take place is done informally by the worker's immediate supervisor. Often the foreman does not even think of it as counseling. The author had this brought to his attention when he spent a day with an industrial supervisor as part of a job-description study that was being made.

During the day, along with giving orders, making inspections, and planning for the next day's work, this particular supervisor helped six of his employees to work out solutions to individual practical problems. The six problems involved such diverse activities as listening to grievances about working conditions and handling a telephone call from the wife of a worker who wanted advice on a domestic problem (which wasn't given, by the way). I mentioned to the supervisor that he was carrying out a good load of counseling during the day. His reply was to the effect that he didn't do counseling because this really wasn't part of his job. He did not regard the six individual problems he gave his time to as counseling. I would, however, for in each instance the foreman let the employee unburden himself by talking through his problem. In three of the cases, I received the impression that the employee *himself* worked out a solution to his problem as he talked and responded to the supervisor's questions. Since another interpreter might hesitate to call these informal instances counseling, let us describe a little more fully what goes on in the counseling situation, beginning our description with the use of professional counselors operating within a formal framework.

Nondirective Counseling. The formal counseling interview is, by its very structure, worker-oriented. The counseler listens, does not argue, records what he hears, and uses the information he gets to try to help dispel anxieties. He does not discipline the worker as the supervisor has to do at times. The counselor presents information to management which he believes is in the interest of the worker, not for use against the worker. Adherents of these formal programs have described them as "adjusting rather than paternalistic," "counselee-centered rather than authoritative," "clinical rather than disciplinary." The method is essentially the nondirective approach described by Rogers [53], where the subject himself does the most talking. Pauses of long duration sometimes occur, but the properly trained person will recognize these pauses to be good omens. Many times during these pauses the counselee is working out solutions to his problems. Often following long pauses the counselee says things which reveal that he is beginning to grope toward understanding.

In essence the nondirective approach in counseling is designed to provide opportunity for the counselee to work through his problems to his own satisfaction without being given advice or guidance. Here the counselor establishes rapport, listens, and talks very little himself. He reflects his acceptance of the client's feelings and attitudes and lets the counselee himself break up the silent intervals, lets him bring out his own problems. Some counselors find the nondirective approach difficult because it does not allow for advice, argument, lecture, or cross-examination. It does not allow the counselor to ride his position of prestige or to take responsibility for final action.

Nondirective counseling demands that the counselor be secure and well adjusted himself and that he be a good and interested listener who can use a language level appropriate to the occasion without losing the dignity of the counseling relationship. If the counselor can get the counselee to state his problem, to give its history, and to develop the problem—without having to ask leading questions—he has developed quite an art.

The counselor helps the counselee get insight into his problem by recognizing mixed emotions and by responding to how the man feels rather than to what he says. He gets the man to restate and discuss his problem without injecting his own personal opinion or experience. The counselor can usually feel that he has succeeded, whether or not a problem was finally solved, if the client feels some accomplishment upon coming out of the session.

Directive Counseling. There are times and places where directive counseling gets best results. Here the counselor takes an active part in bringing about an understanding or solution to a problem. He does not give the man the solution but directs him toward a solution. And it must be remembered that there are times when people need to be told what to do.

Certainly there is little opportunity for most industrial supervisors to get much formal training in counseling. What little they can get, formal or informal, should enable them to do a better job in dealing with their workers. Included somewhere in the training should be the recognition of one of the role conflicts of the supervisor: often his job requires him to function not only as a counselor but also as an evaluator and a disciplinarian, all within a brief span of time.

Mental Health. Meltzer [39], emphasizing the importance of mental health in industry as a continuing process, has described the importance of getting not only factual information about the worker but unstructured responses as well. Through projective interviewing—digging into memories, experiences, and personifications—much can be learned about the worker's attitudes and frustrations that induce problems for the supervisor as well as the worker's sources of pleasure and tension. From his studies Meltzer has concluded that the practice of making rounds, comparable to the rounds a doctor makes in the hospital, can tell us much about the realities of adjustment problems as revealed through daily episodes—problems involving such often overlooked reactions as that of a senior man who is refused a request for a change of shift.

What does the industrial way of life do to, and for, the men who man the machines? Kornhauser [28] concludes from his studies of factory workers in the automobile industry that mental health becomes poorer as we move from more skilled, responsible, varied types of work to jobs lower in these respects. This is not due in any large measure to differences in prejob background or personality of the men who enter and remain in the several types of work; it is more dependent on factors associated with the job. Why do we find poorer mental health in low-level occupations? The author indicates the factors involved are lower pay, economic insecurity, and disagreeable working conditions, on the one hand, and the more intangible influences of status, promotion opportunities, type of supervision, and work-group relations, on the other. The lack of personal control of job operations and the nonuse of abilities, with consequent feeling of futility, add to the picture. It is important to look at the entire pattern of work and life conditions of the people in these occupations, not at single variables.

Tensions of Workers and Supervisors. To fully understand the overall job of the supervisor, we must look at the tensions of his climate. He must live with the worries of the worker, frequently a person with a limited range of abilities, a man often on a highly repetitive, highly paced job, for whom job safety hazards sometimes create special adjustment problems. The production employee has little control over what he does or how he does it or when, and he turns to the foreman for help. Some help may come through job enlargement and job rotation, but basically what management can do for the worker is limited.

The supervisor has his tensions also, a fact sometimes overlooked by the subordinate. A large number of people create problems for the first-line foreman as a matter of routine—inspectors, dispatchers, engineers, stock-room clerks, cost-control analysts, labor relations people, and a host of others. The production-line foreman's job also involves many activities, ranging from "Throw it out" to "I'll see that you get it by noon." In one study of foremen on the assembly line in automobile factories it was found that the number of their activities ranged from 237 to 1,073 for an eight-hour day. The average number of activities was 583 per day, or *1 every forty-eight seconds*. And many of these activities involved decisions. Yes, the foreman has his tensions, also. He may even welcome that conference he has to attend. At least the committee meeting may give some variety to the tensions [61].

GROUP DECISION PROCEDURES

The development of human relations programs in industry has been approached from two directions. The impetus on improving the job satisfaction and morale of workers has come largely through attempts to improve first-line supervision by emphasizing the friendly personal touches. From the direction of the higher and intermediate levels of management has come an emphasis on the techniques of problem-solving conferences. Fortunately, the two approaches have a common base, since they deal with attempts to satisfy such psychological needs as status, recognition, and feelings of personal worth. Group decision procedures, which have been proved so successful at the higher participative-management levels, are being used more and more at the first-line supervisory levels in dealing with a wide range of problems, from the coffee break, desk arrangements, and vacation schedules in the office to overtime work, safety practices, and job modifications in the plant.

Problem-solving Conferences. Some of the very best work in the application of the principles of behavior to group decisions has been conducted by Maier [36]. He has found that group problem-solving conferences are useful in several ways: (1) developing awareness of basic problems, (2) getting different points of view on problems, (3) providing for permissive participation of the people involved in any given problem, and (4) developing approaches to solving problems.

It is important, of course, that any given supervisor work out techniques best suited to his personal mannerisms and the psychological climates in which he finds himself. Conducting an effective problem-solving conference is a skill that has to be learned through experience.

Maier has described four stages of effective group decision-making procedures:

1 *Studying the problem.* In this stage the leader checks his own responsibility to see if this is a problem he should deal with. He analyzes the situation to see if it is a problem to be brought before the group. It is important that the leader check his own attitude to see if he feels the group is capable of solving the problem, if he is willing to encourage the group to solve the problem. Following this comes a plan for presentation of the problem to the group, telling *why* there is a problem.

2 *Sharing the problem.* First comes a statement of the question, presented in positive terms, never in terms of objecting to something. It is presented to the group as "our" problem rather than "my" problem, in a way that will stimulate interest rather than give rise to defense reactions. Facts are presented in this stage.

3 *Discussion of the problem.* This is the stage that requires the leader's skill in human relations. Here he must establish an atmosphere of permissiveness, where everyone must feel free to talk without criticism. Here is where the supervisor pays as much attention to how people feel as to what they say. Every effort is made to get people to talk without putting anyone on the defensive. Even such behavior as eyebrow raising or a shrewd glance on the part of the leader of the session can destroy the atmosphere of permissiveness.

4 *Solving the problem.* Here the supervisor must recognize that group solutions come slowly because each person has to catch up with the other persons' thinking. He must get the feeling of group agreement on a solution without calling for a formal vote. Many solutions do not find everyone agreeing, and they should not be put on the spot by vote. An informal check or agreement can be obtained by such questions as: "We have had some good suggestions here. Do you feel they provide the answer to our problem?" Finally, it is important that each solution should specify some action. Discussion is often concerned with *what* should be done, but unless the *how* is included misunderstandings may occur.

Conference Leadership. Those who have used the group problem-solving procedures point out several do's and don't's that group leaders should follow. Let us list twenty merely to show how important it is to understand how people feel in conference situations and to get an appreciation of why resistance sometimes gets out of hand.

The supervisor who is leading a group-decision conference should:

1 Know the general types of things he intends to include in the discussion.

2 Have something prepared to start the meeting off.

3 Have brief warm-up sessions at the beginning.

4 Present the general problem area and let the participants express their ideas on the way they see the problems involved.

5 Expect some resistance at the beginning of any session.

6 Let the men get aggressions off their chests.

7 Recognize all suggestions, but influence *direction of thinking* by asking further questions.

8 Protect individuals from criticism by other group members by interpreting all remarks in a favorable light.

9 Recognize his own position and prestige and try never to be defensive.

10 Freely admit that he is wrong if he is.

11 Keep the discussion *problem-centered*.

12 Respect minority opinions.

13 Have a recorder keep a list of suggestions.

14 Keep the discussion going by asking such questions as "How do you see the problem?"

15 Not try to come to a solution too soon.

16 Not give personal suggestions as to a solution too soon.

17 Make his objective one of resolving differences.

18 Keep an optimistic attitude that the problem can eventually be solved.

19 Try to round out each meeting with the feeling that something has been accomplished.

20 *Listen*—let the others do most of the talking.

Example of Group Problem Solving. Aside from the more tightly structured group-decision conferences, participation in group problem solving can at times work well without the direct leadership of the supervisor. For purposes of illustration we shall describe a case taken from Maier's book, *Principles of Human Relations,* an excellent source of case studies [36]. The problem presented is a small one, but it shows that group decisions can be made applicable to small as well as to big problems.

This particular office problem involved a change of habits of the office worker. The office in question contained eighty girls divided into four groups, each with a supervisor. The superintendent, Mr. Barr, was in charge of the entire office. The work of the girls was such that it was necessary for some to leave their positions, whereas others were quite stationary and spent a good deal of their time in telephone contacts. However, in taking relief periods, in leaving or

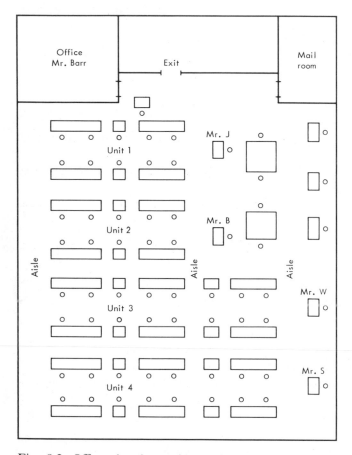

Fig. 8.2. Office plan for problem-solving case. The work positions of the girls, managers' desks, aisles, and exit are shown as related to the case described in the text. (From Maier, N. R. F. *Principles of human relations.* New York: Wiley, 1952.)

returning to the office, all the girls, on certain occasions, had to move through the office to get to the only corridor exit, as shown in the plan of the office in Figure 8.2.

The problem concerned the manner in which the girls moved through the office. Instead of using the outer and center aisles, they cut through various units, and this activity disturbed the work of girls who frequently had phone contacts. Furthermore, the girls went out in pairs or larger groups, and this too caused confusion.

In other offices the same problem had been handled in this way: the supervisors indicated that only aisles were to be used in going from one part of the room to another. Since the regulation had not been favorably received by the workers, violations became so general that management had no choice but to overlook the infraction.

Mr. Barr decided not to make an issue of the problem, but to try a more subtle approach. He noted that girls frequently deposited mail in the mailbox next to the door on their trips out of the office. He reasoned that if he placed the mailbox in the left front corner, it might draw the girls toward the outer aisles and reduce the amount of diagonal traffic through the middle of the room. However, all this planning was a failure. There were complaints about the unhandy position of the mailbox. With this personal experience and the failure to handle the problem in other offices as a background, Mr. Barr made no further attempts to correct the problem for a number of years.

Later, while participating in a human relations training course, Mr. Barr decided to try the democratic method of solving his old problem. He decided to turn the problem over to the girls themselves. They soon made a plan for the correction of the problem and put it into effect almost immediately. Since there was general acceptance of the plan, good morale, and a high degree of execution of the decision reached, the problem solving was considered a success.

Since the solution to the problem had been worked out so easily and continued to work, Mr. Barr was curious to see if the democratic technique should be given the credit. He decided to make a test.

He decided arbitrarily to change the glass in the door at the front of the room from opaque to transparent glass. The change was made on Saturday. The next Monday he watched for reactions. They soon came. By noon he had three complaints.

On the basis of the complaints Mr. Barr put the problem to the group. He pointed out that he had replaced the glass without realizing that it made a difference. He was willing to make changes but wondered what it was that bothered them. The criticism given was unclear until one girl mentioned glare. All the girls now mentioned this. He asked the group to help him find the best way to correct the matter. It was soon agreed that a shade be put on the window. The shade was purchased and installed. Since then no one has taken the pains or the interest to see that the shade is drawn!

Maier reports that two years later the traffic-problem solution was still holding up well and that practically no violations had occurred, despite the fact that several new girls had been hired during this period and management people had given them no instructions. Some way or other the new girls learned. The new manner of leaving the office had apparently become part of the culture of this office.

PROBLEM SOLVING IN HUMAN RELATIONS

The old adage that the best way to handle a problem is to prevent it has merit in supervision. We, of course, cannot prevent many problems from coming up, but we can often lessen them in degree and in frequency of occurrence. This can be accomplished by more self-understanding, by understanding why other people react to us as they do, and by familiarity with and skill at human problem solving.

Let us assume that we are aware of the *understandings* of human behavior. How can we handle the human relations problem when it does come up? There is nothing new or unique about the outline below on problem solving. It phrases questions to "you" as a matter of convenience. An examination of this outline offers one systematic method of working out solutions in human relations problems and often in personal problems as well:

I. *Defining the problem*
   A. First indication that problem exists
      1. What is bothering you?
      2. Is it a real problem?
      3. Is it a problem of your concern?
   OBJECTIVE: To recognize a problem
   B. Selecting the problem
      1. Does the problem need to be solved?
      2. Is the problem made of a number of problems?
      3. Is the problem within your capacity and knowledge?
   OBJECTIVE: To differentiate main problem from subproblems
   C. Stating the problem
      1. Can you write the problem out clearly and accurately?
   OBJECTIVE: To state the problem
   D. Setting up tentative solutions
      1. What ways can be thought of by which the problem can be solved?
      2. Why did you include these tentative solutions?
      3. What outcomes might be anticipated?
   OBJECTIVE: To see several ways of solving problem with possible consequences of each
II. *Working on the problem*
   A. Recalling what you know
      1. What do you already know that is vital to the problem?
   OBJECTIVE: To see what is at hand in the way of information

    B. Getting more information
        1. What additional information is needed?
        2. Where do you get it?
        3. How can you get it?
    OBJECTIVE: To get all the facts
    C. Organizing the information
        1. In what kind of order could you write down the information?
        2. Is any of the information irrelevant?
    OBJECTIVE: To have only pertinent information for use
    D. Interpreting the information
        1. How does the information relate to principles that may be involved?
        2. Does an examination of the information lead to other problems?
        3. If so, what problem should be solved first?
    OBJECTIVE: To see relationships
III. *Coming to a conclusion*
    A. Stating possible conclusions
        1. What are the possible conclusions?
        2. How do these conclusions stack up with your tentative solutions in I, *D*?
    OBJECTIVE: To clarify the alternatives
    B. Determining the best conclusions
        1. What conclusions can you eliminate?
        2. What conclusions do you want to draw?
        3. What conclusions seem most logical?
        4. What conclusions can you draw?
        5. What do you think will happen if you put the first-choice conclusion into effect?
    OBJECTIVE: To draw a logical and reasonable conclusion
IV. *Carrying out the conclusion*
    A. Doing something about the conclusion
        1. What *action,* if any, does the conclusion call for?
        2. If action is indicated, how and when can it be put into effect?
        3. If no action is indicated, what then?
    OBJECTIVE: To act on the conclusion
V. *Learning from above activity*
    A. Reviewing your behavior
        1. Did the problem solving work?
        2. If "yes," what do you think made it work?
        3. If "no," what made it not work?
        4. What would you do or not do the next time you have a problem similar to this one?
    OBJECTIVE: To learn from experience

The effectiveness of the supervisor in his many and varied roles comes down in the final analysis to how well he can solve problems. The person who has a good perception of the problem to be solved, who has an adequate command of the facts and observations that pertain to it, who understands why there is a problem, and who can come up with possibilities of solutions freely and criticize them rigorously is in a favorable position to do effective problem solving. One favorable aspect of problem solving in the area of human relations is that in most instances the supervisor has a ready check on whether or not his solution has been a good one. Feedback to the supervisor of his mistakes is not long in coming—from the individual worker, from the group, from the union organization, or from higher management.

SUGGESTIONS FOR SELECTIVE READING

Argyris, C. *Integrating the individual and the organization.* New York: Wiley, 1964. A "mix-model" conception of a social organization.

Bradford, L. P., et al. (Eds.) *T-group theory and laboratory method.* New York: Wiley, 1964. For general information about sensitivity training.

Corsini, R. J. *Roleplaying in business and industry.* New York: Free Press, 1961. A manual for training in human relations.

Davis, K. *Human relations at work.* (2d ed.) New York: McGraw-Hill, 1962. Extension of the type of material in this chapter.

Davis, K., & Scott, W. G. (Eds.) *Readings in human relations.* New York: McGraw-Hill, 1959. A balance of readings in the general area of human relations.

Fleishman, E. A. (Ed.) *Studies in personnel and industrial psychology.* Homewood, Ill.: Dorsey, 1961. Section V of these readings is on leadership and supervision.

Gardner, B. B., & Moore, D. G. *Human relations in industry.* (4th ed.) Homewood, Ill.: Irwin, 1964. An old stand-by for practical suggestions.

Hersey, R. *Better foremanship.* Philadelphia: Chilton, 1955. An old stand-by giving practical answers.

Homans, G. C. *Social behavior: Its elementary forms.* New York: Harcourt, Brace & World, 1961. On productivity and motivation; by one of the original Hawthorne studies investigators.

Hugh-Jones, E. M. *Human relations and modern management.* Amsterdam: North Holland Publishing Company, 1958. For an intercultural comparison on supervision.

Industrial Relations News. The dollars and sense of human relations in industry. New York: *Industrial Relations News,* 1960. A business guide to human relations.

Kay, B. R., & Palmer, S. *The challenge of supervision.* New York: McGraw-Hill, 1961. A readable book on human relations skills in supervision.

Maier, N. R. F. *Principles of human relations.* New York: Wiley, 1952. An old stand-by on techniques and case materials.

Maier, N. R. F. *Problem-solving discussions and conferences.* New York: McGraw-Hill, 1963. For leadership methods and skills in conferences.

Miles, M. *Learning to work in groups.* New York: Teachers College Publication, 1959. Indirectly related to some of the problems of industry, directly to others on how to work with groups.

Moser, L. E., & Moser, Ruth S. *Counseling and guidance: An exploration.* Englewood Cliffs, N.J.: Prentice-Hall, 1963. Only indirectly related to industry.

Pfiffner, J. M., & Fels, M. *The supervision of personnel: human relations in the management of men.* Englewood Cliffs, N.J.: Prentice-Hall, 1964. Emphasizes the developmental approach rather than the traditional view of the supervisor as administrator.

9

Executive Leadership and Development

Thomas L. Hilton

Who is an executive? Defining the term is a difficult problem, as anyone will recognize who has ever tried to write a formal description for the job. One operational definition is that of the employee who identified executives as "the ones who are allowed to use the private company parking lot." Although this may provide an indication of a man's status in the organization, it is hardly a workable description of the executive's job. Some people view this leadership personality by saying, "He is the executive type; doesn't like to work." We will look at what some people think executives do and then present evidence that indicates what they actually do.

FUNCTIONS OF EXECUTIVES

There are those who picture the executive as a person who sits at a great walnut desk surrounded by telephones, masterminding the fate of his company and its employees. This mythical executive spends his day making split-second decisions and issuing directives, like a master puppeteer who decides what each act shall be and who shall do the performing.

Then there is the conception of the executive, a little more realistic, as the master expediter who is always on the go, never in his office. He has few, if any, scheduled routine responsibilities. If he were suddenly to leave for a six-month tour of Europe, his absence would scarcely be noticed, save by those members of the organization who were perceptive enough to observe that things were not running quite so smoothly as usual and that morale was suffering a little. In general, we might say that in the absence of this executive, communication would be more difficult, objectives not quite so clearly defined. In other words, the primary function of this second mythical person is to maintain a favorable environment for effective work by other people in the organization. This role requires that the executive be an expert in the motivation of human behavior to an almost impossible degree.

The Empirical View. The empirical version of the executive is quite different from those descriptions above. One group of psychologists [59] found through extensive interviews that executives spend their time on the following kinds of activities:

1 Inspection of the organization
2 Investigation and research
3 Planning
4 Preparation of procedures and methods
5 Coordination
6 Evaluation
7 Interpretation of plans and procedures
8 Supervision of technical operations
9 Personnel activities
10 Public relations
11 Professional consultation
12 Negotiations
13 Scheduling, routing, and dispatching
14 Technical and professional operations

These activities are somewhat like those found in organizational descriptions of executive functions, more realistic and less romantic than many popular views.

The origin of the written descriptions of executive functions stated in organization charters and manuals has been lost in antiquity. Many no doubt resulted from the laws, the military practices, the social customs, and even the tribal ways of early history. They have been modified and augmented over the years as the exigencies and opportunities of the changing industrial scene have demanded it. When a sales manager, for example, fails to function effectively within the company, his successor is likely to find a revised specification of his duties, responsibilities, and authority. But this does not mean that we can regard the accumulation of these operational procedures as the best guide for the executive.

Dimensions of Executive Functions. In a similar but more elaborate study Hemphill asked ninety-three business executives to describe their position in terms of 575 items of a questionnaire [30]. The executives indicated the extent to which activities such as "Adjust work schedules to meet emergencies" were a part of their position. An analysis of their responses revealed ten separate factors underlying their responses:

1 *Providing staff service in nonoperational areas.* (Some services falling in this category were gathering information, selecting employees, and briefing supervisors.) The six executives who measured highest on this dimension held the following positions: corporation secretary, engineer of outside plant, assistant treasurer, assistant general purchasing agent, director of personnel services, and supervisor of division of employment.

2 *Supervision of work.* (Includes planning, organizing, and controlling the work of others.) The positions measuring high on this dimension tended to be at the middle-management level or below. Supervision of work did not appear to be characteristic of the highest management positions.

3 *Business control, including cost reduction, preparation of budgets, determination of goals, and enforcement of regulations.* High on this dimension were budget administrators, plant managers, and general sales managers.

4 *Technical concern with products and markets.* Positions high on this dimension tended to be concerned with high-level selling or research engineering.

5 *Concern with human, community, and social affairs, including company good will, promotions, and selection of managers.* High-level sales positions were most frequently found on this dimension.

6 *Long-range planning.* Executives who measured high on this dimension tended not to get involved in the routines or details of day-to-day operations.

7 *Exercise of broad power and authority.* The positions which measured high on this dimension tended to be in upper-management categories such as division management and general sales management.

8 *Concern with company reputation.* Two broad areas of concern were included in this factor—product quality and public relations. The executives best described by this dimension were those who had general responsibility for the company's products or services.

9 *Concern with personal status.* Executives with high scores on this dimension were those who indicated that activities such as gaining the respect of very important persons and refraining from activities which might imply sympathy with unions were important to their position. They tended to be less concerned with maintaining the general reputation of their companies, very likely because their duties seldom brought them into contact with the public, judging from the titles of their positions.

10 *Preservation of company assets.* Executives holding positions high on this dimension were concerned about capital expenditures and large operating expenses and taxes, and they tended not to be involved with activities such as industrial relations or technical operations.

Obviously some positions will have attributes not included in these dimensions, and also the characteristics of a particular executive position will change from time to time.

Hemphill also observed that executives in different companies and at different management levels tended to describe their positions in highly similar ways but that positions in different functional areas tended to be somewhat less similar.

There remain two other conceptions of the executive—the conception which is prescribed by company charters and the conception resulting from theoretical analyses of the position. The first ordinarily consists of a description of responsibilities and duties. These are stated in much the same way as they are stated in the constitution or manuals of nonbusiness organizations like the parent-teacher association and student extracurricular activities. In addition, within every company there are unwritten expectations about the functions the executives should fulfill. These are transmitted to new executives verbally or by the process of imitation, senior executives serving as models for the younger or newer executives. With the high mobility of the contemporary executive there is now probably less tendency for companies to rely on informal, unwritten communication of executive duties and responsibilities.

Theoretical Versions. Written statements of executive-job descriptions and questionnaire results are necessary and helpful to officers, but it is equally clear that they are not necessarily valid prescriptions of efficient executive behavior. We cannot be sure that rules which have resulted from the needs which organizations have experienced in the past are applicable to twentieth-century organizations. A science of administrative behavior is required, one which will provide a framework of propositions by means of which we can test the validity of different conceptions of the role of the executive. Whether it is good to have a given executive spend 15 per cent of his time engaged in public relations activity can only be ascertained by considering the totality of functions which the executive should perform in the organizations. For some executives, in some situations, a 15 per cent bracket of time devoted to public relations may be highly effective, but for another executive, another company, or even another time, it may be a gross misapplication of effort. Important advances in a science of administration have been made, but we are still far from the goal of a science which enables us to answer many practical questions.

One writer on scientific management [5] defines an organization as "a system of consciously coordinated personal activities or forces of two or more persons." This definition brings out three vital elements of an organization—willingness to serve, common purpose, and communication. According to this theoretical conception, the executive must work to secure the willing performance of essential services from individuals and to define the purposes, objectives, and ends of the organization. Furthermore, it becomes the job of executives to develop and maintain the system of communication by selecting men carefully and offering them incentives to do the job. In other words, executives must provide techniques of control permitting effectiveness in promoting, demoting, and dismissing men, and they must understand the importance of the informal organizations within a company in which the essential property is compatibility of personnel.

These are functions of the executive organization, not the functions of any one man. In effect, it is the entire executive organization "that formulates, redefines, breaks into details, and decides on the innumerable simultaneous and progressive actions" of the company.

The Standards of Successful Leadership. Having pictured the difficulty of describing the functions of an executive, let us now raise some other provoking questions. Can successful leadership be attributed to a man? To the situation? To a combination of the two? What kind of man is successful as a leader? Are leaders born? Can leaders be developed?

What evidence do we have that may help us answer these questions?

The success of an executive can only be evaluated *in terms of some criterion*. It is in the light of the functions an executive is called upon to perform that we examine industrial leadership. As we have seen, only a beginning has been made in conceptualizing executive functions; only now are researchers beginning to assemble data with which organizational propositions can be tested.

THE CRITERIA OF SUCCESS

Since we cannot unequivocally specify the proper functions of an executive and, in addition, would be hard put to obtain valid measures of the extent to which any one executive fulfills these functions, we make some inferences. One line of reasoning runs like this: (1) By objective standards organization X is highly successful. (2) Mr. Y is the executive of organization X. (3) Therefore, Mr. Y is a good executive. For example, let organization X be the production department of a paper mill. Mr. Y is the department head. It is observed that the net manufacturing cost per ton of paper produced in Mr. Y's department is less than that produced in any paper-production department known. On these grounds, it is concluded that Mr. Y is a good executive.

Some Faulty Reasoning. In the foregoing example both the logic of the deduction and the validity of the premises are faulty. The argument implies that organizational success results only from executive functions and that Mr. Y is the sole source of executive functions: obviously, we cannot accept these statements as logically valid.

Furthermore, net manufacturing cost per unit is not necessarily an adequate measure of the success of the manufacturing organization. We would want to be sure, for one thing, that the cost included all depletion of resources, including human resources, particularly the resources of the executive himself. In other words, low costs may have been achieved by making such demands on the personnel and rewarding them so little—monetarily and otherwise—that in the next time period, productivity will ebb markedly. Or the executive in question may have achieved a high level of performance at the cost of his own physical and psychic well-being.

The Problem of Delayed Effects. Again, we would want to ask whether organizational success results only from executive functions. In a broad way it does. For example, it can be argued that if production is costly because of defective raw materials or incompetent employees or obsolete facilities, then the executive has failed in so far as it is a responsibility of the executive to obtain these resources. But it is clear that the matter may well be beyond the control of any one executive. In the paper industry, for instance, a year of low rainfall can lower water levels to the point that cheap power is no longer available. Surely an executive cannot be held responsible for the external environment (rainfall, for instance) except in those cases where he can be expected to anticipate changes or to take steps ensuring his organization against unpredictable external factors.

In the long run, a chief executive probably can be held responsible for provision of adequate resources. But what is the length of this time period? This question introduces one of the most perplexing problems encountered in human performance evaluations, the problem of delayed effects.

Salary as a Criterion. Some other indirect measures of executive success are even less defensible. The salary received by an executive frequently has been used as a measure of his effectiveness. This measure can be regarded as a combination of several variables: (1) the worth of the executive as perceived by his superiors, (2) the supply of and demand for similar executive performance within the industry, (3) the ability of the organization to provide incentives, (4) the policy of the organization in regard to executive compensation, and (5) the value the executive places on nonmonetary rewards.

Who knows by what criteria an executive's superiors evaluate his worth? And even if we assume that the superiors do validly appraise his effectiveness, we also have to assume that the other factors mentioned do not influence the executive's salary. As a matter of policy in most organizations, length of service or age is an important determinant of salary. Consequently, in studies of effectiveness which use salary as a criterion, a minimum requirement is that some control or adjustment for age or length of service be made.

Studies of executive success usually employ *ratings* of the executive as criteria. The rating is done by the executive's superiors, by his associates, by subordinates, or by noncompany observers. The ratings vary from global judgments of overall effectiveness to mere checking of whether the executive performs certain actions or not. The global judgments obviously are subject to the dangers already mentioned. At their best, they represent a valid appraisal of the extent to which the executive fulfills the rater's conception of what a good executive is, and thereby they usually tell us more about the rater's conception than about the executive himself. At their worst, they provide an unreliable indication of whether the rater wishes to present the executive in a favorable or unfavorable light for one or another irrelevant reason—personal friendship, animosity, hero worship, paternalism, sycophancy, to name a few.

Clinical Evidences. In spite of our problems with the criteria of successful executive leadership, there have been some studies of the correlates of success. These provide us with some appealing hypotheses in regard to the attributes of successful executives.

In a clinical study of 100 business executives extensive personal data were obtained. Analysis of the data attempted to identify a personality pattern which was common to all the successful executives. These were the executives who had a history of continuous promotion, who were regarded by their superiors as still promotable, and who were at the time in positions of major responsibility and were earning salaries within the upper ranges of the then current business salaries. Executive effectiveness was defined, therefore, primarily in terms of the perceptions and preconceptions of the executives' superiors [32].

The attributes of the successful executives were perceived to be the following:

1 High drive and achievement desire.

2 Strong mobility drives, a need to advance and to accumulate "the rewards of increased accomplishment."

3 A perception of superiors as "controlling but helpful," not as "prohibiting and destructive."

4 High "ability to organize unstructured situations and to see the implications of their organizations." Their time orientation is to the future.

5 Decisiveness—the "ability to come to a decision among several alternative courses of action." It is proposed that the loss of this trait is "one of the most disastrous for the executive; his superiors become apprehensive about him."

6 Strong self-structure. They are able to resist pressure from other people and have high faith in themselves.

7 Active, aggressive striving. The aggression is not necessarily overt, nor is the constant activity physical, for they are mentally active as well.

8 Apprehension and fear of failing.

9 A strong reality orientation. "They are directly interested in the practical, the immediate, and the direct." If sense of reality is too strong, the executive may be handicapped.

10 Identification with superiors and detachment from subordinates. But the successful executive may be sympathetic with many subordinates.

11 Emotional independence from parents but no resentment toward them.

12 Loyalty to overall goals of the company rather than complete concentration on the self.

The author concludes that the successful executive "represents a crystallization of many of the attitudes and values generally accepted by middle-class American society." But, he points out, "he pays for his virtues in uncertainty and fear."

Cultural Patterns and Managerial Talent. Before World War II industrial psychology was largely concerned with the men and women who labor in the factory or keep the books in the office. Since the war there has been a surge of interest in the study of the men who manage, and as a corollary researchers have begun the important task of studying managerial cultural patterns. Haire et al. [28], in an elaborate study of the motivation, goals, and attitudes of over three thousand managers from fourteen countries, found that manager's attitudes toward management in different countries followed a pattern more closely associated with cultural variation than with degree of industrialization, which has frequently been thought of as a determinant of attitudes. For example, managers from Spain and Italy tended to agree more in attitudes toward management, despite their dissimilarity in degree of industrialization, than did managers from Italy and Denmark, where degrees of industrialization are more similar. The goals of Japanese and Norwegian managers are not precisely the same, nor are those of Indian and Italian managers. Nevertheless, these studies found a high degree of unanimity among managers in all countries and at all levels of management. More than anything else managers want the opportunity to use their talents to the utmost in their work, to act independently, to realize themselves as individuals. Self-realization and autonomy universally are more important to managers than prestige, social satisfaction, and even security.

Many studies have pointed to intelligence as a characteristic of successful managers. Harrell [29] found, for example, that the average intelligence-test scores of those who hold positions in the upper and middle levels of management is very high, reported to exceed the scores of about 96 per cent of the population. Ghiselli [23] also found the executive's average score to fall at the 96th percentile. But within this group a critical intellectual level is reached where the careers of those earning the very highest scores were not as successful as the careers of those who earned somewhat lower scores. Individuals who fall among the top 2 or 3 per cent of the population in intelligence are somewhat less likely to be successful managers than those immediately below them. It is possible that those individuals at the very extreme high levels of capacity to deal with abstract ideas and concepts do not find in managerial activities the intellectual challenge they need. They may even see too many alternatives in decision making to come to practical conclusions in time to meet problems. Concludes Ghiselli about managerial talent:

> The talented manager is one who is well endowed intellectually, gifted with the capacity to direct the efforts of others, self-stimulated to action, confident in his activities, and striving for a position where he can most fully utilize them —this picture of managerial talent very likely does not well describe the scientist, the physician, nor the politician.

The above studies found also that at the upper two levels of management there is a positive relationship between initiative and job performance. The greater the individual's capacity for initiative, the more likely he is to be judged as being a good manager. On the other hand, at the lower levels of management and with line jobs there is less relation. While initiative may be rewarded at the higher levels of management, at the lower levels it may even be punished.

Executives versus Supervisors. In another study fifty executives were compared with fifty lower-level supervisors of the same age and occupational history. The authors concluded:

> The executive considers mobility to upper levels essential for success, since his need for esteem and feelings of personal accomplishment can be satisfied *only* by securing a high position. The supervisor, on the other hand, has a much lower level of aspiration and less mobility drive and considers success achieved when he has attained personal and family security, respect, and happiness [52].

Although we are far from being able to spell out with any high degree of confidence the attributes of a successful executive, additional insights can be gained from the studies of leadership in general, by piecing together the accumulated wisdom of those who have worked closely with executives, and from executives themselves. Let us continue by taking a look not only at the individual as a leader but also at the environment which helps make leadership possible.

INDIVIDUAL LEADERSHIP AND THE ENVIRONMENT

Interest in studying the behavior of people in groups began prior to World War II and gained momentum during the war as problems of leadership and communication became vitally important. The researches inspired by Lewin brought new emphasis to an old problem—essentially the point of view that the behavior of a person at any given moment is a function of his individual characteristics and his psychological environment [42, 43].

Individual Differences. The individual characteristics which Lewin had in mind were not traits in the sense of observable uniformities in the overt behavior of individuals, but rather the momentary state of the needs of the person. He argued that the fact that the observable behavior of two people is similar is by no means proof that their individual characteristics are the same. Two people behaving aggressively may be doing so for entirely different reasons. One may have a pressing acquired need to do harm to the lives of other people, and the situation which we observe is perceived by this person as an opportunity to satisfy his aggressive need. The people or objects against which he aggresses are means to an end in the same way that food is a means to a hungry man.

The strongest momentary need of the second person may be a need for autonomy, a need to be left alone. He acts aggressively toward the people in the given situation because he sees them as insurmountable barriers to his achieving his independence. He may be mild-mannered and kind in other situations; here his frustration manifests itself in belligerent acts against the agents of his frustration. Note that the physical environment of the two men is identical but each perceives it quite differently.

Leadership Stereotypes. American efforts to predict human behavior have been dominated by an emphasis on traits and abilities, something of a carry-over from the beginning days of industrial psychology. For instance, several efforts to predict leadership skill have focused on the physical trait of height. To this day there is a popular stereotype of the leader as a tall man. For example, a recent construction job in downtown Pittsburgh was observed to have three different observation windows cut in the tall wooden guard wall along the sidewalk. The lowest window was labeled "Junior Superintendent," a higher window "Assistant Superintendent," and the highest window "General Superintendent."

The evidence for this stereotype is contradictory. Although some studies have found height to be correlated with leadership, other studies have produced negative results. These findings are not surprising. For some groups in certain environments with certain tasks, tall men are perceived by the group as more able to serve its goals; for other groups in different situations they are not. The crucial determinant of successful leadership is not the trait make-up of the leader, but the needs of the members of the group and the nature of the situation in which the potential leader and his potential followers find themselves.

Situations and Leadership. In the furnace room of a steel foundry, a burly, aggressive, outspoken foreman may provide highly successful leadership, but his traits are not likely to further the cooperative goals of, say, a group of physicians. After an extensive survey of personal factors associated with leadership, one investigator has come to this conclusion: "Leadership is a relation that exists between persons in a social situation, and . . . persons who are leaders in one situation may not necessarily be leaders in other situations." [63]

Despite the convincing theory and evidence in support of a situational theory of leadership, many investigations have proved that certain personality variables do differentiate between leaders and nonleaders. Intelligence, for instance, is almost always found to be higher among leaders than among nonleaders. Likewise, such traits as self-confidence, sociability, will (initiative, persistence, ambition), and dominance are generally found to be significantly different.

Do these findings of the researchers who have studied personality variables serve to refute the situational theory of leadership? In one sense they do, for the personality variables mentioned seem to be common to many leaders. On the other hand, it can be argued that there are problems which are common to all situations and that these common problems uniformly require the same characteristics of leadership for their solution. For instance, all group activity has a purpose. This is true by definition; a collection of individuals without a common purpose is just that—a collection of individuals, not a group. It seems likely that the group will appoint or otherwise accept a leader who is superior in those activities, including intellectual activity, which are required for the fulfillment of its purpose.

Social Interaction. A leader ordinarily must have some social interaction with the group or at least some social proximity to it. The more sociable a man is relative to the sociability of the other members of the group, the more likely he is to become the leader. Similar arguments can be proposed for the other personality variables. It is conceivable, however, that exceptions to the usual situations will be found. For instance, it is not overly difficult to imagine a group and a situation in which successful leadership will require a low level of intelligence on the part of the leader. Nevertheless, for practical purposes, we can accept the personality variables mentioned as likely to be found in leaders, provided we are always mindful that group needs and the nature of the situation are the primary variables.

Some Generalizations on Leadership. Psychologists interested in industrial leadership problems have drawn several useful conclusions for industrial consumption:

1 The major problem of leadership is not one of providing inspiration and achieving obedience, but one of creating a situation in which the followers willingly accept the leader as their agent in cooperative endeavor.

2 The major determinant of behavior is how a person perceives the need-fulfilling possibilities of the immediate situation. Achieving changes in the behavior of employees, for instance, is primarily a matter of achieving a change in their perception of the immediate situation.

3 Authority which is maintained by threats of punishment is clearly undesirable; it achieves only acquiescence, not voluntary acceptance.

4 Employees are more likely to accept group or organizational goals as their own when they have personally participated in setting up these goals.

5 The security, support, and, sometimes, anonymity which participating in a group provides, as well as the pressure which group members exert on each other, make groups unusually effective instruments for achieving change.

6 Communication among a number of people is greatest when they face each other as members of one group, provided that the group leader permits free interaction; groups themselves, then, provide the best way to disseminate information, opinion, and ideas.

It is important to recognize that typically the industrial executive is not in the same position as the leader of a small group. A basic distinction which must be considered is the difference between leadership and headship. The executive in the business organization receives his authority from the organization itself. He is appointed from above. By his control of sanctions and incentives he has the power to achieve obedience. In addition, his goals as a leader are not necessarily compatible with the goals of his employees. The group leader, on the other hand, maintains his leadership by virtue of the "spontaneous recognition" of fellow group members when he contributes to group goals. Here the goals are chosen by the group itself.

Fiedler [18], after an eleven-year study of leadership, concludes that *time* is an important dimension in the effectiveness of different leadership methods. When the organization is running well, authoritarian leadership may be quite effective. In essence, there are virtually no problems, and people may be willing to have little to say. Likewise, in times of crisis decisions must be forthcoming, and people expect autocratic decisions. However, in times of change which emerges gradually from growth, people want to be involved. Here permissive leadership proves more effective.

Leadership Methods. The behavior which a leader evokes depends somewhat on his leadership methods. Knickerbocker [40] has proposed that there are four methods a leader may use for directing the activities of people:

1 *Force.* The leader uses his control of means to force the choice of certain activities which he desires as means. The alternative to following him is reduction of need satisfaction.

2 *Paternalism.* The leader provides means and hopes for acceptance of his leadership out of loyalty and gratitude.

3 *Bargain.* The leader may arrive at a bargain, a more or less voluntary choice made by each party to furnish certain means in return for certain means.

4 *Mutual means.* The leader creates the situation in which certain activities of his and of the group, if performed together, will serve as mutual means, means for all to satisfy their own (perhaps different) needs.

Knickerbocker says that the present-day leader is in a dilemma, since "he must succeed as a leader despite the fact that he cannot control the conditions in terms of which he leads." But he believes that "when management successfully creates the necessary conditions, the organization and its objective become a means not only to management but also to labor." In other words, here is expressed the belief that the industrial leader can become the kind of leader that theory and research in group psychology suggest would be highly effective. Our conclusion can only be that this remains to be seen; at present the industrial leader typically is in quite a different position from the small-group leader, and great caution must be exercised in applying the principles of small-group leadership to industrial leadership.

Some of the fads, such as brainstorming, which have come into widespread use in dealing with the dilemmas of leadership have been found wanting. Studies show that brainstorming does not constitute an efficient way of capitalizing on the intellectual resources of different individuals. Once the exact nature of the problem has been defined, possibly in a brief meeting, individual problem solving is better. Dunnette et al. [16] found, for example, that the mean number of ideas produced by advertising personnel groups of four people thinking as individuals was 141; the corresponding mean number of ideas produced by the groups brainstorming as groups was only 97. Holding a brief conference for the purpose of summarizing the results of the problem-solving efforts and communicating the final decision may be far more valuable than brainstorming without structure. One may wonder how often a quickie "think" conference is called just because the boss is lonesome.

A COMPOSITE PICTURE

We have seen that the functioning executive is a complex person in a complex situation. To date there exists no means by which his behavior can be accurately predicted or his effectiveness evaluated. The integration of the myriad of personality, situational, organizational, social, and economic variables still is best performed by the experienced human observer. Melvin Anshen [2], long experienced in the study of executive behavior, has this to say:

Even in a world of incomplete knowledge, we can develop reasonable projections of characteristics which will be useful to strengthen in the next management generation. The following list is offered simply as one man's suggestions, subject to any amendments each one of you may care to add.

1 Knowledge of the technical aspects of the business—as a basis for understanding their meaning in relation to the making and executing of policy.

2 Understanding of the relationships among the functional parts of the business—as a basis for thinking beyond departmental limits.

3 Understanding of the environment in which the business is carried on: economic, social, and political; special emphasis attaches to a grasp of the causes and significance of change.

4 An imaginative approach to management problems, particularly with respect to the ability to think beyond the routines of normal operation both in defining problems and in exploring alternative lines of solution.

5 Courage in making decisions—and equal courage in refusing to make decisions when the time is not ripe, or when decisions should be made by others as part of their own exercise of delegated responsibility.

6 Understanding of the tools of administration and control, and skill in using them to get results.

7 Ability to work with and through other people, individually and in groups: to stimulate their best efforts and to win and hold their confidence and loyalty.

8 Ability to encourage the development of subordinates: to delegate responsibility, to coach effectively, and to provide challenge for growing ability.

9 Power for continuing personal growth in performance and capacity.

Self-evaluation and Leadership. In the book *Executive Ability: Its Discovery and Development,* Cleeton and Mason [11] point out the importance of self-evaluation of one's behavior as he exercises responsibility for the efforts of others, makes decisions on questions of policy and practice, and sees that the decisions are carried out. Executive ability is not an all-or-none quality. It is important to recognize that varying degrees of executive ability are required in the large variety of positions involving administrative and supervisory responsibility.

An unusual kind of evaluative summary of the responsibilities of the leader was given by an industrial psychologist in his farewell presidential message to the faculty, alumni, and friends of Antioch College:

It will require time to think back over the many events that have been crowded into these few years and to draw a proper meaning from them. However, two related convictions have developed slowly but steadily out of this experience.

The first is a conviction which has been derived from my personal struggle with the role of college president. Before coming to Antioch I had observed and worked with top executives as an advisor in a number of organizations. I thought I knew how they felt about their responsibilities and what led them to behave as they did. I even thought that I could create a role for myself which would enable me to avoid some of the difficulties they encountered.

I was wrong! It took the direct experience of becoming a line executive and meeting personally the problems involved to teach me what no amount of observation of other people could have taught.

I believed, for example, that a leader could operate successfully as a kind of advisor to his organization. I thought I could avoid being a "boss." Unconsciously, I suspect, I hoped to duck the unpleasant necessity of making difficult decisions, of taking the responsibility for one course of action among many uncertain alternatives, of making mistakes and taking the consequences. I thought that maybe I could operate so that everyone would like me—that "good human relations" would eliminate all discord and disagreement.

I couldn't have been more wrong. It took a couple of years, but I finally began to realize that a leader cannot avoid the exercise of authority any more than he can avoid responsibility for what happens to his organization. In fact, it is a major function of the top executive to take on his own shoulders the responsibility for resolving the uncertainties that are always involved in important decisions. Moreover, since no important decision ever pleases everyone in the organization, he must also absorb the displeasure, and sometimes severe hostility, of those who would have taken a different course.

A colleague recently summed up what my experience has taught me in these words: "A good leader must be tough enough to win a fight, but not tough enough to kick a man when he is down." This notion is not in the least inconsistent with humane, democratic leadership. Good human relations develop out of strength, not of weakness.

I'm still trying to understand and practice what is implied in my colleague's statement.*

THE SELECTION OF POTENTIAL EXECUTIVES

In view of our paucity of knowledge in regard to the functions and attributes of executives, there appears to be little that can be said with certainty as to which men should be selected as executives. At best, executive selection is, at present, educated guesswork. The research that has been conducted on executive selection suggests some possible profitable

* Reproduced with the permission of the late Dr. Douglas McGregor, formerly president of Antioch College.

variables for which to look. The leadership research likewise provides some hints in regard to the personal attributes which may contribute to successful executive performance. Recent reviews on administrative judgment, research needs in executive selection, and the criteria of executive success indicate there is now a widespread interest in the problem. Observations from experienced observers offer additional cues [31, 35, 60, 69].

Some Major Assumptions. However we slice our problem, selection is still guesswork when the problem is one of selecting young men who are likely to develop into executives ten or more years from now. Knowing the attributes of today's successful executives is of particularly questionable value, since it involves at least the assumption that today's executives have been properly selected, i.e., that today's executives are performing more effectively than other men who might have been selected for their positions. It is conceivable that our present beliefs and stereotypes are resulting in the wrong men being appointed to executive positions, particularly since, as described earlier, we do not fully understand executive functions. Contemporary successful executives may not be as successful as others who might have been selected. Two writers [41] have predicted that by 1980 the requirements of the executive may be radically different from the requirements of today. Computers may well take over some decision-making functions of the executive; they may even reduce the status of the man in middle management to that of a clerk.

Situational Testing. Aside from, or in addition to, the conventional procedures of personnel selection described in Chapter 6, one method of selecting potential executives is situational testing, first used extensively by the Office of Strategic Services during World War II. The first objective of this technique is to envision the kind of problem situations which the executives of the future will be likely to encounter in fulfilling executive functions, e.g., marketing, planning, labor, public relations problems. Next, replicas of these problem situations are devised in the testing center. A large staff, which may even include professional actors, a communications system, and any other equipment needed to simulate operating conditions are required.

The candidates are given "real" problems, which often involve a task to be accomplished with only limited resources. For instance, they are sometimes given a group of "workers" to assist them, but the workers are instructed to obstruct progress as much as possible. The reactions of the candidate—how he handles the "incompetent" workers, how he reacts to frustration, and whether he is able to get the job done—are meticulously observed and recorded [50].

The In-basket Test. A modification of the situational testing technique which has proved useful in management training programs shows some promise as a selection device [20, 21].

The examinee is asked to sit at a desk on which there is an in-basket filled with whatever might typically be found in the in-basket of the administrator in the position for which candidates are being selected. Included may be important memoranda requiring immediate action, routine daily reports requiring no action, and social items (e.g., office trivia, an invitation to play golf). Some of the items can be ignored; others contain significant information about the psychological climate of the setting. The examinee is instructed to go through the items as if he were on the job, handling them by referring, delegating, planning meetings, and in general exercising control and leadership; and he is told that everything he decides or does must be in writing. Whatever memoranda, reminders, or letters he writes become his answers to the test items. A folder of information is given the examinee describing the organization, its structure, history, personnel, and function.

At the end of the allotted time (usually two to three hours) the examinee is given a reasons-for-action form which provides him with the opportunity to express more clearly how he perceived each item and why he took the action he did.

The scoring of the in-basket test, which requires specially trained personnel, produces three types of scores. In the first, the content of the examinee's responses is considered with a view to how many times the examinee makes a "correct" response, or a response exhibiting qualitative characteristics such as decisiveness or imaginativeness. In the second, the focus is on examinee's style, e.g., whether he is courteous to subordinates. In the third, judgments are made about how well the examinee does on the overall task.

Situational testing would still involve the assumption that those men who perform best in the test situation will perform best under actual control-operating conditions, say, ten years later. The validity of this assumption can only be tested by longitudinal investigations. The present need for this kind of investigation is great.

If situational testing is desirable, why not expose candidates to actual operating conditions rather than to costly simulated test situations? Why not let each candidate work for the company for a trial period during which his performance would be carefully observed?

Despite the advantages of this trial-by-fire type of selection, it is questionable whether adequate test conditions can be created on the job. Good selection requires a broad range of test situations and ample opportunity to obtain valid observational data. These conditions are seldom attainable under operating conditions. In addition, an intensive situational testing program lasting, say, two or three days, allows companies to select the successful candidates without any obligation to provide employment for the unsuccessful candidate.

Whether or not we have valid ways of picking the people we wish to groom for executive positions, industry still has to pick somebody. One way or another a man has to be selected as a potential executive. The word "potential" is important because, except for the small minority of experienced administrators who enter companies as higher-level executives, most executives develop within the companies they serve. For example, 90 per cent of 900 top executives studied by *Fortune Magazine* had been with their companies ten or more years. A survey of 1,000 top officials of major United States industrial companies by *Scientific American* says few managers come to the top directly from other firms. Around the age of 50 the executive is promoted to a vice-presidency, becoming the chief executive as he approaches 60 years of age.

EXECUTIVE–DEVELOPMENT TRAINING

Types of Practices. Current practices in executive development vary from complete laissez faire to highly organized systematic training. The former involves no formal efforts on the part of the company. Potential candidates merely mature in the company, picking up from their day-to-day experiences what skills they can. At the other extreme, the early years a potential candidate spends with the company consist of continuous training. His positions are carefully chosen to provide him with the experience he will require as an executive. He is transferred from time to time to provide him with a broad range of experience in all aspects of the company's operations. There are frequent conferences, during the working day and evenings, at which he has the opportunity to learn new skills (often human relations skills), to learn about new technical developments, and to make up for any deficiencies in his educational background. He is asked to attend week-long training sessions and may even be encouraged to attend formal programs given in various schools of business. Even his wife may be given the opportunity to acquire the social skills she will need. He will receive regular reports on his progress and hold extensive discussions with regard to his shortcomings. In some instances, even the services of a clinic will be available to him if personal psychotherapy is necessary.

Whether such an extensive program is justified is, of course, difficult if not impossible to ascertain. The first question is whether the product of such a system is in actuality a more qualified man than the product of a laissez-faire system.

A rigorously controlled study of the value of executive training has, however, never been conducted. There is some reason for this; the situation is like that encountered in mental-health research. To validly test the efficiency of a new method or new mental-health program requires that a comparable control sample be excluded from participating in the new program. But if you are confident that the new program will be highly beneficial, what right have you to deprive a sample of its benefit, particularly if they earnestly seek the benefit? And what effect will the mere act of being deprived have on the control sample? In addition, how do you hold all other things equal, particularly in an industrial setting? As was learned in the Hawthorne experiment, you cannot manipulate the experimental group without influencing the control group. Also there is the problem of criteria. Just how does one measure the value of a training program? Although we do not have an answer to this question, a lot of industrial organizations seem to think their training programs are worth the money they cost.

Educational Programs for Executives. Educational programs for executives have expanded rapidly until at the present time some 250,000 executives go back to school each year. There are three main ways in which the various programs have been run. First, university schools of business have instituted programs that run for periods of about ten weeks during which the executives come and live on the campus. They are taught by the regular faculties and hear lectures by outside experts. Second, there are the company-run institutes, such as the one conducted by General Electric at its own educational center. Here top executives from every G.E. division live together for thirteen weeks; they attend classes together, have their meals together, and sleep in a dormitory. They hear lectures on subjects ranging from geopolitics to economics; they also work on individual projects. Some of the faculty are company executives, and some are brought in from university faculties. Most companies with such programs design their curricula around courses closely related to their particular business.

Third, the American Management Association, along with a number of other management training associations, maintains programs for companies that are too small to run their own show. The training programs last anywhere from five days to several weeks.

In general, these programs cover studies in management principles, the nature of organizations, planning and controlling, and appraisal of operational performance. Some programs set up problem-solving situations where teams of executive students compete in such areas as making decisions on awarding advertising contracts, problems in promotion, and merit rating. Most of the programs include courses or workshops in human relations.

Programs and Personal Adjustment. Somewhat unique have been the studies of experienced executives who have attended university programs. Since the

Harvard Business School initiated the idea in the late 1940s, several thousand executives have participated in some fifty programs sponsored by universities and colleges. Most programs give focus to middle management. Gorsuch [27] and Chowdhry [9, 10] report on studies of the personality and motivational factors of the participants. Many of the men said they had been traveling at such a fast pace that they had given little time to personal planning or cultural pursuits. Some on follow-up reported that on returning to the job they changed their leisure-time habits and basic living plans. One factor reported over and over was that the increased self-confidence that was derived from successfully competing with their peers and the drive felt to improve things back on the job was dampened by "the same old climate." New perspective and novel ideas got lost in the routine of day-to-day activities.

Why did the men attend the program for executives? Answers to this question turned up an interesting finding in one study related to personal adjustment. Of twenty-nine executives who went through one program fifteen were there on their own initiative and fourteen had been sent. About half of the total group had backgrounds of some organizational stress, of being at a critical stage of their career and decision making, and of being involved in dilemmas having polarities. The other half had seemed committed to their professional roles, had backgrounds of success and a sense of achievement. These "unconflicted" executives had the characteristics of the upward-mobile person we described in an earlier chapter. They liked the organization and felt a strong part of it. The "conflicted" executives, most of whom were self-initiated, sought out the programs as a flight from stress and hoped to find ways to resolve their dilemmas and conflicts. These were men in a crucial stage of their careers now considering alternatives in their continuing career development.

Most of the executives selected and sent to the program by their company felt the selection was an indicator of success. These unconflicted men looked upon the program, not as an escape from stress, but as an opportunity to gain knowledge and acquire new managerial skills. Whether the executive uses the program as a psychosocial moratorium or as a platform to launch himself higher may indicate contrasting personality patterns in reacting to stress. Some tension-ridden executives dream of getting out of the race, while others thrive on it.

CONFERENCE GROUPS

Planned work assignments and informal on-the-job training are vital and irreplaceable types of training. Together they include informal instruction, work assignments carefully planned to provide varied and informative experiences, continual observation, extensive opportunity to discuss problems encountered and progress made, and suggestions of ways in which the potential executive can improve himself by the assignment of reading and recommended professional activities.

An important additional type of training involves the structure and operation of the organization—namely, the use of conference groups. The conference method has been widely used in industry. A scheme for the permanent incorporation of conference groups into the organization in such a way that there can be *both formal and informal* communications between various groups has been proposed. This scheme shows how an organization can use its own structure to provide for continuous executive development. Let us include it here as an example of still another way of giving attention to training.

A diagram of organization structure for "optimal communication and perpetual executive training" is shown in Figure 9.1.

A feature of the proposal is the way in which horizontal communication between the groups is achieved by means of a junior-management group composed of selected junior members of the second-echelon groups. These men may be the most outstanding members of their groups, or they may be selected by systematic rotation, staggered to minimize disruption of group operation. This group makes recommendations only. (The other groups are responsible for policy at their level and recommend policy to higher levels.) Not only does the junior-management group provide for coordination between the departments at its own level, but as a result of its several perspectives on company problems it is able to provide original, perceptive suggestions to top management.

Conference groups provide the potential executive with knowledge of the problems and accomplishments of other departments and give him a broader point of view. By freely participating in the group, he learns to contribute to cooperative problem solving, to respect the opinions of his associates, and, frequently, to see the shortcomings and narrowness of his own point of view. In addition the trainee also learns to express himself cogently and confidently. In the course of analyzing problems he acquires relevant incidental information, on accounting techniques and labor relations, for example. Such a conference situation provides all the people concerned with an opportunity to get a global view of problems. Conference groups enable executives to observe their subordinates *actively engaged in management problem solving* and provide a source of valuable data on which to base recommendations for promotion.

We suggest that all conference groups be led in a permissive but controlled way; that is to say, let free discussion be encouraged, let no votes be taken, since the objective is to achieve unanimity—but let the leader maintain orderly discussion. The improvement of employee relations,

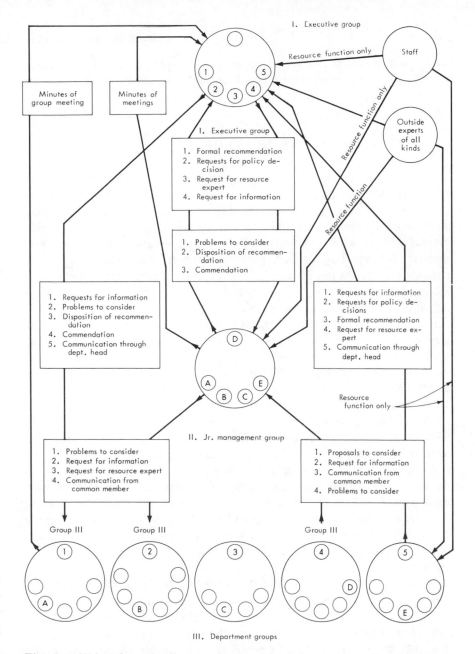

Fig. 9.1. This schematic diagram for organization structure of optimal communication and perpetual executive training shows how conference groups can be organized, providing for both formal and informal communications between executive, junior management, and department groups. Such schemes enable executives to observe their subordinates actively engaged in problem solving. (From Moyer, K. E. *Conference communication and executive development.* Mimeographed edition, 1959, 1–41.)

safety, and selection are suggested as initial topics of discussion. After the ice is broken, many other problems for discussion will flow to the groups.

SUCCESSFUL EXECUTIVE DEVELOPMENT

Currently, executive-development programs consist of planned work assignments, informal on-the-job training, including ideas for self-improvement, and organization aids to development, including formal training classes and conferences. Techniques usually employed incorporate formal lectures with or without visual aids, discussion groups, role playing, and problem solving. Experienced observers report that regardless of its methods and techniques of training, an executive-development program is good and meaningful only in proportion to the degree to which the company is committed to development in general.

If a training program is viewed as a segregated peripheral effort which need not be tied in with the long-term planning and development of the resources of the company, then it may well do more harm than good. What use is there in providing a group of young men with advanced skills and heightened aspirations if their new skills are neither appreciated nor needed and their new aspirations are likely to be frustrated?

The primary opportunity for the development and training of a potential executive is in the work assigned to him; how far he gets is up to him. The key man in his development is his immediate superior.

A superior who is mindful of the future needs of his subordinate and also the future needs of the organization can thoughtfully and systematically assign varied and significant tasks providing invaluable experience for the potential executive. It is important to note that this is not variety simply for the sake of variety. Each new assignment must be selected in the light of the developing needs of the candidate; i.e., it should build on previous experiences and prepare him for the next assignment. In addition, each new assignment must enable the candidate to use his growing skills productively. It is said that some companies rationalize assigning men to menial berths by saying that the different experience is good for them. If this is the only motivation for such assignments, then the practice is, of course, indefensible. On the other hand, it is possible that a sympathetic, penetrating analysis of a candidate's record might indicate that, in the case of this particular man, assignment to a menial task would provide a beneficial experience.

It is important to keep good records on the man being groomed for a higher position. A long-range effort such as this requires that a full description of the candidate's development be kept, including statements of the reasons which motivated his assignments, summaries of experiences and skills acquired, and constructive evaluations of his performances.

It is likewise important that the motivation for development originate in the potential executive himself. The company can provide opportunities, aids, incentives, and, initially, direction. To be fully effective in the long run, however, the guidance of the development process should subtly shift, as time passes, from the organization to the individual. We shall discuss this more in the final chapter of this book.

Portrait of a Successful Executive. The successful executive is usually completely immersed in his work; he identifies himself totally with the organization. At the same time, however, there are many other demands on his time and energy. He is frequently called upon to participate in community work, and he probably has strong family ties. There is, therefore, almost inevitable conflict among his roles, resulting in cross pressures, frustrations, and feelings of guilt and self-incrimination.

The conflict is intensified by many factors. There are the ample monetary awards and status symbols with which the executive's services are purchased. There is, however, no specified contractual relationship between an executive's compensation and the number of hours he works. Surely most executives must feel an obligation to devote a supernormal amount of their time and energy to their work.

Long hours and hard work do not in themselves cause breakdowns. It is probably true, within limits, that hard work never killed anyone. It appears to be the conflict and consequent tension which results from these demands which exhaust an executive, as is the cause with many people in lesser positions.

Another problem is that many executives, particularly lower-level executives, are deprived of the security and support which a stable and settled community life provides. A transferral every two or three years obviously precludes the establishment of deep roots in the community. The frequently moving executive becomes adroit at establishing himself and his family quickly, but his ties are at the same time kept fluid and superficial.

As a consequence of the factors mentioned above, as well as other stresses in any executive's life, it is no wonder that so-called "executive breakdowns" are not infrequent. An executive does not have simpler, less pressing needs than a worker. In fact, his needs are no doubt more elaborate and intense than those of company employees who have less responsibility [3, 6, 15, 18, 36, 62].

Frequently, the executive is viewed as a tower of strength who can adapt to any situation, but he too can be discharged without warning, transferred to a distant office on a moment's notice, capriciously shuffled in the organization, expected to reject all noncompany interests, or humiliated by his superior. It may be true that good executives can withstand all such strains; in fact, at present we tend to use the term "good executive" to define one who can withstand the strains. The question is, "Are these strains necessary and desirable?" The answer seems clear. Surely even the hardiest individuals are not as effective under these conditions as they would be otherwise. We need not, however, lose the services of those executives who cannot function effectively in such an environment. Let us add to the several skills stressed in executive-selection and -development programs one other: the skill of being able to practice good personal adjustments.

SUGGESTIONS FOR SELECTIVE READING

Champion, J. M., & Bridges, F. J. *Critical incidents in management.* Homewood, Ill.: Irwin, 1963. A volume on forty-eight incidents and ninety-four critiques on the incidents.

Collins, B. E. & Guetzkow, H. *A social psychology of group processes for decision making.* New York: Wiley, 1964. For readers interested in group problem-solving research.

Dalton, M. *Men who manage.* New York: Wiley, 1959. A provocative book on the dynamics of the industrial environment.

Dill, W. R., et al. *The new managers.* Englewood Cliffs, N.J.: Prentice-Hall, 1962. A readable study of successful and unsuccessful managers in terms of cases.

Guest, R. H. *Organizational change: The effect of successful leadership.* Homewood, Ill.: Irwin, 1962. Leadership, climates, and change.

Haire, M. *Psychology of management.* (2d ed.) New York: McGraw-Hill, 1964. Covers human needs, leadership, communication, training, pay, and organizations.

Harrell, T. W. *Managers' performance and personality.* Cincinnati: South-Western Publishing Company, 1961. A view of the personality characteristics of men who manage.

Jennings, E. E. *The executive: Autocrat, bureaucrat, democrat.* New York: Harper & Row, 1962. A popular version of the problems and styles of executives written by a college professor.

Kibbee, J. M., et al. *Management games: A new technique for executive development.* New York: Reinhold, 1961. Simulated operating and policy decisions utilizing computers.

Learned, E. P., & Wilson, C. E. (Eds.) *European problems in general management.* Homewood, Ill.: Irwin, 1962. Cases related to business strategy, policy, leadership, and process.

Leavitt, H. J. *Managerial psychology.* Chicago: University of Chicago Press, 1964. People in tens, hundreds, and thousands.

Leavitt, H. J., & Pondy, L. R. (Eds.) *Readings in managerial psychology.* Chicago: University of Chicago Press, 1964. Selected readings from business, psychology, and social science journals.

Likert, R. *New patterns of management.* New York: McGraw-Hill, 1961. Some challenging and controversial views in management theory.

Maier, N. R. F., & Hayes, J. J. *Creative management.* New York: Wiley, 1962. Authors conclude that "the price of every non-conference is a mortgage on the future."

Manley, R., & Manley, S. (Eds.) *The age of the manager.* New York: Macmillan, 1962. A popular book by popular writers.

Schlender, W. E., et al. (Eds.) *Management in perspective.* Boston: Houghton Mifflin, 1965. Readings covering new thinking about problems; only indirectly psychological.

Schultz, G. P., & Whisler, T. L. *Top management organization and the computer.* New York: Free Press, 1960. A description of decision-making problems in a new era.

Sherif, M. (Ed.) *Intergroup relations and leadership.* New York: Wiley, 1962. A book of readings ranging from readable to sophisticated.

Stryker, P. *The character of the executive: Eleven studies in managerial qualities.* New York: Harper & Row, 1961. A readable paperback, popular in content.

Summer, C. E., Jr., & O'Connell, J. J. *The managerial mind.* Homewood, Ill.: Irwin, 1964. Science and theory in policy decisions.

Tagiuri, R. (Ed.) *Research needs in executive selection.* Cambridge, Mass.: Harvard Graduate School of Business, 1961. Some changing views of managerial job performance, readable to technical.

Whitehill, A. M., & Takezawa, S. *Cultural values in management-worker relations: Japan. "Gimu" in transition.* Chapel Hill, N.C.: University of North Carolina, School of Business Administration, 1961. Study of Japanese workers and of management trainees.

10

Attitudes, Job Satisfactions, and Industrial Morale

B. von Haller Gilmer

What does the worker want from his job? How do benefits influence his feelings about where he works? How do attitudes affect the amount and quality of production? How do managers feel about what they do? Where does the scientist get his satisfaction? These and similar questions are raised when we consider human needs and their interaction with organizational climates. In this chapter we shall pull together the several aspects of what people think about their jobs in terms of the *feelings* they have. Understanding feelings provides a base for interpreting a number of problems related to labor relations, work, individual and social adjustments, and career development.

PROBLEMS AND DEFINITIONS

Being satisfied with a job means more than just not being discontented. When several hundred managers and professional people were asked to describe a job experience when they felt exceptionally good or bad about their job, two things turned out to be important. Favorable experiences were associated with job *content,* that is, the task performed by the person. In this the principal sources of satisfaction were feelings of accomplishment, recognition, the work itself, and chances of advancement. Negative feelings mainly centered around job *context,* such things as supervision, company policy, and operating procedures. Individuals tend to perceive satisfactions as coming from within and dissatisfactions as coming from the work environment. A few people, particularly at professional levels, see the problem as an interactional one between individual and environment [11, 18, 35, 41].

The terms "employee attitude," "job satisfaction," and "industrial morale" are in many instances used interchangeably. Blum [5], however, has made the point that they are not synonymous. An attitude may contribute to job satisfaction, since the latter is comprised of a number of attitudes. Similarly, job satisfaction is not the same as industrial morale, although it may contribute to morale.

Job attitude is the feeling the employee has about his job, his readiness to react in one way or another to specific factors related to a job. *Job satisfaction* or *dissatisfaction* is the result of various attitudes the person holds toward his job, toward related factors, and toward life in general. *Industrial morale* is generated by the group. For the individual it is a feeling of being accepted by and belonging to a group of employees through adherence to common goals. In a company, industrial morale is the composite expression of the attitudes of the various individuals in the company.

In this chapter, we shall discuss the ways that attitudes are determined, the extent of job satisfaction and dissatisfaction in representative industries, the factors related to attitudes, and the dimensions of good morale.

INFORMATION ABOUT ATTITUDES

We all have attitudes which govern our tendencies to react positively or negatively to people, to things, to situations. We like or dislike our work in different ways and in different degrees. Our morale may be good or bad depending on the adequacy with which a group functions in carrying out its purposes. Management has several ways of getting information about employee attitudes.

Formal Communication Channels. Higher management depends extensively upon the analyses of foremen and other supervisors to evaluate what the worker thinks. Such reports appear to be a normal method for trying to find out about employee attitudes. Unfortunately, in many places they are an unreliable source of information. The expressions of attitudes are screened on the way up, and false ideas are fostered. Bellows [3] reports that many foremen do not know how to handle men in the first place; hence, how can they effectively interpret workers' feelings? In one study, he found that one-fourth of the foremen felt that the best way to handle tough men was to be tougher than they were and that about 40 per cent of the supervisors erroneously believed that workers were little interested in what others thought of their job so long as the pay was good. Few workers ever see top management. If they depend on their supervisors to interpret how they feel, one can readily see that there is little chance of an objective evaluation of job satisfaction through the normal communication channels.

Grapevine Channels. Rumored attitudes are a part of all organizations. However, the information that rumors carry becomes altered and often distorted as it makes its upward movement. More dangerous still are the attitudes communicated by the grapevine, for they may reflect only the extremes. Within this structure, attitudes of the majoriy of the workers never get impartially expressed.

Behavior Manifestations. Griping on the job, slowdowns, early quits, and excessive absenteeism are true revealers of attitudes, but they come too late. By the time such manifestations are evidenced, damage has been done. All too frequently, however, in some companies this is the only way information about employee attitudes is communicated.

Interviewing. Talking with people has long been used as a means of getting at attitudes. In the guided interview, there is the attempt to get answers to predetermined questions. This is in contrast to the unguided interview, where the employee is encouraged to talk about anything he wishes. In the counseling interview and the exit interview, attitudes may also be uncovered.

The Questionnaire. The questionnaire technique is most economical and has certain advantages of objectivity of measurement providing for a quantitative treatment of responses. Answers may be gotten through checklists, multiple-choice questions, yes-no answers. Space for write-in comments is sometimes included on questionnaire forms. In order to provide for complete anonymity, some blanks have holes that can be punched; some have a tear ballot where one can tear the appropriate arrowhead to indicate an answer. Various attitude scales have been used in practical ways to determine employee feelings.

Many companies keep a running tab on employee attitudes. Typical is that described by Brown from his work in the textile industry [7]. He concludes that the repeated use of attitude measurements makes it possible for a company to compare its level of morale with that of other companies, observe trends over a long period of time, and detect problem areas and situations before they become disruptive. Attitude measurements have proved useful in spotlighting departments where particular morale problems exist and have been effective in determining employee and supervisory training needs. This author reports that repeated attitude measures aid in checking up on the effectiveness of training.

THE EXTENT AND NATURE OF JOB DISSATISFACTION

The average figure of job dissatisfaction found in varying industries is around 13 per cent. Age as a factor here has been shown from twenty-three studies. In general, job satisfaction is high among young workers but tends to go down during the first few years of employment. The low point is reached when workers are in their middle and late twenties or early thirties. Then it increases steadily until a temporary middle-age revolt sets in. Initial enthusiasm for work is apparent among the younger group, but any failure to get ahead lowers job satisfaction for a period. Gradually, really dissatisfied workers are weeded out, and the rest struggle to survive and move ahead. In late middle age, positive attitudes toward the job are found in the man with seniority [20]. Blauner [4] makes the point that from many studies there is a remarkable consistency in the findings that the vast majority of people, in virtually all occupations and industries, are moderately or highly satisfied rather than dissatisfied with their jobs. But what of those who are dissatisfied?

The Dissatisfied Worker. There is considerable evidence that job dissatisfaction is often associated with generalized maladjustment of some kind. People who are dissatisfied with their jobs are less outgoing and friendly, are more emotionally unbalanced, and show more boredom, daydreaming, and general discontent than do their satisfied coworkers.

The dissatisfied worker finds it difficult to adjust to arbitrary standards of work or to rigid requirements of the employer. For example, in one study of nearly fourteen hundred workers, in seven different occupations, it was found that people dissatisfied with their jobs had levels of aspiration far exceeding their levels of ability and opportunity [36]. Many people take jobs on a temporary basis or shift from one job to another. Secretaries often shift jobs. Why does a good secretary quit? Rarely ever is it for real lack of skill. Marriage and family comprise one reason, but after that, according to one study, come the reasons of boredom and "just fed up." The secretary is tired of being troubleshooter, scapegoat, calorie counter, ego soother, work organizer, stand-in researcher, personal drumbeater, and ghost writer—all without portfolio and recognition.

Occupation Level. The literature review of almost two thousand articles reports the unequivocal fact that the higher the level of occupation, the higher the level of job satisfaction. One study, conducted on a large national sample, showed that 25 per cent of unskilled workers were dissatisfied with their jobs compared with 0 per cent of businessmen. Sustained job-interest studies have shown that professional people lead the list in degree of job satisfaction, that salaried workers are next, and that factory workers are least interested in their jobs [20]. Not only is there higher job satisfaction among the better educated, but they worry differently in one respect. A government commission on mental illness reported that college graduates tend to worry more over genuine rather than imagined troubles.

It is not at all uncommon to find low job satisfaction among workers in the lower social strata, where family ties are relatively weak, housing is substandard, and the opportunities for achieving stable work habits are limited. Such habits as shiftlessness, irresponsibility, and lack of ambition are normal responses which the worker has learned from his physical and social environment. The well-educated girl from a professional family may scorn a job as a waitress, whereas someone from a lower social class may be happy with it. There is considerable evidence that the attitude people have toward their jobs is more than just an individual matter; it is related to the value system of the class.

PROFESSIONAL AND MANAGERIAL LEVELS

The chief factor that places the professional man—physician, lawyer, and scientist, in particular—in a somewhat unique category is that his satisfactions come largely from his own efforts. A survey among doctors showed that they were dependent on their organizations (hospitals, medical societies) for operational settings in which to function but that these organizations did little in providing satisfactions per se. In fact, a large number of doctors reported that their hospitals were badly managed. University professors often express the feelings that they are primarily professionally oriented, possibly reflecting one reason why so many shift from job to job, particularly in the earlier years when mobility holds more possibilities. Members of law firms report that basic job satisfaction comes largely from what they do as individuals. To a somewhat lesser degree, staff professionals in industry report that they are professionally oriented in contrast to higher-level managers, who say they are essentially company-oriented.

Kornhauser [28], in describing scientists in industry, points out that often conflict develops over the problem of colleague control versus administrative control of research staff, contributing to dissatisfaction with staff jobs. Management's desire for research supervisors whose primary loyalty is to the organization rather than to the profession conflicts with the scientist's desire for research supervisors whose primary loyalty is to them rather than to management. Interactions between professions and organizations tend to produce competing orientations, career lines, and incentive systems. The scientific profession seeks contributions to knowledge and gets satisfaction from research papers and colleague acclaim. The industrial firm seeks contributions to production and sales, rewarding commercial success with promotions in a hierarchy of status, income, and authority. Sometimes the scientist gets confused as to where he should look for satisfaction.

A survey shows that the vast majority of medical practitioners are satisfied with their profession, but that large numbers are dissatisfied with their specialty. For example, 87 per cent of a group of pediatricians were happy to be medical doctors, but only 63 per cent were satisfied with their specialty. "I like to work with diseases, but not with overprotective mothers," said one.

Hoppock [21], in a twenty-seven-year follow-up on job satisfaction of employed adults, found evidence for increase in satisfaction with age. Vroom [49], in measurement of supervisory personnel, found that persons ego-involved in jobs rated higher in job performance than those not ego-involved; this relationship was greater for those higher in autonomy. Porter [37, 38], reporting on his studies of nearly two thousand American managers, concluded that the vertical location of management positions is an important factor in determining the extent to which managers feel they can satisfy their psychological needs; in general, the higher the level the better. Presidents and vice-presidents had the highest fulfillment in satisfying the need for autonomy. Managers at the upper middle level reported general across-the-board satisfaction of psychological needs, and the middle and lower managers said they obtained from the job more fulfillment of security and social needs. Large companies can produce at least as favorable management attitudes as small companies in terms of job challenges and the kind of behavior seen as necessary for job success and for need satisfaction. In large and small organizations alike, managers' attitudes vary with level of position and with whether the position is described as line or staff. In general, staff managers derive less satisfaction from their job, feel they have to be more other-directed than line managers. Exceptions to this can be found in companies more dominated by research and development than by production.

Perceived Job Satisfaction of Managers. Eran [14], in a study which extended the researches of Porter on job attitudes, found that how a person perceives his own personality traits is important for satisfaction. Figure 10.1 shows vice-presidents compared to lower managers on the five psychological needs called "security," "social," "esteem," "autonomy," and "self-actualization" (broken lines). The solid lines compare two groups of people at the same lower middle-management level. One group consisted

of managers who perceived themselves to possess traits which were characteristic of high-level managers, labeled "highs." The second group included those whose scores on a self-descriptive inventory were below the
average for their own managerial level. This group is labeled the "lows." In
this questionnaire study it was found that the "highs" felt more fulfillment
and satisfaction of needs than did the "lows." Also the "highs" perceived

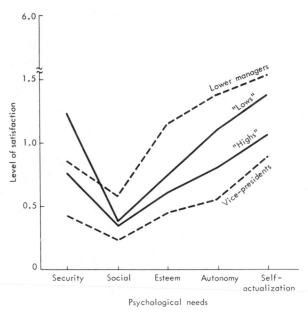

Fig. 10.1. Perceived job satisfaction of managers
shows that those who see themselves possessing
traits characteristic of high-level managers feel more
like them. Solid lines compare these "low" and
"high" perceptions where both groups are actually
at the same job level (After Eran); broken lines
compare vice-presidents with lower managers (After
Porter). A low score indicates high satisfaction.

some of the needs to be more important for their job, and they were more
inner-directed in their orientation toward the importance of personality
traits in their jobs. This study found that job satisfaction may be accounted
for by the interaction of environmental and personal factors. It is also of
interest that the differences between the "highs" and the "lows" in perceived job satisfaction were not as large as the differences between low-level
and high-level managers.

WORKER JOB–FACTOR COMPARISONS

Many studies concerned with job attitudes have dealt with what the worker wants from his job. Table 4 gives a list of ten job factors in order according to the number of times each was mentioned in about 150 studies. Under each heading are listed the specific aspects of the job factors that are related to attitudes.

Table 4 / Specific Aspects of the Ten Major Job Factors

Intrinsic Aspects of Job

Appropriateness to training and preparation and abilities
Appropriateness to aspirations and plans
Opportunity for learning knowledge and skills
Pride in accomplishment and workmanship
Prestige, status, dignity, importance, respect, power
Recognition, public and private, appreciation, fame
Self-respect
Public service, altruism
Service to company
Personal contacts with outsiders
Contacts with management
Freedom and independence of research, action, and planning
Well-defined work project and duties
Creativity and self-expression
Opportunity to participate in decisions
Responsibility and authority
Initiative
Challenge
Thought and attention
Interest
Variety or repetition, specialization
Ease
Opportunity for travel
Opportunity for mobility
Personal convenience and preference
Appeal and desirability of work
Effects on health
Adventure

Tension and pressure
Work load and routine demands, distribution of work
Speed requirements
Distasteful job duties

Supervision

Foremanship
Consideration, fairness
Courtesy, tact
Proper evaluation
Information on status and progress
Appreciation
Credit, recognition, praise
Professional advancement
Economic advancement
Advancement in social position
Aspiration or ambition in relation to advancement
Merit system of advancement, etc.
Promotion from within the company
Promotion policies

Security

Steadiness of employment
Company stability
Continuous work prospects
Self-adequacy
Seniority
Feeling of being valued by firm
Having a trade
Opportunity to learn trade, job, skills, career
Influences of political processes on government positions

Table 4 (*Continued*)

Company and Management

Company attitude toward and coopera-
tion with labor unions
Company sponsorship of athletic teams,
employee home development, candi-
dates for city government, playgrounds
Contributions to charities
Interpreted fairness, intentions, and good
sense of management
Administration cooperation and assist-
ance
Company procedures and policy
Pride in company and product
Company interest in individual worker
Company training program
Meeting of company obligation
Keeping promises, sincerity
Cooperation
Encouragement
Understanding, empathic ability
Ability to handle people
Opportunity for employee decision mak-
ing
Sociability
Availability for assistance and consulta-
tion
Loyalty to workers
Permissiveness, closeness
Personal counsel
Delegation of authority
Manner of criticism and discipline
Consistency of orders, discipline, etc.
Technical competence and aptitude

Working Conditions

Attractive surroundings
Clean and orderly workplace
Adequacy and condition of equipment,
supplies, and tools
Lighting
Temperature and ventilation
Absence of smoke, noise, excessive heat,
odors
Safety conditions
Music
Recreational and food facilities
Medical facilities

Parking facilities
Geographical location and community
Hours

Wages

Pay, income, salary, earnings
Economic factors, motives, values
Economic advantages
Profit
Wage satisfaction
Financial adjustment
Profit sharing
Frequency of raises
Enough to live on
Fairness or equitableness of compensa-
tion

Opportunity for Advancement

Advancement on merit
Advancement on seniority
Structure of organization
Size of organization
Company reputation and public rela-
tions
Management's foresight and planning

Social Aspects of Job

Congenial coworkers, on or off the job
Social approval
Interpersonal relationships
Group dynamics
Team balance
Cooperation and group effort
Size and functions of work groups
Pride in belonging to team, belonging-
ness
Pride in team accomplishments
Inter- and intradepartment relations
Department reputation
Competent coworkers
Prejudices

Communication

Information of employee as to status
Information on new developments
Information on what company is doing
Information on personnel policies, pro-
cedures

Table 4 (*Continued*)

Information on company lines of authority	*Benefits*
Suggestion systems	Retirement provisions
Instructions and orders	Provision for emergencies: illness, accidents, etc.
Annual report	
Company magazine, newspaper	Leave, vacations, holidays

SOURCE: Herzberg, F., Mausner, B., Peterson, R. O., & Capwell, Dora F. *Job attitudes: Review of research and opinion.* Pittsburgh: Psychological Service of Pittsburgh, 1957.

EFFECTS OF ATTITUDES ON PRODUCTIVITY

Within the past thirty years, the writings in the area of worker productivity have shown a shift from an emphasis on wage incentives and environmental working conditions to an emphasis on human relations.

This shift is due, in part, to the fact that working conditions and wages have been improved in recent years. Mainly, however, industry leaders are finding that there is another important side to the economic man. A poll of the executives of several hundred companies emphasized that business leaders are beginning to realize how important worker attitudes are.

What can be done to improve worker attitudes? There are no simple answers. Is music, for example, a legitimate device that gives pleasure to workers and profit to employers? As long ago as 1911 it was reported that six-day bicycle riders can be stimulated to respond with increased effort when lively music is played even though working close to the point of exhaustion [1]. Uhrbrock, one of the pioneers of industrial psychology, has reviewed some four decades of research of music on the job and its relation to worker morale and production [47]. He concludes that many unqualified claims are not proved and that some advertising brochures issued by music merchants are not backed by facts. Attitudinally, the majority of factory workers surveyed prefer working where music is played, but not all workers feel so positively, and some are annoyed by it. Young, inexperienced employees engaged in *simple,* repetitive, monotonous tasks increased their output when stimulated by music, whereas evidence has been presented which demonstrates that experienced factory operators, whose work patterns are stabilized, do not increase their production when music is played, particularly when performing *complex* tasks. Some investigators have found that at times music has had an adverse effect on production. There is a negative correlation between age and preference for work music.

Is the performance-appraisal interview worthwhile in improving worker morale? A study at General Electric showed that most subordinates felt they deserved more favorable appraisals than they received [25]. Criticisms of performance in the single interview typically resulted in defensiveness, and the use of praise had no measurable effect on employee reactions to subsequent job performance. Subordinate participation in goal planning, another aspect of the study, resulted in improved subordinate attitudes pertaining to man-manager relations but little difference in the degree to which goals were achieved. The study showed further that increased subordinate participation in *day-to-day* goal planning was much better in bringing about favorable attitudes and goal achievement.

Work and Attitudes. Do attitudes affect the amount and quality of work production? This is an involved question; what are the facts? In 1957, twenty-six studies were cited in which some quantitative relationship between productivity and job attitudes in a variety of jobs had been measured. Fourteen of these studies found that workers with positive job attitudes showed higher productivity than those with negative attitudes; for nine studies, there was no relationship; and in three studies, workers with positive job attitudes actually showed poorer production records than those with negative attitudes. The contradictions in these studies may be due in part to differences in the research methods involved, in the workers surveyed, or in their work situations. One basic consideration is that high productivity accompanies high morale only when the attitudes of the work group favor maximum output. This is particularly true when the work group is very cohesive, when the atmosphere is friendly, and when belonging to that specific work group is highly desirable to its members. A group of this kind can either restrict or raise output independently of the degree to which its members are satisfied with their jobs. Cohesive groups may be highly productive or highly unproductive, depending on whether the members go along with management goals for high productivity.

The findings of studies relating attitudes to job turnover and absenteeism are in general in agreement. Twenty-one of twenty-four studies cited in the literature report that workers with positive job attitudes have less turnover and absenteeism than workers with negative attitudes [20]. Two studies report no effects, and one study showed workers with positive job attitudes as having more turnover. Wickert [50] has shed some light on the problem in his investigation of telephone-company employees. He found that those who quit their jobs felt they were less personally involved in these jobs than those who stayed; they left, in part, because they had had no chance to help make decisions, and they felt they had not contributed to the success of the company. Another investigator found virtually the same thing with bricklayers and carpenters, who were less likely to leave their jobs when they were given some say-so in the composition of their work groups.

It has been found that the critical employee is not always a poorer producer than the uncritical one, but the preponderance of evidence adds up to the conclusion that workers with positive job attitudes outproduce workers with negative job attitudes when the psychological climates favor high production, where there is good supervision, and where the employee really wants to produce and get ahead.

Aspiration and Productivity. Morse [34] has made the point that employee satisfaction is a function not only of how much a person receives from the job situation but also of where he stands with respect to his level of aspiration. When the environment provides little possibility for need satisfaction, those people with the strongest desires, or highest aspirations, will be the least happy. Or, as she has put it another way, "The greater the amount the individual gets, the greater his satisfaction, and, at the same time, the more the individual still desires, the less his satisfaction." From her interview studies of white-collar clerical workers and supervisors, Morse makes the point that if an employee is in a situation where he is not making any decisions *and does not want to make any,* he will tend to be highly or moderately satisfied with his work, but if he is not making any decisions *and would like to make some,* he will tend to derive little satisfaction from his job.

With satisfaction seen then as a function of both the strength of needs in a particular area and the amount of "environmental return," we can see how education increases the strength of needs for pay and for job status. This factor is of vital consideration to the college student in planning his career. As the person grows older, the need for pay and job status increases. This can lead to job dissatisfaction when the discrepancy between levels of aspiration and possibilities of attainment gets too great.

One way to get an indication of how people feel about their jobs in terms of environmental feedback is to take a look at turnover of people on the job.

Some Generalizations About Job Turnover. In a review of over seven hundred titles dealing with job turnover, Schuh [42] finds that managers tend to remain with their companies longer than professionals and craftsmen. Production workers have the highest turnover rate in industry, surpassed generally only by household employees. North American industry as a whole has a turnover rate around 40 per cent a year. The average person holds a job with the same employer or in the same type of business, in the same locale, for 3½ years. Studies of those who have remained with a given organization ten years or more show ratios of one-third for managers, one-fourth for professionals and craftsmen, and one-fifth for workers. Even within a given employment bracket, differences of turnover are found.

For example, typists have the highest turnover rate, followed by stenographers. Comparatively, secretaries have the lowest turnover rate within the clerical and secretarial occupation. And turnover is costly. One company which spent almost a million dollars to recruit 193 scientists and engineers found only 54 had remained with the organization by the end of one year.

Men at the top of the corporate jobs tend to remain in their positions, markedly in contrast to men of lower rank. Insul et al. [22] found that 120 executives from forty firms, ranging in size from 2,000 to 125,000 employees, had held no more than three management jobs. This particular sample included 34 presidents and 19 board chairmen among some forty job titles.

Study after study in the Schuh review reflects the fact that individuals do very little career planning before seeking a job and industry itself often fails to provide a climate for job satisfaction. Reasons for turnover range widely with most data obtained by exit interview. Employees tend to give polite rather than real reasons when they leave. Typical is one study where over half of the employees said they were leaving for higher pay, while a follow-up study showed the real reason was poor supervision and psychological factors related to job attitudes. Such things as commuting and crowded transportation are frequently mentioned in exit interviews as reasons for absences and for quitting a job. However, one may question these as basic reasons for turnover. A study of over 6,000 white-collar workers in 30 Swedish insurance companies showed no relation between commuting time and absenteeism. Living distance had little to do with turnover. Weather affects tardiness, but not absenteeism. And regardless of weather, tardiness increases toward the end of the week.

Some investigators have related turnover to scores on intelligence, aptitude, personality, and interest tests. These measures predict early quits fairly well but do less well in predicting who will give up a job after about eighteen months. When the employee's job goals are in line with the demands of his position, he has a high probability of staying. Turnover is high among those persons whose positions are below their level of education. On the whole, the weighted application blank has yielded the highest validity coefficients over the greatest number of jobs. But study after study shows that rapid decay in predictability of the blank occurs, necessitating reweighting every two or three years.

In some industries women leave their jobs more frequently than men. In other industries, textile, for example, and certain clerical jobs, they show less turnover than men. In the main, women entering the labor market today stay with the job longer than women who entered it a decade ago. The easing of household duties, better child care, higher cost of living, and more interest of employers in problems of women are contributing to a falling rate of female turnover. Personnel selection and training are also related to this improving situation.

There is a higher turnover among younger than among older people. The older employee often has too much invested in the job situation, whereas the younger person is still exploring the job field and learning more about himself through job trial and error. Handicapped workers have, on the average, lower job turnover.

The probability of leaving a job is directly related to the extent to which a person has failed to relate personal goals to job opportunities. Many people even fail to define their own goals clearly. Coming onto the scene are researches on turnover centering on the interrelationships between the individual and his climate. Important also is the problem of job obsolescence. The United States government estimates that each week some thirty-five thousand workers lose or change their jobs because of the advance of automation.

THE PSYCHOLOGICAL CLIMATE FOR WORK

The social aspects of the job work groups, leadership, and organization of the company all add up to a psychological climate for the person to work in. It is known, for example, that work groups which are cohesive, which have a sort of pride in the group, have higher morale than those which are not cohesive. However, it appears to be substantiated that high morale is not always associated with high productivity. Why? In part, we will get an answer to this question as we take a look at the complexities of how people work together or fail to work together.

Informal Group Structures. Logically we may think that all people are ambitious, but they are not. We may think that people are motivated to keep accidents from happening; statistics show otherwise. We may think that work which is planned for convenience and efficiency will be accepted by the work groups, but experience sometimes proves otherwise.

Both the formal and the informal structures of an organization, as we indicated in Chapters 2 and 3, can be described by the roles that the people play, by the ways in which they communicate, and by the final decisions that are made. Formal structures are, of course, the official way a company is organized. Informal organizations, on the other hand, result from friendships, car pools, nearness of workplaces, community interests, union associations, and the like.

Kinds of Informal Organizations. Brown [6], writing on the social psychology of industry, describes three kinds of informal organizations. First, we find the formation of groups based on some issue. Thus, a revolt in the ranks of the United Steel Workers lined up people for and against existing policy-making groups. Second, we have the clique, which, for example, may be based on a common workplace or on the sharing of some common task. The formation of a group consisting of intimate friends constitutes a third kind of informal organization. How these groups interact determines the morale of an organization to a large extent and often serves as the key element in productivity. Many informal groups have leaders who may actually set production norms. The real power of these informal groups was first adequately observed in the Hawthorne studies. These studies pointed out that such devices as trading jobs, helping one another, talking, engaging in horseplay, and teasing were all prohibited by management rules; but the foremen did little more than wink at them. As a matter of fact, some studies have shown a high degree of labor turnover in jobs where there was little opportunity for conversation among workers.

On mass-production jobs in the automobile industry, one investigator has explained low job satisfaction among the workers on the basis of the lack of social contact due to the impersonal pressure of the assembly line. A number of findings have revealed that work situations in which the formation of informal work groups is inhibited are not conducive to optimal employee morale.

The Sociogram. The sociogram was developed by Moreno in the early thirties to describe relations among people [33]. This unique instrument offers a graphic way to look at communication. One can see how these "who works with whom" structures can have a bearing on morale, either at the worker level or at the management level. Let us illustrate some patterns these relationships can take.

Figure 10.2 shows kinds of sociograms found among workers (modified

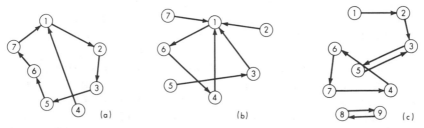

Fig. 10.2. These sociograms represent one way to portray communication between people graphically: (*a*) a cohesive group without a strong leader as contrasted to (*b*) one with a strong leader, and (*c*) an unstructured group with cliques, isolates, and mutual admiration societies. (From Blum, M. L. *Industrial psychology and its social foundation.* New York: Harper, 1956.)

after Blum [5]). A diagram of a cohesive group without a strong leader is shown in (a). The sociogram of a group with a strong leader is represented in (b). An unstructured group with cliques, isolates, and mutual admiration societies is shown in (c).

Figure 10.3 shows a sociogram of a group as found at the management level in a rubber company by Browne [8].

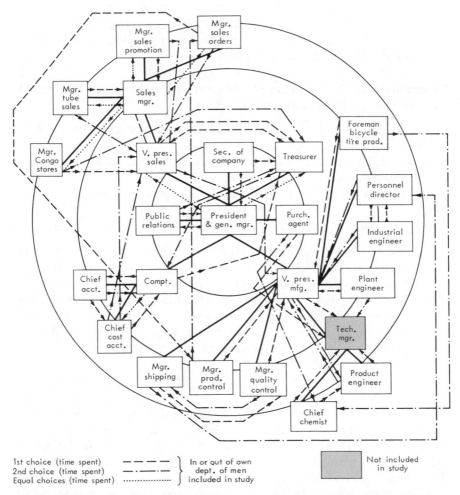

Fig. 10.3. This sociometric pattern for the Congo Tire and Rubber Company is the result of a study of twenty-four executives who were asked to report with whom they spent the most time in the course of business. Note that the "choices" center around the vice-presidents for manufacturing and sales, and the treasurer. (From Browne, C. G. Executive leadership in business. IV. Sociometric patterns. *J. Appl. Psychol.*, 1951, 35, 34–37.)

ORGANIZATIONS AND MORALE

The manipulation of the variables affecting morale in a live business organization has certain limitations as to experimental control. Hence, why not build a miniature organization in the laboratory? True, such laboratory experimentation has limitations when it comes to relating results to real organizations. But the laboratory situation holds the advantage of manipulating one variable at a time, and it is possible to get at some of the relatively isolated factors operating in job satisfaction.

Laboratory Studies. In a series of laboratory experiments [2, 17, 43, 46] answers were sought to such questions as:

• What difference does it make in an organization if communication is limited to certain channels?
• How will the morale and performance of an individual member be affected by the centrality of the position he occupies?
• What is it about a central position in an organization that is so satisfying?
• Does a position of autonomy affect job satisfaction in the individual?

Communication networks were established where subjects in any one group were seated around a circular table separated from each other by radial partitions which extended out so that the subjects could not see each other. They communicated by means of written notes passed through slots in the partitions. The communication network of any group was controlled by having some slots open and others closed. Problems were provided by the experimenter. The groups developed their own system of pooling information and working out answers.

The drawings in Figure 10.4 represent the "organizations," or different groups. In the "star" group all information is sent to a central person, who then transmits the answer back to each individual member. In the "chain" network the information is sent by the end men, the men on the periphery (P), to the middle men (M), and then in turn to the man in the center (C). The "Y" network is a combination of the "star" and the "chain." The "circle" network lacks centralized organization; thus problem solving is made more difficult. In such a network, pieces of information could bounce around for some time before someone accumulated all of them and took the leadership in sending out answers.

Results of the experimentation showed, first, that for efficiency in problem solving the "star" and "Y" nets did better than the "chain" and "circle." Second, the members differed both within and across nets in the

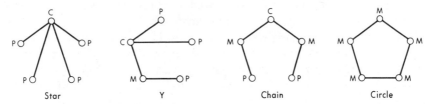

Fig. 10.4. Four communication nets show how the group is hung together. In the "star," the men on the periphery send information to the central person, who then transmits answers back. In the "chain," middlemen are interposed between the center and the periphery. The "Y" network combines the star and the chain. Problem solving is more difficult in the noncentralized "circle" network. (After Leavitt, H. J. Some effects of certain communication patterns on group performance. *J. Abnorm. Soc. Psychol.*, 1951, 46, 38–50.)

amount of satisfaction derived from their jobs in the group and in the amount of status accorded them by other group members, as measured later by questionnaire. Even in these experimental situations, devoid of much reality, the persons occupying central positions expressed greater job satisfaction and were seen as having higher status than the occupants of middle positions. The latter, in turn, expressed more satisfaction than the occupants of the peripheral positions.

Satisfaction of Individual Needs. The descriptions above represent only a few of the experiments on this problem. As far as job satisfaction is concerned, they add up to the following conclusions:

1 A central position in a communication net usually has associated with it a larger amount of autonomy. Its occupant can decide for himself what to do next. The person on the periphery has to be told what to do. In our culture, at least, being able to decide for oneself what to do is more satisfying than having to be told.

2 Being autonomous has more effect on satisfaction than does merely being central.

3 In positions where the person is in a position of being both central and autonomous, satisfaction is highest.

4 Members of the groups whose personalities (measured before the experiment) showed strong psychological needs to be independent were more dissatisfied with positions of low autonomy than were members who had weaker independence needs.

Why do people get together in certain groupings, derive satisfaction from belonging to a particular group, and leave it only with reluctance? It is here that *the individual finds a climate suitable to his individual needs,* where other members of the group help him satisfy his desires for recognition and status, his feelings of being wanted, and most of all, his feelings of security. When these needs in *the individual members of the group* are satisfied, group cohesiveness produces high morale and, in turn, high productivity, especially where leadership and company loyalty are also a positive part of the psychological climate. When there is good reason for suspicion, the group can sometimes limit production *and* get by with doing so. A good example of this can be found in the Hawthorne series of studies [40].

Group Behavior. In the Bank Wiring Observation Room study, an observer was placed in the room to record as much as possible of the group's behavior as the people worked at wiring, soldering, and inspecting switchboard banks. In due course of time it became apparent that the men had become distrustful of the observer. The informal structure of the group began to operate. They set a low standard of output, which was rigorously enforced by group pressures. The men worked hard in the morning and early afternoon until they had reached their informal quota. From then on, the day was filled in with trivial work, helping the slower fellow worker. Social pressure was exerted on the chiselers to maintain their quota by stepping up their work; it was exerted on the rate busters to slow it down.

A number of studies of rate busters have been reported in which it has been shown that the work group can close ranks against these deviates. Dalton [13], in a study of the individual rate buster, describes him as a person who is relatively maladjusted socially and unable to gain acceptance in the work group on a personal basis. Another writer has found that highly cohesive groups tend to enforce the group standard of productivity more rigorously than do less cohesive groups, but high productivity results only where the attitude toward the company is favorable [42].

Resistance to Change. There is some tendency, both within and without industry, for people to resist change even though the change may be best for the individual or for the group. As simple a situation as introducing safety devices on machines to prevent accidents has even caused strikes among workers where the devices necessitated changes in work habits.

One investigator describes how a wage-incentive system was introduced into an automobile factory without any explanation of the reasons for it or of the results it was supposed to produce. The plan was a failure. Others tell of the failure to increase production in coal mines by changing from technical obsolescence to the use of modern machinery which had been shown to be effective in other mines. The workers not only resisted verbally, but they failed to produce with any appreciable change in output. The modern machinery caused the men to lose identification with their jobs.

They had not been consulted about the change, and therefore they were not conditioned to accept it [45].

In a somewhat similar situation in a textile plant, a proposed change in production operations was put to the workers *as a problem*. The workers themselves, thus being involved in a solution affecting them, accepted the change. The workers also increased their productivity during the course of the problem solving [39]. Many people seem to fear change whether it comes as a product of time, as a product of fear, or just because it is different.

EMPLOYEE PARTICIPATION

There are numerous illustrations of how participation on the part of employees can help bring about their adjustment to changing conditions. People tend to support what they help to create. Let us describe one such situation in a small manufacturing company in southwest Virginia where psychologists had virtually a free hand in trying out the principle of participation. The experiments are described by Marrow and French [30] and Coch and French [10], who participated in the projects. In this particular plant, a long-standing prejudice existed among supervisors against hiring older female workers. Exhortation from higher management and from the psychologists did not shake this prejudice. But when the supervisors met in small groups to discuss the problem and their own attitudes, they arrived at the conclusion that their attitudes had been wrong. More important, they changed their hiring practices.

Again in this plant situation, a problem of a different sort of resistance to change was met. The company had especially severe turnover problems among workers who were forced to transfer from one job task to another because of changing market conditions. Many of these workers quit shortly after the retraining started or before they had attained competence at their new jobs. The retraining became a slow and costly process.

Through cooperation with top management, the psychologists set up a controlled experiment. Work groups were established. They were briefed on the problem and asked to plan how the factory could adapt to shifts in the market and in technology. By group discussion, these workers soon arrived at the conclusion that their own retraining was necessary, and they launched into it. Turnover dropped practically to zero, training time was decreased, and the change was made more smoothly. With a control group the picture was different. They were merely told that a change in their job was necessary and that they would have to be retrained for a new job. This group showed high turnover and a longer, more costly training period. Subsequently, this no-participation group was reassembled for participation in the decision-making process. Figure 10.5 summarizes the results, contrasting the response of this group to retraining when they did participate and when they did not participate in the change.

These studies are dramatic, but they also raise a practical question: Is our problem just one of "get in there and participate"? A large-scale survey of General Motors employees indicates that workers do wish to be involved

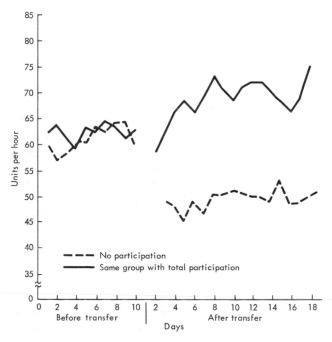

Fig. 10.5. A comparison of the effect of "no participation" with "total participation" on the same group in a decision-making process. Measurements were made in terms of work output in relation to transferral from one job task to another. (From Coch, L., & French, J. R. P., Jr. Overcoming resistance to change. *Hum. Relat.*, 1948, 1, 512–532.)

in day-to-day decisions. In this study, it was found that workers' attitudes toward both the company and the union are strongly affected by the degree to which foremen and shop stewards welcome the participation of the worker. The workers will show a strong attachment to the company if the degree of participation they feel in the decision making with the foreman is more than the participation they have with the shop steward. Since, however, the shop steward is himself a worker, participation is often easier at the union level. Loyalty comes with feelings of participation. Other writers maintain that participation in decision making is a major factor in the morale of all levels of employees [23].

One question to be borne in mind is this: How much participation can be allowed without sacrifice of control?

Participation is not something which can be conjured up or created artificially. You cannot buy it as you would buy a typewriter. You cannot hire industrial engineers to put it in. Participation will not work so long as it is treated as a device to get somebody else to do what you want him to do. Real participation is based on respect; it is acquired when the staff man faces the reality that he needs the contributions of the operating people.

Kolaja [26] studied workers' participation in decision making in a Polish textile factory and found the workers almost untouched by Communist ideology. They worked for the pay envelope, blamed poor output upon technological and managerial deficiencies beyond their control, and sought to relieve the monotony of mass production by activities outside the factory. Little or no benefits were evidenced from the participative management in this situation. In contrast, the same author found a Yugoslav factory displayed a more successful pattern of management-worker cooperation in the sharing of decisions in the enterprise. This was due in large measure to the fact that the employees held more responsibility and had a greater degree of identification with the factory. The Yugoslav factory provided more opportunity to make decisions, thus reducing the *psychological distance* between the man who translates the concept into action and the man who develops the managerial concepts and decisions [27].

There is much evidence to support the position that both attitudes and productivity of employees are geared to the quality of supervision. The morale of the first-line supervisor himself, however, is often neglected. As a foreman, he doesn't belong to the worker group, and often he is not fully accepted as a part of management. He wants to participate in management functions with his supervisor, who in turn wants the same thing from his superior, and so on up the ladder. At all levels in the industrial organization, we find that morale in its simplest terms involves the *feelings* of people.

WORK ENVIRONMENT AND MORALE

What of the feelings of people who are exposed to working conditions deleterious to man's well-being? This is a problem of increasing concern in this day of rapidly advancing technology. Can people be found who will be willing to work in high-noise-level areas around jet aircraft and guided missiles? What about absenteeism and turnover among workers whose jobs can possibly cause illness or even death? Are other factors in the work environment more displeasing to the man than physical discomfort? Are there positive factors in a job situation which counterbalance the negative factors?

Morale and Working Conditions—An Experiment. A series of studies has been made of the morale of workers exposed to high levels of occupational noise and other undesirable work conditions. These studies, reported by Felton and Spencer [15], indicate two important things. First, in this day of technological change more attention than ever needs to be given to the scientific selection of people for hazardous jobs; consideration must be given to both their technical skills and their ability to work with others. Second, in the evaluation of worker morale it is very important to know the psychological conditions of work before predicting that bad physical work conditions per se will cause low morale.

The investigation reported below was made at Tinker Air Force Base in Oklahoma, a jet-plane base, where the noise exposure was at times as high as 140 decibels (db). (For comparison, a pneumatic drill has a loudness level of 80 db, a boiler factory around 100 db, and loud thunder, around 120 db. A level of 140 db can induce severe pain.) In control rooms the noise levels were around 88 db; in the ready room the level reached 109 db; inside the test cell one jet engine at idle speed reached 119 db. The maintenance of jet aircraft just prior to flight reached 140 db. In this study no subjects were exposed to these painful levels at 140 db. The subjects were aware, however, that even medium-range intensities could be a hazard to health.

The problem was simply to determine whether a high degree of morale can be maintained around intense noise, and if so, why? Some previous work of Miles [32], made aboard an aircraft carrier, had shown that maintenance and other personnel engaged in servicing and operating jet planes are efficient in their work and willing to continue in their jobs, even without using earplugs.

The Air Force study was planned so that 100 jet-engine testers could be studied and compared with 100 welders and grinders. The two groups worked under different environmental conditions. The engine testers worked as a team under bad physical conditions. The welders and grinders worked in isolation under less severe physical conditions. The groups were matched for age, race, sex, pay status, and length of service. The experimental design of the study included personal interviews, environmental-noise measurements, psychological tests, sociometric investigations, reviews of absence due to illness, injury experience, and frequency of visits to the industrial medical dispensaries on the base.

The noise to which the experimental engine-tester group was exposed reached a maximum of 119 db. The control group (the welders and grinders) worked in an area with the much less intense noise of 76 db, about the average of factory noise. The skill requirements of the workers were classified as repetitive, average, and diversified, and the "social geography" of the jobs was identified. About three-fourths of the workers had received only a high school education, most of them were born in the state, and they were in the middle-age range.

In the personal interviews the workers were encouraged to talk about their social contacts and their attitudes toward each other, as well as about their jobs. Sociograms were developed which described a knowledge of the group structure, the leaders and dominant figures, the integration and cleavages, the clique formations, the amount of social interaction, and the hierarchic status of each member.

The experimental group (engine testers), because of the very nature of its jobs, was highly integrated; cohesiveness among the members was intense. There was just no place for isolates on the test teams. The job requirements were diversified. On the other hand, the welders and grinders operated alone. They worked in booths, behind protective eyewear, and completed a work assignment on a single engine part. To them, their work seemed unrelated to the engine as a whole. Their jobs, although requiring some skill, were quite repetitive.

The results of the study showed *very high morale* among the engine testers, although these workers were exposed to levels of noise not far below the threshold of pain. The welders and grinders were found to have *low morale,* although their noise-environment level was no more than that of the average factory. Why the difference in morale?

Among the engine testers there was common motivation: the group goals were to turn out good engines which could be sold to the inspector. "Selling an engine" meant protecting a pilot's life, building a stronger Air Force, and making a better country. Leaving the men to work out the details of procedure, supervisors gave the assignments to the workers in groups, but stood by to offer help when needed. Since these workers felt an overall satisfaction at accomplishing something worthwhile, they complained very little about the unpleasant features of the work situation. There was little or no complaint about the exposure to noise and outside temperatures or about the job being greasy and the area slippery. Little was said about the ever-present vibrations, the threat of engine explosions, and the potential danger of hearing loss. Complaints stemmed not from the work per se or from the physical environment. They came from such things as favoritism, inequities in giving raises, ratings, overtime, loan-outs, and demotions.

In short, these engine testers had to work together. Cooperation was basic to getting the job done. The purpose of their job was clear to them; the work itself was tangible, concrete, and easily grasped.

The welders and grinders were physically separated; the work was individual and repetitive and required no cooperative effort in any way. Many of the workers were found to be isolates or near isolates. Their morale was found to be low. Complaints from these men were numerous and centered around their isolation, their being dealt with arbitrarily, or their being discriminated against. They described their work as strenuous, unhealthful, nerve-racking, and fatiguing. They expressed deep feelings of job insecurity. For the most part the sociogram of these people demonstrated a sparseness of friendship choices, tenuous connections. The grinders in particular expressed no satisfaction in their jobs. There was no ego involvement or identification with the work. Although the physical hazards involved in the grinding work were of less potential danger than those involved in engine testing, the dangers here were mentioned more frequently. There were many complaints about dust, flying steel particles, impaired illumination, eyestrain, and standing; and believe it or not, these workers complained far more about noise than did the more cohesive group of engine testers.

Although most of the welders and grinders were highly dissatisfied with their jobs, a small minority were found to have a high morale. These were a group of nine welders who were found to belong to an informal clique. Although their jobs were separated, they got together at lunch and at other times. There was no common goal for these men such as that which existed among the well-integrated engine-testers group. Their clique had a clear status hierarchy dominated by a few individuals; nevertheless, the members of this group complained far less than did their nonclique counterparts.

The Perception of Working Conditions. Several important conclusions can be drawn from these studies for our understanding of industrial morale. First of all, the results substantiated some earlier work that such factors as noise, exposure to bad weather, slippery operational areas, and other undesirable physical working conditions *do not* determine morale per se. Morale results from the worker's *perception* of his working conditions and his job. How the job is perceived is a function of his ego involvement with it. Associated with ego involvement are a feeling of belonging, a sense of responsibility, and an opportunity to contribute knowingly to a worthwhile effort.

There is sometimes a wide gap between the workers' and the supervisor's perception of the work situation. Costello and Zalkind [11] make the point that literally hundreds of times during the day the administrator is perceived and his behavior interpreted by people around him. He, in turn, perceives others and interprets their behavior. The way an administrator is perceived as a leader can determine his acceptance. His own perception will, in part, determine what he does in a superior-subordinate relationship. Perceiving is more than just the input of information; it is the interpretation and feeling that goes along with this.

In making a comparison of supervisors' description of their behavior with employees' description of their experience, Likert [29] found considerable differences in answers to questions. *Asked of supervisors:* "How do you give recognition for good work done by employees in your work group?" *Asked of employees:* "How does your supervisor give recognition for good work done by employees in your work group?" The replies:

- "Give(s) privileges very often": 52 per cent of supervisors say they do this; 14 per cent of workers say they do.
- "Give(s) more responsibility": 48 per cent of supervisors say they do this; 10 per cent of workers say they do.
- "Give(s) a pat on the back": 82 per cent of supervisors say they do this; 13 per cent of workers say they do.

Other questions and answers were similar in pattern. The worker may well define a need as "something you ain't got."

FACTORS RELATED TO JOB ATTITUDES

Through worker selection and placement, adequate programs of training, and work situations favoring cohesiveness, workers' needs have a better chance to get fulfilled. When one feels that he is needed as a part of the organization, then his morale can be high in spite of the undesirable aspects of the physical environment.

But why, we may ask, do men work in the first place? One man may feel that something important needs to be done, that he is the man to do it. He needs no other motive to get the task completed. In the upper levels of the industrial hierarchy we may find economic forces pressuring an executive to work hard purely for financial reward. At another time he may work to avoid penalty for shirking. But generally he works, as do most people gainfully employed at any level, not for some special reward or for fear of penalty, but for a *combination of reasons*. We work for different reasons at different times, but in the main we are all after very much the same things in our work.

Near the beginning of this chapter we listed in Table 4 the specific aspects of the ten major job factors related to attitudes. Let us now consider each of these in a summary way as they contribute to understanding why people work. In terms of overall needs managers and workers differ little in kind, although they may differ greatly in degree and in the hierarchy in which they would place their needs at any given time. Let us present some average ranks as determined by Herzberg et al. [20]. It is possible, of course, that no single individual would rank these factors in the order in which they are presented. We also know that at any given time, for any given person, a certain factor may rank high. With changing circumstances this high factor may shift to a relatively low comparative position. For example, for a man who has just been married wages may be of primary importance. At some other time he might place wages low in his comparisons. For the upward-mobile manager opportunities for advancement may well take first place, even topping security. The man in the wet mines may place working conditions near the top. For most people benefits (hospitalization, holidays) may rank last by comparison because most people already have them in some form or other.

1 *Security.* This factor deals with the steadiness of employment; it is positive where the manager or worker feels he has a reasonable chance of working under conditions of company stability. The man with security feels that he is valued by the firm and that he has the abilities and the opportunity to keep his job. Security is a strong reason for liking a job and is generally mentioned first by both men and women as contributing to job satisfaction. The lower one gets in the occupational scale, the greater the importance attached to the security factor. The greater skill and responsibility demanded in higher-level jobs gives the employee more "salability" and hence creates a demand for his services both within his own company and in others.

Security is a job-attitudes factor which increases slightly in importance with an increase in age. There is evidence that security is less important to employees with more education. It seems to be equally important to employees regardless of their dependents, with the possible exception of the single man who is entirely on his own.

2 *Opportunity for advancement.* What are the chances of getting ahead? This factor ranks high in importance, particularly to the person striving for upward mobility. Opportunity for advancement is quite a different problem for persons at opposite ends of the socioeconomic scale. The professional man and the corporation executive have this factor primarily within their own individual control. To the man in middle management, however, the problem of opportunity is of greater concern, for his future is largely tied in with what happens to and within his company. To the worker, advancement is related to merit, to be sure, but seniority plays a big role where union contracts are in effect. The young, ambitious, good worker may find advancement held back because of seniority agreements.

The results of many attitude surveys show that the lack of opportunity for advancement is frequently a strong reason for disliking a job, but rarely is opportunity for advancement mentioned as a contributor to satisfaction. Men are much more expressive in giving importance to this factor than are women. There is some evidence that there is a decrease in the importance of the advancement factor with increasing age. Once a man has reached his "opportunity level" and becomes adjusted to his situation, other factors become more important to him, length of service in a stable company, for example. Intelligence and education are substantially related to the opportunity factor. As a matter of fact, one serious problem for the bright and ambitious college graduate is to realize that promotional opportunities are often slower in coming than he would like. Some studies show that college seniors select their jobs largely because they think they will have a good opportunity for advancement.

3 *Company and management.* What constitutes a good company and management? To one employee this may mean how well the company gets along with the union. Another man may rate the company on its sponsorship of athletic teams. Whether we are dealing with the size of the organization, reputation, earnings, or public relations, the employee believes that a good company is one which helps him feel some stability in his job. Like security, this job factor is seldom a strong reason for dissatisfaction, but it contributes substantially to the employee's satisfaction.

In terms of occupational level there is some evidence that the higher the skill level, the greater the satisfaction with the company. Older workers show a slightly greater concern for the rating and reputation of the company than young workers do. Perhaps their years of service to the company have made them a little more ego-involved with it.

4 *Wages.* When this factor is ranked with nine other job factors, employees give it fourth place. It is interesting that employers generally rank this factor near the top when they are asked what the employee wants. Although there is some indication that wages and opportunity for advancement are related through the element of money, employees consistently have rated wages as much less important than either opportunity for advancement or security.

Studies show that the factor of wages contributes more to the dissatisfaction than to the satisfaction of the worker. Rarely ever does a man express satisfaction with the amount of money he is making.

Wages are more important to men than to women workers and are generally more important to factory workers than to office workers. Herzberg and his colleagues conclude that there is a tendency for the importance of wages to drop as the employee grows older, at least until the age of forty. After forty, the employee attaches more importance to the factor of wages, whereas the factors of job, company, security, and so on seem to have become fairly well established.

5 *Intrinsic aspects of the job.* There are many reasons why people like their job simply for the sake of the job. One man may like what he is doing because he has just the right ability and training for it. Another may like his job per se because it brings him recognition; a third person may like his job because it is easy, gives him an opportunity to travel, or is free of tension and pressure. Whatever the reason, what the man does at his particular job contributes to both satisfaction and dissatisfaction.

There is an important relationship between a person's skill and education and the requirements of a job. It has been found, for example, that a reduction in the skill requirements of a job increases the dissatisfaction of the more skilled worker, whereas it would not affect the less skilled worker. The higher the occupational and skill level of the person and the higher his education, the more important the challenge of his job becomes. Most people in executive or supervisory positions say they like their job because intrinsically it challenges and stimulates them. One difficult thing for successful leaders to realize is that employees in lower-status jobs often do not like jobs with challenge. For them there must be other things involved if the job is to lead to satisfaction.

6 *Supervision.* To the worker, his supervisor is both a father figure and an irritating boss who is an equally strong contributor to both satisfaction and dissatisfaction. Women seem more sensitive to supervision than do men, but for both bad supervision can be a primary reason for absenteeism and labor turnover.

Supervision seems less important at the high levels in spite of the fact that people in high positions have a greater tendency to verbalize the things that are wrong with their particular supervisory structure. College graduates voice criticism of their supervisors more than less educated people. They are particularly critical at times of the supervisor's ability to handle people. There is some evidence that married workers with dependents are more conscious of the problem of good supervision than are single men. One could interpret this as meaning that the man with family responsibilities feels more necessity for supervisory approval. And, of course, we cannot overlook the fact that the supervisor, in playing his many roles with the worker, is a focal point for attitude formation.

7 *Social aspects of the job.* This is one of the most difficult of the job-attitudes factors to describe. It involves such needs as belonging and social approval. This factor contributes to both satisfaction and dissatisfaction of the employee. A man who feels himself a member of a productive, cohesive group is happier with his job than is someone who finds himself a misfit. The social factor appears only slightly more important to women than to men; it is relatively independent of age and occupational level.

8 *Communication.* An old military expression which says that "there is always someone who does not get the word" is expressive but hardly a complete definition of the factor of communication. The lack of good communication may be a reason for disliking a job, but it is never a specific reason for liking a job. What, then, is really meant by communication? To be sure, it means the formalities of conveying information, giving orders, turning out annual reports. But to the employee it also means being listened to, receiving recognition, and "knowing why." Good communication, as far as feelings go, means the opposite of being ignored. The factor of communication seems to be more important at the higher educational levels.

First-line supervisors list the lack of good communication as one of their chief annoyances. Perhaps this is because they feel that they are "told" by higher management rather than "conferred with." In one company an attitude survey was made among 120 foremen. When asked to describe their biggest problem, most of these supervisors listed communication. In a few months these men were brought together to discuss company policies and problems. After a one-day session they returned to their jobs. One year later when they were asked to identify problems, communication was far down the list. A follow-up study showed that merely being brought together and asked for views on company problems had made the men feel that communication was now good. Recognition that he is a part of management may well be what the supervisor wants when he asks for improved communication.

9 *Working conditions.* Temperature, lighting, ventilation, parking facilities, cafeteria, toilets, and the like are always a place affording criticism when the employee wishes to let off steam. Actually this factor has been found to make an equally low contribution to both satisfaction and dissatisfaction. Working conditions are substantially more important to women than to men, as we shall point out later in the chapter entitled "Women in Industry." Hours are more important to men than any other specific aspect of working conditions; but among women, especially married women, this aspect has even more significance. To the more educated and higher-level employee, hours are almost negligible in importance. Few, if any, executives work the limited hours of the union man! To workers in hazardous jobs, safety conditions are most important; but when they are ranked with nine other job factors, working conditions come in next to last.

10 *Benefits.* Retirement provisions, hospitalization, leaves, vacations, and holidays are now a fairly standard part of most jobs; there is greater uniformity throughout industry in this factor than in any of the other major factors. This factor has not been mentioned as a real contributor either to satisfaction or to dissatisfaction in the many studies of job attitudes. It is interesting to note, however, how much attention is paid by union representatives to fringe benefits at the time of contract negotiations.

The student giving serious consideration to his or her career may find the ten factors described above useful in helping him to establish an individual need hierarchy. He will no doubt find that he wants all these factors in the job that he chooses, but he will want them in different degrees. As time goes on he will find his attitudes shifting, but it is important that he have a base of understanding from which to operate in making decisions about his life's work.

SUGGESTIONS FOR SELECTIVE READING

Atkinson, J. W. (Ed.) *Motives in fantasy, action, and society.* Princeton, N.J.: Van Nostrand, 1958. Only indirectly related to industry.

Berelson, B., & Steiner, G. A. *Human behavior: An inventory of scientific findings.* New York: Harcourt, Brace & World, 1964. A useful reference of generalizations about behavior, organizations, and publics.

Edwards, A. L. *Techniques of attitude scale construction.* New York: Appleton-Century-Crofts, 1957. For the sophisticated reader.

Festinger, L. *A theory of cognitive dissonance.* New York: Harper & Row, 1957. For the sophisticated reader.

Fiedler, F. E. *Leader attitudes and group effectiveness.* Urbana, Ill.: University of Illinois Press, 1958. Research bases for morale.

Goldstein, M. J., & Palmer, J. O. *The experience of anxiety.* Fair Lawn, N.J.: Oxford University Press, 1964. A casebook.

Hersey, R. *The myth of the inscrutable Oriental.* Ocean City, N.J.: Social Science Press, 1965. Comparative attitudes of Asian, German, and American workers toward management.

Herzberg, F., et al. *The motivation to work.* New York: Wiley, 1959. Utilizing research on job attitudes, includes some higher-level executives.

Jones, M. R. *Nebraska symposium on motivation.* Lincoln, Nebr.: University of Nebraska Press, 1965. Some research problems and theories of motivation for the sophisticated reader.

Kaplan, M. *Leisure in America: A social inquiry.* New York: Wiley, 1960. An analysis of the sociology of leisure.

Krech, D., et al. *Individual in society.* New York: McGraw-Hill, 1962. A text treatment of social attitudes, groups, and organizations.

Levinson, H., et al. *Men, management, and mental health.* Cambridge, Mass.: Harvard, 1962. Observations and interviews of 874 employees at all levels by a Menninger Foundation team.

Lifton, W. M. *Working with groups.* New York: Wiley, 1961. Techniques in small-group processes.

Lipset, S. M., & Lowenthal, L. (Eds.) *Culture and social character.* New York: Free Press, 1961. Some questions on the fate of human individuality in a mass society.

Maier, N. R. F. *Creative management.* New York: Wiley, 1962. Conflict between man and the organization.

Munn, H. L. *Partners in production.* Englewood Cliffs, N.J.: Prentice-Hall, 1961. An industrialist writes about interpersonal and group relations.

Remitz, U. *Professional satisfaction among Swedish bank employees.* Copenhagen: Munksquard, 1960. A study of the attitudes of 1,200 bank employees.

Sherif, Carolyn W., et al. *Attitude and attitude change: The social judgment–involvement approach.* Philadelphia: Saunders, 1965. A reference work; only indirectly related to industry.

Zauders, A. F. (Ed.) *Performance appraisals: Effects on employees and their performance.* Ann Arbor, Mich.: Foundation for Research on Human Behavior, 1963. Improving work planning and performance review.

Zweig, F. *The worker in an affluent society.* New York: Free Press, 1962. Aspirations of the British working classes.

IV.

MEN AND MACHINES

11

Work and Conditions of Work

Harry W. Karn

In previous chapters the industrial scene has been examined in terms of the supervisory and management activities related to production goals, the nature of the organizational environment in which these activities occur, and some of the ways people react within the organizational structure. We have been looking at men behaving in an environment that calls for work. Let us now take a closer look at the behavior called work. What is its nature? Does it change over time? If changes occur which result in reduced output, can we do anything to prevent the decrement? Questions and issues of this nature we shall consider in this chapter.

Work, in essence, is the use of a person's physiological and mental processes in attainment of some goal. The goal may be a managerial decision, the sale of an insurance policy, the erection of a stone wall, or the production of a steel ingot. This definition of work is broad, and it is sometimes criticized because of its generality. For example, may we not define play in the same way? Does not the tennis player use his physiological and mental processes in an attempt to attain the goal of winning the game? Indeed he does. But the point to remember is that even though work and play may seem to be extremes of a continuum, the distinction rests primarily upon motivation rather than on any fundamental differences between performance determinants. What is play to some people may be work to others. The basic principles describing and explaining both work and play are the same.

COMMON CHARACTERISTICS OF WORK

As a basis for discussion it will be helpful to examine work performance pictorially in terms of its basic concepts. Suppose we enter a factory or office or a department store for the purpose of studying the output of the workers. By obtaining measures of production and plotting them against time, we come up with a work curve which looks something like the hypothetical curve shown in Figure 11.1.

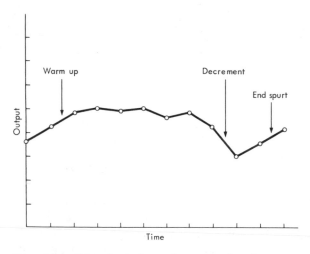

Fig. 11.1. Hypothetical work curve showing common characteristics.

The work curve shows that before peak productivity is reached there is an initial warming-up period. Eventually there is a decrement or falling off in production, but often, in anticipation of the end of the workday, there is an end spurt.

A word of caution about work curves is in order. There are variations in the curves from day to day for the same worker and also variations among workers. Also the different kinds of work—heavy muscular work, light tasks, or work of a clerical nature—do not yield identical curves. The representative curve shown above is the best single description and will serve as a point of departure for our discussion about the causes of change in work activity and what can be done to improve productive efficiency.

REST PAUSES AND WORKER EFFICIENCY

The major characteristic of the work curve that is most disturbing to the industrialist who must keep his business in the black is decrement, or diminishing production. What can be done to prevent this decrement is the critical question. Let us see if an answer lies in the way the work is distributed over time.

Numerous studies in the laboratory and in industry have shown that distributing work through the introduction of rest pauses results in increased output. In a typical laboratory study, subjects lifted weights until they were exhausted. After a five-minute rest they could lift the weights with about 80 per cent of their previous ability. They returned to 95 per cent of their best output after a rest of twenty minutes. In industry the beneficial effects of rest periods on production have long been noted. A historic study conducted by the National Institute of Industrial Psychology in Great Britain in the 1920s is significant because it shows how a work curve may be altered by introducing rest periods. Before the introduction of the rest pause, the work curve, averaged from a number of workers and depicting output for each half hour during the day, rose until 9:30 A.M., remained at the same level until 11 A.M., fell off sharply until noon, then climbed slowly until 12:30, and from 12:30 to 1 P.M. fell off slightly. An hour's lunch break began at 1 P.M. After a rest pause of seven minutes had been introduced at 11 A.M., the work curve throughout the morning was generally at a higher level, the decrement after 11 A.M. being markedly diminished and periodic fluctuations giving way to more uniform output throughout the morning. In the afternoon, when no rest pause was interpolated at 4 P.M., the work curve fell sharply from 4 to 4:30, but after the introduction of a seven-minute rest period at 4 P.M., the work done during the remaining twenty-three minutes of the half hour exceeded that done in the same half hour when no rest pause was interpolated [55]. Many recent human-factors studies have shown the same phenomena as this earlier investigation, and no doubt some readers have experienced something similar in their own work efforts.

Work supervisors sometimes argue that most employees take unauthorized rests when there are no regularly scheduled rest periods. Are there any advantages of authorized rest periods over periods of unauthorized rest? A study of a group of comptometer operators in a government office provides one answer to this question [32]. The operators were observed without their knowledge for a two-week period during which a record was kept of the number and length of their unauthorized rests. Later a rest schedule was formally introduced, consisting of an eight-minute pause in the morning and a seven-minute pause in the afternoon. Because of government regulations, the workday was lengthened by fifteen minutes to make up for the time spent in the regularly scheduled rest periods. Total working time thus remained unchanged. The changed system resulted in a significant decrease in the time spent in unauthorized rest and a 35 per cent increase in work completed.

One reason for the advantage of authorized over unauthorized rest periods is probably better placement of the rest interval during the work period. The best way to determine how rest periods should be scheduled is to plot production records throughout the work period and note drops in production. Consider, for example, the production curves shown in Figure 11.2. Since production is beginning to fall off at point A, this is the logical

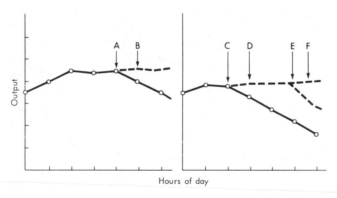

Fig. 11.2. Location of rest pauses.

place to introduce a rest pause. The pause may be introduced at point B if the worker knows when it is coming, because the anticipatory effect is sufficient to keep him going during the interim. The dotted line in the figure shows the effect on production of introducing the rest period. In the afternoon, the pause is introduced at C or D and again at E or F if production falls during the late afternoon.

How can we account for the beneficial effects of rest pauses on production? A number of plausible reasons come to mind, the most obvious being that rest provides the opportunity to recover from fatigue. The physiologist has demonstrated that work causes an accumulation of waste products within the organism which reduce work capacity. Rest provides a period during which the waste products are dissipated and bodily capacity restored. In heavy muscular work, physiological fatigue is unquestionably a major factor contributing to work decrement.

When work does not involve the expenditure of a great deal of physical energy, the beneficial effect of rest periods may be due to relief from a task that engenders in the worker feelings of boredom. The worker is not physically tired—he is irritated, lacks interest, is fed up with his job. He wants a change, a break from what seems to be interminable activity. Rest pauses provide an opportunity to talk and think about nonjob activities. When the worker returns to his job, he is psychologically refreshed, so to speak, and this is reflected in increased output.

The effectiveness of introducing rest pauses may be due to still another factor—a change in attitude toward the company, including, of course, the work supervisor. A worker with a favorable attitude toward his supervisor is much less likely to soldier on the job than the worker who dislikes his boss. The introduction of rest periods may be tangible evidence that management has an interest in the welfare of the worker, and he may respond with more efficient output. On the other hand, the worker may feel differently if the coffee break, for example, is gained through union negotiations. Like other authorized rest periods, the coffee break may lead to abuse, not only in extra time taken out but in psychological time lost in getting back in the full swing of work. It is a loss somewhat related to the unproductive minutes before quitting time. One insurance company, after a study in its nationwide offices, defined the time from 4 to 5 P.M. as "the most expensive hour in America."

REPETITIVE WORK

The introduction of rest periods is not the only way to alter the shape of the work curve in the direction of increased output. The nature of the job itself has a lot to do with how long a person can maintain a high rate of production. We "stay with" interesting jobs a lot longer than with uninteresting jobs, and repetitive jobs appear to be the least interesting. We reflect this lack of interest when we say that the job is boring. Actually the job itself is not boring. Boredom is the worker's reaction to the job. More specifically, boredom arises from a conflict between the necessity for doing a dull job and wanting to turn to more interesting activities.

Attention requirements have much to do with the degree of boredom engendered by repetitive tasks. A highly repetitive job to which the worker becomes habituated elicits relatively little boredom in some workers if they do not have to pay close attention to what they are doing. If the worker can do the job "without thinking," he is free to talk to his fellow workers about yesterday's football game or next month's vacation. Or, if conversation is impossible, he can daydream. Boredom will be pronounced on a repetitive job like an assembly-line operation where the continuous work flow and the task requirements occur over and over again but permit few lapses or shifts in attention. Boredom is not a problem in a complex and varied task which because of its intrinsic nature tends to hold attention.

METHODS OF ELIMINATING BOREDOM

The problem of eliminating the effects of boredom is acute in present-day industry, since there are many repetitive tasks resulting from the fractioning of work into smaller and simpler units. An obvious but naïve answer to the question of how to eliminate boredom is to do away with tasks of a repetitive nature. This is not only impractical but to a considerable extent unnecessary.

A promising lead on how to reduce boredom comes from the finding that repetitive tasks do not give rise to the same degree of boredom in all persons. For example, in an investigation of women sewing-machine operators, those reporting the strongest feelings of boredom disliked routine activity, more often preferred active leisure activities, and indicated lack of satisfaction with their home and personal life. Operators who were least susceptible to boredom were placid and generally contented with the existing state of affairs. Another study of women performing repetitive work in a chemical factory showed that those experiencing the most boredom tended to be more extroverted than introverted, desired opportunities to use their own ideas, and attached great importance to promotions. There is also evidence that persons of low normal intelligence are less bored by repetitive work than persons of higher intelligence. Additional study of the personality characteristics associated with feelings of boredom are necessary, but the available evidence indicates that production decrement resulting from boredom can be reduced by selecting people who will not be bored with the jobs to which they are assigned [53, 54, 55].

Although rest periods tend to reduce the deleterious effects on production resulting from boredom, the effect is not due as much to a need for rest as it is to a need for change. The bored worker is satiated with doing the same old thing. Rest periods provide an opportunity for change, of course, but boredom can frequently be relieved by giving the worker another kind of job. Variety is the spice which makes work interesting, and the interested worker is never bored. Maier reports a practical application of the principle of variation concerned with two types of maintenance jobs, dusters and solderers [34]. The workers complained of overwork and were apparently bored with the tediousness of their routine tasks. They were eventually given the opportunity to exchange jobs, and all of them accepted. Half the workers dusted and half soldered, but every two hours they exchanged jobs. Feelings of boredom were reduced, and, significantly, the dusters now dusted as much on a half-time basis as they had previously on full time.

Exchanging jobs is not a general cure-all for boredom. The effectiveness of the practice depends at least in part on the amount of similarity between the jobs and the frequency with which the exchanges are made. If two jobs are perceived as highly similar, changing from one to the other will do little good. On the other hand, if they are so highly dissimilar that great versatility in skill is required, boredom may be reduced but at a great loss in efficiency. Where there is a moderate degree of similarity which allows the use of the same skills but the experience of doing something different, the beneficial effects will be maximized. Even in this situation confusion in operations can ensue if the jobs are alternated too often.

The bored worker frequently says that he has the feeling of not making any progress. He perceives his work as endless and unmeaningful. Routine inspection of the same kind of machine parts as they come off a conveyor will not likely engender feelings of progress in the inspector. One part is like another, and there are thousands of them. These feelings can sometimes be reduced by the foreman or supervisor who takes time to point out to the worker the relation of his routine or part work to the total job picture. He might explain why, for example, certain tolerances must not be exceeded. Or he might ask for suggestions on the improvement of methods of inspection, or discuss waste costs resulting from the rejection of parts. Giving the worker responsibilities and opportunities for judgment makes his work more meaningful and hence reduces the feelings of boredom which occur when he is looked upon as a robot who is told to do a job and ask no questions. In some situations a technique used to help correct boredom is "batching". No new work is given to the employee until he completes the batch he is working on.

What will *more* leisure do to people? Boredom, even fatigue, may increase with shorter work hours. Many workers are even now taking on second jobs, and for reasons in addition to bringing in more income. Such moonlighting is one way to deal with the problem of additional leisure time, for some perhaps a better way than developing new and more expensive tastes. Boredom is affected not only by individual personality but by job perception and even by mood. On the job, in addition to job rotation and job enlargement, introducing subgoals that allow for task completion sometimes may help to lessen boredom.

In one individual low threshold for boredom may be offset by a low threshold for stimulation; in another, it may be accompanied by a high threshold for stimulation. In the second instance, boredom may become a serious psychological problem for the individual.

LENGTH OF WORK PERIOD—SOME PROBLEMS

In the preceding discussion we have seen that the introduction of rest periods at appropriate times can prevent, to some degree at least, a decrement in production during the working day. We have also examined the adverse effects on production of placing the worker on what he perceives to be a monotonous or boring task. But we have also observed that the problem of preventing work decrement in the repetitive task situation is not a hopeless one. While on the topic of factors which influence output, we should also examine the effect of lengthening or shortening the workday and workweek. Is it a simple problem? No. The subject is particularly pertinent because of the current trend in American industry to shorten the length of the workday and workweek. Do we get more efficient work when hours of work are reduced? Let us examine a few facts which bear on this question. We must turn to old data for comparisons.

One of the earliest studies on the relation between output and length of the work period was conducted by Vernon during World War I [51]. This study showed an increase in hourly output of about 20 per cent in a munitions factory where the workweek was shortened from 58.2 hours to 51.2 hours. A further reduction in the workweek to 50.4 hours brought with it another increase of 17 per cent in hourly output. Viteles [52] reports a study conducted during the Depression of the thirties in the textile industry showing that a reduction from fifty-four hours to forty hours in the workweek resulted in an hourly-output increase sufficient to bring the total weekly output slightly above the level of the fifty-four-hour week. Was fear of job loss involved? Was better equipment a factor? Or what?

Some observers are now of the opinion that output is usually increased if the number of working hours per week does not go much beyond forty. Indeed a survey of over three thousand workers in thirty-four industrial plants in the United States after World War II showed maximal efficiency with an eight-hour day and a forty-hour week [27]. But what will the thirty-hour week show? Some day we may know. Factors enter the understanding of work that go beyond mere physical effort. Studies show, for example, that the modern bricklayer can lay 2,000 bricks per day without undue strain, but at the present time 300 is the maximum allowed by most union contracts. The complexity of such problems is amplified when we look at an old one—time-and-motion study in all of its ramifications.

TIME–AND–MOTION STUDY

One obvious way to maintain production or increase it is to see that the worker is using the best possible method for doing a given job. A worker may get a job done, and the end product of his efforts may be satisfactory. But what about the nature of the various operations performed in getting the job done? Did he waste a lot of time and energy performing unnecessary movements or standing around waiting for a machine to finish an operation? Are the activities of several men working on a job distributed properly? Men left to their own devices on a job seldom consider these questions, with the result that their true job efficiency is never maximized. For example, an analysis of an inspection job revealed that when left to their own devices, most inspectors put their attention on the wrong aspect of the operation. The inspectors' job was to examine a pile of tin plates for defects and to remove any imperfect plates from the pile. They examined each plate as they turned it. Thus as the first plate was being turned, the side coming up was examined, and after the plate was turned, the side going down was examined; then the second plate was picked up, and both of its sides were examined, the one side while it was coming up and the other side while it was going down. Inaccuracies occurred because the inspector was always looking at moving surfaces. A new method was developed in which the inspector ignored the moving plate and examined the one at rest (see Figure 11.3). The new method cut down inspection errors considerably. This illustration shows the importance of investigating the best way to do a job. The general name given to the process of finding better methods for doing a given job is time-and-motion analysis, or study.

In time-and-motion study occupational movements are broken down in order to determine the fewest and simplest movements necessary to do the job and the time required for each movement. The motion picture is now standard equipment in time-and-motion-analysis. Through an examination of the films showing precisely what is done by each of the operator's hands and the time spent on each operation, the analyst rearranges some movements, eliminates others, and comes up with the fastest and least wasteful work pattern.

Time-and-motion analysts are guided by a body of rules and principles which are treated in detail in standard works on the subject. Some examples of the major time-and-motion principles are:

1 Minimize the number of motions by eliminating unnecessary movements.

2 Minimize the length of motions by reducing reaching distances to tools, supplies, and machine operations.

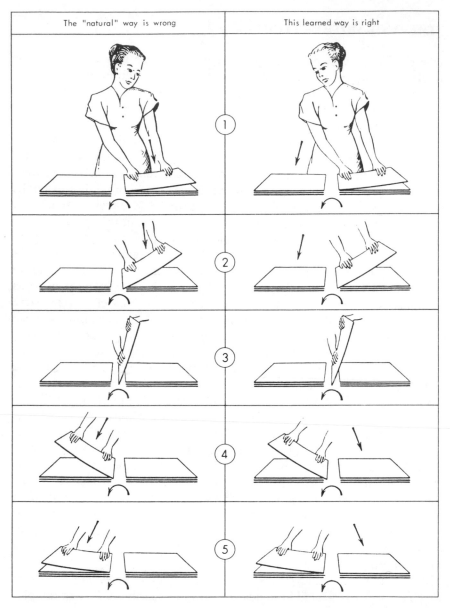

Fig. 11.3. Analysis of two methods of inspecting tin plates. The semicircular arrows show the way in which the sheets are turned over from inspector's left to her right. The straight arrows show where the inspector directs her eyes. (Adapted by permission of the publisher from Joseph Tiffin. *Industrial psychology.* New York: Prentice-Hall, 1952.)

3 Provide for continuous-curved motions instead of ziggy or straight-line motions involving sharp changes in directions.

4 Arrange work to permit an easy and natural rhythm wherever possible.

5 Distribute action among the used members of the body in accordance with the inherent capacities of members.

At first glance time-and-motion analysis appears to be a good technique for maximizing efficiency. Certainly there is considerable merit to the general argument that production is at least to some extent a function of the way the job is done. Even in such a simple physical task as lifting a heavy steel bar, there is a right way and a wrong way. The worker with lifting know-how can lift all day. The worker who does not know how to lift tires quickly and may even injure himself. In more complex manual tasks and also in mental tasks there are poor, better, and best ways of performing jobs. Yet despite the apparently sound case that one can establish for time-and-motion analysis, it has been subject to numerous adverse criticisms as a technique for maximizing production.

One weakness of the technique as generally practiced is the worker's misunderstanding and suspicion of it. The time-and-motion analyst is usually perceived as an outsider who is trying to put something over on the worker. "The trouble with this place is that there are too many efficiency experts," is a common complaint of many workers. Employees fear that the efficiency expert is mainly interested in speeding up production and that if this happens, there will be a drop in rate of pay and probably a dismissal of some workers. With this attitude prevalent in the worker, time-and-motion analysis is not likely to result in improved production.

Another criticism of time-and-motion study, with its objective of discovering the best way to do a job, is the questionable criteria used to determine the best way. Traditionally, time-and-motion analysts have assumed that there is one best way for performing each job. But astute observers of worker performance have learned that what may be the best way for John Doe is not the best way for Bill Smith. Physical and psychological differences among workers must be recognized. For example, there is evidence to show that older workers with declining perceptual and motor skills modify their work methods to compensate for their deficiencies, so that the best way for them is different in many respects from the best way for a younger worker.

Still another criticism of time-and-motion analysis has to do with the validity of the rules and principles that are followed by the analyst. One guiding principle states that "hand motions should be confined to the lowest classification with which it is possible to perform the work satisfactorily." The fingers are the lowest classification, followed by the wrist, forearm, and upper arm. Generally speaking, lower classification requires less time and effort than higher classification. But there are exceptions. Controlled research has shown that in certain kinds of activity wrist motion can be made with less fatigue and more speed than finger motions. There are other studies which point to a need for further research on the rules and principles to be used in time-and-motion study [30].

Despite the criticisms of time-and-motion study, the basic idea of maximizing output through the use of efficient work methods is sound. The opposition to time-and-motion study does not constitute an argument against it but rather is an argument against the way it has been used. When individual differences are recognized and methods developed through careful and complete observation, time-and-motion study can contribute greatly to efficient production. Acceptance of the analyst by the worker can be gained if the time-study department works with time-study stewards selected by union membership and if the worker can make contributions as his own job analyst. This kind of cooperation dispels some of the worker's fear that the time-and-motion analyst is a company man set to get more work for less pay.

THE WORKING ENVIRONMENT

So far, our discussion of how to prevent decrement in the work curve has been focused on conditions or factors that are related to the job itself— how the job should be done, how much time should be spent on the job, and the problems arising when men are put on repetitive jobs. We are now ready to tackle the problem of whether work output can be influenced through alterations in the general work environment. We assume that almost everybody prefers pleasant to unpleasant surroundings. But are we justified in assuming that because the surroundings are pleasant, production will be changed? In the ensuing discussion we shall attempt to answer this question by surveying some of the studies that have been carried out on the effects of noise, illumination, temperature, ventilation, music, and related conditions on work output.

Noise. Noise is usually regarded as a distracter and therefore as interfering with work efficiency. "I can't do my job properly around this place because it's too noisy," is a common worker's complaint. Actually, clear-cut evidence that noise reduces work output is very scant. We do know, of course, that many people find different kinds of auditory stimulation irritating. Thus high tones and very low tones are judged almost universally to be more annoying or irritating than tones in the middle ranges. Unexpected noises, intermittent noises, and reverberating noises are also irritating to most people. Such knowledge as this has made it possible to sound-treat work areas in order to reduce the irritating effects of noise.

An interesting study of the effects of noise in a work situation has been conducted in England in a film-processing plant [10]. Different measures of efficiency were made in untreated workplaces and in the same places after the noise level was measurably reduced by acoustical treatment. The results of this study showed that rate of work was not improved by noise reduction but that error was significantly less frequent when the noise level was less.

Another study had to do with the output of weavers over a period of twenty-six weeks during which the workers wore ear defenders on alternate weeks. The protective devices reduced the noise from 96 to 87 decibels. There was an increase of 12 per cent in speed of production while they were wearing the ear defenders.

In view of the universal dislike of noise it seems probable that deleterious effects exist, but much additional research must be conducted before definite conclusions can be drawn regarding the effects of noise on work output in different jobs [38].

Music. Within recent years, the practice of introducing music in the workplace has become common. Music is alleged to have salutary effects on attitudes, to improve morale, and to increase production. Some of these claims have been subjected to experimental inquiry which we reviewed in Chapter 10. In two investigations significant increases in production were associated with the use of music. In both of these studies the workers performed relatively simple tasks, so before it can be assumed that all productive effort will be enhanced by music, the effects of music on different kinds of tasks must be determined [26, 46].

In one study of the effects of music on a complex industrial task, attitudes were revealed as important. This investigation was conducted in a rug-manufacturing factory and dealt with a task known as setting. Setting is a relatively complex job involving the preparation of material for rug looms. The work requires a high level of mental and manipulative skill and considerable physical endurance. Music was found to have no favorable or unfavorable effects upon the production of workers in the setting operations. Despite these findings, questionnaire results showed that the workers were favorably disposed toward music and, perhaps more significantly, that they believed that it increased their actual production [31].

It is not entirely clear why simple task performance is sometimes improved by music and complex task behavior is not. One possibility is that the workers in the setting operation, being highly skilled and experienced, had developed stable habits of production and adequate adjustments to the work environment and that music effects were not sufficiently strong to break these well-established habit patterns.

Illumination. Despite a voluminous literature on the effects of illumination on work efficiency, solidly established relationships are practically non-existent. Studies have been conducted in actual work situations, and in some cases changes in illumination appear to be related to output, but so many variables have been left uncontrolled that it is impossible to assess the effect of the illumination variable per se. There have been some well-controlled laboratory studies, but in these cases the tasks were often not of the kind that are performed in the industrial workshop. Where there does appear to be similarity between the laboratory tasks and workshop tasks, it is possible to make some educated guesses as to the probable effects of different illumination levels on industrial output. Tentatively, it has been concluded that the majority of industrial operations could be carried out with maximum efficiency in the neighborhood of 10 foot-candles. In exacting visual tasks like drafting and typesetting, as high as 40 foot-candles are required, and spectral qualities are often important [30].

The color dynamics of the workplace is often claimed to be an important determinant of work efficiency, but supporting evidence is conspicuously nonexistent. One of the few experiments related to the color problem is that dealing with the effects of colored illumination upon perceived temperature. This study was prompted by the almost universal tendency to speak of green and blue as "cool" colors and red and orange as "warm." The experimental question: Can a person's judgment of the temperature of the air around him be biased by the hue of his surroundings? Subjects performed a number of tasks illuminated by different spectral lights and were asked to indicate by a switch when the temperature rose to a point when they began to feel uncomfortably warm. The findings showed no change in the levels of heat they would tolerate as a function of the colors of illumination, but nevertheless they persisted in the conventional belief that blue and green are cool colors when asked to rank the colors they had experienced. It appears, therefore, that despite beliefs about color efficiency, any attempt to change the comfort of persons in a work environment through variations in colored illumination may be unsuccessful [7].

Atmospheric Effects. Every worker at one time or another has complained about the "heat" or the "cold" in terms which imply that his efficiency is being affected adversely by the temperature of the working environment. A determination of temperature effects on work efficiency would seemingly be an easy matter. The problem actually is complicated because almost always when atmospheric temperature varies, other conditions such as humidity do not remain constant. There are a few studies which enable us to pinpoint temperature effects uncontaminated by uncontrolled variables. These studies have been summarized by one investigator [5], and he concludes that the desirable temperatures for sedentary work in winter are from 68 to 73°F and for the same kind of work in summer, 75 to 80°; for moderately hard work in all seasons, the desirable temperature is 65°, for strenuous work, 60°. Humidity effects are considered negligible because in the range of temperatures investigated relative humidity is an unimportant variable.

The role of humidity has been demonstrated in a number of studies, so that there is a factual basis for the common expression that "it's not the heat, but the humidity" which causes discomfort. In one of these studies workers were exposed for one hour to different combinations of humidity and temperature. Temperatures as high as 140°F were judged to be tolerable when the humidity was only 10 per cent. On the other hand, when the humidity reached 80 per cent, a temperature of 110° was judged to be intolerable [30].

Besides temperature and humidity, air circulation is another atmospheric condition that is critical in a good work environment. An example is a study in which electric fans were operated on alternate days for a period of six summer weeks and the effects on a weaving operation were observed. For every hour of the working day, production with the fans stopped was less than when the fans were running. The beneficial effects of the fans were greater in the afternoon than in the morning, for the most part, although the third hour of the morning and the second hour of the afternoon showed the greatest production increases.

Altering atmospheric conditions in order to create a favorable working environment is nowadays frequently accomplished through the installation of air-conditioning systems. Indeed, these systems are now under such precise control that humidity, temperature, and air-circulation problems would appear to be amenable to ready solution. However, the problems are not as simple as they appear. The complicating factor is the worker's reaction or perception of the change brought about through the manipulation of physical variables. A case in point is the reaction of workers in a blackout factory built in Texas during World War II [15]. The building contained no windows or skylights but was conditioned to control temperature, humidity, and air circulation. Since the ceiling was 50 feet from the floor, most of the air vents were located near the top of the walls.

From the beginning employees complained about the bad air. It was too hot, too humid, and too close. A thorough check of the system was made, and it was found to be in excellent working order. Complaints persisted until it was recognized that the workers were rural people unaccustomed to industrial work and air conditioning. They felt cooped up in a windowless plant where they could not feel a breeze. Since the vents were too high for the workers to feel the moving air, they needed some visual indication of stirring air. When tissue streamers were fastened to the ventilators high on the walls, the workers could see that the air was moving, and the frequency of employee complaints soon became negligible.

FINANCIAL INCENTIVES AS APPLIED TO PEOPLE AT WORK

Our treatment of the conditions which in many instances enhance production has been largely confined to factors such as rest pauses, noise, work methods, illumination, and the like. Their beneficial effects may be attributed in most cases to the fact that they increase the worker's satisfaction. In one way or another, output is a function of reward. To the production-oriented businessman, our account so far would be conspicuous by the absence of any mention of financial reward as a means of increasing production. The fact that American industrial management has long relied upon extra pay and incentive plans to raise work output calls for an examination of this topic.

Some form of incentive wage is offered to about 60 per cent of all industrial workers in the United States. Let us take a look at the broad outlines of a fairly typical incentive system that has been in operation at the Procter & Gamble Company since 1928 [41]. Consider the case of Frank Handy on his job of sealing boxes of soap in the packing room. Frank's job requires him to put glue on the flaps of the boxes and push them into the sealing belt as they pass down the line. The job has been studied to find both the correct method of doing the work and the average time normally taken to do it. The standard time for this job has been set at thirty-six seconds, or 0.01 hour per box. The rate of 100 boxes an hour means 800 boxes per eight-hour day. However, since Frank can and does seal 125 boxes an hour, or a total of 1,000 boxes, he gets credit for two extra hours for which he receives a bonus of two hours' pay. So much for the overall picture. The kind of job study on which the system is based is worthy of more detailed treatment in view of what we shall say later about some of the shortcomings of incentive systems.

In an actual job study, an examination is made of the various ways or methods of performing the task; this is followed by the selection of the best method. This method is written out in terms of specific job elements, and the employees are trained in this correct method. Next, there is a determination of the average time it takes the employees to do the job. Thus as Frank Handy seals boxes, the job-study engineer records by stop watch the time for each element of the job. The worker's performance is considered in terms of how *smooth* his operations are, how *quickly* he seals the boxes, how *accurate* he is in applying the glue, and how *careful* he is in lining up the flaps. How well he *plans ahead* in filling the gluepot is also considered. Is Frank physically fit to do the lifting required? Is he the right height to reach the machine? All of these factors are critical in the job study.

After studying Frank's job performance, the engineer finds that Frank's skill and effort are above normal. Based on company skill and effort values, it is judged that 16 per cent more time should be added to make Frank's actual time equal to a fair normal time. This addition amounts to 7.2 minutes per 100 boxes.

In addition to the time required to do the work, an allowance is made in the standard for personal needs and tiring. A fatigue allowance is added to compensate the worker for the effects of getting tired when he maintains a consistent work pace throughout the day. By comparing Frank's job with typical fatigue allowances based on company experiences, the job-study engineer determines that this allowance should be 15 per cent of the normal time. This addition amounts to 7.8 minutes per 100 boxes.

When we add together the time for each step in the study of Frank's job, we get the final standard time that is allowed for doing the work:

	Minutes per 100 boxes	Hours per box
1 Frank's actual average time	45.0	0.0075
2 Allowances for skills and efforts	7.2	0.0012
3 Personal needs and fatigue	7.8	0.0013
Final standard time	60.0	0.0100

The analysis described above shows the extent to which a job can be objectified. It sets up a standard and provides the worker an opportunity to earn extra money. The company benefits by employing what seem to be the most efficient work methods. At first glance, some kind of incentive system would seem to be an ideal way to step up production and make more money for both employee and employer. Yet despite the apparent objectivity of an incentive system based on a job analysis, important judgment and value questions enter the picture, which give rise to a variety of problems. What is normal job production? What is a fair rate of pay for achieving it? What about employees displaced by production increases?

When an incentive system fails, the reasons are sometimes psychological. The announcement of an incentive plan based on a job study such as that exemplified in the case of Frank Handy may be reacted to with distrust. As was pointed out in our earlier discussion of time-and-motion study, the job analyst is often seen as a management man who sets arbitrary rates in order to compel the worker to produce more for the same amount of money. Many workers feel that the analyst will establish a standard production rate that is too tight. Hence even though a bonus is provided for exceeding the standard, the extra pay is not worth the effort. Or if the production rate is not too tight and many workers exceed it and thus make more money, the company will cut the rate. This suspiciousness may cause workers to hold back on production. In a nationwide poll of workers, nearly 75 per cent said that a worker should hold back on production because his piece rate would be cut if he worked to full capacity. From a psychological standpoint, it is interesting to note that workers also hold down output in order to protect the less skillful members of their work group. Apparently their loyalties to fellow workers outweigh the desire for financial gain [35].

An overall appraisal of incentive systems in general would be that sometimes they work well and probably just as frequently they do not. The details of the various incentive systems now in operation are probably of minor importance in determining their success. The important thing is how the worker perceives the system in relation to all of his needs, psychological and material. The value of incentive pay cannot be viewed in isolation. Work behavior cannot be manipulated solely by the manipulation of money. Financial rewards are part of a total picture. They are effective when other basic needs are also satisfied.

WORK AND PAY

Vroom in his book *Work and Motivation* [53], which pulls together a vast literature of theory and facts, emphasizes that there are both motivational and nonmotivational determinants of performance. There is an interaction between the ability of the person to do a task and his motivation to get it done. The effects on performance of a given increment in motivation are negligible for those low in ability and positive for those high in ability. Similarly, the relationship between ability and performance varies with the amount of motivation, being negligible for those low in motivation and positive for those high in motivation.

The level of performance of workers is related to the extent to which performance is instrumental in the attainment of higher wages, promotions, and acceptance by coworkers. Level of performance varies directly with the strength of the individuals' need for achievement, how they feel about their pay, the feedback they receive, and the opportunity to make decisions relative to their work. The interrelation between the personality of the worker and his work environment is most important.

In giving an overview of psychological research on pay, Haire et al. [22] assume that pay acts as an incentive to work, but beyond this is a big class of problems dealing with how pay is seen by the recipient and the questions of social comparison. "How does my pay look in comparison to his?" With whom do different groups compare their pay? What groups provide the standard? Below satisfaction, pay can be a dissatisfier, and above some satisfactory level it sometimes seems to add relatively little.

Workers and Pay. If a man is promoted for successful performance and he sees it (or others see it) as simply the result of a tight labor market in his specialty, what becomes of the spur? For many an employee (worker, manager, or scientist) there comes a time when he realizes that he is on a particular lifetime curve—a big-leaguer, a minor-leaguer, or an also-ran. How does he settle with his acceptance of a lesser curve of progression than he may earlier have hoped for? Adams and Rosenbaum [1] found that hourly workers who were made to feel overpaid displayed greater productivity than control subjects who earned the same pay but were made to feel fairly paid. Arrowood [4] conducted an experiment in which subjects paid by the hour worked under overpaid and equitably paid conditions and under public and private conditions. In the public condition, subjects turned in their completed work to the experimenter; in the private condition they mailed it in. Overpaid workers produced significantly more in both conditions. If workers perceive that they are overpaid and other means of reducing dissonance are not readily available to them, they will produce more than the control subjects paid the same wages; conversely, if they perceive their wages as underpayment, they will work less than the control subjects.

Subjects appear to reduce dissonance by increasing the quality of their work. Under some circumstances individuals behave so as to earn less at the cost of greater effort. This finding is contrary to an assumption sometimes held that workers behave so as to maximize their gains and minimize their effort.

Managers and Pay. What do managers think about their pay? Who is the most content with his pay? Andrews and Henry [3] found the comparison between oneself and one's subordinate of critical importance to pay satisfaction. For managers outside the company, pay comparisons seemed to play an important role. People with high expectations reported less satisfaction with their present pay: satisfaction with present pay tended to be inversely related to the amount of pay increase anticipated over the next five years. How the manager feels about his salary depends both on its absolute size and how it stacks up with other salaries. Middle-management people tend to compare their pay with those on a lower level, while members of lower management are more concerned with keeping up with their peers.

Lawler and Porter [29] found that higher-paid managers give less attention to pay and that there were no line-versus-staff differences in either importance attached to pay or satisfaction with pay. At a given management level, as pay increased, satisfaction with pay also increased. These investigators also found that for any given amount of pay, the higher the level of management, the less satisfaction with pay.

What a person does when he works is dependent in part on how important the outcome is. We have seen in the chapters on supervision and executive behavior how difficult it is to evaluate higher-level performance. It is known that surgeons who have done nothing more strenuous than cutting and tying small blood vessels have expended as much energy as welders or drill-press operators.

For the worker, pay and promotions hinge largely on ratings. How well can we do in this area of evaluation?

MEASURING WORKER PROFICIENCY

Now that we have examined most of the major ways and means for preventing work decrement and how people feel about pay, a word is in order concerning individual differences among workers in what they do. The work curve presented at the beginning of this chapter represents the performance of a typical worker. But we know that all workers do not react in an identical fashion. Despite changes in work conditions, there are always good workers, average workers, and those who are below average. Establishing an efficient work program calls for a determination of proficiency among individual workers. How is this accomplished?

On so-called "production jobs," proficiency is usually evaluated in quantitative terms. Quantity is often considered to be the only variable. If Frank produces 100 units per hour, he is viewed as being more proficient than John, who turns out 80 units per hour. But of course, in actual practice, most items vary in quality. Thus in measuring worker proficiency, it is necessary to set up a standard which requires that the product be of specifiable quality in order to be acceptable. If units produced are rejected because of qualitative deficiencies, then these must be considered waste and subtracted from the output measure. Plotting a work curve is meaningful only to the extent that units produced are based on a consideration of both qualitative and quantitative aspects of work performance.

When we come to the problem of measuring proficiency on nonproduction jobs, difficulties arise. Nonproduction jobs are those in which quality plays a predominant role. Quantitative measurement is usually impossible because, although quantity is present, it is in the form of a complex pattern that is not readily amenable to measurement. On nonproduction jobs proficiency is usually measured through the use of human judgment techniques, which, although subject to some degree of human error, have proved useful. Evaluating a worker's proficiency by some qualified second party familiar with the job is termed *merit rating*. There are a wide variety of merit-rating systems being used in industry, each with special features. Tiffin has analyzed the major rating systems which have been in use long enough to be discussed in terms of their practical value. Let us examine three of the most error-free systems [49].

One of the most widely used methods of employee rating is the *employee-comparison* system. In this plan, each employee working under a given supervisor is compared with every other employee. The workers are arranged in pairs. Periodically the supervisor checks the man in each pair who is better in overall performance. Tiffin reports that time and time again this method of rating has shown greater agreement between ratings of the same men by different supervisors than has any other method. The system, however, has limitations. It cannot be used for promotional purposes, counseling, employee improvement, transfer, or layoff, because it cannot show the reasons why a man was rated low. However, in layoffs it may be enough to identify the lowest in the group.

Another system of rating, the *forced-choice* method, requires considerable preliminary work in developing the scale. Pairs of statements about job performance must be found, both of which express equally favorable or unfavorable things about a man; but only one of the statements in each pair actually differentiates between the men known to differ in job performance. The statements are then printed on the rating form in groups of four. Two of the four statements are favorable (and equally favorable), and the remaining two are unfavorable (and equally unfavorable). The rater is asked to check two of the four statements—the one which most accurately describes and the one which least accurately describes the man being rated. The plan has not had widespread use in industry because of the preliminary work involved and the difficulty encountered in keeping scoring secret. It deserves greater consideration because it produces objective evaluations, yields a more nearly normal distribution than most rating methods, can be scored by machine, and yields ratings that are related to valid indices of good and poor performance.

An increasingly popular and useful method for evaluating proficiency is the *critical-incident* technique, in which there is a determination, through interviews of superiors, of those behaviors which workers exhibit or fail to exhibit that are critical to success or failure in a given job. Once such a list is compiled, supervisors are asked to watch for these behaviors during work performance. If a considerable number of good critical incidents are noted about a worker over a given period of time and few negative critical incidents have been observed, the man's rating will be high. Conversely, if most of the incidents observed are negative, his rating will be low. In this rating we are getting reports on actual behavior, not just opinions about behavior.

Although some system of merit rating must be resorted to in evaluating proficiency on nonproduction jobs, performance on production jobs should also be evaluated in terms of merit. Merit is a far more general aspect of proficiency than production in terms of items turned out per time unit. Merit includes a variety of characteristics which make a man a valuable employee, such as his attitude toward other employees and the supervisor, observance of safety regulations, assumption of responsibility, and the like. Systematic merit rating brings to the supervisor's attention many aspects of the employee's performance that can be improved and often suggests the appropriate course of action.

WORKER EFFICIENCY AND THE NEW TECHNOLOGY

The overall purpose of this chapter has been to pinpoint those conditions and principles related to worker efficiency that have not been directly mentioned or have been mentioned only by implication in earlier chapters. One may well ask if what has been said will apply five or ten years from now in view of the rapid technological changes taking place almost daily in most industries. These technological changes are indeed important—so much so that two chapters on human-factors engineering and systems will be devoted to them. The new technology, in general, is leading more and more to the mechanization of jobs that were formerly done by people. Despite the demonstrated efficiency of automated devices, principles of work behavior discussed in this chapter will have to be considered and properly applied as long as there are work tasks for people to perform.

It is perhaps fitting to close this chapter on work and efficiency with a few words about the impact of the rapid rise of automation on present-day workers. It is predicted that automation will eliminate many dreary repetitive jobs which mechanization brought into existence. It will shorten the workweek, slow the work pace, and increase leisure time on and off the job. But there are problems. It will also make dull jobs duller for some people. And it will probably necessitate plant operation over a twenty-four-hour period in order to pay for expensive automated equipment. This will interfere with the workers' home and social life and cause unfavorable worker reaction. And there are strong indications that automated jobs cause worry and anxiety among workers responsible for watching and guarding costly automated devices. Also, some workers fear automation as a mechanical monster that will put them out of a job. To counter the threat they resort to featherbedding and restrictions of output. Social needs are not satisfied in many automated jobs, and worker frustration is the result. On this point Marrow tells of workers in an English oil refinery seeking a raise because the plant was being automated. The extra pay they wanted was referred to as "lonely pay"—a bonus for their losing the companionship of workmates [35].

Popular notions to the contrary, most people do not want freedom from work. They want psychological and financial rewards for their work, to be sure. But they want work. This is indicated by a recent University of Michigan survey in which a national sample of 400 employed men were asked whether they would continue to work if they inherited enough money to live comfortably. Over 80 per cent said they would [36]. There are those who say that work must continue to be a way of life, even if it be featherbedding at the worker level or featherbraining at the professional level.

SUGGESTIONS FOR SELECTIVE READING

Anastasi, A. *Fields of applied psychology*. New York: McGraw-Hill, 1964. Part III covers work methods and working environment.

Barnes, R. M. *Motion and time study*. (4th ed.) New York: Wiley, 1958. A readable book of techniques.

Blauner, R. *Alienation and freedom*. Chicago: University of Chicago Press, 1964. Studies of worker alienation related to the technology involved.

Dankert, C. E., et al. (Eds.) *Hours of work*. Englewood Cliffs, N.J.: Prentice-Hall, 1965. From moonlighting to time on the hands.

Friedmann, G. *The anatomy of work*. New York: Free Press, 1961. The negative aspects in work.

Gaudet, F. J. *Solving the problems of employee absence*. New York: American Management Association, 1963. A research study of how to decrease absenteeism.

Gellerman, S. W. (Ed.) *Motivation and productivity*. New York: American Management Association, 1963. An industrial psychologist looks at practical problems in work, including some selected readings.

Karn, H. W., & Gilmer, B. v. H. (Eds.) *Readings in industrial and business psychology*. New York: McGraw-Hill, 1952 and 1962. Each edition contains four articles on work.

Niebel, B. W. *Motion and time study*. Homewood, Ill.: Irwin, 1963. The place of methods, time study, and wage payment in modern industry.

Patchen, M. *The choice of wage comparisons*. Englewood Cliffs, N.J.: Prentice-Hall, 1961. The kinds of comparisons people make about earned income.

Patton, A. *Men, money, and motivation*. New York: McGraw-Hill, 1961. Compensation plans as incentives in accepting employment.

Ryan, T. A. *Work and effort.* New York: Ronald, 1947. An old stand-by on work productivity.

Saltonstall, R. *Human relations in administration.* New York: McGraw-Hill, 1959. Chapters 11, 12, and 13 show effects of organizational climate on work.

Shils, E. B. *Automation and industrial relations.* New York: Holt, 1963. New problems in design of jobs.

Smith, K. U., & Smith, M. W. *Perception and motion.* Philadelphia: Saunders, 1962. A biopsychological approach to skill performance that differs from time-and-motion study.

Vroom, V. H. *Work and motivation.* New York: Wiley, 1964. Theories and facts about the interrelationship between human motivation and the work that people perform.

Whisler, T. L., & Harper, S. F. (Eds.) *Performance appraisal.* New York: Holt, 1962. A book of readings.

Whyte, W. F. *Men at work.* Homewood, Ill.: Irwin, 1961. Research cases and their analysis.

12

Accidents and Safety

Harry W. Karn

Of the many and varied problems related to men working in industry one of the most costly is industrial accidents. A report of the National Safety Council indicates that industrial accidents cost well over 3 billion dollars a year, with an average cost to industry of about $50 a worker. The monetary cost is enormous, but in terms of life and limb the situation is tragic. Accidents and safety are obviously critically important areas of inquiry for the industrial psychologists. In this chapter we shall describe the nature of the problems leading to accidents and what can be done to improve safety.

Magnitude of the Problems. It is not uncommon to read in the news of someone who has been hurt by walking through a glass door. Markings on the door at adult eye level may not help the small child. Safety glass, of course, can help reduce the severity of the accident. This example illustrates that safety involves both people and things.

The phenomenon of accidents constitutes one of the major human, social, and economic problems of modern times. Jacobs [21] says that gross statistics make clear the magnitude of this problem: in the United States in any given year roughly 100,000 people are killed and around 10 million more injured through accidents. In 1962, for example, there were 97,000 accidental deaths, about half of which were related to motor vehicles, a fourth to the home, and some 15 per cent to work. At work and at home, falls lead in causes, followed by handling objects, being struck by falling objects, and contacting harmful substances. Electricity, heat, explosives, and machinery account for most other accidents. Practically all studies in the field of accidents have indicated that the human factors predominate in their etiology [3, 27, 34].

Engineering and the Human Element. The practical application of psychological principles to the behavior of men at work is a matter of prime concern in the field of accident prevention. For example, some investigators have pointed out that becoming a safe worker is a typical learning function [37]. A case in point is a study of the accident records of streetcar motormen and motor-coach operators in which it was found that accident rates continued to decline throughout the first seventeen months of operation [12]. The operators all had from two to four weeks of training before being put on regular runs and at the end of that time were judged ready for regular operation. Yet learning continued (Figure 12.1).

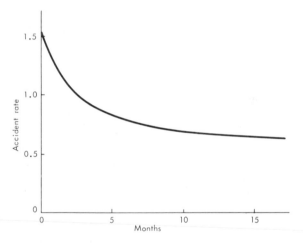

Fig. 12.1. Relation of accident rate among street car operators over 17 months. (After Ghiselli, E. E., & Brown, C. W. Learning and accident reduction. *J. Appl. Psychol.*, 1947, 31, 580–582.)

Despite the psychological ramifications underlying the problem of accident prevention, there is a strong tendency in many quarters to neglect the psychological approach in formulating accident-prevention strategy. This happens because safety engineers charged with safety responsibilities are ordinarily not trained in the field of human behavior. Apparently, accident prevention is looked upon as an engineering problem to be solved through the proper design of mechanical safety devices. It is certainly true that the engineer has a real contribution to make toward achieving the goal of accident-free behavior. But the contribution of the psychologist must not be minimized. Actually, the answer to the question of how to prevent accidents requires a cooperative effort of engineer and psychologist.

Is it possible for an engineer to design a safety device that is foolproof regardless of what the operator does? Generally speaking, the answer is "no"—at least, not one that can be operated efficiently and economically. Foolproof safety devices have an uncanny property of becoming hazardous in the hands of certain operators.

Building a safety device that is foolproof requires sound equipment design plus a careful consideration of the human element. The safety of a mechanical device is to a large degree a function of its meaningfulness to and acceptance by the worker who is operating it. It is particularly difficult to protect the hands. Nearly one-fourth of all on-the-job accidents in the United States result in disabling hand injuries.

THE CONCEPT OF AN ACCIDENT

Having indicated the importance of the human element in accidents, let us now explore the problem of accident behavior more concretely by asking just what constitutes an accident. Curious as it may seem, the layman and many experts in the field of accident prevention define accidents in a variety of ways. If a workman falls off a ladder and is not injured to the slightest degree and does not cause any damage to equipment, is this an accident? Frequently, the answer is "no." Suppose he sprains his ankle in falling off the ladder. Is this an accident? What about the worker who falls off the ladder and rubs the skin from his elbows—shall we call this occurrence an accident? Indeed, in each of these instances we have an act or instance of behavior which we must call an accident. There are of course differences. In one case the results are inconsequential, in another there is a skin abrasion, and in another there is an incapacitating sprained ankle. However, common to each of these instances is the act of falling off the ladder. The differences lie in the *results* of falling off the ladder.

There are instances of behavior involving acts with common features and different results, and, of course, there are other instances where the acts are different but the results are similar. A complete understanding of the nature of accidents and their prevention requires that a careful distinction be made between acts and the results of these acts. The appropriate distinction is made in the descriptive statement that defines an accident as *an unexpected, incorrect, but not necessarily injurious or damaging event that interrupts the completion of an activity.*

Accident Results. Some of the major classes of accident results can be enumerated without difficulty. First, there are results which do not involve injuries of any consequence. These are no-injury accidents. A workman bumps against a piece of moving machinery. Result: just grease on his overalls and a button ripped off his suspenders. Second, there are minor-injury accidents. A workman bumps against the same piece of machinery and suffers a slight laceration of the skin on his forearm. Third, there are accidents involving major injuries. Contact with moving machinery results in a mangled hand which has to be amputated. And of course there are accidents in which there is damage to equipment. A workman bumps into the moving machinery, and his recoil causes a nearby wrench to fall into revolving gears. There is a damaged machine although no bodily injury. Widely different results are apparent in each of these cases, but each result stems from the same or nearly the same happening.

LOST–TIME ACCIDENTS

In studying accidents the importance of distinguishing between acts and their results is brought into sharp focus when we consider the emphasis which industry puts upon lost-time accidents. This emphasis merits special treatment because it confuses the problem of accident prevention, the solution of which is, of course, the aim of all safety programs.

While the elimination of lost-time accidents is a desirable goal, this goal will never be achieved by concentrating only upon those accidents involving loss of working time. Unfortunately, a few safety directors think that it can be. The safety director who boasts of a good record because his company has had relatively few lost-time accidents is typical in some organizations. Some companies do not keep records of accidents which involve no loss of time.

Such emphasis upon lost-time accidents fails to take into account the necessity of concentrating upon the causes of accidents. The results are not unimportant, but they can only be eliminated if we know what causes them. Focusing attention on results will no more solve the accident problem than focusing attention on cancer will lead to its cure. A cure for cancer will come only when the cause of this disease is discovered.

Thus accident prevention must begin with a discovery of causes. These causal factors can be ascertained only through a systematic collection of observations in a wide variety of situations. The act which led to no loss of time today may next week lead to a major injury and the loss of a month's time. Safety programs must be based on information from all accidents regardless of their consequences. If this is done, not only situations that actually result in injury, damage, or loss of time are identified, but also those that have the potential for yielding these consequences. Certainly there is not a sufficient number of lost-time accidents to provide the critical information necessary for an identification of causes. One authority in the field of accident prevention states that non-lost-time accidents outnumber lost-time accidents by a ratio of 29 to 1. To neglect information provided by non-lost-time accidents is to make the whole problem of accident prevention practically insoluble [18].

THE CAUSES OF ACCIDENTS

Every enlightened student of behavior knows that behavior is caused, and accident behavior is no exception. A close examination of accident causes reveals two general categories—unsafe conditions and unsafe acts. *Unsafe conditions* involve some aspect of the physical environment which sets up or makes probable the occurrence of an accident. Cluttered arrangement of machinery, poor lighting, unguarded moving parts, and oily floors are examples of unsafe conditions. *Unsafe acts* are those behaviors which lead to an accident or those failures in performance which result in an accident. In the cases previously cited in which three workers bumped into a piece of machinery, the unsafe act was the act of making contact with the machine. The results were different in each case, but if the act of bumping had not occurred, there wouldn't have been any result to worry about. Failure to engage a safety device is an example of neglectful behavior which frequently leads to an accident.

Interaction of Acts and Conditions. Unsafe acts and unsafe conditions may interact in such a way that an accident may be caused by both. Too, an accident may be caused by a number of unsafe conditions or by a number of unsafe acts. The careful investigator always seeks to determine all the factors which lead to an accident.

Let us now push our analysis of causes a little further and ask what causes the unsafe condition or the unsafe act. Since we are getting further and further removed from the actual accident, we can call these matters indirect causes of accidents. The unsafe-act and unsafe-condition categories we can conveniently call the direct causes of accidents.

What causes a man to perform an unsafe act? A number of possibilities are immediately apparent, such as faulty vision, illness, worry, intoxication, poor coordination, lack of job know-how, and the like. All these states or conditions reside within the individual; they make up the so-called "human element," and we may justifiably call them human factors.

Human Factors in Accidents. Analyzing the nature of causes to the point where we are dealing with human factors is helpful in understanding accident causation because we are now dealing with something which can tell us why the unsafe act was performed. If we can isolate a human element responsible for the unsafe act, we are in a position to do something constructive. Thus if one of the human elements responsible for the unsafe act is lack of job know-how, we may be able to eliminate this causative factor by training. If the cause is faulty vision, corrective glasses may remedy the situation. If the human factor is uncorrectible, the offender can be removed from the job and placed in a less hazardous type of work.

Unsafe conditions usually stem from human factors. A worker overloads a conveyor belt and leaves the same; later the belt breaks, and the result is an accident to someone in the immediate vicinity. The direct cause of the accident, the broken belt, is an unsafe condition caused by an unsafe act. But why did the worker commit the unsafe act of overloading the belt and walking away? Was he distracted by worry over unpaid bills or the illness of a member of his family? If we trace the accident back to its primal source, we find that the worker's state of mind is the indirect cause out of which the direct causes originated.

As a matter of fact it is not hard to present a strong case for the contention that all unsafe conditions have their origin in human factors. Worn-out machinery can create an unsafe condition which might cause an accident. But if the machine had been properly maintained and the wearing parts replaced soon enough, the wearing out would have been avoided, and the unsafe condition would never have occurred. Why did a worker fail to maintain the machine in proper working order? What human factor in him caused the neglect? A steampipe may burst and be the cause of an accident. This looks like an unsafe condition where no human factor is involved. But steampipes are supposed to be periodically tested for stress potential, and failure to do this is an unsafe act by a human operator. Once again we may ask: Why was the operator negligent? Cases like these are frequently classified as unsafe conditions caused by nonhuman factors, but it is obvious that the classification is an arbitrary one. It is used where the causative human agent is not readily identifiable.

If all accidents are caused, then careful analysis and observation should lead to the discovery of the causes. The next obvious step is to remove the causes. Accident prevention has been retarded by the failure to identify in some systematic fashion the conditions which cause accidents [3].

THE ACCIDENT REPORT

Where shall we turn to obtain reliable data or information useful for an accident-prevention program? The basic source of such information is the accident report. A good accident report should include data on such items as the following:

1 *Date, hour of the day, shift, and location.* Working conditions often change, sometimes in a systematic manner from day to day, from hour to

hour, and from shift to shift. For example, the day-shift worker usually comes to work after a full night's sleep and breakfast. The preceding activity of the night-shift worker is usually more varied. Fatigue effects are more pronounced during the latter part of the working day. These and other factors under this category can influence accident behavior.

   2 *Job classification, job operation, and job unit.* These data give specific information about the type of work in which the accident occurs. The hazard potential of different jobs and operations within jobs can thus be determined. Suppose a painter fell from a ladder while descending with his back to the rungs of the ladder. His job classification would be painter; his job operation, using a ladder; his job-operation unit, descending the ladder.

   3 *Accident type.* Information in this category should include an exact description of the nature of the accident including a description of the contact agent. These descriptive data are not necessarily extensive and detailed. For the painter who fell from the ladder, a statement like "fell to the floor" would be sufficient.

   4 *Immediate cause of the accident.* This information covers the cause of the accident in terms of specific unsafe acts or conditions or both. Among other findings we get from this information an answer to the question: What violation of a commonly accepted safety procedure resulted in a particular accident? We need to know what actually was done or was not done that contributed to the accident.

   5 *Results of the accident.* Data under this heading cover bodily location of the injury, description of the injury, and extent of property damage. Frequently the person who fills out the accident report cannot immediately describe the injury or property damage precisely. Medical assistance and help from someone responsible for assessing property damage are needed.

   6 *Experience.* How important experience on the job is in relation to type of accident can only be determined by a careful analysis of reliable data, the source of which must be the accident report. Data of this kind can be of great help in planning a safety training program.

   7 *Psychological data.* Scores on aptitude tests, personality inventories, and achievement tests should be included in the accident report if available. The analysis of such data may provide information for identifying some of the personal factors contributing to accident behavior.

   Complete data within each of the categories discussed above constitute the minimum requirements for useful accident reporting. Large bodies of data carefully gathered on the various items of the report provide the basic information for the design of a successful accident-prevention program. All accidents should of course be reported, not just those involving injury and property damage. From our previous discussion it will be recalled that information about accident type and causes is as valuable for the study and prevention of accidents when no injury or damage occurs as when the opposite is true. Injuries and property damage from accidents are relatively rare events, and a vast amount of data on accident causation is wasted if noninjurious accidents are neglected. Data from noninjurious accidents are easier to obtain than data from injury-producing accidents, for people are more willing to talk about "close calls" and "near-misses" than about injurious or damage-producing accidents in which they are personally involved.

INVESTIGATIONS OF PERSONAL FACTORS RELATED TO ACCIDENTS

Here we shall summarize information about accidents in relation to intelligence, muscular coordination, and other factors, showing in some instances that popular opinion and research evidence do not always agree.

Intelligence. One of the earliest studies on the relation between mental ability and accidents showed no correlation of any significance between scores on intelligence tests and accident frequency among dockyard apprentices. It has been suggested that one should expect intelligence to be related to accidents involving errors of judgment but not to accidents involving manual skills. This suggestion may account for the lack of relationship in the dockyard study. In another investigation there was a much greater incidence of accidents among workers who were below average in traits associated with mental ability than among those who were about average in these traits. These somewhat contradictory conclusions are typical of the literature on the subject. Intelligence may be an important factor in some kinds of work activity and not in others. Very likely a minimum amount of mental ability is necessary for accident-free behavior in all occupations. Accident-prevention programs should include a determination of the critically important mental-ability requirement [3, 8].

Vision. How well a person can see would appear to be a factor contributing to accident susceptibility, and there is some indication that this is so. In one investigation [23] the visual requirements of each worker in twelve groups were determined. The workers were then tested to determine whether or not they met the usual requirements of their respective jobs. Findings revealed that in eleven of the job groups, the percentage of safe workers was higher among those who passed the test than among those who failed it. No differences were found in the one exceptional group, which consisted entirely of laborers. Another investigator found that only 37 per cent of a group of machine operators who passed visual tests had accidents during a given year, whereas 67 per cent of those who did not pass the vision tests had accidents [43].

Coordination. Muscular coordination has been singled out by some investigators as a factor having a bearing upon accident susceptibility. It would seem reasonable to suppose that slowness of response and clumsiness would contribute to accident frequency. Yet speed of reaction in and of itself has been found to have no significant relation to accident frequency in industry. But more complex reaction tendencies are apparently important. For example, one investigator used a battery of tests consisting of a dotting test, a device for measuring speed of reaction to a signal, and a test which required the subject to change his muscular performance in accordance with changing signals. When 500 employees were divided into two groups on the basis of high and low test scores, the poorer performers had 48 per cent more accidents than the better half. Also, the poorer quarter had 51 per cent more accidents than the better three-quarters. These findings have in general been supported by other investigations of muscular coordination and accidents [8, 39].

Personality Characteristics. Many writers in the field of safety have argued that the personality and temperament of the individual have a great deal to do with his susceptibility to accidents, and there is mounting evidence to substantiate this claim.

A relationship between emotional cycles and frequency of accidents has been reported from a study which showed that the average worker is emotionally low about 20 per cent of the time and that more than half of the 400 minor accidents studied occurred during these low periods [19]. On the basis of chance alone, only about 20 per cent of the accidents would have occurred during these low periods. The importance of the worker's emotional state is further attested in another study in which it was shown that production is about 8 per cent higher during periods when the workers were hopeful, elated, and happy than when they were angry, disgusted, apprehensive, or worried [20].

The relationship between accidents and interpersonal preferences has been studied among workers on the finishing end of a steel-mill hot strip [36]. Most of the high accident rates were found among the men most disliked by their fellow workers; men well liked by their fellow workers tended to be accident-free. A recent study of personality dynamics and accident susceptibility utilized a sentence-completion test administered to two groups, one composed of men who had a high incidence of accidents and the other composed of men who suffered no accidents in the same industrial setting. Test results indicated that the high-accident workers, in comparison with the nonaccident workers, were significantly low on the socially desirable personality dispositions of optimism, trust, and socio-centricity [6].

Highly suggestive is the discovery of a relationship between scores on an introversion-extroversion test and performance on an auditory-vigilance task in which the subjects were instructed to detect numerical relationships as they listened to a tape recording of spoken digits. The generally superior performance of the introvert group of subjects is attributed to the fact that they were more alert or attentive in a situation calling for sustained vigilance. This could mean that in jobs with high attention requirements introverts are less likely to have accidents than extroverts [2].

Fatigue. The critical point at which fatigue becomes an accident determinant in any individual has not been ascertained, but we can be fairly certain that extreme fatigue leads to increased accident frequency. For example, in a shell factory in England during World War II the accident rate among women workers was reduced by more than 60 per cent when the factory changed from a twelve-hour to a ten-hour day [39].

Caution must be exercised in attributing accidents to fatigue if there is an accompanying change in production rate. What may seem to be a fatigue factor may really be a tendency to overlook accident dangers because one is working faster. The way to separate these two factors may be illustrated by an analysis of accidents made by the United States Public Health Service in which the effect of production rate was held constant. The technique was to divide the accident index by the production index for a given work period, in other words, to report in terms of accidents per unit of output. Results showed that in the earlier hours of the day the accident index rises and falls with the output rate. Increases in production bring a corresponding increase in the number of accidents. However, this relation breaks down in the closing hours of the working day. Here the accident rate remains high relative to the production rate. Such an analysis makes it possible to show the importance of the fatigue factor.

Experience. Common sense, a knowledge of the psychology of learning, and actual research findings point toward inexperience on the job as a factor contributing to accidents. Table 5 summarizes the data from an English study which shows a close relationship between accident rate and amount of job experience [8].

Another study carried out in England shows that the accident rate continues to decrease among young workers up to eighteen months after employment. Still another analyst reports that accidents among workers on a stamping press dropped from seventy-seven on the first day to an average of thirteen for the next six days [14, 39].

A relatively recent investigation dealt with the question of whether a reduction in accident rate with experience is due to experience per se or to age. For workers operating metal-forming mills there was a sharp decline in accident rate during a three-to-five-month breaking-in period of initial on-the-job performance. Once the breaking point is passed, age exerts a greater influence than does experience; the older, more mature workers have fewer accidents than the younger workers. It is also pointed out in this study that the effects attributable to age and experience may be due in part to the weeding out of workers less fit for the job [37].

Table 5 / Job Experience as Related to Accident Rate

Length of Service	Accident Rate (per cent of total)
Less than 1 month	181
1–3 months	127
3–8 months	87
8–12 months	62
1–5 years	57

The fact that job experience and accidents are related calls attention to the importance of safety training for all new employees. Job know-how is of course usually acquired with experience on the job. But sometimes this know-how is acquired in a trial-and-error fashion as the result of bitter experience. Making the process one of acquiring know-how through training and guidance is clearly a means of reducing accidents. In the study of metal-forming mills referred to previously, a group of workers given safety training prior to actual job performance had significantly fewer accidents during the early period of employment than those workers who had no such training. We shall examine the problem of safety training later in this chapter.

Risk Acceptance. A promising new area of research has to do with the concept of risk as a basic human factor in accident causation. Risk acceptance may be defined as the behavioral trait of an individual to engage in an activity where there is some specific probability of failure.

An exploratory but penetrating and objective study of risk behavior was conducted in which a risk simulator was designed and built in accordance with an operationally defined risk-taking environment. Preliminary research demonstrated that individuals can be differentiated with respect to the reactions to risk opportunities.

Following the preliminary experiments, the simulator was placed in an industrial environment and used on thirty-seven workers. An analysis of observed risk differences among subjects showed that the high-risk group had incurred more industrial accidents, were less skillful, and possessed greater variability in task performance than the low-risk group [32].

ENVIRONMENTAL CONDITIONS RELATED TO ACCIDENTS

Besides personal factors, or conditions within the individual, there are also external or environmental factors which contribute to accidents.

Lighting and Temperature. Scarcely anyone would argue that lighting or conditions of visibility do not effect the accident rate in some situations. Certainly it is true that fewer accidents occur in daylight than in any kind of artificial illumination. One insurance company estimated from survey results that 25 per cent of all industrial accidents were due to poor lighting. In a survey carried out in Great Britain it was found that artificial lighting caused an overall increase in accidents of about 25 per cent [39].

Temperature has an effect upon the worker which can increase his accident liability. The data from one study on factory workers are shown in Figure 12.2. Fewest accidents occur when the temperature is in the vicinity of 70°. The rate is considerably higher when the temperature is below 65° or above 75°.

Another study, made in coal mining, showed a progressive increase in minor accidents as the temperature of the pits ranged from 62° to 85°. In pits having the highest temperature, the minor-accident frequency was

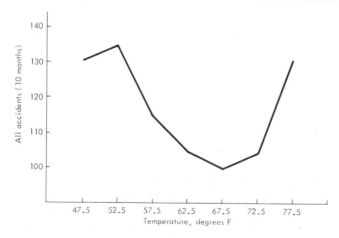

Fig. 12.2. Relation between accident frequency and temperature. (After Vernon, H. M. Prevention of accidents. *British J. Industr. Med.,* 1945, 2, 3.)

three times greater than that in pits having the lowest temperature. The precise optimal temperature for safe work in different occupations is a problem which has not been solved [39].

Severity of Work. Physical demands upon the worker probably contribute to accidents, although substantiating evidence of this is scant. In one of the few investigations of this factor it was found that for factory workers engaged in muscular work the ratio of afternoon to morning accidents did not differ from that of persons engaged in machine work or handwork. The afternoon productivity of the men engaged in the heavier work, however, was less than that of the men engaged in the lighter work. In terms of accidents per productive unit, therefore, the workers on the jobs which were more demanding physically appeared to be at a disadvantage. This conclusion suggests that as the working day proceeds, the number of accidents per unit of production increases in jobs requiring more physical effort [14].

Industrial Climate. The usual approach to the study of psychological and environmental factors related to accidents has been to single out one factor or variable at a time, such as mental ability, experience, illumination, etc. Another, more recent approach is more global in that it involves the simultaneous study of many variables in the belief that this will lead to the discovery of a climatic pattern characteristic of low-accident work environments.

The first study using the global approach was carried out in the Camden works of the Radio Corporation of America [24]. Accidents were found to occur more frequently in those departments with low promotion probability, low intracompany transfer, and high noise level. Greater accident severity was found in departments with a predominance of male workers, low promotion probability, low suggestion record, nonyouthfulness of employees, and high average tenure of workers. Another study conducted along the same lines showed the following climatic factors to be related to accident frequency: seasonal layoffs, other industrial plants in the vicinity, percentage of employees who routinely handle heavy materials, blighted living conditions, garnisheed wages, size of plant, and production rate. The following were found to be related to accident severity: absenteeism, equalitarian eating, national union representation, penalty for tardiness, employee profit sharing, extreme temperature, dirt and perspiration [34].

THEORIES OF SAFETY PSYCHOLOGY

The oldest and best-known theory that has been advanced to explain accident behavior is known as the accident-proneness theory. People who repeatedly have accidents are alleged to be accident-prone; i.e., because of a peculiar set of constitutional characteristics, they engage in unsafe behavior. Despite the popularity of the accident-prone concept, supporting evidence is highly controversial. While it is true that some individuals have accidents repeatedly and that a relatively large proportion of accidents are experienced by a relatively small proportion of individuals, this in and of itself is not proof of accident proneness. Statistical studies of the way accidents are distributed among the worker population show that a concentration of the majority of accidents in a minority of the individuals is a mathematical necessity. Thus the only support for the theory of accident proneness comes from instances of repeated accidents in excess of chance.

A research report of statistical analyses carried out on accident data in which the chance factor was taken into consideration shows that only about 15 per cent of the variance in individual accidents can be accounted for by accident proneness. Furthermore, it is likely that the 15 per cent figure is spuriously high, since nonproneness factors in the environment were left uncontrolled in many of the studies on which the analyses were based. Particularly important in this regard is the failure in many reported studies to take into consideration the extent to which all of those who had accidents had equal exposure to risk [5]. Certain workers may have had an excessive number of accidents because they were exposed to hazard more often than their fellows.

Even if the 15 per cent figure is correct in accounting for accidents due to proneness, there remains 85 per cent unaccounted for. To take care of this large residual two situational or climatic theories have been proposed by Kerr [25].

The Goals-Freedom-Alertness Theory. According to this theory, accidents are regarded as low-quality work behaviors occurring in an unrewarding psychological climate that is not conducive to a high level of alertness. The more rich the climate is in diverse economic and psychological op-opportunities, the higher the level of alertness in the workers and subsequent high-quality, accident-free behavior will be.

Among other things, a rewarding psychological climate must be one in which the worker is encouraged to set up short-term and long-term goals with a reasonable probability of attainment. He must have opportunities to raise problems and participate in their solution. This leads to habits of alertness and high-quality production. The studies on the effect of psychological climate on accident behavior lend considerable support to the alertness theory.

The Adjustment-Stress Theory. This theory, like the previous one, stresses the nature of the working climate as a major determinant of accidents. In essence, it states that a worker under distracting stress is more liable to accidents than a nonstressed worker. At first glance this may appear to be a restatement of the accident-proneness theory, but it is not. Accident proneness has to do with permanent constitutional inadequacies in the individual's make-up, whereas the adjustment-stress theory is concerned with ordinary adjustment to stress resulting from temporary conditions such as illumination, temperature, congestion in the workplace, alcohol consumption, and the influence of disease organisms.

Kerr points out that the alertness theory and the stress theory complement each other as well as the accident-proneness theory. His evaluation and estimates lead him to conclude that "the variance in accident rates among industrial workers distributes in terms of theoretical causation" as follows:

Accident proneness	1 to 15 per cent
Goals-opportunity-alertness	30 to 40 per cent
Adjustment-stress	45 to 60 per cent

THE PROBLEM OF ACCIDENT–PREVENTION TRAINING

From the preceding discussion it is obvious that much remains to be done in isolating the physical and psychological conditions which lead to accidents. Nevertheless a substantial body of fact and theory is known on which to base safety practices and procedures. Not the least of these is a well-designed accident-prevention training program.

Training deals with the applied psychology of learning, as we discussed in Chapter 7. The specific function of training is to cause the trainee to learn some new way of behaving. In the area of accident prevention, the function of training is to reduce accidents. The trainer must bring about a change of behavior in the trainee, and the criterion of success is a change from accident-producing behavior to safe behavior. Everything else is secondary. Apparent cooperation in a safety training program is of little or no importance unless accidents are reduced. Employees may be entertained by safety films and say that they like a training program, but these things are of little consequence unless accidents are reduced. Lectures by safety engineers are largely a waste of time unless they bring about a reduction in accidents. Training in accident prevention must measure up to one basic criterion, namely, accident reduction as a consequence of training effort.

Knowing and Doing. Accident reduction is achieved through training only if the worker learns to behave safely on the job. If a new worker does not know the company safety regulations and he is given this knowledge and demonstrates that he knows it, has he been trained in accident prevention? Not necessarily. Knowing will not always ensure doing. The problem of training clearly involves two phases: first, the worker must learn how to behave the safe way; second, he must be stimulated to do it. Thus the safety slogan of United States Steel—"Knowing's not enough."

When Is Training Indicated? The first step in determining when training is needed is to examine the accident reports. Suppose such an examination reveals that a significant percentage of accidents are associated with a certain kind of unsafe acts. Does a finding indicate lack of knowledge or failure to put that knowledge into practice? We should find the answer to this question, for there is no point in trying to teach a worker something that he already knows.

If the records on unsafe acts do not tell what is known and what is not known, the sensible thing to do is to use some kind of job know-how test. Such a test should cover all aspects of the job which relate to safety. The test should be objective, and it should be so designed that it requires a minimum of time for administration. Relatively few industries use such tests, but they can be clearly helpful, since they tell the safety director where to start in setting up an accident-prevention training program. If the tests reveal lack of knowledge about how to do a job safely, then training should meet this lack. If the workers possess the knowledge but are still having accidents, the problem is one of motivating the worker to put into practice what he knows.

Content of Training Program. Suppose a determination of training needs reveals a lack of knowledge of how to perform a job in a safe way. What kind of information should be given to the worker? A careful examination of a properly executed accident report will answer this question. Good accident reports contain data on the kinds of accidents that are occurring, the type of activity in which the accidents occur, the specific job operations having to do with accidents, the cause or causes of accidents, and the results. Training content should be centered around those specific items. If analyses show operation X to be highly hazardous, then it is only reasonable to spend more training on this operation than on operation Y, which is shown to be a low-hazard operation.

If a training program is starting from scratch, that is, with no accident data available, the content might be determined through a job analysis by a safety-minded industrial engineer. The analyst reviews the job in its entirety, considering each step in the job sequence. He considers each operation in terms of its hazard potential and then formulates a safe way to deal with this hazard. Suppose an operation involves several specific acts, one of which is lifting a heavy steel bar. The engineer asks himself which of these acts is likely to lead to an accident. He may decide that the act of lifting is potentially hazardous. Therefore, in working up training content, he will emphasize the proper way to lift.

The critical-incident technique described in Chapters 6 and 11 is a possible method for obtaining content material for an accident training program. Through interviews, workers would be asked to recall unsafe acts of their own and those they have observed in others. The findings would provide the basic material around which to build training content. The critical-incident technique has been used successfully to determine pilot-error incidents in aircraft operation and in a wide variety of proficiency and performance situations [4, 10].

Executing the Training. Once the need for training has been established and the training content has been formulated, how will the program be carried out? A completely satisfactory answer to this question is difficult because training techniques have seldom been systematically evaluated. There are, however, some general training principles which can be safely followed.

A good way to begin is to have a skilled worker demonstrate to the trainee the safe way to perform the job. Seeing an act performed gives the learner an overall idea of how it should be done. After the demonstration, there should be a question-and-answer session to determine whether the trainee can tell in his own words what he should do.

Following the demonstration the trainee should be called upon to perform the act himself. He should repeat this performance until it is clear that he has mastered it. Too many trainers stop with the demonstration phase of training. Demonstration only shows the trainee what he should do. People learn only when they do something themselves.

Written material, flip-chart talks, and movies can be used to clarify some of the important points in safety training. They can serve the useful purpose of dramatizing the importance of safety. As training aids they are widely used but probably overrated. Certainly they should never be substituted for firsthand information and active performance under the supervision of an experienced trainer.

Who Should Do the Training? The practices that have been recommended thus far will not succeed unless the training job is in the hands of a responsible trainer. Sometimes an outsider who is an expert in the field is assigned the training responsibility. Generally, this is an unwise practice. Outsiders usually do not know the work atmosphere of a particular plant well enough to handle the day-to-day problems peculiar to the plant's operation. Also, outsiders are often looked upon by the workers as disinterested persons who are here today and gone tomorrow.

The safety engineer and his assistants are sometimes given the job of accident-prevention training. This policy also has shortcomings, since safety personnel must necessarily give off-the-job training in capsule form. That is, trainees are taken aside in the classroom and given special instructions in accident prevention. Safety personnel are not sufficiently close to the actual work operation to do the best job of training.

The one man who is closest to the worker is the man's foreman or immediate supervisor. The responsibility for the detection and correction of training deficiencies falls squarely into the hands of the immediate supervisor. Safety department personnel should clearly define step by step the specific responsibilities of first-line supervision and then see to it that the foremen carry out these responsibilities. If the supervisor does not insist upon safe practices from his men, safe practices will not be forthcoming, regardless of what top management or the safety engineer does in the way of promoting accident prevention.

Supervisors are frequently reluctant to accept the responsibility for safety training on the grounds that they already have too much to do. Top management then has the problem of getting foremen to accept the responsibility for safety training. This may require a reorganization of the supervisor's overall duties, or it may mean providing him with assistants.

When supervisors do an inadequate job in the field of safety, it is because upper management tolerates an inadequate job. Reprimand and recognition will usually bring about an improvement in the supervisor who has been lax in his safety duties. If he sends in a poor report, returning it to him for correction will lead to improved reporting in the future. Accident-prevention training can only be effective when there is an insistence upon safe practices from the office of the president all the way down to the front-line supervisor.

TECHNIQUES IN MOTIVATING SAFETY

As we pointed out in the discussion of training, part of the problem is how to stimulate the worker to practice what he knows. The problem of motivation has been repeatedly referred to, but it merits additional treatment because of its complex nature and the difficulty that is often experienced in bringing about the proper degree of motivation in a practical situation.

The Long-range Point of View. Suppose an analysis of accident data reveals that on a particular job a number of accidents are caused by metal dust which gets into the workers' eyes. To eliminate this cause, the safety department issues a regulation stating that safety glasses must be worn. Not wearing the glasses is alleged to be an unsafe act. "But," says the worker who won't wear glasses, "I've been on the job for years, have never worn glasses, and have never had an accident." Suppose there is a safety regulation which says that descending a ladder with the back to the rungs is an unsafe act. Many workers can truthfully state that they have been descending ladders in this way for years and have never had an accident. Automobile drivers are told that driving a car above the speed limit is unsafe, but many people habitually exceed the speed limit and don't have accidents. There would probably be no motivational problem in these examples if an accident occurred every time the glasses were not worn, every time the ladder was descended in the wrong way, every time the speed limit was exceeded.

How shall we convince the worker of the fallacy of his reasoning? The important thing is to emphasize the need to take the long-range view—the point of view that in the long run an accident will catch up with him if he persists in violating safety practices. Pertinent evidence should be presented to the skeptical worker. Every industry's accident files contain cases of individuals who went accident-free for months and years and finally had an accident which could be attributed to a specific unsafe act.

Employee Participation. Within recent years a considerable amount of evidence has been accumulating which shows that employee participation in matters affecting their own welfare is strongly motivating. The principle applies, of course, to the problem of motivating safe behavior. As an example, one writer pointedly notes that if employees are encouraged to participate in defining the safety requirements for jobs, the rules set up will be accepted by them and provide a basis "for the constant retraining and reminding which the workers require" about safety.

As a practical example of the effect of employee participation in decision making, consider a case in which the practice of wearing safety shoes was introduced in a steel-mill operation. Certain workers were selected who were well liked and held in high regard by their coworkers. They were presented with data from accident reports which showed a large percentage of foot injuries and were asked to come up with suggestions or recommendations for preventing such injuries. The supervisors met with the men on company time for several sessions during which the safety problem was discussed from many angles. The practice of wearing safety shoes was brought up, and it was decided to try out different makes of shoes on an experimental basis. During the meetings the safety engineer sat in on all sessions but never made a decision himself. His sole role was to stimulate discussion among members of the group and get them to arrive at a unanimous decision. Significantly, the members of the committee reported that they had from time to time discussed the problem with their fellow workers. Finally, the group decided to institute the practice of wearing a certain kind of safety shoe on the job at all times. The policy was wholeheartedly accepted by the working group with scarcely even a minor infraction of the regulation.

There are a number of reasons why the motivational problem just described was solved so effectively. First, the decision was made by the people who were to be directly affected by the decision. It is becoming axiomatic in psychology that people are more effectively motivated when they are permitted some degree of participation in the determination of their own activity. Contrary to widespread opinion, many people like to assume some responsibility. Allowing a person to make a decision amounts to paying him a compliment, because respect for his judgment is being shown.

A second reason for the effectiveness of the group decision was that, by the very nature of the group process, the change was introduced gradually. Almost everyone resists abrupt changes. Old, habitual ways are highly motivating by the very fact that they are deep-seated or well learned. It requires less time and effort to do something the old way than it does to learn a new way, even though the new way, when learned, will be easier and quicker. The countermotivation needed to offset resistance to change involves, among other things, a gradual introduction of the new way and an avoidance, if possible, of an aribtrary decision by someone who will not be directly affected by the change.

Safety Campaigns and Posters. The use of posters and campaigns aimed at stimulating safe behavior is a common practice in industrial organizations. Their effectiveness is questionable, although under certain conditions they seem to have merit.

Posters which convey a general message, particularly in negative terms, probably do little good. A gruesome picture showing some mutilated part of the body with the caption, "Don't let this happen to you," is of little value in preventing accidents. It creates resentment, fear, and sometimes anger. No one wants to get killed or injured, and it is an insult to a workman to imply that he or anyone else is so motivated. Posters should carry a simple, reasonable, and constructive message in positive terms. Statements like the following, placed in appropriate places, are examples of positive and informative poster material:

- Wear Hard Hats Here
- Deposit Cigarette Butts in This Container
- Cross at This Point
- Lower Safety Guard before Starting Machine

Poster material should be used which attracts the maximum amount of attention. Legibility and proper use of color are attention-getting determinants. Locating the poster so that it will be readily seen is obviously important. And there should not be so many posters that they clutter up the working landscape. The fact that one or two posters are effective does not mean that additional posters will be more effective. A poster which is unique or different catches the workers' attention most quickly. If posters are everywhere, people cease paying attention to them.

Safety campaigns or contests in which workers strive for a safety record over a certain period of time tend to sensitize the worker to be safety-conscious. The best kind of safety campaign is that which never really ends. Rewards of some kind should be given the individual who has a good safety record. Indeed, there is no good reason why a man's accident record should not be a permanent part of his personnel file to be used in determining his fitness for promotion, job transfer, or increase in pay.

THE ENGINEERING PHASE OF THE SAFETY PROBLEM

So far, the discussion in this chapter has been focused on the human element in accident behavior. We have been concerned with understanding the nature of the worker so that we can predict and control his behavior. The mechanical or engineering side of the story should not, of course, be neglected. A well-designed working environment can do much to eliminate accidents in some cases, and in others it can make the handling of the human factor a lot easier. On the latter point, for example, the problem of getting men to wear safety clothing may be largely a psychological problem. Whether it will be a difficult psychological problem or an easy one may depend upon the design of the safety apparel. If the clothing is uncomfortable, the problem will be more difficult. Of course, there are so many different safety devices in use in modern industry that specific treatment of each and every kind is impossible. But we do know that all good safety devices have certain common features.

Foolproof Devices. From the mechanical standpoint, a good safety device should be as foolproof as possible. At the beginning of this chapter it was pointed out that it is probably impossible to create a completely foolproof device. But there are degrees of foolproofness, and the engineer with originality and ingenuity can make fairly accurate estimates on this matter. A rotary saw blade that will not start until a guard is in place is more foolproof than one that can be started with the guard disengaged. An ingenious worker may locate the wiring which leads to the motor and arrange it in such a way as to bypass the safety guard. But this kind of action is much less likely to occur than just starting the saw with a disengaged guard.

Production Interference by a Safety Device. Another major requirement of a good safety device is that it not interfere with production. Devices that interfere with production are resisted by both workers and management. A well-designed device not only does not interfere with production but actually facilitates it. Most unsafe operations are perceived as such to some degree, and the perceived hazard hampers production. When the worker knows he is safe, he is free from worry and strain and has a greater fund of energy available to devote to production.

Proper Maintenance of Equipment. Keeping equipment in good order is an important safety measure. Poorly maintained machinery creates unsafe conditions just as surely as does properly maintained equipment without specifically designed safety devices. The success of the safety department depends upon the cooperation and efficiency of the maintenance department, and the former can do much to ensure prompt repair and maintenance by stressing the safety need.

A common failing is the lag between the time of the report of need for repair and maintenance and the execution of the work itself. Sometimes hazardous conditions are spotted but not corrected for a long time. During the interval the unsafe conditions are often responsible for a rash of accidents. An otherwise good safety program can easily bog down if maintenance men are so overworked that they cannot keep mechanical equipment safe and in good working order. Slipshod and nonprofessional repair and maintenance by the workers themselves are a poor substitute for the work of the maintenance crew. The practice creates a false sense of security which may lead to more accidents than if no attempts at all are made at correction.

Good Housekeeping. Essential for accident-free behavior is orderly housekeeping. Some plants lack adequate storage space for equipment and tools. There are an insufficient number of depositories for waste materials. Windows and floors are not kept clean, and machinery is not properly loaded. All these housekeeping details must be attended to if a safe work atmosphere is to be maintained. One reporter cites a variety of accidents attributable to poor housekeeping—slipping on greasy, wet, or dirty floors; bumping against poorly stacked or misplaced materials; tripping over loose objects on floors, stairs, and platforms; injuring parts of the body on projecting nails, hooks, or sticks [6].

The Need for Research on Design of Equipment. Although it is true that modern industrial equipment incorporates safety devices of one kind or another, there is need for further research on the design of safe machinery and equipment. There are certain subtle features about a piece of equipment which seemingly have little to do with its safe operation but which may actually contribute considerably to unsafe behavior. Thus the faulty design of control levers may contribute to accidents. Or a gauge may be so poorly designed that errors in reading it are frequently made.

The design of safe equipment calls for a careful consideration of the worker's perceptual abilities and his intellectual- and manual-response capacities. Even the automaticity of a piece of equipment should be examined in terms of its safety properties. How automatic should a device be in order to get maximum proficiency from the operator? The obvious answer, "Make it as automatic as possible," is not always psychologically sound; for, if a human operator is needed at all, he must have enough to do so that he will not become bored. Lack of attention may well be the cause of accidents in certain machine operations. The principles underlying good equipment design are covered in the next chapter, on human-factors engineering.

OVERALL ACCIDENT–PREVENTION STRATEGY

The sum and substance of this chapter is a set of facts and principles which form the core of accident-prevention strategy. Strategy is the execution of a plan of attack—a set of guiding principles that are used to solve problems. Solution of a problem can be carried out haphazardly. Such an attack involves a great deal of activity, much of which is wasteful of time, effort, and money. All good problem solvers supplant the hit-or-miss approach with a systematically planned and guided approach. Solution of the accident problem is no exception.

Basic accident-prevention strategy calls for:

1 *A cause analysis of accidents.* Speculation that an accident was the result of worry or lack of attention or carelessness has no place in accident-prevention strategy. Strategy requires observation of men at work and from these observations an identification of unsafe acts and unsafe conditions.

2 *A distinction between accidents per se and their results.* To define an accident as "an act in which someone gets hurt" makes cause analysis difficult if not impossible. It is poor policy to wait for an injury before making a cause analysis. The same principle applies to cause analysis resulting in loss of time.

3 *Elimination of unsafe acts.* When the cause analysis points to an unsafe act, appropriate action must be taken to correct this factor. This may require training, and the nature of the training depends on the need. The trainee may need to know what to do, or he may know and not put into practice what he knows. If the unsafe act cannot be eliminated by training, placement of the employee in a less hazardous job is necessary.

4 *Elimination of unsafe conditions.* If some factor in the physical environment is leading to accidents, steps to nullify it should be taken. Wearing safety equipment may be the nullifying step. Proper maintenance of machinery is another. A guard or other safety device on a piece of machinery is still another. Research on the design of equipment will lead to the discovery of additional unsafe aspects of the physical environment.

Future Research. Wherever the strategic procedures summarized above have been put into practice, the result has been an improvement in the safety record. Where these have not been adopted, as in the case of traffic accidents, the record is poor. Only recently has even a start been made on the basic strategy of accident prevention on highways [42]. Considerable work is now under way to develop new techniques for sampling risk behavior and for inferring changes associated with countermeasures and other activities. There are those who believe that this is one of the most likely payoff areas in accident research. The growth of accident clinics, where emphasis is placed on diagnosis of the particular causes of accidents in particular people, gives indication we are now becoming more concerned with individual behavior. Human performance is related to stimulus level and follows an inverted U-shaped curve. This is to say performance deteriorates if there is either too little stimulation or too much. Both extremes subject the individual to an increase in the potentials of an accident.

Accident frequency and severity rates have been very substantially improved since the early 1900s. However, the rate of improvement during the past thirty years has been slower, and the traditional approaches may be reaching the limits of their effectiveness. We must control the agents of injury, not only by protective devices but also by the original design of equipment in terms of the physical and psychological capacities of the individual [26]. McFarland and Moore [27, 28] conclude that accidents now outrank diseases as a leading cause of death from age one to age thirty-four. Industry is now increasing its attention to the off-the-job accident as a major step in preserving the working effectiveness of its employees. Major strategies include the control of exposure to risk, the reduction of accidents during risks, the prevention of injury when accidents occur, and minimizing the residuals of injury.

SUGGESTIONS FOR SELECTIVE READING

Accidents. *World Health,* World Health Organization, Geneva, 1961. March–April, (Special issue). For an overall view of safety problems.

American Public Health Association. *Accident prevention: The role of physicians and public health workers.* New York: McGraw-Hill, 1961. A book worth study although not completely industrial.

Brody, L. *Human factors research in occupational accident prevention.* New York: American Society of Safety Engineers and New York University, 1962. Bibliography and interpretative literature on safety showing the new emphasis.

De Reamer, R. *Modern safety practices.* New York: Wiley, 1961. Accident prevention methods and management practices.

Haddon, W., et al. *Accident research: Approaches and methods.* New York: Harper & Row, 1964. New views toward a science of accident research; sophisticated reading for the layman.

Heinrich, H. W. *Industrial accident prevention.* (4th ed.) New York: McGraw-Hill, 1959. Practical suggestions on everyday accident prevention.

Karn, H. W., & Gilmer, B. v. H. (Eds.) *Readings in industrial and business psychology.* New York: McGraw-Hill, 1952 and 1962. Each edition contains research and theoretical articles on accident causes and prevention.

Metropolitan Life Insurance Company. *Industrial safety.* A practical look at accident prevention.

National Safety Council. *Accident facts.* (1965 ed.) Chicago: National Safety Council. Readable.

New York Academy of Sciences. Research methodology and potential in community health and prevention medicine. *Ann. NY Acad. Sc.,* 1963, 107. Contains two articles on industrial accidents.

Simonds, R. H., & Grimaldi, J. V. *Safety management.* Homewood, Ill.: Irwin, 1963. A practical book on accident prevention.

13

Human-factors Engineering

Lee W. Gregg

Human-factors engineering has grown out of the professions of engineering and experimental psychology. It constitutes a growing segment of general industrial psychology, along with extended programs for research into human factors in systems generally, and deals with the problems of machine design for optimum human use.

Human-factors engineering, or engineering psychology, as it is also called, is concerned with how people receive information through the senses, store this information, and process it in making decisions, and it deals with how people react. It is also interested in how persons communicate in a man-machine system. For the housewife the researcher has made studies of reaction time and errors in different arrangements of the four-burner stove and has come up with a virtual error-free design where there is compatibility between burner and control knob. The new L-shaped-desk setup for the secretary was designed to bring an enlarged work space within easy reach. Study has gone into the design of automobile seats which must accommodate people of varying shapes and forms. Also, seats must be designed to serve not only the driver who has duties to perform but also the passengers who may wish to relax. New classrooms and auditoriums are now being built providing for better two-way communication. Studies of aircraft accidents have meant newer cabin designs for both comfort and safety [4, 28, 43].

In this chapter we shall discuss the basic principles involved in relating people and things in a harmonious way. These principles have much in common whether the problem is the design of a household appliance or a space capsule. The roles of the engineer and the psychologist overlap in working out solutions to a multitude of man-machine problems. Since we are now familiar with what the psychologist does, let us begin by describing where the engineer fits into our picture.

THE JOB OF THE ENGINEER

Contriving, designing, and producing structures and machines useful to man is the job of the engineer. He applies his knowledge of the mechanical, electrical, chemical, or other properties of matter to the task of creating all kinds of functional devices—safety pins and automobiles, mousetraps and missiles. Since the ultimate user of these devices is man himself, human characteristics must be considered in their construction. Human muscular frailty provided the necessity for and dictated the design of such devices as the lever, the pulley, the screw, and hand tools of all sorts. Similarly, our more complex machines represent a direct outgrowth of human needs.

As more complex tools have been invented, they have become more difficult to manage. Some of the simpler control mechanisms of the earlier machines—levers or wheels—no longer provide the sensitivity required for optimum human use. More important perhaps is the fact that the machines themselves have created new needs that can often be met only by contriving new machines. Man is no longer satisfied with the speeds which earlier automobiles provided; he must go faster. He also wants to be able to do this more easily and more comfortably. Hence we find windows operated by remote control, power steering, fuel injectors, and many, many more of these speeding objects to bump into on the highways.

With the introduction of an independent source of power, the simple and direct link between man and the machine was broken. Very often we know the nature of our environment only in an indirect way. For example, most people traveling in a modern automobile on the modern highway have an inadequate sense of speed. Even though they see the changing roadway, they do not perceive accurately their rate of travel. The engineer must provide the means for transmitting to these people the necessary information for safe and efficient control of the vehicle.

THE PROBLEM OF COMPLETE AUTOMATION

One solution to the problems that arise in dealing indirectly with the environment is to make the machines so fully automatic that no human control of them is ever required. To a limited extent modern industry has been able to eliminate the human element. In certain specialized tools and even in more elaborate systems, automation may be almost complete. A reasonably stable process, such as that exemplified by modern petroleum production, can be carried on in plants which are almost wholly automatic.

But even here we find a few operators watching over the complex instrument panels, monitoring them, and being ready to respond to the automatic warning signals that indicate that conditions have arisen which the machines cannot handle. These men are performing different tasks from the workers before them, but they are nonetheless exercising the ultimate control functions.

Machines and the User. It might be possible to anticipate some of these conditions which the machines themselves cannot handle and build into the systems the means for dealing with them. For example, one could provide auxiliary power units to be used when the primary ones are damaged in a storm. In this way, the *range of environmental conditions* which the machine can cope with is extended—not without cost, however. Adding parts which may be used but infrequently is expensive. We pay for the parts themselves, for the space they fill, and for the increased complexity of the system, because the parts must be integrated into the overall structure.

Moreover, we must remember that the machines are created to satisfy the needs of the user. As the needs change, different functions are required of the machines. The stable processes and products of the refineries will, in fact, be modified as new petroleum products are found. Needs also change in the short run. The automobile which can get you back and forth to work most economically is not necessarily the one which can take you to a distant destination with speed and comfort or provide the needed space for camping and fishing gear on a vacation trip. Flexible and adaptable multipurpose machines are, necessarily, complex machines.

Complexity limits the development of complete automation. Each of the separate quantities that influences the behavior of the complex system must be measurable and subject to physical control. All of the facts about the performance of the separate parts must be linked with one another and related to the goals that the machine must achieve. This can only be accomplished through a very complex central processing unit, a multipurpose control device flexible enough to handle the variety of facts given to it— a giant brain. Some of the high-speed digital computers presently available are beginning to approach the degree of complexity necessary to tie in these many and varied facts. In effect, these machines partially simulate the generalized abilities that man already has [16, 42].

THE FIELD OF ENGINEERING PSYCHOLOGY

The task which confronts engineering psychology is to describe the special abilities and limitations of man in such a way that design engineers can effectively incorporate the human operator as a component in the man-machine system. This requires knowledge about sensation and perception, psychomotor behavior, and cognitive processes.

A Problem in Communication. Communicating with the engineer is also a part of the task. The descriptive material must be presented not necessarily in terms that other psychologists can understand, but in such a way that the design engineer can use it. Only by treating both the animate and inanimate components in terms of common conceptualizations can the psychologist and the engineer attain an understanding of their joint actions. For this reason, the bias that has arisen is to treat people as if they were machines rather than to treat machines as people. As a result, the psychologist working in this field has had to learn the language of physical science.

The field of engineering psychology has evolved only within the past twenty to twenty-five years. During World War II psychologists were called upon to assist engineers in the development of weapons systems. At first this help involved suggestions for the design of knobs, levers, and dials. A number of investigations were concerned simply with the evaluation of these devices in terms of the speed or accuracy of human response. Later the team approach to systems design enabled psychologists to use their knowledge of the various sensory and motor aspects of man's behavior. In the team, the psychologist served as an adviser to the engineer and in some instances participated in designing various components of the systems. At present the field of engineering psychology, while it draws upon findings within the general field of experimental psychology, is basically concerned with specifying, in physical terms, those properties of human behavior which are important for the control of machines. Once these properties have been appropriately specified and mechanical or electronic means for simulating them have been developed, unmanned systems of increasing complexity are possible, as we see demonstrated in the aerospace program.

THE NATURE OF MAN–MACHINE SYSTEMS

What is a system? How does the man fit into it? The systems concept is the basic idea that enables us to put the man and the machine on even terms. The word "system" suggests more than one component part. It is bigger than the elements that compose it. The way the parts act toward one another determines the nature of the system. In Figure 13.1 the elements of a system are represented by the blocks. Let us first look at two systems which involve machines only.

The Open Loop. Suppose that we wish to turn on some outside lights at dusk. In setting up a system to accomplish this, we might use a photocell which would react to the change in the outside level of illumination. The quantity of light entering the photocell is the input variable. Whenever this input falls below some previously established level, a switch is activated. The lights come on and the output of the system, also a quantity of light, is modified. When the general out-of-doors illumination—the input—increases again at dawn, the quantity of light entering the photocell exceeds the level set for turning off the lights, and the control switch is deactivated.

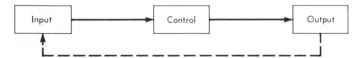

Fig. 13.1. The elements of control systems. In a control system there is an *open* loop when the action follows the path from input through control to output, as represented by the solid arrows. The broken arrow shows the output being fed back into the system so that the output itself is modified; this is called a *closed-loop* system.

The control system, consisting of the photocell and some additional electronic equipment, produces a change in the output which depends on a change in the input. Notice in Figure 13.1 that the action follows the solid arrows from left to right. Once the switch is deactivated, further changes in the input do not influence it. This is the simple open loop.

The Closed Loop. Suppose, however, that we now wish to control the temperature of a room. In this case the input variable is the temperature variation that acts upon a thermostat. Whenever the temperature of the room falls too low, a switch turns on the furnace. The result is a greater output of heat for the room. Is this, too, the open loop? It is not, because here the output quantity acts back on the input element. The broken arrow indicates this fact in Figure 13.1. Feeding back the output or some part of the output quantity so that the output is itself modified is characteristic of the closed-loop system.

Specifications in Control. Both of these examples represent types of control. We can see that the word "control" means holding some specified quantity constant. In the first instance we wish to maintain the conditions of illumination, in the second, to maintain the level of temperature. Open-loop systems, which lack feedback, are necessarily limited in their scope of operation. They must be calibrated to work properly under some particular set of conditions. Of more interest is the self-regulating system which results when we close the loop. Devices of this type provide rather precise control over a wide range of input values. It is not easy to design an instrument which attains this precision, however.

Suppose for the moment that we try to make a closed-loop system out of the photocell and floodlights. We might do this by letting one of the lamps shine on the photocell. If we incorporate a time lag into the control element, a condition of unstable operation is set up. All night long, the lights go on, then off, then on again. The system oscillates or hunts and cannot settle down. This illustration points up problems, some of them not particularly obvious, which confront the design engineer in building complex interacting mechanisms of the self-regulating type. Their design requires the precise specification of many values having to do with time lags, inertia of moving parts, sensitivity of the detector elements, and so on.

These same complications are present in the systems where men perform the controlling acts. It is, therefore, just as necessary to specify human values with precision as it is to do so for the parts of the machine itself. Let us now turn our attention to man as a control system playing his part in the larger man-machine structure.

An Example of a Man-Machine System. In Figure 13.2 we have represented a very small part of an aircraft system. It suggests a single control function, namely, that of regulating the speed of the aircraft. We may think of the first-level control system as the pilot—the human operator himself. Presumably, he too possesses input, control, and output elements, but for the moment, let's keep him intact. The input to the pilot is derived from the airspeed indicator—a pointer reading on a dial. We must specify a quantity to be controlled, a constant value of perhaps 550 miles per hour. It is the same as setting the thermostat at 70° or adjusting the photocell to turn on the lights at a given level of darkness. By convention, any input element that provides the direct sensory stimulus for the human operator is called a *display*. The operator receives information from the display that may lead to a decision to advance the throttle; this is accomplished by a movement on the part of the pilot. The object through which the operator's control decision is carried out is a *control mechanism* or, simply, a *control*. The output at this level is a change in position of the control. In a sense the throttle lever is made to follow inversely the movements of the pointer so that any discrepancy or error is kept to a minimum. It is a closed-loop system, since the output modifies the input.

It is important that we realize that this description is possible only when the particular level is defined. For example, a new set of input and output quantities is indicated in Figure 13.3. At the next higher level, the display, human operator, and control device become the control system which receives information, processes it, and provides an output in a somewhat different form. In some instances the remoteness of the human operator from the environmental variable to be controlled is quite great. At each successive level, time lags are introduced which in general reduce the system's effectiveness.

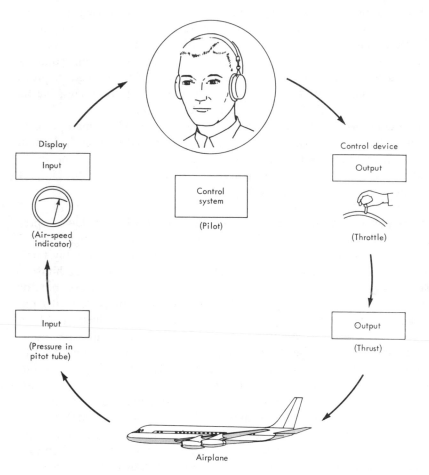

Fig. 13.2. Controlling air speed of an aircraft. The pilot is a control system, receiving inputs from the display (air-speed indicator) and providing outputs to the control device (throttle).

As the number of levels increases, another interesting result can occur. More than one pathway for feeding back information about the output quantities may exist. In the diagram of Figure 13.3 some of the possibilities are shown. Most direct is the feedback which an operator receives as he manipulates the control mechanism itself. He sees and feels the extent

to which a lever is pushed or a wheel is turned. Sometimes the position of
the control is reflected as an integral part of the display. The nature of the
feedback, where it comes from and where it goes, is a very important determiner of the behavior of self-regulating systems [38].

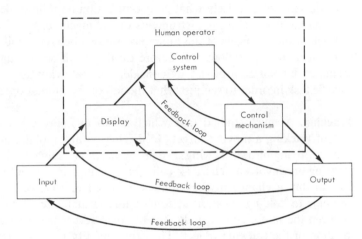

Fig. 13.3. A variety of feedback loops is possible in closed-
loop systems. The human operator may "feel" the position
or resistance of the control device; he may sense the changes
in output directly as increased or decreased pressures; the
state of a control device may be directly displayed on an instrument panel; or the state of the unit on which the control
device acts may be displayed. The basic feedback loop is that
created by the effect of output on input.

THE BEHAVIOR OF THE HUMAN OPERATOR

In observing what the man actually does in his role as controller of the
man-machine system, three aspects of his behavior can be identified. These
correspond to the parts of any generalized control system as outlined in
Figure 13.1. The man, by analogy, is considered to be such a system.

From Information to Action. Man's first act in the control system is to receive information. What information he receives depends on the nature of
his immediate environment or, more specifically, the kinds of machine displays the system provides. Next, he decides what to do—he thinks. Actually it is difficult for us to know exactly what occurs, but we infer that
processing of the information received from the display goes on within the
central nervous structures of the man. In psychology this control activity

has been studied extensively, and is identified as higher mental processes—thinking, problem solving, cognition, reasoning, and the like. We will identify this aspect of the human operator's performance as *complex information processing*. Finally, the man initiates some physical action. His output is in the form of a response or movement by means of which he manipulates the control. Precisely what course of action he follows depends on the decision he makes and the instruments of the machine.

Each of these aspects of the human operator's behavior will be dealt with in the sections that follow. But before turning to these accounts of the elements of human control, let us consider the behavior as it appears in a specific task in order to see just what the job of the human operator is.

Tracking. A much-studied task which arises in many different settings is that of tracking a moving target. In driving an automobile, aiming a shotgun at a flying bird, or sewing a seam by machine, some of the elements of tracking are involved. The task calls for a change in the output of the system so that a change in the input is matched or followed in space. This amounts to holding constant at some value (usually zero) the discrepancy between the target and an indicator of some sort which reflects the spatial location of the tracking object. Thus the quantity to be controlled may be thought of as "error."

In the psychological laboratory, tracking tasks related to certain military systems have been so constructed that they permit us to observe the operator in action and to measure his accuracy. One such arrangement uses the cathode-ray tube for the display. This is an electronic tube used in radar which operates in a fashion similar to the television picture tube. A spot of light moves over the face of the tube in two dimensions. Its movement represents the movement of the target through space. The indicator, or cursor, may be a small lighted circle. The job of the operator is to manipulate a joystick control so that the target is kept within the circle [1, 8, 26].

Some interesting researches on tracking are now under way utilizing cutaneous mechanical vibration, electric pulses, and air-jet stimulation presented in varying sequences and in varying places over the surface of the body. New problems in perception arise as observers are subjected to combinations of these unique spatial-temporal patterns of sensory inputs. For space travel tracking based upon cutaneous stimulation may well find practical use where auxiliary sensory inputs may be required [18].

Pursuit and Compensatory Tracking. If, as suggested in Figure 13.4, the system's input causes the target to move over the face of the screen and the control mechanism permits changes in the cursor so that the operator can follow the target about, the task is referred to as *pursuit tracking*. Contrasted with this procedure is one in which the cursor remains at a fixed place in the center of the screen, and movement of the joystick control counteracts the movement of the target as represented on the face of the tube. This is called *compensatory tracking*. Notice that the difference between these two modes of tracking lies in the way in which the information is presented. In pursuit tracking, the target course can be observed by the operator. He attempts to match the motion of the cursor to that of the target. In the compensatory task, the target course is not so clearly defined. Instead, what the operator sees is the result of the target and the corrective or adjustive effects produced by the control.

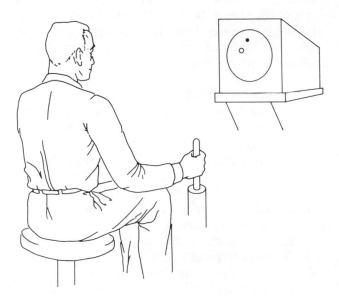

Fig. 13.4. Pursuit tracking. The target (solid dot) moves in two dimensions over the face of the oscilloscope. A cursor (open circle) is controlled by the stick.

Making Corrections. In the analysis of human-operator performance in a tracking task, certain statements can be made about his gross behavior. Anyone who has carefully studied his own behavior in such tasks will probably be able to recall these same features. First, there is an initial misalignment and an attempt to correct it. Generally, accuracy in making corrections is poor in the early stages. It takes more time for the operator to detect the discrepancy, to decide in what direction and by how much the stick should be moved, and even to move it than is required after considerable practice. There is a tendency, in making the corrective movement, to overshoot or undershoot so that, instead of smooth-flowing movements, jerky, discrete adjustments are made. Each attempt represents a separate chunk of behavior rather than a continuous flow. In this way the tracking behavior proceeds. Later on there is a considerable smoothing out of the adjustments because the individual learns to anticipate changes and to organize movements in sequences. This erratic feature of the human operator's behavior led the late K. J. W. Craik, a British psychologist, to apply the term "intermittent" to the definite corrective behavior of the man in this kind of situation [11]. Even personality differences may be related to operator behavior under certain practical conditions. Drew and his co-workers [12] found, for example, that changes in errors and speed in a simulated driving task after various dosages of alcohol were related to personality measures. Individuals with high extroversion scores made more errors and increased errors more with increasing dosage than did those with low extroversion scores.

Transduction. A second characteristic of the human operator's gross behavior is that the man changes the form of the input and output. In physical terms, the energy form which the operator receives is a pattern of light which, during the course of interpretation and processing, comes out as a pattern of movement, i.e., mechanical energy. The engineer's word for this behavior in a machine is "transduction." The radio loudspeaker, for example, is a device which changes electric energy to sound energy. We find that the human operator has special abilities with respect to transducing energy, and systems design requires matching the needs of the system's variables to the abilities exhibited by the man. In other words, certain kinds of inputs from displays lead more readily to certain specific output movements. This problem has been treated in psychology as the *stimulus-response correspondence*.

Amplification. A third important characteristic of the human operator's overall behavior may be called amplification. This means that small amounts of energy give rise to larger amounts when passed through the system. Amplification is basic to almost all control systems whether they include the human operator or not. It is through the expenditure of small amounts of energy that larger energy sources are manipulated in performing the system's work. Relatively little work, in the physical sense, is required in throwing a switch on or off, but the work performed by a motor energized by the switch can be very great. At the level of the human controller, small changes in the discrepancy between target and cursor may give rise to greater changes in his responsive movements.

With these features of the human operator's behavior in mind, we return to the analogy of man as a control system in his own right. Our first concern is with the inputs to the man.

INPUTS AND THE HUMAN SENSORY PROCESSES

The human operator receives information from his environment through the special senses—sight, sound, touch, smell, and taste. The information which he receives is presented by machine displays and thus only indirectly tells him of the changes in the input variables. We do, of course, receive much of the useful information directly. We may observe that the light on our desk is insufficient for reading and may, on the basis of this observation, turn on a lamp. The input variable, level of illumination, is received directly through the visual sense. Sometimes, greater precision is required than is afforded by the unaided visual mechanisms. Perhaps we wish to photograph a scene, and this requires a fairly precise setting of the aperture of our camera. The same input variable is involved when we measure the reflected light from the surface of objects with a light meter. In this case, the information is displayed as a needle deflection. We get information represented by the scale symbols which may be converted readily to the proper setting for the camera. The display is a visual one, but the information presented tells us only indirectly of the input.

Design of Displays. The engineering problem is to determine how to construct displays so that the information required is received quickly and accurately by the machine operator. Thus the engineering psychologist treats the sensory mechanisms of the human being as detector devices.

In designing displays for the more complex systems where many inputs must be represented, it is important to provide as much of the relevant information as possible in a single display. For example, in a task which requires locating objects in space, it is easy to build a display which yields information about a single dimension, say, the distance of an approaching aircraft from the end of a runway. However, to give this information *and* information about its altitude, heading, or speed of approach in a single simple display is very difficult. Hence much of the time and effort expended in display design are directed toward finding ways to simplify the presentation of many separate pieces of information and incorporate them into a single meaningful display.

The problems of presenting information to the operator can be illustrated most easily by a look at the simpler systems where we have single inputs. We have previously suggested that the behavior of the human operator is intermittent. The information provided by a single dial or gauge, with its numbers or other symbols, is attended to by the observer discretely. This means that although the input variable itself may be constantly changing, as in the tracking task, the human observer can grasp the meaning or detect the state of the signal only as a fixed unit in time. For purposes of control action, the information is apprehended as a stationary discrepancy or value. Thus, if two or more displays are presented to the controller, only one of them can be attended to and hence provide a usable signal at one time. In reading, for example, successive fixation of the eyes on separate parts of the written material occurs. Although the better reader exhibits fewer such fixations per line of type, he nevertheless shows the same general pattern. He is able to assimilate a larger number of individual symbols within a single fixation than can the slower reader, but in performance he behaves in essentially the same way.

In the task of presenting information to an operator, the time needed to acquire units of the message contained in the signal must be specified for the many different kinds of sensory inputs that may be used.

Information Theory. In engineering psychology, a convenient analogy has been drawn between the sensory mechanisms of the human being and their counterparts in communication engineering. The concept of a *channel* has come to refer to means by which sensory data are conveyed to the person, just as the television channel stands for the means whereby the audio and video signals are transmitted and received. Information is put into one end of the channel and comes out the other end. This is an almost exact counterpart of the human being receiving information from a display. The display "sends" patterns of light or sound that symbolically denote the changes in the input variable. These patterns are the message. Reception of the message and the perception of its meaning come about through the specialized organs of the man.

Each of the sensory modalities is considered a sensory channel. The sense of sight constitutes the means by which information from visual displays is transmitted to the consciousness of the human controller. The usefulness of this analogy becomes apparent when we recognize that with a suitable measure for the amount of information contained in a display and a procedure for determining how much of the information presented is received by the observer of the display, a precise technique is available to us for improving displays.

The Bit. A measure has been developed by communications engineers called the bit (a contraction of binary digit). A bit is the information in a single choice between two alternatives. Thus if we know that one of two events is to occur but are uncertain which it will be, one bit of information which resolves this uncertainty is transmitted by a signal. Paul Revere's "one, if by land; two, if by sea" signal system transmitted one bit. Any signal, then, that has just two states or any language with only two symbols can provide one bit of information. Now let us suppose that there are eight buttons on a panel before you, and you are to push one of them. How much information must be given to enable you to push the correct one?

If, as in the first row of Figure 13.5, half of the buttons are circular and half of them triangular, the message "Press the circular button" reduces your uncertainty and provides some of the information you need. In fact, it halves the number of alternatives. If the message reads, "Press the circular button that is colored black," the number of alternatives is again halved. You finally know what to do when the message reads, "Press the circular button that is painted black and has a projecting stem." Three bits

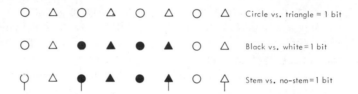

Fig. 13.5. Eight alternatives and three bits. Each of the binary cues—circle vs. triangle, black vs. white, stem vs. no-stem—halves the number of alternatives, so that one of eight alternatives can be selected.

of information are contained in the message; they reduce the eight alternatives to just the one specific object, button number three. This information could have been transmitted in many other ways, of course. Relays that are open or closed, lights that are on or off, or currents that either flow or do not flow are all possibilities. But in a strict sense, precise specification is possible only when information is given in quantitative terms.

Of course the message could have read, "Press button number three." On the surface, this appears considerably easier and more efficient and seems to contain fewer units of information than indicated above. Our language is a highly developed code and provides us with a great deal of flexibility, so that there frequently are many ways of saying the same thing. Notice, however, that in setting up the simple number code, eight possible messages, one for each of the eight buttons, would have to be established in advance; i.e., eight *different* signals would be necessary. From a communication point of view, it is usually easier to think of and provide the means for sending just the three binary symbols. Thus, in teletype, five "on" or "off" punches in a tape can be used to designate thirty-two possible symbols—enough for the twenty-six letters of the alphabet and a few punctuation marks.

Redundancy in Communication. The fact is that messages in our language often contain the same information several times. Constraints of the language (the letter "u" always follows "q") create redundancy in normal verbal communication. The context of speech gives us information about what the next symbol is going to be. Hence, when that symbol occurs, some of the information it would have contained has already been received. Shannon [36] has estimated the redundancy of English based on the statistical structure of the language over distances of about eight letters to be 50 per cent. Students have long known that textbooks need be only half as long as they usually are.

These concepts are valuable for the field of engineering psychology because they help us to devise a means of quantitatively describing inputs to the human operator. Quite apart from language communication as such, we may apply these concepts to any kind of display in which stimulus objects with varying characteristics provide knowledge of changes external to the system. We can compute the capacity of the observer to receive information per unit of time. Or we can find how much information can be transmitted by certain displays if the observer is given sufficiently great amounts of time to observe them.

Amount of Information in a Display. Hake and Garner [21] determined the amount of information transmitted to observers who made judgments about the value represented by a pointer position between scale marks as on an instrument dial. In this experiment, the pointer was allowed to take on five, ten, twenty, or fifty different positions within the interpolation interval.

The greater the number of pointer positions, the greater is the amount of information contained in the display. However, we might reasonably expect that there would be more errors with the larger numbers of values to detect, so that what the observer gets out of the display represents what is there minus the error factors. Hake and Garner found that above a certain minimal number of allowed positions, the amount of information was approximately constant. Very little additional information is transmitted by allowing more than ten pointer positions. For the particular size of scale that they used, slightly more than 3 bits of information per pointer presentation were obtained from the ten, twenty, and fifty positions, whereas only 2.31 bits were transmitted in the five-position case.

Informational analysis of displays is a useful device in treating some of the problems of equipment design for human use. However, a great deal of study devoted to the understanding of the sensory mechanisms—the channels through which the observer picks up the inputs—has yielded basic data about the receptor processes. These results have not often been obtained in information-theory terms. They nevertheless identify important factors that are related to the design of displays and the operator's role in the machine system.

CONTROL AND HUMAN INFORMATION PROCESSING

The human operator serves as a living link between the inanimate parts of the man-machine system. The information obtained from the system displays passes through him, but not in the same way that a message passes through a telephone wire. Such a procedure would be wasteful of man's unique talents as a decision-making machine. Rather, the information presented to the operator is assimilated, processed in the light of previously acquired information stored in memory, and evaluated for future action. In many systems, the amount and complexity of this processing is fantastically great. In other practical situations, man's controlling acts are quite simple, and if it were not convenient to keep the man around for other reasons, his control functions might well be eliminated.

The design engineer needs to know which tasks are best performed by machines and which are best carried out by a human operator. If we are to assist the engineer in this, we must look more closely at the information processing which the operator carries out in his role as the data-transmission link in the system. The operator comes to the system with certain previously learned habits and knowledge. He knows what it is that the system is to do.

In the earlier example of the aircraft pilot, the pilot had to know that he was to maintain an airspeed of 550 miles per hour. He retained this figure in his memory, stored away but available for purposes of comparison with the figure designating his actual airspeed at any time. He received the latter value whenever he directed his attention to the airspeed indicator on his instrument panel. Next, he compared the two values and determined whether his present airspeed was greater or less than the desired value. As a result of this test, or comparison, he made his decision: "My airspeed is greater than the desired value; therefore I will reduce it." The decision he made is neither more nor less than pulling forth certain pieces of information—also stored in memory—associated with the possible outcomes of the test.

Complex Information Processing. The chain of mental acts that leads to the final decision of the operator begins with the *perceptual responses* which enable him to interpret the data of the display. The patches of light and patterns and shapes are meaningful objects or quantities; the operator recognizes them and distinguishes among them pieces of information for subsequent comparisons. For more complex situations, there may be many steps or stages along the way to reaching the decision. For this reason, we will call the final comparison that the operator makes—the one which leads to one of several alternative courses of action—the *decision*. The comparisons that he must make after the recognition or identification of the objects but prior to this final step are *judgments*. The distinction between judgments and decisions is simply that we can make a judgment and not do anything about it; when we make a decision, however, the implication is that some course of overt action will follow.

Perceptions, judgments, and decisions, then, are the kinds of mental activities that are included within the broader framework of complex information processing. All three of these activities require basically the same sort of processing. In general, at least two pieces of information must be appropriately specified, and at least one test comparing the pieces of information must be carried out. The distinctions among perceptions, judgments, and decisions are made in terms of the kinds of information compared, the bases for the comparison, and what happens as a result of the comparison. In the following sections we will present brief descriptions of these activities [37].

Perceptual Processes. We are constantly being stimulated by sights and sounds, of which only a small fraction have significance for our present behavior. What we attend to and how we interpret the stimuli are determined by our perceptual processes. We recognize or identify an object for what it is because, in the past, experiences of a particular kind were associated with the object. A perception, then, comes about when certain aspects of the stimulus are observed and compared with a stored impression. Let's see how this process works.

Scanning. In perceiving, we draw meaning from the sensory impression by first distinguishing the properties, or characteristics, of the objects. We must observe the relevant attributes that will permit us to determine whether or not the object matches the stored representation. Since there are many ways in which any given object may be characterized, we speak of a scanning, or search, process as a part of the general perceptual act. Normally we think of applying this term to a rather broad and vague field of view; for example, we scan an expanse of water or land. But even relatively small displays such as the screen of a radar set can be scanned too. Carried further, the scanning idea permits us to describe the way in which an observer attends successively to input elements whether large or small. In perceiving, we seek distinguishing characteristics of the object by scanning first one property, then another, then still another. Paying attention to the right things enables us to put similar things in the same class and to distinguish other things which do not belong in that class.

The operator, in learning to use the machine, comes to recognize the location of particular instruments. He identifies the uses of the dials and controls. He finds out what they do and how they do it. The sensory inputs that he receives take on meaning as his experience with the machine components broadens. Since our perceptions are based on learning of this sort, we might expect that enough practice would enable us to perform effectively under any circumstances. But this is only partially true. In the more complex systems there are many inputs to the operator—many displays and many input variables denoted by them. There is always the possibility of confusion and interference within the system itself. Moreover, some of our perceptual responses are so well habituated and so continually practiced that to create meanings which oppose them in the design of the system would not only increase training time but would pose an ever-present opportunity for errors in interpretation.

Coding. In engineering psychology, the problem posed by the need to present stimuli in meaningful ways is often called a problem in coding. We want to represent the input variables in such a way that they can make sense to the human operator. One way of doing this is to provide a simple, single cue for the recognition of the stimuli. This method was used in an experiment on a complex job involving the control of air traffic. The study was conducted by investigators at the Ohio State University [34]. The problem made use of a system that was designed to simulate aircraft flying under instrument conditions while being guided into a landing field. The human controller observes the location of incoming aircraft on a radar screen and gives instructions to the pilots so that their aircraft maintain a safe operation in the air and yet are brought into their destination as quickly and efficiently as possible. Usually the targets appear on the radar as small blobs of light, and it is possible to determine which blob stands for which airplane only by remembering the relative positions, headings, and speeds, as obtained from the display. This task is a complex one. The controller must keep in mind a plan of the arrival sequence and guide the flight of the planes to match the sequence that he sets up. He tells the pilots what direction they should go, where they should turn, how fast they should be traveling, and at what altitude they should fly. In the experiment the perceptual task of the controller was made easier by the use of a clock code which served to identify each of the aircraft which entered the traffic patterns. This coding allowed the controller to differentiate among the blips on the radar and in this way gave meaning to each of the individual elements of the display. In terms of such measures as control time and fuel consumption for the simulated aircraft in the problem, the improvement in the overall effectiveness of the operator attributable to the identifying code was quite great.

The Ohio State University experiment demonstrates the principle which applies to the perceptual problem in complex information processing. The perception of an object depends on there being some unambiguous cue which enables the person to distinguish that object from others. Speed of recognition can be increased by reducing the time required for scanning the properties of the object, since only one unequivocal aspect is important.

Processes of Judgment and Estimation. Of great importance in the sequence of the operator's behavior are the judgments and estimates that are derived from consideration of the sensory inputs. As a result of perceptions, things are categorized into classes; objects are recognized or identified as belonging or not belonging to a particular class. Judgments, on the other hand, typically involve comparisons of quantities along a dimension. A few examples will help make this distinction clear. We recognize an object which is before us as a book. This is a perception. We can ask the question, "Is it a long book or a short book?" Our answer is, in effect, a judgment or an estimate. We could also estimate how much the book weighs, or, along another dimension, we could judge the literary merit of the book. Similarly, when we see an object flying through the sky, the categorical answer to the question of whether it is a bird, or a plane, or space vehicle is again found in our perception of the object. But estimating the distance or altitude or size of the object, once it has been identified as an airplane, requires additional processing.

The fundamental comparison between information presented to the senses and information stored in memory is once more called into play in carrying out such estimates and judgments. The outcomes, as before, depend on what has been learned in the past about the properties of objects.

Making Judgments. We can distinguish two methods of making judgments. An *absolute judgment* is one in which a value is assigned to the object; the value represents a point on the dimensional continuum. To say that the book weighs 2 pounds or that the airplane is 3 miles away is an absolute judgment. Stored information is called forth for comparison purposes. *Comparative judgments* make use of information provided by two or more objects. Thus, to judge that one book is heavier than another is a comparative judgment.

Judgments of time, size, brightness, extent, and the like may be required in a variety of systems where such dimensions of the displayed stimuli are utilized by the operator for later decisions. An example of an absolute judgment in the context of a man-machine–system performance is the judgment reached in determining from the pointer position of a gasoline gauge in an automobile that there are 7 gallons of fuel remaining in the tank. Another dial may provide information which leads to the absolute judgment that the engine is hot. These judgments are *not* decisions. They do, however, yield the information necessary for the last step in the complex processing exhibited by the human operator.

Decision Rules. The final step in the sequence of mental events which leads to overt action by the operator is the decision. The pieces of information available in immediate memory which are compared in reaching the decision are the perceptions and estimates which the operator has derived from the inputs presented him by the machine displays. Associated with the alternative outcomes of the comparison are the courses of action that the operator must then follow if he is to complete his role as a transmission link in the system. Depending on what it is that the system is to do, we get relationships, such as, "If this . . . , then I must do that." Essentially, a rule of some sort is established which defines the manner in which the system must behave to accomplish the control function. Such terminal relationships are decision rules.

Consider the tracking problem described earlier in the chapter. The task of the operator is to keep the spot of light centered on the cross hairs of a screen. He is to do this by moving a joystick control that will change the position of the spot of light on the screen. A target generator causes the spot of light to move about haphazardly over the face of the screen. This is the compensatory tracking task. The goal of the operator is to minimize the discrepancy, or error, introduced by the target generator. More specifically, we can formulate a decision rule which states the relationship between the momentary position of the target and the position which is desired and also the required action associated with such relationships. If the target is too far to the right of center, then the operator moves the joystick to the right. As a result of the perceptual acts that define "target and center" and as a result of the judgments or estimates of "too far," he is enabled through the associated spatial relationships to go into action and make the necessary corrective movements.

Making Decisions. The precise statement of the rule depends on how the system actually works. The operator must learn which way the spot will move when he moves the stick in a given direction. He must also become familiar with the rate and extent of movement of the spot on the screen for given amounts of stick displacement. Furthermore, he must gain a general idea of the way in which the target moves—how fast the changes in position take place and the like. The decision rule then expresses the prescribed course of action, so that one of several possible outcomes prevails. Decision rules are not always openly stated in words in the way we have described them here. Very often, in complex and variable situations, people make decisions which lead to effective action and then find it impossible to say just what it was that prompted them to decide to do what they did. Sometimes we find that skilled individuals reach decisions quickly and yet are unable to instruct the novice in their techniques.

Behavior of this sort frequently seems so automatic that it is difficult to conceive of anyone engaging in the elaborate process outlined here. A partial explanation of this observation lies in the fact that the behavior of the operator is intermittent or sequential, as we described earlier. There is a limit to the amount of information that can be held in immediate memory at any one time. To try to think about a problem and *at the same time* to try to make the process that you are going through the object of thought is difficult if not impossible. The skilled performer is not required normally to produce in language form the mental steps that he goes through. In fact, to do so would probably affect the efficiency of his performance. Hence the cues and subtle interpretations of them are lost to immediate recall.

Our description of the decision-making processes, though not complete, nevertheless contains the essential ingredients. If human decisions seem more mysterious, more "human" than this, it is *only* because statements of the rules have not been made formally. Certainly some of these decision rules build up slowly in the course of time. Indeed, they may be modified from time to time as the decision maker acquires greater knowledge of the alternatives and the outcomes to which they lead. It is also true that many decisions must be based on partial and imperfect knowledge. This simply means that the perceptual interpretations and judgments made along the way are themselves fallible.

The implications for equipment and systems design are clear. Don't let situations arise where more than one perceptual interpretation is possible. Keep the cues for recognition unambiguous. Provide an adequate basis for the kinds of judgments or estimates that must be made. Define the decision rules explicitly.

OUTPUTS AND THE HUMAN MOTOR RESPONSES

After the information has been received and processed by the operator, action of some sort is initiated. The operator responds. Responses that involve throwing switches, turning wheels, moving levers, and the like are called *motor responses*. They require the activation of body members through muscular work.

In some systems the responses of interest to the system's designer are verbal responses made by the operator in communicating with others in the system. Since these systems are very much more complex, we still continue to focus our attention on the system in which a single control receives inputs from and provides outputs to machine components. Although some bowlers try to "talk" to the ball after it has been released, we will assume that what is done with hands and arms while the ball is still in contact with the bowler has a greater bearing on the number of pins knocked down than do verbal responses.

The Study of Motor Skills. A great deal of early work in psychology was devoted to the study of psychomotor skills. The word "psychomotor" suggests that some higher activity precedes the motor response, even if it involves only the recognition of a simple signal that initiates action. In early studies, devices of one sort or another were constructed, and the performance of individuals carrying out the tasks was assessed. At first, these tests were very simple; the psychological investigators focused their attention on movements and muscular adjustments alone. Measures of the movements and of their form and accuracy were obtained. Later the devices used to study motor skills became quite complex and, in fact, approximated miniature systems. Such devices called for perceptual and cognitive behavior as well as motor responses, and during World War II many of these complex instruments were developed as selection devices or training aids. Identification of the basic features of motor action becomes difficult when the complexity of the task is increased.

In the field of industrial engineering a somewhat different approach has been used, as we described in the chapter on work and the conditions of work. Time-and-motion studies have led to the isolation of certain basic patterns of movement. These elements are then combined to describe various tasks. The very practical reason for this approach is that it enables us to predict in some quantitative way how difficult the job is, what its time requirements are, and what rest allowances are desirable for it. Such studies give little more than a crude approximation of the nature of the motor responses. The job elements of time-and-motion study are assumed to be independent; it is assumed that recombining the elements in different ways will not change the values assigned to them. That this is not always a safe assumption was demonstrated in an experiment using a device called the Universal Motion Analyzer developed by K. U. Smith at the University of Wisconsin [22].

The Motion Analyzer. The motion analyzer provides time measures for various components of motor behavior. For example, one measure is travel time—the time required in moving the hand from one location to another over the surface of a large panel. On the panel are switches or buttons or other objects that can be manipulated by the operator. Manipulation time, then, is another measure which can be obtained from the device. A number of experiments show that travel time, even though the length of the movement is constant, depends on the terminal manipulation—its kind or extent. This means that allowances for the various elements cannot be set up independently of the context in which the movements are carried out. They cannot be added up as columns of numbers.

Apart from the purely psychological and engineering approaches to the investigation of the motor skills, there is the physiological study in which the structures of the body as separate organs are investigated. Although little is known of the underlying physiology of the higher mental processes discussed in the preceding section, considerably more information is available about muscles and the way they are activated. Hence the knowledge gained from measures of electric activity in muscles, anatomic studies of muscular structure, and biochemical studies of the properties of living tissue provide a foundation for the systematic treatment of motor skills.

The Classification of Movements. Descriptively, the forms of muscular activity that are important to the human operator of the man-machine system include the following. First, we frequently find that the basic movement is that of *simple positioning*. In this movement, the body part moves from one particular spatial location to another. Muscle groups initiate action, and the movement is stopped by opposing muscle groups when the new position in space is attained. A corrective movement in tracking, the act of reaching for an object, and the twisting of a knob from one setting to another are examples of such movements. Of course, the direction, force, or amplitude required by the task may vary. Then measures of the speed and accuracy with which the movement is carried will change. If, for example, the person is called upon to move his hand in the horizontal plane a fixed distance of 14 inches, the accuracy will change with the direction of movement. The relationship between accuracy and angle of movement is shown in Figure 13.6 [10].

Other movements of a similar nature are *tense* and *ballistic* movements. In the tense movement the body member is caused to shift in position, but opposing muscular structures are activated while the movement is carried out. Such movements occur whenever variable forces act upon the body member during the course of the action. In driving an automobile over smoothly paved roads, the corrective steering movements are essentially simple positioning movements; but driving over a bumpy country road, where rocks or ruts may cause forces to be applied that either add to or subtract from the force produced by the driver, leads to the tense kind of movement pattern. The ballistic movement, in contrast, is one in which little or no subsequent forces are applied, either externally or internally, once the initial force is applied. Activation for this type of movement is produced by the sudden, full effect of a well-defined muscle pattern. There is no opposition then from muscle groups that normally in the simple positioning movement would stop the response. Throwing a baseball or swinging a golf club are ballistic movements. The final position of the body member is not quite so important as the initial direction and force, although without the proper follow-through and provision for stopping the body part, the unskilled or unpracticed amateur can "throw his arm out." Although the true ballistic movement is not commonly found in most human-operator performances, it may occur when a person flips on a switch or in the very special case of eye movements.

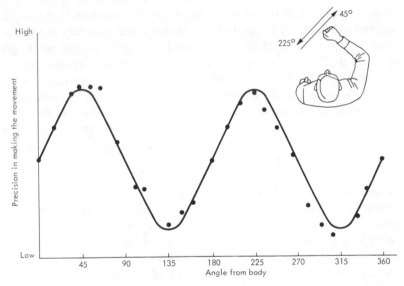

Fig. 13.6. Changes in the accuracy of positioning movements. Depending on the direction of movement, accuracy in tracking a slowly moving target varies. (After Corrigan, R. E., & Brogden, W. J. The trigometric relationship of precision and angle of linear pursuit movements. *Amer. J. Psychol.*, 1949, 62, 90–98.)

Static Responses. Positioning movements are dynamic in the sense that the body member and the control device manipulated by the body member move through space. Static responses are similar to these movements in the patterns of activation, but the extent of movement in the static response is relatively small. These responses produce pressure variations; they are used to exert force on objects—brake pedals and the like—but the movement required is minimal or not present at all. They are extremely important in manipulating objects—in grasping, holding, or picking things up. As much physical energy may be expended in this type of motor response as in the dynamic movement patterns. However, such responses have not been thoroughly observed and studied because there are no obvious ways of detecting them. One approach to a more adequate description of these special muscular patterns is through the use of biological amplifiers that detect the electric activity generated in muscle tissue whenever it is activated. Since the amount of electric activity is proportional to the amount or strength of contraction, description of the patterns of activity and of the extent of energy expended is possible even though work in the physical sense cannot be observed.

The more complex movement patterns are built up from the simple positioning responses. Series of movements can be performed because they are learned as a unit. This chaining of responses becomes very critical in many systems because the relatively independent sequences can be triggered by the operator's decision—once they have been well learned—and can then proceed with little cognitive effort on the part of the operator. The apparent automaticity of certain motor behaviors carries with it both advantages and disadvantages for the design of the man-machine system. The chief advantage, of course, stems from the improved performance which usually results from the reduction of central processing time. The chief disadvantage is the loss of flexibility.

Sequential Movement. The simplest form of sequential movement is the *repetitive movement* in which a unique pattern is itself repeated many times. Tapping tasks and wheel-turning movements are of this sort. When a fairly long sequence of relatively independent movements is carried out as a unit, *serial movements* are being made. It should be emphasized that these movement patterns are descriptive of the human motor output alone and do not refer to the information-processing activities and decision-making acts of the operator. While we are learning to make such responses, we must think a good deal about what we are doing, but once these patterns have been established, they can be carried out as a unit. Central control, thinking about them, is, therefore, unnecessary. Hence, the term "continuous movements" is fallacious. The output of the human system is intermittent. The apparent smoothness results from the integration of varying components into larger and larger units.

HUMAN MOTOR–ABILITY FACTORS

In the psychological study of motor responses, a wide variety of instruments have been constructed; each purports to measure certain aspects of the operator's behavior that might be important in the control of man-machine systems. As we mentioned earlier, some of these psychomotor tests are quite simple; others are extremely complex. Since these tests conform roughly to the kinds of controller activities which may be expected in different kinds of systems, the identification of common abilities which are reasonably independent of one another can provide a useful basis for describing motor behavior.

The technique of factor analysis has been applied to this problem [14]. By obtaining the intercorrelations of performance measures on a large number of these tests administered to the same individuals, psychologists can determine clusters of tests that have similar ability requirements. Inspection of tests which are closely related gives some idea of the common characteristic which underlies good performance on them. Certain abilities have thus been identified and named.

Motor-ability Tests. Among the factors represented in a sample of forty tests was one called *wrist-finger speed*. Tapping tests, which involve moving a stylus back and forth from one plate to another, and aiming tests, which require the person to place pencil marks in small circles, contain this factor. The basic muscular-movement patterns are essentially simple repetitive or serial movements of the fingers or wrist. It was found that this factor reflected primarily the rapidity of movement rather than the careful positioning of the stylus or pencil. In fact, as the circles were made progressively smaller, less and less of this particular ability seemed to be required for high scoring on the tests.

Other factors were found in the study which provide a framework for describing kinds of motor skills. In addition to wrist-finger speed, rate of arm movement was important. The two factors appear to be similar, but the latter involves the larger muscle groups of the arm. Accuracy of the movements did not appear to be critical. Instead, an entirely distinct factor emerged that accounted for the ability to perform quickly and precisely a series of accurately directed movements. This factor was called *aiming*. For other movements in which a number of different muscle groups were employed simultaneously to produce a coordinated pattern of response, the factors of finger dexterity, manual dexterity, and psychomotor coordination were found. These factors seem to be related to the size of the muscle groups which work together in performing the coordinated act. Finger dexterity involves fine manipulation, such as that of the skilled watchmaker who uses the finger tips primarily in executing his task. The gross involvement of the larger muscles of the back, arm, legs, and wrists of the baseball player typifies the factor of psychomotor coordination.

These factors and others, including reaction time and steadiness, help us to understand the outputs of the human operator. In contrast to the job elements of time-and-motion studies, these factors, it seems, may be treated as components of skill. This means that we should not necessarily expect an individual to be able to execute an equally skilled performance in a task involving finger dexterity and in a task requiring psychomotor coordination. What the watchmaker learns to do and what the ballplayer learns are quite different things.

Measures of Motor Performance. Movements made by the human operator are observable. We can measure the effectiveness of the various motor responses by obtaining quantities that reflect speed and accuracy of the movements. These determinations are important in their own right because these human outputs limit the output of the entire system. We can think ahead, for example, faster than we can write down our ideas on paper.

In general, measures of speed and accuracy exhibit a reciprocal relation. What we gain in one typically results in a loss in the other. The generality of this relationship is seen in a unique approach to the problem of determining the limits of motor behavior. In an attempt to provide a more precise, quantitative statement of such a limit, Fitts used ideas taken from the information theory discussed earlier in this chapter [13].

He compared several different tasks that involved the factors we have identified as wrist-finger speed, finger dexterity, and aiming. The difficulty of the tasks was changed by introducing greater or lesser distances over which movements were to be made and by changing the tolerances that were allowable for the accurate performance of the tasks. The subjects were permitted to adjust their rate of working so that a constant level of accuracy was maintained. For the different tasks, approximately the same overall effectiveness was observed when the balance between speed and accuracy was expressed in terms of the information capacity of the motor performance. Thus, when the difficulty of the task was increased, the subjects worked more slowly. But in quantitative terms the measure of motor output was essentially constant.

Just as the engineer evaluates the performance of the machine components by subjecting them to certain standard tests, so too the engineering psychologist evaluates the performance of the man. One such standard procedure by the engineer for testing a variety of mechanical and electric systems is to apply a sudden load on the system and obtain measures of the response. By analogy, such a *step input function* is frequently utilized in evaluating human performance.

Reaction-time Study. One study investigated the reaction time of operators who were to make a simple corrective movement when the step input function consisted of a sudden displacement of a spot of light on a screen similar to those used in radar presentations [35]. Reaction time was essentially constant no matter what the size of the displacement (see Figure 13.7). More surprising, perhaps, was the finding that the time required to make the response itself was much the same for different extents of movement. Changes in the acceleration and deceleration of the movement compensated for the greater length of travel. Whether this knowledge of a fixed time lag is or is not important to the design engineer depends on the other properties of the particular system. However, in some instances, knowledge of the maximum rates of change in the corrective movement becomes critical; in order to keep overeager operators from imposing

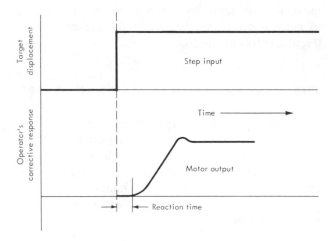

Fig. 13.7. Response to a step input function. Displacement of the target is almost instantaneous, but the operator's response lags in a predictable way in following the target.

changes which are too great or which will produce overcorrection and jerkiness, the design engineer takes special steps to offset these possibilities. For example, the display can be "quickened" so that the effects of the operator's adjustment are fed back faster than the system can respond. Thus the operator actually receives information from the display about the future state of the system.

The System Components. The measures of motor performance are important for reasons other than simply quantifying the controller's output. Since these measures provide our only means of observing the behavior of the man, it is through their relationships to the inputs that we can infer that such processes as perception, judgment, decision making, and many other things psychological exist as we have described them. Learning, for example, cannot be measured directly. We infer that such a process takes place from observed changes in behavior. The nature of these processes is defined in terms of the overt behavior and its relation to changes in stimuli that we provide.

This same methodology permits us to evaluate the effectiveness of the system components—the displays and controls—which the human operator must use. By holding the response constant and varying the input from several displays, we can determine which display is best for a particular system. By holding the inputs and other requirements constant and varying the responses—devising different kinds of control devices or changing the movements in some way—we get the kind of information that permits us to determine the effectiveness of the movements and to evaluate the different controls themselves.

THE ANALYSIS OF MAN–MACHINE SYSTEMS

Although the field of engineering psychology is young and the precise specification of the engineering properties of the human operator is far from realized, enough data are available from studies of the sensory, cognitive, and motor abilities of man to suggest tentative ways of approaching the design of equipment for human use. We at least know what we must look for in any attempt to evaluate the performance of the man-machine system.

What to Look For. At the outset, we identify the control functions of the system. This is roughly equivalent to saying that we must first understand the purpose or goal of the system's performance before we can recommend a way of reaching that goal. Complications may arise because a given system may entail control functions simultaneously directed toward two or more goals. For example, a highway-traffic control system may be required that has as its ultimate purpose moving vehicles through a congested area quickly and safely. But speed of movement and safe operation of the vehicles in the traffic patterns are incompatible.

We next must determine the nature of the input to the operator, the output from the operator, and the knowledge required by the operator if he is to effect the appropriate control decisions. What the operator already knows or can learn in a reasonably short period of time will determine how to best display the operator inputs and provide for his outputs. Any modification that simplifies the conceptual scheme of the operator and thereby allows faster recognition, fewer steps in the central processing, more clear-cut alternatives for decision, or a change that takes advantage of the better-learned motor-response sequences may improve the effectiveness of the system.

Since we are almost always dealing with systems of the closed-loop type, a further consideration is that of identifying the feedback links. These, too, supply input changes to the operator, and may actually be reflected in the primary display of the machine. However, we also recognize that the feedback may be intrinsic to the human operator's behavior itself. For example, both visual and proprioceptive cues, the latter arising within the musculature during performance, provide information to the operator that may be useful in directing his behavior. In many systems we may wish to provide special displays that monitor the internal changes in the system. These displays may be as simple, for example, as a red warning light to indicate when engine temperatures are too high.

How to Look. A system is a complicated mass of interconnected parts. In order to be able to identify the critical elements in meaningful ways, it is necessary to represent the relationships among the parts in some fashion. A device used by the engineer is the flow diagram. Figure 13.1 is essentially a very simple example of such a diagram. The blocks represent physical or sometimes conceptual elements, and the connecting lines indicate the way in which these parts are connected, including the direction of energy flow. In general, such diagrams present only a static picture of the state of affairs existing within the system at a particular point in time. Only by analyzing changes in the flow diagram over a period of time do we obtain some idea of the dynamic picture of the system.

Mathematical representations of a system's operation may give precise statements of the relationships that exist within the system. In order to obtain these equations, ways of measuring the variable quantities must, of course, be known. One kind of mathematical representation which is often employed, for example, is that of determining the *transfer function* of the system. In this particular case, the output quantities, frequently obtained as a time-varying measure, are determined as a function of the input. Since dimensional size of the quantities within the equation must be maintained, one of the basic problems in engineering psychology is that of finding appropriate ways of measuring dimensionally equivalent inputs and outputs. The meaning attached to such mathematical representations of systems then depends on the nature of the dimensions involved.

In a physical system, say the amplifier in your radio, the meaning of the transfer function is fairly clear, since we put in a small voltage and get out a larger one. The gain of the system can be described by the equation that expresses the output as a function of the input. For example, $E_o = KE_I$ tells us that the magnitude of the output is greater than the magnitude of the input by a factor of K. The constant K is the gain of the system and has meaning because we have maintained dimensionality within the equation. There are voltages on both sides of the equals sign.

Such transfer functions have been derived for systems with the human operator imbedded in the system. It is as if both machine and human components were stuck in a "black box." But the task of obtaining transfer functions for the human operator himself—where he alone is in the black box—can only be accomplished when dimensionally equivalent human inputs and human outputs can be found.

GENERALIZED PRINCIPLES OF SYSTEMS DESIGN

There are essentially three things that we must consider in systems design. The first is the loading imposed on the information channels. In the man-machine system we must make sure that the sensory input channels and the motor outputs do not become overloaded. This may be accomplished by appropriately coding the inputs or modifying the task requirements.

A second area of concern is the matching of inputs and outputs throughout the system. In the case of the machine components this may take the form of providing the proper mechanical links, adjusting lengths of lever arms, and the like, or matching the impedance of an amplifier output to the loudspeaker of the radio to obtain maximum power transfer. For the human operator, the matching concept is seen in the problem of choosing appropriate directions of motion for display elements, such as pointers and control devices. The idea of display-response compatibility recognizes the importance of proper choice of these relationships.

Finally, effective systems design requires the adjustment of the time constants of the parts within the system. In the physical realm, inertial and frictional forces govern the motions of objects. A heavy flywheel keeps spinning, but it takes longer to start than does a light wheel. The time constants are here derived from the properties of the objects. The human operator has time constants, too. Other things also get involved when we consider more aspects of the human factors in systems.

SUGGESTIONS FOR SELECTIVE READING

Bennett, E., et al. *Human factors in technology*. New York: McGraw-Hill, 1963. For sophisticated readers.

Borko, H. (Ed.) *Computer applications in the behavioral sciences*. Englewood Cliffs, N.J.: Prentice-Hall, 1962. A collection of readings about how computers are useful in research.

Chapanis, A. *Research techniques in human engineering*. Baltimore: Johns Hopkins, 1959. For the technically qualified reader.

Damon, A., et al. *The human body in equipment design*. Cambridge, Mass.: Harvard University Press, 1965. From the readable to the technical.

Dorian, F. *Commitment to culture: Art patronage in Europe. Its significance for America.* Pittsburgh, Pa.: University of Pittsburgh Press, 1964. Art as an antidote to automation.

Fargus, R. H. *Perception: The basic process in cognitive development.* New York: McGraw-Hill, 1966. Relates perception to the broader cognitive area.

Feigenbaum, E., & Feldman, J. (Eds.) *Computers and thought.* New York: McGraw-Hill, 1963. A collection of papers on information-processing theories; sophisticated reading.

Flaherty, B. E. (Ed.) *Psychophysiological aspects of space flight.* New York: Columbia, 1961. Readings at the sophisticated level.

Geldard, F. A. *The human senses.* New York: Wiley, 1953. A readable description of all of the human senses.

Greenberger, M. (Ed.) *Management and the computer of the future.* Cambridge, Mass.: M.I.T., 1962. Lectures presenting optimistic and pessimistic views of computer usage.

Harper, R. J. C., et al. (Eds.) *The cognitive processes: Readings.* Englewood Cliffs, N.J.: Prentice-Hall, 1964. From readable to sophisticated.

Luce, R. D., et al. (Eds.) *Handbook of mathematical psychology.* New York: Wiley, 1963. Three volumes of sophisticated reference and research work.

McCormick, E. J. *Human-factors engineering.* (2d ed.) New York: McGraw-Hill, 1964. Extensive covering of engineering psychology in a readable text.

Morgan, C. T., et al. (Eds.) *Human engineering guide to equipment design.* New York: McGraw-Hill, 1963. Technical.

Rosenblith, W. A. (Ed.) *Symposium on sensory communications.* Cambridge, Mass.: M.I.T., 1961. Sophisticated papers, from cutaneous communication to involved coding problems.

Sinaiko, H. W. (Ed.) *Selected papers on human factors in design and use of control systems.* New York: Dover, 1961. From readable to technical.

Vygotsky, L. S. (Translated by E. Haufmann & G. Vakar.) *Thought and language.* New York: Wiley, 1962. Development of language and concept formation in children.

14

Human Factors
in Systems

Robert B. Miller

It seems to just come naturally that each person sees his job in relation
to his own experiences and background and within a framework of his
own goals. At the professional level much the same kinds of perceptions
exist as those found at the managerial level. The accountant sees the problems of the organization in terms of profit and loss data, the company
lawyer sees decision making as it may be related to legal restraints, and
the psychologist thinks in terms of the human elements. Within each profession there are specialties. The psychologist may concentrate his efforts
on job analysis, personnel selection, safety training, or something else. Aside
from being a specialist, the industrial psychologist also functions in general
ways. As a consultant to management, he may offer advice from data he has
collected on a specific problem, from general principles, or from a collection of personal observations and wisdom. Occasionally he may have
the time, energy, facility, and support to do experiments in which he tests a
hypothesis or validates a procedure. As the psychologist in industry becomes more involved in research and development, he steps into a newer
role involving systems. Let us look more closely at this role.

EXPANSION OF PSYCHOLOGICAL PROBLEMS

We have already discussed many of the problems with which industrial
psychologists work and have seen how they go about solving them. We
have also mentioned that problem areas are expanding, and we have seen

evidence of how the applications of psychology in industry are branching out. What does this mean for the psychologist? How does he attack problems that seem to be coming from all sides? More specifically, what are the newer roles now appearing for industrial psychologists? Generally, the industrial psychologist has a problem context defined for him when his management thinks that there is something wrong somewhere in company operations and suspects that, somehow, human beings are to blame. The problems are numerous, as we know. Too much labor turnover. Too many accidents. Too many misfits hired. Too few people with managerial talent. Too many troublemakers in plant 4. Too many grievances in plant 6. Too many complaints about the incentive system. Too many complaints about the lighting system, the rest rooms, the dining facilities, the vernier markings on the inspection gauges. The rapid growth of technology in the space age has created new problems for human beings. What can be done about the changing context of our human problems?

There are signs pointing to different kinds of questions that will be asked the psychologist in the future. These will be broader questions demanding of him different working relationships with his associates. We shall begin by looking at two examples.

Effects of Automation. Let us assume that an industry is planning to become fully automated in the next five years. This may mean the elimination of many jobs and major changes in others. The industry wants to avoid imposing major hardships on its employees—on its executive officers, its line workers, and others. How does it go about planning for and carrying out this transition? Clearly, the problem will take several specific forms. The psychological problems will include building up different attitudes in supervisory and working personnel. New skill requirements will have to be predicted for managerial and line workers. New job structures may have to be designed not only for a man's present capabilities but also for the pattern of abilities he must superimpose on what he knows now and is able to learn. Training techniques will have to be developed. In some ways, the new plant facilities may be restricted by policies that permit only the easiest and least costly transition. But most important of all, the entire task must be accomplished within strict budgets of time and money.

Obviously, the psychologist cannot hope to solve such a problem by himself. He will work with associates who have engineering knowledge, cost accountants and economists, market analysts, production specialists, and many others. He will not make decisions by himself, but he will make recommendations as a member of a team. He will arrive at recommendations partly by interacting with other specialists. But on what evidence will he be able to base his suggestions? That is the subject of later parts of this chapter [4, 8, 41].

Operations Analysis. Let us look at another example. A large company believes that the installation of a huge automatic computer will be of benefit. But before committing itself to a costly investment in equipment, it wants to know what such an installation will entail; it wants to be given an estimate not only of the cost of the equipment but of its total demands. The company also wants to know what services the computer can provide, what kinds of data can be profitably analyzed, and how useful the analyses will be. The psychologist may be asked to *participate* in making estimates both of cost and of return. Again, he is a team member, not a lone wolf. Functioning as a member of an operations-analysis group, the psychologist contributes to information technology.

The psychologist will look into the present personnel cost of getting and processing company data; he will make estimates of costs for new or retrained personnel; he will examine supervisory- and maintenance-personnel requirements, potential dissatisfactions, rerouting in the communication system, shifts in supervisory and executive functions, etc. In assessing the potential usefulness of the new equipment, he may have in mind the processing of personnel information which heretofore would have been too costly an operation but which in the future may give him the equivalent of experimental data. However, his thinking cannot be that of the psychologist alone. His ideas will have to be adapted to those of the accounting department, the production department, and the inventory and sales departments, all of which are likely to be represented in the operations-analysis group. And the psychologist will have to be able to converse with these people in some common set of terms [29, 33].

RESEARCH AND DEVELOPMENT

Psychologists have always engaged in research, a fact underlined many times in the preceding chapters. Now something new is being added: certain psychologists are finding themselves on a development team. More and more, the newer roles of the industrial psychologist place him at one time in research and at another time in development. What are the differences between research and development?

Research is the quest for knowledge. *Development* is making something that does something. The remainder of this section will enlarge on this main distinction and on the different roles and operations this distinction implies for the psychologist. Let us begin our discussion with a brief review of what we mean by research so that we may better understand the newer role of the psychologist in development.

Research in Science. Research has many meanings in popular and technical usage. A writer of historical novels says he is doing research when he is reading historical documents of the era about which he plans to write. When a scientist looks into existing references about a scientific topic, he generally feels that it would be pretentious to call this research. Instead, he calls it "literature search." Generally, the term "research" implies that facts are being discovered rather than merely reviewed, although important contributions can be made merely by bringing known facts together.

Research itself can be done in many ways. A researcher may begin by asking the question, "I wonder what will happen if I put object X in situation Y?" He then proceeds to do so and notes the outcome. This approach is *exploratory research* and results in some kind of *demonstration*. A more advanced kind of study may begin with the question, "Is condition A really essential in producing condition B?" The answer requires an experimental group subjected to condition A and a control group in which condition A is presumably absent. The addition of a control group makes it *experimental research*. Experimental research usually aims at testing the validity of a hypothesis, and a hypothesis is a statement of relationships. A group of hypotheses that are logically related to each other is called a *theory*. These are very superficial definitions, but it can be seen that research results in facts producing knowledge. The facts may lead to support or rejection of a hypothesis or theory. Knowledge and trained observation are important requirements for forming hypotheses, but they are not the same things as hypotheses.

Laboratory Research Example. A psychologist in a laboratory observes that the closer hungry rats are to the food box, the faster they seem to run and the harder it is to get them to make detours. The psychologist wonders if people behave in the same way. His wondering brings him nearly to the formation of a hypothesis. He states a hypothesis when he says, "Human beings will crowd each other more when they are closer to a goal (such as food) than when they are more distant from the goal." So he measures the distance between people in line at a cafeteria. He compares distances between people at the entrance to the serving counter with distances between people 20 feet away from it. The reader may try the experimental measurements himself to test the hypothesis that, in this respect at least, people are more like primitive animals. By making observations of the average number of people per foot from the food tray to the edge of the steam table, one can get a continuous or functional relationship between distance from goal and human density. This quantification is often more useful than merely knowing that some relationship exists.

Notice carefully that the facts (in this case the measurements) *test* the validity of the hypothesis. Depending on how the facts are gathered and analyzed, a more or less general statement can be made about the nearness of a goal and crowding behavior. Does the same phenomenon hold true at a box office? For the persons waiting turns in a doctor's office? Qualifications may have to be made in the generalization or in the way in which a term like "goal" is defined.

Applied Research Example. Now let us shift to an experiment which is aimed less at achieving a general statement than at discovering whether object or process A is superior in some way to object or process B. This kind of study is generally thought of as applied research, although the distinction between it and laboratory research is often a small one. We may want to know if test A predicts superior salesmen better than does test B. Or whether a formal training course in the fundamentals of electricity produces more adaptable maintenance men than does a policy of merely shifting them around in a number of jobs. So we set up an experiment and get a body of facts. On the basis of these facts we may or may not recommend to management that alternative A is better than alternative B.

In such exercises, the ingenuity of the psychologist is directed toward efficient ways of reaching a conclusion that will stand up outside the special conditions imposed by his experiment. But his ingenuity may have to be supplemented by sound working knowledge of the probable influence of the many factors and conditions which he has *not* varied in making his experiment. A professional psychologist who has practical and industrial experience in setting up and running an experiment and in drawing conclusions from it is, therefore, more likely to arrive at the correct recommendation than is a layman who is less experienced in these matters.

These conditions should not dismay the prospective researcher; rather they should emphasize the challenge and creative effort that a good research job, like any other nonstandardized situation, calls for. We should bear in mind that creative effort is invariably aided by extensive knowledge, especially if the knowledge can be readily drawn upon while one is setting up the experimental conditions and preparing the conclusions. But we must remember that the knowledge itself does not guarantee that the effort will be creative. A question must be asked and the answer sought.

Research, then, is the process of asking questions and getting sample answers about relationships between events A and B. In general, the better the research, the more certainly can we predict B by efficient control or description of A. Research leads to knowledge.

The Nature of Development. Development, in contrast to research, leads to objects and procedures. For example, we may know, from a body of research, the principles of operating an automobile by gas turbine or by nuclear energy. This does not mean that we would be able to build a workable automobile driven by gas turbine or nuclear energy. Development is hedged by two important considerations—cost and efficiency to produce and cost and efficiency to operate. Development consists of taking knowledge and using it to invent objects or procedures that serve practical purposes and have dollar denominators to them.

Examples of Development. An industrial psychologist is asked by his management, "What can the company do to reduce technological obsolescence of our design engineers?" The company wishes to keep inventors up to date on technical knowledge, but with minimum cost and dislocation both to the men and the company. A completely practical and successful solution still has to be found.

A more modest problem may arise. Because of various accidents, a company has installed safety guards on a number of its machines. But the men on piecework complain that their work rate is reduced and that the safety guards interfere with their ability to see what they are doing. Some men even remove the guards. Disciplinary actions are taken, and grievances arise. The industrial psychologist may be called in to develop the best all-around compromise between safety, work rate, job satisfaction, and cost to the company. This problem is a development problem. There is no formula, no textbook, no standard set of rules for solving this specific problem in its particular context.

In another situation, the psychologist is asked to assist in designing the display control panel for an airplane that the company is developing for commercial use. After studying the problem he prepares a sketch which is submitted to the engineering department. "Look," says the engineer with a good deal of vexation, "this airplane has to fly. Also, it has to carry a cargo. We can give you only 12 inches in height and 29 inches across for the whole panel. The instruments can be only 7 inches deep, and the whole business can't weigh more than 44 pounds." The psychologist says, "I can't give you a device that will meet the requirements for the pilot to operate the aircraft and still fall within your limits." To which the engineer will reply, "Look, bub, people have been flying airplanes without your help for fifty years. This airplane is going to be designed and ready to fly in nine months—with or without your assistance. You get back and work out a panel 12 by 29 by 7 inches, weighing no more than 44 pounds, and there will be a bonus for every pound less. Oh, yes, I forgot to mention that the cost of the panel, including instruments, controls, and accessories, must be less than $950 for production items. This includes development costs, and *that* includes your salary. Incidentally, I hear our competitor has a control panel that meets these specifications and costs less; the Navy is getting ready to buy it. Better get busy, son."

The Variables in Development. The engineer's hard-boiled speech sums up practically all the variables that go into development. It should be clear that development, like any form of practical inventing, proceeds by a series of compromises with competing factors. An object that is ideal with respect to any single set of principles—psychological, engineering, or other—is a fantasy. The professional man responsible for human factors must, of course, maintain the goal of perfection in his job, but he must recognize that his demands must be coordinated and compromised with those of others who may have equally lofty aspirations similarly compromised.

The point at which the psychologist feels that management demands more compromise than his ingenuity can overcome or his integrity can tolerate rests in the area of professional ethics. The question of whether to keep on and be satisfied with small gains and contributions or to throw in the towel and seek another job may be going on continuously until the psychologist becomes identified with team effort and objectives.

At present, the majority of professional psychologists, especially those with new Ph.D.s, tend to be oriented toward research and experimentation rather than development and application. It is, of course, essential that we have good research, or the wellsprings of our science will dry up. On the other hand, it is equally necessary that we have highly competent professionals dedicated to development. More and more psychologists are entering industry each year in this new role.

The Role of Consultant in a Development Project. Sometimes the professional researcher may undertake the temporary role of consultant in a development project; under these circumstances he generally offers advice but does not identify himself with a project and its outcome. He risks only a second fee, rather than his job in a company. Furthermore, he may find the role of critic more congenial than that of responsible collaborator. Thus he will make surveys and field studies, or experimental evaluations, of objects and procedures already designed. This is important work, too, and it is not so risky as trying to design and install an incentive plan which is acceptable both to management and the union as well as effective for the worker, or designing an airplane control panel which suits the engineer as well as the pilot, or creating a training device which is guaranteed to develop skills that will transfer to the job situation. The researcher is more interested in getting information than in having to make decisions based on given information. His professional training, by and large, teaches him how to hedge against making decisions.

Intermesh of Research and Development. It is not impossible, however, for the person who directs or conducts research to put the knowledge thus gained to practical use through inventiveness in development. These functions may merge, for example, when, through the study of job requirements of maintenance mechanics, sets of troubleshooting principles or strategies are devised, and these become incorporated in special training devices. Or research into the factors that influence the fastest and most error-free translation of information by the human being when he uses a keyboard as in typing may lead to a new concept in keyboard design. Obviously, the extent to which research and development can be made to intermesh is limited by the way in which and by the breadth with which the research problem and development problems are stated. In the behavioral sciences some effort is beginning that may lead to a language and a theory which will more readily permit translation of specific development objectives into broad-scale research activities *and* the translation of research into development. Some writers believe that a step in this direction will be made when we have a good means of classifying and showing relationships among human tasks in objective as well as in psychological terms.

Research without development can at times lead to a cultural lag. Paterson [39] illustrates this with his description of the history of a typewriter keyboard. In 1932 Dr. August Dvorak developed a simple typewriter keyboard with improvements on the standard keyboard arrangements designed by Sholes in 1873. Research on the older design showed the keys to be in bad arrangement for the modern touch typist, having been developed for use with the hunt and peck system. The new keyboard was based on an analysis of letter sequences of the 3,000 most frequently used words in English. In all, 36 million two-letter sequences were found, and the frequency with which each two-letter sequence occurred was recorded. Thus the most common letter patterns were revealed for the first time. The letters were then placed in the most effective and least fatiguing positions on the keyboard. Research showed that the new arrangement minimized the energy cost of continuous work, eliminated excessive and awkward reaches of the fingers, and balanced the work loads carried by the two hands.

The results obtained by the new keyboard were spectacular. Students trained on the simplified keyboard won many awards. The Carnegie Foundation made large grants to Dr. Dvorak to carry on the research. Paterson, writing in 1960 about the striking cultural lag in the history of psychology that ensued, concluded: "In spite of the fact that the general adoption of the simplified keyboard in the United States would bring to business and government an annual saving of well over one billion dollars in stenographic costs cultural lag has thrown up its road blocks. Dvorak's contribution remains today as merely a spectacular localized success."

As the reader may guess from the foregoing discussion, there is at present a considerable gulf between theoretical research in psychology and so-called "applied experimentation and development." Some of the reasons for this gulf have been proposed above. Let us turn now, however, to some growing problem areas for the industrial psychologists.

THE INDUSTRIAL PSYCHOLOGIST AS PROBLEM SOLVER

The industrial psychologist has for a long time addressed himself to specific applied problems and/or to general applied problems. More recently some psychologists have become concerned with what we will call *systems problems*. A few examples will illuminate the differences between specific, general, and systems problems, as they involve research and development.

Specific Applied Problems. These problems can be exemplified by a hypothetical case. The personnel director of the Ace Box Factory asks the industrial psychologist to "find out what accounted for the high turnover rate of women in the factory during 1963 as opposed to the low turnover rate in 1962." Without stirring from his seat, the psychologist could reply, "More women wanted to do something other than work in the Ace Box Factory in 1963 than in 1962." This answer is quite incontrovertible, so why is the personnel director unlikely to accept it? The reason is that he can't do anything constructive with such an answer. The first requirement in finding the answer to an applied problem is (or should be!) to uncover information which permits a *decision* to be made and some constructive *action* to be taken by the person who asks the question.

In general, the first step is to test the validity of the question. *Did* more women leave Ace during 1963 than in 1962? Did Ace perhaps employ twice as many women in 1963 as in 1962, and was this accompanied by double the turnover? If this was the case, then the turnover *rate* was the same for both years even though the absolute number that left doubled.

If an inspection of the records indicates that the actual turnover rate *is* increasing, then the personnel manager should be shown the actual figures. A judgment should then be made as to whether the problem is of practical importance; that is, will management spend money not only to find out what the causes of the increase are but also to underwrite some remedial action? Let us assume that the answer is "yes" to both questions.

The next logical step would be to determine how many women left voluntarily and how many were fired, and compare 1963 with 1962 rates. After this step, the inquiry would radiate out to matters over which the company has immediate control—the procedures by which the women were selected, indoctrinated, trained, assigned, supervised, grouped, motivated to work, communicated with by management, etc. A sample of those who quit and of those who did not quit would be questioned. Perhaps the questions would include background and precipitating incidents that led to quitting or to near quitting.

Let's suppose that the actual quit rate increased 20 per cent in 1963 over 1962—this is something about which to worry. But it is discovered that in 1963 about 30 per cent of the quits left in order to go to work for Zantex Electronics, a new firm that was hiring young engineers, many of whom were probably bachelors. Most of these girls who went to Zantex quite frankly said that they went there not because that firm paid more money (it paid less) but in order to be near eligible men. These and other findings are reported to the personnel manager. It is at this point that *research* ends. Development *begins* with the question, "What can we do about it?"

The study could easily be broadened. Why didn't the married women also quit? Were there some conditions at Ace that were particularly discouraging for the unmarried girls? Yes, there were: there was a tightly knit married women's club in the plant, but none had been organized by or for unmarried women; furthermore, it was Ace policy to send all young unmarried men out on the road for training in sales immediately after hiring. This often resulted in their courting and marrying girls they met in their sales territory. Examination of the causes behind the causes may reveal a good many more alternatives than appear on the surface. This study so far has been specific to conditions at Ace; hence we would classify it as a *specific applied problem*.

As you might expect, the approach to a solution, or a development, for a situation revealed by specific research would also be specific. Ace might organize and support a young unmarried men's and women's club, with the help of an energetic entertainment chairman, and bring its men in from the road for regular club affairs. Or if the company could hire enough married women, it might reduce the hiring of unmarried women in 1965. Of course, by doing this, it might invite a new family of troubles, but one always takes some risk when trying a new development.

General Applied Problems. Dealing with general problems gives us another view of the psychologist's role. An industrial psychologist working for Acme Industrials proposes a plan for studying the relationship that fatigue, stress, and incentives have to various kinds of work decrement in industrial situations. The plan is to get data from a *variety* of existing and experimentally controlled work situations, tasks, and task settings, such as wire winding, punch-press operations, routine operations, semiroutine operations, and even problem-solving situations such as tool and die design. The major task variables may include difficult or complex discriminations and perceptions, human information processing and decision making, and manipulations; or the scope may be restricted to any one of these psychological factors. But whatever activities are studied, the problem is a general one.

Psychological Variables. It should be noticed at once that the above proposal is couched primarily in terms of psychological variables rather than in terms that the company might use, such as the question, "Why can't we get more sustained productivity out of the wire winders?" To the extent that the psychologist will examine a sufficiently broad sample of situations, he may arrive at general conclusions relating fatigue, stress, and incentives to falling off of productivity during the daily and weekly cycle. Such conclusions, if stated in operational terms, may lead to constructive development not only by Acme but other companies as well.

It is not likely that a company will gamble the amount of time and money that such a study will take unless it has considerable confidence in the researcher and his ability to translate at least some of his findings into worthwhile developments. The fact that the researcher may be reluctant to accept responsibility for converting findings into developments useful to the company is often a realistic reason for the company's reluctance to foot the research bill. Moreover, even though the salary of the researcher is paid by a university, the company must provide one or more persons to show him around, and it may also have to accept interference with the normal flow of production. These things are costly.

Systems Problems. Systems methods are ways of stating, thinking about, and solving problems that take into account *complex interrelationships*. Among these interrelationships are those of objects, processes, and human components. Since a description of systems approaches is contained in the following section, we will merely point out here that the industrial psychologist's role in industry is not necessarily that of a solver of either specific or general problems. To the extent that he is designing something useful as a team member working with architects, engineers, accountants, production specialists, mathematicians, and operating and maintenance personnel, he will be engaged in a systems enterprise.

Such a "systems man" will generally not be in a staff position that provides direct recommendations or information to management. He will, instead, tend to be closely associated with a company project such as the development of a new aircraft for military or commercial use. If he is responsible primarily for human factors, he will have to think about the interplay of all human factors with the equipment and the requirements imposed on the man-machine team. These considerations will cover a wide range. He may be concerned with the selection and training, say, of the pilot, copilot, and flight engineer, as well as with the design of facilities for the elimination of body wastes of passengers. Coping with unusual but possible contingencies during operation and the predicting of kinds and amount of human error and undependableness call for team action. In general, the psychologist who, through interest or opportunity, elects to follow the systems approach thereby becomes a more active collaborator with other research and development specialists, such as physicists and design engineers. Furthermore, his responsibility will entail across-the-board consideration of the many human factors that affect the eventual operation and maintenance of the man-machine organism [1, 6, 14].

THE GENERAL SYSTEM

The student can get a unique global view of an industrial organization from studying the blueprint of a general system.

In order for the industrial psychologist to participate effectively in the planning or redesign of a system, he must have a thorough knowledge of it and all its parts. In some respects, he may have to know more about it than do the planners of equipment and facilities. Such knowledge permits him to suggest what activities are best assigned to machines and what functions should be taken over by human beings. He may help to show how human beings can be used to best advantage in the enterprise, but he can do so only through thorough familiarity with system requirements as well as with human capabilities and limitations. At later stages of participation and development he can use information about the system in determining precisely and concretely what the human work requirements will be. He can then frame selection procedures for the various tasks and jobs assigned to human beings and proceed to the design of training, training devices and job aids, and evaluation procedures. He can also play a vital role in conducting tests of the adequacy of *the system as a whole* to perform its intended purposes.

Human-factors Specialists. Because of his varied roles and his integration with the design team, the psychologist may even change his title to that of human-factor specialist. His decisions cannot be based solely on what is optimum for the human beings in the system; they must be tempered by what is good (that is, economical and efficient) for the system as a whole. The following sections describe how this newer type of industrial psychologist becomes informed so that he can play his complex role effectively.

System Requirements and Definition. A system may be described in any one of a number of ways, depending upon the purpose that the description is to serve. In its broadest sense, the description should aid in obtaining and recording information about the existing or proposed system in terms that will aid in planning, designing, or modifying it. The description should permit maximum freedom in suggesting alternatives; at the same time it should express the various restraints and fixed conditions imposed upon and accepted by designers.

The description should permit:

1 Maximum freedom in suggesting alternatives in design and the implications of these alternatives

2 Reminders of all the kinds of information which it is important to have for planning and design purposes

3 Ease in expanding the description to permit coupling of subsystems descriptions into broader systems

4 Ease in coupling the description of the system with descriptions of functionally or physically interconnected systems

5 Differentiation of functions that can be performed by human beings from functions that can be performed by machines

6 Ease in determining similarities to and differences from other systems

7 Quantification of operations

The main purpose of the description is to keep all pertinent information in view at the same time so that ideas can be readily shifted around like building blocks.

The definition of a general system is really very simple. We can define a general system roughly as *any planned group of man and machine entities and procedures that convert input signals or materials to output signals or materials according to some human purpose.*

GENERAL–SYSTEM FACTORS

The factors in a system contain some two dozen kinds of information. Rarely can all of this information be obtained at one time; rather, the information tends to grow and be filled in as the system becomes designed or invented. Let us describe the various factors below. We shall use an automobile service station as our illustration, since most readers are familiar with the nature of this business.

Purposes, Functions, Processes, Process-links. All four of these terms are related to each other in common usage. *Purpose* is what the system should accomplish, stated in simple, general terms. Thus the function of a service-station system is to provide gasoline, water, and oil to automobiles with a minimum of average waiting time. *Function* may refer to the purpose of the overall system or the action of some part of the system. It is the most flexible of all terms used in the description, because functions can always be divided into subfunctions. Function names are arbitrary. Thus, a pump may perform a sucking-up function and a pushing-out function, as well as a measuring function. The measuring function may be divided into a flow-sensing function and a flow-indicating function, and each of these may be divided into rate of flow and absolute amount. A function is an abstraction, but since a function may be thought of independently of the object which performs it, the concept of function is perhaps the most powerful of all concepts for human inventing purposes.

Process is identified by change in a signal or substance, usually in the context of the instrument effecting or responsible for the change. Inflating a tire with air is a process, as is also the condensation of moisture in a gasoline-storage tank. *Process-links* are sequences of changes and activities.

Outputs, Criterion Variables, Criterion Tolerances, Waste. These terms describe what comes out of a system. An *output* is information, material, or an object that comes out of a system or one of its components. The gross outputs of a filling station include gasoline in gas tanks, oil in crankcases, water in batteries and radiators, compressed air in tires, and—not altogether incidentally—satisfied customers. Output is a convenient term because it can be used in so many different contexts.

A *criterion variable* is some factor of an output that identifies a quantity or quality to be controlled. Thus the amount of time that a customer must, on the average, wait for service is likely to be one criterion variable of some importance to a service station. Another may be the cost of the gasoline. Another may be the customer's notion of how well the gasoline performs.

A *criterion tolerance* is the range through which values of a criterion variable may fluctuate and still result in an acceptable output. A customer may accept an average three-minute wait for service, but perhaps he is unlikely to return if he has to wait more than seven minutes. A criterion tolerance may also be thought of as a working limit of some variable.

Waste is a form of output for which there is no customer or which is an annoyance or disturbance. Waste may be in the form of energy, objects, or interference with gainful outputs. Gasoline slopped over from a filled tank is a loss either to the customer or to the station owner or both. A leaking air hose creates waste. So do the errors of the tire changer who occasionally punctures an inner tube through carelessness or lack of skill. Waste can be measured as the ratio of costs of useless output to costs of useful output.

Environments, Inputs, Contingencies, Emergencies, Noise. An *environment* is a context of conditions that has some more or less general effects on system operation. Thus a filling station may be on a side road or a main road, near a city, or out in a desert. All of these and many more environmental conditions will affect the number and kind of customers, demands, distribution of busy and slack periods, length of waiting periods that will be acceptable, and so on.

Environmental conditions change. Some changes are slow, some are rapid. Some are progressive, some are cyclic, some are temporary and intermittent. A slow, progressive change occurs when a residential community becomes a business community. A more rapid change is that from one season to another when buying habits and demands for services change. A rapid, temporary change in an environment occurs when the first heavy snowfall brings a demand for chains and their installation and for being towed out of snowdrifts, in addition to the regular demand for gasoline and oil. Although immediate returns may not compensate for the heavy investment required to keep everything running smoothly under extraordinary demands, the services provided at such a time may result in additional permanent customers for the gasoline station.

Some environments, such as that of a punch press, are relatively unchanging or undergo only subtle changes such as those accompanying progressive deterioration of air-conditioning equipment and increase of dust. But a systems planner will attempt to predict and identify as many of these changes as he can in order to provide for them or be aware of their possible cost if he does nothing about them.

An *input* is anything that comes into the objective parts of the system. It may be the customers and their cars coming into the gasoline station, the materials to be sold, replacement parts for the pumps, or the people who come in to operate and maintain equipment and provide services. An environment is a very general form of input. Somewhat more specifically, an input is information which the system senses or material which the system can accept for processing. Inputs have variables and tolerances just as outputs do, and some inspection arrangement is usually provided. The food and drink tasters used by the Medicis to determine if poison was present is a medieval example of testing the input to the system.

A *contingency* is a generally unscheduled event which demands some unusual mode of operation for the system. A contingency may arise from an *environmental* condition such as a heavy snowstorm, or it may be a large load of cheap tires that the dealer can buy if he has ample credit and storage space. It may come about through equipment *malfunction,* such as a pump failure. Contingencies also arise through *human error,* such as the failure to note the amount of gasoline pumped into a customer's car registered on a pump before returning the register to zero.

People who plan systems generally pay less attention to the ways in which contingencies can arise and how to cope with them than they do to normal situations. This deficiency is one reason why the development of systems is so costly; it also accounts for the great number of trial-and-error corrections which, from hindsight, seem unwarranted. This deficiency may also be one reason why, once a system is fixed and manages to survive, it is difficult to introduce major changes in concept—such changes, for example, as the drive-in, the self-service store, the assembly line, or the recent trend toward automation.

It is especially important for persons who deal with human factors to anticipate as thoroughly as possible the contingencies and *emergencies* that may beset a system, because ordinarily the human operator, considering "operator" in the broad sense, will have to fill in the gaps left by planning. Whatever the machine will not do automatically must obviously be done by the human beings. Improvising to meet unexpected conditions almost certainly will be less efficient in the long run than preparing to meet conditions through planning. A trade-off against planning time is budgeted for learning how to adapt a new system to the stresses imposed on it or arising from within it. When the human beings in the system must cope with a large variety of contingencies, the situation may be taken care of by selecting personnel for intelligence and aptitude and by training.

The description of a contingency should include answers to these questions:

1 How is the contingency detected and identified?

2 What is the likely consequence if the contingency or emergency is not detected?

3 What corrective action can be taken? What standby is needed?

Many of these data will be difficult to collect. The information they provide will be of substantial assistance in preparing training content or in making special provisions in the design of the equipment or facilities whereby the operator can cope better with situations that otherwise might be catastrophic.

Noise is any disturbing or irrelevant signal, object, or process. It is the input counterpart of waste. The concept of noise includes not only an auditory disturbance, but any kind of disturbance, actual or potential, to operations. With this broader definition, it is a convenient term to have. An example of noise in the filling station may be the presence and activities of young loafers who congregate and perhaps the passing motorist who stops in merely to get route directions. Glare on display panels is a form of visual noise. Noise may not only be a system input but may arise within or between components in a system. Noise, like waste, can sometimes be converted to gainful use. Usually, however, it is a nuisance, and provisions may have to be taken against it.

Area and Physical Locations of the Installation. These are relatively permanent parts of the system's environment and constitute the space and physical support for the installation of the system. The area available for off-street parking may be an important factor in designing a filling station. Whether the storage tanks must be dug into rock or soft earth is another.

Objects, Equipment, and Materials. These are the factors most self-evident in a system, and attention is characteristically concentrated almost exclusively on them. Important as they are in planning and operations, let us defer their implications for human factors to a later section of the chapter, "Task Analysis."

People. We are now ready to add to our general system the all-important factor of people. We can approach the problem of dealing with people as if they were individuals or as if they were teams. Both viewpoints are important to system design. The features about people which are of most interest to us in this chapter are:

Aptitudes. What the individual can learn in given periods of time and under given training conditions.

Knowledges. The range of actual and symbolic situations to which the individual can make symbolic (thinking or verbal) responses and the range of these symbolic responses.

Skills. The abilities of the individual to perceive and to make appropriate muscle and work responses.

Motivations. The incentives that induce the worker to give some quantity and quality level of work and also enable him to resist distractions.

Attitudes. Relatively persistent and habitual patterns of like and dislike (as of approach and avoidance) that the individual has for various objects, symbols, and states of affairs.

Role. Whether supervisor, peer, or subordinate. There are many other kinds of roles that people assume, but these are of main interest to us here.

Procedures, Rules, and Strategies. *A procedure* is some routine way of responding to a more or less standard or normal situation. A *rule* is a procedure that must not be changed under any circumstances or practically any circumstances. A *strategy* is a procedure which has alternatives at various steps, and the choice of the alternatives depends on what shows up at each step. Familiar examples appear in games. A less familiar example, but extremely important for systems work, is the troubleshooting technique in which a strategic selection of check points will speed up the location of a defective part.

The human-factors specialist may often make substantial contributions to the design of a system by helping specify work procedures and strategies. This is an extension of the kind of work done by methods engineers, or time-and-motion people.

Values. As we continue with our service-station illustration, we soon come face to face with values. These are the priorities and relative weights given (under various conditions) to such system factors as different inputs, system components, or different outputs. For example, for some customers, checking the radiator or battery may be given less priority than cleaning the windshield during rush periods. Value priorities usually show up when the system is under stress and something has to give. However, values also appear under normal operating conditions in the decision as to what kinds of error can occasionally be tolerated without redesigning some part of the system. Values are often contained in the operating policies of a company, department, or supervisor.

Monitoring Arrangements. Monitoring is the comparison of some actual input or output with a criterion input or output, plus a mechanism for action if the actual value disagrees with the standard value. Monitoring is the attempt to maintain the operating integrity of the system as it was designed to operate. It may detect emergency conditions and switch to alternative modes of action; the monitoring function may also extend to coordinating the action of the system as a whole with input availability and output demands. Subfunctions of monitoring include: (1) data sensing (inspection), (2) data storing (records), (3) data interpretation, and (4) channels for executive response and control. There are optimal points in a system where inspection should be performed.

Monitoring may be as informal as a foreman looking over the shoulders of his employees or as formal as the elaborate mechanisms in an automated chemical industry. A term in common usage that, in a restricted way, is related to the function of monitoring is "process control."

Research and Development (R&D). These are, in part, an extension of the monitoring function. But in this function, data are ordinarily stored for longer periods of time and analyzed with the intent, not of maintaining the *status quo* of the system, but of introducing improvements in equipment design, operating procedures, training or selection of personnel, or monitoring procedures. The more precisely errors and waste can be analyzed, the more likely it is that a useful by-product can be found, or that means can be invented for reducing waste. The identification of the variables constituting errors and waste is therefore highly important to the efficiency of the research and development function of the system. Without suitable data channeling, however, the function becomes impotent.

It is axiomatic that systems left to run by themselves become progressively degraded. The better their design and monitoring, of course, the more gradual the degradation. R&D activity can resist and reverse this trend of systems toward death.

R&D may, like monitoring, be formal or informal. Observant individuals within the system may think of ideas for improvements and carry them out; or a huge agency may be established for this function.

Parenthetically, the reader should notice that monitoring and R&D are not factors in a strict sense; they are really a combination of factors already mentioned in the text. Their importance and the fact that they are so often neglected in thinking and working with systems justify mentioning them somewhat out of context.

Suppliers of Inputs and Buyers of Outputs. In some cases, such as that of the filling station, the buyer of the output also supplies some of the input. But the dealer also has to get his pumps, gasoline, tires, tools, and personnel from the outside. The buyer of the output is only partially controlled by what the system does for him. He looks for competing prices and services, or may dispense with all filling-station outputs if he rides by public transportation.

Probabilities of Occurrence and Recurrence. These are the probabilities that, under any particular set of conditions or within some time period such as an hour, day, week, or year, some event will occur which demands system action. The decision to install one, two, or three sets of gasoline pumps will depend in part on the peak demands for gasoline, how often these peaks occur during a day, the chance of one or more pumps going bad and requiring a standby, or the frequency with which a profitable repair job is missed when the one mechanic is off duty. These frequencies and probabilities have to be weighed in two ways. One is the cost of providing against losing a sale, customer, or other benefit. The other is the profit to be obtained from the provision that is made.

As can be seen from the examples, probabilities influence what should be done under normal and exceptional circumstances and in fact are the main determiners of what will be normal and what will be exceptional. These factors are reflected directly in the kind of personnel who are hired and the training that is given to them.

OVERLAP WITHIN A GENERAL SYSTEM

It should be noted that the factors of a general system as described above overlap in many ways. This overlap is inescapable in any plan based on things, ideas, and processes that interact with each other.

Whether designing a new system or redesigning an existing one, it is almost a practical necessity to itemize on paper the kinds of information described above. A convenient way of doing so is to begin with the general

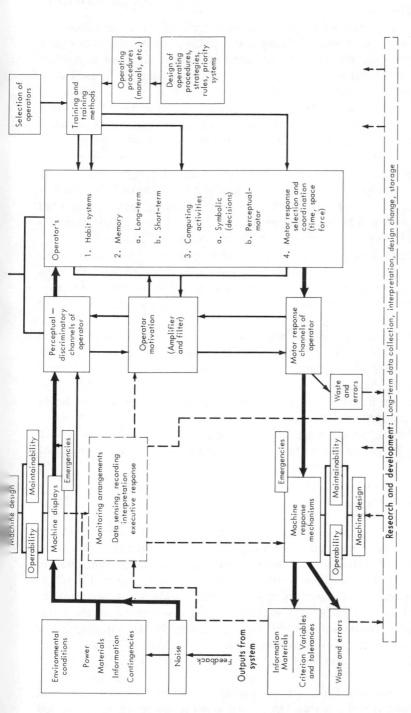

Fig. 14.1. Flow chart of variables in a single-operator man-machine system. One can get a total picture of the system by beginning with the INPUTS in the upper left-hand corner and following the solid arrows clockwise to MACHINE, to HUMAN OPERATOR, and around to OUTPUTS. The PROCEDURES in the upper right-hand corner support the human-operator part of the system. The broken arrows indicate where the results of research and development influence the system.

and fill in the particulars to trace a typical cycle of the system from beginning to end. In planning a filling station, this cycle would start with a potential customer driving along the highway and looking for a gasoline station. It would end with the customer back on the highway. At each stage between these extremes, one would list the variety of input variables and environments and the contingencies which might occur in the particular locality in mind. Then one would itemize what provisions might be taken against them. The end product of such a procedure will be a systems flow chart that can be used as a master-planning document. It will help in remembering what goes with what, and in checking the consequences of any particular development that is proposed. The preparation of this chart is no simple exercise even for a relatively simple system, such as may exist between a man and his secretary or in a telephone intercommunication network linked to outside telephone service in a five-office company.

The systems flow chart may or may not be prepared by a psychologist. It certainly cannot be prepared by one man alone. As we will see in the next section, much of the information it contains will be vital to the psychologist in determining the human needs imposed by any system that has gone beyond planning stages.

If all else in this section is forgotten, the reader should remember that *every* industrial and business system includes men and procedures; some systems also include machines. Let us take a look at one way a general system can be charted by giving some study to Figure 14.1. We suggest to the reader that he not try to absorb this diagram all at once. This figure appears quite complicated when first viewed. However, it is really no more complicated than an organizational flow chart such as the one we described in Chapter 2. As a matter of fact, one may think of this as a man-machine flow chart.

TASK ANALYSIS

Task analysis is a procedure for describing in specific terms what the human operator is required to do. In many respects, it is like a very complete manual of instructions, although it includes information not found in such manuals. Task analysis is most important for the industrial psychologist. A statement of job requirements is the backbone of any work in human factors. The extent of completeness and concreteness of the statement of job requirements is the limiting factor in the directness and efficiency with which *any* personnel work can be done. Without such information, human-factors work is shooting in the dark [15, 23]

Pitfalls in Analyses. There are several major pitfalls in making job and task descriptions and analyses. One is that general statements about the job may lead to assumptions that are not valid. Thus some toolmakers must use numbers in their work. The assumption that the toolmaker requires a thorough grounding in mathematics is invalid if it means that he must know math up to and through differential equations and calculus. Actually, he may do no more than compute angles and surfaces, for which rather simple procedures in geometry may suffice. It would then be improper to say that he needs to "know" geometry. In fact, he may be able to do quite well with simple skill in arithmetic and the proper tables to consult. This is the pitfall of *irrelevant job requirements*. It comes from superficial and general statements.

A second pitfall is the converse of the first. A job may seem to be made up of a number of simple steps or elements. But in practice the trick is to figure out how to do these steps in the right order on a particular occasion and use judgment as to which steps should be omitted. This is like assuming that playing chess is no more than knowing the rules of the game. The result is an *underestimation of the job requirements*.

A third pitfall arises from paying too much attention to normal operating conditions and *failing to identify contingencies, emergencies, and other situations* that are out of the routine. This will inevitably result in training people who have to have additional years of on-the-job experience before they can be trusted to work without close supervision.

The fourth pitfall is the opposite of the third. This consists in *overemphasizing the occasional situation* which might occur on the job. No doubt occasions arise when it would be helpful if a carpenter also knew how to wire a house, but the cost of carpenters would be much higher than it is if a knowledge of house wiring were made a standard requirement for them. Similarly, there are circumstances when the ability to make any kind of repair on a machine would be an asset, but paying for an additional skill that is used very infrequently may not be worth the asset it provides. Furthermore, an infrequently practiced skill gets rusty and unreliable, and a half-learned skill may be worse than none at all. These considerations should temper the tendency to emphasize the "might be helpful" skill or knowledge (which can be multiplied infinitely for any job). This emphasis should be especially deplored if training on the more frequent and essential job requirements is thereby penalized. This pitfall accommodates many professional educators who go into the field of industrial training.

Kinds of Tasks. No classification scheme exists whereby one task can be absolutely distinguished from another task on psychological grounds. However, it is convenient to make various differentiations on grounds of utility.

A *tracking task* is one in which continuous adjustments are made to a continuously changing signal. Aiming a gun at a moving target or from a moving platform is an example of a tracking task. Many lathe operations have tracking components. So does steering a vehicle or controlling its rate according to some perceived relationship. The chapter on human-factors engineering discussed at greater length the characteristics of tracking tasks.

Procedural tasks are those which are performed more or less one step at a time. They can be broken into separate units of action; examples are punch-press operations and assembling a relay. Most of the tasks in our daily work are procedural tasks. Procedural may range from highly stand-ardized routines, where the same series of responses is invariably made to the same series of signals or cues, to nonstandardized procedures such as troubleshooting and other forms of problem solving on the job. Fighting a fire will have both standard and nonstandard ingredients.

The importance of making at least a rough classification of tasks in this way is that different aptitudes may be tapped in selection of personnel and different training conditions will have to be set up. Problem solving and other nonroutine tasks may call for special knowledge that will not be re-quired of standard routines. And whereas one can learn to perform quite a complex number of things at about the same time if they occur in the same order every time (as in piano playing), one must be more careful of piling up simultaneous activities which are nonroutinized. Laying one task on top of another, for example, watching a radarscope at the same time that the functioning of the equipment is being monitored, is called *time sharing*.

The modern trend in equipment design is to reduce the extent to which the human being does tracking and standard routine tasks and to increase the extent to which he makes complex decisions. In other words, the human being is a problem solver in contingencies and emergencies and can take over from the machine.

Task Description. In its simplest terms, a task description is a statement of the cues or signals that are the stimulus to a required action, and of the required action that results in work being done. For example, "When the lamp turns red, turn switch X to the right as far as it will go." This is a fairly simple statement of a signal-response relationship. When all these individual signal-response relationships are described in the order in which they are properly done, the result is a task description.

Let us look more carefully, however, at the elements within the example cited. We find on the stimulus or signal side two components. One of these is the lamp itself. Call this the *indicator*. The state of the lamp (whether on or off) is the *indication*. On the response side of the statement we also find several elements. Switch X is the *control object*. Turning it to the right is the *control response*. In addition there is another signal element in the example. This is the phrase "as far as it will go." Let us think of this as an *indication of response adequacy,* or response feedback. Its function is to inform the operator that he has or has not made the correct response. Many tasks, of course, have action steps that have no direct indications of response adequacy. These tasks or task elements are usually more difficult to learn than those which have immediate, continuous, and unambiguous response feedback. The immediacy of response feedback in bicycle riding may be one reason why it can be learned rather rapidly as compared with riding a horse. (There may be some who dispute the example.)

Notice that the ingredients of a task description are those of any good instruction—what will give the signal, what the signal will be, what to do, and what to do it with. Also, how to know when the correct response has been made. Many of our everyday instructions take some of these ingredients for granted. Such ambiguity has its hazards in everyday life and in task description.

Special Circumstances and Contingent Conditions. It is now time to recall the section in system description that stressed the importance of identifying contingencies, emergencies, special environmental conditions, and other abnormal situations. Failure to include such information in a task description is like giving a person a pictorial description of the inside of a strange house without telling him he will have to find his way around in it in total darkness. Thus pouring liquid from a can into a receptacle may be a simple task indoors but a difficult one outdoors in a strong wind. Putting a nut on a bolt is a fairly simple operation unless it has to be done in a space barely large enough to accommodate two fingers. It is easy enough to learn to drive down a road without traffic; it is another matter on city streets during rush hours.

Task descriptions should therefore be accompanied by statements of the environmental conditions and the range of circumstances that may complicate performance. A clear statement of the cues that indicate when a task is or is not to be performed is also necessary. Failure to indicate this is a pitfall with obviously serious consequences for personnel planning.

Work-cycle Analysis. The following procedure is proposed for completeness in job-task description. It consists of tracing through a typical work cycle from the beginning of a sequence to its end. It is important to go back to the real beginning of the cycle, rather than somewhere along in it. For example, the work cycle of flying an airplane mission begins not on the starting ramp or even in the hangar, but back in the briefing room. It ends when the pilot turns in his flight papers or is debriefed. The start of a maintenance work cycle begins with a work order of some kind. Thence to selection of tools and perhaps of diagrams and proper work manuals. Then transport to the site of the job. And so on to the turning in of a completed work order and the replacement of tools and disposal of parts.

It is good policy to list the gross tasks in sequence in a work cycle before making a step-by-step description of activities within each gross task. Contingencies and special circumstances may be listed under each title of a gross task. It should be remembered that the title of gross tasks and the number of behavior activities that get lumped into a gross task are quite arbitrary. Different persons making the same analysis will have different gross-task titles. But the heart of the description is finally in the detailed, step-by-step activity description of indicator, indication, control response, and feedback. Skilled individuals should prepare quite similar descriptions of the same tasks.

Task descriptions can be made from direct observation. But they can also be made from blueprint descriptions of equipment or equipment prototypes and information as to how the equipment should be operated, plus systems data.

Let us presume that a work cycle has been sketched out in the form of a series of gross-task titles and that these in turn have been filled in with detailed descriptions of the activities that compromise the task. We also have identified the varieties of contingencies and malfunctions, environmental conditions, and other factors that may complicate the task requirements. All of the work thus far could be done quite well by a nonspecialist in human factors, such as an engineer or operations analyst. The next phase undertakes a behavioral analysis of this description.

Although the human being acts as a unified entity, it is nevertheless useful to distinguish, at times, various kinds of psychological function. These have been divided into perceptual processes, recall processes, problem-solving (decision-making) processes, and muscular (motor) processes. It should be underscored that these divisions are for convenience in analysis. Perceptual processes, for example, are strongly influenced by recall from previous experience and even from motor processes. Each task as a whole, as well as each group of specific activities, is studied with each of these functions in mind. The patterns of events likely to produce errors in perception, recall, decision making, or responses on the machine controls are noted, and the nature of the expected error is described. Time-shared activities are scrutinized with particular care, especially where the signal-response patterns are not precisely the same from one work cycle to another [40, 43, 45].

THE HUMAN–FACTORS SUBSYSTEM

Now that we have a system description and a comprehensive set of job-task requirements through task description and analysis, what can be done with the information? A number of scattered examples were cited, but they

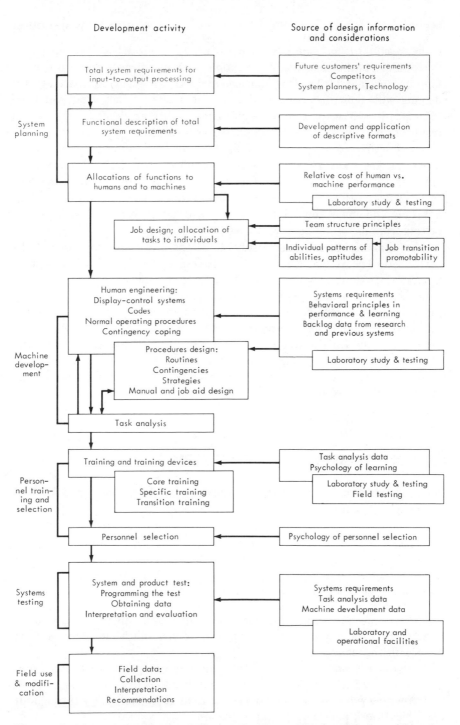

Fig. 14.2. Map of the human factors subsystem. The breakdown within the system can be seen by following the arrows, beginning with "system planning" in the upper left-hand corner.

were specific to the context in which they were given. We are now in a position to put the elements of the human-factors subsystem into a general map (see Figure 14.2). This map can be used for planning a strategy for dealing with human factors. It should also make explicit what will have to happen with respect to human beings, whether the outcome is the result of an explicit plan or of implicit improvisations.

The big map is an extension of the systems approach to laying out the most efficient route to a distant but identified goal. It is also the most efficient way of bearing in mind and selecting alternative routes for either small or large detours. The principal advantage of maps is that they present not only the main route but also other options that are available for getting from a starting point to a destination.

The ultimate objective in personnel actions is getting jobs done, tasks performed. The system descriptions, and especially the task descriptions, identify the overall task requirements for a given stage of system development. From these descriptions comprehensive plans can be formulated for job design, human engineering of the work environment, proficiency testing, training and training aids, selection procedures, and other areas within the province of industrial psychology. These factors are interrelated like the roads on a road map and the segments of a route to a destination. Changes in any of these factors inevitably cause changes in the other factors. Some of the changes may be inconsequential; others may have practical importance.

DESIGN VARIABLES OF A SUBSYSTEM

The following outline contains the design variables that make up the personnel subsystem.

Job Design. Let us here define a job as all the tasks that will be assigned to a man holding a given job title. Job design has practical meaning when there are two or more persons interacting in a system. Relevant considerations in job design are:

1 *Task rate and frequency.* Can one man handle all that needs to be done? Will a standby be required for peak loads, and what else should be done with the standby?

2 *Physical location.* One man can be in only one place at one time, and time is required to transport him from one location to another.

3 *Keeping busy.* A job should keep a man reasonably busy throughout the typical work period of system operation.

4 *Common knowledges and skills.* In general, the tasks given to one position should be "psychologically homogeneous"; that is, they should require about the same level and pattern of ability. This will help both in selecting and in training personnel.

5 *Compatibility with existing job structures.* This will help persons who are making a transition from a previous system to the new system.

6 *Supervisory positions.* These require special attention and skills quite different from technical abilities.

7 *Opportunity for advancement.* Planning for career structures within a system will provide incentives.

8 *Special overriding factors.* There will be cases where all the foregoing considerations may have to be violated in fulfilling a given set of system requirements. Notice also that many of the considerations above are in conflict with each other. This conflict is resolved by the principle of trade-offs: factors have to be juggled until you get the best with what you have to work with.

Manpower Development. The renewed emphasis now being given problems of selection, training, and proficiency criteria is coming more within the framework of systems. Job and task requirements are being used in devising procedures for selecting personnel for jobs, cutting down on the error in prediction in many selection tests. Training is being looked at, in a few quarters, with a view to providing the least costly way to bring a job novice to the point of meeting the proficiency criteria for his job. Training ordinarily includes much education in irrelevant knowledges, and it often neglects teaching the person how to meet the practical contingencies of his job. And more attention is being given to proficiency criteria. Ideally, these are performance tests of the actual tasks where a wide sampling of environmental conditions, contingencies, and malfunctions (including human errors) is introduced into the tests.

THE ADVENT OF THE COMPUTER—A PROJECTION

Automatic data processing is changing both the anatomy and the physiology of much of industry. The higher speed and greater flexibility in handling, abstracting, storing, and retrieving information of many kinds will change not only the mechanics of organizational life in industry. They will also change power structures and attitudes of those within industry. The nature of control will shift somewhat (not entirely) from authoritarian cut-and-try intuition or decisions by committee. The shift will be to adroitness in tapping stores of information and logically manipulating it. We should expect, as a consequence, changes in the organizational climate and the locations of prestige. The psychologist who is sensitive to these changes and their implications may help to steer them to balance the needs of the employees and of the company.

Automatic data processing also can (and will, we predict) alter the way the industrial psychologist does his job. It will be practical to keep, process, make decisions with, and do research with records in ways hitherto impossible. The number of variables and the buckets of data which in seconds or minutes can be processed into multiple regressions, factor analyses, and solutions to simulation models is fantastic when compared with manual calculation. Almost continuous automatic research can be maintained as live data are fed into the system. This makes it possible for an organization to become highly informed not only about the consequences of its behavior as an entity but also about the behavior of its parts, including personnel subsystems. The setting up of a categorical and processing structure to realize these possibilities requires knowledge in depth and breadth both of the operations to be studied and of data-processing capabilities.

The industrial psychologist is therefore well advised to acquire some working knowledge of what computers can and can't be programmed to do. Of more importance than skill in actual computer programming is the ability to design the application problem and flow-chart it so that a specialist in computer programming can convert the problem statement into language that speaks to the computer. Many of the analytic concepts presented in this chapter are applicable as approaches to application flow charting. We believe it is safe to predict that industrial psychologists who can claim familiarity with automatic data-processing procedures will have ample job opportunities in the decade ahead.

The human factors in systems require the psychologist to function in the varying roles of critic, specific problem solver, and general problem solver and in systems where he is concerned with interrelationships among people, work environments, and the processes whereby they interact.

SUGGESTIONS FOR SELECTIVE READING

Bennett, E., et al. *Human factors in technology.* New York: McGraw-Hill, 1963. A variety of writers with differing technical backgrounds and interests discuss theory and data on human performance in a range of contexts.

Cherry, C. *On human communication.* New York: Wiley, 1957. Interdisciplinary studies of communication for the sophisticated reader.

Dreyfuss, H. *The measure of man: Human factors in design.* New York: Whitney Library of Design, 1960. For the sophisticated reader.

Flagle, C. D., et al. *Operations research and systems engineering.* Baltimore: Johns Hopkins, 1960. Systematic approaches to the planning and use of resources for complex enterprises.

Fogel, L. J. *Biotechnology: Concepts and applications.* Englewood Cliffs, N.J.: Prentice-Hall, 1963. Fitting men and machines.

Gagné, R. M. (Ed.) *Psychological principles in systems development.* New York: Holt, 1962. Twenty psychologists talk about systems, computers, tasks, selection and training, performance appraisal, and experimental design.

Hall, A. D. *Handbook of instruction for aerospace personnel subsystem designers.* Wright-Patterson Air Force Base, Ohio: Air Force Systems Command, AFSC Manual 80-3, 1961. A broad and detailed definition of the personnel subsystem and of procedures for designing and evaluating it—primarily military but with parallels for industry.

Hall, A. D. *A methodology for systems engineering.* Princeton, N.J.: Van Nostrand, 1962. Treats the scope of systems engineering and includes sections relevant to the "human component" and rational approaches to values in systems.

Johnson, R. A., et al. *The theory and management of systems.* New York: McGraw-Hill, 1963. A rather technical treatment of the application of systems logic and techniques to management enterprises, including organizational structures.

Kuhn, A. *The study of society: A unified approach.* Homewood, Ill.: Irwin, 1963. Decisions, communications, and organizations.

McMillan, C., & Gonzalez, R. F. *Systems analysis: A computer approach to decision models.* Homewood, Ill.: Irwin, 1965. A systems view of the firm, methods, concepts, and models; sophisticated.

Mann, F. C., and Hoffman, L. R. *Automation and the worker.* New York: Holt, 1960. A study of social change in a plant brought about through automation.

Nadler, G. *Work design.* Homewood, Ill.: Irwin, 1963. Work factors and equipment in systems.

Orth, C. D. *Administering research and development.* Homewood, Ill.: Irwin, 1964. Scientists and engineers in organizations.

Philipson, M. (Ed.) *Automation.* New York: Random House, 1962. A collection of insightful articles for the layman on computer applications including industry and research.

Rice, A. K. *The enterprise and its environment.* London: Tavistock Institute, 1963. A systems approach in studying organizations.

Rubenstein, A. H., & Haberstroh, C. H. (Eds.) *Some theories of organization.* Homewood, Ill.: Dorsey, 1960. For the sophisticated reader.

Sells, S. B., & Berry, C. A. (Eds.) *Human factors in jet and space travel: A medical psychological analysis.* New York: Ronald, 1961. From readable to sophisticated.

V.

SPECIAL GROUPS
IN INDUSTRY

15

Labor-Management Relations

Myron L. Joseph

The American industrial scene is pervaded by the image of the rugged individualist and by a strong concept of private property rights. It is difficult for many employers to accept the fact that they are not completely free to run their own plants and that their employees are unwilling to rely on competition among themselves to uncover and reward the most productive. The current institutional pattern is the culmination of a long period of development and change. Taking a look at the ways of union organizations helps to give us a perspective for understanding the many problems of psychological conflict found within labor-management relations.

THE GROWTH OF UNIONS

Even before the spread of industrialization, workers in this country were banding together in organizations to protect themselves against the competitive pressures of expanding markets. This was not the action of oppressed workers against their exploiting employers; rather, it was the reaction of the skilled craftsmen against economic forces which threatened to dilute their skills and lower their wage scales. In the American environment, with its rapidly expanding economic opportunities, the new labor organizations had a difficult time taking root. The legal, political, and social forces were extremely antagonistic to organizations that interfered with the "natural" laws of competition and constituted a threat to private property.

Early Hardships of Labor Unions. In prosperous times, when their bargaining power was high, the labor unions had some success, but prior to 1880 they virtually disappeared during periods of depression. Their susceptibility to economic reversals was due in part to the attractiveness of the political movements of the period, each of which had its own answer to the worker's depressed conditions. Programs for education, homesteads, easy credit, and producer cooperatives attracted the efforts and loyalty of workers, who could not see any hope in the more mundane direction of improving their working conditions. They could escape the risk of unemployment and low wages if they could become self-employed.

In spite of these difficulties unions managed to find a pattern for survival. In the latter half of the nineteenth century, paralleling the growth of industrial markets, national unions grew in number and in strength. The newly organized American Federation of Labor formalized a philosophy which enabled the movement to overcome some of its major obstacles in this country. The leaders recognized the necessity of following the narrowly defined interests of their members, and they vowed to avoid the alliances, political panaceas, and internal disputes which had weakened the earlier organizations. Union membership continued to grow slowly and fluctuated as in the past with economic conditions. However, unionism was not wiped out again in periods of depression, and each revival of industry brought new growth.

Fights against Unions. In these days the industrial and legal environment remained basically antagonistic to organized labor. The earlier conspiracy trials were succeeded by prosecutions under the antitrust laws and the free use of a powerful antiunion weapon, the injunction. With the threat of unionism spreading to the newly developing mass-production industries, management waged a furious battle to keep its plants nonunion. Employees suspected of union sympathies were discharged without hesitation. The weapons brought into play against labor organizers included the so-called "yellow dog" contract, which was an agreement to stay out of unions as a condition of employment, the black list, private police, barbed wire, and tear gas. At the same time company welfare plans and new approaches to individual employees were instituted in the hope of eliminating the attraction of the unions. In the face of this vigorous campaign and in a unique period of declining living costs despite prosperity and high employment levels, union membership fell from 5 million in 1920 to less than 3 million in 1933. The leaders of the labor movement were not successful in breaching the walls of the mass-production industries, which employed large numbers of semiskilled and unskilled workers. Their efforts were hampered by the fact that each craft union wanted to make sure that it would not lose potential members in newly organized plants to any other organization. The drive for unionization seemed to have lost its steam.

Depression Stimulates Union Membership. The Depression of the thirties brought about a dramatic reversal of the declining trend of union membership. Unemployment and declining wage levels made workers less willing to depend upon employer generosity for satisfactory working conditions. The political atmosphere reflected a general disillusionment with the business leadership of the community and produced legislation which protected labor's right to organize. With the mass of workers ready for unionization and a favorable government administration, labor unions grew rapidly. Dissatisfaction within the labor movement with the old-fashioned organizing techniques and an internal power conflict produced a split in the ranks of labor. Far from slowing down the process of organization, the rivalry between the newly formed CIO and the older AFL stimulated a race for new members.

The Mass-production Industries. One by one the mass-production industries succumbed to the organizing drive; new unions were formed; the older organizations grew, though unevenly. By 1937 more than 7 million workers had joined labor unions, a figure which increased to more than 14 million in 1949. In 1955 the two labor federations joined together to form the AFL-CIO, and by 1960 over 18 million workers were labor-union members, about 2 million of them white-collar. Union membership is heavily concentrated among various blue-collar workers in manufacturing, a sector of the labor force which has been declining in relative importance for over a decade. Largely as a result of this trend union membership fell to a little below 18 million in 1962. Membership in the United States in 1962 was about 30 per cent of those employed in nonagricultural establishments. By contrast, in 1954 some 35 per cent of all nonagricultural workers were union members.

The future of the labor movement will depend on its ability to attract members in the expanding sectors of the economy. Some students of labor allege that unions have lost their missionary zeal, that they are fighting a rear-guard action to preserve the *status quo* and to defend the narrow interests of a membership who are no longer the deprived in the economy. However, labor unions are still a potent economic and political force. They are working hard to organize white-collar employees and to expand their membership in nonmanufacturing industries. One strong white-collar union is the American Federation of Television and Radio Artists. The American Federation of Teachers (AFL-CIO) is expanding both in secondary schools and in universities.

UNION CONSTRAINTS ON MANAGEMENT

Almost by definition unions constitute an interference with managerial freedom of action, but that does not explain the violent rejection of unionism by employers when the problem first faced them and the continued emo-

tional antagonism displayed today by many management people who have
dealt with unions for years. Management works to achieve its objectives in
a generally restrictive environment. Competitors, banks, suppliers, customers, and the government place constraints on business decisions. Some
of these groups enter directly into the decision process through representation on boards of directors, whereas others control parts of the environment
within which the firms must operate. Although business organizations are
usually reluctant to accept any of these restrictions, their strongest reactions
have been traditionally against the intrusion of labor organizations.

A Challenge to Management. After a plant is organized, the paths through
which management achieves its goals depend upon the reactions and
cooperation of union leaders. To management, the goal of economic security is threatened by the impact of unions on the efficiency of operations and
by shifts in the organizational structure that make the path to advancement
less clear. The union-enforced constraints and the fact that the labor
leaders are not within their span of control interfere with the desire of
management to control its own affairs. This restriction is particularly disturbing because it is exercised by "outsiders." Union actions challenge
many of the folkways that serve as guides for management decision.

In spite of the fear they have evoked, unions now constitute an important part of the industrial environment. Many managers may have to
redefine some of their goals, but they will also find new ways to achieve
satisfaction in the new organizational context. An important step in this
direction is to develop an understanding of the internal bonds of labor
unions. As we discussed in the chapter on the structure of organizations,
union officers and members do not function within the familiar hierarchic
pattern of the firm.

WHY WORKERS JOIN UNIONS

Why do workers join unions, and what satisfactions do they derive from
their membership? The motives for joining a union vary with economic
conditions and the circumstances of the individual plant. Positive reasons
include the desire for greater security, the liking for such an organization,
and a feeling that a union is the only way to get results. On the other hand,
many workers join because of contract requirements, social expediency, or
informal group pressures from their fellow workers. The evidence suggests
that irrespective of the immediate reason for joining, most workers accept
unions with some degree of conviction. In one study of the situation it was
found that 46 per cent of the members joined because of the union-shop
requirements, but 93 per cent of the workers reported that they needed a

union to buck the employer. A wage problem or some other specific grievance may serve as the last straw, but the act of joining a union usually
reflects some more basic need, such as seeking job security [30, 35, 36, 37].

PROBLEMS WITHIN THE UNION

Although an organization does not exist apart from its members, its behavior must be examined independently. In order for a labor union to
advance the goals of its members and officers, it must be able to make
decisions, take actions, and overcome its internal organizational problems.
The labor union's organizational needs and problems constitute an important factor in determining its behavior. To survive, a union must be
able to maintain its strength and resist the multiple dangers of an antagonistic environment.

Threats to Survival. Labor unions feel that employers remain a strong
potential threat to their survival. The continuing resistance to organization
in many industrial areas and the reluctant acceptance of collective bargaining in industries that have been organized for many years serve to reinforce
the still vivid memories of the violent antiunion campaigns of the past.
Today's union officers and staff workers are drawn for the most part from
the ranks of the early organizers and activists. They retain much of the
suspicion and antagonism which developed out of their experience and
help maintain a word-of-mouth tradition of the hostile employer based on
the period of struggle.

Value Conflicts among Workers. The absence of a strong working-class
identification in our society has increased the difficulties of recruiting and
maintaining union membership [27]. The middle-class values of many
American workers are in conflict with union objectives and methods. In
rural areas and among some white-collar groups this has made organization
a slow and difficult process. In established unions, the younger workers
cannot compare the preorganization working conditions with their present
state, and they may not see any important reasons for paying union dues.
Even if the worker recognizes the benefits of collective bargaining, union
membership is not required for him to share the negotiated improvements.
In organized plants, the collective agreement covers all employees without
regard to membership, and in many nonunion firms employers follow a
pattern of matching the wage increases obtained through collective bargaining in the organized sector of the industry.

INSTITUTIONAL GOALS

How does the labor organization function to further its objectives of survival and growth? To a limited extent the members will accept union policies which strengthen the organization in so far as they see union strength as a means to the fulfillment of their needs. The connection, however, is not always clear, and in some cases may not exist. The members may not understand the economic and political forces which would threaten the union if their contract demands were too extreme. The time period within which the danger exists is likely to be much longer than the span of the members' immediate interests. They may be reluctant to sacrifice an immediate gain for a long-run advantage. In addition, the members may not feel that their own objectives are related in any way to the growth of the organization. They may be more interested in results than in continuing any particular organization as their representative.

Union-leadership View. It is the union officials whose goals are much more closely linked to the organizational needs of the union. The leader's position depends on its survival, and his status is a function of the size, power, and reputation of the union. The difference between the leaders and members is illustrated by their perception of strikes. Union officers often tend to justify strikes and strike threats as a means of increasing the union's power in the long run; inactive members weigh the issues and the chances of success more pragmatically. From the union leader's point of view, even an unsuccessful struggle proves willingness to fight, and will give greater weight to future strike threats. In addition, the conflict may solidify the membership behind their leader and provide evidence that the organization is fighting vigorously for the workers' interests. It may be particularly important to demonstrate this if the union is threatened from within by member apathy or from without by a rival organization [3, 22, 28].

Union Organizational Needs. The fact that union demands and the actions of union officials are frequently related to institutional goals provides an important source of misunderstanding and conflict. In the case of a hopeless strike, the union's behavior is considered irrational by management standards. It is difficult to see why a union will be willing to strike for a union-security agreement when 90 per cent of the employees are already members unless the union's perception of a threatening environment is taken into consideration. Similarly, collective bargaining can become hopelessly bogged down over very small differences because management does not understand that the importance of the union's figure is based upon its organizational needs.

The union may not be able to accept any contract which provides less than that won by a rival union without losing members or even the local. It might be safer for the union to risk a strike than to sign a contract which could be compared unfavorably to its rival's. The demands for industry-wide bargaining are more likely to increase the security of union organizations than to enhance their bargaining strength. The increased scope of the bargaining relationship would protect them against internal comparisons and raids by other unions and would make it more difficult for individual employers to eliminate the union from their plants [19].

The importance of institutional objectives is painfully illustrated when changing technology or shifts in demand threaten the existence of a labor organization. Disputes over the need for flight engineers on modern airplanes and the use of railroad firemen on diesel freight locomotives were severely complicated by the organizational implications of proposed settlements that would have protected the interests of individuals but would not have preserved existing jobs. The arbitration award of the Seward board in the railroad-firemen dispute protects the jobs and incomes of most of the affected workers. But as fireman positions are vacated through attrition, the union will shrink. This dispute, which has been boiling for a number of years, led to the first peacetime Federal compulsory arbitration legislation. The issues are so important to the union, however, that the dispute is far from over in spite of the arbitration award.

THE UNION ORGANIZATION

A factor which must be considered in dealing with a union is the nature of the organizational constraints within which union officers function. Unlike the hierarchic management structure, a union is a political organization.

Power Delegation. The authority for the decisions of the officers comes from the members as delegated by the organization's constitution and by-laws. Authority may be withdrawn through the election process, and there is always the possibility of rival claimants for the leadership roles. Even while the officers are advancing the organizational goals of the union, then, they must protect their own positions in the official hierarchy. Compared with the survival problems of management personnel, the cost of repudiation for a union officer is high. His only alternative, particularly at the local-union level, may be to go back to his job in the shop. The greater the status difference between his office and the available job, the heavier the penalty for losing the political struggle.

It is true that the national officers of the union are better insulated against the attitudes of the members, but internal revolts occur with sufficient frequency to affirm the necessity of protecting their political positions. Lack of opposition in elections does not demonstrate the absence of potential threats or a lack of responsiveness to membership pressures. As long as the path of democratic process remains open, as it does in most unions, even the top leadership must answer to the members. The revolts within the ranks of the United Steelworkers in 1965 illustrate this point [10, 32].

Power of Union Officers Is Limited. Union officers are constrained not only by the power of the ballot but also by the fact that the members constitute the basis for their power. The ability of the union leader to gain concessions from management, the keystone on which his status depends, is a function of the support his members are willing to give. We are not suggesting that the union policies, which are for the most part formulated by the leadership, are identical with those which would have been established by a membership referendum. We are saying, however, that the officers must estimate the amount of pressure behind various membership demands and the possibility that they could be used as a steppingstone for a potential rival. They must also base their decisions on the willingness of the members to take strike action for a set of demands and to abide by the negotiated agreement. The power of union leaders to enforce their decisions on their members is very weak. Union officers can refuse to support grievances which are not based on current agreements and can withdraw official sanction and financial support from unauthorized protests. Rebellious officers at the local and intermediate levels can be disciplined by supporting rival candidates or, in extreme cases, by removing the dissident from office. However, if these rebels have any substantial support from the rank and file, intervention of this type can be extremely dangerous because it may serve to stir up potent political opposition. As a result most cases of disciplinary action by national unions are for the purpose of protecting their locals against dishonest, dictatorial, or negligent local union officers.

Action against rank-and-file members who do not cooperate with union policy is difficult. The most extreme penalty that the union can impose is loss of membership. But this is a realistic alternative only against individuals or very small groups unless the principle involved is worth the loss of a local.

Dependency on the membership forces labor leaders to keep one eye on their political fences. Unlike their management counterparts, there is no single measure, like profits, which can be used to evaluate their performance [28, 43].

Behavior in Negotiations. Collective bargaining differs markedly from other commercial negotiations in that the union officials are communicating with their constituents through their preparations for bargaining, their behavior at the bargaining table, and their comments on the course of the negotiations. Table thumping and complaints that management representatives are not acting in good faith are often part of the process of gaining membership acceptance of the eventual agreement. Some unions formalize the process by requiring membership ratification of the terms of the collective agreements. It is ironic that the union officers who protest bitterly when management bargaining representatives do not have sufficient authority to make concessions must themselves be extremely wary that they do not accept an offer which the members would reject or which could serve as a weak spot in their political armor. On occasion, seemingly innocuous issues are very difficult to resolve because they are important to a group of workers who hold a strategic position in the local's politics or because the officer is afraid that a concession can be twisted about by his opponents in such a way as to endanger his position. This unbusinesslike and illogical behavior of union officers, which is a cause of considerable friction, results from the fact that the pressures under which they function produce a different logic from that of management. Nevertheless, the labor leader's interaction with his members serves an important management function. The working conditions arrived at through negotiation will probably constrain management more than it would like, but the process of collective bargaining increases the probability that the employees will accept such conditions. Since there is no simple way to define what is right or what is best, employees are more likely to accept conditions which were arrived at through a process in which their interests were adequately represented [1, 2, 4].

LABOR–UNION MEMBERSHIP

"The interest of the members" is as difficult to define as the public good. The membership ranks of labor unions are homogeneous only in the sense that they are employees. At the national level one union will represent a variety of occupations in several industries working throughout the country. Even within a local the members' interests and attitudes will vary in accordance with their racial and ethnic backgrounds, levels of skill, age, years of service with the company, and social groups, to mention just a few of the variables by which union members can be stratified. Each group has its own set of priorities for the demands to be made on management. Within the limits set by management's willingness to make concessions, more for one group means less for the others. On some issues the interests of different classifications of members are diametrically opposed. Better opportunities for promotion for one group will make it more difficult for some others to move ahead; more job protection for older workers often makes the younger workers less secure.

Union Democracy. Union constitutions and bylaws formalize the process of membership participation in union decisions, and they usually follow a very democratic pattern. The leaders will generally arrange for the major interest groups to be represented on the committees which determine the collective-bargaining demands and conduct the negotiations. If the pressure is strong enough, a group may be given the right to negotiate a separate contract or to be represented in the union organization by a department of its own. In one instance a major industrial union was forced to give more autonomy to its skilled members after a series of wildcat strikes demonstrated their unwillingness to accept the terms of a contract that had been approved by the general membership.

In spite of the formal provisions, bargaining policy tends to be a leadership function. The demands that are formulated by the rank and file cover too wide a range to serve as a realistic guide, although they provide a useful sounding board for the officers, who cannot ignore an issue for which there is widespread support. Frequently the demands are initiated by members under the guidance of the officers or their representatives. They are then funneled through leadership committees which formulate bargaining policy in the light of the political and strategic needs of the organization. In many cases where the industry's products compete in national markets, union bargaining decisions must be controlled at a level far removed from the local unions and their members. In addition, the increasing complexity of negotiations places a premium on expert knowledge and bargaining skill.

An Organizational Paradox. The competing forces within the labor-union organization create an organizational paradox. In order for the union to respond to the needs of its members, each member or group of members must be free to influence decisions and participate in the political process. However, the ability of the union to force concessions from management is a function of its bargaining strength, which in turn is closely related to the ability of the organization to maintain a solidly united front. Although it has many other functions, a union is basically a fighting organization, and anything which limits its ability to stand up to management in a crisis will weaken its ability to advance the interests of its members. Consequently, union constitutions and mores enforce the requirement of individual loyalty to the organization, and it is difficult to draw the line between dissent and disloyalty. The individual's right to defend his own interests must therefore be tempered in the light of the effect of protest on the ability of the organization to function in the interest of its members.

Sections of the Landrum-Griffin Act of 1959 were designed to protect union democracy and to weaken the control of union leaders over local unions and members. In some situations, however, weakening the national union may endanger mature and stable bargaining relationships. Recently a major union negotiated what was considered to be a generous wage increase for its members in a large local. Partly because of internal political conflicts, the local members rejected the contract. A rival union was waiting in the wings, anxious to replace the incumbent union as bargaining representative if the local members were not satisfied. The union negotiators had to return to the bargaining table to try to improve on a contract which they had already recommended to the membership. This example of democracy in action will probably result in a serious strike. It is inevitable that legislation designed to correct extremes has broader and often unanticipated consequences.

OFFICERS OF THE UNION

The forces leading to centralization and the loyalty requirements for organizational strength tend to protect the national union officers from membership political pressures. Other characteristics of labor unions increase their independence. Probably the most significant is the relative indifference of most union members to the government of their organization. Very few feel any need to participate in the functioning of the union. There are typically large membership turnouts at meetings called to consider a new contract or to conduct a strike vote, but extremely small attendance at all other times. This should not be taken as a sign of indifference to the organization but rather as an indication that the union is perceived as performing a particular function for its members and that as long as there is general satisfaction with the results, the members have little reason to participate in its affairs [15].

Protection for Union Officers. The officers are protected from the rank and file by the power which their tenure in office gives them over strategic parts of the organization. The loyalty of the paid staff of the organization, who owe their jobs to the incumbent officers, provides the leaders with an effective political machine. The international representatives who service the local unions constitute the only direct contact which most union members and local officers have with the national organization. They can give support to local leaders friendly to the administration and make things difficult for their opponents. As long as the union staff remains loyal, it is difficult to break the rule of the incumbent officers.

National Union Officers. The preponderant position of the national officers in determining union policy facilitates their implementation of the organizational objectives, which are tied more closely to the personal goals of the leaders. As union leaders gain more experience and develop a more sophisticated understanding of their economic environment and the problems of the companies with whom they deal, their perception of the collective-bargaining situation will tend to deviate more and more from the view held by the rank and file.

The officers' continuing relationships with management representatives take on value, both in terms of long-run bargaining strategy and the personal need to hold their respect. The further removed from the rank and file the leaders are, the more their behavior is conditioned by the values of other groups in the society with whom they have increasing contact. The net result of the relative independence of the national union officers are labor unions that are more stable and responsible and less responsive to membership attitudes. It should be noted that policies designed to force purer democratic behavior on labor organizations may entail a social cost in terms of less stability and responsibility [7, 35].

Local Union Officers. At the local level, the political potency of membership pressures is less easily confined. A candidate can make himself known to the members with relative ease. Handbills, personal contacts, and informal communications within the plant minimize the electioneering advantage the incumbents may have. The campaign issues are likely to be very personal ones, relating to the personalities, behavior, and reputations of the candidates. Anything can be picked up by an opponent and blown up into a damaging accusation. Between elections, dissident groups can always pack a local union meeting as a means of putting pressure on the officers. When a local president finds a large turnout from a particular department at a meeting, he knows he is in for trouble. If one officer is unwilling to support a grievance, the member may be able to find another who is willing to build his own political strength by pushing it [33].

The fluidity of the political situation forces the local officers to devise techniques to protect themselves as best they can. The widespread "rule of two" serves to discourage accusations and rumors of selling out to management. This custom requires that no union officer will meet with a company representative unless at least one other officer is present. A local officer can be criticized if he does not win enough grievances, but it is politically difficult to refuse to accept grievances that have little chance of being granted. Partial protection is gained by establishing a committee which passes on the merits of grievances. Although this takes the blame away from any one individual, it does not prevent factions within the group from claiming that they would have pushed the grievance but that others prevented it. The record of wins and losses can be improved by taking credit for concessions and passing the less hopeful cases on to the next step in the grievance process. The less insulated an officer is from membership pressure, the more difficult it is for him to explain to a grievant that his claim is unwarranted. Consequently, many cases are appealed to the international representative and even to arbitration although they are basically without merit. The effectiveness of this relief will depend on the relations between the local officers and the international representatives, and this is one of the tools that the latter can wield to exert influence at the local level. Even if the case is not passed on to the next level, the local officer may soften the blow by going through the motions of arguing a hopeless case, so that he will receive some credit for supporting his members.

The political advantage to be gained from winning concessions is hotly contested. A cooperative international representative will be careful to give credit to the local officers even if he conducted all the negotiations. Opponents, on the other hand, may try to undermine an officer by claiming that he is too dependent on the international representative and has accomplished nothing on his own. To prevent this situation, some locals handle all of their own cases, taking their chances on losing cases but claiming all the credit for the successes.

It is difficult for management to be neutral in this situation because its behavior can be very influential in determining the political success or failure of the local officers. A policy of making important concessions only at the top local level can give the officers at that level more security in their positions and more influence on union policies. The timing of concessions can be very important to the outcome of local elections. Local union politics frequently reflect management's industrial relations policies.

MANAGEMENT MEETS THE UNION

When faced with the prospect of unionization, employers have a wide range of possible response. Federal legislation does not permit interference with the free choice of the employees, but management may express its attitudes toward unionization with reasonable freedom as long as no promises or threats are implied. Even if an employer would rather not deal with a union, a policy of opposition frequently carries considerable risk. In the heat of an organizing campaign, grievances are magnified, and charges are pressed by union representatives in order to gain adherents. Attempts to correct any unsatisfactory conditions at such a time would simply provide the organizer with proof of the union's effectiveness, and answering exaggerated or fabricated charges might embroil the employer in an emotional interchange in which the objective situation played only a minor role. If the employees did not already have the information which would demonstrate the exaggerated nature of the organizer's claims, it would be very difficult to communicate it to them in an objective way without having the attempts turned around to the union's advantage. Many employees would say, "After all, if the employer is so anxious to keep the union out, perhaps it can really help us!" The greatest dangers of opposition are the implications of failure.

Behavior Patterns. The behavior patterns of the union leaders are developed in this formative period, as are the attitudes of the management organization. If the union succeeds, the employer must treat union officers as representatives of his employees. The type of leadership which succeeded in overcoming the employer's opposition is not likely to have the qualities he would like to meet over the bargaining table. If exaggerated promises and emotionally charged accusations were the path to victory, as they may well be in a hotly fought contest, the new officers will be expected to make good on their claims. If the employer escapes the danger of having to deal with overly aggressive or irresponsible leaders who were trained in combat, he must still face the problem of developing in his own ranks, trained in the same school, the attitudes necessary to maintain a stable bargaining relationship. Although for many employers the economic and noneconomic costs of unionization may be high, the costs of opposition should be fully realized.

A number of authors have categorized management policies along a continuum which is closely related to the conflict-cooperation classifications used to describe patterns of union-management relations. At one extreme there is forceful and open resistance to unionization through the use of coercive techniques which shade into the various forms of agressive persuasion of which employers may avail themselves within the constraints of the Labor-Management Relations Act. Further along the continuum are the employers who reluctantly accept the legal obligation to bargain with unions but who do everything possible to restrict the influence of the unions with at least the hopeful expectation that someday they will be eliminated. In such situations there is a continuing struggle over the loyalty of the employees, and the unions will have to act to guard their institutional security. There is a better chance of a stable relationship when employers are willing to accept unions and collective bargaining as a permanent part of their decision process and guard against actions which would threaten the unions' survival. Here again there are degrees of acceptance ranging up to a level of cooperation which includes the recognition of many joint problems and the establishment of a decision process in which the responsibility for many decisions is shared [14, 38, 40].

LABOR–MANAGEMENT BARGAINING

As we know, *bargaining is basically a power relationship*. Each side must consider the costs and gains of alternative bargaining positions. The ability to inflict penalties and the capacity to survive penalties are implicit in the bargaining process. If a union could not strike or inflict damage on management through such techniques as the slowdown, it would have no strength as an organization to enforce costly demands on management. Similarly, management would be unable to resist union demands if withholding agreement did not inflict monetary or organizational costs on the union.

Commitments as Strategy. If one of the parties can succeed in convincing the other that it is unable to retreat from a solution within the acceptable range, the act of commitment will force the opponent to accept the offer [18]. Management and unions go to great lengths to convince each other that they are firmly committed to particular positions. Employers make public statements and establish a situation in which their status would clearly be in jeopardy if they retreated. Strike votes by union members and strike deadlines are among the techniques used by union negotiators to cut themselves off from retreat. Part of a good strategy would be to help the opponent to rationalize his retreat from a committed position so that he does not lose the ability to commit himself in the future. The difficulty of accurately comparing the multiple issues covered in negotiations makes it easier to compromise issues because the compromise need not be interpreted as a retreat.

The Limited Use of Facts. The nature of bargaining helps explain the limited function of facts. They may be used to support demands or to help establish patterns, but they are infrequently used as a basis for agreement. If the parties could agree on the principles which should determine the outcome of bargaining, recourse to facts could settle the issue. The nature of the power conflict is such, however, that each side will support those principles which favor its own cause, and disagreement over facts usually disguises a more basic disagreement [5].

Working toward the Contract. The negotiation of labor agreements differs in a critical aspect from the process by which most other contractual arrangements are reached. Unless one of the parties fails to survive, agreement must be reached eventually. The alternative of simply breaking off relations if negotiations are not successful and seeking a more satisfactory agreement with another organization is not available. Most strikes are not aimed at the destruction of the union or the company, but are simply moves in the process of reaching an agreement. This mutual interdependence of labor and management serves as a major constraint on bargaining behavior. For one thing, the negotiators must provide a basis for the continuing relationship, recognizing and adjusting to the existing conflicts of interest. In attempting to agree on mutually acceptable working conditions for the period of the agreement, they must recognize the impossibility of covering the multitude of specific problems which will be the content of disputes that will arise. If we think of collective bargaining as an orderly process for adjusting conflicts of interest, it must include both the negotiation of a contract as general or as specific as the parties feel will meet their needs and a continuing method for handling disputes and issues which arise within the framework of the collective agreement.

Contract Violations. Damage suits are rarely a satisfactory remedy for breach of labor agreements—unlike most other contracts. The parties must consider the impact of their actions, including legal action against each other, on the quality of the ongoing bargaining relationship. An antagonistic bargaining committee may be a heavy penalty to pay for the satisfaction of proving damages against the union, and, in fact, most such suits seem to be withdrawn as part of the general settlement of disputed issues. More important is the fact that most of the problems which arise during a contract period will not involve a formal breach of the agreement by the union. The failure of individual members to abide by the contract does not automatically make the union liable for damages, and frequently the union officers are as anxious as management is to bring the dispute to an end. In any event, so long as the union officers disavow the actions which violate the contract and make some attempt to obtain compliance, management is left with disciplinary action against the individual employees as their only recourse.

The working conditions described in collective-bargaining agreements are constraints on management. They establish employees' rights and the limits of managerial control of the work force. Normal court procedures would not be a very effective means for protecting employees against labor-contract violations by management. The courts are time-consuming and expensive, and the legal tribunals are generally unfamiliar with the complexities of labor relations. But more importantly, the parties require a procedure that will help them work together under the contract, that will enable them to apply the labor agreement equitably to a continuously changing set of circumstances. In recognition of this, most labor contracts are to a considerable extent self-enforcing. A formal grievance procedure enables an employee to appeal managerial decisions to higher levels of the management hierarchy through his union representative. Typically the union steward, the grievance committee, and the staff representative servicing the local will meet with their respective counterparts in the management organization at the different steps in the grievance procedure. If the union is not satisfied with the results of the last stage of consultation, most contracts provide that the grievance may be appealed to arbitration.

THE SETTLEMENT OF GRIEVANCES

Some firms stress the *judicial function* of the grievance process and insist on a strict legalistic interpretation of the labor contract. This tends to curtail the number of grievances and places emphasis on the formal procedure. At the other end of the spectrum is the *clinical approach,* which recognizes the dynamic nature of industrial relations and the need for adjusting the problems which arise out of the process of change. Although a legalistic approach may keep complaints which are not covered by the contract out of the grievance machinery, it will not eliminate the sources of conflict, which may well find less desirable outlets for expression [18].

First Level of Grievance. In most cases the vast majority of grievances are settled at the first step, involving the shop steward, the foreman, and the grievant. At this level, the process is very informal, and settlements which do not cause trouble for the higher levels of either organization are unlikely to be scrutinized with any care. In fact, such scrutiny would be impossible in many cases because of the inadequacy of the records. Even in companies which attempt to maintain a policy of strict contract interpretation at higher levels, the first informal stages of the process are characterized by rule and contract evasion by stewards and foremen. They make informal concessions to each other which help meet their respective needs. The steward is able to meet his political commitments, reward his followers in the shop, and minimize the danger of costly appeals and less favorable contract interpretations from higher-level management. The foreman gains greater flexibility, fewer bad grievances, and guards himself against the actions his superiors might take if he were not able to handle his own problems. This informality helps to stabilize industrial relations, but the higher levels of both organizations may have a completely erroneous conception of relations in the shop [8].

Liabilities of the Grievance Process. The existence of a grievance procedure does not, of course, ensure a frictionless adjustment of difficulties. A problem of growing importance is the delay between the time of filing a grievance and its final disposition. If the employees are frustrated in their expectations of obtaining a fair handling of their cases in a reasonable time, the grievance process may create more problems than it solves. The delays are partly the fault of management and partly the result of the political nature of the union. If answering grievances is not given sufficient priority by the employer, the union committee may be forced, in response to pressure from interested members, to accuse management of stalling tactics or at least of negligence. This is a particularly frustrating situation because, short of direct action, there is no practical way for a union to force management to answer a grievance. The contract provisions which specify that a grievance must be answered in a particular period of time serve only as evidence of good faith and a standard for normal procedure. Union officers are often reluctant to put too much pressure on management to answer a grievance because, as one officer said in explaining delay to his members, "It is always easy to get a 'no' answer." Membership discontent may build up to the point where the local officers are forced to prefer any answer to a continued delay, since the delay is interpreted as weakness on their part.

The effectiveness of the grievance process is hampered by the fact that it is unavoidably an integral part of the internal political process of the local union. Particularly in the industrial unions, where national or pattern bargaining plays a major role in contract negotiation, grievance handling and contract administration become the primary function of the local officers. As a result, the stage at which the grievance is won or lost becomes political currency. If the answer is to be favorable, the steward, grievance chairman, or local president would like to get the credit. If the grievance is denied, they would like to appeal it to another step so that the final negative answer will not be attributed to them. It takes a strong local officer to explain to a member that his grievance has no basis and that he will not process it. It is not unusual for the number of grievances and the level of aggressiveness with which they are argued to jump markedly in the period before a local election.

Arbitration. Arbitration should be considered an integral part of the grievance procedure. In addition to providing a method of disposing of unresolved issues of contract interpretation, arbitration helps to make the grievance steps more meaningful. Management and union officers are better able to eliminate unwarranted complaints, since the final result does not depend on relative force or the effectiveness of the pressure. Without arbitration, the balance of rights, as seen by the employees, is uneven. In the process of performing managerial functions, the employer could violate employee rights at will, and the only effective employee protest would be force. Arbitration provides a fair method of determining whether or not rights have been violated and makes the contract something more than a temporary halt in the power struggle [16, 20].

Arbitration is not universally accepted, and many contracts exclude certain areas, such as production standards, from their mandatory arbitration provisions. In such cases the union is free to strike if it is unwilling to accept management's answer at the highest level of consultation in the grievance process. From the employer's point of view there has been a great reluctance to allow an outsider to make a decision which is not in the strictest sense an interpretation of the provisions of the contract.

THE CONTRACT ISSUES

The collective-bargaining agreement is a contract between management and the union as the representative of all the employees in the bargaining unit. It represents the only enforceable constraints, other than those which are a part of our legal structure, on the personnel and labor relations activities of management for the period of the agreement. Many contracts make this explicit by including a "management rights" clause which states in various ways that the restrictions on management are limited to those contained in the contract.

Each contract is the product of its own environment. The extent to which different issues are important to the parties, the arrangements which are available to meet their needs, and their relative power to obtain their demands vary. Control of hiring has been extremely important to the unions in the construction industry but of no significance in the industrial unions; their attitudes toward seniority provisions show the reverse pattern. Each collective-bargaining situation should be examined in the light of its own economic and organizational pressures.

Major Bargaining Issues. Some of the provisions of a labor contract can be identified as primarily union-oriented. They do not relate directly to the employee's working conditions but serve to strengthen and stabilize the organization.

One example is the checkoff clause, which requires that management deduct union dues from the members' wages and remit them directly to the union. This cuts down the manpower necessary to administer a large union, but more importantly it makes it more difficult for a member to resign, since the positive act of revoking the checkoff authorization would be required. When collections were made by hand, each dues date presented the possibility of nonpayment, and the local officers had to do a continuous job to keep up the resources of the organization.

Compulsory union membership is the most controversial union-security issue. Management resistance is based in part on a reluctance to strengthen the union's position by requiring employees to join, and in part on a genuine belief that compulsory union membership is an infringement on employees' freedom. Unions believe that all employees should support and participate in the organization that is responsible for representing them in negotiations, and argue that if the majority of workers select a union, compulsory membership does not violate individual rights.

Unions try to protect their members against the unilateral control of management. In part this is a conflict between management's need for flexibility for efficient production and the employees' desire to determine their own work behavior and to understand and control working conditions. The union seeks to protect its members against arbitrary or unfair decisions and to use the force of the union to balance the interests of the individual workers against the interests of the company. These issues are resolved through contract clauses relating to discipline, work assignments, layoff, promotion, and transfers. These restrictions give protection against anti-union discrimination and make it more difficult for the employer to put pressure on his employees to increase their level of output.

Technological Change and Job Security. In recent years job security has become an increasingly important issue. The high average rate of unemployment has caused unions to seek job protection for their members and in some cases to push for arrangements that spread the available work. The pragmatic, membership orientation of labor unions helps to explain the fact that the fight for job security frequently becomes a dispute between unions for the available work. Industrial unions try to restrict management's right to subcontract work to outside employers. Craft unions try to use their economic power to obtain more of the industrial construction and maintenance work for their own members. This conflict is being fought by negotiations, by arbitration, in the courts and within the AFL-CIO.

Another aspect of the drive for job security is the attempt of many unions to obtain protection for their members against the displacement caused by technological change. In many cases companies have been able to program the installation of new equipment so that normal attrition absorbs the displacement. The Kaiser Steel agreement reached in the early sixties provided for a guarantee against technological displacement, and other contracts have included income guarantees, company-financed retraining for displaced workers, and liberal severance allowances. Many unions have turned to the shorter work week as a means of increasing employment opportunities for their members. The extended-vacation provisions of the basic steel contracts are another response to persistent unemployment. When aggregate demand does not increase fast enough to absorb the workers displaced by advancing productivity, unions accelerate their efforts to protect their members against the human costs of technological change. In automation, its most recent form, technological advance has become a major source of concern for the labor movement. When unemployment is high, it is difficult for the labor movement to remember that technological change is the major source of our high standard of living.

Wages. Wages are, of course, a major focus of labor agreements. In spite of the fact that current research has been unable to demonstrate that unions have succeeded in gaining any substantial comparative advantage for their members through collective bargaining, the bargained increases are perceived by officers and members alike as a measure of the success or failure of the union organization. There is no union-management agreement on the appropriate criteria for wage determination, and the factors stressed by the parties change as changing conditions make them more or less consistent with the interests of either side. An additional problem is that some of the factors which influence a union's wage position are perceived by management to be irrelevant. Coercive comparisons with wages in other areas, other industries, and other unions are a function of the organizational pressures on union leaders and may be as important to them as the economics of the firm [23, 32, 44].

The Costs of Collective Bargaining. Labor contracts contain a great variety of employee benefits, ranging from holidays and vacations to supplementary unemployment compensation. Although negotiations are primarily a union-leadership function, the political nature of the organization suggests that in most cases the contracts correspond in a general way to important needs of the members. In some areas the resulting patterns may help achieve management goals as well. For example, a rational job-evaluation program may be as important to an employer as to the union, and the positive implications of improved morale for increased productivity should not be neglected. However, in many cases union gains are made at the cost of some efficiency. Even if management responds by improving in other directions, the restrictions enforced by collective bargaining limit the efficiency of production.

When bargaining breaks down, the resulting strikes curtail production, and may, on occasion, cause the general public considerable inconvenience. However, our acceptance since the 1930s of collective bargaining as a process for determining wages and working conditions is based on the judgment that the resulting social benefits and balance of interests outweigh the social costs. Collective bargaining has remained primarily a private institution. Recently unions and companies in several industries have experimented with new bargaining techniques to reduce the possibility of strikes. They have established committees to study and discuss major problems on a continuing basis, in some cases with the aid of neutral consultants, in the period between contract negotiations. The parties believe they will be able to agree on solutions to complex issues more effectively if they are not faced with the pressing deadline of contract expiration. Collective bargaining can be expected to adjust to the changing institutional and economic environment [4, 5, 11].

As job security gains prominence as a union demand, it runs headlong into management's need to increase efficiency. The problem of industrial harmony will not be solved until we develop better techniques for sharing certain ego goals, says Stagner in his writings on industrial conflict [40]. Human values must be equated with the economic facts of life, and for psychology labor-management relations may have profound implications [13, 22]. Both individual and environmental variables are important, and modern researches are now pointing in this direction.

SUGGESTIONS FOR SELECTIVE READING

Banks, O. *The attitudes of steelworkers to technical change.* Liverpool, England: Liverpool University Press, 1960. The perceptions of workers after the fact of change.

Barbash, J. (Ed.) *Unions and union leadership.* New York: Harper & Row, 1960. Readings helping with the understanding of the labor movement.

Berle, A. A., Jr. *Power without property.* New York: Harcourt, Brace & World, 1959. The author predicts collective bargaining will move more into the corporation's external power.

Bernstein, I. *The lean years.* Boston: Houghton Mifflin, 1960. History of the American worker from 1920 to 1933.

Bierne, J. A. *New horizons for American labor.* Washington, D.C.: Public Affairs Press, 1962. Labor unions have some reluctance to meet some questions.

Cole, D. L. *The quest for industrial peace.* New York: McGraw-Hill, 1963. Some new thinking about labor-management relations.

Eby, K. *Protests of an ex-organization man.* Boston: Beacon Press, 1961. Big unionism as big business.

Form, W. H., & Miller, D. C. *Industry, labor and community.* New York: Harper & Row, 1960. A sociological book about power structures.

Galenson, W., & Lipset, S. M. (Eds.) *Labor and trade unionism.* New York: Wiley, 1960. Some trends in labor-management relations.

Hoffer, E. *The ordeal of change.* New York: Harper & Row, 1963. Essays by a union official on social change.

Jacobs, P. *The state of unions.* New York: Atheneum Publishers, 1963. Unions and their problems in adapting to change.

Karn, H. W., & Gilmer, B. v. H. (Eds.) *Readings in industrial and business psychology.* (2d ed.) New York: McGraw-Hill, 1962. Section XI includes five articles on labor-management relations.

Karsh, B. *Diary of a strike.* Urbana, Ill.: University of Illinois Press, 1958. Problems of pluralism, fed by rising educational levels.

Kornhauser, A. W., et al. *Industrial conflict.* New York: McGraw-Hill, 1954. A classic on the practical aspects of industrial relations.

Lesieur, F. G. (Ed.) *The Scanlon plan.* Cambridge, Mass.: M.I.T., 1958. Articles on success and failure in one approach to labor-management relations.

Nestor, A. M. *Women's labor leader.* Rockford, Ill.: Bellevue Books, 1954. Autobiography of a woman labor leader.

Peterson, Florence. *American labor unions: What they are and how they work.* New York: Harper & Row, 1964. An academically oriented view of unions.

Purcell, T. V. *Blue collar man.* Cambridge, Mass.: Harvard University Press, 1960. A study which shows dual loyalty of workers is possible.

Ross, A. M., & Hartman, P. *Changing patterns of industrial conflict.* New York: Wiley, 1960. Decline in frequency and duration of strikes and lockouts in northern Europe and North America.

Seidman, J., et al. *The worker views his union.* Chicago: University of Chicago Press, 1958. What workers think about unions.

Shostak, A. B. *America's forgotten labor organization.* Princeton, N.J.: Princeton, 1962. A survey of the role of the single-firm independent union in American industry.

Stagner, R. *The psychology of industrial conflict.* New York: Wiley, 1956. Union-management relations as a psychological problem.

Stagner, R., & Rosen, H. *Psychology of union-management relations.* Belmont, Calif.: Wadsworth, 1965. A small volume on a rapidly growing field of psychology.

Widick, B. J. *Labor today.* Boston: Houghton Mifflin, 1964. Union goals and organization.

16

Handicapped, Unemployed, and Aging Persons

B. von Haller Gilmer

The leaders of industry in recent years have shown an increasing awareness of the psychological as well as the economic problems of the handicapped individual, the unemployed, the migrant worker, and the worker approaching retirement. The social community and local and national government agencies are likewise showing concern over such questions as: Does the handicapped person make a reliable, productive worker? What are the effects of unemployment on the individual? What of the insecurities of the migrant worker? Are our age criteria for retirement from industry sound? These questions are of interest to each of us as individuals who may, at some time or other, be faced with one or all of them.

THE HANDICAPPED WORKER

In one sense of the word we are all handicapped. There is no job that really demands all our capacities. This is fortunate in that no one of us is physically, mentally, and emotionally anywhere near perfect. Thus we are normal workers in relation to the jobs we can do successfully and handicapped workers in relation to the jobs we are physically, mentally, or emotionally unable to perform satisfactorily.

Productivity of the Handicapped. Through adequate job analysis, physical and psychological measurement, training, and job orientation, it has been shown that the vast majority of handicapped people can be placed on jobs where they can produce as well as nonhandicapped workers. Fortunately, attitudes toward the handicapped are beginning to shift away from emphasis on what the person cannot do to what he can do, away from the idea that the handicapped individual is a charity case to the belief that he is an economic asset.

The handicapped worker is very much like the nonhandicapped worker in many ways. The loss of an arm, leg, or eye does restrict the number of things a man can do. But a poor aptitude for mathematics or a lack of mechanical skill is also a restraint. If we possessed all these things, we would have a wider range of jobs to choose from. Physical defects in themselves do not destroy working capacity; they merely make the person incapable of performing certain jobs. In fact, the handicapped worker may be outstanding in some jobs.

The Polaroid Corporation uses blind people for loading film, and there are some epileptics who have proved to themselves and to industry that they can man an assembly line. Abilities, Inc., a subcontracting profit-making company that pays the prevailing wage scale, has had over a decade of success in employing the physically handicapped. Stress is put on abilities, not inabilities. A one-armed man, using a special jig, performs a delicate soldering job. Women with arthritis-weakened wrists wind wires with the aid of a machine. Other employees work in pairs, matching their abilities and disabilities to the job. Much of the ancient art of weaving is being kept alive in the Hawaiian Islands by the part-time employment of arrested TB cases, and the industry has for years proved to be profitable.

Statistical surveys and clinical case studies by local and state governments, the Veterans Administration, the U.S. Department of Labor and Civil Service Commission, the United States Chamber of Commerce, the National Association of Manufacturers, labor unions, and private companies have been published on the various behavioral aspects of the physically handicapped worker.

Typical of the findings is one report from over a hundred corporations involving thousands of workers which states that about two-thirds of the physically handicapped workers produce at approximately the same rate as their able-bodied fellow workers and that 24 per cent produce at a higher rate. Only 10 per cent of the handicapped are reported lower in production than their nonhandicapped counterparts. Accident rates, absenteeism, and turnover are frequently lower for the handicapped [46].

The Handicapped as an Economic Asset. Several factors favor the physically handicapped worker as a good economic bet. In the first place, handicapped employees usually have been screened, and their abilities have been matched with job requirements. Often more attention has been given to training and job orientation than among able-bodied workers. Moreover, individual motivational factors often operate in favor of the handicapped person. He is conscious of his handicap and often has feelings of job insecurity. He may well put forth more effort to hold his job, to report for work, or even to excel at his job. Other things being equal, the handicapped worker holds a very favorable attitude toward his job.

Although some information shows that handicapped workers occasionally are problems to an employer, the consensus of professional publications favors employing the handicapped person who has been properly rehabilitated. Success depends on finding out accurately the person's potentials and preparing him physically, vocationally, and psychologically for the job he will do. It also depends on helping the man find the right job—not just a job which he can do but a job in a place where the work climate is such that he will be accepted. Appropriate job analysis may well show that the handicapped have many usable assets. Many jobs do not require the "whole," healthy person.

Effects of Rehabilitation. Under the right kind of rehabilitation, the handicapped person is "adaptable, productive, careful, regular, reliable, and capable," concludes the National Rehabilitation Association from its study of thousands of cases. Evidence of adaptability is shown by the way the handicapped adjust quickly and satisfactorily to the conditions of the job. Where productivity can be objectively measured, handicapped workers are equal to and sometimes superior to other workers in job performance. They are careful workers, showing safety records equal to or superior to those of their fellow workers. Their handicaps seem to make them want to be safe. Unless there is something unusual about the nature of the handicap, regularity on the job is as good as and sometimes better than that of the other workers on the same job. Statistics indicate the reliability of the handicapped; they are not job hoppers. The handicapped are capable of doing superior work where they have skill to meet the job demands.

Who are the handicapped? They include young people, grownups, and elderly men and women. Some are clerks, others are executives; some are farmers, and others are machinists and housewives. The handicapped are veterans and nonveterans, college graduates and illiterates, blue-collar and white-collar workers; they may have a high IQ or be mentally retarded. In short, the handicapped are a fair cross section of the American people. An analysis of 66,000 persons rehabilitated during one typical year showed that 56 per cent were disabled by disease, 30 per cent by accidents, and 14 per cent by congenital conditions. Of this total the greatest single group had lost the use of arms, legs, or back. Next in order came amputees and blind or visually impaired workers [46].

The United States Public Health Service reports that in any given year there are about 20 million persons living outside of institutions who are handicapped by chronic ailments. Of these about 4 million cannot work, keep house, or go to school. Almost half of the noninstitutionalized population in the sixty-five-plus age group is physically or mentally impaired.

One of the principal results of the progress of automation has been to stimulate a nationwide reassessment of the manpower needs and resources of our economy. As a part of this reassessment, the special needs of the handicapped are being given increased consideration. Employment of handicapped workers demands intensified efforts toward enlarging their skills and improving guidance facilities. Changes are slowly taking place in certain practical situations involving community attitudes toward the handicapped. For example, there is a more favorable attitude toward renting to blind couples because the data have shown that they are not an undue accident risk.

Studies of adult industrial workers who have suffered sudden disablement show that they have to adjust not only to physical limitations but also to psychological disturbances which may be more crippling than the physical disabilities. In many respects the rehabilitation of the mentally and emotionally handicapped person is more difficult than is that of the physically handicapped.

The industrial worker who becomes handicapped may be able to find placement within the same company and sometimes at the same job. The man who becomes a heart case may be able to carry on his regular duties within limits.

The Job Climate. The psychological climate of the job is important to the handicapped man. Some counselors feel that it is important to impress upon the men on the job that a handicapped worker should be treated in a normal, matter-of-fact way. More than average curiosity, undue cheerfulness, or excessive helpfulness may indicate to the handicapped person that his colleagues are sensitive to his condition. Once fellow workers become accustomed to seeing the handicapped worker around, they will accept him, handicap and all. Fortunately, the recognition that the handicapped worker can be an economic asset to society and to himself is gaining ground.

Employing the Handicapped. Much has been written on the pros and cons of employing the physically handicapped. One opinion holds, for example, that the impaired person is more likely to be injured, since his actions and movements are hampered by his handicap. An opposite view is held by those who believe that the impaired person is less likely to be injured because he tends to be more safety-conscious. What are the facts?

Neither of these statements is completely accurate in light of accident studies, yet there is some truth in each. The answers depend in great measure on how well handicapped persons are fitted to their jobs and their work environment. One study in the Western Electric Company of 685 handicapped workers well matched to their jobs found that 23.5 per cent became injured at work, compared with 39.1 per cent of the control normal group. In this same study it was found that there were 7.9 per cent more resignations among the normal workers than among the handicapped workers; 7 per cent more absences occurred among the normal workers; there were 5.6 per cent more discharges for just cause among normal workers; and 4.6 per cent more earnings were received by the handicapped workers [31].

The Pennsylvania State Bureau of Rehabilitation found that less than 1 per cent of 29,000 physically handicapped automobile drivers were involved in accidents one year as against 4½ per cent of 2 million drivers of normal physical fitness. Superior selection, training, and attitude may have favored the handicapped group. It is also possible that the handicapped did less driving, but even so, they appear to be good risks [37].

The many successes achieved in the rehabilitation of war veterans have opened up for the handicapped a number of areas generally thought to be the exclusive province of normal people. For example, 388 totally blinded veterans were put into new occupations never before open to the blind. They soon became highly successful in these jobs, which ranged from technical occupations and industrial management to sales and service-type work. At present, there are more than 6 million known handicapped workers; most of them are employed in factories, in offices, and on farms—in situations similar to those held by nonhandicapped persons [46].

THE PSYCHOLOGICAL ASPECTS OF UNEMPLOYMENT

One way to appreciate, at least to some extent, the place of work in the lives of all of us is to get a view of the man who is out of work. Who is he? How does he feel? What can we learn from studying the behavior patterns of the unemployed?

Unemployment Is Always Present. Unemployment has a serious impact not only on the individual but also on society, and nowhere is this impact felt more, economically or psychologically, than in the industrial community affected. Unemployment exists in good times as well as during recessions and depressions. In a study sponsored by the Twentieth Century Fund, it was found that the United States has not been free of unemployment since the turn of the century; it never disappears and rarely falls below 5 per cent of the labor force. Unemployment includes both those workers who are out of jobs for short periods of time when changing jobs and those who are forced into longer periods of unemployment by seasonal variations and depressed market conditions. Only a few of the unemployed really do not want to work. There are around 250,000 domestic migrant workers in any normal year. Migrants appear to be more influenced in making their decisions to move by good conditions in the host country than by bad conditions at home. For the most part, migrants have an indigenous disadvantage wherever they go unless they are highly skilled [53]. Technical advances, although beneficial to employment in the long run, contribute to temporary loss of jobs. Since 1900 unemployment of 1 to 3 million people at any one time has been considered normal. At one time during the Great Depression of the thirties, unemployment in the United States reached a total of 10 million men and women either partially or totally out of work. One-third of all those normally employed were out of work in 1932 [48]. The United States Department of Labor in 1965 estimated that one million man-years of productive time were being lost each year because of unemployment of persons over 45. Age discrimination in employment is on the increase.

Seasonal Unemployment. Cyclic and seasonal unemployment is a menace to stable career patterns. Although it hits hardest at semiskilled and unskilled workers, it touches others indirectly. Style changes and model innovations affect production schedules; holidays influence consumer buying patterns; the supply of young, school-age workers fluctuates. All these factors contribute to the up-and-down swing of employment here and there.

Seasonal-unemployment patterns differ for men and women, for the young and the adult. During the first four months of the year, unemployment is higher among men over twenty-five years of age. It reaches a peak in February because of reduced activity in the construction industry and in agriculture. Unemployment for this group is below the annual average for the remainder of the year. Men and women under twenty-five years of age find jobs harder to get during the summer school-vacation months because of the influx of young people into the labor market. For the most part, women over twenty-five years of age find employment relatively stable.

Psychologically, seasonal unemployment comes to be accepted, and hence the unemployed seasonal worker does not lose status; on the other hand, the worker who is accustomed to steady employment may fear a great loss of status when he is confronted with prolonged unemployment. Unemployment insurance has come to be a part of the normal pattern in our society and hence different from being on relief.

The percentage of workers affected by seasonal layoffs varies. In the beet-sugar industry, canning, and ice manufacture, 50 per cent or more of the workers may be off during the slack time. About 25 per cent of automobile workers may be laid off temporarily during model change-overs.

Such industries as the manufacture of fertilizers, woolen goods, and furniture are quite sensitive both to seasonal effects and to economic depressions. On the other hand, employees of telephone companies, electric-power industries, and the like enjoy more stable employment.

For the young person getting started, the lack of work is common even in prosperous times. For teen-agers ready to begin careers, unemployment often runs as high as 10 per cent. However, little or no psychological damage normally results from these conditions.

Prolonged Unemployment and Status. But what happens to the individual as a result of prolonged unemployment? A few studies were made of this problem during the Great Depression in both the United States and in England. From these studies, which are summarized below, we will get a descriptive picture of the changes which take place in the individual, as well as an insight into the nature of human needs and the place that work holds in the routine of modern living.

Unemployment, of course, affects individuals differently, but there is a general pattern in the way the unemployed feel and act. Two major factors govern both individual and general behavior among the unemployed—the cultural background of the person and the length of time he has been out of work.

A man from middle-class circumstances may find his ego deflated sooner and more deeply than will the laborer who has always lived on the borderline of poverty. The unemployed man from the poorer environment probably has more associates who are also out of work than does the person who lives in a better community. In the former environment, contrast may not be so noticeable. But middle-class people live in a psychological environment where the incentive to independence and self-support prevails. When economic opportunity is lacking, not only does the individual feel it directly, but he feels the social sanctions that his neighbors apply. Although the man from the lower-class group may be worse off economically, the social pressures on him are less. Ginsburg [17] summarized this status problem. "The unemployed were able to adjust to the loss of their jobs, the exhaustion of their savings accounts, even to the cashing in of their insurance policies, but they broke down on the day they asked for relief."

Stages of Behavior of the Unemployed. For most people the course of unemployment runs through three stages, according to Blum [9]. First, there comes the feeling of shock regardless of any forewarning that the loss of the job was imminent. In this stage, the individual reviews the sequence of events leading to his unemployment and rationalizes about the wisdom of having taken the job in the first place. He soon settles for the idea that he can use a much-needed vacation. This is followed by an appraisal of his abilities and the formation of plans to get another job.

The second stage includes the active search for a job. Most people begin looking for one better than the one they had, and then for a similar one, if unemployment continues. As time passes, they begin to look for work anywhere doing almost anything. "During this period," Blum says, "the individual is rather unresigned. His spirit is unbroken, and although he is unhappy about his predicament, he is still hopeful of success."

The final stage in unemployment involves the breaking down of the individual. Failing to find a job, he becomes anxious and pessimistic and begins to lose hope.

Some people pass through these stages rapidly, particularly the person who has experienced more failure than success. Each stage lasts longer for the individual who has had more success than failure in the past.

Effects of Prolonged Unemployment. There are several aspects of the psychological effects of prolonged unemployment:

1 There is a loss of the sense of security, both economic and psychological.

2 The worker comes to blame himself for his condition; then he takes an aggressive attitude toward the situation.

3 There is the problem of time. For the man who has a job the day's activities center around that job because it takes the greatest share of his time. For the unemployed man, time hangs heavy.

4 Daily routines of the household become interrupted. Regular hours of getting up or going to bed, of eating or performing chores are disrupted. This adds to the feeling of being lost.

5 Early in unemployment, the individual attempts to conceal his status from others. He may even leave for his "job" at the regular time and return home at the usual time at night. He fills in this time by job seeking, watching movies, or just loafing around. Bakke [3] reports that in England during the Great Depression, the unemployed did not frequent the pubs during working hours but rather at the closing time of the factories—when those who were employed went in for their beer.

6 Irrational spending has been noted among the unemployed; they often spend their money on luxury items instead of on necessities; some even take up relatively expensive hobbies which rapidly deplete unemployment-insurance funds or the relief check. This is one reason why relief is often given in goods rather than in money.

7 Some unemployed attempt to retreat from their situation through fantasy and dreaming. Others escape through psychosomatic illness. Some seek illegal outlets; others become radicals. But in the main, most unemployed men remain good citizens. Suicide and drinking are apparently not common escapes.

8 The unemployed man becomes excessively depressed if his family, relatives, and friends change their attitude of sympathy and understanding to one of criticism of the former breadwinner.

9 One of the most interesting psychological changes that occurs with prolonged unemployment is the intensification of daily habits. For example, the person who has read extensively when employed reads even more when unemployed. The person who reads only a little while holding a job will probably read even less when out of work. Those who were religious while employed become more religious during unemployment, whereas those people normally not very religious become even less so during unemployment.

10 The effects of prolonged unemployment of parents soon show up in the insecurities and anxieties of their children. This throwback to the parents reinforces all the other effects on the head of the family, lowering the morale as well as the authority of the father.

11 Personality changes related to unemployment show up eventually in irritability, new faults, a breakdown in morale, and loss of emotional stability. Prejudices may increase, and scapegoats are sometimes set up as a defense for the position the person finds himself in. Unemployment may well bring out into the open a person's previously concealed feelings of inferiority.

Aspiration and Unemployment. Although the unemployed do show behaviors in common, the *degree* to which unemployment affects the individual depends upon past experience and individual aspirations. The migrant worker without a home comes to expect less than the person who has seen better times. One study of over four thousand migrant families made in 1932 showed that 69 per cent were on the move because of economic distress. Some were following the seasonal-employment route; some were looking for a permanent home; all hoped for little more than a place where body and soul could be held together. In another study of some twenty-six thousand migrants, made in a prosperous year, the goal was essentially the same—economic survival. Ambitions for the children and hopes of becoming a part of some community were further goals, but little was expected. Aspirations of community status could not be verbalized too well by these people because most of them had never experienced it. In many ways they could best be described as the culturally handicapped [2].

Somewhat in contrast to this group who "had little to lose psychologically" is a group of established families in New York City who "had more to lose." A psychiatric study of the latter group revealed that most of these people had been established in jobs, carried life insurance, and were on the way up when the Depression put the breadwinner out of a job. To these people, the emotional experience of losing a job may be compared to the loss of love which a child suffers from a rejecting parent, especially a child who has done nothing to deserve the loss. This feeling of rejection was especially strong among men who had worked long, arduous years for one employer, to whom, as well as to the job, they had understandably formed real attachments. "Deprived of 'love,' their first reaction was one of fear and bewilderment, combined with optimism, born of wishful thinking, obviously over-compensatory in nature" [16].

It was found that the shame and embarrassment of being on relief was so great that a number of families persisted in hiding the fact for years. They refused to use commodities which would at once identify them as relief recipients. This study further reports that many of the children refused to eat the hot lunches provided for them at school, since this would identify them as reliefers. In some cases there were attempts to cheat on relief investigators in petty ways affording the recipients some slight ego gratification of the kind a child gets from teasing teacher or pilfering his mother's purse for pennies.

Lasting Effects of Unemployment. The jobless man who eventually gets employment is not the same man he was before his unemployment experience. He has different attitudes, often colored by bitterness and disillusionment. His skills are lessened, his self-discipline relaxed, and often his habits of neatness, punctuality, and getting along with others have to be relearned. He has acquired fears that may remain with him a lifetime.

Studies show that women suffer less than men during unemployment. This may well be related to the fact that, generally speaking, women have never really been accepted in industry, that they often work on a temporary basis, or that they resign to have babies. Although unemployment can hit the woman worker just as hard economically as it does the man, psychologically women seem to be exempt from many of the problems which face men who are out of a job.

Of the many writings on the psychological effects of unemployment on the individual, practically all focus upon one basic problem: satisfaction in life comes from the feelings of accomplishment that the person gets from work. This fact was central in the national economic-opportunity legislation passed in the mid-sixties.

AGING AND WORK

"I was classified as a has-been. Instead of 'How's business?' the question was 'When are you heading for the warm climate?' What am I expected to do?"

"I am 55, an accountant displaced by a computer. My company has made adequate economic provision for me in my early retirement, but what will I do with my time?"

"If my husband retires now, what will I do with him around the house all day? I hate to think about those extra 20,000 hours I'll have him on my hands in the next ten years."

These people have in large measure raised questions about age, ability to be productive, problems of adjustment, leisure time, and the criteria involved.

The Criteria of Aging. When is a man old? "Aging, true physiologic aging, is not determined by the time elapsed since birth, but by the total amount of wear and tear to which the body has been exposed. There is, indeed, a great difference between physiologic and chronologic age." These words of Hans Selye [43], who has worked on the problems of aging and the stress of life for some three decades, give us a key to the problem of how long any given individual should continue to work.

Among the unskilled and semiskilled workers, work accomplishment is primarily of a physical nature. Some get old in their thirties; others are capable of work into their sixties. Among skilled workers in our industrial society productivity continues as long as general health and opportunity permit. Little information is available from which it is possible to determine the role of age per se in industrial output. On the whole, there is little evidence that the output of older workers is less than that of younger ones.

In other areas, age is a factor in productivity. Lehman [28] has shown that the age for winning championships in sports comes early, often in the teens. The peaks for notable intellectual creativity come a little later but fall off rapidly during and after middle age. In contrast, professional recognition and leadership status in business, education, medicine, law, and politics tend to come in later life. In Figure 16.1, taken from the data of Lehman, we see the ages at which a sample of 2,795 commercial and industrial leaders became outstanding represented by the solid line. The broken line of the figure is the same as the solid line with the exception that it makes allowance for population differences at successive age levels.

Figure 16.2 gives an overall view of the physical and psychological growth of man in relation to age brackets.

Effects of Age Sometimes a Myth. Before we conclude too hastily that "the scientist is through at forty," let us examine the kind of change that frequently takes place in a creative field. The physicist, for example, becomes personally involved in some technical problem and produces numerous research papers. As he gains in professional stature, his interests broaden, graduate students require more of his attention, and administrative problems become more demanding. Gradually our scientist moves from a do-it-yourself role into one of leadership in science.

In studies of age differences in happiness and life adjustments of 257 workers in one work setting, Meltzer [34, 35] found the feeling of the employee that he has his "share of happiness" increases with age. The belief of the worker that he has received his "share of recognition" does not seem to differ from age group to age group in terms of statistical significance, although the trend seems to be negatively associated with age.

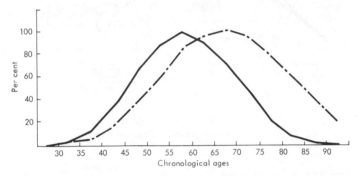

Fig. 16.1. Age and industrial leadership. The solid curve shows the ages of 2,795 outstanding commercial and industrial leaders. Higher executive posts are most likely to be filled by 57-year-olds; only 80 per cent of 66-year-olds are as well placed. The broken curve corrects for the fact that young people exceed older people in our population but that, proportionately speaking, older men are more favorably placed. (From Lehman, H. C. *Age and achievement*. Princeton: Princeton University Press, 1953.)

In general work takes on more significance with age, and spare time decreases in significance. With increased age there is increased interest in "steady work" and decreased interest in "advancement." In a study of 141 male workers comparing best and worst years for self and others, Meltzer found the most preferred years are twenty through thirty-five for self and under twenty for others. Periods already passed are regarded as happier than those yet to come. It was the workers with more than ten years seniority who favored older years more often. Just being old, as such, carries prestige, the amount and nature of which depend on the characteristics of the person, his history in the plant, and the nature of the organizational policy toward age.

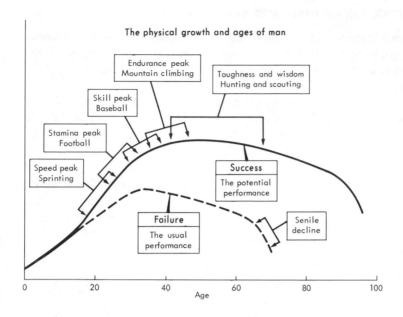

The physical growth and ages of man

Endurance peak
Mountain climbing

Toughness and wisdom
Hunting and scouting

Skill peak
Baseball

Stamina peak
Football

Speed peak
Sprinting

Success

The potential
performance

Failure

The usual
performance

Senile
decline

0   20   40   60   80   100
Age

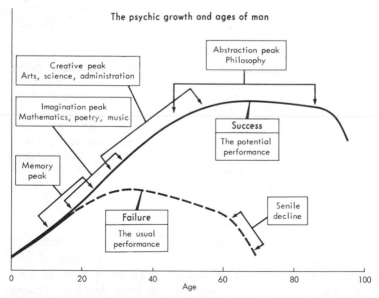

The psychic growth and ages of man

Abstraction peak
Philosophy

Creative peak
Arts, science, administration

Imagination peak
Mathematics, poetry, music

Memory
peak

Success

The potential
performance

Failure

The usual
performance

Senile
decline

0   20   40   60   80   100
Age

Fig. 16.2. Possibility and actual performance. In these two graphs the solid curve indicates the physical or psychological potential of normal people, with peak periods for various activities. How most people fail to measure up to these potentials is indicated by the broken curve. (From Still, J. W. Man's potential—and his performance. *The New York Times,* Nov. 24, 1957. Cited by Hurlock, E. B. *Developmental psychology.* New York: McGraw-Hill, 1959.)

Compensation takes place for every deviation in age; often, if certain capacities diminish, others are enhanced. Older people may make up for slowness in some job through steady work and good attendance. Since the greatest occupational mobility takes place under age thirty-five, older workers are an asset in terms of continuance on the job. This factor of stability, often enhanced by stronger loyalty, is of considerable importance in those industries where training periods are long and expensive.

Age is a convenient factor on which to attach status differentials. The young beginner on a job has little or no status; the older worker may be called Pop and treated with a certain deference. Some popular opinions about age are supported by research evidence; others are found wanting. For example, in general, research supports the opinion that people become more conservative as they grow older. On the other hand, a reason commonly offered for discrimination against the older worker is that he is more of an accident risk than the younger worker. This view is not justified in light of the facts. Tiffin [47], for example, in a study of 9,000 steel workers, has shown that older people are even better accident risks than younger workers. Although statistics in general favor safety in older workers they have more accidents than expected when placed on "young workers' jobs."

Another measurable aspect of industrial behavior is absenteeism. Let us cite one typical study showing again that we should be careful in selling the oldsters short. This study was made in the Baker Chocolate Division of the General Foods Company. It will be noted from Table 6, which gives a summary picture of the number of absences and days lost, that workers over 45, the traditional dividing line between young and old, show

Table 6 / Number of Absences and Days Lost, by Age, Sex, and Length of Absence

	All Employees			Male			Female		
	Total (619)	Under 45 (330)	45 and Over (289)	Total (479)	Under 45 (250)	45 and Over (229)	Total (140)	Under 45 (80)	45 and Over (60)
I Number of absences:									
Total absences	1,624	1,061	563	1,162	748	414	462	313	149
1 day	960	683	277	703	486	217	257	197	60
2–5 days	498	307	191	337	206	131	161	101	60
6 or more days	166	71	95	122	56	66	44	15	29
II Days of absence:									
Total days	4,931	2,845	2,086	3,394	1,962	1,432	1,537	883	654
1 day	960	683	277	703	486	217	257	197	60
2–5 days	1,520	930	590	1,027	615	412	493	315	178
6 or more days	2,451	1,232	1,219	1,664	861	803	787	371	416

SOURCE: Kahne, H. R., Ryder, C. F., Snegireff, L. S., & Wyshak, G. Don't take the older workers for granted, *Harv. Bus. Rev.*, 1957, 35, 90–94.

up well in comparison with workers under 45 years of age. Actually, total absence per employee is a shade less among the older workers [25].

When we examine absence rates for the total firm in relation to age and length of absence (Table 7), we see that the 45-to-55 age bracket has a decidedly better absence record than either those older or those younger. In fact, it will be noted that the under-35 group has the worst record of all. It is important to note the distinction between kinds of absenteeism. Older workers are absent *for longer periods* (severity rate) but younger workers are absent *more often* (frequency rate).

Table 7 / Absence Rates for Total Firm, by Age and Length of Absence

	Disability Rate*				Frequency Rate†				Severity Rate‡			
	All Absences	1 Day	2–5 Days	6 Days	All Absences	1 Day	2–5 Days	6 Days	All Absences	1 Day	2–5 Days	6 Days
All employees	3.4	0.6	1.1	1.7	1.1	0.6	0.3	0.1	3.2	1.0	3.2	15.2
Under 35	4.0	1.2	1.3	1.5	1.7	1.2	0.4	0.1	2.4	1.0	2.9	18.3
35–44	3.4	0.6	1.0	1.7	1.1	0.6	0.3	0.1	3.3	1.0	2.9	15.6
45–54	2.9	0.4	0.9	1.6	0.8	0.4	0.4	0.1	3.5	1.0	2.5	14.8
55 and over	3.6	0.3	0.9	2.2	0.7	0.3	0.2	0.1	4.8	1.0	3.8	18.3

* Average number of days absent per 100 scheduled workdays $(DR = FR \times SR)$.

† Average number of absences per 100 scheduled workdays $(FR = DR/SR)$.

‡ Average length of time lost per absence $(SR = FR/DR)$.

SOURCE: Kahne, H. R., Ryder, C. F., Snegireff, L. S., & Wyshak, G. Don't take the older workers for granted, *Harv. Bus. Rev.*, 1957, 35, 90–94.

The results of this study are important in raising the practical question: Are different kinds of absences important? We need to know answers to this question when considering how suitable older people prove themselves to be on the job. Certainly, if frequent short absences, particularly of the unexpected and unnecessary kind, are annoying to management or impede production seriously, the older workers are preferable. If, on the other hand, staffing is not flexible enough to fill in for workers justifiably absent for several days at a time, then younger workers may be preferred by management.

Older people may be less adaptable to changes in job assignments; they may be more set in their ways; they may show less muscular strength and agility than younger people. But at the same time, experience and judgment may compensate for these things. Just as the handicapped worker may be an asset to business if he has been adequately analyzed as to what he can best do, trained to take advantage of his assets, and properly oriented and placed on the job, so can the older worker become an asset. Greater attention should be given to aptitude tests and to measurement of physical reserve in placing the older worker on the right job.

PSYCHOLOGY OF AGING

Research on the psychology of aging is older than the formal beginnings of industrial psychology. In his history, Birren [5, 6] speaks of three phases: the early period from 1835 to 1918 when the nature of aging came to be regarded as a problem to be solved by observation; the beginning of systematic studies, 1918 to 1940, followed by a gap during World War II; and the period of expansion from 1946 to 1960. Current research centers on the industrial or occupational aspects of aging, the clinical problems, and the problems of adult education and training. Public interest in the problem is increasing, and becoming more vociferous, reflecting perhaps a change in society, which is now asking questions about how individuals can live better, if not also longer; questions to which there are sometimes no answers.

In general terms aging is associated with a gradual decrease in the performance of most body organs. The speed of this change varies, however, from one organ system to another, even in the same individual. For example, muscle strength decreases 50 per cent between age thirty and ninety, while the speed of an impulse passing down a nerve fiber is reduced only 15 per cent in this same time span. Researchers looking for any suggestions of changes in mental function resulting solely from age have found virtually no changes in the fifties that were inevitable. Some persons in their sixties and seventies show loss of memory, reasoning, and decision-making ability, but many do not. It may be that the brain does not get exhausted by overwork so much as that the individual is worn out from the emotional stress accompanying the effort. Older individuals tend to be slow in their behavior, younger adult subjects more task-specific in their response speed [7, 12, 19]. In summarizing investigations in the various fields of creative work, Dennis [13] points out that spurious factors may account for a considerable part of the apparent decline in the output of significant works of art, literature, and science in the later years of life. It is possible that historians and critics show a bias in favor of citing works from an artist's earlier period, so that the apparent decline in creative output is merely a reflection of this view. Output may decrease with age, but there are exceptions. "It may be that man runs out of energy before he runs out of creative power."

Age and Speed. Turner [49] has emphasized the point that individual differences in performance increase with age. Almost always there are some older people whose performance equals or surpasses the average performance of the younger group. There is a tendency for older people to place more emphasis on accuracy and less on speed. However, surveys show that comparatively few older people are placed on jobs where there is unusual pressure for speed or where the pace of working is mechanically determined, as on a moving assembly line. It is important to ask: Decline in what? For example, studies of intellectual functioning have shown that different subfunctions decline at different rates. Throughout middle age vocabulary-test scores show practically no decrement, and motor-skill loss is small, but visual perception and spatial-relations ability show sharp declines [30].

RETIREMENT

The worker, the manager, and the professional man, if they live long enough, must each face the problem of quitting work. What are the problems of retirement?

The Magic Age of Sixty-five. For most workers there is no retirement, because they either are forced out of work or die before retirement age is reached. In the United States, the age for industrial retirement is widely assumed to be sixty-five for men and in some industries as low as sixty for women. The magic age of sixty-five for retirement seems to have come about when the Federal government originally selected a base for paying old-age and survivors insurance, that is, Social Security. Although it has been an age generally accepted by both business and union officials, sixty-five is still a controversial figure. Everyone seems to agree that some people are old at forty and that others are still young at seventy. Until there are good, measurable, and acceptable criteria of physiological and psychological age, it can be expected that the retirement age will be determined chronologically. There does seem to be some relaxation of retirement age during periods of labor shortage for skilled workers. Executives who are still productive may be carried on as consultants, or in some instances optional age levels for retirement may be put into effect, such as is now being done among college teachers, who are in short supply.

It is believed that the number of retired workers will increase at an accelerating rate until at least 1980. A fair assumption may be made that there will be steps taken to lower retirement age if the supply of workers is adequate, to adjust it upward when there are labor shortages.

Individual Differences in Aging. Individual differences among older people are enormous, both mentally and physically. That our bodies gradually wear out during life has always been known. The sensory processes decline, motor skills slow down, and attitudes change. With advancing years, people require increasingly more rest, but the process of aging does not progress at the same speed in each person, nor does each need the same amount and type of rest. Many a man who could still have given numerous years of useful work has been made physically ill and prematurely senile by enforced retirement at an age when his requirements for activity were still high and his ability to produce was still ample. This psychosomatic illness is so common that it is now called "the retirement disease." Every person has his own individual requirements for rest and activity. And certainly to lie in bed all day is no relaxation for an active man.

Studies of the reactions of older people can teach us much about energy conservation. Experiments on animals have clearly shown that excessive stressful activities use up reserves of adaptability which cannot be replaced. Selye [43] has stated the concept thus: "Vitality is like a special kind of bank account which you can use up by withdrawals but cannot increase by deposits. The only control is the rate that withdrawals are made."

When we consider the problems of personality changes that take place in older persons, let us bear in mind that chronological age per se should not be the criterion for judging when the person is past his prime.

The Loss of Status. In our culture the person who has reached retirement loses status. He may be treated as a has-been, consciously or unconsciously, through overattention or neglect. The man of status who has made decision after decision as a daily routine gets retirement shock when he is no longer called on for decision making or even for advice. This has been such a serious problem for management personnel who have reached retirement age that some companies now have planned programs of preretirement counseling and of easing-up practices over a period of time. The person gradually gets used to doing less; it is a sort of "job decompression" program.

Aside from the economic burdens of the retired person, he experiences some of the losses felt by the unemployed—feelings of not accomplishing anything through work. This comedown was described by a retired executive, formerly a vice-president and treasurer of a large corporation, who said he looked forward each month to a meeting of his local shuffleboard club. Much discussion of finances was always in order—what to do with a balance of $35 in the treasury!

No Typical Pattern in Old Age. Time hangs heavy on the retired individual's hands. Although some take up hobbies, these activities do not seem to relieve tensions as they formerly did. Working in a woodshop may be good to take the executive's mind off his office problems, but without these problems, the hobby may become only a time killer.

For those elderly people who become somewhat senile, the clinical picture is not good—mental rigidity, suspiciousness, hoarding, overtalkativeness, untidiness, and the like give a pessimistic picture of growing old. But this picture is not completely typical of old age. There are many oldsters who remain in good health and avoid the crisis of retirement. It may well be that we have not given enough attention to the proper placement of the reasonably healthy retired person. Why shouldn't he resent made work that just keeps him busy? A retired business executive could hardly get much satisfaction from building furniture all day in his hobby shop or from helping his wife around the house.

Aging may come gracefully, or it may come in anger. In one study of male aging and personality, five clusters of persons were found [41]. Among the well adjusted were the "mature" men, relatively free from neurotic conflict, able to accept themselves realistically and to grow old without regret for the past. Next in order came the "rocking chair" type, who welcomed freedom from responsibility and the opportunity provided by old age to indulge their passive needs. In the middle came the "armored" men, who maintained a well-functioning system of defenses against anxiety by keeping active. Among the poorly adjusted were the "angry" men, who were bitter over failures to achieve their life goals and who blamed others for their disappointments. Finally, the study described the "self-haters," who had turned their resentments inward, blaming themselves for their misfortunes; these men were depressed rather than angry. These types emerged, not from an *a priori* typology, but from a statistical analysis.

A PERSPECTIVE

When we look at the various needs for adjustment in middle age and old age, the overall problems related to work may become more meaningful to us. In one sociological study [11] word portraits were made of various people as they reached the time of retirement. As we take a look at these eighteen descriptions, it is possible to see at a glance the different kinds of problems arising from age. The descriptions show that individual differences exist and that they may even be greater in maturity than they are in childhood, adolescence, and middle age. Industry is coming to recognize this more and more as our expanding economy places additional demands upon the effective uses of human resources. Some men must retire, some can work part time, and some can keep going strong.

A is getting along in years but has good health. He has had to give up his more vigorous activities but still attends clubs and parties and looks after his business. Or, if he has retired, he carries on with hobbies and other interesting activities. His sight and hearing are not as good as formerly but do not give him any great troubles. He has faced the fact that he is not as strong as he was and has adjusted his activities accordingly.

B is definitely showing his age. He walks slowly and lets his shoulders sag.

There is nothing very much the matter except that he doesn't get around as fast as he once did. He can't do his work very well, and he tires easily. He is content to sit quietly and let others carry on.

C has definite physical ailments characteristic of old age (such as high blood pressure or partial blindness or deafness). These interfere greatly with both work and recreation. He is inclined to complain.

D has not had to make any upsetting changes in his way of living. The family is still intact, and when members are absent, they keep in touch by correspondence. Finances are still adequate for the usual standard of living. No unusual or sudden illness has come either to D or to his immediate family.

E has had to meet some sharp changes. He has lost a member of the family dear to him or has had a moderate decrease in income or has been retired before he was ready for it. He has shown normal sorrow and the ability to accept his losses fairly well.

F has had to make drastic changes in living. The death of a dear family member has left him desolate. Or he has had to give up his home and go to live with a relative or in a home for the aged. He says he sees no reason to go on living.

G talks occasionally about his adolescence. When he does, it is to relate some humorous incident or some exciting or interesting adventure. This was apparently a good period in his life.

H reminisces about adolescence along with other earlier periods of his life. His comments are neither doleful nor thrilling but simply matter of fact.

I dwells much more upon his adolescence and the difficulties he had then. He tells of the unjust severity of his parents, the unfair treatment he received from brothers and sisters, the troubles he had at school, among friends, and at work. He remembers adolescence as a very difficult period when he was not well treated by others.

J has achieved a comfortable position for his old age. He is respected by his family and his friends. He has no financial worries. He has retained his old friends and enjoys their respect. He lives in as good a house as when he was younger.

K lives in his old neighborhood or one of the same type, but he has to struggle to keep up appearances. His clothes are shabby, and his house and furniture need repairs. He tries to keep up his contacts with old friends and succeeds by working hard at it.

L has had to accept an unsatisfactory standard of living. He has parted from his old friends and seldom sees those who knew him in better days. He is quite sensitive about his situation. His former friends feel that he has gone down since they knew him.

M has always been a cheerful, happy person. He has met his problems courageously and has worked out the best solutions possible for his situation.

N has always been inclined to be a worrier and to look on the gloomy side. Nevertheless, he has met his small problems fairly well and has been only mildly unhappy. He has had to have help from family and friends to face major problems.

O has never been able to face his problems. He has always gone to pieces easily, blamed others for his troubles, and complained a great deal. He is nervous and unstable. In a severe crisis he would probably have a complete breakdown.

P has led a successful life. He has done as high a type of work as he was capable of doing and has met his family responsibilities. He has been interested in the welfare of his community and his fellow workers. He feels satisfied.

Q has never been able to meet his own standards. He has tried to reach good standards but has never been quite able to make it. He therefore looks on his past life as a failure and is either bitter or full of excuses for his failure.

R has been a failure through and through. He has had low standards and has failed miserably to do what the community expects in the way of regular work and family responsibilities. But since his standards are low, he does not express any regret.*

Attitudes toward the Aged. Another point concerns the importance of part-time work for older people. There are a number of people beyond the age of retirement who are willing and able to work part time. What should be employment policy in such cases? This question is not so simple to answer. Just as we have seen that individual differences exist among older people, so do individual differences exist among companies. Let us describe two particular firms. In company A, no one apparently has to retire or wants to. In company B, retirement is compulsory at age sixty-five, and apparently no one wants to stay on the job even that long [49].

Company A has 650 employees, of whom 307 are 55 years of age or older. There are 99 employees between 60 and 70 years old, 46 over 70. The company manufactures small metal products and machinery. The philosophy of the company is, in effect, that there is no age barrier to employment. "We have never believed that a man in good shape at 59 or 64 becomes suddenly useless the day he is 60 or 65," said the superintendent. It is the feeling among the younger men in the company that "older men are kept on too long." Among the older workers the attitude is that "a man should be allowed to work as long as he is able." This company is described as never having adopted modern personnel and safety practices, and many of its methods are old-fashioned. But it makes money, and older people like to work there.

Company B is an automobile-assembly plant where the entire working environment puts a premium on youth. Retirement is compulsory at age sixty-five. The attitudes of the men are that there is a "compulsion to keep the line moving." Even the younger men believe that as they get older they will not be able to keep up with the pace of their jobs. A prevalent belief is, "They have no use for you when you get older."

These two cases illustrate the point that uniformity in retirement policy cannot effectively take care of individual differences either among individ-

* Cavan, R. S., Burgess, E. W., Havighurst, R. J., & Goldhamer, H. *Personal adjustment in old age.* Chicago: Science Research Associates, Inc., 1949. Reproduced by permission of Science Research Associates, Inc.

uals or among companies. More and more, both management and labor unions are recognizing the fact that responsibility toward the older employee does not begin and end with a retirement plan. There seems to be a movement in some places toward job analysis and job reassignment for the older worker. This philosophy is not unlike that of personnel selection and placement now in common use for the new employee. In some places, procedures have been carried an additional step, and the reengineering of jobs for certain older workers is going on.

Redesigning the Job. Abrams [1] reports an interesting case of a factory in Syracuse where older women working as clay-press operators were turning out a diminishing amount of work. Rather than get rid of these older workers, the company reengineered the job by installing special hydraulic and pneumatic presses which decreased physical demands and awkward working conditions. With these modifications, the workers were quite capable of keeping up with the work.

In another case, older employees working on an operation in a shirt factory, which required them to match materials, were found to be losing their visual acuity. The firm rescheduled their work so that they did not receive any material which was hard to match by color or design. The same company, when confronted with workers who had developed arthritis or heart disease, redesigned machine controls or relocated workers' lines to better fit the job to the employees' physical capacities.

In his survey of over two hundred companies Abrams found a number of techniques employed in job engineering for older workers, such as:

1 Rescheduling the pace of production to eliminate fatiguing "quick sprints"
2 Reshuffling work so that the older worker receives large, easier-to-handle materials
3 Reducing production rating on incentive positions filled by oldsters
4 Providing better leverage for tools and controls
5 Relocating control levers and wheels
6 Providing power tools
7 Rearranging work area to bring motion into normal working area
8 Providing power feed of stock to machines
9 Substituting pull motion for push motion
10 Providing better grip on tools

Some of the effects of such changes were most encouraging. The job engineering had helped combat declining production in certain places. Labor turnover was reduced, and savings on costs enabled management to retain experienced workers.

Job Reassignment. Where job reengineering may not be practical, some companies have found it profitable to reassign a worker to a job within his capacity. It was reported by Abrams that large concerns usually have such a diversity of available positions that they can find some suitable post for an aging worker without much difficulty [1]. Job reassignments have included shifting older workers to jobs outside the line of production, to jobs requiring custom or quality work, or to jobs calling for part-time work on a more desirable shift. The following reassignments are typical of those made in different industries which have worked well for older employees.

The Blackstone Corporation employs workers on incentive or day rate and transfers aging men who request it from incentive pay to daywork.

At the National Biscuit Company, operations must keep pace with the ovens; on most positions paced with the ovens there can be little slowing down. So the aging man who can't maintain the pace is shifted outside the sphere of jobs revolving about the oven.

At the Republic Steel Company, operators of mobile equipment whose eyes are failing are shifted to other types of work not requiring visual acuity.

General Mills, Inc., reports switching aging workers from nightwork to daywork and bringing outside salesmen into the office.

The General Motors Corporation, through its Chevrolet Central Office, says, "Size and diversification of the Chevrolet organization has in the past made it possible to move the aging and physically impaired employee to a job which he could do. A review of this matter shows the older workers gravitate to the less arduous tasks in the plant. As a result we have not found it necessary in many cases to engineer the job to the older worker." This is the refrain heard commonly from big industry: "Transfers are no problem; we transfer aging personnel quite regularly."

The Kroehler Manufacturing Company reports having "many workers over 65 and even beyond 70," but it has numerous jobs that can be handled by older men without undue fatigue.

Sylvania Electric Products, Inc., similarly reports that it is "fortunate in being able to reassign older employees to jobs fitting their capacities." The operations in the radio and television plant are such that subassembly and inspection departments are capable of handling aged people.

The H. J. Heinz Company and the General Electric Company both report that job transfer is a commonly used technique. The food concern says it has been "very successful" in solving its problems of making adjustments for older workers by transferring them to different jobs, "in most instances without down-grading." Therefore it reports not engaging in job engineering for declining capacities.

The International Business Machines Corporation also reports that a "great diversity" of jobs enables it to transfer workers easily.

The Procter & Gamble Company since 1923 has had a guarantee of regular employment which assures workers forty-eight weeks of work a year. The company reports that this has resulted in a low turnover, with a consequent aging of the labor force. The company says that it has developed an understanding among its workers that successful operation of the plan depends in part on willingness of the employees to accept occasional transfers which may be necessary because of schedule changes, installation of technological developments, or physical or mental impairments which may arise.

The American Sugar Refining Company, Link Aviation, Inc., and Winthrop Stearns, Inc., also report that transferring is common. The last transfers employees by using a "limited service" category. "When we have a square peg and a round hole, we simply shift the peg to where it fits rather than re-design it," the firm reports.

The National Cash Register Company, with almost thirteen thousand employees, has one department especially arranged to take care of those with declining physical capacities, so that they can sit at a bench and perform work which does not require much physical effort. There are sixty workers in this department who sit at benches and disassemble registers, and the parts disassembled are sold as scrap. The company transfers aging employees to small assembly jobs, such as light filing of metal, and also arranges for a shorter workday if necessary.

A large perfume company hiring a high proportion of persons fifty to seventy years of age says that age doesn't severely handicap their workers. Most work is done by hand, and few operations are paced by machines. Nor are there many heavy lifting operations. "We find we have a sufficient variety of these operations for us to set up our incentive groups in such a manner that those who by reason of age have lost the necessary rhythm required for the machine operations can perform certain of the necessary hand operations on the final assembly line," the company reports. Having a variety of shipments, it uses younger personnel on the heavier freight shipments and older workers on light mailings and shipments.

The United States Gypsum Company prefers to shift an older employee to a lower-level job than to hire a new employee, because his experience will allow him "to handle it more efficiently."

Moore Business Forms, Inc., reports that transfers are made to similar types of presses if operating complicated large presses becomes too much for older workers.

"Closely allied with the relocation of an employee who is unable to perform his primary job is the matter of wage rates to be paid on the new job," points out the Rochester Community Survey. It found that it is customary in Rochester plants to pay the employee the rate of his assigned occupation. In some instances this results in a lower rate, but occasionally the amount earned is increased.

Prejudice against Older People. In spite of what industries and some unions have been able to do for the aged person, there still exists much prejudice against older people. In a study of a nationwide sample of elderly people, Barron [4] found that 53 per cent of them lacked any club or other organizational affiliation, and 40 per cent were rarely asked for advice by their family and friends. About a third claimed to have no really close friends. Social isolation was found to be most conspicuous among the unemployed aged. The aged tend to demonstrate such typical minority-group reactions as hypersensitivity, low morale, defensiveness, self-hatred, and isolation.

Of the aged unemployed, 70 per cent who had tried to secure reemployment reported that they were unsuccessful, largely because of "prejudice against older workers." Barron concludes that the social isolation of the older person is a basic factor in the tension which exists between the young and the chronologically aged in our society. Unless people have frequent and meaningful contact with each other, they build up stereotypes of each other and develop prejudiced attitudes.

Some Facts Worth Noting. Bowers [10] made a study of 3,162 men and women workers ranging in age from 18 through 76 years who performed various duties in an organization that included a variety of operations. Data were gathered on each worker from personnel records. Supervisors made appraisals of the person's work, of any administrative actions taken affecting the employees, of any completion of training courses, of grievances, and of any similar information important to the study. Men and women in the age groups 18 to 29, 30 to 44, 45 to 50, and 60 and up were compared in ability, character, and faults. Included were such traits as accuracy, initiative, job knowledge, efficiency, cooperativeness, dependability, attendance, thoroughness, steadiness, tactfulness, slowness, and instability.

The results of this study indicate that age differences in traits were relatively small. Older workers of both sexes with over two years' service were reported to learn less readily and to be slower; on the other hand, they more frequently showed good attendance, steadiness, and conscientiousness. These trends were reported by Bowers to be quite consistent. In other traits covered in this study, age differences appear to be negligible or not consistent. For example, the difference in efficiency between the oldest and youngest groups of men was 9 net percentage points favoring the younger, but there was only a 1 per cent drop between the 30-to-44 group and the 60-and-up group. Of interest is the finding that the oldest women were considered more efficient than the younger by 7 percentage points, although women under 30 years of age were fairly often mentioned as rapid workers. No consistent age differences were found in job knowledge, accuracy, dependability, or emotional stability. Physical differences were not mentioned often enough, even for the oldest group, to indicate that such handicaps were of importance. In this company, attitudes favorable to older people were evidenced by the fact that it employed new people over 45 and that several were hired as new employees who were over 60 years of age.

The author concludes with the following statement:

> Quite evidently workers should be employed and retained on the basis of merit without reference to age. Biases and misconceptions limiting the use of older persons should be replaced by facts. Oldsters can maintain productivity, thus making an extended productive life worth while, strengthening manpower resources, and lessening possible economic burdens which often result from dependency of large numbers of non-productive older persons.

Job Demands and Age. McFarland [32], who has studied the psychophysiological problems of aging in air-transport pilots and the age problems of professional truck drivers and who has reviewed the overall psychological aspects of aging, concludes that aging is a highly individual matter; chronological age alone, he says, is rarely a reliable index of a person's physical or mental development and adjustment. He points out that the natural process of aging is of more significance for some occupational groups than others by virtue of differences in the demands made upon individual abilities. A defect in vision or hearing may be important for one occupation but not for another. Slowing reaction time may lead to loss of confidence where a task requiring quick responses is involved. The problem is one of matching the abilities of workers to the requirements of their job *throughout the life cycle.*

PLANNING

Attitudes toward older people and their role in society have tended to force them into corresponding behavior patterns. There is evidence that as people age, individual differences tend to become more marked. Instead of retiring people arbitrarily when they reach a given chronological age, we might better think in terms of helping to place them in jobs more suited to their abilities. Today there is a growing interest in the problems of old age on the part of medical people, social scientists, governments, forward-looking industrial leaders, and responsible union leaders. A number of industries are keeping good workers on the payroll through programs of job engineering, job reassignment, and job counseling. In others, where it is uneconomical to keep the oldsters working, unions and management are working out plans allowing early retirement with benefits. These programs, limited as they may be, denote a favorable trend toward dealing with some of the problems of the aging worker. For the retired executive some plans are in operation promoting part-time consulting. For example, in Pittsburgh there is an organization called Associated Senior Executives. The members are retired professionals in administration and research and development. A small company, for example, which cannot afford a full-time man in their product development may call on a senior associate for assistance. Between jobs he returns to his retirement activities.

The trend toward shorter hours of work, as well as toward earlier retirement, may have an important influence on attitudes toward work versus leisure. The week of labor, sixty or seventy hours for the last generation, is now in some quarters less than forty, and for the person in retirement much less, of course. Leisure time, that is, free time after subtracting working time, sleeping, eating, and other essential activities, has increased from three hours in 1870, to five hours in 1910, to around eight hours in 1960, according to Kaplan [25]. What are people currently doing with this time? Most surveys show entertainment to be well in the lead, upward of three-quarters of leisure time being so invested. To some, "leisure" is a myth. It may perhaps be better thought of as a time for creative expression. Dorian, in his stimulating book *Commitment to Culture* [14], points out that the modern world may offer opportunities never before afforded for patronage of the arts. ". . . we need art—today more than ever before. We need art as an antidote against automation. We need the aesthetic enchantment of art, its creative illumination, to contrast the push-button emptiness of our mechanical life."

Planning for leisure may be psychologically comparable to planning for retirement. It could involve the small business as a rehabilitative technique for aging, or perhaps participation in The Association of Retired Persons, a country-wide organization of around a million members. It could also involve spending the later years in planned communities where useful activities are a part of the climate [26, 42].

Many industrial organizations are now providing opportunity of retirement readiness. The Bell Telephone Company, for example, provides seminars in some divisions for both husbands and wives months in advance of actual retirement. Here they get ready for meeting physical, economic, and psychological problems of retirement by participating in sessions with professional specialists including Social Security officers, trust officials, real estate men, lawyers, physicians, economists, and psychologists.

Attitudes about spending less time at work depend, in part, on whether leisure is brought on voluntarily or involuntarily. Effectiveness of retirement adjustment is related to "adequate psychic resources." Lacking such resources before retirement means most people are unable to develop them after retirement.

While the trend for fixed retirement ages continues to increase, data show most Americans still retire only when they have to. In Great Britain, it was found that 70 percent of men compulsorily retired at 65 declared they would have gone on working if possible. However, only 25 percent actually tried to find new work. Researchers are becoming concerned with appropriate psychological climates for aging persons. Some individuals may find the retirement community matches their needs; others may think that these rapidly growing real-estate developments encourage segregation by age, and so react negatively to them. One conclusion from research is emerging—the need for interpersonal relationships for most people does not abate with old age.

SUGGESTIONS FOR SELECTIVE READING

Beaumont, R. A., & Tower, J. W. *Executive retirement and effective management.* New York: Industrial Relations Counselors, 1961. Questions of when the manager should be retired.

Birren, J. E. (Ed.) *Handbook of aging and the individual.* Chicago: University of Chicago Press, 1960. Readings ranging from readable to technical.

Birren, J. E. *The psychology of aging.* Englewood Cliffs, N.J.: Prentice-Hall, 1964. For an overall view of the psychological problems of aging.

Crook, G. H., & Heinstein, M. *The older worker in industry.* Berkeley, Calif.: University of California, Institute of Industrial Relations, 1958. Attitudes toward aging and retirement.

Cumming, Elaine, & Henry, W. E. *Growing old.* New York: Basic Books, 1961. A general theoretical interpretation of the psychological nature of aging.

Ginsberg, E. *The unemployed.* New York: Harper & Row, 1943. What unemployment means to the man of middle-class status.

Kastenbaum, R. (Ed.) *New thoughts on old age.* New York: Springer, 1964. Some clinical aspects of aging.

Kleemeier, R. W. (Ed.) *Aging and leisure.* Fair Lawn, N.J.: Oxford University Press, 1961. The use of leisure time in later years.

Larrabee, E., & Meyersohn, R. (Eds.) *Mass leisure.* New York: Free Press, 1958. Some views of the psychological problems that come with less time spent at work.

Lawton, M. P., & Lawton, Fay G. (Eds.) *Mental impairment in the aged.* Philadelphia: Philadelphia Geriatric Center, 1965. Research conference summary, readable to sophisticated.

Lowenthal, Marjorie F. *Lives in distress.* New York: Basic Books, 1964. Analyzes the decision-making process involved in admitting elderly persons to the psychiatric ward.

Morris, W. *When you've lost a job after forty.* Englewood, N.J.: Knabe-North, 1963. Written by a white-collar man who has been through the mill and survived.

Musson, N., & Hensinkveld, Helen. *Buildings for the elderly.* New York: Reinhold, 1963. Architectural aspects of building design for the aged—a unique equipment-design problem.

Orbach, H. L., & Tibbits, C. (Eds.) *Aging and the economy.* Ann Arbor, Mich.: University of Michigan Press, 1964. A collection of papers discussing income, employment, and the older person as consumer.

Retirement Council, Inc. *One hundred one ways to enjoy your leisure.* Stamford, Conn.: Retirement Council, Inc. Some practical suggestions about retirement.

Samuelson, P. A., et al. (Eds.) *Readings in economics.* New York: McGraw-Hill, 1964. Six papers on economic problems of unemployment.

Schneider, B. V. H. *The older worker.* Berkeley, Calif.: University of California, Institute of Industrial Relations, 1962. A pamphlet (98 pages) on the role of workers forty-five and over in the labor market today and tomorrow.

Shannon, D. A. *The great depression.* Englewood Cliffs, N.J.: Prentice-Hall, 1960. A legacy from the 1930s for those "too young to remember."

Social Security Administration. *If you become disabled.* Washington, D.C.: GPO. A what-to-do pamphlet.

Social Security Administration. *Your social security.* Washington, D.C.: GPO. Answers to questions about social security.

Stern, Edith M. *Notes for after fifty.* New York: National Association for Mental Health, 1955. A series of pamphlets on the problems of preretirement.

Stern, Edith M. *A full life after 65.* New York: Public Affairs Pamphlets, No. 347, 1963. Practical answers to practical problems on aging.

Stevens, H. A., & Heber, R. *Mental retardation.* Chicago: University of Chicago Press, 1964. A review of current research, some parts for the sophisticated reader. Some material on vocational problems.

Tibbetts, C., & Donahue, W. (Eds.) *Social and psychological aspects of aging.* New York: Columbia University Press, 1962. Readings covering areas from housing to living patterns.

Williams, J. M. *Human aspects of unemployment and relief.* Chapel Hill, N.C.: University of North Carolina Press, 1933. Written about and during the Great Depression.

Wright, Beatrice. (Ed.) *Psychology and rehabilitation.* Washington, D.C.: American Psychological Association, 1959. The problems and progress in rehabilitation.

17

Women in Industry

B. von Haller Gilmer

"It would not be much of an exaggeration to say that if all women who are employed in industry stayed home on Monday, our economy would suffer a headache," said one industrialist. And he added, "If they stayed out for the remainder of the week, we would suffer an economic disaster." However one may interpret such expressions of opinion, it is certainly true that women are playing increasingly significant roles in industry. But how are they accepted? Why have they been treated as a necessary but nevertheless special group?

When equal pay for women was made law in 1963 in the United States after two decades of legislative debate, reactions ranged from "It's about time" to "It's truly revolutionary." One memorandum from an industrial advisory service said in part:

> Avoid any hasty *actions* at this time.
> • If *productivity* of men and women is really different for the same job, you may eventually decide to put piece-work, or incentive factors into your pay plan —to eliminate any doubt.
> • If *absenteeism* is higher among women, you may end up with a system of bonuses or penalties to reflect the added costs.
> • If *turnover* is lower among men, you'll want to explore a seniority pay setup—to compensate for training costs, etc.

History tells us that when Henry VIII had trouble about a wife, it shook Oxford and Cambridge to the core, but there is scant evidence to show that women in industry constitute an unusual problem. What is their role there?

ONE–THIRD ARE WOMEN

Almost one-third of the total labor force in our country is made up of women. By labor force we mean all people who work for pay, whether as production workers in a plant, as office managers, or in professional jobs, as doctors or engineers. Figure 17.1 shows the relative numbers of women working in various types of jobs in the United States.

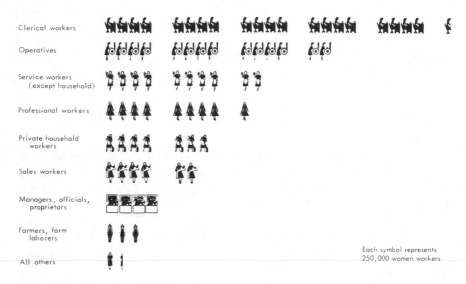

Fig. 17.1. Relative number of women in various types of jobs. Of the women working in the United States, the largest single group is in clerical work. Relatively few are found in managerial positions. (Courtesy U. S. Department of Labor.)

The subject of women in industry is more interesting to college students today than it has ever been before. An increasing number of young women, both married and unmarried, are entering industry after graduation from college. Older women, including many who do not need to work for a living, are coming into or returning to industry after their family responsibilities become less demanding. The number of working wives in the United States has risen from around 4 million in 1940 to some 15 million in 1965.

At the present time there are about 50 per cent more women at work than there were just before World War II. It has been predicted that by 1975 our total labor force will be about 90 million persons [27]. Where will these people be found? In any good business year, women comprise about 90 per cent of the total labor reserve, and here we find the answer to this question. Of necessity about half the growth will be made up of women, largely from the married group in the age bracket from thirty-five to fifty-four.

Much has been written about women in industry, but there are few scientific studies of the subject [15]. We shall approach the psychological problems peculiar to the woman worker and manager by looking back a few years into our industrial history.

A HISTORICAL BACKGROUND

The rapid progress of women in industry has been contemporaneous with the growth of our mass-production economy. The accompanying changes in customs and modes of living have been important to women workers. The social revolution at the turn of the century which brought the young single woman into the office gave her some economic independence. It also brought new life to a host of industries, such as garment factories, beauty shops, and women's magazines.

The expansion in manufacturing, construction, and transportation was followed by growth of commerce, trade, and service industries. But the dramatic appearance during World War II of Rosie the Riveter, of the woman welder, truck driver, and lathe operator, directed attention to the abilities of women in occupations which had never before been considered suitable for them. Mechanical power has made difference in strength between the sexes less important in many jobs. For example, the use of fork trucks allows women to accomplish much of the heavy lifting which was once performed solely by men. In the three years following Pearl Harbor, over 6 million women entered the labor force for the first time.

Women in World War II. Before World War II, it was generally accepted in steel mills that "skirts are bad luck"; this kind of work was the province of men. But at the height of the war, women were performing every job formerly done by men in ore mines, steel mills, and shipyards except jobs requiring heavy physical exertion or calling for many years of training and experience. During the year 1944, for example, about 40,000 of the total of 315,000 employees of one large steel corporation were women. Approximately 15,000 of these were in office occupations, and 25,000 were working directly in war production. These women came from all walks of life; formerly they had been housewives, saleswomen, stenographers, teachers, musicians. One subsidiary of this corporation listed 275 different jobs filled by women.

By conveyorizing operations, one plant of the United States Steel Corporation was able to increase its number of women employees to 48 per cent of the total. Overhead cranes and electrically driven dinkeys carried materials from department to department, thus obviating the need of lifting heavy material. Of the 153 crane operators in this plant, 79 were women. In the chemical laboratory, 80 per cent of the personnel were women who had not gone beyond elementary chemistry, taken either in high school or college; they were given on-the-job training [12].

Women in steel mills broke tradition and gave to their sex a power status never before experienced in heavy industry. Their presence introduced many changes, such as the installation of modern sanitary facilities and the employment of women counselors to guide new employees into the strange world of the steel mill. After the war the mills gave up the women workers.

Changes in Cultural Attitudes. In the half century since 1910, there have been significant changes in terms of the socioeconomic groups to which women workers belong. Whereas only about a quarter of all working women were nonmanual workers in 1910, the proportion has now risen to about one-half. The number of women in nonagricultural work has increased nearly 100 per cent in the past half century. This increase has been due to changes in cultural attitudes as well as to economic influences. The breakup of the old middle-class pattern of respectability in which the wife did not work if her husband could afford to keep her at home has affected all levels of society. Apparently women need the feeling of accomplishment which comes from earning money. In one survey 74 per cent of the women said they would continue to work even if they inherited enough money to live comfortably [2]. In terms of "job satisfaction," a survey of college-educated married women showed that those who were gainfully employed were more satisfied with their marriages than those who were "only homemakers." [49]

For many years, domestic service remained the largest single occupation for women. The rise in new mass-production industries and the vast technological changes taking place in more recent years have brought clerical workers and machine operators into the pattern.

At the professional level, teaching and nursing are still the most obvious choices of careers for women, although business, engineering, and the sciences are gaining in proportion as women's status changes.

Various factors have affected a change in women's occupations. The change-over from an agricultural to an industrial economy created the need for a new labor supply; this supply of new workers became available as women became less tied down with household duties.

The rise of our highly industrialized economy has been accompanied by social changes. During pioneer days most women directed their efforts to production and service for the family. Later, as a result of new inventions, spinning, weaving, sewing, laundering, and many personal services were taken over by commercial companies. As the luxuries of living came more and more to be necessities, there was an increasing need for women to help with the family budget. Thus the status of both the part-time and the full-time woman worker was raised considerably. Gradually women were offered more extensive opportunities to obtain education and specialized training. Some companies claim that although they originally put women into certain jobs because of a manpower shortage, they have found that special characteristics of women make them better suited to some tasks than men. These changes have been coming about slowly and are still in process.

Intercultural Roles. In a review of writings about the jobs of women in other countries Wickert points out that the notion of women's roles versus men's roles is primarily cultural rather than biological in origin [50]. Among the Australian aborigines women take the initiative. In the Philippines, who are the gossips The men! In the U.S.S.R., who are the doctors? Women constitute 70 per cent of the physicians, compared with some 5 per cent in the United States. In India it is general practice for the male to prove his manhood in the home rather than in his occupation. In many cultures women are scapegoats reflecting broader cultural problems. In the United States as well as elsewhere, absenteeism, for example, is actually shown to be an economic rather than sex-related problem.

When a sample of fathers, mothers and daughters in this country were brought together to discuss appropriate topics in mixed triads (rather than triads composed of family members), traditional sex-role differentiation became evident. When people who didn't know each other were put together, the males were task-oriented, displaying a strong attitude of "getting on with the job." Women tended to be expressive, emotional, and human relations–minded. But once the family was put together as a triad free from outside surveillance, the male showed much emotion, and the woman became very businesslike in solving the practical problems. The stereotype of male and female roles in our society is often not as clear-cut as in other cultures. Perhaps we should be cautious in assuming too quickly who is limited and who best suited to different jobs in industry. This is particularly important where technology is opening up new jobs not yet stereotyped. Telephone-operator jobs from the beginning were essentially "women only." A spokesman for the telephone industry says that were it not for automation, at the present time the phone companies alone would need the services of nearly all the working women in the country as operators to handle their increased business load [50].

Technology Opens Up Jobs. The increase in the number of public service and welfare agencies has opened up new opportunities for women in such areas as social work and government offices. Since there was little or no traditional competition from men in these occupations, they, like teaching and nursing, have become known as women's work. Technology, with such inventions as the typewriter and the telephone, created new kinds of jobs which went mostly to women. As automation increased, more new places appeared for women. In the craftsmen's occupations the traditions of long apprenticeships and prejudices against women began to give way as machines eliminated the necessity for physical strength on the job. Both the public and employers have gradually been changing their common belief that certain types of work are not appropriate for women. Jobs in electronic data processing are opening up for women, but in competition with men.

The Majority Minority. In an article in a technical journal dealing with the subject of women in industry, one writer [39], concluded, ". . . women are a *minority* group, in the social sense of the term, regardless of what percentage of the population they may actually make up." *Business Week* summed up what many statistics bear out in America. "Despite an increasing interest among women in returning to work after raising a family, business isn't eager for them." Yet, as stated above, women constitute almost one-third of our total labor force; 13 million households find women working to help support the family budget. They constitute one-sixth of the 18 million members of the nation's 184 labor unions, take 17 per cent of all higher degrees, make up 4 per cent of the listings in *Who's Who,* and own more real estate and stocks and bonds than do men. They spend more of the consumer dollar and inherit more business property.

Women can retire on Social Security earlier than men, but outlive the male by four years. There are more women voters than men voters. The first woman vice-president of a national broadcasting chain was appointed in 1962, and in 1964 the Harvard Business School opened its doors to women in the M.A. program for the first time. One company employing a minority number of women, with only a few in supervisory positions, made an attempt to better integrate these people into the organization. "We will never make it," reported one woman supervisor of some thirty male and female clerks. "The company is man-oriented."

Much has been written on women in industry, and many of the writings point to the prejudices involved. In one survey of over two thousand male managers conducted in the early sixties, four out of five responded that women are always at the top in absenteeism regardless of status. "Are women more neurotic than men?" "Yes," said 52 per cent. Two-thirds of the respondents said women make poor supervisors, and three-fourths said there are more problem workers among women than men. One woman vice-president said she was always put with the executive wives at social functions, "although I own the majority of stock in the company."

DIFFERENCES BETWEEN WOMEN AND MEN AT WORK

Do women like their jobs? Do they have the same job dissatisfactions as those expressed by men? Do they have much interest in unions? Do they make good managers? Questions like these are important not only to personnel people but also to college students who are trying to decide what kind of job to prepare for or what particular job offer should be accepted.

Differing Attitudes. Of several questionnaire-type studies reported in the literature comparing men and women in job satisfaction, some indicate that women are more satisfied than men; others show the reverse; and still others show no differences. Qualitatively, women seem to express themselves more freely, either by written comments or in interviews, about such things as cleanliness of working conditions, pleasantness of social relationships on the job, and treatment by supervisors. Women verbalize loyalty more than men but show less interest in pay, benefit programs, and opportunities for advancement. The author had the opportunity to make a good comparison between the attitudes of men and women working together on the same types of jobs in a company employing about equal numbers of each sex. A questionnaire was used. When asked what they liked least about their jobs, two-thirds of the men mentioned low pay, but very few women mentioned money in spite of the fact that their rate of pay was below that of the men. On an item concerned with cafeteria conditions, 600 women made a specific complaint which only 2 men mentioned. Noticeable differences between men and women in their questionnaire responses were found in areas involving supervision and cleanliness in working conditions; the women were more sensitive than men. On questions involving a proposed installation of automatic laborsaving machines, the men expressed fear of losing their jobs, but the women were apparently not interested in the problem [15]. In one study of men and women over an age range from 21 to 65 years the need for achievement among men dropped with age, but the need for power rose. Among women, need for achievement and need for power both dropped.

Problems of Adjustment. The employed woman who has to divide her energies between the working world and her traditional role as a woman faces adjustment problems peculiar to her sex. The married woman has both home and job responsibilities somewhat different from those of her male counterpart. The social and psychological pressures on the single woman complicate her attitudes toward marriage, toward her job, and toward her associates. A major consideration of the young single woman in selecting a job may well be the opportunities which it offers her to meet elegible men of marriageable age.

The woman who works does have problems of both physical and psychological adjustment. Hilliard [18], in her studies of women and fatigue, says we have recently created further stresses: to adolescence, pregnancy, and menopause are added the varied role of wife, mother, homemaker, and career woman. In a study of 116 men and 96 women in the New York Telephone Company, higher incidence of illness absenteeism was reported by women. This study, which was equated for age, social and economic position, and other variables, concluded that there was a cultural attitude present in that the women used different criteria from the men in determining what constituted illness; they also showed a greater readiness to report illness. Age and marital status per se are not related to absenteeism in women, but number of dependents is [11, 19, 28, 37, 38].

Married and Part-time Workers. Women differ from men in their original attitudes toward work. Most young women today take a job until marriage or a few years after. The married women are more likely to leave the labor force during the years when their small children require care. Many return to jobs when their children are partly grown and no longer need constant attention. Because of this cycle, the largest proportion are in the labor force between the ages of twenty and twenty-four. The proportion declines in the age range from twenty-five to thirty-four and increases again around thirty-five. In 1890 one wife in twenty worked, in 1965 one in three.

Statistical surveys show that an increasing number of married women are going into industry. Part-time work is more likely to be sought by women than by men, since women frequently need to combine a paid job with household cares. Data show that 60 per cent of all part-time workers are women, most of them married and over thirty-five years of age. They usually do the same type of work as full-time employees. Apparently part-time work has resulted from the normal needs of management and is not merely a by-product of full employment. Women work part time because of a need to increase or supplement the family income or to have outside interests. Management uses them during busy periods, for relief schedules, or for temporary peak loads. Organizations such as the Kelly Girl Service, which provides part-time secretaries, are on the increase. The Polaroid Corporation reports good results in keeping on skilled women part time after they have had their children; thus they become available for full-time work later without the necessity of retraining. Women help to fill the labor demand during the peak periods of sugar-cane harvesting throughout most of the world, a situation favoring the desire for part-time work and compatible with plantation management.

Barriers to Employment. Women must face age barriers to employment earlier than men. Opinions of employment-service personnel indicate that women around thirty-five years of age meet difficulties in getting jobs equivalent to those met by men of forty-five to fifty years of age. Figure 17.2 shows the kind of shifting in jobs for women that takes place by age group.

In 1955 a study was reported by the Women's Bureau of the U.S. De-

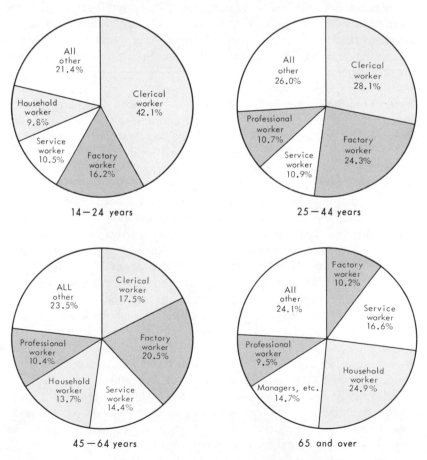

Fig. 17.2. Most common jobs for women by age group. These graphs illustrate the relationship between age and types of jobs held by women workers. (Courtesy U. S. Department of Labor.)

partment of Labor on twenty-three training programs for middle-aged and older women looking for work [48]. The programs included such items as industrial sewing, institutional housekeeping, domestic work, selling, and production work in the electronics industry. Without exception, the instructors and administrators of the training programs stressed the fact that learning proficiency in these highly practical jobs depended on individual ability regardless of age. There was some evidence that older women did not do as well as younger students in classwork and theory but were better in demonstration and practice work. The instructors felt that since the mature women had been away from school for several years, they were no longer accustomed to studying. One important finding of the study was that mature women had a great need for individualized counseling and guidance. Their self-confidence had to be developed. The overall results achieved in these twenty-three training programs showed clearly that women who have never worked or have not worked for several years can, with proper counseling, training, and placement, become both productive and satisfactory employees.

Some Traditional Beliefs Are Wrong. It has been a generally accepted idea that certain kinds of work are unsuitable for women. Many groups and agencies concerned with problems of social welfare have condemned nightwork as being bad for women. Before World War I, it was commonly believed that working at night was dangerous to the health of women. As scientific evidence failed to support this view, more attention was given to the idea that nightwork for women created a social hazard, disrupted family living, and deprived the workers of recreation and participation in community life. The pressure of public opinion led a number of states to pass laws regulating or prohibiting certain kinds of night employment for women. Some industries tried to prevent "the possibility of annoyance or criminal assault" by ending the swing shift an hour earlier for women than for men, so they could leave the plant at a separate time.

But what of the facts? Do women object to nightwork more than men do? One study may help to give a new perspective to this problem. A total of 270 men and women who worked nights in hotel and restaurant occupations were asked about their views on nightwork for women [46]. A preponderance of the women found nightwork acceptable. Some had chosen it deliberately because they liked the night shift or because it was the most convenient time to work. Others had taken a night job because this was the only thing they could find. In contrast, the men who were interviewed expressed more objections to nightwork.

Equipment Redesign. Society's concern for protecting the woman worker has had a long history; it has been expressed through the enacting of state laws and varying social customs. In recent years, however, an even more significant change in industry has occurred because of the influence of the woman worker herself. Some of the initial work of human engineering in industry—fitting the machine or job to the worker—began with women. Since they are shorter than men, women had to use platforms when standing at machines. With the large influx of women into industry during World War II, many plant changes were brought about which were good for men as well as for women. More and more frequently levers and pulleys were substituted for muscles. Rest rooms were modified, and lunch-rooms were improved. More safety practices were introduced. It even became fashionable for a woman worker to dress to suit her job.

Facts versus Opinions. A great deal has been written about the physical limitations of women for various jobs. For example, a Soviet Russian commission reported an investigation which revealed that almost three-fourths of the women required to do heavy lifting in such industries as coal and steel had menstrual troubles, twice as many as had similar troubles when engaged in lighter work [33]. It has generally been assumed that women are more susceptible to fatigue than men. One finds statements that overtime work causes more accidents among women than men. It has also been reported that absenteeism is as much as 100 per cent higher among women than among men. Such statements are often made without citing valid statistical data, and one should use caution in generalizing from them. Some authorities attempt to prove that women are more accident-prone than men; others claim the reverse. When adequately documented studies are considered, the evidence indicates that in the areas of safety, absenteeism, and general adjustment to the job situation, factors other than sex differences are often more likely to be the reasons for variations in human behavior. Some writers maintain that it is woman's psychic dependency on man and her feeling of inferiority engendered by male domination which cause her to be less successful in the industrial world. But we would do well to consider their statements to be opinions only, not evidence.

Again, public opinion expresses the view that age does not favor the working woman. The U.S. Department of Labor says training is the primary requirement for employment, particularly for technicians. And many women stay on the job. In 1920 the average age of the American working woman was 28. In 1940 it was 32; in 1950 it was 40, and in 1964 it was 42.

It is difficult to separate facts from opinions in what has been written about women workers. To say, as several writers have, that women are not as good long-term investments as men is indulging in hasty generalization. In some kinds of clerical positions they have been shown to be better investments. It may be true that a smaller proportion of women than men qualify for upgrading or advancement to supervisory jobs in manufacturing industries. But what criteria are used here for upgrading or advancement? Maybe our stereotyped conception of the woman has placed her in such a role that she cannot meet the standards for promotion. In universities there are few women in the sciences who hold the rank of professor. This may change with the growing need for college teachers.

WOMEN'S JOBS

About two-thirds of all women in industry are employed in manufacturing, retail trade, or personal services. The largest numbers are in clerical and operative jobs; only a few are in executive positions. Somewhere around one-fourth of all women workers are in factories, primarily those manufacturing apparel, textiles, or foods. About one-fourth of the workers in the executive branch of the Federal government are women, but only 4 per cent are in science and engineering. The first woman employed by the government worked in the Treasury Department in 1861, and she served in a clerical capacity.

Traditions and Discriminations. There are still many prejudices and traditional discriminations against women in factory-type jobs, but enough traditions have been broken to show that changes can be made. Even such small things as changing physical working conditions and introducing schedules which allow the women time to get their housework done can reduce women's absenteeism below that of men. In the more professional types of jobs (accounting, science, engineering, mathematics), once thought to be the exclusive province of men, women are being accepted in many quarters. Some writers feel that our shortage of scientists and technologists can be partially overcome by selecting and training more women.

Although women are going into many "men's" professions, the proportions are still small. Most female college graduates who work go into traditional women's jobs. Women constitute about 90 per cent of all librarians, 60 per cent of all welfare workers, and 80 per cent of all public school teachers. For many jobs women must deemphasize the traditional homemaker roles.

At another level, women have a hard time fitting into some of the skilled trades. Lack of training facilities is a part of their problem, but their greatest difficulty is that they have to fight tradition and union politics, even at times of peak employment. For example, studies have shown that among tool and die makers two out of three men entered the trade through apprenticeship; among molders 57 per cent entered this way [44]. During the peak employment of the middle 1950s there were only 9 apprentices for every 100 journeymen tool and die makers employed in the metal-working industries, and none were women. In many trades women apprentices are unheard of. In another way women have not quite fitted into the union picture. Whereas women may be aggressive and courageous in emotional situations like strikes, they take little interest in the day-to-day business routine of the union. They are apathetic about paying dues and fighting for fringe benefits. Some union leaders have expressed concern about the possible dangers to unionism in this feminine attitude, and well they might.

In one small industrial community elections were held to determine if the union would represent the workers. One plant, composed mostly of male workers, voted the union in. Another, owned separately, but in the same textile industry, turned the union down. Said an organizer—"We couldn't get the women interested in unionism." This latter plant employed mostly women.

Higher-level Positions. Apparently it takes a long time to establish a tradition favorable to women within the higher-level positions in industry. In the home offices of insurance companies, women hold only about 20 per cent of the supervisory positions; in banks, the figure is even lower. Both of these industries employ large proportions of women. Two-thirds of all insurance-company employees are women. Women constitute about one-half of the number of employees in banks. Only in department stores does one find an even distribution among women and men in the so-called "higher level" positions. Here women make up about two-thirds of all employees [2, 13].

Women officers in industry are no more than 4 per cent of the total. Only a handful hold board directorships. In production operations in manufacturing, few women are found above the level of forewoman. Aside from prejudice, lack of education and training has been cited as one of the principal reasons women do not advance. One writer summed the problem up well by pointing out that the young woman does not take specialized training because she fears it will be wasted in a hostile market, and she has little chance for advancement because she lacks the training. This circular dilemma must surely be avoided if our economy is to continue along its predicted course. The women in middle-management brackets with no more than a high school education are usually older than those in the general labor market, and more of them are single. Women in personnel work, training, publishing, job testing, social service, science, and engineering are usually college graduates [51].

The opportunities for women at the administrative level are increasing in such positions as research analysts in banks and insurance companies and in merchandising, public relations, advertising, and personnel work. However, very few women in any field occupy the top executive jobs. One business magazine estimated that not over five thousand women could be found among the quarter-million "real" executives. A market analysis of women holding positions of responsibility in industry and commerce indicated that the way women behave on the job rather than the way they perform the technical operations of their position is a chief determinant of their acceptance as administrators. Apparently there is a widespread belief that women are "too emotional" or "too personal" to hold down supervisory jobs or executive positions. Most evidence that seems to point in this direction, however, is more subjective than objective [2].

Opportunities in Administrative Jobs. One of the most illuminating studies on opportunities for women in administrative jobs was conducted by the Harvard Business School. In effect, the study was a market analysis to find out what women do if they hold responsible positions in business and how they are accepted. Of particular interest to the college girl thinking about a business career were the findings on the kinds of jobs opening up for women, what things are in their favor, and what barriers to advancement must be met [13].

The research team interviewed 175 persons in ninety-five organizations. Forty-seven of the administrative people interviewed were women, and the fields represented included accounting, advertising, banking, credit, food, government, heavy industries, hospitals, insurance, law, management consulting, manufacturing, publishing, retailing, textiles, utilities, and wholesaling.

There was a general acknowledgement of the increasing importance of women in business, but very few women were found to be holding top executive jobs. "Second in command" was the way several executives described the highest level that a woman could hope to attain. One management-consulting firm expressed a prevailing sentiment that the highest position women are going to reach in the foreseeable future in any large numbers is that of assistant to a top executive, primarily an expansion of the secretarial function. Exceptions to this apparent limitation on women's advancement were found in the more creative fields, such as merchandising, promotion, public relations, and magazine publishing. In the more specialized positions, such as home economist for large food companies and women's magazines, the field is wide open, as are such comparable areas as the fashion industry. Working as a buyer for a department store was strongly emphasized as a lucrative occupation for women.

New Opportunities. The study showed further that there is a growing place for women in certain types of research jobs—as investment analysts in banks and insurance companies, in technical research positions in laboratories of food and chemical companies, and in statistical jobs in nearly all large organizations, regardless of their business.

The job area of consumer contact seems to be opening up for women. One bank executive expressed the general idea in this way: "A woman would rather talk to a woman about financial matters, particularly if she is afraid she'll ask a foolish question." Similarly, in fields such as retailing, merchandising, and promotion, it was pointed out that women have long been used in jobs requiring a knowledge of the woman consumer as well as of the product.

Many executives who were interviewed regarded personnel work as a natural field for women. An important consideration should be included here, however. The study pointed out that the level to which women can rise in this field seems to depend on the kind of business they choose. Where women constitute a major part of the working force, there is apparently more chance of a woman's becoming head of the personnel department than in companies where men predominate. Strongly unionized industries and those requiring a large number of skilled employees, such as engineers, offer less chance for women to become head of personnel. Heavy industry, steel, for example, is a most unlikely place for a woman to become an executive.

Limitations to Advancement. With women entering the sciences, law, and other professions in greater numbers than ever before but without full recognition, we find a warning sign for those college women planning careers in industry. There are barriers to the success of women in business —barriers which are mostly psychological in nature. What are these barriers?

The Harvard study of ninety-five organizations showed that the limits on women's advancement to the administrative level as imposed by the general attitudes of the business community vary from industry to industry. In certain fields, where the primary function is to serve other businesses, a woman is at a disadvantage. One businessman summed the attitude up by saying, "While a woman performs very effectively *within* the walls of many banking organizations, the prospect of her representing the organization to business units outside is still unacceptable to most businessmen."

In nearly every line of business represented by the interviews, the comparative shortness of a woman's stay in an organization was pointed out. Among the common opinions expressed by men on the limitations of women in business were: "She is barred from executive dining rooms." "She doesn't play golf with customers." "Women regard their jobs as of secondary importance in life." "Women do not really want careers." "Women do not like to assume responsibility." From the women interviewed came such statements as: "Women are too ready to attach themselves to a pleasant working situation and to refuse advancement opportunities because their current situation is so nice and easy." "Women do not choose a career but fall into one."

The analysis of other attitudes frequently expressed in the interviews pointed out that men resent working for a woman and that women do not like to work for other women. Apparently, both men and women feel there is less status in working for a woman than in working for a man. Most negative sentiments concerning women in supervisory positions seemed to be based on the belief that women "are more emotional than men" and "take everything too personally." Several men in top positions acknowledged that there was very little difference between men and women so far as emotional attitude toward their jobs was concerned, but held that women were less likely to hide their feelings and keep them from influencing business decisions.

Attitudes toward Married Women. Attitudes toward married women working in business fall into two schools of thought. The older, more traditional businesses, such as banking, have only recently begun to hire or retain married women. Adherents of one school hold the belief that a married woman shifts her allegiance from her job to her home. In contrast, there is the idea that marriage is a stabilizing factor which makes the woman more confident and dependable.

One interesting aspect of the executives' discussions was the frequent reference to the fact that administrative training and business experience should make a girl a much better wife for a businessman.

Wives of Men in Industry. Another important aspect of the industrial environment to which industry, as well as other kinds of organizations, has given some attention in recent years is the part played by the wives of men in industry. Consideration has been given to educating the families of workers in such company matters as health and safety. In selecting Americans for government assignments overseas consideration is given to the adaptability of the wife of the technician as well as to the technician himself. However, the most elaborate attempt to bring wives onto the industrial scene has occurred in the management structure. No picture of the psychological climate of modern industry would be complete without some description of the role played by executives' wives. This is a subject of particular import to the young man who is planning a career with some companies (and to his wife also).

Surveys concerning management wives have been conducted across the United States. The interviews were made on the basis of a rough sampling of management by age and business (size and type); they were supplemented by interviews providing a cross section of particular corporation communities. Interviews were held with executive wives themselves, with executives as corporation officials, and with executives as husbands; they were held with management consultants, sociologists, and psychologists. The husbands of the wives in question were in the age range of twenty-five to forty and in junior and middle management or with aspirations for getting there.

Corporation officials sketched the ideal management wife as one who is highly adaptable, is gregarious, and realizes that her husband belongs to the corporation. As the wife sees herself in this corporation culture, she is judged "good" by what she does *not* do: she is not to complain when her husband works late; she is not to fuss about a transfer; she is not to engage in any controversial activity. Above all, the wife feels that she is expected to be a good listener, to serve as the sounding board for her husband's frustrations. In a subtle sort of way the good management wife is expected to be a valuable publicity agent for the husband. Of course, in many organizations, wives do not get involved in the company at all. A manager's wife can affect her husband's performance more often in a small "company town" or an overseas location than in a large-city complex.

There is enough evidence to conclude that attitudes of women and about women can and do change. It may well be that the wise personnel man should take a hard look to see just where he may profit by employing women even though men may be available for the job. The woman worker, the woman executive, and the professional woman may hold the key to our expanding economy.

WOMEN IN AN EXPANDING ECONOMY

Technological innovations are expected to continue. They will bring the development of new skills, some of which may be generally accepted as women's work. Witness, for example, how women have moved into the relatively new field of electronic-computer operations as programmers. Curricula and subject matter in our schools are beginning to be attuned less to older patterns of women's employment and more to meeting the needs of modern technology.

Let us examine several of the reasons given by employers in the past for hiring or refusing to hire women.

In certain manufacturing fields, in professional service, and in sales work, some jobs are often closed to women because it is taken for granted that they should be held by men. This belief has been so generalized that some employers say women would induce negative reactions not only among male supervisors, fellow employees, and customers but also among the public at large. The mere fact that a particular job has traditionally been held by a man or by a woman often determines who will get the job when a replacement is needed.

Certain cultural patterns help to decide who will get what job. The idea that women should have easier, cleaner, and lighter tasks has been a part of the pattern of male chivalry. Some employers frankly admit that the economic factor operates in job assignments. Women can be hired for less money than men; hence certain jobs get labeled as women's, and men tend to avoid them.

With employers setting higher educational requirements for their new employees, many men are failing to qualify for jobs that women are prepared for. The realities of meeting labor competition at the more technical levels, plus the fact that women now have a better opportunity to get into the newer technical jobs, make job opportunities for women better now than at any other time in our industrial history.

A Changing Pattern. Another factor which favors the entry of more women into industry is "age acceptance." Although there are still prejudices against hiring the older female worker, the percentage of older women in the labor force has been increasing [4, 27]. Over one-half of the working women are married and over forty years of age. We now find the working wife in all communities and among all social, racial, and ethnic groups. An increasing number of women now remain in the labor force for most of their adult lives, save for short periods taken out to bear and raise children. In some circles this work pattern is even becoming fashionable for wives of economically secure husbands.

Several circumstances have been responsible for this change. The employment of women in wartime had the effect of breaking, at least in part, certain attitudinal barriers against women in industry. But more important, our expanding economy has put new demands on the labor supply, and technological changes have created a need for more highly skilled people. Whereas automation will probably have little effect on the major fields of women's employment (teaching, nursing, service, sales, the apparel industry), it is opening up many new jobs for women in the electronics industry and microtechnology.

The National Manpower Council predicts that the reason for the employment of women will bear less and less relationship to their low income and social status. The number of middle-income families continues to grow, and women in the middle- and upper-income groups have been going to work in steadily increasing numbers. In the future, fewer women may be working because of economic necessity, and more and more because they choose to. Women, although still restricted, are finding greater freedom to choose for themselves the particular pattern of employment which best satisfies their own needs.

Education. There is some evidence to support the position that girls are discouraged from intellectual excellence by our society and that this discouragement operates most strongly in the areas of science and mathematics and in those activities involving decision-making processes. One research study concludes that as girls grow up, they discover that women are not supposed to excel intellectually. By the twelfth grade something in their growing concept of the women's role prevents them from competing with men in our North American culture. Social pressures by her peers help mold the girl student into a stereotype of feminine charm that is not yet completely removed from the old notion that to be feminine, a girl must quake at a column of figures. For the young girl in our culture the marriage go-round is a primary goal.

Currently there is movement in the United States to take stock of our need for women's brain power. Continuing-education programs especially designed for women in their thirties and forties who want to complete or update their education are now receiving support in many quarters. In the past girls have been penalized in their initial employment opportunities because of a lack of education and cultural stereotyping or because of the movement to early marriage. Since growing demand for "split level" education for women will probably manifest itself more prominently in the coming decade, we may witness changes in the education of women [10, 25].

Womanpower in the Future. There is certain to be more effective utilization of womanpower in the future, and we dare say it will be accompanied by a number of adjustments:

1 Attitudes about women working and attitudes of women working in industry will undergo more change.

2 Many women appear to get satisfaction from combining work for pay with homemaking functions. Adjustments will be made to allow for this.

3 Discontinuity in employment poses a problem of skill maintenance when women temporarily leave the labor force to raise families. Provision will be made for retraining the older woman when she returns to work.

4 Shortages of highly trained personnel will bring about excellent opportunities for women who are prepared for a specific job or profession.

5 Sex labels of jobs will tend to disappear as women are allowed to show what they are capable of doing. Advancing technology will help give them the chance.

6 Nonindustrial jobs in government and the armed forces will help to break the barriers of tradition unfavorable to women.

7 The increased emphasis by union organizations on raising pay for women will tend to level women with men in certain jobs in keeping with legislation of equal pay for equal work.

8 The increasing fear of insecurity may motivate women to develop some kind of employment skill even though they plan to marry.

9 The growing independence of women will expand opportunities for them in industry.

10 The current strong pull toward early marriage will lead more women to work to help support the family budget.

Of the several factors related to the prediction that women will play more and more important roles in industry, we believe three are primary. First, except in periods of economic adjustment, women will be needed in industry more than ever before. Second, technological advances will create many jobs highly suitable to women. Finally, women are acquiring more status in industry, and this in itself will induce more women to work.

SUGGESTIONS FOR SELECTIVE READING

Beauvoir, Simone de. *The second sex.* New York: Bantam, 1961. Biological and psychological nature of woman in her climate.

Bernard, Jessie. *Academic women.* University Park, Pa.: Pennsylvania State University Press, 1964. The range of problems of the woman scholar.

Cassara, Beverly B. (Ed.) *American women: The changing image.* Boston: Beacon Press, 1962. Chapters deal with workers, unions, and professional women.

Cussler, Margaret. *The woman executive.* New York: Harcourt, Brace & World, 1958. A sociologist looks at the woman in middle management.

Farber, S. M., & Wilson, R. H. L. (Eds.) *The potential of women.* New York: McGraw-Hill, 1964. The role of woman from many points of view.

Friedan, Betty. *The feminine mystique.* New York: Norton, 1963. A popular book about women at home and at work.

Harrison, Evelyn. *The working woman: Barriers in employment.* Chicago: American Society for Public Administration, 1964. Influence of President's Commission on changing status of women.

Hilliard, Marion. *Women and fatigue.* Garden City, N.Y.: Doubleday, 1960. A woman physician's answer to practical questions of interest to personnel managers (and husbands).

Jephcott, Pearl, et al. *Married women working.* London: George Allen and Unwin, Ltd., 1962. Two studies of social results of married women going out to work.

Leonard, Eugenie, et al. *The American women in colonial and revolutionary times,* 1565–1800. Philadelphia: University of Pennsylvania Press, 1962. A syllabus of over 1,000 items providing a picture of colonial women in life and work.

Long, C. *The labor force under changing income and employment.* Princeton, N.J.: Princeton, 1958. Contains material on women in industry.

Manle, Frances. *Executive careers for women.* New York: Harper & Row, 1961. A popular book about our crisis in brain power.

Mead, Margaret, & Kaplan, Frances B. (Eds.) *American women: Report of President's Commission.* New York: Scribner's, 1965. An overall view of the status of women, with recommendations.

Miqueli, Violeta. *Women in myth and history.* New York: Vantage Press, 1962. The long struggle to attain emancipation.

Myrdal, Alva, & Klein, Viola. *Women's two roles.* London: Routledge, 1956. Work and the home—a British view.

National Manpower Council. *Womanpower.* New York: Columbia, 1957. Present and future status of women in our industrial society.

National Manpower Council. *Work in the lives of married women.* New York: Columbia, 1958. Problems of the married woman worker.

Nye, F. I., & Hoffman, Lois W. (Eds.) *The employed mother in America.* Chicago: Rand McNally, 1963. A profile of the employed mother by several behavioral scientists.

Paradis, Adrian A. *The new look in banking.* New York: McKay, 1961. Stories of famous women bankers.

Rheingold, J. C. *The fear of being a woman.* New York: Grune & Stratton, 1964. A book on mental and physical health which adds to an understanding of the varied roles of the woman; nothing specific on industry.

Rogers, E. *Human ecology and health.* New York: Macmillan, 1960. Has a section on women at work.

Smuts, R. W. *Women and work in America.* New York: Columbia, 1959. The effects of changing popular opinion about women at work.

Sudlow, Elizabeth. *Career women of the Bible.* New York: Pageant Press, 1951. Historical view of careers of women.

Turner, Marjorie B. *Women & work.* Los Angeles: University of California, Institute of Industrial Relations, 1964. A good summary, in 80-page booklet, of women in industry.

U.S. Department of Labor. *Woman's handbook.* Washington, D.C.: Author, Women's Bureau, 1963. Working papers of the President's Commission on the status of women.

Winter, E. *A woman's guide to earning a good living.* New York: Simon and Schuster, 1961. A popular how-to book.

Zapoleon, Marguerita. *Occupational planning for women.* New York: Harper & Row, 1961. A how-to book addressed to counselors.

SOCIAL INTERACTION AND ADJUSTMENTS

18

The Industrial Community

B. von Haller Gilmer

With the increasing effort of states and local communities to obtain new industries and with the desire of industry to improve its public relations within the local community, a new emphasis is being given to industry-community cooperation. The problem, however, is not simple, for we must remember that the union also enters the picture in the struggle for power and status. What kind of people does industry like to see in a community? Why do communities seek certain types of new industries? How have technological changes affected community living? Does absentee ownership lead to bad labor relations? Is a man's work affected by the community in which he lives? Should the local plant manager strive for leadership within the community? These are the types of questions we will deal with in this chapter. Modern industry can no longer ignore the fact that how a man lives is related to how he works.

IMPORTANCE OF KNOWING THE COMMUNITY

Social scientists have long been interested in the human problems of industry-community relations. Psychologists are interested not only in the man at work but also in how the place where he lives affects his work, his attitudes, and his productivity. With the increasing diversifications within industry, with the dispersion of plants into the rural areas, and with the growth of the new suburbia, understanding the industrial community itself is becoming more and more important to the psychologist.

American industry is becoming increasingly aware of the importance of the human relations factors in seeking plant locations. To indicate this growing awareness, let us quote a portion of a letter from the president of a medium-sized corporation to an industrial consultant.

Our industrial engineering department is favorably disposed to having us locate our new processing plant just outside of the town of Middlebrook. The town is well located in terms of raw materials, transportation facilities, and markets. We are told that we can be given favorable tax rates. Before we take option on various properties in the region, we would like to have you survey the community and get us answers to such questions as: What is the potential labor supply of men in the age bracket of 20 to 50? What is the potential supply of women for seasonal and part-time employment? What kind of people live there? What are the attitudes of these people toward organized labor? Who runs the town? What are the prevailing wage rates for skilled and unskilled labor? How prosperous are the nearby farmers? Are there enough people we could select locally who could fill our needs for foremen within a reasonable period of time?

The letter continued with the request that if the labor supply looked good and if a program of selection, training, and orientation of workers could be worked out, the consultant also try to determine what the company would need to do in the way of public relations in order to gain acceptance in the community.

Searching out new plant sites for corporations and advising job-starved towns on what sort of new industries they are best suited to attract now engages both local and international organizations.

Why is industry paying more attention to the human environment? Although answers to this question depend on many circumstances and change with different locales, one historical example can give us a conceptual base for better understanding the problems of industrial behavior, namely, the Yankee City studies [44].

THE YANKEE CITY STUDIES

Yankee City is the fictitious name given to a real town founded early in the 1600s at a harbor on the mouth of a large river in New England. When these studies began, during the early thirties, there were some seventeen thousand people living there. Slightly over half of the population were born in or near the town; a little less than a quarter of the population were foreign-born; and the remainder were born elsewhere in the United States. About one-fourth of the employable population worked in the shoe industry.

The purpose of the studies was to find out, through the gathering of economic data, through the observations of individual and group behaviors, and through intensive interviewing, how the worker in the plant, his activities, and his attitudes are related to the total community in which he lives. The worker brings his outside life with him into the factory; when he returns home at night to his family and friends, he takes part of his factory life with him. How do these two lives influence each other?

An Old Community. Yankee City's social make-up had become firmly organized over a long period of time, and the relations of the various members of the society were exactly placed and known by the individuals who made up the group. The town had a life of its own; it was not a satellite of a large metropolitan area. An intensive study of the total community was made by putting field men in various strategic places. Some went into factories to observe the behavior and relationships there; others were placed among the workers at home. Still others conducted interviews and collected budgets. Some men were put to work studying associations; others investigated the churches. The community gave wholehearted cooperation to the researchers. Personal data were gathered on practically all of the seventeen thousand men, women, and children of Yankee City.

In Yankee City's social system, economic wealth did not guarantee the highest social position. People were ranked by the members of the community into socially superior and socially inferior positions. Members of a class tended to marry within their own group, although marriages up and down did occur. One could better himself by a "fine marriage" or lower his status by "marrying beneath himself." Some wealthy families were found outside the top-status class because "they do not belong to the right families," "they do not go around with the right people," "they don't know how to act." The researchers found that if a man's education, occupation, wealth, income, family, intimate friends, and clubs and fraternities and his manners, speech, and general outward behavior were known, it was not difficult for his fellow citizens to give a fairly exact estimate of his status. It was easy to classify the whole community in terms of a status hierarchy.

The profile of Yankee City, then, could be said to be like that of many other towns of its size, age, and location; it had its "old families" and "new families," "the people on the 'hill' and those who live in the 'flats,' " those who were "going up in the world" and those "on the way down."

The largest and most important industry in Yankee City was shoe manufacturing. Other industries included building trades, transportation, clamming, and silverware manufacturing. At the time of the studies, a number of workers classed as auto-body and cotton-textile employees were unemployed, since these industries had left the city and surrounding areas. Farming was a negligible pursuit in the economic life of the town. Four different faiths cared for the religious needs of the Yankee City community; the majority of the population were of the Protestant faith. The schools were typical of those in a New England community of this size.

Although the voters among the lower classes far outnumbered those in the higher classes, they had a disproportionately small percentage of officers in the political hierarchy.

The Community's First Strike. This was Yankee City in March, 1933, the year of the strike. As strikes go, it was a small one, involving only seven shoe factories and 1,500 workers. It involved little money; and it was not a rough strike in terms of people getting physically hurt or property being damaged. The strike did not even last long, only a month. But at Yankee City it was important because it occurred at a time when the city was being studied by a team of social anthropologists. The record of the dramatic conflict in this small town represents the most complete and definitive study we have of the factory in the community and what the problems of *people* are during a community crisis. It tells us about the nature of human needs and how people in groups react to frustration. It gives us at least some insight into the nature of industrial behavior.

Here in the worst year of the Great Depression all the workers in all the factories of the principal industry in the Yankee City community walked out. They struck with little or no warning. Management had said the workers would never strike, for they were sensible and dependable, and through a long peaceful history had proved they would always stay on the job. Even union men outside the city agreed that the workers could not be organized. Most of the townspeople said the workers would never strike—but they did.

The strike went through three phases. First, the workers organized themselves, joined an industrial union, and became strong union members. Management was unsuccessful in regaining control over the workers. The second period began with frontal attacks on management. The union won the support of the public, and most of Yankee City sided with the strikers. Finally, mediation and peace negotiations began when the government stepped in and, after a series of negotiations, helped end the strike.

The researchers talked with people all over the city and questioned them about the strike. The answers tended to reveal more about the life and status of the men who talked than about the causes of the strike. The secrets of the strike seemed to lie in the whole life of the community in which the workers and owners were but a part. Five "why" questions basic to the whole problem soon came out.

Why the Workers Struck. In a community where there had been very few strikes and *no* successful ones in a three-hundred-year history, why did the workers in *all* the shoe factories strike, win all their demands, and, after a severe struggle, soundly defeat management?

Why in a "nonunion community" could a union be successful in separating the workers from management?

Why was the union successful in organizing *all* the workers in *all* the shoe factories in the community?

Why was the union successful despite efforts to break it up?

Why did Yankee City change from a nonunion to a union town almost overnight?

All groups in the Yankee City community became involved in the strike. Each person interviewed had his own version of the cause of the crisis. The people blamed economic factors associated with the Depression; they blamed minority groups; and they blamed a dozen other things. One old lady put the problem in a nutshell: "Our todays are made out of yesterday. In fact, sometimes I think we are yesterday."

Technology and Social Change. For some three hundred years, Yankee City had grown slowly, and rigid class structures had become ingrained in the community. Status differences were apparent at every level. In the nineteenth century, the worker accepted the role of dependent child, and the owner or the manager played the role of humanitarian or kind father who knew what was best. By the early part of the twentieth century, the managers of industry acted like gods. "They had become the heroes to labor as well as to management." In short, Yankee City had come to accept paternalism as the normal pattern of human relationships, not only in the shoe industry, not only in worker-employer relationships, but also in the totality of community life.

Following the long history of Yankee City paternalism came the influence of technological development and economic change. Shoemaking had progressed from the early times when the family was the productive unit through the periods of early and late small-city capitalism. By the beginning of the 1930s, mass production was in effect, the machine dominated the industry, *and* control had shifted to the new owners in New York City. The Depression was on, and before national relief appeared on the scene, fears and antagonisms raised among the workers by their economic *and* psychological position helped to precipitate the strike, a community strike as it were.

Local townspeople contributed to strike funds. Sympathy with the strikers came from small merchants and other business people of comparable status with the workers. Technological changes had hampered the chances of a man's working his way up. Instead of a simple, universally agreed-upon hierarchy of statuses in technological jobs, the researchers found the situation to be confused and tense; there was suspicion and conflict between workers and managers. Confusion spread into the community itself. More than just a skill hierarchy was lost when the manufacture of shoes shifted from a craft industry into the mass-production pattern. A feeling of worker pride was lost. The skill hierarchy which had dominated the very lives of the workers and helped establish their place in the community was gone.

The workers had many frustrations in common. They dismissed small differences among themselves and united in one industrial union, national in scope. They were now part of a growing labor movement.

In the early days of the shoe industry, the owners and managers were residents of Yankee City. Their loyalties were in the community. There were feelings of neighborliness and friendship between worker and manager and feelings of mutual community responsibilities. The local owners were accepted leaders of the community.

When absentee ownership took over Yankee City and manufacturers' associations and labor unions grew strong, the "local boy" managers who remained on their jobs lost both power and status. In the eyes of the workers, the father figure had changed. In the days before big-city financiers took control, the local enterpriser was financed by Yankee City banks. The people made their investments locally. These local leaders of finance who were subject to local control, influenced by sentiments within the community, lost status also. There was a resentment on the part of these nonworker groups against the outside operators.

The extension of the industrial hierarchy to the big city reduced the local leaders to inferior positions in the hierarchy where they were incapable of making decisions and could not initiate actions which would give them the power to lead the workers and the rest of the town.

Thus Yankee City offers us one picture of a way in which business and industry were closely integrated with the community. Time changed a way of life. What happened in Yankee City gives us an idea of the importance of community human relations as well as individual human relations.

DIFFERENT TYPES OF COMMUNITIES

Paternalism has very few advocates today. Its decline has been due to the breakdown in the isolation of industrial villages. Industrial plants have grown in size and organization to such an extent that paternalism would be most impractical. With the growth of unions, the worker is no longer suited to the role of the dependent child.

The Boom Town. Much of the global picture of human relations problems in industry can be seen through descriptions of various types of industrial communities. The company-dominated community has its advantages and disadvantages for worker-manager relationships. Boom towns and mush-room communities have their peculiar problems. A different pattern of community living was established at Oak Ridge, Tennessee, in 1942: in three years, 75,000 people gathered to live in this town in a "semi-hush-hush" atmosphere, in which special-interest clubs became a basis for social relationships.

Cape Kennedy represents a type of boom town that is most likely to endure, having sprung up from an original town of 22,000 people. More questionable is the town that develops around defense plants whose con-tracts could be canceled with little warning. Some say that community growth is related not only to the section of the country being developed but to community brain power. For example, the gaps left in the New Eng-land economy by the wholesale departure of the textile industry are being filled by electronics, spurred on through research and development.

A Steel Town. Another community, described by Walker in the book *Steeltown,* gives us a somewhat different picture of the social variables in the industrial community. Here is a steel town of 14,000 people, Ellwood City, Pennsylvania, where there are few status differences of importance. In contrast to the three hundred-year-old Yankee City, this steel town was established around the turn of the century. People had moved there vol-untarily to work in steel plants. The managers always lived near workers, and still do. Worker-manager relations are a part of "big steel"; few real decisions are made at the local level. It is most unlikely that Ellwood City will ever show community behavior similar to that of the Yankee City crisis. The communities are just different and always have been [42].

New Industrialization. Urban and regional planning is now a profession, a subject in which one can receive a Ph.D., and much of the curriculum involves work in the behavioral sciences. The classical pattern of job hunters ranging widely on their own is giving some ground to "jobography," some of it planned and some of it just happening. Communities are fight-ing to keep industries from moving out of town as well as putting on drives to bring new industries into the community. The industrial community, says Hunter [19], is often the hundreds or thousands of people who are held together by a single enterprise. One community may be labor-oriented and another spurn the big unions. The recent industrialization of the South has led to labor being accepted in government-contract industries and often rejected when the industry is locally owned and operated. Decentralization of the meat-packing industry in the Midwest is causing union organizational problems that did not exist in the larger urban areas.

Blumer [3], in taking a look at the researches dealing with industrially retarded regions of the world, challenges the view that the early stages of

industrialization inevitably lead to frustration, aggression, and rebellious-
ness on the part of the workers. Empirical evidence shows that wide variations in working conditions, rewards, and worker-management relations
are more important than industrialization per se. Social and cultural factors
and accelerated social change are important. Studies of several Texas
communities, embedded in the sociocultural matrix of natural settings rather
than the artificial environment of the laboratory, show that it is quite possible to reduce intergroup hostility and conflict within such communities,
providing cooperation favorable to industrial development [40].

The New Suburbia. What may be a threat to one community, such as the
moving in of a minority group, may prove to be an asset to another. Racial
or ethnic discrimination and social or economic stratification, with their
related fears and resentments, help determine community patterns. The
community not only contributes to the security or insecurity of the individual but is a place where behaviors can be manifested through informal
organizations. One interesting description of how this can occur is found
in some examples of the new suburbia described in Whyte's *Organization
Man* [46].

In contrast with the rigidities of the traditional community, where inter-
locking family relationships fix the individual's position and where he can
move upward only by sanction of the next upper group, we find that the
new suburbia offers more in the way of classlessness.

Levittown, Pennsylvania, is representative of a type of the new suburbia
where the goal is not to keep up with the Joneses; rather, it is, as Whyte
puts it, to "keep down with them." Conspicuous display is frowned upon.
Even in a single neighborhood, an item which would be quite acceptable in
one block might be regarded as flagrant showing off in another. True, the
new suburbia is fraught with problems and conflicts as is any other community, but here a man is more on his own in his chances for upward mobility. This melting pot of people from many industries, of men with many
interests and varied backgrounds, is a growing pattern of a community life
which contrasts with the Yankee Cities and Steeltowns. The more education the person has, the more mobility he shows. The higher the educational
level, the more extensive is the migration.

One study shows, for example, that of those who worked their way
through college outside their home state, 69 per cent did not return. And
it is of interest that long-distance movers report that almost half of their
business is composed of company people being transferred from one place
to another. Although over one-half of the United States population do not
live in the houses in which they were born, many people do not get far
away from home. A survey made by the Federal government in the middle
sixties showed that 50 per cent of Americans have not traveled more than

200 miles from home, some 60 per cent have never spent a night in a hotel, and 80 per cent have never taken a trip in an airplane.

As the seats of economic power continue to shift from local institutions to national organizations, the middle-management group of people will move more often, some up and some out. The new suburbia provides something of a temporary home, not unlike army-post life for the family.

The Large City. For the middle-aged people whose children are grown there is some movement back to the city. For those who can afford it the movement is into downtown luxury apartments. Just as electricity made the once lowly candle a symbol of gracious living, so a fireplace in the new apartment dwelling represents middle-age success for many of those who say they are tired of fighting freeway traffic. But for the most part the large city, save for certain isolated high socioeconomic sections, is composed of many and varied middle to poor neighborhoods. Miller and Form [31] have shown that the uneven distribution of rent and occupations in the large city supports the notion that the city is made up of a lot of local and self-contained industrial neighborhoods which are relatively isolated from one another. The lack of interaction among these neighborhoods reinforces the prejudices that each group has toward the others. Some of the tensions of work may well be related to the fact that the larger the city, the less its different segments appreciate the lives, habits, institutions, and culture of those in other areas.

How a man lives may well be related to the way he works, thinks, and acts. In one large city, there are two railroads belonging to a steel empire. One railroad, which serves a number of steel mills, is located within city boundaries, and most of its workers live in crowded, run-down, tough neighborhoods. This railroad has a history of frequent labor complaints, strikes, and threats of strikes. The other railroad, owned and managed by the same people, serves as a connection between the steel mills and ore supply. It employs about the same number of people. This railroad has a history of good labor relations and few strikes. Its workers live in small settlements along the railroad and, for the most part, own their modest homes and a couple of acres of land. Although the workers of both railroads receive the same pay rates and belong to the same national union, their behavior on the job is different. One reason for this difference seems apparent to the common management of the two railroads: the community way of living affects job satisfactions.

POWER STRUCTURES IN THE COMMUNITY

We have seen in the Yankee City studies how power in the community shifted away from industry as paternalism died out and absentee management took over; in its place, the union found acceptance and power. Variations of this power shift and struggle in the last two decades have been duplicated all over the country. As communities have grown in size, common participation by the entire population has decreased. Businessmen who long held an advantage over the workers through organization, legal knowledge, and resources have found that national unions can now compete with them on even terms. Both power groups have become public relations conscious. They vie for community approval and compete with each other in providing community service programs, athletic teams, and youth organizations. But out of this power struggle has come much good. As one looks at the successful growth of community charities, one sees that they have been made possible by labor and management organizations joining in harmony with each other and with the rest of the community. Both the union and industry have learned the importance of good community relations. Social welfare has developed as one area in which the two can cooperate *and* compete. National union leaders have extended their welfare activities beyond union membership. In the struggle for power, the "lack of welfare" can become a threat to union loyalty and allegiance.

Competition for Power. Both management and labor are conscious of trying to win the loyalty of the workers. They struggle for the confidence of both the workers and the community. One's loss may be the other's gain. We have seen industry lose the power struggle in Yankee City, and we have examples of the difficulties of unions in organizing small, rural area plants.

Labor and management both have a stake in education and in local, state, and national politics. Labor-union attempts to influence formal education have been limited primarily to participating in educational conferences at the college level and trying to influence local school systems to abstain from antilabor teaching at the high school level. Industries, on the other hand, have become a primary source of support to independent colleges and for years have supplied funds for huge college scholarship and fellowship programs. At the secondary school level, particularly in the vocational skills, industry has had a marked influence on education. The Du Pont Company, for example, has an elaborate program for supplying educational information on our free-enterprise system; this information has been successfully integrated with the regular courses in a number of schools. At the higher-education level, the Standard Oil Company of New Jersey has been most progressive in setting up top-level conferences between college teachers and industrial leaders. Such programs, of course, are not antilabor in any sense, but are designed to acquaint educators with the philosophies of industry. Fortunately for education, the public schools have not become an area where labor and management have fought for power.

In the area of leisure and recreation, labor is going all out to win community support in its power struggle for the workers' loyalty. During working hours, industry has control over the worker. A good work situation itself can provide an excellent medium for building up loyalty to the company, and this threatens loyalty to the union. To combat this, union locals have turned their attention to getting the workers together for cards, beer, athletic events, and family picnics, since they have long since found out that, save for emergency situations, union meetings themselves draw small audiences of members. So successful have the unions been in using the leisure time of workers that management is beginning to support more of what once were regarded as recreational frills. Businessmen are learning that cliques formed at work often feed back into community activities in ways that reinforce group ties between industry and the community.

THE BUSINESS CLIMATE

The business climate has been defined as the net result of all outside conditions affecting the cost and ease of operating a business in a community. These conditions may be social, economic, or political, and they may have their origin at the local, state, or national level. These conditions represent such tangible things as tax rates and such intangible things as the general attitude of the community toward the business.

The success of any industry depends upon employees, customers, stockholders, and related businesses; and management has long been conscious of this. More recently, however, the business climate has come to be a new dimension of management responsibility.

Business-climate Elements. The General Electric Company has been in the forefront in applying survey methods to appraise the business climate in the community. Some of the questions used in its appraisal guide require answers based on observation and judgment. Others require extensive investigation to come up with accurate facts and figures [16].

General Electric has determined that a favorable business climate is a composite of some eight elements:

1 *Community progressiveness:* A realistically progressive attitude on the part of political, religious, and professional leaders toward sound community growth and city planning, along with citizen understanding of community and business problems.

2 *Government:* Honest and efficient government, supported by a safe majority of alert, intelligent voters who have the balanced best interests of the community at heart, with an absence of unreasonably restrictive regulations or financial handicaps imposed by the local, state, and federal governments.

3 *Labor relations:* A sound working relationship between employers and employees as evidenced by an absence of unwarranted strikes and slowdowns over a number of years and, where collective bargaining contracts are in effect, a constructive and fair union leadership which acts as the servant rather than the master of its membership.

4 *People:* An adequate supply of people to fill employment needs who have a good work attitude, who are properly educated, who are in good physical condition, and who have a good understanding of how our business system operates and their stake in its success.

5 *Labor costs:* Wage and salary rates and payment methods which are fair to employees, and at the same time provide an opportunity for employers to operate profitably in competition with other manufacturers of their product lines.

6 *Community services & facilities:* Adequate community services and facilities such as banks, hotels, utilities, shopping facilities, health facilities, and the required commercial services needed in operating businesses.

7 *Social, cultural & educational institutions:* A social and cultural atmosphere that will attract and hold good professional employees, including good and adequate schools, an enlightened press, radio and TV, and an abundance of healthful recreational opportunities.

8 *Business citizenship:* A serious-minded assumption of business citizenship responsibilities on the part of all employers in the community as evidenced by consistently good employee relations and courageous leadership in civic and political affairs.*

General Electric reports that the payoff in business-climate research is somewhat analogous to the payoff in product research: both are long-term propositions. Years of time, effort, and money may be required before an investment in product research begins to net a return in sales and profits, and so it is with business-climate research. The same sustained effort is required in evolving marketable products from research. After years of experience General Electric finds that every community it has studied harbors within it untapped resources of skills, intelligence, energy, and dedication which, if mobilized in a common effort, could make it a better place in which to live, work, and do business. A good business climate is also an environment conducive to community progress and prosperity. "As a concept, business climate is a 'philosophy' of business conduct in its community relations—a way of life."

Many companies have formulated programs of community service. Pollard, in writing on the emerging pattern in corporate giving in the *Harvard Business Review* [34], concludes that investments in communities and, particularly, in higher education are investments in the companies' tomorrow. Today's new managers know that companies must help to nourish the main sources of educated manpower. It is estimated that by 1970 a total of

* Reproduced here by permission of the General Electric Company.

800,000 American business concerns will be contributing to higher education.

THE MEDIANA STUDY

One of the changes taking place in the growing industrial towns across America is the increasing role being played by business itself in community affairs through local voluntary associations. These community projects are frequently initiated outside the framework of local government. Often the mayor and city council appear to be dragging their heels while organized groups of citizens exhort the community to push toward progress. These voluntary associations include the chamber of commerce, the community chest, service clubs, and various kinds of citizens' committees. Their influence ranges from stimulating local authorities to take various actions to virtually running the town.

Characteristic of this contemporary American community, in contrast to that of the past, is the status gap between the personnel of the local government and the community leaders. The elective, or appointive, offices of municipal, county, and even state governments are manned mostly by people whose social positions may be below those community leaders who belong to the country club, Rotary, and the chamber of commerce. The city fathers and county commissioners are usually recruited from among local lawyers of uncertain income, small proprietors, courthouse politicians, and similar miscellaneous persons. Political control in the town seems to be with one group, while money, status, and intellect are with the other.

What Is Expected? The business climate is a question of growing interest to more and more of the large industrial organizations that are moving into these communities with their branch operations. What is expected of them?

We wish to report here a description of the organizational structures of an American community, a description sponsored by the American Telephone and Telegraph Company and presented by Rossi [37]. The study was made in a midwestern industrial town of some forty-five thousand population, with the code name of Mediana. Data were collected through personal interviews with community leaders and businessmen and from a sample of the general population.

Why is there a strong drive among businessmen toward participation in community activities? What functions are served for business itself? This study concludes that we must look beyond the manifest or surface motivations to view the community as a system performing various types of functions for the participating organizations and for individuals. Not only do community organizations provide a framework for social life, for gregarious pleasures, but participation provides a context in which businessmen get access (in varying degrees) to those who control the economic aspects of the community.

For the telephone business, Mediana Bell found it important that its commercial managers have access to government officials, to other businessmen, and to the local newspaper. Says the report:

> Although the traffic in favors among businessmen and between businessmen and community leaders is not a traffic in heavy goods, it does constitute a steady flow of considerable magnitude. The stream of favors is a lubricant, making the conduct of business in Mediana much easier than it would be if every request had to go through official channels and be subject to bureaucratic scrutiny.

The community participation system provides a means for ordering firms and individuals who have no intrinsic ordering relationships among themselves. The reputation of a firm, as well as the borrowed prestige that may go with it for the individual, is in part determined by the extent to which its managers participate in community affairs, providing the managers are not allowed to participate beyond what is their "proper level." The primary determiner here is size and wealth, and some large companies encourage their high-level officials to manage the united fund drive, thus functioning as a prestige broker.

Businessmen prefer to participate in a community climate free of opposition. Participating in political affairs is acceptable only when the elements of hostility and possible opposition are moved from the scene, preferably in advance. Hence there is a preference for citizens' committees which give equal representation to prestigious minority groups.

It is important also that community projects be well scouted in advance when an organization man may be involved. The failure of a high-level manager to put across his project would not only lower his prestige in the community but actually give cause for the home office to question his managerial ability. Hence local small businessmen often become the leaders of many community projects. They have less to lose in the event of failure. Although leadership is open to the larger outsider firms, it is not expected of them as much as it is of the locally owned large company.

Another illustration of the dimension of company size in community leadership is the readiness with which the recent arrival in town is accepted. The new manager of a large organization can find leadership acceptance more quickly and more easily than the new manager of a small enterprise. All the outsider from the prestigious firm has to do is give in to the many invitations he will receive.

Roles within the Community. Such studies as this one offer guides to both the industry planning to operate in the smaller community and the individual in his career development. Certain expectations help define the roles to be played within the community system. Companies are expected to make financial contributions varying according to the size and prosperity of the enterprise and to supply personnel to help man committees. Those firms that perform in gracious style get more recognition than do those that perform out of duty and with reluctance. Rossi describes the nature of this style element with the following examples.

Two companies received commendatory recognition from the united fund. Mediana Power's manager was praised because he had worked out a method, through cooperation with the Utility Workers' Union, of getting around the company's stricture against payroll deductions for the fund. Union representatives and company personnel men stationed themselves at the pay office on payday and solicited contributions from the power-company employees.

Another company received special praise because of its policy of permitting its workers to put in some four hours of overtime at time and a half, the wages so earned to be contributed to the united fund. The overtime is now worked on a particular day each year, designated as Good Neighbors Day. Employees get special stickers for their cars and for windows of their homes as status symbols.

The business managers themselves have somewhat less spelled-out expectations other than "to do their share." Included, besides a reasonable corporate contribution to the united fund, is allowing fund solicitors to have access to the firm's workers. The company should send some of its managerial personnel into the various clubs and its younger executives into the Jaycees. And, of course, some member of the firm should be in the country club.

Expectations of a company held by the general public show the public to be more interested in the problems of everyday life. Typically, the average citizen of Mediana was concerned with such problems as parking, street conditions, and adequate recreation for children. When asked what should be the obligations of a business to the city where it is located, respondents indicated the company should pay a decent wage, provide good working conditions, and have a fair attitude toward labor unions.

Among the various management levels within a particular firm, each gradually shakes down into its own niche in the community organizational structure. In Mediana, the chamber of commerce took people from the top levels, the chief executive of a firm often being on the board of directors. There was found to be a rank order of service clubs as well. A district commercial manager will be in Rotary, the local commercial manager in Kiwanis, and lesser officers in the lower-ranking clubs. There is a saying in Mediana to the effect that Rotary owns the town, Kiwanis runs it, and the Jaycees do all the leg work.

THE FOREIGN BUSINESS CLIMATE

Of recent interest has been the study of business climates overseas. Robinson [36] says it is essential that the company operating on the international frontier learn to appreciate those aspects of the foreign environment that differ significantly from the domestic environment where business decisions are concerned. Ability to project oneself into the position of a potential foreign associate or government leader requires sensitivity to his motives, interests, and habits. Old stereotypes are out.

Economic development through private enterprise and the research programs associated with it have gone far in helping us appreciate and to some extent understand cultural differences. Considerable care must be taken in selecting people to represent American enterprises overseas. Operations that send misfits and playboys to their foreign offices and create living conditions that isolate them do not create an appropriate image. In contrast to the ugly image, let us give a few examples of community acceptance in foreign countries [6, 7, 8, 14, 18].

One company working with the Venezuelan Ministry of Education has made possible extensive programs of teacher education and has helped to create an entirely new school so situated that it serves not only for the children of its own employees but the general public as well. Sears, Roebuck, which has effected a highly successful operation in Mexico, attributes much of its acceptance to what was learned through application of its social science research [48].

How can quiet little towns set in a lovely and historic countryside preserve their cherished values when industrialization begins? And what, if anything, can industries do to help them? In particular, can an American-based company gain acceptance in this foreign setting?

The prospect of industrialization at first aroused mixed feelings in Stenungsund, Sweden. It was a town already in economic decline. Its population was down to some two thousand inhabitants; people had been leaving to look for jobs elsewhere. The local city fathers proposed to make the town into an industrial center, and Jersey Standard wished to build a chemical plant there. Studies of site resulted in a book some 3 inches thick, but equally important was a study made of the people and their attitudes. A series of surveys, paid for by the company and the town, were made. Even Swedish noise specialists were called in for their advice, and the local citizenry participated in the planning of parks and housing from the beginning. The enterprise has been a success both economically and in terms of community acceptance. Community leaders and company management working together supplied positive answers to the questions. The countryside still has its old churches, forests, fields, and sunshine. It has both the sense of the past and the promise of the future, says one observer [41].

To a large extent the measure of any business climate is a measure of people's behavior. And the attitudes and behaviors of people are related to community classes. Let us now take a look at this aspect of the industrial community.

COMMUNITY CLASSES

Much has been written about classes of people by anthropologists, sociologists, psychologists, and other behavioral scientists. In the following sections of this chapter, we wish simply to present those descriptions which we feel are relevant to understanding some of the human problems of the industrial community. These descriptions have been selected from many scholarly writings.

White-collar Workers and Wageworkers. Any small industrial community may be divided, in general terms, into three social classes—the manager group, the wageworkers, and, somewhere in between and sharing characteristics of both, the white-collar workers.

White-collar people share with wageworkers the characteristic that they both rely on occupation rather than property for their source of income. Mills [32], in his book *White Collar,* points out that in the early nineteenth century probably four-fifths of the occupied population were self-employed enterprisers. At the present time, only about one-fifth of the people come within this category. The four-fifths of the people who now earn a living do so by working for the 2 or 3 per cent of the population who own 40 or 50 per cent of the private property in this country. This four-fifths includes both wageworkers and white-collar workers. The importance of the white-collar worker may be indicated partly by the fact that the selling of services, which determines the livelihood of most white-collar workers, has grown until the money now paid out for services exceeds that paid out for things.

Though white-collar employees and wageworkers are alike in that they are both without income from property, their characteristics differ in other respects. In terms of prestige, white-collar employees claim higher status than wageworkers. Partly this is assured, because their income in general is higher. But they also gain status because they live on prestige borrowed from the firm itself; they are the assistants of authority and hence exercise a derived power. Psychologically, white-collar groups have successfully claimed and maintained more prestige than wageworkers. How permanent this position will remain is in question. Its defense is a part of the power struggle now going on between management and labor organizations.

White-collar workers are themselves divided into two groups, particularly in a smaller community. The higher group includes high-income salesmen and professional and managerial employees. The lower group includes clerks and salespeople. Despite this clear distinction, members of the wageworking class blend all white-collar workers, both higher and lower, into a group called "business" and make little distinction between them. To them, these business people are all "pencil pushers who sit around and don't work."

Views about the Management World. The white-collar workers and the wageworkers have diverse pictures of management. To the worker, management is "something one reports to in the office," "the printed instruction," "a sign on the bulletin board." To the white-collar group, management is "one part people who give you the nod, one part system, one part yourself." Mills makes the point that, as one of the managed sees it, "you are on view from above. The money you handle is somebody else's money, the papers you sort and shuffle already bear somebody else's marks. You are the servant of decision, the assistant of authority."

Of course, to the people at the top, management is the place where power is concentrated. Management sees its job as one of making both wageworkers and white-collar workers feel a part of the organization and willing to carry out company policy and procedures. Communication between top and bottom must be so structured, management believes, that commands can go down and be understood and accepted and that information can come up and be understood and acted upon. Thus the image of itself which management presents to each of the other groups is very important.

Influences within the City. In the city, industrial influence is different. Human relations are more impersonal. White-collar workers live apart from wageworkers as well as from top-management people. They tend to live around those plants which employ them.

This isolation and the communication patterns which grow up may account for the tension between industry and various parts of the community, conclude Miller and Form [31]. They go on to generalize that the larger the city, the less its different segments appreciate the lives, institutions, and culture of those in other areas.

Resistance to Change. When work and residence are in the same neighborhood, the community is more family-oriented than in those instances where the breadwinner has to travel distances to work. There is evidence

to show that a man may be unhappy about a promotion if it means breaking into established habit structures. The author is familiar with one such
case which led one man to ask for his old job back.

Jack was a general supervisor for a railroad. He had worked his way up
from trainman over a period of twenty years. He had lived in the house where
he was born nearly forty years earlier. Jack was a respected white-collar
leader in the community of 25,000 inhabitants and enjoyed his businessman's
status. Promotion into headquarters of the railroad in a city of some 1.5 million
people was offered Jack, and he accepted the new job. He was quite successful
as far as the technical aspects of the job were concerned, but he was very unhappy about being in a new suburbia of the city. In less than two years he
asked for a transfer back to his old supervisory job in his home town. When
I asked him why he was willing to give up status and more pay to return home,
his answer was simple—"I liked my old way of life better."

No doubt there are those who would dislike moving from the city to the
country. People resist change, and perhaps they resist change in community
living habits as much as or more than changes in habits of work. This
is a problem that has to be reckoned with in moving industries. Industrial
decentralization may mean changing the routines of the city dweller as
he moves to the smaller town. Here he finds things "too small." It may
mean just as big a change for the farmer who turns to the factory to supplement his income. He finds things "too large." We can see how, apart
from uprooting both groups from their past social patterns, the rural-urban
conflict can become a morale problem within the plant itself.

Resistance to change takes many forms. Researchers have found that
some people reject the idea of using salt-free sea water, and complaints
have been numerous. In one coastal town it was found necessary to secretly
feed parts of the saline conversion into the water system for weeks to prevent resistance to its use for research purposes. The British Ministry of
Housing found that when it tried to move working-class families from grimy,
overcrowded, urban slums to a well-planned garden city with good schools
and no heavy traffic, resistance developed. Used to the grubby intimacy of
city life, transplanted urbanites missed the profusion of corner pubs,
neighborhood dance halls, and the ready help of neighbors and friends.

Work Shifts. With the decline in agriculture many rural workers are
virtually forced into industry. Although a few divide their time between
working on the farm and in the factory, more and more are migrating to
industrial communities. Here they find almost everything different from
their previous mode of living. One of the biggest problems in adjustment
is having the workday come in the middle of the night. The U.S. Department of Labor points out that more and more industries are employing
second and third shifts during good times. One-third of the production

workers in the automobile industry normally work other than in the day-time.

With the growth of continuous-process manufacturing, many machines have to be manned around the clock. In the plastics industry, for example, it is not economically feasible to shut down certain machines. It costs too much to get them heated up properly, and stopping the operation gums up the liquid materials. Again, many plants are so costly to build that they have to be kept going two or three shifts to justify the capital expenditures.

For men on the second or third shift, family life is all but disrupted. Particularly is this true where more than one member of a family works. Coordinating shifts, or turns, within a family is almost impossible, since turns for any one man change so often.

COMMUNITY TIES

Arensberg [1] emphasizes the importance of knowing how people live in order to understand the relationship between community and industry. Although the tie between work and community may often be indirect, it is most important. He illustrates the point through a firsthand observation of the behaviors underlying a paper-mill strike. Fortunately for his study, he was accepted by both union and management. Each gave him access to records and allowed him to hold interviews both on and off the job.

The strike, it turned out, had been called by the paper-machine crew. To management it seemed strange, since this particular department was not involved in an incentive scheme which had been introduced in the cutting room. The incentive scheme was said to be the reason for calling the strike. But why would another department, seemingly unaffected, call the men out? To management, unaccustomed to thinking about the close relationship between the work situation and the community, it seemed incomprehensible that men in no way connected during working hours with the crucial department should feel themselves aggrieved.

On investigation it was found that the company's incentive scheme had its effects at a level, as Arensberg put it, "far beyond the formal industrial relationships prescribed by the company's organization chart." The two sets of workers were bound by ties of kinship and by traditional patterns of age and occupational prestige, entirely outside the factory. The company's engineers had done far more than merely provide a better output in a single working department. They had, in fact, reversed the customary patterns of authority. The new incentive scheme had set juniors and inferiors to hurrying up their seniors and superiors. The machine-room men had struck against the disturbance of their community.

This incident brings out another important point when we consider problems of classes. Here we find illustrated the lack of perception on the part of management of the way the workers look at problems. Differences in class perception often underlie industrial conflict even though something more specific may be named as the cause.

SOCIAL FORCES WITHIN THE COMMUNITY

Whether one comes from the city, the town, or the rural community, he is aware, somewhat at least, of the system of caste and class which governs American life. He is interested in getting a picture of the social influences shaping his own career. The college student has no doubt seen, firsthand, instances where some families have stayed at one level for generations, while others have risen to the top and stayed, and others have fallen to the bottom. What are the factors that determine social position? What is the subtle interplay of education, money, profession, and club and business associations that builds the social pyramid? What are the secrets which have made some men victims of downward mobility and carried others to high places of power and prestige? Such were the questions that led to Warner's study of a representative community in the Midwestern part of the United States. Warner, in his book *Democracy in Jonesville* [43], describes the social forces that make the American community run. He and his associates began their study during World War II; they continued for most of a decade. In the pages to follow we shall summarize some of the findings of this unusual study.

The Jonesville Study. Jonesville (a code name) has a population of a little more than six thousand people. It is a town where, in terms of social hierarchy, "everybody knows everybody's place." The upper class divides into old families and new families. The first group includes those who have enjoyed wealth and position for several generations and those who have managed to retain their social position despite loss of much of their wealth. The new families include those who have climbed into top position and have succeeded in being accepted by those already there. Not every wealthy family reaches the top position. This upper class constitutes less than 3 per cent of the population in Jonesville.

The upper middle class, active in all community activities, has less wealth than those at the top. The members of this class are the prominent, substantial people to whom common men often pay deference. But they are anxious people, fearful of doing something wrong and ruining their chances for advancement. They are constantly on the alert to enter into worthy civic enterprises, particularly those of which the elite are active sponsors.

Among the people who "belong to nice families but are nobody socially" are the small shopkeepers, the skilled workers, and the clerks. Below these are the "little people," the "poor but honest" workers who live around the mill in the less well-kept part of town. Finally comes a fifth, lower lower class, the people who live "across the tracks."

The young people of each class tend to marry at their own level. Their children acquire the status of the parents, learn their way of life, and help ensure the permanence of the class system. The citizens of Jonesville know and think about class behavior, and this knowledge is one of the basic guides to proper and adaptive behavior for them all.

In Jonesville, as in all American communities, the class structure is fluid. Families or individuals may not remain in one class. Mobility may be up or down. People do not quite openly admit that there are different classes, yet through their actions they place themselves and each other in a social class. While the boy from across the tracks does not often reach the mansion, he frequently ends up with a small business on Main Street. On the other hand, there is also downward mobility. Whether movement is up or down, in or out of social groups, the social class of a person's family is the zero point for indicating a change in status.

Mobility Indicators. Eight categories of indicators of mobility emerged from the studies. First comes "educational difference." This is a prerequisite for mobility into or through the middle classes. Second comes "occupational variance," where a person is in an occupation which is evaluated as different from that of his father's status. This is basic to socioeconomic status. "Membership transference," for example, becoming a member of the Rotary Club, indicates a movement into upper-middle-class status. A fourth area of change seen in upward mobility Warner has called "activity deviation," exemplified by the man who changes his church affiliation to improve prestige.

A fifth pattern of mobility up and down is the "clique change," where the mobile person meets socially with individuals who have a different status from the one he or his family held originally. Related to this is a sixth factor, "role revision," which signifies that to move upward a person must be accepted and evaluated positively by others; he must adapt the roles he plays to his new social position.

"Interclass marriage" is a seventh aspect of mobility, which more often results in a change of social status for the woman than for the man. Acceptance of a woman who marries a man of high status doesn't always come easily. Her behavior is carefully observed and related to her background.

The eighth factor related to mobility is the "residential movement." Choice of location can be a very strong symbol of status.

THE STRUGGLE FOR UPWARD MOBILITY

What makes people want to move up? Certainly upward mobility is related to progress at both the individual and the group level; but at what price? Some psychiatrists have voiced the opinion that the struggle for upward mobility is one of the big contributing causes of mental illness in the United States.

There are two aspects of mobility. The *situation* the person finds himself in is of importance. The person is given opportunity to move ahead employmentwise by the offer of a job, or he finds himself trapped in a situation where he has to work his way out and up. The situational conditions favoring or hindering upward mobility are many. As a rule, they are easy to spot. It is more difficult, however, to get at the second aspect involved in mobility, *personal motivation*.

Levels of Aspiration. Before we go on with the subject of mobility, however, let us consider some experimental studies on levels of aspiration. Here, in a simpler setting, we can find some useful facts for our consideration. Lewin et al. have discussed the many facets of the subject. They pose the following simple problem: A person has scored 6 in shooting at a target with ring 10 at the center. He decides the next time to try for 8. He attains 5, is much disappointed, and decides to try the next time to reach 6 once more [25].

Within such a sequence there are four main points, as illustrated in Figure 18.1.

Here in our level-of-aspiration situation, the subject begins a typical sequence of events. His last performance ("has scored 6") has set his level of aspiration for the next performance ("try for 8"). The new performance was below what he tried for ("attains 5"); hence there is a "goal discrepancy." The difference between the goal level and that of the new performance is the "attainment discrepancy." This difference is one of the bases of the reaction at point 4 in the figure.

In our example the subject is really trying to hit center. This is his ideal goal. Knowing that this is too difficult for him, at least at the present, he sets his goal at 8, his "action level." It is the level of the action goal which is usually taken as the criterion for the level of aspiration for an individual at a given time. It has been found that nearly all individuals of Western culture, when first exposed to a level-of-aspiration situation, give initially a level of aspiration which is above the previous performance and under most conditions tend to keep the goal discrepancy positive.

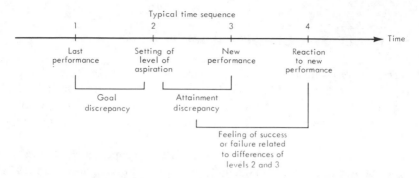

Fig. 18.1. Level of aspiration. Four main points are distinguished in a typical sequence of events in a level-of-aspiration situation: (1) last performance, (2) setting of level of aspiration for the next performance, (3) new performance, and (4) psychological reaction to the new performance. The difference between the level of the last performance and that of the new goal is called "goal discrepancy." The difference between the goal level and that of the new performance is called "attainment discrepancy." This difference is one of the bases of the reaction at (4). (From Lewin, K., Dembo, T., Festinger, L., & Sears, P. S. Levels of aspiration. In Hunt, J. McV. [Ed.]. *Personality and behavior disorders.* New York: Ronald, 1944, Vol. I., pp. 333–378.)

Generalizations about Aspirations. Being a realist about it, the individual will place his expectation somewhere within the boundary zone of his ability. Three facts we know from experiments:

1 People tend to seek a relatively high level of aspiration.

2 There is a tendency for the level of aspiration to go up only to certain limits.

3 There is a tendency for the person in his level of aspiration to stay out of an area too difficult or too easy.

The judgment of the probability of success or failure on a given level is determined by past experiences, by certain realistic situations, and, in addition, by wishes and fears. A recent failure will tend to lower the level of aspiration, and the level will decrease more after resounding failure than after a near success. Success and failure also have their cumulative effects. Experiments show that the feeling of success and failure does not depend on the absolute level of achievement. What may mean success for one person may mean failure for another; and even for the same person, the same achievement will lead sometimes to feelings of failure and sometimes to feelings of success.

Factors in Mobility. Let us now return to the question of individual motivation and upward mobility. In his studies of community life, Warner points out that the primary factor for upward mobility is a high achievement level. What is expected of a person in relation to his age level sets a standard. Traditionally, there are two basic areas for achievement. The first involves obtaining an education, and the second involves finding a place in the occupational hierarchy. Says Warner [43], "Success in one or both of these areas is almost a basis for achievement in other aspects of living. It is an expression of the ambition drive of an individual."

Achievement level is, of course, dependent upon individual ability, a special talent for science, athletics, art, and so forth.

A third factor in mobility concerns an individual's social techniques. This means behaving in ways that fit the situation. And the ability to perceive the situation and react appropriately to it is important in upward mobility.

A fourth factor that emerged from the Jonesville studies concerns the person's ambitions for getting ahead. This has been called "status anxiety." Here the person places too high a value on status symbols, seeks recognition from those in superior positions, or strives for roles which may bring prestige. The person who overreacts in trying for status lowers his chances for upward mobility.

A fifth factor in evaluating potential mobility involves what Warner has called "situational responses"—a sort of "How do other people evaluate us?" kind of thing. We are all familiar with the words used to describe the man with this asset—"knows what to do," "has a pleasant personality," "always says the right things."

Club Status Symbols. In any community one can find the club status symbols that go with upward mobility—country club, hospital charities, Daughters of the American Revolution, Rotary. Of the upper-class families in Jonesville, three-fourths belonged to at least two, and half belonged to three or all four of these clubs. In the Lions, Masons, and Eastern Star, the majority of the members came from the upper middle and lower middle classes. For the lower lower class of the Jonesville community "there isn't much."

Associations are very important for upward mobility. For some the old school tie has its importance. Membership in women's clubs, the PTA, and the Red Cross provide associations at another level. Individuals at the top of the social ladder are ready to identify with their own social status; those at the bottom derive little ego satisfaction from such identification. At the bottom of the socioeconomic hierarchy there is less feeling of belongingness. Maybe belongingness is *the* basic need underlying the struggles for upward mobility.

Study of a High-status Community. Lest one conclude that the struggle is over when high socioeconomic status has been attained, he should take a look at what is involved in staying up there. The sociological study of a high-status suburban community of 17,000 people has been described in the book *Crestwood Heights*. Here is pictured the community of material abundance, the "dream community where many aspire to live, but only a few can," populated to a large extent by those who have achieved rapid personal mobility. Here is described a community where the child, who in more static social situations might be permitted to take certain aspects of the common life for granted, is made to "appreciate" the close connection between effort and achievement; it is a community where one cannot take anything for granted [38].

The person who aspires to the Heights in his upward mobility must be prepared to follow the highly developed pattern of movement from one job to another, from one place of residence to another, from one city to another, from one class position to another. The man and woman of Crestwood Heights have few bonds that cannot be broken at the promise of a promotion. They have been prepared for this from the cradle if they were born into this society.

Mobility must be matched by opportunity for training, for employment, and for advancement. To the man bent upon an executive career, training includes both the necessary technical skills and the social graces, plus the strong desire to manage. The executive or professional man of the Heights must be ready to abandon cherished usages and techniques as new ones arise. He must be willing to acquire new conceptions of life and organization and to revise constantly in later life his procedures within his chosen field.

The authors make the point that the differences between the careers of the person who has risen by his own effort and the person who has been born and brought up in Crestwood Heights have a relation to the flexibility which is so essential to the executive in a rapidly changing society. The person who is "born into a good start" is more likely to accept current techniques and practices than is the individual who is struggling upward. Psychologically, in work or in play, the key to survival in the Heights is *competition*. Success in making the Heights or staying there may well depend upon how well the person is prepared for competition at this high level, particularly in the more subtle phases of the status struggle.

SOCIAL CLASS AND PERSONALITY

Many of the problems found in industry and in the industrial community are related to social classes and to the individual behavior of each person in the lower class, the middle class, and the upper class. In their book on the psychology of adjustment, Shaffer and Shoben [39] have presented a summary picture of how social-class membership determines in large measure personality traits. The neighborhood in which he lives, the groups to which he belongs, and the rewards and punishments to which he is exposed determine in large part the child's learning environment and what he becomes as an adult.

The Lower Class. These authors describe the mother in the lower class as being closer to her baby in many ways than the mother in the middle and upper classes. Nursing continues longer, and weaning is far less abrupt than is usual in the middle-class home. Toilet training is delayed, and infantile genital play is not inhibited. The child is permitted greater freedom in his explorations and given more prompt and affectionate attention when he gets into difficulty. On the other hand, the lower-class parents are quick to anger. As the child grows up these parents resort to ridicule, shaming, whipping, and other forms of physical punishment. It is easy to see that growing up under both economic and psychological privation conditions one to belonging to protective groups and to exhibiting "irrational" behavior (from the viewpoint of higher classes) such as overeating when food is abundant or overheating the home when fuel is plentiful. When viewed from above, these people are often considered shiftless and lacking in thrift and foresight. Their behavior in spending is as irrational as that of the person who has been under the strain of prolonged unemployment. Because they are generally deprived of "things," lower-class people have a strong urge to overbuy when they get money. These have-not frustrations tend to strengthen the drives for immediate gratification. Not only is there an attitude of seizing upon the pleasures of the moment, but these people tend to react with a greater freedom of emotional expression than is found among the middle class.

Children and adolescents from the lower class are less inhibited in their expression of sex and anger. Fights of a physical nature between husband and wife are frequent. Parents even teach their children to fight with fists and knives and to hit first. Dirty fighting appears to be one way of attaining considerable status both within the family and from one's peers. Interestingly enough, seeking protection from parents and fellow gang members is quite acceptable, in contrast to the middle-class emphasis on self-reliance.

Through connections with industrial supervisors in several different kinds of industries, this writer has accumulated a number of instances of "low-class behaviors" of workers which by middle-class standards would be regarded as crude. One of the most difficult tasks with which the industrial supervisor has to contend is trying to break through the barriers of low-level behavior. One foreman expressed it thus: "These people don't know any better and don't want to know better." [2, 4, 22]

The Middle Class. Unlike lower-class parents, middle-class parents make a great effort to get the child to "live right," do well in school, and to think in terms of long-range goals and delayed rewards. A conscious effort is often made to subdue immediate gratifications and learn to discipline oneself. Education is designed to facilitate future achievement. In contrast to their lower-class counterparts, the children from the middle classes are taught responsibilities, independence, and self-reliance. Physical aggression is frowned upon, overt sex expression is regarded as indecent, courtship and marriage are regulated by rules of right and wrong conduct.

The middle-class person develops within a pattern of denying impulse gratifications in favor of developing initiative. He strives to learn appropriate social as well as technical skills. He struggles for improvement, but at some risk. With attainment being a dominant goal, failure becomes an ever-present threat.

The Upper Class. What of the upper class? Here, with a strong emphasis on taste, manners, good form, and family reputation, a child is taught that he is superior. This may be an asset to the person if he does not have to face too much of the reality of rough and tough competition. It can be a liability where exaggerated values are overly stressed. The secure status of an upper-class member is somewhat automatically conferred by his family, and it can be retained so long as the person does not step out of line. Sometimes the individual brought up in the protection of his upper-class standing finds the going rough when finances become depleted and "family security" is gone.

Achievement Needs. Modern-day industrial communities offer a ready-made laboratory situation for studying achievement needs. The industrial worker who has grown up in a lower-class society is not interested in long periods of preparation and work which will lead to later rewards. He wants his rewards now. Pension plans and programs of future security have little or no motivational value for this person.

To the middle-class person in industry, achievement needs are most important. Sacrifices for education are willingly made; marriage may be delayed to provide for the period of professional training. But these achievement needs come at a price. The struggle for achievement often brings on anxiety which leaves in its wake compulsions to hard work or rationalization to cover up failures.

The attitudes, the feelings, the strivings, and the complacencies of many people at the same or at different levels in industry are more easily under-stood when we analyze their class background. One complaint frequently heard from the successful man with a high achievement drive is that "so many people in industry do not want responsibility." And there are those, perhaps, with a low achievement drive, who wonder "why so many people in industry want to be president."

INDUSTRIALIZATION AND THE FAMILY

The man at work, be he an executive or a laborer, does not function alone in his industrial environment. It is almost inevitable that his problems of work are shared with his family, and the feedback from family life affects his work. Essential to the study of the whole man in his total community is the study of the family. About two-thirds of families have one or more members earning a wage or salary in a nonagricultural industry [12, 24].

Socioeconomic Environment. Industry directly and indirectly helps estab-lish the socioeconomic environment within the community, even to the extent of influencing marriages. In their jobs, large numbers of men and women become acquainted. Several studies have shown that one of the primary factors related to who marries whom is proximity. Men and women who live within relatively short distances of each other tend to marry. People who live in the same neighborhood usually come from the same class and often from the same status groups. Marriages occur between people who are thrown together at work or who meet through their posi-tions in the social structure.

   The modern industrial-urban family has a high degree of equality among its members. The father is less of an authoritarian figure than in the patriarchal family, particularly where the wife and/or children work for pay. Although those who work may leave their problems at the office or not talk about their work at home, much about these problems is revealed by attitudes, particularly where feelings are involved. Men at all levels of society concentrate daily at their place of work, leaving their homes for a world of often different values and traditions. In all levels of society, says our industrial sociologist, the husband is but a part-time member of the family who must somehow adjust his work life to the demands of the family life. Some men succeed here, but many fail. One man may see his "work self" dominate; another may see the "family self" win out. Here one may find a key to personal adjustment. How a man behaves with his family often reveals something about how well his needs are being satisfied at work.

Work and the Family. To the man in the upper levels of society with prestige and authority gained at work, there may be little carry-over into his family life. The pressure of life at the high occupational levels may mean the man has little time to devote to his family. In either case the work self differs from the family self. This is particularly true where the wife has adequate funds of her own to allow her some independence.

To the middle-class white-collar man, the situation is often different. The income of the white-collar worker is usually superior to his wife's; hence the family is wholly or in part dependent on the husband's wages. But still his family has not a complete idea of what the man has to put up with in his work. He has difficulty transferring his feelings of accomplishment or lack of accomplishment to his family. The family may observe the strains of his failure or try to share in his victories, but with little real success.

The status position of the worker may be as low within his family as it is at work. If the wife or the children work as wage earners, they may make out as well as or better than the husband. This very weakness of the father's position may cause him to play an authoritarian role in the family as a defensive behavior. For the unemployed father, with the mother as breadwinner, there is often role shifting. Some studies of the family as a unit of interacting personalities conclude that we must ask how the child is socialized into a particular family, how he develops life roles, for example, as a scapegoat, that may keep him culturally handicapped [17].

For the worker, the manager, or the professional man there is a total environment. To put it simply, the total environment for the individual consists of "problems in the office and the factory" and "problems where we live." Automation, technological changes, world conditions—all impinge upon the individual, often creating a climate of uncertainty. Invention has a way of opening up opportunities for some and denying them to others; perhaps we should remember, along with Thoreau: "The mass of men lead lives of quiet desperation."

SUGGESTIONS FOR SELECTIVE READING

Abegglen, J. C. *The Japanese factory.* Glencoe, Ill.: Free Press, 1958. Organizations whose goals are divergent from comparable North American plants.

Dahl, R. A. *Who governs?* New Haven, Conn.: Yale University Press, 1962. A case study of New Haven, Connecticut, and theories of political behavior.

Freedman, L., & Cotter, C. P. (Eds.) *Issues of the sixties: VI. The changing American character.* Belmont, Calif.: Wadsworth, 1963. A collection of readings about urbanization, family, and education.

General Electric Company. *Business climate: A handbook of effective business climate programming.* New York: Author, 1963. Gives details of the practical study of communities.

Hagen, E. E. *How economic growth begins: A theory of social change.* Homewood, Ill.: Dorsey, 1962. Economic growth in Asia and Latin America.

Havighurst, R. J., et al. *Growing up in River City.* New York: Wiley, 1962. Readable report of a longitudinal study of youth in a small Midwestern community.

Hershey Chocolate Corporation. *The story of Hershey: The chocolate town.* Hershey, Pa.: Author, 1960. The growth of a community around an industry.

Hodges, W. *Company and community.* New York: Harper & Row, 1958. A study of success and failure in community projects.

Horowitz, I. L. (Ed.) *The new sociology.* Fair Lawn, N.J.: Oxford University Press, 1964. Essays dealing with social science and social theories as seen by sociologists.

Joshi, B. L., & Rose, L. E. *Political change in Nepal.* Berkeley, Calif.: University of California Press, 1966. A socio-psychological study of politics and personality in a transitional society.

Lindzey, G. *Projective techniques and cross-cultural research.* New York: Appleton-Century-Crofts, 1961. Uses and misuses of projective techniques in psychological and anthropological research.

Lynch, K. *The image of the city.* Cambridge, Mass.: M.I.T., 1960. A study of the visual quality of Boston, Jersey City, and Los Angeles.

Marrow, A. J. *Changing patterns of prejudice.* Philadelphia: Chilton, 1962. A study of the antagonisms that keep people apart in New York City.

Mills, C. W. *White-collar: The American middle-class.* Fair Lawn, N.J.: Oxford University Press, 1951. A provocative book about business and community.

Mowitz, R. J., & Wright, D. S. *Profile of a metropolis.* Detroit: Wayne State University Press, 1962. A case-method study of Detroit beset with problems.

Mumford, L. *The city in history.* New York: Harcourt, Brace & World, 1961. A biological and social entity in which people lead vicarious lives.

Organization for European Economic Co-operation. *Social research and industry in Europe.* The Hague: W. P. Van Stockum & Zoon N.V., 1960. Problems and perspectives; in English translation.

Rand, C. *Cambridge, U.S.A.* New York: Oxford University Press, 1964. Growth of a new type of intellectually oriented industrial community.

Robinson, R. D. *Cases in international business.* New York: Holt, 1962. Discusses social traditions and how they are changing throughout the world.

Seeley, J. R., et al. *Crestwood Heights.* New York: Basic Books, 1956. Life in a high-socioeconomic-class living community—the problems from split-level adjustments to child guidance.

Srole, L., et al. *Mental health in the metropolis: The midtown Manhattan study.* New York: McGraw-Hill, 1962. Views of large-city subculture.

Warren, R. L. *The community in America.* Chicago: Rand McNally, 1963. A textbook on community study.

Zelomek, A. W. *A changing America: At work and play.* New York: Wiley, 1959. A view of changing community life.

19

Individuals
in Organizations

Robert B. Miller and B. von Haller Gilmer

A business is made up of people, and people are human. Within the framework of this theme we have described in the preceding chapters the nature of organizational environments and problems related to need achievement and to the selection and training of men and women for job assignments. We have detailed many of the human factors surrounding the interrelationships of men and machines and have said some things about the behavior of people in groups. All organizations, regardless of type, size, or function, have in common the human element. For the organization these human resources must be programmed to perform tasks, produce and distribute goods, or serve in a variety of other ways. For the industrial organization it is axiomatic that the business exists for, or by, financial profit, functioning in a climate demanding some social responsibility. Organizations can both help and hinder the satisfactions of human needs. In some ways both individuals and organizations are known by their needs. For the individual, adjustment within an organization involves an understanding of personal aspirations in relation to a social environment, where success depends both on individual effort and the climate. In some respects, organizational environments emphasize dependency, but at the same time they value independence, thus creating a dilemma for the individual.

In this chapter we shall talk about the individual in the organization, beginning with some generalizations about people and jobs and the alternatives involved in career decision making. Attention will be given to the patterns of careers and to the development of personal skills. The chapter raises some questions as to the ways people react to stress where there are no nostrums, no panaceas, and no gimmicks that can be offered the individual for his psychological survival in the organizational complex. For some individuals, charting a road map from the vanishing *now* to the inevitable *then* is challenging; for others, change may be projected with a short planning horizon; and for some, communication may mean no more than sharing inadequacies.

A Point of View. This chapter is addressed for the most part to the person who is thinking about a managerial or professional career in industry and who is concerned about problems in self-development. Our aim is to raise questions for the individual who is considering how he may relate his abilities, habits, personality, and skills to environmental situations. And questions are raised concerning criteria of success and failure. This chapter also has been prepared with the recognition that there are gaps in researches that might be helpful in career decision making.

In the preceding chapters we have talked about behavior problems related to the worker, the supervisor, the executive, and, to a lesser extent, the professional man. Some of the questions we raise here are based on researches described previously, and some have been gathered from the tangential references listed in the bibliography. The eighteen preceding chapters were based on a review of over fifteen thousand publications in the several areas. In preparing this final chapter the authors have sought out experimental and clinical studies and professional descriptions, both in behavioral science and managerial literature, related to the problems of higher-level careers. We have interviewed a number of people about these problems and have reviewed hundreds of case histories recorded in books. We have no doubt exposed some of our personal biases in selecting the topics to be covered. The authors have adopted here the point of view that self-development involves asking questions in an area where there are no easy answers and possibly, for some at least, no answers. We hope the chapter provokes questions for the reader in considering organizations and men. In effect, this implications chapter tries to pull together some views on what life in organizations is like and what psychology may have to offer the individual. We should also like to point out that we do not wish to pass judgment on the value of the situations and behaviors we will describe. The facts are that they exist in some places and at some times. Observers of individual behaviors in organizations have pointed out the negative and costly aspects of many of these situations to organizations as well as to individuals. Much attention was given in the preceding chapters to how best to solve some of these human problems of organizations. The reader, no doubt, has his own solutions. The authors are also aware that the presentations here may not contribute to the serenity of some readers.

SOME ELEMENTS IN CAREER PLANNING

As the individual reflects back to the days when his interests changed from wanting to be a fireman, then a lawyer, doctor, or businessman, to the decisions related to pursuing his education at some higher level, chances are he will remember having first gone through the *fantasy* stage of early childhood, where his interests were transitory and for the most part unrelated to any potential capacities. Following this came the stage of *tentative choices*. Here capacities vaguely became related to interests, and vocational preferences were established in a dreamy sort of way. In the late teens came a third stage of more realistic *planning*. Here, in this chapter, we wish to discuss a fourth stage along the route from fantasy to reality—*career development*—bearing in mind that not all people have a choice in selecting their careers and jobs. Opportunity and circumstances enter in large measure. It may be well to remember also that throughout a lifetime a person may have several careers [52, 63, 64].

Generalizations about People and Jobs. Let us begin with a few generalizations, some of which have been formally studied and have been found useful in preparing for career planning:

- People differ in their abilities, interests, personalities, and desires.
- Organizations differ in the opportunities they can provide for taking care of individual differences.
- Companies, even local plants or offices, differ in their psychological climates.
- Selection of the career job is an experience that cannot readily be undone. It produces changes in the individual through his investments of time, of money, and of ego.
- The perfect job does not exist. Somewhere compromise has to be made between capacities, interests, values, and opportunities.
- With few if any exceptions, each person has the potential for success and job satisfaction in a number of different occupations.
- Childhood and adolescent identifications play some part in shaping vocational interests, provided that the required abilities and opportunities are present.
- One will always be faced with possibilities for making job changes throughout life—particularily the upward-mobile individual.
- Work is a way of life. The most effective personal adjustment comes where the nature of the work itself and the way of life that goes with it—community, home, leisure-time activities, friends—are congenial to the aptitudes, interests, and values of the person in question.

• No job provides for complete satisfaction. No person completely fits the job. The interaction of the individual and his environment determines career patterns and career changes.

Levels of Information. From the vast literature on job counseling come suggestions that career planning should start early for each individual, when a wide variety of questions can serve as starting points. Frequently mentioned are: Do you want to work mostly with people or with things? Do you want to work for yourself or for an employer? What are the requirements of the kind of job you would prefer most? It is reported that few people seeking jobs through employment agencies have considered these and some dozens of other questions of this nature. It is also reported that in one survey of over one hundred popular books and writings on the techniques of job seeking, emphasis was placed, for the most part, on approved ways of behaving, wearing proper clothes, and presenting a good front. Little was included to suggest that career planning goes deeper than the veneer of do's and don't's.

At a somewhat more sophisticated level comes literature dealing with sources of information on communication letter-writing, how to prepare for interviews, and what is involved in moving ahead on the job.

The levels of information and counseling about jobs and careers center largely on occupational groups, differing widely between the worker and the executive. For the former, job opportunities and placement center largely on the employment office, for the latter on programs of self-development.

Occupational Groups. From many studies on vocational development come the conclusions that the nature of work is a most important determiner of social status. In Figure 19.1 Super presents a useful scheme for classifying occupations by "level," "field," and "enterprise." "Level" is identified with such variables as income, prestige, intelligence, education, degree of authority, and responsibility for decision making. "Field" is closely related to differences in aptitude patterns and in interests, and ranges widely from the outdoor occupations to the fine arts. "Enterprise" is a dimension that refers to the setting in which the work is performed, such as agriculture, manufacturing, or government. Jobs in the same field and at the same level may have appeal for different persons when performed in different settings. One person may prefer the specifics of a setting which provides the mobile activity found in some selling jobs, while another person may feel more comfortable in the office; and if the growth in the number of government employees is any indication, there are many people who do not have deep aversions to bureaucratic climates.

Career planning varies in amount and in sophistication largely in relation

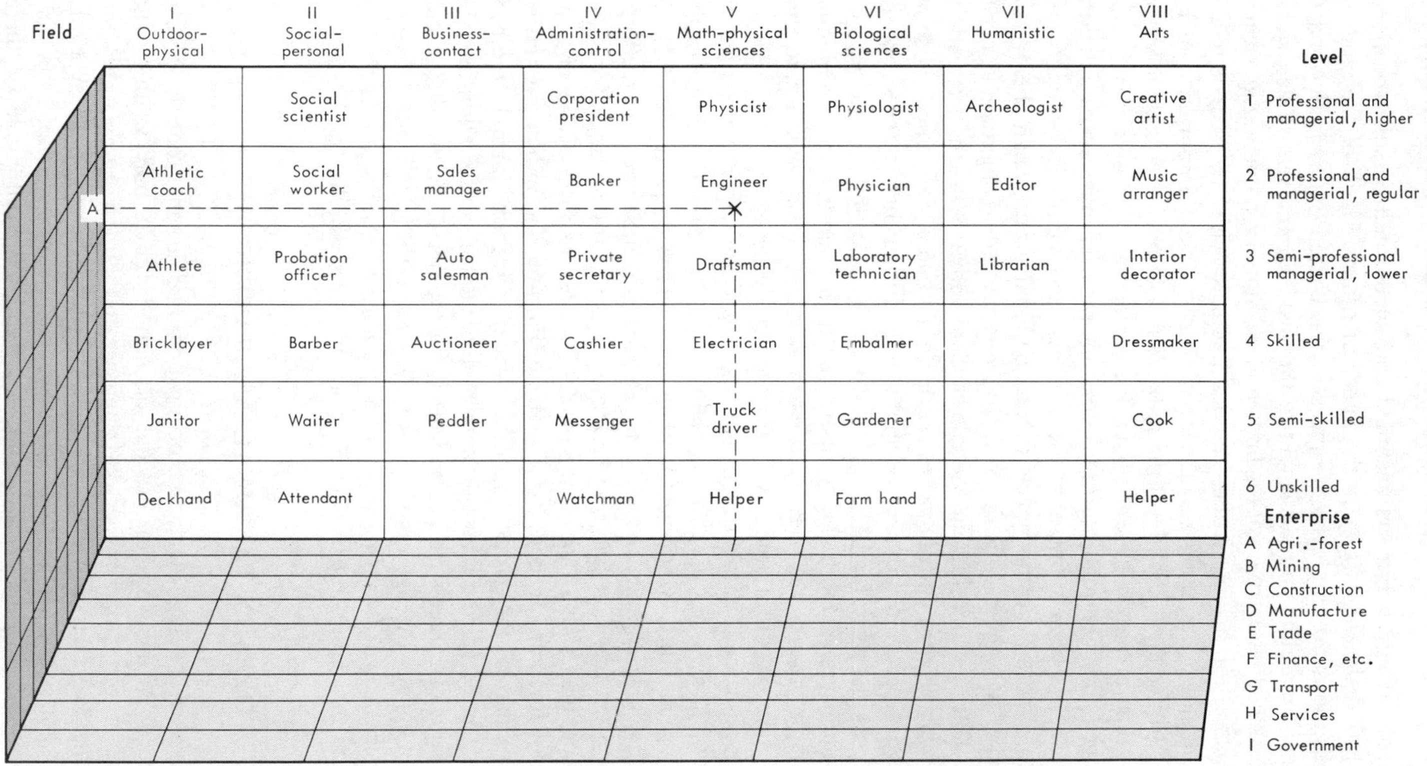

Field

Level	I Outdoor-physical	II Social-personal	III Business-contact	IV Administration-control	V Math-physical sciences	VI Biological sciences	VII Humanistic	VIII Arts
1 Professional and managerial, higher		Social scientist	Sales manager	Corporation president	Physicist	Physiologist	Archeologist	Creative artist
2 Professional and managerial, regular	Athletic coach	Social worker		Banker	Engineer	Physician	Editor	Music arranger
3 Semi-professional managerial, lower	Athlete	Probation officer	Auto salesman	Private secretary	Draftsman	Laboratory technician	Librarian	Interior decorator
4 Skilled	Bricklayer	Barber	Auctioneer	Cashier	Electrician	Embalmer		Dressmaker
5 Semi-skilled	Janitor	Waiter	Peddler	Messenger	Truck driver	Gardener		Cook
6 Unskilled	Deckhand	Attendant		Watchman	Helper	Farm hand		Helper

Enterprise

A Agri.-forest
B Mining
C Construction
D Manufacture
E Trade
F Finance, etc.
G Transport
H Services
I Government

Fig. 19.1. A scheme for classifying occupation by level, field, and enterprise. (Adapted from Super, D. E. *The psychology of careers.* New York: Harper, 1963.)

to occupational level. For the unskilled and uneducated person, vocational planning is slight and largely in the hands of others. Much of the work of over four thousand employment offices in the United States is devoted to vocational counseling and placement of the unskilled and semiskilled workers. The skilled industrial worker finds himself more of a commodity where the demands for his particular abilities fluctuate with the economy and with technological change, and the union is of primary importance in his security. Above the skilled level the individual is in many respects more on his ōwn. The manager does not have the protection of a union, but if he has reached a high enough position, economic security may not be a serious problem. It has been shown that there is less career mobility among those in the top and the bottom levels of occupational groups than there is in the middle. It is most difficult to move from manual to nonmanual occupations. During work life individuals tend to move between occupations on the same level or into adjacent occupational categories. There is some tendency for people to advance occupationally during their careers, but for most people not very far [43, 52]. And some people find themselves culturally handicapped from the beginning even in a university community. For example, a study reported in 1964 in Berkeley, California, found that some 15 per cent of all adults were functionally illiterate [36].

Recent researches emphasize that upward mobility depends not only on aspiration but also on opportunity. Many people do not get or perceive the chances for mobility. Many people at the managerial or professional levels in industry have confidence they can get ahead through their own efforts. Workers often feel that pull and luck are necessary for advancement, and study after study shows that most workers have few aspirations beyond the position of foreman. In contrast, for the upward-mobile individual getting ahead is a part of the game, a game in which education, formal or otherwise, is essential for the understanding of alternatives in aspiration and the requirements of career survival, as well as for the development of personal skills. Sometimes the aggressive person fails to consider the psychological and physical costs of moving upward. Sometimes he finds stress caused by excitement more pleasant than stress caused by less activity [6, 29, 54].

ALTERNATIVES IN PERSONAL ASPIRATION

The individual, having selected an occupation, may assume that the course of his career in the world of practice is charted. Or he may visualize the first steps on the career ladder and then see the ladder disappearing into the clouds. The facts, however, are different. Nearly every high-level job, or profession, if one wishes to use the term, has a gamut of choices in personal objective and aspiration. Almost certainly the full range of these choices will not be present in any single organization or organizational complex. But before we get too specific, let us look at some broad preferences, particularly those that younger people may wish to take a look at.

Kinds of Activities. We all engage in a variety of activities involving choice. Let us illustrate how important this kind of choosing may be. One kind of choice is between sedentary and mobile activity. This is a matter of temperament and probably not a trivial issue. Some persons face a permanent desk job with horror. Sitting at a desk for eight hours a day is, indeed, an insult to natural mobility. But within many professions there are alternatives. A librarian may be a cataloger, and indeed this is a desk job. Or he may be a desk librarian, which, paradoxically, requires considerable movement during the day—going to the catalog, searching the shelves, moving books, and so on. A teacher generally leads a fairly active physical life, standing, walking, gesturing, speaking, drawing on the blackboard, as compared with a dean, who frequently spends his day almost entirely sitting at his desk or at the conference table.

A scientist may elect to be a theories and data analyzer, in which case his work is done mostly from a chair. Or he may be active in data collection, in which case he is likely to have considerable physical activity during the day [18, 66].

In general, however, the higher a man rises in his profession, the more deeply he settles into chairs behind desks, at conference tables, and in vehicles of transportation from one conference setting to another. This progression into sedentary life may not be inescapable, but the pressures toward it become greater with successful achievement.

Another major dimension in early choice of work situation is between independence of the time clock and a schedule of activities laid out by others. The salesman is an example of relative independence. The appointments he keeps are usually of his own choosing and setting. His effectiveness is measured by results and not by the instructions he follows in getting them. The consultant and the physician in private practice are other examples. In even these cases, of course, independence is a matter of degree. The customer or client may be more capricious and exacting than any shop foreman or petty manager. Independence is sometimes confused with irresponsibility. But successful independent work (as authors and musicians will point out) requires substantial psychological reserves of energy to enable one to keep going during the dreary days; it requires self-confidence even in adversity, and self-discipline or work habits that can be generalized. By definition, the independent man has no buffers to cushion the inevitable shocks and disappointments of the job. If he tends to procrastinate unpleasant but necessary chores, he will become crushed under backlogs. He must also be able to teach himself through his mistakes. The free life is seldom an easy one. But to some it is worth the price to avoid the breath of authority close to one's neck. And some people view the free life in others as not involving work [37, 38]. One novelist reports that her gardener remarked on one occasion that it must be nice not to work—"All I see you do is sit in the shade and write."

In contrast, there are jobs that relieve the person of continuous choice and self-prodding. They are not necessarily routine except that they require presence during the workday, and are examined as much in how the task is done as in its results. A standard work environment tends to induce at least the motions of work, and these often become work. The accomplishment cycle is the hour, the day, or the week, rather than the month, the quarter, or the year. Of course, a cushion against laziness, mental or physical depression, disappointment, and procrastination is also likely to be a cushion against spectacular achievement. The size of the penalties tends to balance the size of the rewards, and this truism applies to practically all choices.

Signs in Choosing Goals. A desk job versus a mobile job and independence from management surveillance versus accommodation to it deal with aspects of job settings. Within these settings let us now look at some different kinds of personal objectives in work.

The test of a personal aspiration has two parts. One is the kind of assignment and goal result for which a person will work harder than for alternatives. The other part of the test is what kinds of accomplishment provide the greatest satisfaction. From what does the individual get his kicks? Conversely, we can apply the test by finding out where his greatest capacity for frustration and disappointment lies, what kinds of failure make him feel most keenly the pangs of worthlessness.

A more subtle way to test for type of aspiration is by observing what situations and goals evoke *initiative* action. Does the student, for example, spontaneously seek out political power among his associates in social contact and in societies? Does he read deeply into subject matter that is outside specific assignments? Does he recognize the social influences on his goals? Does he get into money-making enterprises beyond the requirements of necessity? Does he express compulsions to project order and structure into his own and neighboring operations, whether for study, for conducting lab activities, or for making procedural rules in a campus organization? Does he contrive to get himself into the position of giving service to others through informal tutoring or writing communications or setting up entertainments? These may be signs that some fundamental goals have already been tentatively chosen. Or the student may ask himself what kinds of activities he tries to avoid.

Let us examine some of these alternatives in greater detail.

The Quest for and Use of Knowledge. In its formal sense, this is the quest of science. But the formal scientific method of hypothesis formation, hypothesis testing, and induction into theory can be made impersonal and informal. The key idea here is the act of discovery as the goal condition.

This search may in some individuals be restricted to technical discoveries within formal disciplines, the so-called "pure" and so-called "applied" science. But the urge to discover and to know the answer may also apply to any other kind of problem solving starting with the "what," the "how," and the "why."

What is the best number and composition of personalities and talents to assemble in the formative stages of developing a new product? How should this mix change at different stages? Are these differences of mix for different kinds of product? How can one account for the empirical outcome of a study into this problem?

Obviously we have two parts in each of these sample problems. What works? Why does it work? Some persons may generally be satisfied with answering the first question. Others may be dissatisfied until they also reach some answer to the second question.

The world is generally not favorable to subsidizing the individual quest for knowledge and understanding, although obviously the material plight of the scientist as such has vastly improved in the last two decades, not only in industry but also in universities. But even today, careful search must be made for a setting—even in colleges and universities—where self-directed inquiry for its own sake will be an acceptable part of the climate [2, 6].

Let us say that one is not only skilled (and lucky) at getting insights but also versatile and willing to tackle any of a wide range of problems with equal enthusiasm. Almost inevitably he is recognized by his associates as "an intellectual." In practically every industrial and business setting, including those devoted to technology, he may come under personal suspicion and at least mild ostracism unless he has considerable offsetting charm and is willing to edit down his ideas from the way he thinks them to the way he says them. The stereotype generally prevails that intellectuals, individually or collectively, are impractical, and this attitude often persists despite individual evidence to the contrary. There are exceptions, found both in colleges and in industries, but they are rare. Put in capsule by Whitehead [69], " . . . a university is imaginative or it is nothing, at least nothing useful."

Let us equate the person who seeks knowledge and discovery with the idea man. An idea man may enter an organization bringing with him considerable prestige from a previous environment. Let's assume that he deserves it. The honeymoon with the organization may last a year or so. After this his successes in the new organization become taken for granted; his failures or partial successes are better remembered. But also, when he ceases to be a stranger, he ceases to be a prophet. He finds that strangers to the organization now tend to be called in as consultants even on topics on which he may be a renowned specialist to the outside world. The organization finds many rationalizations for doing this, if in fact it recognizes the paradox it creates. But it is as if work organizations, like family organizations, unconsciously think to themselves, "If he's one of us, can he really be *that* good?"

One who is on the quest for knowledge and discovery will frequently lead a lonely life in industrial and bureaucratic organizations save in certain special situations. He must be able to get his satisfactions mainly from the joy of discovery, not from the social and material results of discovery. If his personal frustrations in the organization make him crotchety, his fortunes and opportunities for discovery may spiral downward. Certainly his quest for a happy job environment will be a difficult one. But let his children cheer up: the long trend seems favorable.

The Quest for Power. This is the quest for control over other people, for the satisfactions of that control, or for control over activities or property. These are generally the primary aspirations of those who seek positions as managers and executives. There are vast needs for people with the ability to direct, organize, and supervise, in one way or another, the work of employees. Debate is current as to whether it is better to have a professional manager who is not knowledgeable and skilled in the work done by the people he manages or to have a manager who has such knowledge and skill but lacks professional training in management. Although the issues are not quite so clear-cut as this, the debate has a practical as well as a philosophical basis.

The person who deliberately sets his goal as management has many more factors in his favor today than thirty years ago. Rapid changes and expansion in business, industrial, and almost all other work organizations are providing opportunity for many kinds of manager. Although in some organizations the criteria for management may be severe, they are almost never precise or fixed [3, 60, 71].

After the individual passes from the lowest levels of management, he inevitably comes into the competition for special considerations from his organization; he also comes into competition with his peers for promotion and choice assignments. Aggressiveness becomes important not only for success but sometimes for survival. Aggressiveness may be more important in action than in personal conflict with people. One can be aggressive without being a table thumper. Success in the conflicts entailed in higher levels of management generally requires an enjoyment of fighting, the psychological resources to take even extended losses (being in the doghouse occasionally for a year or two, for example), and decisiveness in seeing and following up a personal advantage [13].

The upward-mobile manager must indeed be willing to go where advantage lies for advancement. He cannot be tied to any particular work interest. He may be trained as a physicist and find himself the manager of a personnel department one year and of a patent department the next. His attachments to people and organizations generally need to be flexible. He must have or acquire the signs of and skills for social acceptability to management at least two levels above himself. This may mean poker playing in one environment, easy conversance with the stock market in another, cocktail-party small talk in a third, and, in some situations, knowing what to be against. The exceptions merely demonstrate that one can win against long odds. But as for an actor, no single success or string of successes is a guarantee of a successful career for a manager.

The ambitious manager has pressures from above and below and from the flanks. Because of the unclear and varying criteria of job competence, he is often unsure as to whether his work is being viewed as good, bad, or mediocre. He can rarely see a clear-cut edge or conclusion to a task, so he has little opportunity to take direct satisfaction from what he does. His signs of success are related to promotions; he depends not only on the perceptions and interpretations of others for his job satisfaction but in varying degree also on their favor. If he does not fit a vice-president's image of what a higher-level manager and executive should be, he may not move forward. Assignments may even be chosen for him that will guarantee his failure. There are always such assignments available in any organization, and the astute manager learns to recognize and avoid them, however glamorous they may seem on the surface.

The manager's career tends always to be in unstable equilibrium; it balances on a knife-edge. Success may bring reward after reward, but one failure can do away with years of hard work. Small wonder that these pressures sometimes select out or foster political ruthlessness and self-centered opportunism in upward-mobile managers [42]. The manager's "product" is credit for a job considered well done or avoidance of blame for a job considered poorly done by higher management. The ruthless manager (possibly in the minority) sets up fall guys to blame and contrives to get his name identified with successful outcomes no matter who has done the work. Considerable degrees of skill are required to secure hostages both for failure and for success; he must do this with people, and people are not completely passive to manipulation. Some may feel it has been aptly said that there is no purity in power [25, 26, 30].

Perhaps we can think of the quest for money as a psychological problem similar in certain respects to the quest for power. We should distinguish between aspiration for money because of what it will purchase for the individual and the pursuit of money and property as a career in itself. At some levels this distinction may be blurred. But obviously the person who sets off for millions of dollars does not do so because he hopes to spend them on himself and his family. His interest (oversimplified) is in acquiring the equivalent of a material empire. Likewise, the quest of the discoverer in ideas may be for knowledge itself. The aspiration of the inventor may be to design something that works on its own terms. The interest of the newly appointed dean may be in changing the curriculum. We may be wise in realizing that no behavior can be limited by any set of motivational categories or goal classifications. Motivations and goals are always mixed, usually confused, and both action and reward often come with compromise and change. Human relationships frequently vary along some power dimension.

PATTERNS OF CAREER SURVIVAL

If the classical view of organizational theory is in effect, one attitude of management toward employees is that their individual and collective abilities, motivations, and incentives are commodities. This attitude may be distasteful to some people, but it is a realistic point of view in profit enterprise. And if the industrial enterprise is to survive, employees must recognize this viewpoint as basic and fundamental. It is also true that progress of the organization is dependent on the policy that programming for profit must also be administered with humaneness and with recognition of the needs of individuals. Any individual is either a profitable resource to the company or a philanthropy. This realistic attitude raises a question for the individual—what must *I* do to survive?

Organizational Practices. What are the requirements for an employee who aspires to move upward? With whom should he identify himself? What rituals should he observe? We introduced versions of these questions in the chapter on organizational climates, and no doubt to some the questions were revolting, while to others they were symbolic of understanding what is required for upward mobility. Some people are active with respect to history, some seek the protective umbrella of higher management, and perhaps some just stumble over themselves.

In any organization, a man tends to get tagged by the company he keeps. If his major social contacts are underdogs, he will tend to be known as an underdog. The opposite is not necessarily true, however. It is, of course, characteristic of social behavior to try to find out, "What side are you on, theirs or mine?" as well as "What is your status?" The pattern of social loyalties in a company may be highly complex and may shift rapidly. It can affect whom you go to for advice and counsel in the organization, whom you express your gripes to, and whom you lock horns with in conference debates. Every organization has its ingroups and its outgroups.

Being a member of an out-of-favor group is not necessarily fatal, but it can be a temporary handicap if you are competing with others for a promotion. Adapting to the social realities may be hypocrisy, but it is not necessarily so. It can also be forbearance. Companies in stages of vigorous growth are less likely than more stable companies to constrain their choice of assignments and promotions because of social and group identifications of candidates; in relatively stable companies, where there are many to compete for few positions and where subgroups are likely to be better defined, social nepotism is more likely. An older university campus could serve as a model!

Organizations, like other social groups, have "up-words" and "down-words." An up-word may evoke sentiments favorable to the speaker and to the subject he speaks about; it may even help maintain solidarity and enhance uniqueness of the group. In certain circles during the early 1960s there was such a thing as being "hip," but today it is not hip to be hip. Ideas may be ageless, but words become dated. The use of yesterday's up-word is worse than using no words; it brands the user as out of style, and to be out of style is as bad for an employee as for a woman's hat unless he is eligible for granddad treatment. It takes time and acclimatization to learn an organization's (and profession's) up-words, to use them in proper context, and, especially, to get over feeling uncomfortable every time one says them.

"Scientific management" is a powerful up-word these days; a few years ago it was in disrepute because it implied depersonalization. In effect, the expression "scientific management" generally means making decisions from data plus intuition. ("Seat of the pants" is an up-word of the last decade that is going out, and "cognition" is once again becoming respectable.) "Unscientific management" is management by intuition. The word "planning" is going out of style in favor of "programming." Soon only the unsophisticated will be planning, whereas scientific management will be programming the next year's objectives, actions, resources, and dollars. This word lends a flavor of logical precision and impeccability, plus the charged aroma of the computer. Let us watch to see how soon "city planning" will become "city programming." Even the scientist seeking his contracts must keep abreast of word usage in playing the game of grantsmanship. One difficult task is to figure out what new up-word will replace some current one, such as "model."

It is generally wise to watch one's language in business and industry, as well as in the professions. Polysyllables may be even more dangerous than unpressed pants, even, says one experienced industrial consultant, bringing under suspicion the motives of the self-styled intellectual. This is less true today than some twenty years ago, perhaps because of the large influx of scientists and academic people into business and industry.

In all honesty it must be said that it is easy to lampoon many organizational practices and to make the situations appear more grim than they actually are. Some people make a living at it. This intent has not motivated the preparation of this text or any portions of it. Making money, as well as the productivity that goes into money, is a serious matter. Losing it may be even more serious. When a company hires an employee, it enters into a legal and usually a moral contract with him. It undertakes to pay him for actual and often for potential productivity. Part of an employee's productivity is the avoidance of friction and disturbances that interfere with organizational productivity. Organizations adopt protective devices and attitudes against disturbances just as individuals do. This applies to universities, as well as to companies, and to fraternal organizations also.

It is important to know about organizational protocol. These are the forms for getting things done. Some managements will take no action on anything unless there have been some conferences preceding the decision. The conferences may or may not have been productive. In some cases even the conferees may know that their task is a ritualistic formality. The executive's decision may be independent of, even contradictory to, the recommendations of the committee. But committee action is protocol; it's the thing to do, like wearing a black tie with a dinner jacket or getting faculty concurrence with some university planning already nearing the action stage.

There are many examples of rituals in organizations. Some of them are specific to the organization. Some kinds of safety campaigns, slogans, and memos after an accident in the plant or lab are rituals. Some award programs may fall in the class of ritualistic practices. Promotions and disciplinary actions are often surrounded with rituals. The ritual may arise from an incorrect or outdated assumption about what is good to do, or it may be a gesture after the meaning has passed out of it. Organizations, like societies, develop and preserve rituals for the comfort of having *some* kind of response to situations that seem to demand response. Frequent rehearsal provides the reassurance of stability and structure.

Like the dinner jacket, organizational rituals that have meaning for or at least are accepted by some persons seem silly to others. To ridicule them publicly may be sacrilege. At the least, it is a discourtesy. At the worst, it may brand the scoffer as an outsider to the organization or perhaps categorize him as playing some defensive role.

Organizational Conventions. Every culture has its rituals and compulsions which outsiders may ridicule, sometimes at their peril. These may range from the number of lines to put on an easel chart to methods of reaching a decision. There will be taboo words and up-words. Most of the conventions that affect the newer employee are customary within the organization and may seem strange to the newcomer. The student who has learned that he gets an A if he writes up an idea in a thousand words, but a D if he writes the same idea in fifty words, may be severely handicapped in the organization where brevity is a totem. Sometimes brevity is silly. Generally it has survival value.

Organizational protocol, usually unwritten, tends to specify many of the relationships between employee and manager. These may differ at different levels in the organization. Every person in the organization may automatically be on a first-name basis with every other, but this does not necessarily mean that the interactions don't have formal rules. Many of these rules apply to what kind of initiatory actions may properly be taken by whom and under what conditions. It may be as bad to be too reticent as too forward, but this depends on the climate as well as on the individuals.

In many organizations, ethics do not forbid the manager taking credit for the work of the subordinates, even to the exclusion of their names on reports of achievements. Protocol also tends to establish whom an employee may and may not properly see without his manager's approval. An organization on the surface may seem very democratic, but hierarchic levels defend themselves from impromptu intruders, and with good cause. Going over a manager's head can lead a man into political exposures and even into embarrassing some close associates.

THE PROFESSIONAL CAREER

Let us agree that by professional we mean any person dedicated to the continuous acquisition of knowledge that can be applied to his tasks at work. He performs his tasks from knowledge; that is, he knows in some degree why he does what he does and the implications of doing it differently. He is in a continuous state of learning, not only from his task experiences but through outside sources of education. In some respects a professional is one who makes other people's problems his own.

There are a variety of career patterns which the professional, dedicated to his subject matter, may follow or have thrust upon him [5, 48, 49].

Contract Research. The professional may remain in the sanctuary of a laboratory for the thirty-five to forty years of his professional lifetime, emerging only through his publications and seminars. There are few environments today, however, university or industrial, in which a sphere of influence and substantial dollar support are provided even to brilliant research with no strings attached. Those rare cases of inspired and sustained genius may find them, but there are likely to be deadly rivalries for them. They will be, most likely, housed in universities [67].

It is more likely that the scientist will become part salesman-business-man and learn the art of selling research contracts. He may or may not have skillful assistance from the controller's office, though chances are he learned something about grantsmanship in graduate school. But he will learn the meaning of overhead, contract monitors, budgets, and schedules, progress reports, and expense accounts. He will most likely deal with one or more government agencies. Like any other commodity, the contract scientist faces competition, and he will be lucky if his professional con-science is not occasionally put under some strain—not so much, perhaps, in fulfilling contracts as in promoting and selling them. If his career is tied to contracts, he finds that not only his income but also the incomes of a pyramid of assistants are tied to his continued ability to keep old contracts and get new ones. He often finds himself either shifting to the role of busi-nessman at the expense of research participation or failing to provide a steady stream of income to his dependents in the laboratory. If the latter is the case, he is on a down escalator which is not easily reversed. And there are instances where research has been oversold in the beginning, resulting in pressures being put on others to come through with fulfilling the promises.

The Dramatic Achievement. A professional man may ride on the tails of a single dramatic and well-publicized achievement for a decade, especially if the achievement gets a distinctive name. Finally, the title of the achieve-ment ceases to be capitalized and enters the public domain. When this happens, the identity of the originator becomes blurred and coupled with the past rather than the present, unless he has produced other achievements with equal notoriety in the meantime. The single achievement may have put him into a position of eminence where he has authority to command larger audiences; thus he has greater promotional opportunities for his later work. In this respect, a professional man may treat his career as a business enterprise and his aura of authority as an asset with which to confound his rivals, develop a coterie, and promote his aspirations.

The Lone Wolf. Some organizations may permit and even foster a few lone wolves if they are prolific with ideas which they readily discuss. These are people who are restless in an extended routine responsibility. The lone wolf will have to have initiative in focusing on trouble spots and willingness to roll up his sleeves and do at least some of the dirty work, such as first-hand data collection and analysis. The help may be of a short-range nature, or it may lead to a longer-range change in a policy, procedure, or product.

The lone-wolf kind of problem solver should have a wide range of in-formation about the many facets of work in the total organization even though that information may be only a few molecules thick and lie at the surface. He must have the professional respect of those he wants to help or those who have the problem he wants to work on. He must also be facile in providing some immediate answers even though he may take longer to work out the total problem. He is likely to be energetic, to be quick to pick up an enthusiasm (and perhaps to put it aside, too), and to exude a confidence that may even be arrogant at times. Some people have parlayed a little talent and a lot of arrogance into considerable prestige, but this gets exhausted after they have made the circuit a few times with disappointing results. Obviously the lone wolf must be able to organize a problem and its context quickly and incisively.

The lone wolf sometimes may feel frustrated because of lack of tangible achievements in his own right. Even if his achievements have had success, his management will tend to think of him as a dilettante rather than a versatile expert. Thus in important decision-making conferences his knowledge may be discounted in favor of the knowledge of outside consultants [27, 32, 73].

The Staff Assistant. The professional staff assistant is attached to a middle- or higher-level manager and serves as troubleshooter, data collector, worker on quick assignments, and, on occasion, buffer for aggressive attacks. He may have many of the qualities described for the lone wolf. There is one important exception: he should not be outwardly arrogant. His skills with people are a major asset to him. He must be able to enter departmental trouble spots as an emissary of his manager, get enough confidence to learn the truth even from defensive individuals, and use the truth generally to help rather than destroy. His major asset in avoiding hypocrisy is a genuine motivation to help the people he investigates as well as his manager.

It is proverbial that the best staff man is one who can help get jobs done anonymously. This contradiction in behavior is difficult and requires personal maturity. How dare he use overtly the authority of the manager in carrying out his job! He must be persuasive rather than dictatorial. Other requirements are a realistic knowledge of how the organization works and who are the sources of political strength. He must display the ability to convey an attitude of objectivity framed in friendliness. Generally, the staff assistant is a man with considerable depth of knowledge in some one field. In addition to being a specialist he must also be a generalist, one who knows the important things about a variety of fields. As a staff assistant to a technical manager, he might be a mechanical engineer with some knowledge of operations research, methods analysis, and cost accounting. Staff assistants may have improbable clusterings of knowledge. A primary specialization may rarely or never be of more use than giving a sense of how a technical task is done and the difficulties in doing one well. The staff assistant rarely retains the professional identity of his field, which at times can be a handicap.

The staff man must be prepared to take practically any kind of assignment he is given. Many assignments are passed to him in emergency status. His manager senses or receives an edict to deliver a statement to an executive by a certain date, usually measured in days, occasionally in weeks, and rarely in months. If he is lucky, the staff man will get a helpful briefing from his manager on the assignment. Then he goes to the files and the library for a week end and spends some nights of study. He may have some trustworthy friends who will help him in orientation. He will have a sense of the major issues before he makes his first interview. His official product will be a written report. His unofficial product will be suggestions to department people that often have a greater chance of being followed than if they come as management directives.

The staff man usually has one or two long-term projects punctuated by quick assignments. His jobs may vary from technical to organizational and from departmental or interdepartmental troubleshooting and fixing to personnel evaluation. He tries to shun the last kind of assignment if it seems that someone is going to get hurt, because such news will spread and impair his rapport. His manager may come to depend on him for knowing the "real world" in the organization rather than the façade it presents to management and for anticipating trouble before it becomes a crisis. In a very real sense a good staff assistant has a lot of interaction perception.

Because staff work permits working close to management, it is often used as grooming for a relatively high-level managerial position, but only if the man has already demonstrated managerial capability. Because of the increasing complexity of modern management, professional staff assistants are becoming a necessity to middle and upper levels of managers. There are too many dimensions to know about and control. The executive who must spend much of his time in negotiations and putting out political fires with his peers in the organization is especially pressed for help that he can trust professionally and personally.

Many of the satisfactions and opportunities in any staff work come from the personality and ability of the manager who is served. The defensive manager may use his staff privately as whipping boys for his anxieties and frustrations. The capricious manager may forget about his staff people for months at a time while they fret in a broom closet. The open, confident manager greets his staff assistants as intimate parts of a team effort, extensions of his own eyes, brain, and voice. Since they lack vested authority, he does not demand results without the aid of his personal authority but is grateful when results do not require his intervention. There is evidence of growing opportunity for professional staff work in many kinds of organizations. The rewards are moderate to substantial, and security is relatively high as long as the manager stays on top. Managers frequently take able assistants with them when they are promoted; thus salary increases may occur in tandem. When managers fall, assistants may also.

The administrative assistant and the executive assistant are quite different entities, in much the same ways that executives and administrators are different. The executive assistant has the authority of his manager to put policy and directives into action; he may also be a hatchet man. Only very high levels of management in large, stable organizations have them. The administrative assistant, as such, is a filter of information to the manager, keeps track of budgets and other controls, and generally tries to protect the manager from needless or irrelevant harassment. He may sometimes also play the role of staff assistant, but he is usually too busy to be away from his office for very long.

Innovators. Although statistics on this matter are not likely to be available, most people completing professional training probably take it for granted that they will be creators of new things. Undeniably there are creative acts in everyone's daily life. But nearly all of these acts have little more consequence than transient dust motes that glint and disappear. Most of us, practically all of the time, perform formulated tasks—tasks for which rules cover nearly every contingency, including when to hand the task over to some other specialist with his own set of rules. This applies to professional as well as to clerical tasks.

It would be futile to attempt here an analysis of the variables that make up creativity and its product, innovation. It can be said that even a brilliant innovator has no guarantee of an easy road. What he tries to do must be timely. If his products are too far ahead of the technological culture, he and his work will be neglected. He produces in a cultural context, and that context must be so developed and oriented as to be receptive. If he happens to be in a field at a time when there is motion, agitation, his inventions may have lively appreciation and even adoption. Current examples of such fields are molecular genetics, operations research, information retrieval with symbols (not yet with "intelligence" or meanings), extremely small solid-state switches and amplifiers, and economic decision making—to name a few [15, 24, 49, 70].

The professional innovator, the person with the talent and drive to proceed from one new idea to another, rarely has the temperament or interest to follow through into the details of practice. He may work through a pilot model to show the principle, but usually he is content to get his idea down on paper in the form of lines, flow diagrams, equations, or sentences, depending on his field. When this has been accomplished and the innovator feels assured that the idea is workable, he generally gets restless and wants to move on. But this stage, even if it has resulted in a pilot model, is still far from application.

In some fields and work contexts, the gifted translators of new ideas and format writers are well rewarded. In others they are not. Frequently their contributions are not recognized, or they become overworked managers. Perhaps when their technical function becomes well enough realized that criteria develop for distinguishing brilliant from mediocre performance, more consistent reward patterns will follow. Today, it is often necessary for the man who gets the idea to reduce it to near practice and application in order to get a business acknowledgement of the validity of the idea. The innovator must also be aware that at times trying to induce change can have much the same emotional impact as trying to move an old cemetery [17, 33].

Our appreciation of innovators is often reserved for those long dead. Even in prediction, standardized tests of intelligence are not effective in identifying creative individuals. So often, one finds a relatively thin line of innovative individuals, on the cutting edge of discovery, who have behind them an army of competent people doing routine work.

FROM PROFESSIONAL TO MANAGER

The competent professional man—the man who gets things done and done on time—in almost any field will have pressures to become a manager. These pressures may occur early in his career. In the past and present, acceptance of these pressures has been irreversible. Once he has been a manager, a man automatically loses prestige if he becomes a nonmanager even though his salary may remain the same or increase. And if in a given company a man turns down an offer of promotion to manager once, or twice at the most, he may never again get the invitation. His lack of eagerness is interpreted as evidence that he isn't "managerial material." And if he has not become a manager by his early thirties, he probably never will [60].

Many companies have attempted to reduce the gulf between the professional and the managerial roles. In some, salary scales and job titles are matched. So are such perquisites as type of furniture, office size, carpets, water carafes, and so on. Nevertheless, the attitude of employees (and sometimes of their wives) is that a manager is more important than a nonmanager. And when the chips are down, the management of the company generally shares this point of view in its behavior if not in its speech. The chips consist of the major and many minor decisions of any kind.

The transition from professional to manager in the industrial organization generally happens early, by the late twenties or early thirties. This may be due more to selection procedures than to evaluation of later capabilities and interests. It is true that the attitudes of the experienced manager and those of the experienced professional differ in many ways. Ideas as to what is important also tend to differ in many ways. As a man gets older and deeper in his professional tasks, changes in his attitudes and values may become more difficult to bring about. This may be the point of view of higher management. On the other hand, some persons become dissatisfied with their profession as such, and seek a change. Management promises such a change. So they may seek management jobs that do not entirely forfeit their training and experience.

The signs used to select managers vary all over the landscape, and may be inconsistent even within the same organization. So only the most general comments can be made here. May we suggest they should be taken with some reservations. Perhaps the most general requirement is that the candidate has shown ability to "get assignments done." This may mean at a high level of quality, but more usually it means getting them done on time. Another factor is that the person "knows what he is doing" or at least can convey that impression. This gives his management as well as his associates confidence in him and his assignment.

The aspirant to management should become sensitive and perceptive to the management climate in his own environment. He may show interest, but he should not be too eager in his wooing. One asset is a detailed working knowledge of the entire organization, including its financial structure and behavior. Another is evidence of identification with the schedules, budgets, and costs of his immediate management. Sensitivity to costs is perhaps another major sign of management potential [41, 46].

Much has been written and dramatized about the social difficulties in making the transition from worker to manager. Less has been said about the problems in shifting from professional to manager. If the employee has had personal attachment and commitment to his professional aspirations, he has trouble in viewing these same goals in terms of company profit. Acquiring a new set of values may be more difficult (it may sometimes be impossible) than learning to greet his old associates a little differently or learning another set of work habits. It may be hard to realize, for example, that time spent in not taking action may favor the competitor. Let us look at some of the requirements of managers in more detail.

THE MANAGERIAL CAREER

The manager is primarily an initiator with people rather than of ideas, and he behaves in ways characteristic of his job [13, 19, 72, 74].

The manager must live with constant and diverse pressures without being continuously compressed. He does not work by assignment or by standard periodicities, as nonmanagers do. Almost never does he have all the resources (men, materials, space, dollars) at all times to meet all explicit demands. He also has implicit demands, such as getting more work done from the same resources available to him, getting a higher level of reliability in the work output, cutting costs without reducing output, diversifying the capability of his organization. He has these pressures whether he is a foreman of a spool-winding department in a factory or the director of research in a large foundation. In addition, he has pressure from his employees wanting more pay for less production (at least as he sees it).

A major condition of the manager's survival is the way he spends his time and energy. If he, with the help of his competent secretary, can organize and budget his time effectively, he has one protection against ulcers. Organizing and budgeting time means setting priorities and limits on what he tries to do and how much effort he spends in each activity. Without organization he will be swamped by trivial and alluring distractions. He has to learn how to make a five-minute conversation and a fifteen-minute conference pay, hopefully conserving his physical energy and his psychological reserves.

For long-term survival the man in management must acquire flexibility in accepting changing organizational objectives and policy rules. It is as bad for a manager to be out of date *in his work environment* as for a woman's hemline to be out of style at a party. This does not imply that he has to be docile to caprice; but he must at least *appear* to have a mind open to change, and not resistant to it just because it *is* change. It will make his life easier if he can differentiate mere statements of change in policy and procedure from definite decisions by higher management to monitor and enforce change. Perhaps he himself should be heard in an occasional proposal that does not challenge the habits and attitudes of his superiors too severely.

He will live in and depend on negotiation with subordinates, peers, and superiors. In rapidly shifting and growing organizations, he is likely to spend a major amount of time and effort negotiating for services from his peers in an attempt to get priority over the contesting claims of others. He learns to repay favors in kind in order to maintain a good bargaining position or to build up influence reserves. One characteristic of the effective manager is his ability to handle conflicting roles. The *manner* in which the individual resolves conflict is more important for good mental or emotional health than the *degree* to which internal conflict is experienced [45].

The manager must learn to edit what he says. It is human to take at least some people into complete confidence. Managers learn the danger of confidences. They also learn the dangers of misquotation and overinterpretation of what they say. Thus as they grow older, managers tend to say less and less except when making speeches. Experience seems to teach that organizations cannot be run for long on gusts of emotion.

DEVELOPMENT OF PERSONAL SKILLS

The individual may restrict his effective work environment to the cubbyhole in which he performs assigned tasks. He may keep his nose to the grindstone. He may learn little more than the marks on the surface of the grindstone and its creaks and wobbles and gain a bit of practice in shaping and sharpening the scissors. Or he may learn how to grow.

Expansion of Interests and Knowledge. The starting condition for growth is interest in a greater range of the work environment than is ordinarily given by the task assignment. This interest can be in professional, interpersonal, and organizational relationships and in the product or service produced by the company as a whole. As is well known in psychology, learning is most rapid and best remembered and generalized when there is the set to learn—the active searching for knowledge and its application.

The individual is not a victim of the adjustment process if his thinking and behavior occur through continuous intellectual choice, when he perceives alternatives and their implications, when he looks objectively at the stimulus and purpose of action as well as his response alternatives.

Rarely does the new employee seek to learn about the products and services which characterize the purpose of the organization as a company. The hour or so of indoctrination and the little pamphlet he gets on being hired are relatively trivial for this objective. By knowing the company's product, he can better fit together the various operating parts of the company. The product can be understood in terms of what it provides the customer. This knowledge can assist, develop, and evaluate innovations at any level of activity. Knowledge of liabilities in the products and their use should be included. The nature of competition, its strengths and weaknesses in what it offers to customers, is a part of understanding the product in the market.

Learning about the product will help in understanding the key issues in technology, development, manufacturing, servicing, and marketing the product. Knowledge of these issues enables the employee (on occasion) to interpret management actions that otherwise would seem arbitrary. Being up to date on the key issues and trouble spots in technology and operation also confers the practical advantage of knowing where the hot assignments are or soon will be and thus the field upon which heroes will be made or broken.

Expansions of Organizational Skills. A major criterion of personal development in organizations is the number of roles which a person can successfully play. The playing of a role is a skill which includes a pattern of appropriate attitudes, plus reading and interpretation of signs and actions fitting to that role. A family of skills that is certainly related to varied role playing is comprised of mastery of styles of communication and mastery of communication routes for effective initiative, negotiation, and defense [21, 22].

The employee often learns to think, feel, and act differently in different organizational contexts. For some the range of role playing is very narrow. Roles are limited to three—that in the company of management, that in the company of peers, and that in the company of subordinates. For these employees, attitudes and behaviors become stereotyped within each of these roles. This is what is meant by a narrow range of role playing.

Others manage a greater flexibility within roles. With their managers they can shift the role from dutiful employee to aggressive persuader to confidante and sympathetic pal, and they can make these and other shifts through reading the signs in the manager's behavior. With peers, the range of roles may be from tough bargainer to collaborative conniver and from friendly associate to aggressive rival. There is no necessary implication of subterfuge in these shifts of role playing. They may be spontaneous or deliberate alternatives in responding to situations, climates, personalities, and objectives. Some people, of course, look askance at too wide a divergence of role playing, and no doubt some are unaware of their own role-playing behaviors.

For a supervisor, the range of roles will include fatherly counselor, teacher, guide to action, and objective but firm disciplinarian. Many variations and extensions may occur within each of these roles. Again, these variations will depend on perceptions of situation, climate, personality, and objective. Some of these roles cannot effectively be played at the same time. They may be psychologically incompatible in terms of "audience reaction." Thus it is almost impossible to act as objective presenter of facts at the same time that one is the impassioned proposer of a course of action. One may be each at different times, however, and be effective.

The conference offers opportunity for different roles to be assumed, and some shifts may occur without loss of effectiveness. There are the devil's advocate, the organizer of the proceedings, the impartial judge, the "here are the facts," and the "I challenge any other course of action" roles, as well as the difficult-to-maintain role of objective expert. Each of these roles calls for sensitivity in perceiving not only what to say and when to say it but also when to remain silent even when ideas and emotions are boiling inside. The old hand at conferences senses what can and cannot be accomplished in a conference as it proceeds.

Role playing can be deliberately learned by watching the behavior of others and noting the consequences. And, like any form of rational behavior, it can be practiced through learning to hold thought and impulse in rein before they burst into speech and action. This may be likened to the intervention of an intellectualized superego between impulse and overt behavior. For disturbed personalities this kind of intervention may put rage into the mind and acid into the stomach. The frustrations from the inhibition of powerful compulsive drives over long periods of time may produce apathy, on the one hand, or bursts of manic violence, on the other (recall Pavlov's frustrated dogs). But disturbed or immature personalities have a difficult time in any social environment, sometimes, finding they are more successful in arguing with themselves than with others.

Variation in role playing is properly regarded as a skill. This skill can be advanced by observation, social sensitivity, and the more or less habitual exercise of an editing intellectual function between impulse and expression. One professional mediator described his role thus: "I'm in the business of hearing 'no,' while working quietly to hear 'yes' " [42, 47, 71].

Negotiation and Bargaining. These skills are central to organizational life and fundamental to most managerial effectiveness. Like other social skills, they require sensitivity to and knowledge of individual differences in motivations and behavior. Perhaps the only general rule that can be offered is that of concluding a transaction by leaving the other person with a sense of satisfaction in the bargain he has made.

The best opportunity to learn the art of negotiating is by observing it in practice by persons who are successful at it. This must be done at first hand because their post-mortems are likely to be unreliable. Skilled negotiators often seem to use even casual conversations as an opportunity to put a person in a position requiring either defense or offense, then to release the person from that position, and then to reestablish it in another way. If this is done crudely, the victim becomes uncomfortable or annoyed. If it is done adroitly, the victim becomes grateful for "concessions" that are offered to him. The highly skilled negotiator learns how to use what the other person says as coin for barter.

Defensive Ploys. The word "ploy" combines the meanings of tactic, stratagem, gambit, and gimmick. People learn to reduce their vulnerability to unwanted assignments, overwork, the criticisms of others, running short of funds, association with disliked persons, and a host of other disturbances. They invent or copy mechanisms for handling these risks and avoidances. The trick, of course, is to reduce vulnerability without at the same time inviting a worse situation.

The best defense is preparation. Budgets are protected against cost overruns by contingency funds. These may not be identified as such; they may be items budgeted but without intent of use, so that the funds may be transferred. The risk of punishment for delayed schedules can be reduced by having some extended supply lines for pseudocritical items, some of which the manager knows cannot be delivered in time. Recalcitrant employees are given the isolation treatment by the manager. A difficult but hot project is assigned to two different groups known to be deadly rivals.

The battle-scarred old-timer who has been successful in maneuver is the best source of help to the novice. He may have to be asked for help in so many words: "Mac, how do I keep from hanging myself in this assignment?" It may be good to check independently with several veterans of organizational wars. It is curious how few employees ever ask direct questions about survival in their wilderness—and listen to the answers. Perhaps there is too little time left after making complaints.

Organizing Tasks. A solid dimension of growth is learning how to organize tasks and time and to plan work flow in widening circles of effect. This theme returns to the heart of the new requirements in professional and managerial employees. The complexity of operations, interactions, and decisions in all phases of industry and business needs both greater depth and greater breadth in planning and in organizing work, ideas, information flow, and resources. The up-word expression that in some quarters summarizes the person who can fulfill these requirements is "systems man." He learns to prepare and work from broad maps rather than from a chain of route markers. He is versatile in knowledge of the contexts of ideas, decisions, and operations.

The mammoth organism of men and machines never for long remains static. There is the increasingly heavy pressure of technological change that demands that the organism alter itself rapidly both in structure and habit.

The new world of computers, programming, simulation, business gaming, automation, information retrieval, operations research, decision modeling, communications, and so forth, is tearing open work compartments. Many men will have to know much more about many more things in order to control these dinosaurs. Education begins with the first day on the job, not the first day at school. It should also involve the knowledge that as things recede in time, there is a tendency to take a different perspective.

SUCCESS AND FAILURE

A person's criteria of success may be greatly different from those of his colleague. We cannot establish such criteria. The generally accepted definitions of success seldom satisfy any one person, and sometimes a man's criteria for personal success do not satisfy society in its abstract, mass personality. A man may hold a position of authority with responsibility and prestige and be making a good salary yet in his own judgment consider himself a failure. In contrast, the world at large may think a man a virtual failure, while he himself has reached a peace of mind which can fairly be called success.

The modern professional man or manager must balance the level of his ability and the level of his aspirations within a very critical set of limits to achieve success in his business and in his personal life. Repeated frustrations in his work efforts, as well as in other aspects of his life, usually result in lowering a man's aspirations. But when the levels of ability and of aspiration are not too far apart, occasional frustration or occasional failure can be the spur to drive a person on to his best efforts. It certainly helps shape him to take frustration in his stride. This is the tightrope to success.

The confidence that comes in this way, confidence to take planned managerial risks in spite of the possibility of rejection, reprimand, or even loss of job, is the confidence which makes a psychologically resilient and imaginatively successful manager. A man with this approach to life sees himself as an agent in his own progress, not as a tool of outside forces. Studies show that a change is beginning along the road to success—a change favoring the man of creative, autonomous thought and action [13, 74]. He is not willing to leave his life or his career to the manipulation of some superior officer, and he expects the rewards for his ideas and his actions. And he knows he must have the skills to go along with his drives. If he does not like his organizational climate, he will try to change it; however, his loyalty is strong because he is actively involving himself in the operations of the company. For another man success may involve a different set of values, a different way of living. Some people, as they come near the end of a career, may speak of themselves as did Abbé Sieyes. When asked, after the French Revolution, what he had done to distinguish himself during its most crucial period, he replied, "I survived."

Stress. In his writings on stress, Selye [55] highlights the importance of considering the wear and tear of life when one sets up his short-range, long-range, and ultimate goals. He maintains that stress is a normal counterpart of living. How we react to it is important. When he kept his experimental rats immobilized for extensive periods, they struggled desperately to get free so that they could engage in all the activities that normally provided them with their required quota of stress. Deprived of these activities, they actually made themselves ill in their efforts to maintain health. Often our tensions, conflicts, and frustrations stem from our struggles to play the role of someone we are not, and often we fail to heed our own cues of when we are exceeding our individual stress levels.

Selye emphasizes the fact that we must keep our smallest needs and greatest aspirations in harmony with our hereditary makeup. He points out that when each individual chooses his goals, he should not attempt primarily to avoid stress, which is a natural part of life, but rather to watch his individual stress level. Excessive stress over a period of time may cause such a depletion of energy that success in terms of status, productivity, and money loses its meaning.

In one study of over three thousand business executives aged between thirty-nine and fifty-nine, and employed in eleven northern California corporations, it was reported that the hard-driving manager with a pressing sense of the urgency of time is more likely to suffer a heart attack in his middle years than his more complacent colleague [53]. But it would be erroneous to conclude that stress is limited to high-level managers; evidence is to the contrary. For example, studies at Du Pont comparing the occurrence of heart attacks and other stress diseases in the executive group with the same disease entities in the general company population show almost exactly the same rate of incidence [23].

With increased emphasis being placed on executive responsibilities, managerial stress has recently been receiving study. Is there any relation between the amount of responsibility that a person carries and the psychological problems to which this exposes him? Yes. But again a number of studies support the conclusion that executives do not have a disproportionate amount of stress disorders compared to those down the line. One answer may be related to the findings from a ten-year study by General Motors Research Institute of men in various occupations [20]. It was found that as men advanced to positions of increasing responsibility, their mental and emotional stability increased, as did their ability to withstand strain. There was evidence that men who did not rise appreciably in occupational status during the ten-year period showed no improvement in personality adjustment.

It must be remembered that there are some people who enjoy the exhilaration of time-stress and choose jobs accordingly. Some may lose perspective as to the range of realistic alternatives in staying within individual stress levels, even when abetted by wife and family.

The Public Health Services report on a twelve-year study of business executives shows that their average life span is above normal. It could well be that the worker who worries about a layoff feels more stress than the vice-president whose job is in jeopardy. For one man a performance review may be a threat, and for another it may be a promise. Patterns of reaction to stress are as multidimensional as the organizational factors in absenteeism. The unconflicted executive expresses much the same dislikes for his job as does the conflicted manager. Whereas the former accepts the isolation of his position, including being treated as an office instead of a person or as a scapegoat for pressure groups, as a part of the game, the latter individual tries to fight the windmill. One explanation for the fact that top organizational people can withstand stress lies in natural selection. Many of those whose stress levels do not favor survival as executives do not reach this position [11, 32, 51, 62].

Longitudinal studies, using the Minnesota Multiphasic Personality Inventory (MMPI) and the Thurstone Temperament Schedule, found that those who developed coronary heart disease 14 years later had originally held higher scores on "hypochondriasis," "masculinity," and "activity."

It was found in a nationwide sample of people at different occupational levels that tension increases with rank and with income. The gradual increase in tension as one moves upward is represented by such instances as the proportion of persons reporting that pressures on them went up markedly with both the number of persons supervised and the number of levels of subordinates for which they were responsible. Coordinating the work of others is a factor in management stress, as is the mediation of differences between organizational departments. There is a relationship between a person's rank in an organization and the amount of pressure from associates. Pressure to *act* differently (pressure on activities) is highest among the upper groups, while pressure to *be* different (pressure on conduct) is highest in the middle-management group [31, 32].

Toward Personal Problem Solving. The adjustment problems of the unpromotable executive and the unappreciated scientist, the unclear frustrations of the supervisor, the secretary's hurt feelings, and the anxieties of the grimy-faced miner have something in common. They are statistics that do not get tabulated. For the individual, mental health involves the study of oneself.

Dollard and Miller [14] have stated the problem of self-study for normal people as ". . . a chance to think . . . for most people, life goes by too fast." For the person nearing the end of some formal education self-study may mean the chance to program a variety of disparate information. For the individual already along the way in his career development there may be more understanding that to know is to experience and that programmed activity may drive out unprogrammed behavior. It may be well to add the thought, however, that understanding the problem can sometimes destroy a satisfying feeling of confidence.

One portrait of Western man is that of adventurer, entrepreneur, risk taker. We know from experience and from studies that there are individual differences in risk taking [51]. The same environment which seems oppressive to one person may be a challenge to another. Intellectual risk taking involves having hypotheses and testing them, but at times it is difficult to unwind ideas from emotional attachments. It has been fashionable in some quarters to make the organization the whipping boy for mental ills, for anxieties and for the life that ranges from the quiet to the desperate. Industry may be less a maker of unhappy people than a place which fails to satisfy them.

Problem solving involves goal alternatives, and good mental-health practice means that one should choose knowing the probable costs of reaching his primary goals—costs in terms of personal and domestic insecurity from time to time, struggle against indifference, and the threat of failure that goes with the promise of success. Sometimes the alternative is to recognize the possibility of satisfaction in secondary goals. At least it may be well to be alert to their existence.

Information, relevant and available, is essential to effective adjustment, yet at times one may suffer from too much information. Involved are problems of personal evaluation looked at in terms of the kinds of climates most suitable for individual development. Of importance are the problems of one's own criteria of success and failure in terms of levels of aspiration and levels of stress. In the process of organizing information and setting up decision rules along several dimensions, the relevant facts that have been selected stand a better chance of filtering through for attention. Problem solving may be spurred on by considering what things come in what order and why; learning what things are personally frightening and why; what things bring on excitement, what things evoke procrastination, and what kinds of risks are enjoyable, and why. One may even question how far organizations can or should go in helping provide a climate for good mental health. Effective problem solving behooves each of us to look at our own personality and motivational characteristics, our own level of need achievement, and our own tolerance of ambiguity, uncertainty, and hostility. Habits of searching for alternatives in decision making and of anticipating the consequences are important not only for career survival but also for good health as well.

It may be good—at least it is realistic—to say there is no simple life for individuals in organizations.

SUGGESTIONS FOR SELECTIVE READING

Barron, F. *Creativity and psychological health.* Berkeley, Calif.: University of California Press, 1963. A study of 5,000 men and women on creativity, from ego strength to violence and vitality.

Bartels, R. (Ed.) *Ethics in business.* Columbus, Ohio: Ohio State University, Bureau of Business Research, 1963. Includes some nonpsychological examples of complications in decision making within a legal system.

Bennis, W. B., et al. (Eds.) *Interpersonal dynamics.* Homewood, Ill.: Dorsey, 1964. Readings on human interactions, from needs to skills of survival.

Biddle, B., & Thomas, E. (Eds.) *Social role: Readings in theory and application.* New York: Wiley, 1964. Readable to sophisticated articles.

Blake, R. R., & Mouton, Jane S. *The managerial grid.* Houston: Gulf, 1964. A view of the theories, façades, and deceptive strategies in some organizations.

Bloomberg, W., & Sunshine, M. *Suburban power structures and public education.* Syracuse, N.Y.: Syracuse University Press, 1963. A study of various types of community leadership.

Borow, H. (Ed.) *Man in a world at work.* Boston: Houghton Mifflin, 1964. Papers related to individuals and their problems at work.

Burns, T. & Stalker, G. M. *The management of innovation.* Chicago: Quadrangle, 1961. Some problems of communication in R&D organizations.

Collier, A. T. *Management, men, and values.* New York: Harper & Row, 1962. Through dramatic dialogue, a vice-president writes about the principles that underlie executive decision making.

Eckert, J. P. The integration of man and machine. *Proc. IRE,* 1962. Deals with the growing problems of technological and professional obsolescence.

Flanagan, J. C., et al. *The talent of American youth.* Vol. I. Boston: Houghton Mifflin, 1962. A large follow-through research study.

Gardner, J. W. *Excellence.* New York: Harper & Row, 1961. Excellence at all levels.

Gardner, J. W. *Self-renewal: The individual and the innovative society.* New York: Harper & Row, 1964. One reviewer describes as a "why-to-do-it" book; a sequel to *Excellence.*

Goffman, E. *The presentation of self in everyday life.* Garden City, N.Y.: Anchor Books, Doubleday, 1959. The various roles that people play.

Gross, Nancy E. *Living with stress.* New York: McGraw-Hill, 1958. A popular writer interprets the theories and experiments of Hans Selye.

Heath, D. H. *Explorations of maturity: Studies of mature and immature college men.* New York: Appleton-Century-Crofts, 1965. For the student interested in some of the criteria of adjustment.

Kahn, R. L., et al. *Organizational stress: Studies in role conflict and ambiguity.* New York: Wiley, 1964. Within the framework of role theory examines personal and social costs of working in modern organizations.

Kogan, N., & Wallach, M. A. *Risk taking: A study in cognition and personality.* New York: Holt, 1964. Psychology of thinking and the study of risk taking; sophisticated.

Kornhauser, W. *Scientists in industry: Conflict and accommodation.* Berkeley, Calif.: University of California Press, 1962. Adjustments of scientists in industrial research.

Lazarus, R. S. *Psychological stress and the coping process.* New York: McGraw-Hill, 1966. An overall picture of psychological research on stress; chapters range from readable to sophisticated.

Marcson, S. *The scientist in American industry.* Princeton, N.J.: Princeton University Press, 1960. Extension of material covered in this chapter.

Presthus, R. *Men at the top.* Fair Lawn, N.J.: Oxford University Press, 1964. Structure of influence in two communities in New York State.

Randsepp, E. *Managing creative scientists and engineers.* New York: Macmillan, 1963. A growing problem in R&D-emphasis industries.

Selye, H. *The stress of life.* New York: McGraw-Hill, 1956. Portions of book dealing with practical aspects of stress studies very readable.

Selye, H. *From dream to discovery.* New York: McGraw-Hill, 1964. A researcher on human stress looks at the scientists in terms of what they are and what they ought to be.

Shartle, C. L. *Occupational information: Its development and application.* (3d ed.) Englewood Cliffs, N.J.: Prentice-Hall, 1959. A practical book about jobs.

Smith, G. A., Jr., & Christensen, C. R. *Policy formulation and administration.* Homewood, Ill.: Irwin, 1962. A casebook of top-management problems in business.

Smith, L. J. *Career planning.* New York: Harper & Row, 1959. A readable book on careers.

Super, D. E. *The psychology of careers.* New York: Harper & Row, 1963. An overall view of both research and practical problems of careers from worker to professional.

Taylor, C., & Barron, F. (Eds.) *Scientific creativity: Its recognition and development.* New York: Wiley, 1963. Expands on some of the questions about career development for artist and manager, for the scientists, and for the innovators.

von Neumann, J., & Morgenstern, O. *The theory of games and economic behavior.* Princeton, N.J.: Princeton University Press, 1953. A sophisticated, mathematical classic that relates to some practical strategies.

Warner, W. L., & Martin, N. H. (Eds.) *Industrial man: Business men and business organizations.* New York: Harper & Row, 1959. A collection of articles about outstanding people.

Wepman, J. M., & Liebenson, H. A. *The psychologist as a witness.* Chicago: Callaghan, 1964. Some of the problems of the professional psychologist.

Worthy, J. C. *Big business and free men.* New York: Harper & Row, 1959. An industrial psychologist writes of organizations and men.

Wylie, Ruth C. *The self concept.* Lincoln, Nebr.: University of Nebraska Press, 1961. A critical survey of research; sophisticated.

Zaleznik, A., & Moment, D. *Casebook on interpersonal behavior in organizations.* New York: Wiley, 1964. Case studies illustrating some of the content of this chapter.

Bibliography

This bibliography includes some tangential background references which are not specifically cited in the text. These references are included for those who may wish to expand their reading beyond the limits of the book in following the development of problems.

CHAPTER 1

1. **Albee, G. W.** American psychology in the sixties. *Amer. Psychologist,* 1963, 18, 90–95.
2. **Ash, P., et al.** Industrial psychologists and their professional association. Special committee, Div. 14, American Psychological Association, April, 1963.
3. **Bennis, W. G.** A new role for the behavioral sciences: Effecting organizational change. *Admin. Sci. Quart.,* 1963, 8, 125–165.
4. **Berelson, B. (Ed.)** *The behavioral sciences today.* New York: Basic Books, 1963.
5. **Boynton, P. W.** *So you want a better job?* New York: Socony-Vacuum Oil Company, 1947.
6. **Brady, J. V.** Ulcers in "executive" monkeys. *Scient. Amer.,* 1958, 199, 95–99.
7. **Brainard, R. W., et al.** Design and interpretability of road signs. *J. Appl. Pyschol.,* 1961, 45, 130–136.
8. **Brown, C. W., & Ghiselli, E. E.** *Scientific method in psychology.* New York: McGraw-Hill, 1955.
9. **Clark, K. E.** *America's psychologists.* Washington, D.C.: American Psychological Association, 1957.
10. **DuBois, P. H.** A test-dominated society: China 1115 B.C.–1905 A.D. Invitational Conference on Testing Problems, New York, Oct. 31, 1964.

11. **Dunnette, M. D., & Kirchner, W. K.** *Psychology applied to industry.* New York: Appleton-Century-Crofts, 1965.
12. **Farmer, E.** Early days in industrial psychology: An autobiographical note. *Occup. Psychol.,* 1958, 32, 264–267.
13. **Ferguson, L. W.** Industrial psychology and labor. In Gilmer, B. v. H. (Ed.) *Walter VanDyke Bingham.* Pittsburgh, Pa.: Carnegie Institute of Technology, 1962.
14. **Ferguson, L. W.** *The heritage of industrial psychology.* Hartford, Conn.: Finlay Press, 1963.
15. **Gilmer, B. v. H.** Industrial psychology. *Annu. Rev. Psychol.,* 1960, 11, 323–350.
16. **Greenley, R. J.** Job training. *Labor Relat. Bull.,* National Association of Manufacturers, 1945, No. 35.
17. **Haire, M.** Business is too important to be studied only by economists. *Amer. Psychologist,* 1960, 15, 271–272.
18. **Haire, M.** The social sciences and management practices. *California Mgmt. Rev.,* 1964, Summer, 3–10.
19. **Havemann, E.** The age of psychology in the U.S. *Life,* Jan. 7, 1957, 68–82.
20. **Henderson, J. M., & Quandt, R. E.** *Microeconomic theory.* New York: McGraw-Hill, 1958.
21. **Hovland, C. I.** Two new social science research units in industrial settings. *Amer. Psychologist,* 1961, 16, 87–91.
22. **Katzell, R. A.** Industrial psychology. *Annu. Rev. Psychol.,* 1957, 8, 237–268.
23. **Kendall, W. E.** Industrial psychology. *Annu. Rev. Psychol.,* 1956, 7, 197–232.
24. **Klineberg, O.** Psychology on the international scene. *Psi Chi Newsltr,* 1963, Fall, 1–4.
25. **Krampen, M.** Storia dei segnali stradali. *Stile Industria, Milan,* 1961, 32, 23–24.
26. **Landsberger, H. A.** *Hawthorne revisited: Management and the worker, its critics, and developments in human relations in industry.* Ithaca: Cornell School of Industrial and Labor Relations, 1959.
27. **Leavitt, H. J., & Whisler, T. L.** Management in the 1980's. *Harv. Bus. Rev.,* 1958, 36, 41–48.
28. **Levinson, H.** The psychologist in industry. *Harv. Bus. Rev.,* 1959, 37, 93–99.
29. **Lindzey, G. (Ed.)** *Handbook of social psychology reading.* Reading, Mass.: Addison-Wesley, 1959.
30. **McCollom, I. N.** Psychologists in industry in the United States. *Amer. Psychologist,* 1959, 14, 704–708.
31. **McCollom, I. N.** Psychologists in industry in the United Kingdom and Western Germany. *Amer. Psychologist,* 1960, 15, 58–64.
32. **McGregor, D.** New concepts of management. *Technological Rev.,* 1961, 63, 2–4.
33. **Mayo, E.** *The social problems of an industrial civilization.* Cambridge, Mass.: Harvard University Press, 1945.

34. **Miner, J. B.** Psychology and the school of business curriculum. *J. Acad. Mgmt.,* 1963, 6, 284–289.
35. **Münsterberg, H.** *Psychology and industrial efficiency.* Boston: Houghton Mifflin, 1913.
36. **Ogg, E.** *Psychologists in action.* Washington, D.C.: Public Affairs Press, American Psychological Association, Public Affairs Pamphlet No. 229, 1955.
37. **Osgood, C. E.** *Method and theory in experimental psychology.* Fair Lawn, N.J.: Oxford University Press, 1953.
38. **Petz, B., et al.** Industrial psychology in Yugoslavia. *Bull. Int. Ass. Appl. Psychol.,* 1964, 13, 21–39.
39. **Roethlisberger, F. J., & Dickson, W. J.** *Management and the worker.* Cambridge, Mass.: Harvard University Press, 1939.
40. **Rosen, N. A., et al.** Motivational constraints in an individual retraining program. *Personnel Psychol.,* 1965, 18, 65–79.
41. **Smith, M.** *An introduction to industrial psychology.* London: Cassell, 1952.
42. **Solomon, D.** The effect of better width and spacing on night legibility of highway signs. *Publ. Roads,* 1956, 1, 1–11.
43. **Spence, K. W.** *Behavior theory and learning.* Englewood Cliffs, N.J.: Prentice-Hall, 1960.
44. **Stagner, R.** Some problems in contemporary industrial psychology. *Bull. Menninger Clin.,* 1957, 21, 238–247.
45. Symposium: Blueprinting the next ten years of industrial psychology. *Personnel Psychol.,* 1959, 12, 29–48.
46. **Taylor, F. W.** *The principles of scientific management.* New York: Harper, 1911.
47. **Townsend, J. C.** *Introduction to experimental method.* New York: McGraw-Hill, 1953.
48. **Tuddenham, R. D.** Psychological tests in historical perspective. Conference on Psychological Testing, San Francisco, Feb. 12–13, 1965.
49. **Viteles, M. S.** *Industrial psychology.* New York: Norton, 1932.
50. **Viteles, M. S.** Postlude to the application of psychology in industry. *J. Consult. Psychol.,* 1944, 8, 182–186.
51. **Vroom, V. H., & Maier, N. R. F.** Industrial social psychology. *Annu. Rev. Psychol.,* 1961, 12, 413–446.
52. **Wallace, S. R., Jr., & Weitz, J.** Industrial psychology. *Annu. Rev. Psychol.,* 1955, 6, 217–250.
53. **Watson, R. I., & Campbell, D. T.** *History, psychology, & science: Selected papers by Edwin G. Boring.* New York: Wiley, 1963.
54. **Webb, W. B. (Ed.)** *The profession of psychology.* New York: Holt, 1962.

CHAPTER 2

1. **Anderson, T., & Warkov, S.** Organizational size and functional complexity: A study of administration in hospitals. *Amer. Sociol. Rev.,* 1961, 26, 23–28.

2. **Bennis, W. G.** Leadership theory and administrative behavior. *Admin. Sci. Quart.*, 1959, 4, 259–301.

3. **Bennis, W. G.** Organizational developments and the fate of bureaucracy. Paper at American Psychological Association Annual Meeting, Los Angeles, Sept., 1964.

4. **Berne, E.** *The structure and dynamics of organizations and groups.* Philadelphia: Lippincott, 1963.

5. The "black box" plant is coming. *Dun's Rev. and Modern Industry,* March, 1965, 114–117, 185–194.

6. **Blake, R. R., et al.** Breakthrough in organization development. *Harv. Bus. Rev.,* 1964, 42, 133–155.

7. **Cooper, W. W.** Some implications of the newer analytic approaches to management. *California Mgmt. Rev.,* 1961, 4, 51–64.

8. **Cornell, W. B.** *Organization and management in industry and business.* New York: Ronald, 1958.

9. **Cyert, R. M., & March, J. G.** *A behavioral theory of the firm.* Englewood Cliffs, N.J.: Prentice-Hall, 1963.

10. **Englehart, D. C.** *Augmenting human intellect: A conceptual framework.* Menlo Park, Calif.: Stanford Research Institute, 1962.

11. **Evan, W.** Indices of the hierarchical structure of industrial organizations. *Mgmt. Sci.,* 1963, 9, 468–477.

12. **Gardner, J. W.** *Excellence.* New York: Harper & Row, 1961.

13. **Gilbreth, F. B., & Gilbreth, L. M.** *Applied motion study.* New York: Sturgis & Walton, 1917.

14. **Grusky, O.** Corporate size, bureaucratization, and managerial succession. *Amer. J. Sociol.,* 1961, 67, 261–269.

15. **Hale, E. G., & Almquist, J. O.** Relation of sexual behavior to germ cell output in farm animals. *J. Dairy Sci.,* 1960, 43, 145–169.

16. **Harvey, O. J., & Consalvi, C.** Status and conformity to pressures in informal groups. *J. Abnorm. Soc. Psychol.,* 1960, 60, 182–187.

17. **Janney, J. E.** Company presidents look at themselves. *Harv. Bus. Rev.,* 1952, 30, 59–70.

18. **Jones, E. G.** *The administration of industrial enterprises.* New York: Longmans, 1925.

19. **Langer, J., & Rosenberg, B. G.** Non-verbal representation of verbal referents. *Percept. Mot. Skills,* 1964, 19, 363–370.

20. **Lazarsfeld, P. F.** Latent structure analysis and test theory. In H. Gulliksen, & S. Messick (Eds.), *Psychological scaling: Theory and application.* New York: Wiley, 1960.

21. **Leavitt, H. J.** Management according to task: Organizational differentiation. *Mgmt Int. J.,* 1961, 2, 29–34.

22. **Leavitt, H. J.** Toward organizational psychology. In Gilmer, B. v. H. (Ed.) *Walter VanDyke Bingham.* Pittsburgh, Pa.: Carnegie Institute of Technology, 1962.

23. **Leavitt, H. J.** Unhuman organizations. *Harv. Bus. Rev.,* July–August, 1962.

24. **Leavitt, H. J. (Ed.)** *The social science of organizations: Four perspectives.* Englewood Cliffs, N.J.: Prentice-Hall, 1963.

25. **Mansfield, E.** Technical change and the rate of innovation. *Econometrica,* October, 1961.
26. **March, J. G., & Simon, H. A.** *Organizations.* New York: Wiley, 1958.
27. **Marcus, S.** New weapons against bigness. *Harv. Bus. Rev.,* 1965, 43, 100–108.
28. **Marx, M. H., & Hillix, W. A.** *Systems and theories in psychology.* New York: McGraw-Hill, 1963.
29. **Merton, R. K.** Bureaucratic structure and personality. *Soc. Forces,* 1940, 57, 560–568.
30. **Porter, L. W.** Where is the organization man? *Harv. Bus. Rev.,* 1963, 41, 53–61.
31. **Porter, L. W., & Lawler, E. E., III.** The effects of tall vs. flat organization structures in managerial job satisfaction. *Personnel Psychol.,* 1964, 17, 135–148.
32. **Porter, L. W., & Lawler, E. E., III.** Properties of organization structure in relation to job attitudes and job behavior. *Psychol. Bull.* 1965, 64, 23–51.
33. **Purcell, T. V.** *Blue collar man.* Cambridge, Mass.: Harvard University Press, 1960.
34. **Rasch, G.** *Studies in mathematical psychology.* Copenhagen: Danish Institute for Educational Research, 1960.
35. **Sayles, L. R.** *Behavior of industrial work groups: Prediction and control.* New York: Wiley, 1958.
36. **Schoen, D. R.** Human relations: Boon or bogle? *Harv. Bus. Rev.,* 1957, 35, 41–47.
37. **Shostak, A. B.** *America's forgotten labor organization.* Princeton, N.J.: Princeton University Press, 1962.
38. **Stryker, P.** Can management be managed? *Fortune,* July, 1953, 100–101.
39. **Taylor, F. W.** *The principles of scientific management.* New York: Harper, 1911.
40. **Walker, C. R. (Ed.)** *Modern technology and civilization.* New York: McGraw-Hill, 1962.
41. **Warner, W. L., & Abegglen, J. C.** *Occupational mobility in American business and industry.* Minneapolis: University of Minnesota Press, 1955.
42. **Worthy, J. C.** Organizational structure and employee morale. *Amer. Sociol. Rev.,* 1950, 15, 169–179.
43. **Zald, M.** Decentralization: Myth vs. reality. *Personnel,* 1964, 41, 19–26.

CHAPTER 3

1. **Abelson, P. H.** The appropriate function of a university. *Science,* 1964, 143, 11.
2. **Allport, G. W.** *Personality: A psychological interpretation.* New York: Holt, 1937.
3. **Argyris, C.** Some problems in conceptualizing organizational climate: A case study of a bank. *Admin. Sci. Quart.,* 1958, 2, 501–520.
4. **Balyeat, R. E.** Perceptions of industrial relations policies and practices:

A development project involving a pilot study in selected forms. Unpublished dissertation, University of Minnesota, 1961.

5. **Barnes, L. B.** *Organizational systems and engineering groups: A comparative study of two technical groups in industry.* Boston: Harvard Graduate School of Business Administration, 1960.

6. **Bass, B. M., & Berg, I. A. (Eds.)** *Conformity and deviation.* New York: Harper & Row, 1961.

7. **Baumgartel, H.** Using employee questionnaire results for improving organizations. *Kansas Bus. Rev.,* 1959, 12, 2–14.

8. **Bavelas, A.** Some problems of organizational change. *J. Soc. Issues,* 1948, 4, 48–52.

9. **Blau, P. M.** Cooperation and competition in a bureaucracy. *Amer. J. Sociol.,* 1954, 59, 530–535.

10. **Brogden, H. E.** Primary personal values measured by the Allport-Vernon test: A study of values. *Psychol. Monogr.,* 1952, 66, 1–31.

11. **Buchele, R. B.** Company character and the effectiveness of personnel management. *Personnel,* 1955, 31, 289–302.

12. **Bundy, McG.** The blessing that is federal aid. *Princeton Alumni Weekly,* Feb. 1, 1963, 6–13.

13. **Chapple, E. D., & Sayles, L. R.** *The measure of management.* New York: Macmillan, 1961.

14. **Clark, J. S.** *The increasing role of government.* New York: Fund for the Republic, May, 1963.

15. **Clem, J. E.** *Techniques of teaching typewriting.* (2d ed.) New York: McGraw-Hill, 1955.

16. **Crutchfield, R. S.** Detrimental effects of conformity pressures on creative thinking. *Psychol. Beit.,* 1962, 6, 463–471.

17. **Dalton, M.** Conflict between staff and line managerial officers. *Amer. Sociol. Rev.,* 1950, 15, 342–351.

18. **Derber, M., et al.** Environmental variables and union-management accommodation. *Industr. & Labor Relat. Rev.,* 1958, 11, 413–428.

19. **Deutsch, A.** *The management of scientific talent.* New York: American Management Association, 1963.

20. **Dill, W. R.** Environment as an influence on managerial autonomy. *Admin. Sci. Quart.,* 1958, 2, 409–443.

21. **Editors.** Executive staff and distaff. *Dun's Rev. and Modern Industry,* 1957, 69, 70–75.

22. **Etzioni, A.** *Complex organizations.* New York: Holt, 1961.

23. **Evan, W. M.** Indices of the hierarchical structure of industrial organizations. *Mgmt. Sci.,* 1963, 9, 468–477.

24. **Fleishman, E. A.** Leadership climate, human relations training, and supervisory behavior. *Personnel Psychol.,* 1953, 6, 205–222.

25. **Forehand, G. A., & Gilmer, B. v. H.** Environmental variation in studies of organizational behavior. *Psychol. Bull.,* 1964, 62, 361–382.

26. **Forehand, G. A., & Guetzkow, H.** The administrative judgement test as related to descriptions of executive judgement behaviors. *J. Appl. Psychol.,* 1961, 45, 257–261.

27. **Forehand, G. A., & Guetzkow, H.** Judgment and decision-making activities of government executives as described by superiors and co-workers. *Mgmt. Sci.,* 1962, 8, 359–370.
28. Fund raising practices. *Amer. Ass. Fund Raising Council,* 1962, 8, 1–4.
29. **Gellerman, S. W.** *People, problems and profits.* New York: McGraw-Hill, 1960.
30. **Ghiselli, E. E.** *The concept of role and theoretical basis for understanding organizations.* Bologna: University of Bologna Publications in Business Science, 1963.
31. **Gilmer, B. v. H., & Forehand, G. A.** Recent research on organizational climate. *Training Directors J.,* 1964, 18, 2–8.
32. **Glaser, E. M. (Ed.)** Psychologists in administration: A symposium. *Personnel Psychol.,* 1960, 13, 261–300.
33. **Golembiewski, R. T.** *The small group: An analysis of research concepts and operations.* Chicago: University of Chicago Press, 1962.
34. **Gorsuch, J. H.** Good management men delegate authority. *Advanc. Mgmt,* September, 1954, 5–8.
35. **Gouldner, A. W.** *Patterns of industrial bureaucracy.* New York: Free Press, 1954.
36. **Haire, M.** Size, shape, and function in industrial organizations. *Hum. Organization,* 1955, 14, 17–22.
37. **Helson, H.** Current trends and issues in adaptation—level theory. *Amer. Psychologist,* 1964, 19, 26–38.
38. **Hollander, E. P.** *Leaders, groups, and influence.* Fair Lawn, N.J.: Oxford University Press, 1964.
39. **Hovland, C. I.** Two new social science research units in industrial settings. *Amer. Psychologist,* 1961, 16, 87–91.
40. **Hunt, E. L.** *The revolt of the college intellectual.* New York: Human Relations Aids, 1963.
41. **Irwin, Mary. (Ed.)** *American universities and colleges.* Washington, D.C.: American Council on Education, 1960.
42. **Jackson, J.** *The normative regulation of authoritative behavior.* Lawrence, Kans.: Comparative Studies of Hospital Organization, September, 1962.
43. **Jacques, E.** *The changing culture of a factory.* London: Tavistock Press, Tavistock Institute, 1951.
44. **Katzell, R. A., et al.** Job satisfaction, job performance, and situational characteristics. *J. Appl. Psychol.,* 1961, 45, 65–72.
45. **Kerr, C.** *The uses of the university.* Cambridge, Mass.: Harvard University Press, 1963.
46. **Lea, T.** *The King ranch.* Boston: Little, Brown, 1957, 2 vols.
47. **Lewin, K., et al.** Patterns of aggressive behavior in experimentally created social climates. *J. Soc. Psychol.,* 1939, 10, 271–299.
48. **Likert, H.** *New patterns of management.* New York: McGraw-Hill, 1961.
49. **Lurie, M.** Professors, physicians, and unionism. *AAUP Bull.,* September, 1962, 272–276.
50. **McMurry, R. N.** Recruitment, dependency, and morale in the banking industry. *Admin. Sci. Quart.,* 1958, 3, 87–117.

51. **Mailick, S., & Van Ness, E.** *Concepts and issues in organizational behavior.* Englewood Cliffs, N.J.: Prentice-Hall, 1962.

52. **Mandell, M. M.** The effect of organizational environment on personnel selection. *Personnel,* 1953, 30, 13–16.

53. **Morgan, L. H.** *Ancient society.* New York: Holt, 1877.

54. **Pace, C. R.** Five college environments. *Coll. Bd. Rev.,* 1960, 41, 24-28.

55. **Pace, C. R., & Stern, G. G.** An approach to the measurement of psychological characteristics of college environments. *J. Educ. Psychol.,* 1958, 49, 269–277.

56. **Palmer, G. J.** *Test of a theory of leadership and organizational behavior with management gaming.* Baton Rouge, La.: Louisiana State University, ONR Contract Nonr 1575 (05), 1961.

57. **Paterson, D. G.** The conservation of human talent. Walter VanDyke Bingham Lecture, Ohio State University, Apr. 17, 1956.

58. **Penny, R.** Organizational structures in experimental groups. *Acta Psycholog.,* 1964, 22, 3–24.

59. **Porter, K. H.** Department head or chairman? *AAUP Bull.,* 1961, Winter, 339–342.

60. **Presthus, R.** *The organizational society.* New York: Knopf, 1962.

61. Problem for the front office. *Fortune,* May, 1951.

62. **Rosecrance, F. C.** *The American college and its teachers.* New York: Macmillan, 1963.

63. **Sanford, N. (Ed.)** *The American college.* New York: Wiley, 1962.

64. **Sayles, L. R.** *Individualism and big business.* New York: McGraw-Hill, 1963.

65. **Schein, E. H.** Interpersonal communication, group solidarity, and social influence. *Sociometry,* 1960, 23, 148–161.

66. **Scott, C.** Behavior factors in success and failure: A long range study. Paper presented at Pennsylvania Psychological Association, Lancaster, Pa., 1963.

67. **Sofer, C.** *The organization from within.* London: Tavistock Press, Tavistock Institute, 1962.

68. **Sutherland, R. L., et al. (Eds.)** *Personality factors on the college campus: Review of a symposium.* Austin, Tex.: University of Texas, Hogg Foundation for Mental Health, 1962.

69. **Thomas, E. J., & Fink, C. F.** Effects of group size. *Psychol. Bull.,* 1963, 60, 371–384.

70. **Vale, R. B.** *Efficiency in Hades.* Philadelphia: Stokes, 1923.

71. **Vollmer, H. M.** *A preliminary investigation and analysis of the role of scientists in research organizations.* Menlo Park, Calif.: Stanford Research Institute, SRI Project No. IMU-3580, February, 1962.

72. **Vollmer, H. M.** *Adaptation of scientists in an independent research organization: A case history.* Menlo Park, Calif.: Stanford Research Institute, 1963.

73. **Vroom, V. H.** The effects of attitudes on perception of organizational goals. *Hum. Relat.,* 1960, 13, 229–240.

74. **Walker, E. L., & Heyns, R. W.** *An anatomy of conformity.* Englewood Cliffs, N.J.: Prentice-Hall, 1962.

75. **Warner, W. L., & Abegglen, J. C.** Successful wives of successful executives. *Harv. Bus. Rev.,* 1956, 34, 64–70.
76. **Willis, R. H.** Conformity, independent, and anti-conformity. *Hum. Relat.,* in press.
77. Wives learn executive worries. *Business Week,* 1962, Jan. 13, 1962, 46–48.
78. **Zerfoss, L. F., & O'Connor, R. F.** The atmosphere in which people grow. *Atlanta Econ. Rev.,* 1960, 10, 11–14.

CHAPTER 4

1. **Alexander, R. S.** *Marketing definitions.* New York: American Marketing Association, 1960.
2. **Bayton, J.** Motivation, cognition, learning: Basic factors in consumer behavior. *J. Marketing,* January, 1958, 282–289.
3. **Becknell, J. C., Jr., & McIsaac, R. W.** Test marketing cookware coated with "Teflon." *J. Adv. Res.,* 1963, 3, 1–8.
4. **Bell, M. L.** *Marketing: A maturing discipline.* New York: American Marketing Association, 1960.
5. **Blackelock, E.** A look at the new leisure. *Admin. Sci. Quart.,* March, 1960, 446–467.
6. **Blankenship, A. B.** *How to conduct consumer and opinion research.* New York: Harper & Row, 1946.
7. **Bliss, P. (Ed.)** *Marketing and the behavioral sciences.* Boston: Allyn and Bacon, 1963.
8. **Britt, S. H.** Four hazards of motivation research: How to avoid them. *Printers' Ink,* 1955, 250, 40–48.
9. **Brooks, R. C.** Relating the selling effort to patterns of purchase behavior. *Business Topics,* 1963, Winter, 73–79.
10. **Brown, L. O.** What motivation research is and how it works: Its advantages and shortcomings. *Adv. Age,* 1955, 26, 65–69.
11. **Burtt, H. E.** *Psychology of advertising.* Boston: Houghton Mifflin, 1938.
12. **Buzzell, R. D.** Is marketing a science? *Harv. Bus. Rev.,* 1963, 41, 32–48.
13. **Cash, H. C.** Old research technique turns out to be "motivation" study. *Printers' Ink,* 1955, 40–41.
14. **Cash, H. C., & Crissy, W. J. E.** *A point of view for salesmen.* New York: Personnel Development, Inc., 1957.
15. **Cash, H. C., & Crissy, W. J. E.** *Managing sales resistance.* New York: Personnel Development, Inc., 1962.
16. **Cash, H. C., & Crissy, W. J. E.** *Tactics for conducting sales call.* New York: Personnel Development, Inc., 1964.
17. **Caswell, W. C.** Marketing effectiveness and sales supervision. *California Mgmt. Rev.,* 1964, 7, 39–44.
18. **Cochran, Betty, & Thompson, G. C.** Why new products fail. *Conf. Bd Rec.,* 1964, 1, 11–18.

19. **Committee Appointed by Advertising Research Foundation.** *Copy testing.* New York: Ronald, 1939.

20. **Cox, D. F.** Clues for advertising strategists. *Harv. Bus. Rev.,* 1961, 39, 160.

21. **Crissy, W. J. E., & Cash, H. C.** *Motivation in selling.* New York: Personnel Development, Inc., 1958.

22. **Crissy, W. J. E., & Cash, H. C.** *Guiding buying behavior.* New York: Personnel Development, Inc., 1965.

23. **Cunningham, R. M.** Brand loyalty: What, where, how much? *Harv. Bus. Rev.,* January, February, 1956, 116–128.

24. **Dichter, E.** Public relations and mass motivations. *J. Communication,* 1953, 3, 90–96.

25. **Dix, A. H.** Here's what happens when Starch scores are checked by mail. *Printers' Ink,* 1955, 257, 24–27.

26. **Evans, F. B.** The brand image myth. *Business Horizons,* 1961, 4, 19–28.

27. Factors related to success in the last sales interview. *Life Insurance in Focus,* Life Insurance Agency Management Association, Hartford, Conn., 1963, 3, 1–78.

28. **Ferber, R., & Wales, H.** *Motivation and market behavior.* Homewood, Ill.: Irwin, 1958.

29. **Flynn, J. E.** Some do's and don't's for test marketing. *Mgmt. Rev.,* 1960, 49, 38–41.

30. **Frederick, J. G.** *Introduction to motivation research.* New York: Business Bourse, 1957.

31. **Frey, A. W.** *Advertising.* (2d ed.) New York: Ronald, 1953.

32. **Gold, J. A.** Testing test market predictions. *J. Marketing Res.,* 1964, 1, 8–16.

33. **Gray, J. S. (Ed.)** *Psychology in use.* New York: American Book, 1941.

34. **Guest, L.** Consumer analysis. *Annu. Rev. Psychol.,* 1962, 13, 315–344.

35. **Haire, M.** Projective techniques in marketing research. *J. Marketing,* 1950, 14, 649–656.

36. **Hattwick, M. S.** *How to use psychology for better advertising.* Englewood Cliffs, N.J.: Prentice-Hall, 1950.

37. **Henell, O.** *Some science in personal selling.* Stockholm: Esselte Reklam, 1961.

38. **Hepner, H. W.** *Modern advertising: Practices and principles.* (3d ed.) New York: McGraw-Hill, 1956.

39. **Hepner, H. W.** *Psychology applied to life and work.* Englewood Cliffs, N.J.: Prentice-Hall, 1965.

40. **Herzog, H.** Behavioral science concepts for analyzing the consumer. In D. J. Duncan (Ed.), *Proceedings, conference of marketing.* Berkeley, Calif.: University of California Press, 1958.

41. **Husband, R. W.** *Applied psychology.* New York: Harper & Row, 1949.

42. **Husband, R. W.** *The psychology of successful selling.* New York: Harper & Row, 1953.

43. **Ivey, P. W.** *Successful salesmanship.* Englewood Cliffs, N.J.: Prentice-Hall, 1947.

44. **Jones, E. H., & Sumner, F. C.** Relation of the brightness differences of colors to their apparent distances. *J. Psychol.*, 1948, 26, 25–29.
45. **Katona, G.** *The powerful consumer.* New York: McGraw-Hill, 1960.
46. **Kleppner, O.** *Advertising procedures.* Englewood Cliffs, N.J.: Prentice-Hall, 1950.
47. **Krugman, H. E.** The learning of consumer preference. *J. Marketing,* April, 1962, 31–33.
48. **Kuehn, A. A.** Consumer brand choice as a learning process. *J. Adv. Res.,* 1962, 2, 10–17.
49. **Kuehn, A. A., & Day, R. L.** Strategy of produce quality. *Harv. Bus. Rev.,* 1962, 40, 100–110.
50. **Lazer, W.** The role of models in marketing. *J. Marketing,* April, 1962, 9–14.
51. **Levitt, T.** Marketing myopia. *Harv. Bus. Rev.,* July–August, 1960, 45–56.
52. **Lucas, E. B., & Murphy, M. J.** False identification of advertisements in recognition tests. *J. Appl. Psychol.,* 1939, 23, 264–269.
53. **McKinney, F.** An empirical method of analyzing a sales interview. *J. Appl. Psychol.,* 1937, 21, 280.
54. **McNiven, M. A.** Advertising research. Paper presented before Philadelphia Operations Research Society, October, 1964.
55. **Martineau, P.** *Motivation in advertising.* New York: McGraw-Hill, 1957.
56. **Moyer, K. E., & Gilmer, B. v. H.** Attention spans of children for experimentally designed toys. *J. Genet. Psychol.,* 1955, 87, 187–201.
57. **Nafziger, R. O.** Problems in reader-interest surveys. *J. Marketing,* April, 1945, 359–363.
58. **Newman, J. W.** *Motivation research and marketing management.* Boston: Harvard Business School, Division of Research, 1957.
59. **Nixon, H. K.** *Principles of advertising.* New York: McGraw-Hill, 1937.
60. **Ostwald, Rosemarie.** Fat content and fatty acids in some commercial mixes for baked products. *J. Amer. Diet. Ass.,* 1963, 42, 32–36.
61. **Perloff, R.** The work of the industrial psychologist in relation to consumers and the public. *Business Soc.,* 1964, 4, 23–34.
62. **Poffenberger, A. T.** *Psychology in advertising.* (2d ed.) New York: McGraw-Hill, 1932.
63. **Politz, A.** Science and truth in marketing research. *Harv. Bus. Rev.,* 1957, 35, 117–126.
64. **Reynolds, W. H.** The role of the consumer in image building. *California Mgmt. Rev.,* 1965, 7, 69–76.
65. **Roper, E., et al.** *A study among buyers of Woman's Day.* Greenwich, Conn.: Fawcett, 1960.
66. **Rudolph, H. J.** *Attention and interest factors in advertising.* New York: Funk & Wagnalls, 1947.
67. **Smith, G. H.** *An introductory bibliography of motivation research.* New York: Advertising Research Foundation, 1953.
68. **Spires, A. M., & LeBlanc, A. G.** The relative effectiveness of absolute size in advertisements: A pilot study. *Bull. Maritime Psychol. Ass.,* 1956, 5, 16–20.

69. **Starch, D.** Testing the effectiveness of advertisements. *Harv. Bus. Rev.,* 1923, 1, 464–474.
70. **Starch, D.** What is new about motivation research? *Printers' Ink,* 1955, 252, 58–61.
71. **Starch, D.** How well do people read long advertisements? *Advertising Agency,* 1956, 49, 66–67.
72. **Starch, D.** How well-read are comic strip ads? *Advertising Agency,* 1956, 49, 72–74.
73. **Strong, E. K., Jr.** *Psychology of selling and advertising.* New York: McGraw-Hill, 1925.
74. **Strong, E. K., Jr.** *Psychological aspects of business.* New York: McGraw-Hill, 1938.
75. **Trenchard, K. E., & Crissy, W. J. E.** Trends in the use of certain attention-getting devices in newsweekly advertising. *J. Appl. Psychol.,* 1951, 35, 287–288.
76. **Tucker, W. T., & Painter, J. J.** Personality and produce use. *J. Appl. Psychol.,* 1961, 45, 325–329.
77. **Twedt, D. W.** Consumer psychology. *Annu. Rev. Psychol.,* 1965, 16, 265–294.
78. **Van Bortel, F. J.** Motivation research and the confusing consumer. *J. Home Econ.,* 1956, 48, 22–24.
79. **Weilbacker, W. M.** The qualitative values of advertising media. *J. Adv. Res.,* 1960, 1, 12–17.
80. **Weitz, J.** A study of trade name confusion. *J. Marketing,* 1960, 25, 54–56.
81. **Westfall, R.** Psychological factors in predicting product choice. *J. Marketing,* April, 1962, 34–40.
82. **Wiseman, M.** *The anatomy of advertising.* New York: Harper & Row, 1942.
83. **Wolf, H. A. (Ed.)** *Motivation research, a new aid to understanding your market.* Boston: Motivation Research Associates, 1955.
84. **Wolfe, H. D., et al.** *Measuring advertising results.* New York: National Industrial Conference Board, 1962.
85. **Woods, W. A.** Psychological dimensions of consumer decision. *J. Marketing,* 1960, 24, 15–19.
86. **Wulfeck, J. W., & Bennett, E. M.** *The language of dynamic psychology as related to motivation research.* New York: McGraw-Hill, 1954.
87. **Zubin, J., & Peatman, J. G.** Testing the pulling power of advertisements by the split-run copy method. *J. Appl. Psychol.,* 1945, 29, 40–57.

CHAPTER 5

1. **Allport, G. W.** *Pattern and growth in personality.* New York: Holt, 1961.
2. **Appel, K.** Where do they go for help? *Amer. Psychologist,* 1963, 18, 167–168.
3. **Atkinson, J. W.** *An introduction to motivation.* Princeton, N.J.: Van Nostrand, 1964.

4. **Baldamus, W.** Type of work and motivation. *Brit. J. Sociol.,* 1951, 2, 44–58.
5. **Bergler, E.** *The revolt of the middle-age man.* New York: Wyn, 1954.
6. **Bowers, D. G.** Self-esteem and the diffusion of leadership style. *J. Appl. Psychol.,* 1963, 47, 135–140.
7. **Brayfield, A. H., & Crockett, W. H.** Employee attitudes and employee performance. *Psychol. Bull.,* 1955, 52, 396–424.
8. **Clark, F. L.** *Growing old in a mechanized world.* London: Nuffield Foundation, 1960.
9. **Dill, W. R., et al.** How aspiring managers promote their own careers. *California Mgmt. Rev.,* 1960, 2 (4), 9–15.
10. **Dublin, L. I.** *Suicide: A sociological and statistical study.* New York: Ronald, 1963.
11. **Eaton, W. H.** Hypotheses related to worker frustration. *J. Soc. Psychol.,* 1952, 35, 59–68.
12. **Gardner, J. W.** *Excellence.* New York: Harper & Row, 1961.
13. **Gellerman, S. W.** *People, problems and profits.* New York: McGraw-Hill, 1960.
14. **Goetz, B. E.** Avoiding managerial obsolescence. *California Mgmt. Rev.,* 1965, 7, 91–96.
15. **Halliday, J. L.** *Psychosocial medicine.* New York: Norton, 1948.
16. **Harlow, H. F., & Harlow, Margaret K.** Social deprivation in monkeys. *Scient. Amer.,* November, 1962, 3–10.
17. **Havemann, E.** *They went to college.* New York: Harcourt, Brace & World, 1952.
18. **Homans, G. C.** The Western Electric researches. In G. C. Homans (Eds.), *Fatigue of workers: Its relation to production.* New York: Reinhold, 1941.
19. **Homans, G. C.** *The human group.* New York: Harcourt, Brace & World, 1950.
20. **Hoos, Ida R.** *Automation in the office.* Washington, D.C.: Public Affairs Press, 1961.
21. **Jellinek, E. M.** The estimate of the number of alcoholics in the U.S.A. for 1949 in the light of the sixth revision of the international lists of causes of death. *Quart. J. Stud. Alcohol,* 1952, 13, 215–218.
22. **Jones, M. R. (Ed.)** *Nebraska symposium on motivation.* Lincoln, Nebr.: University of Nebraska Press, 1965.
23. **Kasl, S. V., & French, J. R. P., Jr.** The effects of occupational status on physical and mental health. *J. Soc. Issues,* 1962, 18, 67–89.
24. **Keller, M., & Efron, C.** The prevalence of alcoholism. *Quart. J. Stud. Alcohol,* 1955, 16, 619–644.
25. **Kubie, L. S.** Psychiatry in industry. *Personnel J.,* 1945, 24, 50–55.
26. **Leavitt, H. J.** *Managerial psychology.* Chicago: University of Chicago Press, 1964.
27. **Lewin, K.** Forces behind food habits and methods of change. *Bull. National Res. Council,* 1943, 108, 35–65.
28. **McClelland, D. C., et al.** *The achievement motive.* New York: Appleton-Century-Crofts, 1953.

29. **McGregor, D., & Knickerbocker, I.** Industrial relations and national defense: A challenge to management. *Personnel,* 1941, 18, 49–63.
30. **Maier, N. R. F.** *Principles of human relations.* New York: Wiley, 1952.
31. **Mann, F., & Williams, L.** Some effects of the changing work environment in the office. *J. Soc. Issues,* 1962, 18, 90–101.
32. **Marcus-Steiff, J.** *Les études du motivation.* Paris: Hermann & Cie, 1961.
33. **Meade, R. D.** Time on their hands. *Personnel J.,* 1960, 39, 130–132, 142.
34. **Moore, H.** Basic needs of industrial workers. *Personnel J.,* 1949, 27, 344–348.
35. **Page, R. C., et al.** The problem drinker in industry. *Quart. J. Stud. Alcohol,* 1952, 13, 370–396.
36. **Rosen, H., & Weaver, C. G.** Motivation in management: A study of four managerial levels. *J. Appl. Psychol.,* 1960, 44, 386–392.
37. **Sampson, E. E.** Status congruence and cognitive consistency. *Sociometry,* 1963, 26, 146–162.
38. **Srole, L., et al.** *Mental health in the metropolis: The midtown Manhattan study.* New York: McGraw-Hill, 1962.
39. **Stagner, R.** Psychological aspects of industrial conflict: II. Motivation. *Personnel Psychol.,* 1950, 3, 1–5.
40. **Stern, G. G.** Student ecology and the college environment. *J. Med. Educ.,* 1965, 40, 132–154.
41. **Taylor, Janet A.** Drive theory and manifest anxiety. *Psychol. Bull.,* 1956, 53, 303–320.
42. **Thompson, G. N. (Ed.)** *Alcoholism.* Springfield, Ill.: Charles C Thomas, 1956.
43. **Tuddenham, R. D.** The influence upon judgment of the apparent discrepancy between self and others. *J. Soc. Psychol.,* 1961, 53, 69–79.
44. **Vernon, J.** *Inside the black room.* New York: Potter, 1964.
45. **White, R.** Motivation reconsidered: The concept of competence. *Psychol. Rev.,* 1959, 66, 297–333.
46. **Wittmer, J. J.** Alcoholism in industry: New policy of the Consolidated Edison Company of New York. *Quart. J. Stud. Alcohol,* 1949, 10, 376–379.
47. **Wyatt, S., et al.** *Incentives in repetitive work.* London: Industrial Health Research Board, No. 69, 1934.

CHAPTER 6

1. **Barrett, R. S.** Guide to using psychological tests. *Harv. Bus. Rev.,* 1963, 41, 138–146.
2. **Biesheuvel, S.** Personnel selection. *Annu. Rev. Psychol.,* 1965, 16, 295–324.
3. **Buckner, D. N.** The predictability of ratings as a function of interrater performance. *J. Appl. Psychol.,* 1959, 43, 60–64.
4. **Buros, O. K.** *The sixth mental measurements yearbook.* New Brunswick, N.J.: Rutgers University Press, 1965.

5. **Crissy, W. J. E.** Who's watching the watcher of watchers? *Contemp. Psychol.*, 1963, 8, 228–229.
6. **Cronbach, L. J., & Gleser, Goldine C.** *Psychological tests and personnel decisions.* Urbana, Ill.: University of Illinois Press, 1965.
7. **Crow, K., & Crow, Alice.** (**Eds.**) *Educating the academically able.* New York: McKay, 1963.
8. **Daniels, H., & Otis, J.** A method of analyzing employment interviews. *Personnel Psychol.*, 1950, 3, 425–444.
9. **DuBois, P.** *Multivariate correlational analysis.* New York: Harper & Row, 1957.
10. **Flanagan, J. C.** The critical incident technique. *Psychol. Bull.*, 1954, 51, 327–358.
11. **Flanagan, J. C., & Krug, R. E.** Testing in management selection: State of the art. *Personnel Admin.*, 1964, 27, 3–5, 36–39.
12. **Flanagan, J. C., et al.** *The American high school student.* Pittsburgh, Pa.: University of Pittsburgh, Project TALENT Office, Technical Report U.S. Office of Education, Project 635, 1964.
13. **Ford, J. S., et al.** *Employee aptitude survey: A battery of practical employment tests.* Los Angeles: Psychological Services, Inc., 1960.
14. **Forehand, G. A.** Comments on comments on testing. *Educ. & Psychol. Measmt,* 1964, 24, 853–859.
15. **Gagné, R. M., & Fleishman, E. A.** *Psychology and human performance.* New York: Holt, 1959.
16. **Ghiselli, E. E., & Haire, M.** The validation of selection tests in the light of the dynamic character of criteria. *Personnel Psychol.*, 1960, 13, 225–231.
17. **Greene, E. B.** *Measurements of human behavior.* New York: Odyssey, 1952.
18. **Gross, M. L.** *The brain watchers.* New York: Random House, 1962.
19. **Guilford, J. P.** The structure of intellect. *Psychol. Bull.*, 1956, 53, 267–293.
20. **Habbe, S.** The controversy over psychological testing. *National Industr. Conf. Bd Mgmt Rec.*, 1963, 25.
21. **Horst, A. P.** A technique for the development of a differential prediction battery. *Psychol. Monogr.*, 1954, 68, No. 9.
22. **Hudson, W., & Kruger, C. F.** The selection of African supervisors by leaderless group tests. *Inter-African Labour Inst. Bull.*, 1958, 5, 1–10.
23. **Kennedy, J. E.** A general device versus more specific devices for selecting car salesmen. *J. Appl. Psychol.*, 1958, 42, 206–209.
24. **Litton, G. W.** It's a job—sorting heifers you'll keep. *Livestock Breeder J.,* October, 1962, 16–17, 140.
25. **Locke, E. A., & Hulin, C. L.** A review and evaluation of the validity studies of activity vector analysis. *Personnel Psychol.*, 1962, 15, 25–42.
26. **McGehee, W.** And Esau was a hairy man. *Amer. Psychologist,* 1964, 19, 799–804.
27. **McKee, J. P., & Sherriffs, A. C.** The differential evaluation of males and females. *J. Personnel,* 1957, 25, 356–371.
28. **Miner, J. B.** Personality and ability factors in sales performance. *J. Appl. Psychol.*, 1962, 46, 6–13.

29. **Nagle, B. F.** Criterion development. *Personnel Psychol.,* 1953, 6, 271–289.
30. **Primoff, E. J.** *Test selection by job analysis.* United States Civil Service Commission Assembled Test Technical Series, No. 20, May, 1955.
31. **Ruch, F. L., & Ruch, W. W.** Predicting success in draftsman training with short time limit aptitude tests. *Educ.-Psychol. Measmt,* 1960, 20, 827–833.
32. **Sayigh, Y. A.** *Entrepreneurs of Lebanon: The role of the business leader in a developing economy.* Cambridge, Mass.: Harvard University Press, 1962.
33. **Schwarz, P. A.** *Development of manpower screening tests for the developing nations.* Pittsburgh, Pa.: American Institutes for Research, 1964.
34. **Shriver, S.** Two years of the Peace Corps. *Foreign Affairs,* July, 1963.
35. **Sisson, D. E.** Forced-choice: The new army rating. *Personnel Psychol.,* 1948, 1, 365–381.
36. **Stagner, R.** The gullibility of personnel managers. *Personnel Psychol.,* 1958, 11, 347–352.
37. **Taylor, E. K., & Nevis, E. C.** Personnel selection. *Annu. Rev. Psychol.,* 1961, 12, 389–412.
38. **Taylor, H. C., & Russell, J. T.** The relationship of validity coefficients to the practical effectiveness of tests in selection: Discussion and tables. *J. Appl. Psychol.,* 1939, 23, 565–578.
39. **Thorndike, R. L.** *Personnel selection.* New York: Wiley, 1949.
40. **Thorndike, R. L., & Hagen, Elizabeth.** *Measurements and evaluation in psychology and education.* New York: Wiley, 1955.
41. **Uhrbrock, R. S.** The personnel interview. *Personnel Psychol.,* 1948, 1, 276.
42. **Wallace, S. R., Jr.** Criteria for what? Paper read to Div. 14 of American Psychological Association, Los Angeles, September, 1964.
43. **Weiss, D. J., & Davis, R. V.** An objective validation of factual interview data. *J. Appl. Psychol.,* 1960, 44, 381–384.
44. **Weitz, J.** Criteria for criteria. *Amer. Psychologist,* 1961, 16, 228–231.
45. **Wherry, R. J.** Criteria and validity. In D. H. Fryer and E. R. Henry (Eds.), *Handbook of applied psychology.* New York: Rinehart, 1950. Vol. 1, chap. 27.
46. **Wherry, R. J.** *A comparison of various rating methods.* Washington, D.C., Adjutant General's Office, PRB Report No. 921, February, 1952.
47. **Wherry, R. J.** The past and future of criterion evaluation. *Personnel Psychol.,* 1957, 10, 1–5.
48. **Whisler, T. L., & Harper, S. F. (Eds.)** *Performance appraisal.* New York: Holt, 1962.

CHAPTER 7

1. **American Management Association.** *Teaching machines: Selected references.* New York: Author, 1961.
2. **Bandura, A., & Walters, R. H.** *Social learning and personality development.* New York: Holt, 1963.
3. **Birmingham, H. D., et al.** *Demonstration of the effects of quickening in*

multiple-coordinate control tasks. Washington, D.C.: Naval Research Laboratory, 1954.

4. **Braun, H. W., et al.** The effect of an irrelevant drive on maze learning in the rat. *J. Exp. Psychol.*, 1957, 54 (2), 148–152.

5. **Bruner, J. S.** *On knowing: Essays for the left hand.* Cambridge, Mass.: Harvard University Press, 1962.

6. **Bryan, G. L.** Empirical evaluation of various job-analysis methods. In *Symposium on Electronics Maintenance.* Washington, D.C.: GPO, August, 1955.

7. **Bryan, G. L., & Nagay, J. A.** Use in the military and government agencies. In R. Glaser (Ed.), *Teaching machines and programmed learning: II. Data and directions.* Washington, D.C.: National Education Association, 1964.

8. **Campbell, Iva.** *Teaching machines and programmed learning: A bibliography.* New York: Teaching Materials Corporation, 1961.

9. **Chalupsky, A. B., & Nelsen, D. D.** Programmed learning: Better than regular text books? *Personnel J.*, 1964, 43, 542–547.

10. **Coulson, J. E. (Ed.)** *Teaching machines and computer-based programming.* New York: Wiley, 1962.

11. **Cummings, T. F., et al.** *The development and use of three self-teaching books.* Poughkeepsie, N.Y.: International Business Machines Corporation, 1962.

12. **Dolmatch, T. B., et al. (Eds.)** *Revolution in training.* New York: American Management Association, 1962.

13. **Ebel, R. L.** Obtaining and reporting evidence on content validity. *Educ. Psychol. Measmt,* 1956, 16, 269–282.

14. **Frederiksen, N., et al.** The in-basket test. *Psychol. Monogr.,* 1957, 71, No. 9 (Whole No. 438).

15. **Fryer, D. H., et al.** *Developing people in industry.* New York: Harper & Row, 1956.

16. **Gagné, R. M.** Training devices and simulators: Some research issues. *Amer. Psychologist,* 1954, 9, 95–107.

17. **Gagné, R. M.** Methods of forecasting maintenance job requirements. In *Symposium on Electronics Maintenance.* Washington, D.C.: GPO, August, 1955.

18. **Gagné, R. M.** Military training and principles of learning. *Amer. Psychologist,* 1962, 17, 83–91.

19. **Gagné, R. M.** Simulators. In R. Glaser (Ed.), *Training research and education.* Pittsburgh, Pa.: University of Pittsburgh Press, 1962.

20. **Gagné, R. M., & Bolles, R. C.** A review of factors in learning efficiency. In E. Galanter (Ed.), *Automatic teaching: The state of the art.* New York: Wiley, 1959.

21. **Gilmer, B. v. H.** The third crisis in industrial training. *Training Directors J.,* 1962, 16, 4–11.

22. **Glaser, R.** Learning and the technology of instruction. *Audiovisual Communication Rev.,* 1961, 9, 42–55.

23. **Glaser, R. (Ed.)** *Training research and education.* Pittsburgh, Pa.: University of Pittsburgh Press, 1962.

24. **Glaser, R.** Instructional technology and the measurement of learning outcomes: Some questions. *Amer. Psychologist,* 1963, 18, 519–521.
25. **Glaser, R.** *Teaching machines and programmed learning: II. Data and directions.* Washington, D.C.: National Education Association, 1964.
26. **Glaser, R., & Klaus, D. J.** Proficiency measurement: Assessing human performance. In R. M. Gagné (Ed.), *Psychological principles in system development.* New York: Holt, 1962.
27. **Glaser, R., et al.** The tab item: A technique for the measurement of proficiency in diagnostic problem solving tasks. *Educ. Psychol. Measmt,* 1954, 14, 283–293.
28. **Guthrie, E. R. (Ed.)** Conditioning: A theory of learning in terms of stimulus, response, and association. *Yearb. Nat. Soc. Stud. Educ.,* 1942, 41, 17–60.
29. **Haggard, D. F.** *The feasibility of developing a task classification structure for ordering training principles and training content.* Ft. Knox, Ky.: U.S. Army Human Research Unit, January, 1963.
30. **Harlow, H.** The formation of learning sets. *Psychol. Rev.,* 1949, 56, 51–65.
31. **Hartley, J.** Programmed learning in emerging nations. *Bull. Brit. Psychol. Soc.,* 1964, 17, 19–23.
32. **Hughes, J. L.** *Programmed learning: A critical evaluation.* Chicago: Educational Methods, Inc., 1964.
33. **Keller, F. S., & Schoenfeld, W. N.** *Principles of psychology.* New York: Appleton-Century-Crofts, 1950.
34. **Kendler, H. H.** Drive interaction: I. Learning as a function of the simultaneous presence of the hunger and thirst drives. *J. Exp. Psychol.,* 1945, 35, 96–107.
35. **Lindahl, L. G.** Movement analysis as an industrial training method. *J. Appl. Psychol.,* 1945, 29, 420–436.
36. **Lumsdaine, A. A.** Experimental research on instructional devices and materials. In R. Glaser (Ed.), *Training research and education.* Pittsburgh, Pa.: University of Pittsburgh Press, 1962.
37. **Lumsdaine, A. A.** Instruments and media of instruction. In N. L. Gage (Ed.), *Handbook of research on teaching.* Chicago: Rand McNally, 1963.
38. **Lumsdaine, A. A., & Glaser, R. (Eds.)** *Teaching machines and programmed learning.* Washington, D.C.: National Education Association, 1960.
39. **Miller, R. B.** *Psychological considerations for the design of training equipment.* Pittsburgh, Pa.: American Institute for Research, Wright Air Development Center Technical Report 54-563, 1954.
40. **Miller, R. B.** Analysis and specification of behavior for training. In R. Glaser (Ed.), *Training research and education.* Pittsburgh, Pa.: University of Pittsburgh Press, 1962.
41. **Miller, R. B.** Task description and analysis. In R. M. Gagné (Ed.), *Psychological principles in system development.* New York: Holt, 1962.
42. **Murphy, J. R., & Goldberg, I. A.** Strategies for using programmed instruction. *Harv. Bus. Rev.,* 1964, 42, 115–132.
43. **Shoemaker, H. A., & Holt, O. H.** Use in industry. In R. Glaser (Ed.),

Teaching machines and programmed learning: II. Data and directions. Washington, D.C.: National Education Association, 1964.

44. **Skinner, B. F.** *Science and human behavior.* New York: Macmillan, 1953.

45. **Skinner, B. F.** Teaching machines. *Science,* 1958, 128, 969–977.

46. **Skinner, B. F.** The programming of verbal knowledge. In E. Galanter (Ed.), *Automatic teaching: The state of the art.* New York: Wiley, 1959.

47. **Spence, K. W.** *Behavior theory and conditioning.* New Haven, Conn.: Yale University Press, 1956.

48. **Taylor, H. C., & Russell, J. T.** The relationship of validity coefficients to the practical effectiveness of tests in selection. *J. Appl. Psychol.,* 1939, 23, 565–578.

49. **Taylor, Janet A.** Drive theory and manifest anxiety. *Psychol. Bull.,* 1956, 53, 303–320.

50. **Thorndike, R. L.** *Personnel selection.* New York: Wiley, 1949.

51. **VanCott, H. P., & Altman, J. W.** *Procedures for including human engineering factors in the development of weapon systems.* Wright Air Development Center Technical Report 56-488, October, 1956.

52. **Wolfle, D. L.** Training. In S. S. Stevens (Ed.), *Handbook of experimental psychology.* New York: Wiley, 1951.

CHAPTER 8

1. **Arensberg, C. M., & McGregor, D.** Determination of morale in an industrial company. *Appl. Anthrop.,* 1942, 1, 12–34.

2. **Argyris, C.** *Integrating the individual and the organization.* New York: Wiley, 1964.

3. **Baumgartel, H., & Sobol, R.** Background and organizational factors in absenteeism. *Personnel Psychol.,* 1959, 12, 431–443.

4. **Beuge, E. J.** Morale of supervisors. *Advanc. Mgmt,* 1959, 24, 17–19.

5. **Bingham, W. V.** Making work worthwhile. In E. M. East (Ed.), *Biology in human affairs.* New York: McGraw-Hill, 1931.

6. **Bomholt, N.** *Supervisors performance reports in Scandinavia.* Standard Oil Company of New Jersey, Report III, 1963.

7. **Bradford, L. P., et al. (Eds.)** *T-Group theory and laboratory method.* New York: Wiley, 1964.

8. **Day, R., & Hamblin, R.** Some effects of close and punitive styles of supervision. *Amer. J. Sociol.,* 1964, 69, 499–510.

9. **Deutsch, A. R.** Non-union grievances. *Industrial Relations News,* May, 1962, 1–3.

10. **Dunnette, M. D., et al.** The effect of group participation on brainstorming effectiveness for two industrial samples. *J. Appl. Psychol.,* 1963, 47, 30–37.

11. **File, Q. W., & Remmers, H. H.** *How supervise?* New York: Psychological Corporation, 1948.

12. **Fleishman, E. A., & Harris, E. F.** Patterns of leadership behavior related to employee grievances and turnover. *Personnel Psychol.,* 1962, 15, 43–56.

13. **Fleishman, E. A., et al.** *Leadership and supervision in industry: an evaluation of a supervisory training program.* Columbus, Ohio: Ohio State University, Bureau of Educational Research, No. 33, 1955.

14. **Fraser, R.** *The incidence of neurosis among factory workers.* London: Industrial Health Research Board, No. 90, 1947.

15. **Habbe, S.** Job attitudes of life insurance agents. *J. Appl. Psychol.,* 1947, 31, 111–128.

16. **Hatch, R. S.** *An evaluation of a force-choice differential accuracy approach to the measurement of supervisory empathy.* Englewood Cliffs, N.J.: Prentice-Hall, 1962.

17. **Hedberg, M.** *Labour turnover.* Stockholm: Swedish Council for Personnel Administration, 1961.

18. **Henderson, R. M., & Bacon, S. D.** Problem drinking: The Yale Plan for business and industry. *Quart. J. Stud. Alcohol,* 1953, 14, 247–262.

19. **Hersey, R.** *Better foremanship.* Philadelphia: Chilton, 1955.

20. **Herzberg, F., et al.** *Job attitudes: Review of research and opinion.* Pittsburgh, Pa.: Psychological Service of Pittsburgh, 1957.

21. **Jacobs, T. O.** *Basic problems in small-unit leadership.* Ft. Benning, Ga.: U.S. Army Infantry Human Research Unit, February, 1962.

22. **Jarrard, L. E.** Empathy: The concept and industrial application. *Personnel Psychol.,* 1956, 9, 157–167.

23. **Kay, B. R., & Palmer, S.** *The challenge of supervision.* New York: McGraw-Hill, 1961.

24. **Kay, E.** An experimental study of some methodological and psychological aspects of industrial absenteeism. Unpublished doctoral dissertation, Carnegie Institute of Technology, 1956.

25. **Kennedy, J. L.** A "transition-model" laboratory for research on cultural change. *Hum. Organization,* 1955, 14, 16–18.

26. **Kerr, W. A., & Speroff, B. J.** *The empathy test.* Chicago: Psychometric Affiliates, 1951.

27. **Korner, I. N.** Of values, value lag, and mental health. *Amer. Psychologist,* 1956, 11, 543–546.

28. **Kornhauser, A. W.** *Mental health of the industrial worker: Detroit study.* New York: Wiley, 1964.

29. **Lawrence, P., et al.** *Organizational behavior and administration.* Homewood, Ill.: Irwin, 1961.

30. **Life Insurance Agency Management Association.** *Buddy ratings: A technique for supervisory selection.* Hartford, Conn.: Author, Research Report No. 10, 1957.

31. **Lindauer, M.** *Communication among social bees.* Cambridge, Mass.: Harvard University Press, 1961.

32. **Ling, T. M.** *Mental health and human relations in industry.* London: H. K. Lewis, 1954.

33. **Maccoby, N. A.** A quantitative comparison of certain psychological conditions related to group productivity in two widely different industrial situations. Unpublished doctoral dissertation, University of Michigan, 1950.

34. **McKersie, R. B.** Avoiding written grievances by problem-solving: An outside view. *Personnel Psychol.*, 1964, 17, 367–379.
35. **McMurry, R. N.** The problem of resistance to change in industry. *J. Appl. Psychol.*, 1947, 31, 589–593.
36. **Maier, N. R. F.** *Principles of human relations.* New York: Wiley, 1952.
37. **Mann, F. C., & Dent, J.** *Appraisals of supervisors and attitudes of their employees in an electric power company.* Ann Arbor, Mich.: University of Michigan, Survey Research Center, 1954.
38. **Mann, F., & Williams, L.** Some effects of the changing work environment in the office. *J. Soc. Issues,* 1962, 18, 90–101.
39. **Meltzer, H.** Mental health realities in work situations. *Amer. J. Orthopsychiat.,* 1963, 33, 562–565.
40. **Miles, M. B.** Human relations training: Processes and outcomes. *J. Counsel. Psychol.,* 1960, 7, 301–306.
41. **Muller-Thym, B. J.** Reconstructing the supervisory job. *Personnel,* 1954, 30, 396–405.
42. **Nagle, B. F.** Productivity, employee attitude, and supervisor sensitivity. *Personnel Psychol.,* 1954, 7, 219–233.
43. **Neel, R. G.** Nervous stress in the industrial situation. *Personnel Psychol.,* 1955, 8, 405–415.
44. **Newton, R.** An investigation of certain personality factors in relation to industrial absenteeism. Unpublished thesis, Pennsylvania State University, 1950.
45. **Oriorne, G. S.** The trouble with sensitivity training. *Training Directors J.,* 1963, 17, 9–20.
46. **Parker, W. E., & Kleemeier, R. W.** *Human relations in supervision.* New York: McGraw-Hill, 1951.
47. **Patton, W. M., Jr.** Studies in industrial empathy: III. A study of supervisory empathy in the textile industry. *J. Appl. Psychol.,* 1954, 38, 285–288.
48. **Pelz, D. C.** Influence: A key to effective leadership in the first-line supervisor. *Personnel,* 1952, 29, 209–217.
49. **Pfiffner, J. M.** The effective supervisor: An organization research study. *Personnel,* 1955, 31, 530–540.
50. **Plummer, N., & Hinkle, L.** Life stress and industrial absenteeism: Concentration of illness and absenteeism in one segment of a working population in New York Telephone Company. *Industr. Med.,* 1952, 22, 363–375.
51. **Remmers, L. J., & Remmers, H. H.** Studies in industrial empathy: Labor leaders' attitudes toward industrial supervision and their estimates of management's attitudes. *Personnel Psychol.,* 1949, 2, 427–436.
52. **Roethlisberger, F. J., & Dickson, W. J.** *Management and the worker.* Cambridge, Mass.: Harvard University Press, 1939.
53. **Rogers, C. R.** *Client-centered therapy.* Boston: Houghton Mifflin, 1951.
54. **Scott, W. G.** *Human relations in management.* Homewood, Ill.: Irwin, 1964.
55. **Siegel, A. I.** An experimental evaluation of the sensitivity of the empathy test. *J. Appl. Psychol.,* 1954, 38, 222–223.

56. **Stagner, R.** Psychological aspects of industrial conflict. *Personnel Psychol.,* 1950, 3, 1–15.
57. **Thorne, F. C.** Directive counseling in psychotherapy. *Amer. Psychologist,* 1948, 3, 160–165.
58. **Triandis, H. C.** Some determinants of interpersonal communication effectiveness. *Hum. Relat.,* 1960, 13, 279–287.
59. **Viteles, M. S.** *Motivation and morale in industry.* New York: Norton, 1953.
60. **Walker, C. R.** The problem of the repetitive job. *Harv. Bus. Rev.,* 1950, 28, 54–58.
61. **Walker, C. R., et al.** *The foreman on the assembly line.* Cambridge, Mass.: Harvard University Press, 1956.
62. **Wallen, R.** Improving supervision by reducing anxiety. *Personnel J.,* 1951, 30, 9–13.
63. **Weitz, J.** Selecting supervisors with peer ratings. *Personnel Psychol.,* 1958, 11, 25–35.
64. **Weschler, I. R., et al.** *Yardsticks for human relations training.* Berkeley, Calif.: University of California, Institute of Industrial Relations, No. 66, 1957.
65. **Whyte, W. F.** *Human relations in the restaurant industry.* New York: McGraw-Hill, 1948.
66. **Wilson, R. C., et al.** An iterative analysis of supervisory and group dimensions. *J. Appl. Psychol.,* 1955, 39, 85–91.
67. **Wray, D. E.** Marginal men of industry: The foremen. *Amer. J. Sociol.,* 1949, 55, 298.
68. **Yanauzas, J. N.** A comparative study of work organization and supervisory behavior. *Hum. Organization,* 1964, 23, 245–253.

CHAPTER 9

1. **Ahren, E.** Executive appraisal: a new approach. *Mgmt News,* American Management Association, Mar. 31, 1950.
2. **Anshen, M.** Management development. Western Electric Company, Skytop Conference, May 23, 1957.
3. **Anshen, M., & Bach, G. L. (Eds.)** *Management and corporations 1985.* New York: McGraw-Hill, 1960.
4. **Argyris, C.** *Executive leadership: An appraisal of a manager in action.* New York: Harper & Row, 1953.
5. **Barnard, C. I.** *The functions of the executive.* Cambridge, Mass.: Harvard University Press, 1950.
6. **Bennis, W. G.** Revisionist theory of leadership. *Harv. Bus. Rev.,* 1961, 39, 26–40.
7. **Carlson, S.** *Executive behavior.* Stockholm: Strömbergs, 1951.
8. **Cattell, R. B., & Stice, G. F.** *The psychodynamics of small groups.* Urbana, Ill.: University of Illinois Press, 1953.
9. **Chowdhry, Kamla.** Management development programs: Executive needs. *Industr. Mgmt Rev.,* 1963, Spring, 31–40.

10. **Chowdhry, Kamla.** Management development programs: Moratorium for executives. *Hum. Organization,* 1964, 23, 254–259.
11. **Cleeton, G. U., & Mason, C. W.** *Executive ability: Its discovery and development.* Yellow Springs, Ohio: Antioch Press, 1946.
12. **Coates, C. H., & Pelligrin, R. J.** Executives and supervisors: A situational theory of differential occupational mobility. *Soc. Forces,* 1956, 35, 121–126.
13. **Crissy, W. J. E., et al.** Field assignments for individual managerial development. *Business Topics,* 1963, Winter, 49–63.
14. **Dill, W. R., et al.** *Conference on business games.* New Orleans: Tulane University Press, 1961.
15. **Dubin, R., & Spray, S. L.** Executive behavior and interaction. *Industr. Relat.,* 1964, 3, 99–108.
16. **Dunnette, M. D., et al.** The effect of group participation on brainstorming effectiveness for two industrial samples. *J. Appl. Psychol.,* 1963, 47, 30–37.
17. **Feinberg, M. R., & Lefkowitz, J.** Image of industrial psychology among corporate executives. *Amer. Psychologist,* 1962, 17, 109–111.
18. **Fiedler, F. E.** The contingency model: A theory of leadership effectiveness. In H. Proshansky & B. Seidenberg (Eds.), *Basic studies in social psychology.* New York: Holt, 1965.
19. *Fortune* Editors. The nine hundred. In W. M. Fox (Ed.), *Readings in personnel management.* New York: Holt, 1957. Pp. 18–25.
20. **Frederiksen, N.** Factors in in-basket performance. *Psychol. Monogr.,* 1962, No. 541.
21. **Frederiksen, N., et al.** The in-basket test. *Psychol.-Monogr.,* 1957, 71, No. 9 (Whole No. 438).
22. **Gardner, B. B.** Executives: Their personality and its appraisal. *Advanc. Mgmt,* January, 1953, 13–15.
23. **Ghiselli, E. E.** Managerial talent. *Amer. Psychologist,* 1963, 18, 631–642.
24. **Gibb, C. A.** Leadership. In G. Lindzey (Ed.), *Handbook of social psychology.* Reading, Mass.: Addison-Wesley, 1954.
25. **Ginzberg, E.** *What makes an executive?* New York: Columbia, 1955.
26. **Goetz, B. E.** Avoiding managerial obsolescence. *California Mgmt. Rev.,* 1965, 7, 91–96.
27. **Gorsuch, J. H.** Executive growth: Making better use of university programs. *Business Horizons,* 1963, Spring, 57–62.
28. **Haire, M., et al.** Cultural patterns in the role of the manager. *Industr. Relat.,* 1963, 2, 95–117.
29. **Harrell, T. W.** *Manager's performance and personality.* Cincinnati: South-Western Publishing Company, 1961.
30. **Hemphill, J. K.** *Dimensions of executive positions.* Columbus, Ohio: Ohio State University Press, 1960.
31. **Hemphill, J., et al.** *Administrative performance and personality.* New York: Teachers College, 1962.
32. **Henry, W. E.** The business executive: The psychodynamics of a social role. *Amer. J. Sociol.,* 1949, 54, 286–291.

33. **Hilton, T. L., & Dill, W. R.** Salary growth as a measure of career progress. *J. Appl. Psychol.,* 1962, 46, 153–158.
34. **Homans, G. C.** *The human group.* New York: Harcourt, Brace & World, 1950.
35. **Hulin, C. L.** The measurement of executive success. *J. Appl. Psychol.,* 1962, 46, 303–306.
36. **Hulin, C. L.** The dimensions of executive success. Paper read at Midwestern Psychological Association, Chicago, May, 1963.
37. **Johnson, E. P.** A new kind of performance review emphasizes executives' development. *Personnel J.,* 1954, 33, 131–133.
38. **Kazmier, L. J.** The psychologist as a behavioral scientist in the business school. *Amer. Psychologist,* 1962, 17, 253–254.
39. **Kellogg, M. S.** Appraising the performance of management personnel: A case study. *Personnel,* 1955, 31, 442–455.
40. **Knickerbocker, I.** Leadership: a conception and some implications. *J. Soc. Issues,* 1948, 4, 24–41.
41. **Leavitt, H. J., & Whisler, T. L.** Management in the 1980's. *Harv. Bus. Rev.,* 1958, 36, 41–48.
42. **Lewin, K.** *A dynamic theory of personality.* New York: McGraw-Hill, 1935.
43. **Lewin, K.** *Field theory in social science.* New York: Harper & Row, 1951.
44. **Mace, M. L.** *The growth and development of executives.* Cambridge, Mass.: Harvard University Press, 1950.
45. **Machaver, W. C., & Erickson, W. E.** A new approach to executive appraisal. *Personnel,* 1958, 35, 8–14.
46. **McMurry, R. N.** The executive neurosis. *Harv. Bus. Rev.,* 1952, 30, 33–47.
47. **Mahler, W. R., & Guyot, F.** Appraisal of executive performance, the "Achilles heel" of management development. *Personnel,* 1955, 31, 429–441.
48. **Nash, A. N.** Vocational interests of effective managers: A review of the literature. *Personnel Psychol.,* 1965, 18, 21–37.
49. **Neel, R. G.** Nervous stress in the industrial situation. *Personnel Psychol.,* 1955, 8, 405–415.
50. **OSS Assessment Staff.** *The assessment of men.* New York: Rinehart, 1948.
51. **Peck, R. F., & Thompson, J. M.** Use of individual assessments in a management development program: a case study. *J. Personnel Admin. Industr. Relat.,* April, 1954, 79–98.
52. **Pellegrin, R. J., & Coates, C. H.** Executives and supervisors: Contrasting definitions of career success. *Admin. Sci. Quart.,* 1957, 1, 506–517.
53. **Planty, E. G., & Efferson, C. E.** Counseling executives after merit rating or evaluation. *Personnel,* 1951, 27, 384–402.
54. **Ramfalk, C. W.** *Top management selection.* Stockholm: Swedish Council for Personnel Administration, 1957.
55. **Randle, C. W.** How to identify promotable executives. *Harv. Bus. Rev.,* 1956, 34, 122–134.
56. **Schein, E. H.** How to break in the college graduate. *Harv. Bus. Rev.,* 1964, 42, 68–76.

57. **Schleh, E. C.** Make your executive merit rating realistic. *Personnel,* 1953, 29, 480–484.
58. **Schneirla, T. C.** Social organization in insects as related to individual function. *Psychol. Rev.,* 1941, 48, 465–486.
59. **Shartle, C. L.** *Executive performance and leadership.* Englewood Cliffs, N.J.: Prentice-Hall, 1956.
60. **Spaulding, G. E., Jr.** The "effective" executive: What qualities make the difference? *Mgmt. Rev.,* 1964, 53, 4–15.
61. **Standard Oil Company of California.** *A practical approach to executive development.* San Francisco: Author, 1948.
62. **Stark, S.** Executive foresight: Definitions, illustrations, importance. *J. Business,* 1961, 34, 31–44.
63. **Stogdill, R. M.** Personal factors associated with leadership: A survey of the literature. *J. Psychol.,* 1948, 25, 35–71.
64. **Stryker, P.** On the meaning of executive qualities. *Fortune,* 1958, 57, 116–119.
65. **Tagiuri, R. (Ed.)** *Research needs in executive selection: A symposium.* Boston: Harvard Graduate School of Business Administration, 1961.
66. **Ward, B.** Worker's management in Yugoslavia. *J. Political Econ.,* 1957, 45, 373–387.
67. **Whyte, W. F.** *The organization man.* New York: Simon and Schuster, 1956.
68. **Williams, E. H.** Business games: Their use for the training of managers. *Personnel Mgmt,* 1961, 43, 239–244.
69. **Wilson, A. T. M.** The manager and his world. *Industr. Mgmt Rev.,* 1961, 3, 1–26.

CHAPTER 10

1. **Ayres, L. P.** The influence of music on speed in the six day bicycle race. *Amer. Physical Educ. Rev.,* 1911, 16, 321–324.
2. **Bavelas, A.** Communication patterns in task-oriented groups. *J. Acoust. Soc. Amer.,* 1950, 22, 725–750.
3. **Bellows, R. M.** *Psychology of personnel in business and industry.* Englewood Cliffs, N.J.: Prentice-Hall, 1963.
4. **Blauner, R.** Work satisfaction and industrial trends in modern society. In W. Galenson & S. M. Lipset (Eds.), *Labor and trade unionism.* New York: Wiley, 1960.
5. **Blum, M. L.** *Industrial psychology and its social foundations.* New York: Harper & Row, 1956.
6. **Brown, J. A. C.** *The social psychology of industry.* Baltimore: Pelican Series. Penguin, 1954.
7. **Brown, R. L.** New methods help management to measure employee morale. *Amer. Textile Reporter,* May, 1962, 1–5.
8. **Browne, C. G.** Executive leadership in business: IV. Sociometric pattern. *J. Appl. Psychol.,* 1951, 35, 34–37.

9. **Chinoy, E.** The tradition of opportunity and the aspirations of automotive workers. *Amer. J. Sociol.,* 1952, 57, 453–459.

10. **Coch, L., & French, J. R. P., Jr.** Overcoming resistance to change. *Hum. Relat.,* 1949, 1, 512–532.

11. **Costello, T. W., & Zalkind, S. S.** *Psychology in administration: A research orientation.* Englewood Cliffs, N.J.: Prentice-Hall, 1963.

12. **Costello, T. W., et al.** An analysis of attitudes toward a planned merger. Paper presented at the Eighth Annual International Meeting of The Institute of Management Sciences, Brussels, August, 1961.

13. **Dalton, M.** Worker response and social background. *J. Political Econ.,* 1947, 55, 323–332.

14. **Eran, M.** The relationship between self-perceived personality traits and job attitudes in middle management. Unpublished doctoral dissertation, University of California, Berkeley, Calif., 1965.

15. **Felton, J. S., & Spencer, C.** *Morale of workers exposed to high levels of occupational noise.* Norman, Okla.: University of Oklahoma School of Medicine, 1957. Pp. 1–59.

16. **Friedlander, F.** Job characteristics as satisfiers and dissatisfiers. *J. Appl. Psychol.,* 1964, 48, 388–392.

17. **Guetzkow, H., & Simon, H. A.** The impact of certain communication nets in task-oriented groups. *Mgmt Sci.,* 1955, 1, 233–250.

18. **Guion, R. M.** Industrial morale: The problem of terminology. *Personnel Psychol.,* 1958, 11, 59–61.

19. **Hawaii Visitors Bureau.** *Visitor Reaction Survey.* Honolulu: Author, 1964.

20. **Herzberg, F., et al.** *Job attitudes: Review of research and opinion.* Pittsburgh, Pa.: Psychological Service of Pittsburgh, 1957.

21. **Hoppock, R.** A twenty-seven year follow-up on job satisfaction of employed adults. *Personnel Guid. J.,* 1960, 38, 489–492.

22. **Insel, S. A., et al.** The turnover of corporate executives. Paper presented to California State Psychological Association, 1964.

23. **Jacobsen, E. H.** Foreman-steward participation practices and worker attitudes in a unionized factory. Unpublished doctoral dissertation, University of Michigan, 1951.

24. **Katz, D.** Employee groups: What motivates them and how they perform. *Advanc. Mgmt,* 1949, 14, 119–124.

25. **Kay, E., et al.** *A study of the performance appraisal interview.* New York: General Electric Company, Employee Relations, 1963. Pp. 1–36.

26. **Kolaja, J.** *A Polish factory: A case study of worker's participation in decision making.* Lexington, Ky.: University of Kentucky Press, 1961.

27. **Kolaja, J.** A Yugoslav workers council. *Hum. Organization,* 1961, 20, 27–31.

28. **Kornhauser, W.** *Scientists in industry.* Berkeley, Calif.: University of California Press, 1962.

29. **Likert, R.** *New patterns of management.* New York: McGraw-Hill, 1961.

30. **Marrow, A., & French, J. R. P., Jr.** Changing a stereotype in industry. *J. Soc. Issues,* 1945, 3, 33–37.

31. **Meltzer, L., & Salter, J.** Organization structure and the performance and job satisfaction of physiologists. *Amer. Sociol. Rev.,* 1962, 27, 351–362.

32. **Miles, W. R.** *Immediate psychological effects in an exploratory study of the biological effects of noise.* Benox Report. Chicago: University of Chicago Press, 1953.

33. **Moreno, J.** *Who shall survive?* Washington: Nervous and Mental Diseases Publishing Company, 1934.

34. **Morse, Nancy C.** *Satisfactions in the white collar job.* Ann Arbor, Mich.: University of Michigan, Institute for Social Research, 1953.

35. **Mulder, M.** Power and satisfaction in task oriented groups. *Acta Psychol.,* 1959, 16, 128–225.

36. **Paterson, D. G., & Stone, C. H.** Dissatisfaction with life work among adult workers. *Occupations,* 1942, 21, 219–221.

37. **Porter, L. W.** Job attitudes in management: Perceived satisfaction and importance of needs. *J. Appl. Psychol.,* 1962, 46, 375–397.

38. **Porter, L. W.** *Organizational patterns of managerial work attitudes.* New York: American Foundation for Management Research Association, 1964. Pp. 1–61.

39. **Rice, A. K.** Productivity and social organization in an Indian weaving shed. *Hum. Relat.,* 1953, 6, 297–329.

40. **Roethlisberger, F. J., & Dickson, W. J.** *Management and the worker.* Cambridge, Mass.: Harvard University Press, 1939.

41. **Rosenberg, M. J., et al.** *Attitude, organization, and change.* New Haven, Conn.: Yale University Press, 1960.

42. **Schuh, A. J.** *Labor turnover: An individual, industrial, and national problem.* Personal communication, 1965.

43. **Shaw, M. E.** Some effects of unequal distribution of information upon group performance in various· communication nets. *J. Abnorm. Soc. Psychol.,* 1954, 49, 547–553.

44. **Teel, K. S., & Kinkade, R. G.** Attitudes of production workers toward closed-circuit television. *Personnel Psychol.,* 1964, 17, 1–6.

45. **Trist, E. L., & Bamforth, K. W.** Some social psychological consequences of the long-wall method of coal-getting. *Hum. Relat.,* 1951, 4, 3–38.

46. **Trow, D. B.** Autonomy and job satisfaction in task-oriented groups. *J. Abnorm. Soc. Psychol.,* 1957, 54, 204–209.

47. **Uhrbrock, R. S.** Music on the job: Its influence on worker morale and production. *J. Appl. Psychol.,* 1961, 14, 9–38.

48. **Viteles, M. S.** *Motivation and morale in industry.* New York: Norton, 1953.

49. **Vroom, V. H.** Ego-involvement, job satisfaction, and job performance. *Personnel Psychol.,* 1962, 15, 159–177.

50. **Wickert, F. R.** Turnover and employees' feelings of ego-involvement in the day-to-day operations of a company. *Personnel Psychol.,* 1951, 4, 185–197.

51. **Worthy, J. C.** Factors influencing employee morale. *Harv. Bus. Rev.,* 1950, 28, 61–73.

CHAPTER 11

1. **Adams, J. S., & Rosenbaum, W. B.** The relationship of worker productivity to cognitive dissonance about wage inequities. *J. Appl. Psychol.*, 1962, 46, 161–164.
2. **Adams, O. S., & Chiles, W. D.** *Prolonged human performance as a function of the work-rest cycle.* Marietta, Ga.: Lockheed Aircraft Corporation, TR ORD 273, 1961.
3. **Andrews, I. R. & Henry, Mildred M.** Management attitudes toward pay. *Industr. Relat.*, 1963, 3, 29–39.
4. **Arrowood, A. J.** Some effects on productivity of justified and unjustified levels of reward under public and private conditions. Unpublished dissertation, University of Minnesota, 1961.
5. **Baetjer, A. M.** Light, temperature and humidity. *Industr. Med.*, 1944, 13, 11–112.
6. **Barnes, R. M.** *Motion and time study.* New York: Wiley, 1958.
7. **Berry, P. C.** Effect of colored illumination upon perceived temperature. *J. Appl. Psychol.*, 1961, 45, 248–250.
8. **Best, W. H.** Some new directions in personnel appraisal. *Personnel*, 1957, 34, 45–50.
9. **Blaire, R. N.** A fresh look at the principles of motion economy. *J. Industr. Engng*, 1958, 9, 3–5.
10. **Broadbent, D. E., & Little, E. A. J.** Effect of noise reduction in work situation. *Occup. Psychol.*, 1960, 34, 133–140.
11. **Burnham, R. W.** *Color: A guide to basic facts and concepts.* New York: Wiley, 1963.
12. **California Institute of Technology.** *Shorter work week.* (Pamphlet.) Pasadena, Calif.: Author, 1963.
13. **Chalupsky, A. B.** Comparative factor analysis of clerical jobs. *J. Appl. Psychol.*, 1962, 46, 62–66.
14. **Cleeton, G. U.** *Making work human.* Yellow Springs, Ohio: Antioch Press, 1949.
15. **Davis, K.** *Human relations in business.* New York: McGraw-Hill, 1957.
16. **Flanagan, J. C.** A new approach to evaluating personnel. *Personnel*, 1957, 34, 45–50.
17. **Floyd, W. F., & Welford, A. T.** *Symposium on fatigue.* London: H. K. Lewis, 1953.
18. **Friedlander, F., & Walton, E.** Positive and negative motivations toward work. *Admin. Sci. Quart.*, 1964, 9, 194–207.
19. **Ghiselli, E. E., & Brown, C. W.** *Personnel and industrial psychology.* New York: McGraw-Hill, 1955.
20. **Glorig, A., et al.** Hearing loss in industry. *Laryngoscope*, 1958, 68, 447–465.
21. **Gregg, L. W., & Jarrard, L. E.** Changes in muscle action potentials during prolonged work. *J. Comp. Physiol. Psychol.*, 1958, 51, 532–535.

22. **Haire, M., et al.** Psychological research on pay: An overview. *Industr. Relat.,* 1963, 3, 3–8.
23. **Harris, C. M. (Ed.)** *Handbook of noise control.* New York: McGraw-Hill, 1957.
24. **Hill, J., & Trist, E.** A consideration of industrial accidents as a means of withdrawal from the work situation. *Hum. Relat.,* 1953, 6, 357–380.
25. **Judd, D. B., & Wyszecki, G.** *Color in business, science, and industry.* New York: Wiley, 1963.
26. **Kerr, M. D.** Effects of music on factory production. *Appl. Psychol. Monogr.,* 1945, No. 5.
27. **Kossoris, M. D., & Kohler, R. F.** *Hours of work and output.* U.S. Bureau of Labor Statistics Bulletin, No. 917, 1947.
28. **Langdon, D. E., & Hartman, B.** *Performance upon sudden awakening.* Brooks Air Force Base, Tex.: School of Aerospace Medicine, Report 62–17, 1961.
29. **Lawler, E. E., III, & Porter, L. W.** Perceptions regarding management compensation. *Industr. Relat.,* 1963, 3, 41–49.
30. **McCormick, E. J.** *Human factors engineering.* (2d ed.) New York: McGraw-Hill, 1964.
31. **McGehee, W., & Gardner, J. E.** Music in a complex industrial job. *Personnel Psychol.,* 1949, 2, 405–417.
32. **McGehee, W., & Owen, E. B.** Authorized and unauthorized rest pauses in clerical work. *J. Appl. Psychol.,* 1940, 24, 605–614.
33. **Mackworth, N. H.** The breakdown of vigilance during prolonged visual search. *Quart. J. Exp. Psychol.,* 1948, 1, 6–21.
34. **Maier, N. R. F.** *Psychology in industry.* Boston: Houghton Mifflin, 1965.
35. **Myers, M. S.** Who are the motivated workers? *Harv. Bus. Rev.,* 1964, 42, 73–88.
36. *National Observer,* Mar. 9, 1964.
37. **Nealey, S. M.** Pay and benefit preference. *Industr. Relat.,* 1963, 3, 17–28.
38. **O'Connell, M. H.** *Aircraft noise.* Brooks Air Force Base, Tex.: School of Aviation Medicine, Review 3–60, 1960.
39. **Patchen, M.** *The choice of wage comparisons.* Englewood Cliffs, N.J.: Prentice-Hall, 1961.
40. **Patton, J. A., & Littlefield, C. L.** *Job evaluation.* Homewood, Ill.: Irwin, 1957.
41. **Procter & Gamble Company.** *Time bonus.* Cincinnati: Author, 1946.
42. **Rothe, H. F.** How much incentive in incentive pay? *Supervisory Mgmt,* 1960, 5, 11–15.
43. **Ryan, T. A.** *Work and effort.* New York: Ronald, 1947.
44. **Schwab, R. S., & Prichard, J. S.** Neurologic aspects of fatigue. *Neurology,* 1951, 1, 133–135.
45. **Seyle, H., & Heuser, G.** *Fifth annual report on stress.* Montreal: Acta, 1956.
46. **Smith, H. C.** Music in relation to employee attitudes, piece-work production and industrial accidents. *Appl. Psychol. Monogr.,* 1947, No. 14.
47. **Smith, P. C.** The prediction of individual differences in susceptibility to industrial monopoly. *J. Appl. Psychol.,* 1955, 39, 322–329.

48. **Solomon, R. L.** The influence of work on behavior. *Psychol. Bull.,* 1948, 45, 1–40.
49. **Tiffin, J.** Six merit rating systems. *Personnel J.,* 1959, 37, 288–291, 300.
50. **Vasilev, I. E., et al.** Diurnal rhythm of working efficiency in man. *Sechenow J. Physiol.,* 1957, 43, 755–785.
51. **Vernon, H. M.** *The speed of adaptation of output to altered hours of work.* London: Industrial Fatigue Research Board, No. 6, 1920.
52. **Viteles, M. S.** *Science of work.* New York: Norton, 1934.
53. **Vroom, V. H.** *Work and motivation.* New York: Wiley, 1964.
54. **Wyatt, S., et al.** *Fan ventilation in a humid weaving shed.* London: Industrial Fatigue Research Board, No. 37, 1926.
55. **Wyatt, S., et al.** *The effects of monotony in work.* London: Industrial Fatigue Research Board, No. 56, 1929.
56. **Wyatt, S., et al.** *Fatigue and boredom in repetitive work.* London: Industrial Health Research Board, Report No. 77, 1938.

CHAPTER 12

1. **Arbous, A. G., & Kerrick, J. E.** Accident statistics and the concept of accident proneness. *Biometrics,* 1951, 7, 370–432.
2. **Balkan, P., et al.** Extraversion-introversion and decrement in an auditory vigilance task. In D. N. Buckner, & J. J. McGrath (Eds.), *Vigilance: A symposium.* New York: McGraw-Hill, 1963.
3. **Brody, J.** *Human factors research in occupational accident prevention.* New York: American Society of Safety Engineers and New York University, 1962.
4. **Chapanis, A.** *Research techniques in human engineering.* Baltimore: Johns Hopkins, 1959.
5. **Crawford, P. L.** Hazard exposure differentiation necessary for the identification of the accident-prone employee. *J. Appl. Psychol.,* 1960, 44, 192–194.
6. **Davids, A., & Mahoney, J. T.** Personality dynamics and accident-proneness in an industrial setting. *J. Appl. Psychol.,* 1957, 41, 303–306.
7. **Drake, C. A.** Accident-proneness: An hypothesis. *Charact. & Pers.,* 1940, 8, 335–341.
8. **Farmers, E., & Chambers, E. G.** *A psychological study of individual differences in accident rates.* London: Industrial Fatigue Research Board, No. 38, 1926.
9. **Fisher, B.** *Mental causes of accidents.* Boston: Houghton Mifflin, 1922.
10. **Fitts, P. M., & Jones, R. E.** *Psychological aspects of instrument display: I. Analysis of 270 "pilot error" experiences in reading and interpreting aircraft instrument.* Dayton, Ohio: U.S. Air Force Memorandum, Report TSEAA-694-12A, 1947.
11. **Flanagan, J. C.** The critical incident technique. *Psychol. Bull.,* 1954, 51, 327–358.
12. **Ghiselli, E. E., & Brown, C. W.** Learning and accident reduction. *J. Appl. Psychol.,* 1947, 31, 580–582.

13. **Gimbel, M. A.** Industrial safety. In R. P. Blake (Ed.), *Industrial engineering.* Englewood Cliffs, N.J.: Prentice-Hall, 1943.
14. **Goldmark, J., et al.** Studies in industrial psychology: Fatigue in relation to working capacity. *Publ. Hlth Bull.,* 1920, No. 106.
15. **Goldstein, L. G.** Whither accident research? *Traffic Safety Res. Rev.,* 1963, 7, 1–3.
16. **Gordon, G.** Industry's problem children. *National Safety News,* February, 1953, 32–33, 81–84.
17. **Griew, S.** A study of accidents in relation to occupation and age. *Ergonomics,* 1958, 2, 17–23.
18. **Heinrich, H. W.** *Industrial accident prevention.* (2d ed.) New York: McGraw-Hill, 1941.
19. **Hersey, R. B.** Rates of production and emotional state. *Personnel J.,* 1932, 10, 355–364.
20. **Hersey, R. B.** Emotional factors in accidents. *Personnel J.,* 1936, 15, 59–65.
21. **Jacobs, H. H.** Research problems in accident prevention. *Soc. Probl.,* 1961, 8, 329–341.
22. **Katz, D.** Employee groups: What motivates them and how they perform. *Advanc. Mgmt,* 1949, 14, 119–124.
23. **Kephart, N. C., & Tiffin, J.** Vision and accident experience. *National Safety News,* 1950, 62, 90–91.
24. **Kerr, W. A.** Accident proneness in factory departments. *J. Appl. Psychol.,* 1950, 34, 167–170.
25. **Kerr, W. A.** Complementary theories of safety psychology. *J. Soc. Psychol.,* 1957, 45, 3–9.
26. **McFarland, R. A.** Human factors engineering. *ASSE J.,* 1964, 9, 9–20.
27. **McFarland, R. A., & Moore, R. C.** Accidents and accident prevention. *Annu. Rev. Medicine,* 1962, 13, 371–388.
28. **McFarland, R. A., & Moore, R. C.** The prevention of accidents in the armed services. *Milit. Med.,* 1963, 128, 1190–1195.
29. **Metzger, R.** A verification of the Drake hypothesis of accident proneness. Unpublished thesis, Carnegie Institute of Technology, 1953.
30. **Mintz, A., & Blum, M. L.** A re-examination of the accident proneness concept. *J. Appl. Psychol.,* 1949, 33, 195–211.
31. **Osborne, E. G., & Vernon, H. M.** *Contributions to the study of accident causation.* London: Industrial Fatigue Research Board, No. 19, 1922.
32. **Rockwell, T. H.** Some exploratory research on risk acceptance in man-machine setting. *Amer. Soc. Safety Engr.,* December, 1962.
33. **Schwartz, R. L.** *The case for fast drivers.* New York: Harper & Row, 1963.
34. **Sherman, P. A., et al.** A study of accidents in 147 factories. *Personnel Psychol.,* 1957, 10, 43–51.
35. **Snow, A. J.** Tests for chauffeurs. *Industr. Psychol.,* 1926, 1, 30–45.
36. **Speroff, B., & Kerr, W. A.** Steel mill "hot strip" accidents. *J. Clin. Psychol.,* 1952, 9, 89–91.
37. **Van Zelst, R. H.** The effect of age and experience upon accident rate. *J. Appl. Psychol.,* 1954, 38, 313–317.

38. **Vernon, H. M.** *Accidents and their prevention.* New York: Cambridge, 1936.
39. **Vernon, H. M.** Prevention of accidents. *British J. Industr. Med.,* 1945, 2, 3.
40. **Walker, W. S., & Potter, C. J.** Worker participation in safety through job analysis. *Personnel,* 1954, 31, 141–147.
41. **Whisler, T., & Harper, Shirley F. (Eds.)** *Performance appraisal: Research and practice.* New York: Holt, 1962.
42. **Whitelaw, J. L.** *Highway traffic safety.* East Lansing, Mich.: Reprinted from United States Public Health Service, May, 1964, 1–103.
43. **Wirt, S. E., & Leedke, H. N.** Skillful eyes prevent accidents. *Industr. Newsltr.,* National Safety Council, 1945.

CHAPTER 13

1. **Adams, J. A.** Human tracking behavior. *Psychol. Bull.,* 1961, 58, 55–79.
2. **Adams, J. A., & Creamer, L. R.** Data processing capabilities of the human operator. *J. Engng. Psychol.,* 1964, 1, 150–158.
3. **Ashby, W. R.** *An introduction to cybernetics.* New York: Wiley, 1956.
4. **Benson, O. O., Jr., & Strughold, H. (Eds.)** *Physics and medicine of atmosphere and space.* New York: Wiley, 1960.
5. **Bruner, J. S., et al.** *A study of thinking.* New York: Wiley, 1956.
6. **Chapanis, A.** Men, machines, and models. *Amer. Psychologist,* 1961, 16, 113–131.
7. **Chapanis, A., & Lindenbaum, L.** A reaction time study of four control-display linkages. *Human Factors,* 1959, 1, 1–7.
8. **Chernikoff, R., & Taylor, F. V.** Effects of course frequency and aided time constant on pursuit and compensatory tracking. *J. Exp. Psychol.,* 1957, 53, 285–292.
9. **Clark, B., & Graybiel, A.** The break-off phenomenon: A feeling of separation from the earth by pilots at high altitude. *J. Aviat. Med.,* 1957, 28, 121–126.
10. **Corrigan, R. E., & Brogden, W. J.** The trigometric relationship of precision and angle of linear pursuit movements. *Amer. J. Psychol.,* 1949, 62, 90–98.
11. **Craik, K. J. W.** Theory of the human operator in control systems: II. Man as an element in a control system. *Brit. J. Psychol.,* 1948, 38, 142–157.
12. **Drew, G. C., et al.** Effect of small doses of alcohol on a skill resembling driving. *British Med. J.,* 1958, 2, 993–999.
13. **Fitts, P. M.** The information capacity of the human motor system in controlling the amplitude of movement. *J. Exp. Psychol.,* 1954, 47, 381–391.
14. **Fleishman, E. A.** Dimensional analysis of psychomotor abilities. *J. Exp. Psychol.,* 1954, 48, 437–454.
15. **Frey, A. H.** Human behavior atmospheric ions. *Psychol. Rev.,* 1961, 68, 225–228.
16. **Garvey, W. D., & Mitnick, L. L.** Effect of additional spatial references on display-control efficiency. *J. Exp. Psychol.,* 1955, 50, 276–282.

17. **Geldard, F. A.** *The human senses.* New York: Wiley, 1953.
18. **Gilmer, B. v. H.** *Research problems in cutaneous communication.* Report to National Institutes of Health, B2022-06, May, 1965.
19. **Green, B. F., Jr.** *Digital computers in research.* New York: McGraw-Hill, 1963.
20. **Gregg, L. W.** Psychological evaluation of work capabilities. *Arch. Environ. Mental Hlth,* 1961, 2, 335–338.
21. **Hake, H. W., & Garner, W. R.** The effect of presenting various numbers of discrete steps on scale reading accuracy. *J. Exp. Psychol.,* 1951, 42, 358–366.
22. **Harris, S. J., & Smith, K. U.** Dimensional analysis of motion: VII. Extent and direction of manipulative movements as factors in defining motions. *J. Appl. Psychol.,* 1954, 38, 126–130.
23. **Hartley, R. V.** The transmission of information. *Bell Sys. Tech. J.,* 1928, 17, 535–550.
24. **Henneman, R. H.** Vision and audition as sensory channels for communication. *Quart. J. Speech,* 1952, 38, 161–166.
25. **Jarrard, L. E.** The role of visual cues in the performance of ergographic work. *J. Exp. Psychol.,* 1960, 60, 57–63.
26. **Kreudel, E. S., & McRuer, D. T.** A servomechanisms approach to skill development. *J. Franklin Inst.,* 1960, 269, 24–42.
27. **Lansdell, H.** The effect of form on the legibility of numbers. *Canadian J. Psychol.,* 1954, 8, 77–79.
28. **Lippert, S.** Designing for comfort in airport seats. *Aeronaut. Engng. Rev.,* 1950, 9, 39–41.
29. **McCormick, E. J.** *Human factors engineering.* (2d ed.) New York: McGraw-Hill, 1964.
30. **Mackworth, N. H., & Mackworth, J. F.** Visual search for successive decisions. *Brit. J. Psychol.,* 1958, 49, 210–221.
31. **Melton, A. W., & Briggs, G. E.** Engineering psychology. *Annu. Rev. Psychol.,* 1960, 11, 71–98.
32. **Miller, G. A.** What is information measurement? *Amer. Psychologist,* 1953, 8, 3–11.
33. **Reitman, W. R.** Heuristic programs, computer simulation and higher mental processes. *Behav. Sci.,* 1959, 4, 330–335.
34. **Schipper, L. M., et al.** *The use of displays showing identity versus no-identity.* Wright Air Development Center, Technical Report, 57–12, February, 1957.
35. **Searle, L. V., & Taylor, F. V.** Studies of tracking behavior: I. Rate and time characteristics of simple corrective movements. *J. Exp. Psychol.,* 1948, 38, 615–631.
36. **Shannon, C. E.** A mathematical theory of communication. *Bell Sys. Tech. J.,* 1948, 27, 379–423, 623–656.
37. **Simon, H. A., & Newell, A.** Information processing in computer and man. *Amer. Scient.,* 1964, 52, 281–300.
38. **Smith, K. U.** *Delayed sensory feedback and behavior.* Philadelphia: Saunders, 1962.

39. **Spragg, S. D. S., & Rock, M. L.** Dial reading performance as a function of brightness. *J. Appl. Psychol.,* 1952, 36, 128–137.

40. **Taylor, F. V.** Psychology and the design of machines. *Amer. Psychologist,* 1957, 12, 249–258.

41. **Tonge, F. M.** *A heuristic program for assembly line balancing.* Englewood Cliffs, N.J.: Prentice-Hall, 1961.

42. **Weinberg, E.** Social implications of automation. *Computers and automation,* 1960, 9, 31–32.

43. **Welford, A. T.** The measurement of sensory-motor performance: Survey and reappraisal of twelve years progress. *Ergonomics,* 1960, 3, 189–230.

CHAPTER 14

1: **Allison, R. B.** *Learning parameters and human abilities.* Princeton, N.J.: Educational Testing Service, 1960.

2. **American Management Association.** *Operations research applied: New uses and extensions.* New York: Author, 1957.

3. **Barish, N. N.** *Systems analysis for effective administration.* New York: Funk & Wagnalls, 1951.

4. **Bowman, E. H.** Assembly-line balancing by linear programming. *Operations Res.,* 1960, 8, 385–389.

5. **Case Institute of Technology.** *Proceedings of the conference on operations research.* Cleveland: Author, 1951.

6. **Charny, E. J., & Carroll, E. J.** General systems theory and psychoanalysis. *Psychoanal. Quart.,* 1966, 35, 377–387.

7. **Churchman, C. W., et al.** *Introduction to operations research.* New York: Wiley, 1957.

8. **Churchman, C. W., et al. (Eds.)** *Management sciences, models and techniques.* London: Pergamon, 1960.

9. **Dean, B. V.** *Operations research in research and development.* New York: Wiley, 1963.

10. **Elkind, J. I., & Forgie, C. D.** Characteristics of the human operator in simple manual control systems. *IRE Trans. Automatic Control,* May, 1960, 44–55.

11. **Emery, F. E., et al.** *Information, decision, and action.* Melbourne, Australia: University of Melbourne Press, 1958.

12. **Ferguson, R. O., & Sargent, L. F.** *Linear programming: Fundamentals and applications.* New York: McGraw-Hill, 1958.

13. **Finch, G. (Ed.)** *Educational and training media: A symposium.* Washington, D.C.: National Academy of Sciences, 1960.

14. **Flagle, C. D., et al. (Eds.)** *Operations research and systems engineering.* Baltimore: Johns Hopkins, 1960.

15. **Folley, J. D., Jr. (Ed.)** *Human factors methods for systems design.* Pittsburgh, Pa.: American Institute for Research, 1960.

16. **Garner, W. R.** *Uncertainty and structure as psychological concepts.* New York: Wiley, 1962.

17. **Gauer, O. H., & Zuidema, G. D. (Eds.)** *Gravitational stress in aerospace medicine.* Boston: Little, Brown, 1961.
18. **Goode, H. H., & Machol, R. E.** *System engineering.* New York: McGraw-Hill, 1957.
19. **Grabbe, E. M. (Ed.)** *Handbook of automation, computation, and control.* New York: Wiley, 1958.
20. **Grether, W. F.** Psychology and the space frontier. *Amer. Psychologist,* 1962, 17, 92–101.
21. **Headquarters Ballistic Systems.** *Personnel subsystem reliability for aerospace systems.* Los Angeles: Air Force BSREP, April, 1962.
22. **Jacobs, H. H., et al.** Mathematical, psychological, and engineering aspects of accident phenomena. *Trans. NY Acad. Sci.,* 1956, 18, 261–277.
23. **Janitz, A. E., et al.** Engineering psychology and human factors in design. *Electro-Technology,* 1961, 5, 107–130.
24. **Jordan, N.** Motivational problems in human-computer operations. *Human Factors,* 1962, 4, 171–175.
25. **Katzell, R. A.** Contrasting systems of work organization. *Amer. Psychologist,* 1962, 17, 102–108.
26. **Kennedy, J. L.** The system approach: Organizational development. *Human Factors,* February, 1962, 25–52.
27. **Kidd, J. S.** A new look at system research and analysis. *Human Factors,* 1962, 209–216.
28. **Lackman, R.** A model in theory construction. *Psychol. Rev.,* 1960, 67, 113–129.
29. **McCloskey, J. F.** *Operations research for management.* Baltimore: Johns Hopkins, 1956.
30. **McKean, R. N.** *Efficiency in government through systems analysis.* New York: Wiley, 1958.
31. **Mackworth, J. F., & Mackworth, N. H.** The overlapping of signals for decisions. *Amer. J. Psychol.,* 1956, 69, 26–47.
32. **Macy, J., Jr., et al.** Coding noise in a task-oriented group. *J. abnorm. Soc. Psychol.,* 1953, 48, 401–409.
33. **Mayer, A., & Herwig, B. (Eds.)** *Betrielispsychologie 9. Band: Handbuck der Psychologie,* Gottingen, 1961.
34. **Miller, I., et al.** Evaluating intellectual abilities of man undergoing acceleration. *Amer. Psychologist,* 1960, 15, 481.
35. **Miller, R. B.** Some working concepts of systems analysis. *Amer. Inst. Res.,* February, 1954, 1–6.
36. **Miller, R. B.** *A study of the developmental history of selected complex electronic systems.* San Antonio, Tex.: AFPTRC TR56-1, PBI25975, 1956.
37. **Miller, R. B.** *Task and part-task trainers.* Wright-Patterson Air Force Base, Ohio: Wright Air Development Center Technical Report 60–469, ASTIA, No. AD245652, 1960.
38. **Milligan, J. R.** The hidden value packaging for appearance. In G. A. Walker (Ed.), *Advances in electronic circuit packaging.* New York: Consultants Bureau Enterprises, Inc., 1962. Vol. 2, pp. 299–308.

39. **Paterson, D. G.** Cultural lag in psychology. Paper prepared for Minnesota Psychological Association Meeting, Minneapolis, May, 1960.
40. **Porter, E. H.** *The system thinkers: Parable and paradigm.* Santa Monica, Calif.: System Development Corporation, SP-285, 1961.
41. **Siegel, A. I., & Wolf, J. J.** A technique for evaluating man-machine system designs. *Human Factors,* 1961, 3, 18–28.
42. **Taylor, F. V.** Psychology in the design of machines. *Amer. Psychologist,* 1957, 12, 249–258.
43. **Tilles, S.** The manager's job: A systems approach. *Harv. Bus. Rev.,* 1963, 41, 73–81.
44. **Warren, N. D.** Automation, human engineering, and psychology. *Amer. Psychologist,* 1956, 11, 531–536.
45. **Wissel, J. W., & Hall, S. A.** Human engineering research: Who should do it and why. *Amer. Psychologist,* 1957, 12, 92–94.

CHAPTER 15

1. **Ash, P. (Chairman.)** Psychology in labor relations: A symposium. *Personnel Psychol.,* 1964, 17, 361–383.
2. **Bakke, E. W.** *Mutual survival, the goal of unions and management.* New York: Harper & Row, 1946.
3. **Brooks, G. W.** *The sources of vitality in the American labor movement.* Ithaca, N.Y.: Cornell University, School of Industrial and Labor Relations, 1960.
4. **Brooks, G. W., & Koons, G. R.** Bargaining table techniques. *Amer. Mgmt Ass. Personnel Ser.,* 1957, No. 172.
5. **Chamberlain, N. W.** *Collective bargaining.* New York: McGraw-Hill, 1951.
6. **Chase, S.** *A generation of industrial peace.* New York: Standard Oil Company of New Jersey, 1947.
7. **Coleman, J.** The compulsive pressures of democracy in unionism. *Amer. J. Sociol.,* May, 1956, 519–526.
8. **Dalton, M.** Unoffical union-management relations. *Amer. Sociol. Rev.,* 1950, 15, 611–619.
9. **Dean, L.** Union activity and dual loyalty. *Int. Labor Relat. Rev.,* 1954, 7, 526.
10. **Edelman, M.** Concepts of power. *Labor Law J.,* September, 1958, 623–628.
11. **Feinberg, M. R. (Chairman.)** Implications of psychology in labor-management relations: A symposium. *J. Appl. Psychol.,* 1961, 14, 239, 284.
12. **Gingerich, O.** The computer versus Kepler. *Amer. Scient.,* 1964, 52, 218–226.
13. **Gitlow, A. L.** *Labor and industrial society.* Homewood, Ill.: Irwin, 1963.
14. **Grosset, S., & McDermott, T. J.** Labor-management cooperation in Switzerland. *Labor Law J.,* March, 1963, 1–27.
15. **Herberg, W.** Bureaucracy and democracy in labor unions. *Antioch Rev.,* 1943, 3, 405–417.

16. **Joseph, M. L.** An experimental approach to the study of collective bargaining. *Industr. Relat. Res. Ass. Proc.,* 1961.
17. **Joseph, M. L.** Protect your freedom to subcontract. *Harv. Bus. Rev.,* 1963, 41, 98–102.
18. **Kennedy, V. D.** Grievance negotiation. In A. W. Kornhauser et al. (Eds.), *Industrial conflict.* New York: McGraw-Hill, 1954.
19. **Kerr, C., & Fisher, L.** Multiple-employee bargaining: The San Francisco experience. In R. A. Lester and J. Shister (Eds.), *Insight into labor issues.* New York: Macmillan, 1948. Pp. 25–61.
20. **Killingsworth, C.** Arbitration as an industrial relations technique: The Bethlehem experience. *Proc. IRRA,* 1954.
21. **Lester, R. A.** The changing nature of the union. *Mon. Labor Rev.* August, 1960, 843–845.
22. **Levine, S. G., & Karsh, B.** Industrial relations in the next generation. *Quart. Rev. Econ. & Business,* 1961, Feb., 18–29.
23. **Levinson, H. M.** *Unionism, wage trends, and income distribution, 1914–1947.* Ann Arbor, Mich.: University of Michigan Press, 1951.
24. **Lurie, M.** Professors, physicians, and unionism. *AAUP Bull.,* 1962, 48, 272–276.
25. **McCord, M.** Industrial relations party line: Are you on it? *Personnel J.,* 1962, 41, 281–282.
26. **McDermott, T. J.** Use of fact-finding boards in labor disputes. *Labor Law J.,* April, 1960, 285–304.
27. **Periman, S.** *A theory of the labor movement.* New York: Macmillan, 1928.
28. **Petro, S.** *Power unlimited: The corruption of union leadership.* New York: Ronald, 1959.
29. **Purcell, T. V.** *The worker speaks his mind on company and union.* Cambridge, Mass.: Harvard University Press, 1953.
30. **Rose, A. M.** *Union solidarity: The internal cohesion of a labor union.* Minneapolis: University of Minnesota Press, 1952.
31. **Rosen, H., & Rosen, R. A. H.** The union business agent's perspective of his job. *J. Personnel Admin. Industr. Relat.,* 1957, 3, 49–58.
32. **Ross, A. M.** *Trade union wage policy.* Berkeley, Calif.: University of California Press, 1948.
33. **Sayles, L. R., & Strauss, G.** *The local union: Its place in the industrial plant.* New York: Harper & Row, 1953.
34. **Schelling, T. C.** An essay on bargaining. *Amer. Econ. Rev.,* 1956, 46, 281–306.
35. **Seidman, J.** The labor union as an organization. In A. W. Kornhauser et al. (Eds.), *Industrial conflict.* New York: McGraw-Hill, 1954.
36. **Seidman, J.** Some requirements for union democracy. *Proc. Amer. Econ. Ass.,* May, 1958, 35–43.
37. **Seidman, J., et al.** *The worker views his union.* Chicago: University of Chicago Press, 1958.
38. **Selekman, B.** Varieties of labor relations. *Harv. Bus. Rev.,* 1949, 27, 175–199.

39. **Stagner, R.** Dual allegiance. *Personnel Psychol.,* 1954, 7, 41–47.
40. **Stagner, R.** *The psychology of industrial conflict.* New York: Wiley, 1956.
41. **Stagner, R.** Union-management relations in Italy: Some observations. *Current Econ. Comment,* 1957, 19, 3–15.
42. **Stagner, R., et al.** Dual allegiance to union and management: A symposium. *Personnel Psychol.,* 1954, 7, 41–80.
43. **Taft, P.** *The structure and government of labor unions.* Cambridge, Mass.: Harvard University Press, 1954.
44. **Wagner, L. A., & Bakerman, T.** Wage earners' opinions of insurance fringe benefits. *J. Insurance,* 1960, 27, 17–28.
45. **Wilensky, H. L.** The moonlighter: A product of relative deprivation. *Industr., Relat.,* 1963, 3, 105–124.

CHAPTER 16

1. **Abrams, A. J.** *Job engineering and job re-assignment for the older worker in American industry.* New York State Legislative Committee, 1954, 99–107.
2. **Anderson, N.** *Men on the move.* Chicago: University of Chicago Press, 1940.
3. **Bakke, E. W.** *Citizens without work: A study of the effects of unemployment upon the workers' social relations and practices.* Fair Lawn, N.J.: Oxford University Press, 1940.
4. **Barron, M. L.** *Attacking prejudices against the aged.* New York State Legislative Committee, 1954, 56–58.
5. **Birren, J. E.** A brief history of the psychology of aging. *Gerontologist,* 1961, 1, 127–134.
6. **Birren, J. E.** *The psychology of aging.* Englewood Cliffs, N.J.: Prentice-Hall, 1964.
7. **Birren, J. E., et al.** Age differences in response speed as a function of controlled variations of stimulus conditions: Evidence of a general speed factor. *Gerontologia,* 1962, 6, 1–18.
8. **Block, Jean L.** The American association of retired persons. *Empire,* Dec. 8, 1963.
9. **Blum, M. L.** *Industrial psychology and its social foundations.* New York: Harper & Row, 1956.
10. **Bowers, W. H.** An appraisal of worker characteristics as related to age. *J. Appl. Psychol.,* 1952, 36, 296–300.
11. **Cavan, R. S., et al.** *Personal adjustments in old age.* Chicago: Science Research, 1949.
12. **Chown, Sheila M., & Heron, A.** Psychological aspects of aging in man. *Annu. Rev. Psychol.,* 1965, 16, 417–450.
13. **Dennis, W.** The age decrement in outstanding scientific contributions: Fact or artifact? *Amer. Psychologist,* 1958, 13, 457–460.
14. **Dorian, F.** *Commitment to culture: Art patronage in Europe. Its significance for America.* Pittsburgh, Pa.: University of Pittsburgh Press, 1964.

15. **Gibson, D.** Psychology in mental retardation: Past and present. *Amer. Psychologist,* 1964, 19, 339–341.
16. **Ginsburg, S. W.** What unemployment does to people. *Amer. J. Psychiat.,* 1942, 99, 439–446.
17. **Ginzberg, E.** *The unemployed.* New York: Harper & Row, 1943.
18. **Griew, S.** Complexity of response and time of initiating responses in relation to age. *Amer. J. Psychol.,* 1959, 72, 83–88.
19. **Griew, S.** Age differences in the performance of extended perceptual tasks. *Ergonomics,* 1962, 5, 165.
20. **Griew, S.** *Designing work for the disabled.* London: Department of Scientific and Industrial Research, 1962.
21. **Hall, Harold R.** Company stimulation of individual retirement programming. In *Some observations of executive retirement.* Cambridge, Mass.: Harvard University Press, 1953.
22. **Hoch, P. J., & Zubin, J. (Eds.)** *Psychopathology of aging.* New York: Grune & Stratton, 1961.
23. **Jacobs, A. T.** *How to use handicapped workers.* New York: National Foreman's Institute, Inc., 1946.
24. **Jaffe, A. J., & Milavsky, J. R.** *Unemployment, retirement, and pensions.* New York: Columbia University, Bureau of Applied Social Research, 1960.
25. **Kaplan, M.** *Leisure in America.* New York: Wiley, 1960.
26. **Kleemeier, R. W.** *Aging and leisure: A research perspective into the meaningful use of time.* Fair Lawn, N.J.: Oxford University Press, 1961.
27. **Komarovsky, M.** *The unemployed man and his family.* New York: Dryden Press, 1940.
28. **Lehman, H. C.** *Age and achievement.* Princeton, N.J.: Princeton University Press, 1953.
29. **Leviton, Gloria.** *The relationship between rehabilitation and psychology.* Washington, D.C.: Office of Vocational Rehabilitation (Clark University Conference, June, 1959).
30. **McClearn, G. E.** Psychological research and behavioral phenotypes. *Proc. Borg-Wartenstein Sympos.,* Vienna, September, 1964.
31. **McFarland, R. A.** Physically handicapped workers. *Harv. Bus. Rev.,* 1944, 23, 1–31.
32. **McFarland, R. A.** The psychological aspects of aging. *Bull. NY Acad. Med.,* 1956, 32, 14–32.
33. **Markowe, M., & Barber, L.** Psychological handicap in relation to productivity and occupational adjustment. *British J. Industr. Med.,* 1953, 10, 125–131.
34. **Meltzer, H.** Age differences in status and happiness of workers. *Geriatrics,* 1962, 17, 831–838.
35. **Meltzer, H.** Age differences in happiness and life adjustments of workers. *J. Geront.,* 1963, 18, 66–70.
36. **Miller, D. C., & Form, W. H.** *Industrial sociology.* New York: Harper & Row, 1951.
37. **Pennsylvania State Bureau of Rehabilitation.** Harrisburg, Pa.: Author, 1955.

38. **Pressey, S. L.** The new division of maturity and old age: Its history and service. *Amer. Psychologist,* 1948, 3, 107–109.
39. **Pressey, S. L.** Certain findings and proposals regarding professional retirement. *AAUP Bull.,* 1955, 41, 503–509.
40. **Pressey, S. L., & Kuhlen, R. G.** *Psychological development through the life span.* New York: Harper & Row, 1957.
41. **Reichard, Suzanne, et al.** *Aging and personality: A study of eighty-seven older men.* New York: Wiley, 1962.
42. **Saleh, S. D.** A study of attitude change in the preretirement period. *J. Appl. Psychol.,* 1964, 48, 310–312.
43. **Selye, H.** *The stress of life.* New York: McGraw-Hill, 1956.
44. **Shaffer, Helen B.** Retirement age. *Editorial Res. Rep.,* 1961, 1, 1–17.
45. **Stanton, J. E.** Some factors affecting employment in relation to age. *Ohio State Univer. Press, Abst. Dissertation,* 1955, No. 66, 337–343.
46. **Switzer, M. E., & Rusk, H. A.** *Doing something for the disabled.* Washington, D.C.: Public Affairs Press, Public Affairs Pamphlet No. 197, 1953.
47. **Tiffin, J.** *Industrial psychology.* Englewood Cliffs, N.J.: Prentice-Hall, 1941.
48. **Travis, H.** The structure of unemployment in recent years. *Mon. Labor Rev.,* 1956, 79, 1147–1151.
49. **Turner, A. N.** The older worker: New light on employment and retirement problems. *Personnel,* 1955, 32, 254–257.
50. **U.S. Department of Education.** *Education in the aging: a selected annotated bibliography.* Washington, D.C.: Author, No. 11, 1958, 1–145.
51. **United States Rehabilitation Service.** *Psychological aspects of physical disability.* Washington, D.C.: GPO, Rehabilitation Service Series, No. 10, 1957.
52. **Walters, J.** A review of family research 1959, 1960, and 1961. *Marriage Fam. Living,* 1962, 24, 158–178.
53. **Wells Fargo Bank.** The Canadian economy: Immigration and prosperity. *Business Rev.,* December, 1964.

CHAPTER 17

1. **Baetjer, A. M.** *Women in industry: Their health and efficiency.* Philadelphia: Saunders, 1946.
2. **Bell, D.** Women and business: II. The great back to work movement. *Fortune,* July, 1956.
3. **Bingham, June R.** *The courage to change.* New York: Scribner, 1961.
4. **Bloom, G. F., & Northrop, H.** *Economics of labor relations.* Homewood, Ill.: Irwin, 1961.
5. **Davis, N.** Some psychological effects on women workers of payment by industrial bonus method. *Occup. Psychol.,* 1944, 18, 53–62.
6. **Deutsch, H.** *The psychology of women.* New York: Grune & Stratton, 1944.
7. **Dieken, Gertrude.** Farm women. *Farm J.,* November, 1963, 67, 88.
8. **Dyer, F. C.** Myths about women bosses. *Supervision,* 1959, 21, 18–20.

9. **Ellis, A.** *The intelligent women's guide to man-hunting.* New York: Lyle Stuart, 1963.

10. **Eyde, Lorraine D.** Work values and background factors as predictors of women's desire to work. *Ohio State Studies in Personnel,* 1962, Res. Monogr. No. 108, 1–88.

11. **Farber, S. M., & Wilson, R. H. L. (Eds.)** *The potential of women.* New York: McGraw-Hill, 1964.

12. **Fisher, D. A.** *Steel in the war.* New York: United States Steel Corporation, 1946.

13. **Fuller, F. M., & Batchelder, M. B.** Opportunities for women at the administrative level. *Harv. Bus. Rev.,* 1953, 31, 111–128.

14. **Geister, Janet.** Our new young are different. *Amer. J. Nurs.,* 1964, 64, 102–104.

15. **Gilmer, B. v. H.** Psychological aspects of women in industry. *Personnel Psychol.,* 1957, 10, 439–452.

16. **Hacker, Helen M.** Women as a minority group. *Soc. Forces,* 1951, 30, 60–69.

17. **Higgins, Lois.** Policewomen. *Police,* 1962, 6, 46–49.

18. **Hilliard, Marion.** *Women and fatigue.* Garden City, N.Y.: Doubleday, 1960.

19. **Hinkle, L. E., et al.** Women in industry: II. An examination of the relation between symptoms, disability, and serious illness in two homogeneous groups of men and women. *Amer. J. Publ. Hlth,* 1960, 50, 1327–1336.

20. **Hunter, Thelma.** Industrial courts and women's wages in Australia. *Econ. Rec.,* 1962, 38, 438–447.

21. **James, R. C.** Discrimination against women in Bombay textiles. *Industr. J. Labor Relat. Rev.,* 1962, 15, 209–220.

22. **Johnson, W. L.** Personnel shortages in the health field and working patterns of women. *Publ. Hlth Rep.,* January, 1957.

23. **Kehoe, K.** *Woman's place in tomorrow's workforce.* American Management Association, Personnel Series, No. 165, 1955, 24–26.

24. **Livingston, E.** Attitudes of women operatives to promotion. *Occup. Psychol.,* October, 1953, 191–199.

25. **Lloyd, Betty J.** Womanpower: Key to management manpower shortage. *Personnel J.,* 1962, 41, 180–182.

26. **Miller, F. B., & Coghill, Mary Ann.** Sex and the personnel manager. *Industr. J. Labor Relat. Rev.,* 1964, 18, 32–44.

27. **National Manpower Council.** *Womanpower.* New York: Columbia University Press, 1957.

28. **Naylor, J. C., & Vincent, N. L.** Predicting female absenteeism. *Personnel Psychol.,* 1959, 12, 81–84.

29. **Peterson, E.** Are women taking men's jobs? *Personnel J.,* 1962, 41, 83–84.

30. **Phelps-Brown, E. H.** Equal pay for equal work. *Econ. J.,* 1949, 59, 384–398.

31. **Rheingold, J. C.** *The fear of being a woman.* New York: Grune & Stratton, 1964.

32. **Rockmael, Valerie.** The woman programmer: A subjective reflection. *Datamation,* 1963, 9, 41.

33. Russia: Medical aspects of women in industry. *J. Akush. i. Zhensk. Boliez.*, 1932, 43 (Translation).
34. **Slote, Claire T.** Woman executives: Fact and fancy. *Dun's Rev. and Modern Industry,* December, 1958, 72.
35. **Smuts, R. W.** *Women and work in America.* New York: Columbia, 1959.
36. **Spiegel, Rose.** Women's quest for identity. *AAUW J.,* May, 1962, 244–247.
37. **Spiro, E. S.** Women in industry: I. Patterns of women's work and occupational health and safety. *Amer. J. Publ. Hlth,* 1960, 50, 1318–1326.
38. **Stein, R. L.** Married women and the level of unemployment. *Mon. Labor Rev.,* 1961, 84, 869–870.
39. **Steinberg, E. R.** What about womanpower in the space age? *Space Dig.,* August, 1962, 56–58.
40. **Strong, E. K. J.** *Vocational interest of men and women.* Stanford, Calif.: Stanford University Press, 1943.
41. **Tataninova, T., & Korshunava, E.** Living and working conditions of women in the USSR. *Int. Labor Rev.,* 1960, 82, 341–357.
42. **Turner, Marjorie B.** *Women and work.* Los Angeles: University of California, Institute of Industrial Relations, 1964.
43. **United Nations.** *Status of women in Japan.* New York: United Nations Seminar, 1962.
44. **U.S. Department of Labor.** *Fact book on manpower.* Washington, D.C.: Author, Bureau of Labor Statistics, September, 1954, 1–88.
45. **U.S. Department of Labor.** *Handbook on women workers.* Washington, D.C.: Author, No. 255, 1954, 1–75.
46. **U.S. Department of Labor.** *Night work for women.* Washington, D.C.: Author, Women's Bureau, No. 233, 1949.
47. **U.S. Department of Labor.** *Older women as office workers.* Washington, D.C.: Author, Women's Bureau, 1953, No. 248, 1–64.
48. **U.S. Department of Labor.** *Training mature women for employment.* Washington, D.C.: Author, Women's Bureau, 1955, No. 256, 1–46.
49. **Warren, J. R.** Vocational interests and the occupational adjustment of college women. *J. counsel. Psychol.* 1959, 6, 140–147.
50. **Wickert, F. R. (Chairman.)** Women in industry: a symposium. Papers presented by Dorothy Clendenen, B. v. H. Gilmer, Evelyn Perloff, Anne Roe, and F. R. Wickert at Annual Meeting of the American Psychological Association, Div. 14, Philadelphia, September, 1963.
51. **Wolfle, D. L.** *Commission on human resources and advanced training.* New York: Harper & Row, 1954.
52. **Zapoleon, M. W.** Working girl: Bibliography. *Personnel Guid. J.,* 1953, 32, 68–71.

CHAPTER 18

1. **Arensberg, C. M.** Industry and the community. *Amer. J. Sociol.,* 1942, 48, 1–12.

2. **Bendix, R., & Lipset, S. M. (Eds.)** *Class, status, and power.* New York: Free Press, 1961.
3. **Blumer, H.** Early industrialization and the laboring class. *Soc. Quart.,* 1960, 1, 5–14.
4. **Bott, Elizabeth.** *The family and social network.* London: Tavistock Press, Tavistock Institute, 1953.
5. **Brehm, J. W., & Cohen, A. R.** *Explorations in cognitive dissonance.* New York: Wiley, 1962.
6. **Chowdhry, Kamla, & Tarneja, R. S.** India. In *Developing better managers: An eight-nation study.* New York: National Industrial Conference Board, 1961.
7. **Clee, G. H., & Lindsay, F. A.** New patterns of overseas operations. *Harv. Bus. Rev.,* 1961, 39, 65–73.
8. **Collado, E.** Economic development through private enterprise. *Foreign Affairs,* July, 1963.
9. **Davies, J. C.** *Human nature in politics.* New York: Wiley, 1963.
10. **Dennis, W.** Cross-cultural studies of values. Falk Lecture, Carnegie Institute of Technology, Oct. 9, 1961.
11. **Faris, R. E. L.** The middle class from a sociological viewpoint. *Soc. Forces,* October, 1960, 1–5.
12. **Flanagan, J. C., et al.** *Studies of the American high school.* Pittsburgh, Pa.: University of Pittsburgh, Project TALENT Office, 1962.
13. **Form, W. H., & Stone, G. P.** Urbanism, anonymity, and status symbolism. *Amer. J. Sociol.,* 1957, 62, 504–514.
14. **Gardner, G. H.** The Arab Middle East: Some background interpretations. *J. Soc. Issues,* 1959, 15, No. 3.
15. **Gardner, J. W.** The relation of certain personality variables to level of aspiration. *J. Psychol.,* 1940, 9, 191–206.
16. **General Electric Company.** *Guide to making business climate appraisal:* Schenectady, N.Y.: Author, 1955 and 1963.
17. **Handel, G.** Psychological study of whole families. *Psychol. Bull.,* 1965, 63, 19–41.
18. **Hsu, F. L. K. (Ed.)** *Psychological anthropology.* Homewood, Ill.: Dorsey, 1961.
19. **Hunter, G.** *Studies in management.* London: University of London Press, 1961.
20. **Judge, G. G., & Chuang, Y. H.** The flow of feed grain changes. *Livestock Breeder J.,* February, 1962, 102–107.
21. **Kantner, J.** *The relationship between accessibility and socio-economic status of residential lands.* Ann Arbor, Mich.: University of Michigan Press, 1948.
22. **Kent, H., & Davis, D. R.** Discipline in the home and intellectual development. *Brit. J. Med. Psychol.,* 1957, 30, 27–33.
23. **Knox, J. B.** *The sociology of industrial relations: An introduction to industrial sociology.* New York: Random House, 1955.
24. **Langner, T. S., & Michael, S. T.** *Life stress and mental health.* New York: Macmillan, 1963.

25. **Lewin, K., et al.** Levels of aspiration. In Hunt, J. McV. (Ed.), *Personality and behavior disorders.* New York: Ronald, 1944. Vol. I, pp. 333–378.
26. **Life Insurance Agency Management Association.** *Research on persistency.* Hartford, Conn.: Author, No. 720, 1960.
27. **Lipset, S. M.** Social stratification and right-wing extremism. *Brit. J. Soc.,* 1959, 10, 1–38.
28. **Lipset, S. M.** A changing American character. In S. M. Lipset & L. Lowenthal (Eds.), *Culture and social character.* New York: Free Press, 1961.
29. **Lumsdaine, A. A., & May, M. A.** Mass communication and educational media. *Annu. Rev. Psychol.,* 1965, 16, 475–534.
30. **McCord, J., et al.** Effects of maternal employment on lower class boys. *J. Abnorm. Soc. Psychol.,* 1963, 67, 177–182.
31. **Miller, D. C., & Form, W. H.** *Industrial sociology.* New York: Harper & Row, 1951.
32. **Mills, C. W.** *White collar: The American middle class.* Fair Lawn, N.J.: Oxford University Press, 1951.
33. **Phillips, H. P.** *Thai peasant personality: The patterning of interpersonal behavior in the village of Bang Chan.* Berkeley, Calif.: University of California Press, 1965.
34. **Pollard, J. A.** Emerging pattern in corporate giving. *Harv. Bus. Rev.* 1960, 38, 103–112.
35. **Riesman, D.** The study of national character: Some observations on the American case. *Harvard Librarian Bull.,* 1959, Winter, 5–24.
36. **Robinson, R. D.** *Cases in international business.* New York: Holt, 1962.
37. **Rossi, P. H.** The organizational structure of an American community. In A. Etzioni (Ed.), *Complex organizations.* New York: Holt, 1961.
38. **Seeley, J. R., et al.** *Crestwood Heights.* New York: Basic Books, 1956.
39. **Shaffer, L. F., & Shoben, E. J., Jr.** *The psychology of adjustment.* Boston: Houghton Mifflin, 1956.
40. **Sherif, M., et al.** *Intergroup conflict and cooperation: The robbers cave experiment.* Norman, Okla.: University of Oklahoma Press, 1963.
41. A town in Sweden plans ahead. *The Lamp,* Standard Oil Company of New Jersey, 1962, Winter, 8–13.
42. **Walker, C. R.** *Steeltown.* New York: Harper & Row, 1950.
43. **Warner, W. L.** *Democracy in Jonesville: A study in quality and inequality.* New York: Harper & Row, 1949.
44. **Warner, W. L., & Low, J. O.** *The social system of the modern factory. The strike: A social analysis.* Yankee City Series IV. New Haven, Conn.: Yale University Press, 1947.
45. **Warner, W. L., & Lunt, P. S.** *The social life of a modern community.* New Haven, Conn.: Yale University Press, 1941.
46. **Whyte, W. H., Jr.** *The organization man.* New York: Simon and Schuster, 1956.
47. **Wolpert, H. W.** The image of American firms and brands in the European common market. *Publ. Opin. Quart.,* 1960, 24, 519–521.
48. **Wood, R., & Keyser, Virginia.** *Sears, Roebuck de Mexico.* Washington, D.C.: National Planning Association, 1953.

CHAPTER 19

1. **Abrahamson, M.** The integration of industrial scientists. *Admin. Sci. Quart.,* 1964, 9, 208–218.
2. **Barron, F.** *Creativity and psychological health.* Berkeley, Calif.: University of California Press, 1963.
3. **Bellows, R., et al.** *Executive skills: Their dynamics and development.* Ann Arbor, Mich.: University of Michigan Press, 1962.
4. **Bennis, W. G., et al. (Eds.)** *Interpersonal dynamics.* Homewood, Ill.: Dorsey, 1964.
5. **Berenson, C. (Ed.)** *Administration of the chemical enterprise.* New York: Wiley, 1963.
6. **Berlyne, D. E.** *Conflict, arousal, and curiosity.* New York: McGraw-Hill, 1960.
7. **Blatt, S. F.** An attempt to define mental health. *J. Consult. Psychol.,* 1964, 28, 146–153.
8. **Boynton, P. W.** *So you want a better job?* New York: Socony-Vacuum Oil Company, 1947.
9. **Chase, W. H.** Management of change: The dilemma of public relations. Address before Fifteenth Annual Social Science Seminar for Public Relations Leaders, Menlo Park, Calif., February, 1965.
10. **Cloninger, J. R.** A new deal for drop-outs. *Friends,* 1964, December, 20–23.
11. **Cobb, S., et al.** An environmental approach to mental health. *Bull. NY Acad. Sci.,* 1963, 107, 596–606.
12. **Dankert, C. E., et al. (Eds.)** *Hours of work.* Englewood Cliffs, N.J.: Prentice-Hall, 1965.
13. **Dill, W. R., et al.** How aspiring managers promote their own careers. *California Mgmt Rev.,* 1960, 2, 9–15.
14. **Dollard, J., & Miller, N. E.** *Personality and psychotherapy.* New York: McGraw-Hill, 1950.
15. **Forehand, G. A.** Assessments of innovative behavior: Partial criteria for the assessment of executive performance. *J. Appl. Psychol.,* 1963, 47, 206–213.
16. **Franco, S. C.** Problem drinking and industry: Policies and procedures. *Quart. J. Stud. Alcohol,* 1954, 15, 453–468.
17. **Gardner, J. W.** *Self-renewal: The individual and the innovative society.* New York: Harper & Row, 1964.
18. **Gerard, H. B., et al.** Self-evaluation and the evaluation of choice alternatives. *J. Pers.,* 1964, 32, 395–410.
19. **Ghiselli, E. E.** Maturity of self-perception in relation to managerial success. *Personnel Psychol.,* 1964, 17, 41–48.
20. **Gibson, J. E.** Science looks at your job: A ten-year study at General Motors. *Today's Hlth,* 1960, 38, 14–15.
21. **Goffman, E.** *The presentation of self in everyday life.* Garden City, N.Y.: Anchor Books, Doubleday, 1959.

22. **Goffman, E.** *Behavior in public places: Notes on the social organization of gatherings.* New York: Free Press, 1963.
23. **Gordon, G.** *How to "live" with your job.* Montreal: National Office Management Association Conference, May, 1960.
24. **Gruber, H. E., et al. (Eds.)** *Contemporary approaches to creative thinking.* Englewood Cliffs, N.J.: Prentice-Hall, 1962.
25. **Haire, M.** The concept of power and the concept of man. In G. Strother (Ed.), *Social science approaches to business behavior.* Homewood, Ill.: Dorsey, 1962.
26. **Hancock, J. G., & Teevan, R. C.** Fear of failure and risk-taking behavior. *J. Pers.,* 1964, 32, 200–209.
27. **Hughes, E. C., et al.** *Twenty thousand nurses tell their story.* Philadelphia: Lippincott, 1958.
28. **Jackson, J.** Are professional societies an escape hatch? *Modern Hospital,* 1962, 98, 87–92.
29. **Kahn, R. L.** Organization des rapports humans et motivations ouvrières. In Charmont, C. (Ed.) *Psychsociologie industrielle.* Paris: Briende, 1959.
30. **Kahn, R. L.** *Power and conflict.* New York: Basic Books, 1963.
31. **Kahn, R. L., & Katz, D.** *Social psychology of organizations.* New York: Wiley, 1964.
32. **Kahn, R. L., et al.** *Conflict and ambiguity.* New York: Wiley, 1964.
33. **Katz, E.** The social itinerary of technical change: Two studies on the diffusion of innovation. *Hum. Organization,* 1961, Summer, 70–82.
34. **Kubie, L. S.** Socio-economic problems of the young scientist. *Amer. Scient.,* 1954, 42, 104–112.
35. **Levinson, H.** Reciprocation: The relationship between man and organization. *Admin. Sci. Quart.,* 1965, 9, 370–390.
36. **Likins, R. C.** *Literacy program in your community.* Berkeley, Calif.: Laubach Literacy Center, 1964.
37. **McLean, A. A., & Taylor, G. C.** *Mental health in industry.* New York: McGraw-Hill, 1958.
38. **Marcson, S.** *The scientist in American industry.* Princeton, N.J.: Princeton University Press, 1960.
39. **Menninger, W. C.** Men, machines, and mental health. *Ment. Hyg.,* NY, 1952, 36, 184–196.
40. **Menninger, W. C., & Levinson, H.** Psychiatry in industry: Some trends and perspectives. *Personnel,* 1955, 32, 90–99.
41. **Meyer, H. H., et al.** Motive patterns and risk preferences associated with entrepreneurship. *J. Abnorm. Soc. Psychol.,* 1961, 63, 570–574.
42. **Miles, S. B., Jr.** The management politician. *Harv. Bus. Rev.,* 1961, 39, 99–104.
43. **Miller, F. W.** *Introduction to guidance.* Columbus, Ohio: Charles E. Merrill Books, 1961.
44. **Mindus, E.** *Industrial psychiatry in Great Britain, the United States, and Canada: A report to the World Health Organization.* Stockholm: Institute of Applied Psychology, 1954.

45. **Moment, D.** Partial performances and total effectiveness: The resolution of the specialist-generalist dilemma in managerial and professional development. Center for Research in Careers, Harvard University, Mimeographed edition, 1965, Mar., 1–51.
46. **Opinion Research Corporation.** *The conflict between the scientific and the management mind.* Princeton, N.J.: Author, 1959.
47. **Orzack, L. H.** *Role implications of change in a new organization.* Washington, D.C.: Fifth World Congress of Sociology, Industrial Sociology Subcommittee, September, 1962.
48. **Pyke, M.** *The science myth.* New York: Macmillan, 1962.
49. **Randsepp, E.** *Managing creative scientists and engineers.* New York: Macmillan, 1963.
50. **Rathbone, M. J.** Three men in a boat: Government, labor and business in a world of rapid change. Address to Harvard Business School Club, Washington, D.C., Nov. 28, 1962.
51. **Rim, Y.** Risk-taking and need for achievement. *Acta Psychol.,* 1963, 21, 108–115.
52. **Roe, Anne.** *The psychology of occupations.* New York: Wiley, 1956.
53. **Rosenman, R. H., et al.** A predictive study of coronary heart disease. *J. Amer. Med. Ass.,* 1964, 189, 15–22.
54. **Sayles, L. R.** *Individualism and big business.* New York: McGraw-Hill, 1963.
55. **Selye, H.** *The stress of life.* New York: McGraw-Hill, 1956.
56. **Shaffer, L. F., & Shoben, E. J., Jr.** *The psychology of adjustment.* Boston: Houghton Mifflin, 1956.
57. **Shepard, H. A.** Nine dilemmas in industrial research. *Admin. Sci. Quart.,* 1957, 1, 295–309.
58. **Siegel, S., & Fouraker, L. E.** *Bargaining and group decision making.* New York: McGraw-Hill, 1960.
59. **Simon, H. A.** *Models of man: Social and rational.* New York: Wiley, 1957.
60. **Sloane, A. P.** My years with General Motors. *Fortune,* 1963, 68, 145–148.
61. **Smith, G. A., Jr.** *Business, society, and the individual.* Homewood, Ill.: Irwin, 1962.
62. **Speisman, J. C., et al.** Experimental reduction of stress based on ego-defense theory. *J. Abnorm. Soc. Psychol.,* 1964, 68, 367–380.
63. **Super, D. E.** Some unresolved issues in vocational development research. *Personnel Guid. J.,* 1961, 11–15.
64. **Super, D. E.** *The psychology of careers.* New York: Harper & Row, 1963.
65. **Tannenbaum, R., et al.** *Leadership and organization.* New York: McGraw-Hill, 1961.
66. **Taylor, C. W.** *Research findings on the characteristics of scientists.* Salt Lake City: Bulletin of University of Utah, No. 110, 1961.
67. **Taylor, C. W., & Barron, F. (Eds.)** *Scientific creativity: The recognition and development.* New York: Wiley, 1963.
68. **Thompson, A. S.** Psychology and the dilemma of modern industrial society. *Bull. Int. Ass. Appl. Psychol.,* 1964, 13, 69–77.
69. **Whitehead, A. N.** *The aims of education.* New York: Macmillan, 1929.

70. **Wilensky, H. L.** Mass society and mass culture: Interdependence or independence. *Amer. Sociol., Rev.,* 1964, 29, 173–197.
71. **Wolfe, D. M., & Snoek, J. D.** A study of tensions and adjustment under role conflict. *J. Soc. Issues,* 1962, 18, 102–121.
72. **Wright, M.** *How do people grow in a business organization?* New York: General Electric Company, 1963.
73. **Zaleznik, A., & Moment, D.** *Casebook on interpersonal behavior in organizations.* New York: Wiley, 1964.
74. **Zander, A., & Curtis, T.** Effects of social power on aspiration level and striving. *J. abnorm. Soc. Psychol.,* 1962, 64, 63–74.

NAME INDEX

SUBJECT INDEX